7TH EDITION

REAL ESTATE

PRINCIPLES and PRACTICES

ALFRED A. RING

Independent Land Economist
and Real Estate Consultant
Former Chairman, Department of Real Estate
and Urban Land Studies
University of Florida

Prentice-Hall, Inc.   Englewood Cliffs, N.J.

© 1922, 1938, 1947, 1954, 1960, 1967, 1972 by
PRENTICE-HALL, INC.
ENGLEWOOD CLIFFS, NEW JERSEY

PRINTED IN THE UNITED STATES OF AMERICA

*Library of Congress
Catalog Card Number: 74–168486*

ISBN: 0–13–765800–1

10   9   8   7   6   5   4

PRENTICE-HALL INTERNATIONAL, INC., *London*
PRENTICE-HALL OF AUSTRALIA, PTY. LTD., *Sydney*
PRENTICE-HALL OF CANADA, LTD., *Toronto*
PRENTICE-HALL OF INDIA PRIVATE LIMITED, *New Delhi*
PRENTICE-HALL OF JAPAN, INC., *Tokyo*

CONTENTS

4. REAL ESTATE OWNERSHIP AND INTERESTS 47

5. CONTRACTS 65

6. LAND SURVEYING AND PROPERTY DESCRIPTIONS 90

7. TRANSFER OF TITLE 103

8. MORTGAGE INSTRUMENTS 123

9. DEEDS 142

Guardian's deed, 155. Committee's deed, 155. Cession deed, 155. Deed of trust, 155. Deed of confirmation, 156. Deed of surrender, 156. Deed of release, 156. Taxation, 157.

10.   LEASES   158

Landlord and tenant, 158. Leases, 158. Essentials of a valid lease, 159. Types of lease, 159. Rent, 161. Term of lease, 162. Oral and written leases, 162. Kinds of tenancies, 163. Long-term leases, 164. Ground leases, 165. Termination of leases, 166. Dispossess proceedings, 168. Form of lease, 168. Covenants by tenant, 169. Repairs, 169. Improvements, 170. Liens, 170. Security furnished by the tenant, 170. Additional charges paid by tenant, 171. Sale and leaseback, 171. Fire clause, 172. Assignment, subletting, and mortgaging of lease, 172. Use of the premises, 173. Compliance with orders of governmental authorities, 173. Guarantors and sureties, 173. Tenant liable after re-entry, 174. Right of redemption, 174. Tenant to indemnify landlord for damages, 174. Leases subordinate to mortgages, 175. Covenants by landlord, 176.

11.   OTHER REAL ESTATE INSTRUMENTS   177

Satisfaction of mortgage, 178. Extension of mortgage, 179. Assignment of mortgage, 181. Release of mortgage, 182. Subordination of mortgage, 184. Certificate of reduction of mortgage, 185. Estoppel certificate, 185. Mortgage share (participation) agreements, 186. Party wall agreement, 187. Beam right agreement, 187. Agreements creating driveway easements, 188. Power of attorney, 189. Affidavit of title, 189. Bill of sale, 190. Restriction agreement, 190. Affidavit of heirship, 190. Consolidation agreement, 190. Spreading agreement, 190. Collateral bond, 191. Boundary line agreement, 191.

12.   TITLE CLOSING   192

Preliminary requirements, 192. The title search, 193. Survey, 193. Inspection, 194. Riparian rights, 194. Report of title, 195. Encumbrances subject to which the purchaser takes title, 195. Encumbrances to be removed, 196. Instruments to be delivered, 196. When title passes, 196. Delivery in escrow, 197. Types of title closing, 197. Adjustments and closing statements, 206. Rejection of title, 208.

13.   REAL ESTATE FINANCING   210

Importance of real estate credit financing, 210. Extent of mortgage financing, 211. Trading on the equity, 212. Economic basis for mortgage financing, 212. Kinds of mortgages, 213. Types of mortgages, 216. Mortgage pattern variations, 225. Second mortgages, 225. Equity financing, 226. Individual financing, 226. Group financing, 226. Partnership, 226. Corporation, 227. Tenant ownership corporations, 227. Condominium financing, 228. Syndicate ownership, 229. Sale and leaseback, 229.

14.   REAL ESTATE INVESTMENT   231

The nature and character of real estate investments, 231. Required quantity and safety of initial capital outlay, 231. Quantity and quality (safety) of periodic annual income, 232. Degree of inflationary protection, 233. Liquidity of invested capital, 234. Capital appreciation, 238. Income tax shelters, 238. Mortgage lending project requirements, 241. Real estate investment securities, 242.

15.   THE MORTGAGE MARKET   245

Kinds of mortgage markets, 245. The role of lenders, 246. Individual lenders, 246. Institutional lenders, 246. The secondary mortgage market, 253. The Federal National Mortgage Association, 253. Government National Mortgage Association, 257. Other secondary market facilities, 257. Safety in mortgage lending, 258. Mortgage lending procedure, 259. Closing of the loan, 262. Setting up the loan for supervision, 262. Supervision of the loan, 264. Servicing of the loan, 266.

PREFACE

This book is designed to help those who seek a business career in the broad field of real estate and others who for personal reasons wish to obtain a clear understanding of the facts of real property ownership, as well as of the principal commercial and financial transactions involved in the ownership and transfer of real estate. Further, this book is intended to lay a foundation for study and research of the various fields that comprise real estate as an important area of concentration in community schools of higher learning and in colleges of business administration. A clear understanding of the principles that underlie real estate transactions should also accelerate the conversion of the real estate business to the status of a profession. Substantial progress has been made toward this goal, as explained in the various chapters of this book, in specialized areas such as real estate financing, real estate investment and counseling, real estate management, real estate development, regional planning, and property appraising.

The seventh edition of *Real Estate Principles and Practices* has been revised thoroughly to take into account the continuous complex and important developments in real estate education that have taken place since the first edition, by Philip A. Benson and Nelson L. North, was published in 1922. Although the fundamental features of real property laws have not changed significantly, a number of important changes have occurred in areas affecting real estate domestic and foreign investment, urban renewal, housing legislation, housing of the elderly, real estate financing, and subsidized rentals and housing facilities for displaced persons and indigents. Reinterpretation of basic and common laws has established new principles and practices in the important field of real estate finance and the general field of real estate as a business enterprise. This seventh edition reflects these recent developments and offers guides to their application as tools of learning, both in the classroom and in the field of practice.

The author is greatly indebted to the late Philip A. Benson, president of the Dime Savings Bank of Brooklyn, New York, and president of the American Bankers Association, and to the late Nelson L. North, LL.M., real estate attorney and Lecturer in Real Estate, American Institute of Banking, for their past and substantial contributions to this writing and to their guidance and enthusiastic support which made application of their ideas and molding of real estate thought a reality.

The seventh edition is an outgrowth of the evolution of real estate thought that has been channeled to the author from leading teachers of real estate courses in more than one hundred institutions of higher learning. To these teachers, who have so generously offered their constructive criticism, go the author's grateful thanks. No small credit for the success of this and the previous editions of this book goes to the thousands of students who through diligent text reading and study have offered valuable suggestions for further clarification and refinement of subject matter.

Grateful acknowledgment is made for valuable assistance and continued encouragement and support over more than a a quarter of a century to a great teacher and friend, Dr. Herbert B. Dorau, former chairman of the Department of Public Utilities, Real Estate, and Transportation at New York University. To this outstanding scholar goes much of the credit for introducing real estate as a social science to the colleges of business administration in leading institutions of higher learning throughout America.

For valuable assistance during the manuscript stages of this seventh edition gratitude is expressed to the dedicated members of the Florida Real Estate Commission teaching staff who under the direction of the Division of Continuing Education of the University of Florida have exposed the concept and materials of this book to more than fifteen thousand students and practitioners who enrolled in partial fulfillment of the educational requirements for a real estate salesman's or broker's license. For contributions to the chapters on real estate mortgage financing and investment, the author's thanks go to W. V. Register, member and long-term chairman of the board of the Bank of Dunedin in Florida. For constructive comments and contributions to materials on building cost estimating and construction, appreciation is extended to North Florida's largest developer, Mr. Hugh Edwards of Gainesville. Grateful acknowledgment is also made for valuable help received from the following readers of the manuscript: Dr. Byrl N. Boyce, School of Business Administration, The University of Connecticut, and Dr. Stephen Dale Messner, Center for Real Estate and Urban Economic Studies, The University of Connecticut.

Finally, and with deep sincerity, credit for manuscript reading, text styling, and readability is given to my conscientious home editor, partner, and wife, Elsie.

Since all knowledge is sharpened by mutual expression and field testing of ideas, I wish to dedicate this book to the thousands of alumni who graduated with a major in real estate during my years of tutelage at New York University and the University of Florida.

ALFRED A. RING

INTRODUCTION:
CURRENT FORCES INFLUENCING PROPERTY OWNERSHIP, USE, AND CONTROL

The decade 1970–80 is destined to bring about important changes in the ownership, use, and control of real property. These changes are wrought by deep-seated and intense socioeconomic forces that continue to compel families and individuals to migrate from rural communities to congested, politically unstable, and atmospherically polluted urban centers in search of work and opportunities for higher income. The socioeconomic forces that pressure urban life will undoubtedly cause matters to worsen in the short run before the impending breakthrough of coordinated federal, state, and county government assistance will promote conditions of law and order and implement regional planning which will mitigate, if not solve, the problems of congested urban life.

The expressed hope, following World War II, that the development, production, and ready ownership of the automobile, as an economical mode of mass transportation, would counteract the forces of intense urbanization and bring about a decentralization of industry and urban life has unfortunately not been realized. Although a few industrial corporations and some large warehouse centers have attempted to decentralize operations at opportune times of plant modernization, such attempts have generally met with failure because of the lack of skilled workers, technicians, and professionals at the new locations. As a rule, blue- as well as white-collar workers were unable or unwilling to sever their deep-set social roots or family ties that bound them to urban community life. Generally, too, decentralized areas lacked adequate cultural opportunities, such as good schools, universities, libraries, sports centers, museums, and theaters, which the suburban or rur-urban areas could ill afford to duplicate.

As a consequence, continued and accelerated technological developments spurred by computerized sciences and business opportunities have resulted in further crowding of population into urban centers that show evidences of forming a *megalopolis* (thickly populated urban region) anticipated to stretch uninterruptedly along the eastern seaboard from Boston to Washington, D.C. As of this writing, urbanization has reached a point where 85 percent of the world's population live on less than 2 percent of the available and usable land. The concomitant problems that beset and affect the health, welfare, and safety of people who live in densely crowded urban areas have reached worldwide significance. These problems are aggravated by high costs and insufficient civic services and encompass such difficulties as urban decay, slum districts, hunger, poverty, inadequate public transportation, and inequitable property taxes, as well as the impact on individual health of air, water, and sound (excessive noise) pollution. Now is the time to effect a solution, or at least a mitigation, of these urban problems through a more effective government-supported study of *ecology*, the science that deals with the interrelationship of man and his geographic environment as molded by community development and urban structures.

Environmental problems, among which waste of natural resources and pollution (air, water, sound, etc.) head the list, will undoubtedly cause society at large through more stringent and forceful regulations to limit still further individual proprietary rights in order to promote the social ends of effective land utilization. The tools to achieve and exercise social control of land utilization are well known, and government in its aim to promote and protect the common (populous) weal can legislate land use controls through exercise of its sovereign powers: police, taxation, and eminent domain. Each of these powers will be described in detail in Chapter 4, "Real Estate Ownership and Interests." Recent court cases demonstrate that judicial interpretation of the *spirit* rather than the *letter* of the law has widened the power of government on a state, county, and municipal level to limit and regulate the use of private property for personal or corporate gain where the social costs in all their forms, whether expended or accrued, are deemed excessive in relation to economic gains.

The private sectors of our economy, however, look with concern upon the inroads of socialism and fear conditions that may lead to complete state ownership of land and its resources as it exists in socialist countries behind the iron and bamboo curtains. Strenuous efforts are therefore being made to resist and to forestall a similar fate which is deemed detrimental to the heritage of private land ownership in this country. Yet even the most individualistic laissez faire-minded owners of real estate have come to realize that effective but equitable control over land use, where intended to promote and protect the health, safety, and welfare of society, must inevitably preserve if not enhance private measures of property values by retarding the pressure of socioeconomic forces that cause functional and economic obsolescence.[1]

---

[1] *Obsolescence*—a loss in value from social or economic causes. See Chapter 23 on property valuation for a more detailed explanation.

The past decade has witnessed a gradual and ever more perceptible shift from a largely business-oriented economy dominated by producers and distributors of goods to a consumer protective economy which in recent years has won the support of legislative bodies and the sanctions of courts who now judge on the basis of the spirit and intent as well as on the letter of the law. A case in point is the shift in the entrenched doctrine of *caveat emptor*, "let the buyer beware," to the doctrine of *caveat venditor*, "let the seller beware." This reinterpretation of legal concepts has already significantly affected the respective responsibilities of buyers and sellers in the fulfillment of their contracts and the real estate broker in his role of an agent acting in a fiduciary capacity. The effects of such reinterpretation of both common and statutory law will be given further treatment in Chapter 5, "Contracts."

In recent years, too, real estate as a form of wealth and as a tax preferential investment has grown significantly in popularity, primarily because of two developments. First, the authorization granted under the Internal Revenue Code for the formation of real estate investment trusts[2] has enabled the small investor to participate in tax-favored high-interest-yielding real estate investment ventures and to avoid dilution of trust-earned income by double taxation, since the investment trust in paying out 90 percent or more of its earned income is exempt from federal taxation on its net real estate earnings.[3] Second, and of more recent origin, are the significant dollar amounts of real estate owned by overseas investment funds. These foreign funds, though wholly incorporated in overseas countries, chiefly Europe, acquire principally nonresidential real estate through wholly owned management (operating) companies. Since net-net earnings accruing to these offshore trust funds are not taxable in the United States, this form of investment has proved highly attractive throughout the Western-oriented European continent. It is estimated that offshore investments in the United States will average from $300 million to $500 million worth of real estate annually in the 1970–80 decade.

The importance of real estate, too, as shelter for the expanding population and as a facility to house the developing needs of business and industry has caused Congress annually during the past five years to amend and enlarge statutory housing acts that are designed to stimulate new construction through loan subsidies, grants, and accelerated depreciation allowances that yield tax-sheltered income to real estate equity investors. Next to law and order and peace in the world, housing is recognized as this country's number one problem. A rate of construction reaching three million housing units each year, over at least a ten-year period, is deemed essential to replace substandard housing and to meet the minimum needs of newly formed families. To a greater extent the housing need will be filled by relatively large numbers of apartment dwellings because less land per dwelling unit is required to provide the shelter and also because construction

---

[2]The Real Estate Investment Trust Act became law effective January 1, 1961.

[3]See the chapter on real estate investment for a full discussion of tax-sheltered income.

cost savings derived from mass production can lower the acquisition price per unit of housing.

As noted above, real estate as a factor of production and as one of the indispensable needs of man is of vital importance to everyone, and a study of real estate principles and practices is deemed fundamental to all economic activity and to basic scientific knowledge itself. The writing of a comprehensive text on the fundamentals of real estate poses the important question as to which philosophical approach is to be selected as a guide and in what order and length of socioeconomic decision-making problems the subject matter is to be stressed. There are those who hold that there cannot be any other except the sociological or institutional approach to a study of real estate principles and practices. To them a world without mankind is unthinkable, and thus those phases of knowledge that deal with the interrelation of man to his physical environment are deemed primary. This approach would focus analytically on the principles of urban growth, community development, regional planning, and highest and best land use, as well as on problems related to housing, transportation, utilities, waste disposal, pollution, recreation, and so forth. Others maintain that a study of real estate fundamentals can logically and comprehensively be presented only from a legal and historical point of view. This approach is generally advocated by and widely published under the authorship of writers legally trained and professionally active as attorneys or teachers in schools of higher learning, and these legally oriented publications stress the orderly development of property rights from custom through stages of common, old English, equity, constitutional, and statutory law, as modified by judicial rulings and landmark court decisions. The importance of this approach to a study of real estate is not questioned. However, what is legal may not necessarily be economically feasible or socially compatible at a given time or place. A third and somewhat hybrid approach to a study of real estate has been selected to assist the lay reader and owner of real estate as well as the professional practitioner in understanding the fundamentals of real estate as best applied in day-to-day practice.

The study of real estate as presented herein begins with a discussion of the nature, importance, and character of land. The purpose of Chapter 1 is to establish a framework for the field of study and to analyze the legal, physical, and economic bases of land classification and the role of realty as a commodity. The role of land in the development of the real estate business and in the operation of the real estate market is discussed in Chapters 2 and 3. These chapters introduce the reader to the relationship of real estate transactions to other professional and business activities as well as to the role of government and other forces that influence real estate supply and demand. Still introductory to ownership and use of real estate is the discussion presented in Chapter 4. In this chapter the legal rights of ownership as well as private and governmental limitations controlling the use of real estate are fully outlined.

Chapters 5 through 12 deal with the acquisition, sale, and transfer of real estate by individuals, groups of individuals, or corporations. Successively the reader is introduced to the purpose, meaning, and essentials of the real estate contract, the clauses that govern contracts, and the manner in which contracts are executed. The purpose and necessity for clear and definite identification of real property and the various modes of land description are given full consideration. This is followed by recommended methods of transferring title, title protection, purpose and essentials of a valid deed, and types of deeds that serve specific individual and legal objectives. Recommended title-closing procedures and standardized accounting, closing, and settlement statements are fully explained and demonstrated.

Financing, investment, the documents used to evidence indebtedness, the operation of the mortgage market, and related documents that affect or limit use of real estate are dealt with in Chapters 13 through 15. Because most real estate transactions are made possible through O.P.M. (other people's money), these chapters are of prime importance to students of real estate as well as to those professionally concerned with property financing.

The power to tax and the placement and enforcement of other liens on real estate are discussed in Chapters 16 and 17. Since real estate is the principal source of revenue for operations of local (county and community) government, the means for assessing, levying, and enforcing of tax liens are given full consideration.

The business functions and fields of service that have become professionally recognized are detailed in Chapters 18 to 25 inclusive. Persons who are active in, or who seek to engage in, the practice of real estate on their own, or as a service to others, will find these chapters most useful and informative. The prevailing practices of brokerage, marketing (selling), advertising, management, insurance, valuation, and appraising, as well as land subdividing and developing, are presented as they generally apply in the various states. Customs as well as operation of state and local laws do cause variations in field practice, and the reader is advised to verify laws and procedures as they apply in a specific location.

The city, county, state, and federal roles and interests in promoting and enforcing desirable community planning, zoning, and housing legislation are discussed in Chapters 26 and 27. Government has long since been recognized as the fifth, or steering, wheel that directs the other wheels of production—land, labor, capital, and entrepreneurial management—to effect desirable social goals. These subjects, too, deserve careful study and detailed consideration.

Finally, the mobile home and modular construction as modes of housing, and the principles that guide successful home ownership, are explained in the concluding Chapters 28 and 29. These and the foregoing chapters are intended to guide the reader in a simple but logical manner to a meaningful understanding of the complexities of real estate as a commodity worthy of possession and as a business and professional occupation that has proved both exciting and economically most rewarding.

1

NATURE, IMPORTANCE, AND CHARACTER OF LAND

Realty as a commodity consists of the physical components of land, as nature provided it, and all man-made permanent or "fixed" improvements, "on" and "to" the land, which have been added below or above the surface of the earth or which have affected the utility of a given parcel of land. Since all land has been directly or indirectly modified by man (directly by the construction of buildings, fences, or conversion of forests into grazing, farming, or building sites and indirectly by the construction of access roads, bridges, canals, modes of transportation, and other means of public improvements which increase land utilization), the term *realty* rather than land is appropriate in describing the commodity with which real estate as a business is concerned.

Improvements that are intended to be permanent (permanent for the life of the improvements) convert, when affixed, the commodity of land into the commodity of realty. Yet land remains basic, and the characteristics of land, to a large extent, control the characteristics and utilization of the improvements that are placed upon it. Although realty and real estate are deemed synonymous terms in practice, an important distinction needs to be made between the physical and economic characteristics of realty and the legal rights in real estate which ownership of realty confers. These rights in realty and property interests will be more fully discussed in Chapter 4.

1

The important and basic role of land in the formation of realty, in the development of real estate as a major business, and as a resource in the building of nations and giant cities warrants a careful study and analysis of land as a commodity and factor of production.

Land defined

The layman generally considers land as consisting of the "crust" of the earth, including the underlying soil which supplies us with the fertility for life-sustaining vegetation and provides supporting power for structures and other man-made land improvements. Legally, nevertheless, unencumbered ownership of land includes possession and control of the minerals and substances below the earth's surface as well as of the space and air above the ground. Thus boundaries of any tract or parcel of land extend in the shape of an inverted pyramid from the center of the earth upward to the limits of the sky as shown in the figure below.

LEGAL BOUNDARIES OF LAND

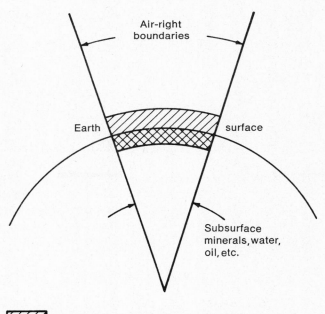

As defined by classical economists, land, in its broadest meaning, is considered synonymous with "nature," including "the material and forces which nature gives freely for man's aid in land and water, in air, light, and heat." This broad definition, although useful in economic analysis where a scientific distinction is to be made between land as a factor of production and the capital improvements superimposed by man, no longer is deemed consistent with the practical application of economics as a useful business tool.

Land, in its narrower definition, fits more nearly the common everyday meaning as consisting of building lots or rural acreage, together with trees, vegetation, minerals, and man-made improvements. This narrower definition of land is deemed more practical for purposes of our study and is accepted as a basis for further discussion.

Land characteristics

The special significance that attaches to land, which warrants treatment of land as a factor of production distinct from other marketable goods and commodities that are classified as capital, is due to the peculiar attributes, both physical and economic, that characterize land. For ease of study, these attributes or special characteristics of land are classified as *physical* and *economic*. In practice, however, the line of demarcation is difficult to ascertain, because the physical characteristics of land directly and indirectly influence the economic behavior of man toward land. These characteristics are as follows:

Physical	*Economic*
Immobility	Scarcity
Indestructibility	Modification (improvements)
Nonhomogeneity	Fixity of investment
	Situs

Physical characteristics of land

Land is physically *immobile*. It is true that some of the *substance* of land—its topsoil, surface minerals, or products—may be transported to more strategically located marketplaces, but the *extent* of land—its geographic location—is rigidly fixed. Even if an atomic bomb should destroy an entire city, the geographic location of each parcel of land would be determinable by minutes and degrees from measures of latitude and longitude in relation to internationally accepted meridians and parallels. It is the immobility of land that caused it to be classified as *real estate*, a term that denotes an owner's right in land and the *permanent* improvements attached thereto. Because of immobility, too, the market for land is *local* in character. To some extent the necessity to guide and facilitate local market transactions accounts for the multitude of brokers and specialists needed to serve adequately the real estate business in each community.

A second and important physical characteristic of land is its *indestructibility*. This physical quality of *durability* has popularized land as a mode of investment. Care, however, must be taken to distinguish physical from economic (value) durability. Physically, land may be accounted for forever, but obsolescence may destroy its value; for instance, the importance of certain locations, as has happened in "ghost towns," may wholly disappear.

Nonhomogeneity is the third important physical characteristic of land. No two parcels of land are ever alike. There may exist a high degree of similarity in land substance and location, or parcels of land may be economically alike and substitutable one for another, but geographically all parcels differ. This nonhomogeneous character of land has legally caused it to be declared a "nonfungible" (not substitutable) commodity requiring *specific* performance (see Chapter 5, page 86) in contractual agreements involving the use or sale of land.

Economic characteristics of land

Although the physical supply of land is fixed, there is no *scarcity* of land as such. Only certain types of land of given quality and location are in comparative short supply. The fear that pressure of an ever-increasing population and the consequent need for more productive land may exhaust the available limited physical supply has caused periodic land "booms and busts," many with disastrous social and economic results affecting entire communities and even nations.

Land in the United States today is relatively less scarce than it was a decade ago, and this despite an unexpected growth in total population and ever more extensive utilization of land and its mineral resources. The reason for this phenomenon rests upon both American inventive skill and the greater and more intensive use of land as a factor of production. The increase in the economic supply of land has had the practical effect of land *production*. This may be demonstrated as follows:

At one time, cattle raising in many states required two or more acres of ground for each head of cattle. Improved pastures and the planting of better and more nutritious grasses have made it possible to graze two animals where only one could profitably roam before. Assuming that formerly two hundred acres of pasture land were needed to maintain a head of one hundred cattle, the discovery of improved grasses thus doubled the economic land supply for this purpose. In cities, too, use of steel and elevators made possible the skyscraper and multistory apartment structures that literally created a city in the sky. The prospects for further and still greater intensive utilization of land make the scarcity of land of only relative importance, an importance dependent more on the economic than on the physical limitations of land.

A second economic characteristic of land is found in the influence or *modification* that the improvement of one parcel or tract of land has on the value and utilization of another. These modifications of land carried out on an area or community scale are classified as improvements *to* the land as distinguished from improvements *on* the land. Whereas the latter include buildings, fences, and fixtures that comprise an integral part of a given site, the former improvements *to* the land refer to access roads, utilities, transportation, school, shopping, and recreational facilities that are essential in the "production" of land for private use or public purposes. The influence of these improvements *to* the land is directly measurable in the increased value of the parcels of real estate benefited, based on the increased utility or amenity derived from a given site through more intensive utilization of the land.

A third economic characteristic is the *fixity* of land investment. Once labor and capital expenditures have been committed for improvements *on* the land, the investment becomes peculiarly "set" or fixed. Drainage, sewage, electric, water and gas facilities, or buildings cannot as a rule be dismantled and shifted economically to locations in which they would be in greater demand. The investment "sunk" in the land is slow in returning during the economic life of the improvements; furthermore, the immobility and fixity of land and land investment make real estate vulnerable to rigid controls for taxation or various other social or political purposes.

Situs, or location, is a fourth important economic characteristic of land. Situs, which refers to economic rather than to geographic location, is a result of individual or group choices and preferences for given areas. It is the quality of situs that gives different valuations to otherwise similar units of urban and rural land. Thus, land values on one side of a street or city square may be double or more of like parcels across the street or square. The economic difference is solely accounted for by people's preference for given site locations which contribute to such favored areas a measurable "situs" quality. The quality aspects of location are importantly affected not only by geographic phenomena such as the direction of prevailing winds or the presence or lack of sunshine or shade but also by population growth or decline, shifts in production or trade centers, and changes in the standard of living that influence modes of urban, suburban, or rural land utilization. The trend toward suburban living and the consequent development of neighborhood and regional shopping centers have caused, in many instances, a lowering of land values, particularly in cities of over one hundred thousand, and many communities fear severe financial consequences if a solution is not soon found to stem the outward flow of population. Thus, though land is immobile and physically indestructible, it is *situs* that gives land the quality aspects of location.

Factors controlling land utilization

A parcel of land at a given time is estimated to have only one *highest and best use*. By highest and best use is meant that possible and legal use or employment that will preserve the utility of the land and yield a net income flow that forms, when capitalized, the highest present value of the land. This concept of highest and best use is of great importance, for upon a proper understanding of it depends good city planning, profitable subdivision and development-of-land policies, and wise site utilization by individual or corporate owners. Since the highest and best use of land at any given time is determined by the estimated quantity and quality of the anticipated net income flow that accrues to land under existing or alternative uses, it is of interest to examine briefly the factors that control land utilization and cause land income to be secondary or *residual* in character.

For land to be productive and income yielding, it must be coordinated (improved) with capital and labor. Since these latter factors of production are relatively mobile, they cannot be attracted to the land under development unless an adequate return or compensation is assured to them. Labor must be compensated first or it may cease to operate. Further, labor, or mechanic's, liens, as provided by law, may be pressed against the owner's property as payments become due. This important provision will be further discussed in Chapter 16, "Liens."

Capital, too, must be compensated adequately, otherwise it will be attracted by equally good and more certain investment opportunities. It is true that once capital is committed to land it becomes semifixed, but capital can be withdrawn in one form or another through lack of property maintenance or accelerated depreciation charges.

The coordinator or entrepreneur renders a personal service, akin to labor. His claim for compensation is next in line. Without the services of the entrepreneur, land improvements cannot take place profitably or economically. Someone must assume the responsibility for combining the warranted proportions of the factors of production that will compensate (competitively) the factors of production and will yield a residual return to land that reaches a maximum under the planned program of highest and best land use.

Because wages of labor, interest on, and recapture (depreciation) of, capital, and costs of coordination have prior claims on income derived from use of land, only the balance of net income remaining represents the income-producing power of the land. It is this "residual" income of land that forms the basis for the computation of land value.

It can be proved, however, that different uses of land will affect the amount of residual income attributable to land. Income, even under the highest use of land, will vary with capacity and efficiency of land utilization—to wit, the number of floors in a skyscraper structure. The greatest residual land income can thus be attained only when a site is improved both under *the highest and the best possible use.* Any other use will diminish the residual income, but such income losses are attributable to the faulty use of land and are reflected in the diminished value of the improvements as functional or economic obsolescence (depreciation) as will be illustrated below.

The determination of the highest and best use of a given site at a given time requires careful study and expert analysis of the social, economic, and political forces that influence land utilization and land income over the estimated life of the proposed improvements. Value, as will be shown more fully in later chapters, is the "present worth of *future* rights to income," and great care must be taken to employ land in such a manner that these future rights will be maximized if discounted to a sum of present worth. It is not unusual to find that the highest and best use of a property may be to leave it as a vacant site until such time as it "ripens" into more productive use. This may be the case in cities that undergo rapid growth, where future demand will warrant the construction of bigger and better improvements than those that current market conditions would justify.

Generally, too, improvements erected many years ago rarely constitute the highest and best use of land. This is due to changes in the arts, in design, and in modes of community living. Where land is committed to a faulty or other than optimum use, it appears logical to charge the error in utilization against the value of the man-made improvements and not against the "passive" land which must be acted "on" to yield an income. Most land, as other scarce resources, is in competitive demand, and the prices bid for units or parcels of land reflect the varied uses to which land can be put under alternate development. Since logically there can be but one optimum use of land, at a given time, under which the average net return to land as forecast over a period of years is highest, a choice must be made to determine which of alternate or optional land uses constitutes the "highest and best use." The concept of highest and best use in relation to land value and the economic law of increasing and decreasing returns can best be illustrated as follows:

Suppose a building site in a given community can be developed under existing and reasonably anticipated zoning restriction for residential purposes only. Suppose further that preliminary study and analysis of neighborhood characteristics and of housing demand narrow the choice of possible and profitable site improvements to one of the following type structures:

1. A single-story duplex building, each rental unit containing two bedrooms, dining-living room, kitchen, and tiled bath. Total improvements cost, $27,500.
2. A three-family apartment building, each apartment containing two bedrooms, dining-living room, kitchen, and tiled bath. Total improvements cost, $37,500.

Since the *highest* use of the building site was prescribed by zoning law for residential purposes, the determination still to be made is which of the alternate types of improvements described above constitutes the *best* use. Under the definition of highest and best use, it is necessary to ascertain the income-producing capacity of the land under the alternate types of improvement and to find by the process of capitalization which income yields to land its highest present value. Based on prevailing rentals of similar residences in comparable neighborhoods of $225 a month per four-room and bath duplex unit and $200 per month per four-room and bath apartment unit, the procedure to derive land income and land value is as follows:

ANALYSIS OF LAND INCOME AND LAND VALUE
UNDER ALTERNATIVE TYPES OF IMPROVEMENTS

	Single-Story Duplex	Three-Family Apartment
Gross annual income:		
Duplex units $225 x 2 x 12 (months) =	$5,400	
Three-family apartment $200 x 3 x 12 (months) =		$7,200
Less vacancy and collection losses @ 5%	270	360
Effective gross income	$5,130	$6,840
Less operating expenses:		
Management 10% (entrepreneur)	$ 513	$ 684
Property taxes	650	900
Maintenance and repairs	300	400
Hazard insurance	100	120
Utilities (hall lights)		24
Cleaning service		150
Total operating expenses	$1,563	$2,278
Operating income	$3,567	$4,562
Less capital costs:		
Interest—duplex $27,500 @ 9%	$2,475	
apartments $37,500 @ 9%		$3,375
Amortization—duplex $27,500 @ 2%	550	
apartments $37,500 @ 2%		750
Total capital costs	$3,025	$4,125
Net income residual to land	$ 542	$ 437
Value of land @ 9% rate of capitalization:		
Duplex $542 ÷ .09 =	$6,022	
Apartments $437 ÷ .09 =		$4,855

The valuation procedure outlined is one generally practiced by informed investors to determine the present worth of land under the income or earnings residual approach to land value. Based on the analysis, as illustrated, the conclusion can be drawn that the highest and best use of the building site under value study is a single-story duplex to be constructed at a cost of $27,500 and renting at $225 per month per dwelling unit. Under this highest and best use the land warrants a present value of $6,022. Under the next best type of improvement or utilization both land income and land value diminish.

Suppose now that the building site in question is not put to its highest and best use and that the three-family apartment building was placed on it at a cost of $37,500. What then is the land value of the site under study and how is the total property value to be allocated between land and building improvements? It appears logical to assume that land can have only one value at any given time and place and that losses due to overimprovement and underimprovement are properly chargeable as depreciation (functional obsolescence) against the building. To state it differently, when the land is misimproved, the building value is said to be residual in character. The mechanics of applying the building value residual procedure is more fully explained in Chapter 24 on appraising. Briefly, the method involves a determination of the value of the property as a whole (land and building) and the subtraction of the capitalized land value from this total as found under the highest and best land use.

For a three-family apartment building, as shown above, construction costs amounted to $37,500 for building improvements and land equaled a value of $4,855, a total of $42,355 under this type of building improvement. However, since land under the highest and best use as demonstrated is worth $6,022, this amount must now be subtracted from the total property value of $42,355 to derive the value of the building improvements. Subtracting $6,022 from $42,355 leaves a building value of $36,333. The difference between building cost of $37,500 and building value of $36,333, or $1,167, is a measure of building depreciation caused by an overimprovement of the building site.

To restate the land utilization principle: Land value is based on residual land income under the highest and best use of the land. Under any other use both income and value diminish and the loss caused by either overutilization or underutilization is classified as depreciation and more specifically as a loss in value due to functional obsolescence. Only under the highest and best land use and at a time when improvements are new are costs and property value the same.

Since the value of a given parcel of land, as demonstrated above, is based on the income attributable to land under its highest and best use, it is important that care be taken to differentiate between (1) income derived under a specific use or agreed-upon rental and (2) income that is warranted and residual to land when put to its optimum use and remains after due economic shares have been allocated to labor (wages), coordination (entrepreneur costs or sacrifices), and capital (interests and capital returns).

The income that is ascribable to land under its highest and best use is referred to as *economic rent*. It is that rent that the land does or will produce if employed to its optimum capacity. Any other income agreed upon or arbitrarily assigned to land is classified as *contract rent*. To the extent to which a contract rent fails to equal the economic rent, to that extent a proportional share of land value is transferred from the owner to the user or tenant.

A thorough understanding of the concept of *highest and best use* is of great importance in the effective and wise utilization of our land resources. Care must be taken in studying the alternative long-term uses to which land may be put to select that possible, legal, and economically warranted use that will preserve the utility of the land and yield the highest possible present value.

The classification of land

A guide to the effective utilization of land and an aid in the study of factors that should be observed in determining its highest and best use are presented in the following classification of land based on legal, physical, and economic considerations:

I. *Legal basis of land classification*:
   A. Publicly owned land—highways, streets, parks, public building sites, harbor and dock sites
   B. Privately owned land—all land not publicly owned and which is used for or held for potential use in agriculture or for residential, commercial, industrial, and institutional purposes
II. *Physical basis of land classification*—elevation, fertility, subsoil conditions, mineral deposits, water table, topography, drainage, climate
III. *Economic basis of land classification*:
   A. Agricultural land—farming, grazing, forestry, wildlife, hunting, and fishing
   B. Residential land—single family, two family, apartments
   C. Commercial land—retail, wholesale, warehousing, financial, amusement
   D. Industrial land—extracting, light manufacturing, heavy manufacturing
   E. Highways and transportation right-of-way

The classification of land and the determination of its highest and best use are generally based on a study of the socioeconomic factors that are deemed beneficial or detrimental for each of the possible and legal alternative uses under which a site may be developed. A full discussion of each of the land uses and classifications presented above is beyond the scope of this text, but an attempt is made to generalize the principles and forces that guide and control land utilization in practice today.

Land use competition

The competition for land use is motivated by the coordinator's or owner's desire to maximize the net return that is attributable to land as a factor of production. Estimates, generally, are made of the probable net returns that may be anticipated under alternative land uses, and value bids and offerings reflect the highest and best use which the market forces bring about through competition. Competition for land, however, because of (1) the localized need for and trading in it and (2) the larger number of misinformed buyers and sellers that comprise the market, is significantly unorganized and all too often it is "cutthroat" in character.

Substantial efforts have been made during the past two decades to make land and its improvements as a commodity more marketable by simplifying the legal phases of title transfer, by improved methods of financing, and by disseminating knowledge which makes possible more accurate forecasting as to the probable income yield of given acreage or urban sites under alternative means of land utilization. Most large state and private colleges and universities have organized departments in real estate or fields of land economics or offer courses in these fields through their departments of economics.

Schools and colleges of agriculture, too, have taken a widespread interest in soil studies and soil analyses, and field experiment stations offer generous aid in land culture and utilization. The Department of Agriculture and the Department of Commerce, through special studies, publications, and field experimentation, have further aided the farmer and urban consumer in the search for higher and better utilization of his realty holdings.

General guides to more profitable employment of farms and urban realty, as offered and published by the educational and governmental institutions named above, have been available for more than half a century, but the application of these guides and principles to effective land utilization is slow in taking hold—particularly in urban centers where the benefits resulting from effective city planning are recognized but relatively little practiced. Farmers, generally, have been quick to realize the benefits to be gained from a long-range land-plan program; today *contour* farming, crop rotation, organic and chemical fertilization, draining and irrigation are the rule rather than the exception in farmland utilization.

In urban areas, public officials recognize the benefits to be derived from effective urban land use under a long-range master city plan. The difficulty rests, however, in popularizing and selling these plans to normally phlegmatic citizens who may view with alarm a change from the "good and old" *status quo*. The change from haphazard to planned city growth and rural redevelopment may be quickened in the future due to growing interest and application of national, regional, state, and county planning activities under directives and guidance of the eleventh Cabinet post representing a new Department of Housing and Urban Development as authorized by Congress and signed into law by President Johnson in September 1965. Although the subject of land use and planning will be more fully covered in a later chapter, a brief presentation of the factors that influence land use and real estate development may be of interest at this point.

Among the more important considerations that govern, for instance, the parts of an urban area to be developed for residential, commercial, or industrial uses we find the following: (1) land contour and elevation; (2) the direction of prevailing winds; and (3) access roads, public improvements, and public means of transportation which connect the community with the environing farms and adjacent urban centers. The importance of physical land contour and elevation appears obvious. People generally like to live in homes that are situated high and dry and which overlook vistas of natural beauty. On the other hand, wise business and commercial undertakings prefer level areas where foot or mobile shopping may be accomplished with a minimum of effort and expense. Steep grades impede the traffic flow, cause parking difficulties, and make foot shopping more hazardous—hence, less attractive. Industrial enterprises, too, seek flat building terrain and land areas that are generally unsuitable for higher uses and which can economically be secured at minimum prices.

Another powerful location force governing the competitive uses of urban land is found in the direction of prevailing winds. Exclusive residential developments, as a rule, seek sites that are favored by prevailing winds. Location in western parts of urban areas, for instance, where winds are westerly, protects the homes from industrial or other undesirable wind-carried odors and minimizes hazards from conflagration which may be fanned by prevailing winds. It is thus no accident that in great cities such as Paris, London, Berlin, and Washington where prevailing winds are westerly, the best and most fashionable residential homes are also to be found in the western part of the metropolis. Once a given area is recognized for this and similar favorable marks of distinction, the geographic location takes on the quality of "situs." To this day, reference to residential addresses in west Berlin, west London or northwest Washington is deemed as indicative of being on the proverbial "*right* side of the tracks." In cities where prevailing winds are easterly or southerly—as is the case in most of Florida—the finer and more costly residential developments will also, as a rule, be found in these sections of the community. Exceptions, of course, are many, for there may be other and more compelling reasons, such as soil qualities, geographic elevation, river or mountain vistas, which outweigh the benefits to be derived from those attributable to prevailing winds.

Prevailing winds, too, affect the location of industrial sites. Even where zoning regulations do not control industrial site location, owners are conscious of the importance of public relations and generally do everything possible to win and retain the public goodwill. Since soot, smoke, odors, and even plant noise are readily transmitted by prevailing winds to areas lying in the path, efforts are made to select sites for industrial plants that will minimize social costs and protect to the highest possible degree the health and safety of the surrounding population. The selection of industrial sites, which are normally unwanted or unsuited for residential use and are deemed situated best in relation to prevailing winds, conforms to sound standards that should guide the competition of urban land uses. Commercial and business operations that aptly locate in the buffer zones that separate the industrial and residential areas are little, if at all, affected by the directions of prevailing winds.

Governmental agencies from federal to community and county levels are becoming increasingly conscious of air and water pollution problems. To cope with these problems, industry performance standards are now being incorporated in zoning regulations. Expenditures to correct existing air and water pollution problems that endanger public health are as a rule subsidized, where warranted, by federal funds on a dollar-matching basis to encourage agencies of the various states to improve the health standards of the public domain.

Improvements to the land in the form of access roads, shopping centers, public utilities—including safe, efficient, and economical means of public transportation—constitute the third important factor that influences the competition for urban land uses. Residential sites invariably cluster about these facilities and urban residential growth takes place along the roads of convenient access and egress and where essential public services contribute to greater amenities of living.

A more detailed analysis of the improvements and facilities that contribute to better living will be found in Chapter 29, "Home Ownership."

Good access roads, parking facilities, and adequate means of public transportation affect also to an important degree the site locations for commercial and industrial purposes. Despite the significant role that truck and auto traffic currently plays in plant and industrial expansion, the railway system still constitutes the backbone of intercity and interstate commerce, and the presence of railway and siding facilities is deemed a prime requisite for industrial or commercial site location. Since railroads, too, seek flat and well-drained land that can be secured at the lowest prices, industrial and commercial users in a given market area find land in the vicinity of railway rights-of-way generally well adapted for their plant location and business market operations.

Land use regulation and control

Since faulty or improper land use may endanger the health and welfare of an entire community, regulation and control over subdivisions and real estate developments have been sought and strengthened by private groups and civic-minded public authorities since colonial days in the United States. Land, because of its fixity in location, is peculiarly subject to environmental influences that make or break the value of a site. This value interdependence of one site or location on another has caused individuals directly and groups collectively, through community action, to establish safeguards and control over current land uses and future land use patterns. Although effective land use control is brought about in many communities and even in large rural areas by mutual consent, by formal agreement among large tract owners, or by pressure on, or moral suasion of, individual users, principal reliance to assure proper land uses and real estate developments is placed today upon direct or indirect public (governmental) controls and upon private, contractual, and legally enforceable land use regulations.

The means for controlling and regulating land use may be grouped as follows:

Direct Public Ownership
Streets and highways (usually)
Public parks and recreation centers
Public buildings and civic centers
Public (government owned) housing
Public Land Use Controls
State, regional, and city planning
Zoning
Building codes and housing regulations
Housing subsidies and mortgage loan facilities
Taxation and assessments
Private Land Use Restrictions
Deed restrictions
Lease restrictions
Contract limitations

The application of the above land use restrictions will be discussed more fully in chapters dealing with property interests, taxation, housing, city planning, and zoning. It is of interest, however, to stress here the problems that underlie the need for public and private land use regulations and controls.

If economic considerations alone governed the highest and best use of land, few difficulties would be encountered in scientifically channeling land into uses from which the greatest monetary gains over the greatest number of years would accrue to a private owner. The competition of land uses based solely on economic calculations would satisfactorily determine the appropriate use of each site or area, and price competition would guide the effective and profitable employment of land as a factor of production.

Economic considerations, however, are not guiding where the interest in and the ownership of land are diversified. All land though privately owned must be considered a public trust and utilized in a manner that will maximize the social gains and enhance the social welfare of the community in accordance with the utilitarian principle of the greatest good for the greatest number of people. It is because of the conflict between private gains and social objectives that land use controls had to be devised to check gains to the former in the interest of the latter and of the larger good embracing an entire community. The following illustrations under which land use controls should be considered may demonstrate the merits of private versus public interests here involved:

Case A. A large laundry and dry-cleaning establishment seeks to locate near a residential market and is offered a tract of undeveloped land between two "A" rated residential subdivisions. The location appears suitable and the site value to the enterprise exceeds the market value of the land which is based on future demand for quality residential sites in the environment. There is no zoning in effect and the laundry, based on its highest and best land use consideration, acquires the tract and begins construction of its plant and equipment.

The residential developments on either side of the proposed laundry plant are also in an unzoned county area, but within their respective subdivisions they have a measure of land use control through deed restrictions which the subdivider wisely recorded to protect the homesites from immediate environmental nonconforming uses or substandard housing.

The laundry and dry-cleaning establishment, soon after completion, proved financially successful, and the owners felt justified in their belief that the land was put to its highest and best use. The noise of plant operation, however, together with increased truck traffic and accompanying hazards to school children and pedestrians, caused a drop in demand for high-class homes in the bordering residential areas and a concomitant lessening of home and site values in the neighborhood. A before-and-after survey of home site values disclosed that the aggregate losses incurred by the many homeowners far outweighed the benefits derived by the sole operators of the laundry and dry-cleaning enterprise.

Case B. A large cement factory located recently near a small Atlantic Ocean resort town when it was discovered that certain lime and shell deposits in the area were ideally suited as ingredients for cement production. The town officials and local chamber of commerce members welcomed the plant owners with open arms and even caused tax concessions to be made to attract the firm to the specific site location. The economic dream of the town fathers came true. The plant within a year of completion employed seventy-five local residents, and anticipated expansion promised employment to many more.

As a result of the cement plant operations, however, industrial smoke, soot, and odors filtered through the clear ocean air. Old-time residents were slow to notice the effect, but seasonal visitors and older people who had sought retirement in this quaint and quiet town soon became aware of the disturbance and the ill results of the polluted air.

The plant is now in its second year of operation. Land values surrounding the plant area have tripled in amount. But to the consternation of the town fathers, the gain in this one area was disastrously offset at a ratio of more than two to one by losses in homesite and recreational property values elsewhere.

The above cases are not isolated instances, but rather are representative of the land use pattern found everywhere where little or no thought is given to the problem of balancing private gains versus social costs. All private gains by necessity incur social costs, and where the latter exceed the gains of the former, measures to protect the general welfare through public and private land use restrictions and controls are in order.

Summary and conclusions

A study of real estate principles and practices cannot successfully be undertaken without a broad understanding of the nature, importance, and character of land upon which all real estate is founded. "Under all is the land." This phrase, taken from the preamble of the Code of Ethics of the National Association of Real Estate Boards, gives further evidence of the importance of land as a commodity in real estate transactions. A practical definition of land includes not only the surface of the earth and the improvements "on" and "to" the land but also the minerals and substances below and the air rights above the ground.

Land, because of its special and peculiar physical and economic characteristics, serves as a *passive* agent which must be utilized locally and combined with other agents of production—labor, coordination, and capital—to be productive and income yielding. Since labor coordination and capital are relatively *mobile* agents that must be compensated first, land income is said to be *residual* in character; provided, however, that land is put to its "highest and best use." An error in land utilization that may cause a reduction in residual income is logically chargeable against the man-made improvements and not against the land. The highest and best use of land is controlled by the law of increasing and diminishing returns. As more and more agents of labor and capital are combined with land, the residual income attributable to land will increase to an optimum under permissible (legal) use and then gradually decrease with intensity of utilization until a point is reached where the total income to land or its economic rent is maximized. It is at this point of maximum income—over the life of the improvements—that land value is established. To guide land into its highest and best use, a study should be made of the socioeconomic factors involved under alternative land uses. For this purpose, a classification of land based on legal, physical, and economic considerations proves helpful.

The competition for land uses, particularly in urban areas, is keen. This competition, because of the large numbers of uninformed buyers and sellers that comprise a real estate market, is largely unorganized and often "cutthroat" in character. To minimize the harmful effects through faulty land utilization upon urban growth and development, studies have been made and aid is available in the establishment of master land use plans through private and governmental agencies. Among the most important considerations that guide appropriate community land use are such factors as soil contour and elevation, directions of prevailing winds, access roads, established school, shopping, and recreational facilities, and public means of transportation.

Fixity of location causes land to be peculiarly vulnerable to surrounding social and economic influences. To safeguard the interests of the many against the selfishness or avarice of the few, public land use controls and private land use restrictions have successfully been invoked. Though land, by and large, is privately owned and utilized for private gain, it is vested with a public interest of sufficient magnitude to warrant use of legal means and moral suasion to bring land into its highest and best use as measured by the maximum good to the greatest number of people.

READING AND STUDY REFERENCES

1. BROWN, ROBERT K., *Real Estate Economics,* Chapter 1. Boston: Houghton Mifflin Company, 1965.

2. CLAWSON, MARION, *Man and Land*, Chapter 10. Lincoln: University of Nebraska Press, 1964.

3. HEBARD, EDNA L., and GERALD S. MEISEL, *Principles of Real Estate Law*, Chapter 2. New York: Simmons-Boardman Publishing Corporation, 1964.

4. HUSBAND, WILLIAM H., and FRANK RAY ANDERSON, *Real Estate*, Chapter 2. Homewood, Ill.: Richard D. Irwin, Inc., 1960.

5. KRATOVIL, ROBERT, *Real Estate Law* (5th ed.), Chapter 2. Englewood Cliffs, N.J.: Prentice-Hall, Inc., 1969.

6. RING, ALFRED A., *Questions and Problems in Real Estate Principles and Practices* (rev. ed.), Chapter 1. Englewood Cliffs, N.J.: Prentice-Hall, Inc., 1972.

7. WEIMER, ARTHUR M., and HOMER HOYT, *Real Estate* (5th ed.), Chapters 4 and 6. New York: The Ronald Press Company, 1966.

2

THE REAL ESTATE BUSINESS

Importance of real estate

Real estate plays a vital part in our national economy. More than two-thirds of the total national wealth is represented by land, land resources, and real estate improvements.[1] The value of all real estate is estimated to be in excess of $1,900 billion, or nearly six times the worth of all mechanical and other equipment of factories and utility industries, including the railroads and airlines. The significant increase in the value of real estate as a factor of production and as a source of governmental revenue is apparent from the latest census studies, which report increases in aggregate local real estate nonexempt assessed valuations for the United States as shown on the following page.[2]

The real estate business engages the attention of many people. It concerns the millions who purchase a home or acquire real estate for business purposes, as well as those who devote their entire time to real estate on

---

[1]Percentage distribution of national wealth indicates the following: structures, 51 percent; land, 16 percent; all other wealth, 33 percent. Source: *Finance Magazine*, January 1967, and U.S. Department of Commerce reports based on John W. Kindrick's unpublished estimates.

[2]U.S. Department of Commerce, Bureau of the Census, *Census of Governments*, Vol. II, 1967.

Year	Assessed Value[3] (Billions)
1860	12
1890	25
1922	125
1957	280
1961	354
1966	499
1971	623 (est.)

their own behalf or on that of others. As a resource and commodity, real estate affects the welfare of all. It is continually being bought, sold, improved, financed, leased, managed, appraised, and otherwise dealt in by related businesses and professions.

Although business generally implies transactions in a commodity for profit, many concerned with real estate are not primarily interested in real estate transactions for profit. Each person requires shelter. Everyone is affected, directly or indirectly, by governmental policies involving housing, taxation, assessment, and regulation of real estate.

The importance of real estate as a source of annual business income can readily be judged by the rising volume of residential construction. On the average each new home sets off a chain reaction affecting the ownership or occupancy of ten existing homes. Not all of these transactions are cleared through business channels. Many homes are retained for investment purposes, rented, or exchanged under private and personal agreements without professional or business aid. Nevertheless, the majority of real estate transfers are reflected in the sizable dollar volume which measures real estate business activity.

More than four million nonfarm real property sales have been closed annually since 1965, according to estimates based on studies of the *Real Estate Analyst Report*.[4] Although the projection upon which these estimates are based is from real estate activity in only about one hundred cities, it gives, nevertheless, a fair picture of the magnitude and scope of the real estate business. Transfer by sale of rural and farm property also contributes notably to the total volume of the real estate business. It is interesting to note that while the average size farm grows larger because of mergers, the value per farm, per acre, has also increased significantly. The April 3, 1970, *Real Estate Analyst Report* indicates average farm size and value per acre for selected years as follows:

Year	Average Farm Size	Average Value per Acre
1950	215 acres	$ 80
1960	298 acres	115
1969	377 acres	187

[3]The ratio of assessed value to sales value of real estate varies from state to state. Latest census studies indicate an average assessment-to-market-value ratio slightly in excess of 55 percent for 1970.

[4]Published by Roy Wenzlick Research Corporation, St. Louis, Missouri.

Development of the real estate business

Although real estate transactions can be traced to biblical days, the real estate business as we know it today is a product of the twentieth century. Early bargain and sale transactions were carried out directly between the owner and purchaser of real estate; lawyers rather than brokers were sought out to safeguard the rights of the parties and to attend to the details involved in property transfer.

Industrialization, urbanization, migration, and territorial settlement made it profitable to subdivide large land holdings into smaller and smaller tracts (standard lots in most of the older and congested cities are still twenty-five feet in width by one hundred feet in depth). Subdividers, developers, and builders were quick to recognize the potential business opportunities and actively encouraged home ownership. Land and home acquisition was wisely urged upon buyers as an investment in the future of the country and a "stake" in the home community.

As steam, electric power, and the automobile increased the mobility of people, property transfers among intercommunity and intracommunity migrants also increased rapidly. There arose the need for specialists who were familiar with the law and requirements for property transfer and who were skilled and able to expedite the buying, selling, renting, financing, appraising, and managing of real estate.

The real estate business at the beginning of this century was largely unorganized and competition was "cutthroat" in character. The *caveat emptor* spirit of the time—"let the buyer beware"—prevailed. No state license laws existed governing activities of real estate brokers and their salesmen until 1917, when California pioneered in the field of legislation.

Urged by the need for establishment of trade ethics, standardization of real estate brokerage practices, commission charges, and servicing fees, leading real estate brokers in the larger communities took steps, during the latter years of the nineteenth century, to organize trade organizations known as *real estate boards*. Unity brought strength. Activities of the boards and those of individual board members were advertised. Publicity given to standardized trade practices increased public trust and confidence in real estate brokerage and related business activities. The success of these individual real estate boards soon attracted the attention of other brokers in the larger communities, and by 1908 a total of forty-five real estate boards were organized.

Exchange of real estate practice and business trend information among the individual real estate boards instilled the need for unity in the real estate business on a national scale and led in 1908 to the formation of the National Association of Real Estate Boards with headquarters in Chicago. Through intelligent leadership and well-organized support on a local board level, the national association grew rapidly in the number of local real estate boards and in individual membership. It is recognized today as being among the leading and most influential trade organizations in the country.

The extent of the growth of the National Association of Real Estate Boards may be best judged by the membership data noted for selected years as follows:

NUMBER OF REAL ESTATE BOARDS AND ACTIVE REALTOR MEMBERS OF THE NATIONAL ASSOCIATION OF REAL ESTATE BOARDS
(*Established in 1908*)

Year	Number of Boards	Active Members
1911	43	3,000
1915	91	6,000
1920	225	10,077
1930	608	18,916
1940	458	14,162
1945	718	24,336
1950	1,100	43,990
1955	1,214	57,240
1960	1,370	68,818
1965	1,518	82,234
1970	1,590	93,400

As a trade organization, the National Association of Real Estate Boards wields a wholesome influence. Among its many accomplishments, the Association points with pride to the following:

1. The drafting and adopting in 1913 of a comprehensive Code of Ethics which has contributed greatly to the transition of real estate from an unorganized business to its current status of a semiprofession.
2. The adoption of the association's emblem and the coining in 1916 of the trademark *Realtor* which is reserved for sole use by the association's active members. The right of the members of the national association to this term has been upheld repeatedly in the supreme courts of the various states.
3. The promotion and standardization of Real Estate License Laws. At present, through association action, license laws are effective in all the states.
4. Broadening and encouraging real estate education through its Committee on Education. This was brought about by promoting the writing of trade and real estate textbooks and the training of members and future Realtors through extension classes and seminars and through courses of study at institutes of higher learning. Today some of the leading colleges in the United States and Canada have active Departments of Real Estate, offering a four-year curriculum leading toward a bachelor of science degree with a major in real estate education. At latest count, 178 universities and colleges were offering one or more of the following courses: Fundamentals of Real Estate, Brokerage, Real Estate Finance, Property Management, Property Valuation, Urban Land Utilization, City Planning, Real Estate Appraising, Real Estate Law, and Housing and Home Ownership.
5. Encouraging home ownership and safeguarding private rights in realty from harmful and unwarranted encroachment by federal legislation. The national association, through its Washington Realtor Committee, has gained great prominence in legislative circles and is now recognized as the authoritative spokesman in all matters concerning real estate.

The national association's greatest single contribution to the furtherance of the real estate business was the drafting, distribution, and enforcement of the Realtor's Code of Ethics. This code, succinctly worded (see Appendix, page 604),contains thirty articles under three major parts which establish:

1. The Realtor's professional relations
2. The Realtor's relation to clients
3. The Realtor's relation to customers and the public

The preamble to the Code of Ethics sets forth that "Under all is the land. Upon its wise utilization and widely allocated ownership depend the survival and growth of free institutions and of our civilization. The Realtor is the instrumentality through which the land resource of the nation reaches its widest distribution. He is a creator of homes, a builder of cities, a developer of industries and productive farms."

In relation to the profession, the code states that the Realtor should willingly share with his fellow members the lessons of his experience. Further, a "Realtor should never publicly criticize a competitor; he should never express an opinion of a competitor's transaction unless requested to do so by one of the principals, and his opinion then should be rendered in accordance with strict professional courtesy and integrity."

In relation to clients a "Realtor should endeavor always to be informed regarding the law, proposed legislation, and other essential facts and public policies"; further, the "Realtor pledges himself to be fair to purchaser or tenant, as well as to the owner whom he represents and whose interests he should protect and promote as he would his own." Also "before offering a property listed with him by an owner, it is the Realtor's duty to advise the owner honestly and intelligently regarding its fair market value."

In relation to the public, the code sets forth that "It is the duty of every Realtor to protect the public against fraud, misrepresentation, or unethical practice in connection with real estate transactions." Furthermore, "A Realtor should never be instrumental in introducing into a neighborhood a character of property or use which will clearly be detrimental to property values in that neighborhood."

Since less than one-third of all active real estate brokers are members of boards of Realtors that are affiliated with the National Association of Real Estate Boards, the real estate trading public must look to the state legislators for enactment of laws that will foster ethical and lawful conduct upon all who engage in real estate business transactions. All states have enacted legislation controlling real estate practices. Most of the states vest authority in real estate commissions that supervise the licensing of qualified real estate brokers and salesmen and enforce commission rules and regulations in the interests of the public. More detailed reference to these license laws and their operations will be made in Chapter 18, "Brokerage."

Since the establishment of the National Association of Real Estate

Boards in 1908, many branches of the real estate business have developed into fields of specialization to a degree that the need for distinct trade and professional organizations has arisen to serve the institutional and professional requirements of those real estate practitioners who choose to specialize.

The associations that were sponsored by, and still are under the jurisdiction of the National Association of Real Estate Boards, are as follows:

Name of Organization	Year Founded
National Institute of Real Estate Brokers	1923
American Institute of Real Estate Appraisers	1932
Institute of Real Estate Managers	1933
Society of Industrial Realtors	1940
Women's Council	1940
Institute of Farm Brokers	1944
Real Estate Counselors	1953
International Real Estate Federation	1956

Other business and professional organizations wholly or partially concerned with real estate activities, but not affiliated with the National Association of Real Estate Boards, include the following:

Name of Organization	Year Founded
The American Title Association	1907
National Association of Building Owners and Managers	1908
Mortgage Bankers Association	1914
American Society of Farm Managers and Rural Appraisers	1929
National Association of License Law Officials	1929
American Right of Way Association	1934
Society of Real Estate Appraisers	1935
Mobile Homes Manufacturers Association	1936
National Apartment Owners Association	1938
Urban Land Institute	1939
National Association of Home Builders of the U.S.	1942
American Society of Appraisers	1952
American Real Estate and Urban Economics Association	1964
National Association of Industrial Parks	1967

Many of the persons engaged in specialized areas of the real estate business have joined these professional organizations in order to improve their standards and practices in the field, to have access to a clearinghouse for information, and to further and protect the interests of the group. It follows, therefore, that the professional associations seek to serve the interests of their members. They keep them informed of developments in the field, sponsor educational meetings and courses of instruction, edit and publish professional publications, publicize the services that the group is prepared to render, and, in general, coordinate promotional activities.

Scope of the real estate business

Although most people think of real estate brokerage when the term *real estate business* is used, the greater part of real estate activity initiates in other areas of real estate specialization. Many who are actively or inactively engaged in real estate are not in the brokerage branch of the business and therefore are not negotiating real estate transactions for others and for a commission but are investing in real estate or mortgages, buying and selling an interest in real estate on their own account, appraising real estate, constructing buildings, or working in a government agency that owns, manages, regulates, taxes, finances, or seeks to stimulate the economic use of real estate. The following outline of the divisions and branches of the business will help to clarify a conception of the real estate field in its broadest sense.

DIVISIONS OF THE REAL ESTATE BUSINESS

I. *Agency*
   1. Brokerage—sales, leases, and mortgages.   2. Management.   3. Appraising.   4. Advisory.   5. Property insurance.
II. *Investment*
   1. Equity.   2. Mortgage.   3. Leasehold.   4. Other interests in real estate.
III. *Operations*
   1. Equity.   2. Mortgage.   3. Leasehold.   4. Miscellaneous.
IV. *Building Construction*
   1. Contracting.   2. Building.   3. Developing.   4. Altering and modernizing.
V. *Government Service*
   1. Taxation and assessment.   2. Acquisition, sale, management, and leasing of government property.   3. Building and land use regulations.   4. Financing.   5. Economic land conservation and use.

Agency

This division of the real estate business is concerned with real estate for or on behalf of others by an agent and for a fee. Agency is further subdivided into specialized services classified as brokerage, management, appraising, advisory, and property insurance. Since the agent does not deal with his own money or property, his compensation is usually based on a percentage of the amount involved in the transaction. For appraising and advisory services the fee depends on time, work details, and degree of responsibility of the assignment. More persons by far are engaged in agency than in any other branch of the real estate business.

In *brokerage* the agent, by reason of his business acquaintances and knowledge, is engaged in the task of bringing together persons desiring to make transactions in real estate, whether to buy, sell, exchange, lease, lend, or borrow on mortgage. The rapid growth of the brokerage business may be ascribed to public realization that the broker is a specialist who can facilitate real estate business transactions at considerable savings of time and expense. Were it not for the fact that the real estate agent renders an essential and economic service, the brokerage business, in this age of enlightenment, would have long since ceased to exist. Compensation for brokerage services are generally established by custom or agreement, and service charges are usually borne by the seller or owner requesting sale or lease transactions, or by the mortgagor (borrower) seeking mortgage funds.

Management is the phase of the real estate business in which the agent takes charge and control of real estate for the owner. He collects rents, leases space, arranges for and superintends repairs, and attends to the general upkeep of the property. His aim is to maintain full occupancy by reputable firms or individuals at maximum rentals consistent with market conditions. A competent manager will keep carrying charges as low as proper care of the property will permit, and protect wisely the owner's interests and investment.

Management as a profession has grown considerably since World War II. This growth can be ascribed partially to increased popularity of real estate as a form of investment and the consequent increase in absentee ownership. Then, too, owners of large buildings have found it profitable to entrust their holdings to management firms. It soon became apparent that a trained manager could cope more effectively and efficiently with the ever-increasing complexities of building equipment and operation. In fact the manager would do all the owner would do himself if able—only better. Management contracts are usually drawn for a period sufficiently long to provide a reasonable opportunity for managerial policies to be placed into effect, and during which the overall return will prove compensatory for the extra efforts expended in the initial year or two of operation. This return or compensation as a rule is based on a percentage of the amount of rents collected. In most real estate offices, the management business is under the supervision of a trained specialist who is aided by a skilled force of employees.

Appraising is that branch of agency in which qualified persons give considered opinions of the value of real estate for others for a fee. Although brokers and managers must be familiar with the principles of property valuation and be able to apply them in their daily work, they will recommend the services of an experienced appraiser whenever value opinions are deemed important. Gone are the days when oral judgments and quick "guesstimating" proved acceptable. Today, appraisal opinions must be substantiated and embodied in a narrative report containing a complete listing and analysis of all pertinent data and a full explanation of the reasoning that led to the appraiser's opinion.

Appraising today is recognized as the most specialized field of the real estate business. In practice this art requires not only broad training in economics, finance, and political science but also ability (gained by experience) to note all the pertinent data that influences value of a given property. The appraiser too must be fully conversant with the legal framework of our capitalistic institutions, including the laws of property and contract. An appraisal opinion, if carefully formulated, will be the logical result of considered judgment of the economic, social, and governmental factors which limit or affect the utility of the property under study. The appraiser's fee, contrary to common belief, should not be based on a percentage of value found. To do so, in fact, is deemed illogical and is ruled unethical by the leading appraising societies and the American Institute of Real Estate

Appraisers. Fees generally are determined in advance and in proportion to time and skill required in the discharge of the assignment. A detailed discussion of the subjects of real estate valuation and appraising will be found in Chapters 23 and 24.

Advisory services are increasing in demand. The complexity of real estate transactions faced by millions of added home and equity owners, and increasing government control of property and its operation, have given rise to a specialist who can evaluate alternative possibilities and suggest a wise course of action. Many brokers, managers, and appraisers act in an *advisory* capacity on real estate matters. This service to owners, investors, mortgage lenders, housing agencies, builders, and developers usually takes the form of an analysis of a particular real estate problem and recommendations for its solution. An agreed fee, as a rule, is charged for such service.

Property insurance is a highly specialized branch of business which is vested with a public interest sufficiently different from real estate brokerage to necessitate separate licensing laws and training requirements in most states. Because of this some may question the inclusion of property insurance as a division of the real estate business. However, service requirements of property owners created a need for effective cooperation between property insurance and real estate brokers. As a result, most real estate brokers and property managers either serve as insurance brokers or include as an integral part of their business organization a special insurance department staffed by trained personnel.

Property insurance, because of its continued need, annual premiums, and relative stability as a source of income, is a welcome partner in the real estate brokerage business. The functions of an insurance broker include study of insurance needs and preparation of complete schedules showing the kinds and amounts of insurance to be carried. The insurance broker generally investigates the physical condition of the properties and recommends changes to reduce hazards, if any, to secure the lowest rate. In fact, the broker acts as the expert adviser to his client in regard to his insurance problems. For this he is customarily paid a commission on the premium by the company with which he places his client's insurance business.

Investment

The investment division of the business may be divided into the three branches of equity, mortgage, and leasehold. In addition, a number of real estate men specialize in miscellaneous kinds of investments, such as tax liens, mortgage bonds, rent loans, and similar transactions.

Equity investments in real estate may take the form of purchase for the individual's use or purchase for dollar income on the investment. Purchase for own use occurs when a business, store, or factory property is acquired by a business concern for business purposes, or when a residence is purchased for the use of the buyer. When such equity investments are made, the first consideration should be the suitability of the property for the intended use. At the same time the soundness of the investment and the possible resale value of the property should not be overlooked.

If equity investments are made for the purpose of getting dollar income, care should be exercised in selecting the investment. The property should be carefully inspected with regard to the safety of the investment and to the extent to which the income is likely to be certain and satisfactory. Location, kind of property, condition of the property, rental conditions, actual and prospective rents, as well as actual and prospective operating expenses, amount and terms of mortgage, and amount of equity investment required are important considerations.

A real estate *mortgage* investment is a loan secured by a mortgage against the property. Such investments are made by individuals or by lending institutions such as savings banks, insurance companies, savings and loan associations, and commercial banks. The mortgage investor is primarily interested in the safety of his investment and in getting a certain and satisfactory return on it. The safety of principal depends upon the kind, location, and condition of the property, upon the amount of income it is capable of producing, upon the percentage ratio of the loan to the value of the property, upon the rate of amortization, and upon real estate market and rental conditions.

The extent to which the mortgage investor is able to get a certain and satisfactory return on the investment is determined by the capacity of the property to earn enough continuously to pay fixed and carrying charges, fair amortization, and a satisfactory contractual rate of interest.

Those engaged in the mortgage investment branch of the business usually have preferences as to the geographical areas in which they will lend, the kinds of property on which they will take mortgages, and the priority of the mortgage lien. Some lenders by preference or law make only first mortgage investments. Others are willing to make second and third mortgage investments so as to get a higher rate of return on the investment even though the risk is greater.

Those who are engaged in the mortgage investment branch of the business make

1. Permanent loans (with or without amortization)
2. Building or construction loans
3. Combination building and permanent loans

A permanent loan is made for a definite period (usually with amortization) at a fixed rate of interest, upon the security of a mortgage on improved property. A building loan is made, as the name implies, to supply all or part of the funds with which to erect a building. The building loan agreement provides usually that the borrower is to erect a certain kind of building on the property covered by the mortgage and that the amount of the loan is to be advanced to him in installments as the building progresses, each installment bearing interest from the time it is advanced. When the building is completed, the loan is payable to the lender, the theory being that the builder will sell the building as soon as completed and repay the loan from the proceeds of the sale. In most instances, the purchaser of the building wants the loan to remain on the property. This situation has resulted in the combination building and permanent loan, which is exactly the same as a building loan except that, like a permanent loan, it is not payable until the expiration of a fixed period. Thus the builder can obtain funds to finance his building operation and continue the loan for the benefit of his purchaser.

The *leasehold investment* branch of the real estate business engages the interest of persons who lease property from the owner for the purpose of securing a rental income from subtenants sufficiently large to yield them a profit over and above required operating expenses and rental payments due the owner on the underlying lease. Some leasehold investors rent improved real estate, modernize it, subdivide it, manage it, and sublet it at a profit. Others lease vacant land, erect a building thereon, and then rent the space in the building at a profit.

Other interests in real estate include investments in tax liens, rent loans, real estate mortgage bonds, notes and certificates, mortgage participations, debentures, preferred stock, and land trust certificates. The persons who are active in this branch of the business are often operators or speculators rather than investors, because they are usually more interested in possible turnover at a profit than in income.

Operations

The operation division of the real estate business embraces those activities that are intended to produce trading profits. The objective of the operator is to buy and sell some interest in real estate for the purpose of making a profit on the transaction. The operator buys and sells, using his own or borrowed capital in successive transactions. His success depends upon rapid turnover at a profit. Some operators are called equity operators because they deal in equities; others are mortgage, leasehold, or mortgage bond operators because they confine their activities to those types of real estate interests. The equity operator may deal in land or in improved real estate. He may also be a builder or developer.

The *operator in land* acquires it either as a speculation for resale at a profit as it stands or for development and resale. In the first instance, the operator has no intention of holding the land for any great length of time but expects a rapid rise in value and believes he can find a purchaser at once for a higher price than he paid. If such rise in value does not occur, he will sell to release his money for another use. The operator will often develop the unimproved land that he has purchased. He subdivides it into building lots of marketable size, lays out streets, curbing, and sidewalks, and installs water, gas, and electricity. Having done so, he hopes to sell the lots for an aggregate amount sufficient to net him a profit over the original cost of the ground plus the expenses of the improvements.

Operation in buildings may be one of the following:

1. Speculative erection, for sale at a profit
2. Speculative buying and selling for profit
3. Buying in order to make alterations and then sell at a profit

In speculative erection, the operator purchases one or more lots and erects a building or buildings thereon, with the expectation of being able to sell the land and buildings at a profit.

Speculative buying and selling of buildings is similar to speculation in land. The operator either thinks he can buy the building for less than he can get for it on immediate resale or believes the price will soon rise, enabling him to sell at a profit.

Many operators have, in recent years, engaged in alteration work. An old building is purchased which, by reason of obsolescence, produces little or no profit. The operator improves and modernizes the building so that it will produce much higher rents. He is then in a position to sell it at a profit over the original cost plus the expense of alteration.

Mortgage lending as an operation in real estate must not be confused with mortgage investing. In the investing branch the lender makes the loan with the expectation of getting an adequate return on the investment. As an operator he expects to sell the mortgage at a profit or gain from servicing the mortgage (accounting, collecting, and record keeping) for the benefit of the investor-lender such as insurance companies, savings banks, trust companies, pension funds, and fiduciary organizations. Mortgage brokerage is compensated at the rate of 1 to 2 percent of the face value of the mortgage loan. This constitutes a "finder's fee" or mortgage initiation charge plus a servicing charge typically computed at the annual rate of 0.5 percent based on outstanding debt balances. Mortgage brokerage has developed into a separate, sizable, and respected branch of the real estate business. The mortgage broker, though he initiates the loan, has no intention of holding the mortgage for income but expects to sell it to an investor, thus releasing his capital for further use.

The *leasehold operation* branch of the business differs from the leasehold investment branch in that the operator expects to make a profit on the sale of the lease, whereas the leasehold investor expects to get a satisfactory return on his leasehold investment. The leasehold operator may get an option on a lease and then sell the option at a profit. Or he may lease property, modernize or subdivide it, and then sell the lease. Some operators are skillful at negotiating leases on partly rented property. Then they rent the vacant space so that the lease is attractive as an investment. And, finally, they sell the lease at a profit.

Building construction

Although many may not agree that building construction is a division of the real estate business, it must be conceded that contractors, builders, developers, and those who alter and modernize buildings are actively engaged in the very important business of improving real estate, of course for profit.

Building construction has therefore been included as one of the main divisions of the real estate business.

The *contracting* branch of the business is conducted by persons who build for others on contract and for a profit. Contractors study the plans and specifications drawn by the architect. They estimate what it will cost to construct the building, and then they bid on the construction job. They include in their bid an amount to cover their overhead and a profit on the job. They may bid a fixed amount for the job or may bid on the basis of the cost plus an amount to cover their overhead and profit.

The *building* branch of real estate is engaged in by persons who use their own capital and borrowed funds to finance the construction of buildings. The builder expects to sell the building that he has built soon after it is finished (at a profit) and then go on to other building ventures. He usually employs contractors to do the actual building for him.

The *developing* branch of the business includes those who buy vacant land or lots for the purpose of erecting thereon private residences. The developer is really an operator who specializes as a builder of homes.

The *altering and modernizing* branch of the business is engaged in by builders who specialize, not in constructing new buildings, but in altering or modernizing old buildings. A profit is made if the altered or modernized building can be sold for more than its cost plus expenditures for altering and modernizing.

Government service

Many departments and agencies of the federal, state, and local governments are concerned with the taxation, purchase, sale, management, regulation, financing, and stimulation of the economic use of real estate. Government service is therefore included as one of the main divisions of the real estate business, even though service at a salary and not for profit is the practice of those who are engaged in the government service division of the business.

One of the oldest government service branches of the real estate business is the *real property taxation* branch. It has to do with the administration of real property tax laws, with the valuing of real estate for tax purposes (assessing), and with the collecting of real estate taxes.

The second government service branch has to do with *acquisition, sale, management, and leasing* of government property. Governments have always bought or acquired by condemnation, sold, leased, managed, or operated property. During World War II, the military went into real estate extensively so as to have adequate bases for military operations, later disposing of such land when no longer required.

The third government service branch of real estate is charged with the responsibility of administering laws that *regulate land use* and govern the kind, quality of construction, and safety of buildings. The regulation of land use is accomplished by means of planning and zoning ordinances, subdivision regulations, and through housing agencies. Building, fire, sanitary, plumbing, tenement house, multiple-dwelling, and housing laws and regulations enforce healthful, safe conditions.

The fourth government service branch of real estate has to do with the *financing* of real estate. Although government agencies are not mortgage lenders in the strict usage of the term, they do subsidize low rental housing construction and operation and have pledged government credit by directly or indirectly guaranteeing certain real estate mortgage loans—directly under local, state, and federal housing legislation; indirectly under the loan guarantee provisions of the Federal Farm Loan Act, the National Housing Act, and the GI Bill of Rights. As a result of the latter forms of legislation, farmers and homeowners find it possible to get lower mortgage interest rates. As will be noted in Chapter 13, "Real Estate Financing," veterans and farmers—on a limited basis—are able to secure direct farm and mortgage loans from governmental agencies. Most of the persons employed in this branch of the business administer the laws and regulations under which the particular agencies operate.

The fifth branch of government service in real estate is concerned with government activities that encourage, stimulate, or regulate the *economic use* of real estate. Laws and ordinances have been enacted and government agencies and departments have been set up for this purpose. The government has created departments of commerce, industry, and economic development which, among other things, encourage and stimulate the economic use of land and the development and preservation of natural resources. Many of these agencies seek to attract commerce and industry to areas that offer particular advantages for the conduct of certain businesses. This promotes economic use of real estate. In addition to performing the function of directing economic use, some of the governmental agencies also regulate land use in order to attain the same objective. Most of the planning boards, zoning commissions, and housing agencies aim to stimulate and regulate the economic use of real estate.

Real estate as a profession

The real estate business in many of its phases of operation, including management, appraising, financing, and advisory consulting, has achieved professional status. In a true sense the real estate expert or agent does not sell anything except his professional "know-how." His skill enables interested parties to come to terms with confidence, each resting assured that expert opinions are based on unbiased consideration of pertinent data. The real service of the professional agent lies in his knowledge of facts as well as law and his specialized experience in matters concerning property value, ownership rights, managerial policy, and financing of total or fractional interests in realty as a commodity.

Relationship of real estate transactions to other professional and business activities

Transaction in and utilization of real estate generally call into play activities of related professional and business enterprises. Although much real estate is still bought and sold without professional aid of any kind, such practices are decreasing as is indicated by real estate brokerage activity reports. Successful acquisition and use of real estate requires not only the services of competent brokers, appraisers, managers, or real estate consultants but also professional or business aid in matters that are legal, technical, or financial in character.

Since real estate, because of its fixity and immobility, cannot be transferred physically by delivery, *rights* in realty and site utilization are conveyed by mutual and contractual agreement between seller and buyer, and transfer of title is symbolized by delivery of a deed. Transfer of rights means transfer of *legal* rights to own, use, and dispose of property; therefore, accurate determination is essential regarding quantity and quality of rights to be conveyed. It is for this reason that legal aid should be relied upon. Essential as may be the services of the real estate broker in speeding the sale for an owner or the selection of a suitable site which he can secure for a buyer at a fair market price, contractual obligations, whether to lease, buy, or sell, should not be undertaken without aid from a legal expert, a real estate attorney.

Abstract and title companies, too, play an important part in real estate transactions. Ownership of record must be traced, and use limitations that former owners imposed upon the property must be determined. Assurance of a good and marketable title, one that a recognized title company is willing to accept for guarantee, should be made a prerequisite of title closing. Often title companies make insurance subject to exceptions and qualifications enumerated in their policies. These exceptions should be considered by competent attorneys to determine whether they affect marketability or otherwise impose objectionable burdens on the property. Title insurance is advisable, and few real estate loans are made without it. The reason is that a title may be perfect according to the record but still prove defective because of facts that records fail to disclose, such as forgeries or missing heirs.

Increased governmental regulations affecting income and taxation make it advisable to seek the services of qualified accountants and tax experts. The accountant is especially trained to ascertain the kind of record system best suited to the enterprise and one that yields comparative cost and income data readily. The tax expert should be consulted on deductions from income attributable to real estate and income and capital gain taxes. His conclusion may influence the time of sale and the method of payment for real estate sold or rented. It may be advantageous to postpone a deal to a later date when the income tax burden may thus be lightened. This expert is familiar with the deductions applicable to real estate ownership, such as taxes, interest, and depreciation.

Surveyors, too, are generally called upon to ascertain encroachments and the physical limits to which property rights extend. Legal descriptions contained in prior deeds are checked, and stakes as a rule are driven to provide markers (monuments) that circumscribe the property. These markers, too, aid real estate brokers when showing the site to a prospect.

Counsel on the physical aspects of buildings is essential at times, especially on new construction or where building alterations are contemplated. In such instances, the services of architects or builders should be engaged. An owner or lessee must make certain that contemplated reconstruction or alteration does not impair the safety of the structure or violate the safety codes or applicable city ordinances.

Banks and trust companies also may furnish sound advice regarding such matters as business trends, interest rates, mortgage and other financing, soundness of the economic situation, and other questions and influences relating to real estate.

The services detailed above, and others, as well as the attending social, economic, and governmental forces that affect the real estate business, will be discussed more fully in succeeding chapters.

READING AND STUDY REFERENCES

1. CASE, FREDERICK E., *Real Estate*, Chapter 1. Boston: Allyn & Bacon, Inc., 1962.
2. HEBARD, EDNA L., and GERALD S. MEISEL, *Principles of Real Estate Law*, Chapter 18. New York: Simmons-Boardman Publishing Corporation, 1964.
3. RING, ALFRED A., *Questions and Problems in Real Estate Principles and Practices* (rev. ed.), Chapter 2. Englewood Cliffs, N.J.: Prentice-Hall, Inc., 1972.
4. UNGER, MAURICE A., *Real Estate* (4th ed.), Chapter 1. Cincinnati: South-Western Publishing Co., 1969.
5. WEIMER, ARTHUR M., *Business Administration; An Introductory Management Approach*, Chapter 1. Homewood, Ill. Richard D. Irwin, Inc., 1966.
6. WEIMER, ARTHUR M., and HOMER HOYT, *Real Estate* (5th ed.), Chapter 2. New York: The Ronald Press Company, 1966.

3

THE REAL ESTATE MARKET

Definition and nature of market

The term *market* has many meanings. As commonly defined, a market may be:

1. A meeting of people (buyers and sellers) who wish to exchange goods and money
2. A public place (as in a town) or a large building where a market is held
3. The region in which any commodity can be sold
4. The course of commercial activity by which the exchange of commodities within a market area is affected; as, "The market is active"
5. A body of goods; as, "the stock market," "the beef market"

The term *market* as applied to real estate transactions is a title conferred by general usage rather than one of precise economic meaning or measurement. Of the market definitions enumerated above, only the fourth one can be applied with any assurance to real estate and then only because of the broad and all-inclusive conception that a market is a "course of commercial activity by which the exchange of commodities within a market area is affected."

The market for real estate thus cannot be described accurately as a meeting of buyers and sellers who truck and barter for commodities which are readily measurable as to quality and quantity, nor can it be described as a public or trading place for commodities such as produce, cattle, stock, or bond securities.

In the early history of land development and community settlement, it was a practice to sell through voluntary auction entire farms, parts of, or entire estates, and even building sites in areas under planned development. These voluntary auctions, which were local in character, did not prove satisfactory as marketing methods. The discontinuance of the voluntary land auction practice has severed the weak link by which real estate as a commodity was traded at a given place in terms of "bargain and sale" which the average person has in mind when speaking of a *market*.

Function of market

The function of a market is to facilitate the exchange of goods. Goods are exchanged when market operations establish a price at which buyers and sellers find it mutually advantageous to trade. The market thus provides a medium for the balancing of supply and demand at prevailing price levels. The higher the degree of standardization of the goods marketed and the greater the mobility of transfer to the various market outlets, the quicker the forces of supply and demand come into balance at prices that reflect competitive values.

Markets generally function as distribution centers and as a rule are highly organized. Modern means of transportation and communication have facilitated central and efficient control of market operations on a regional and national scale. Uniform pricing and trading terms evidence the existence of market controls, and the effectiveness of such controls is amply illustrated in the marketing and distribution of such commodities as automobiles, tobacco, steel, chemicals, and drugs.

Characteristics of the real estate market

Real estate as a commodity has distinct and peculiar characteristics that affect its ownership and transfer by sale. Because of these characteristics and the nature of real estate, as explained in Chapter 1, the real estate market differs from other markets as follows:

1. Market is local in character
2. Transactions are private in nature
3. Commodity is not standardized
4. Market is unorganized and lacks central control
5. Absence of short selling
6. Poor adjustment of market supply and demand

Market is local in character. Fixity of location causes the market for real estate to be *local* in character. As a commodity real estate cannot be moved from place to place. An oversupply of land or land improvements in a midwestern state is of no avail to fill a market demand for like land or improvements in another region or metropolitan center. Real estate must be employed where it is, and because of its fixity in geographic location it is extremely vulnerable to economic effects caused by shifts in local demand.

Fixity in location, too, creates the need for a real estate specialist who is familiar with local and environmental market conditions and with the applicable physical, economic, and legal characteristics of real estate as a commodity. A real estate broker in Los Angeles, California, cannot well advise a homeowner or businessman seeking a site in Atlanta, Georgia. It's possible, of course, that the California broker is familiar with real estate market conditions in Georgia, but absence from the scene of local market operations, if only for a few days' time, may be an interval long enough in which revolutionary changes in the supply-demand relationship of local real estate could take place. As noted in Chapter 2, the business of real estate requires the services of approximately one-half million brokers and brokers' sales personnel in order to meet the *local* needs of real estate buyers and sellers.

Real estate transactions are private in nature. Real estate transactions are principally private in nature. Buyers and sellers meet in confidence and their bid and offering prices are rarely publicized. Even to this date the practice of not disclosing the transaction price is generally followed. Deeds of record do not specify the actual dollar exchange, and secrecy is attempted by the legal phrase that the transfer of real estate was in "consideration of one dollar and other good and valuable considerations." Documentary stamps, required by law, and based on dollar value of the transaction, do give a clue to the transaction price, but the possibility of understating or overstating the stamp requirements must be considered in weighing documentary tax data as evidence of market prices. Privacy in transaction is directly attributable to the specialized nature of real estate as a commodity which requires personal business meetings between the seller and buyer, or agents authorized to act on their behalf.

Commodity is not standardized. Lack of similarity in kind is another real estate characteristic which imposes special marketing conditions. No two parcels of real estate are geographically alike. In respect to location, each parcel of real estate is unique. Even where physical similarity seems apparent, legal and situs characteristics may affect the relative value of each. On the other hand, physically different parcels of real estate may serve economically identical purposes and be exactly exchangeable in value. To illustrate, two residential sites equal in width and depth may support identical buildings, similar not only in floor plan and building material but also as to details of building construction and time of completion. Still these two real estate properties, equal as far as inspection may disclose, may warrant different values or permit different uses because of intangible legal or economic limitations. One property may be zoned residence "A" and the other "B," permitting different site utilization for one but not the other. One property may be subject to deed restrictions limiting its use for high-class residential purposes; the other may be free of any contractual limitations and thus subject to any legal use. Easements, utility rights-of-way, or any of many legal encumbrances may affect the title of one and not the other property.

Lack of standardization, principally, is caused by the nature of land location. Each parcel of land is geographically fixed and has distinct legal descriptions which, as a rule, are accurately set forth in public tax, plat book, or land map records. Because of specific geographic location, no one parcel of real estate may legally be substituted for another without the purchaser's consent, and specific performance on the seller's part may be enforceable by law.

Market is unorganized and lacks central control. Attempts to centralize or organize real estate activities on a large scale have failed because of the nature of the commodity traded. Fixity in location and lack of standardization of real estate as a commodity account for the wide fluctuations in value and number of transactions that characterize the real estate market. Such fluctuations are notable not only in different regions throughout the nation but also within a state or single community. The market for U.S. farmland, for instance, may be judged good or active when based on number of sales and increase in overall and relative values. But this overall "favorable" average may be a composite derived from an extraordinary demand and increase in value of farmland in the wheat, corn, tobacco, or cattle-raising regions, as well as from substantial softening in demand and decrease in value of farmland traded in the cotton belt region. Similar divergent real estate activity is experienced in urban areas. Whereas average national real estate activity may favorably advance, individual cities may show increases in varying degrees or even record notable decreases in real estate business activity. Thus real estate activity in Phoenix, Arizona, Los Angeles, California, or Miami Beach, Florida, may record index sales 200 percent or more above the national average while sales in Tacoma, Washington, and Portland, Maine, may experience over the same period notable declines in real estate activity. The fixity of real estate as a commodity thus not only prevents the transfer of real estate from an area of low demand to one of high demand but makes centralized control of market transactions or the equalization of supply and demand beyond the limits of a local market area inoperative.

Absence of short selling. Dissimilarity of real estate as a commodity and the legal right to specific performance discourage speculation and prevents market operations known as "short selling." Short selling is the practice of selling, when prices are high, securities or commodities that the speculator does not own. Anticipating a drop in market prices, the speculator hopes to cover these short sales by purchasing at lower prices the quantities previously sold. This he expects to do at the time when delivery of the securities or commodities is due and as a rule days or weeks later. The speculator hopes that the time interval will create a market favorable to him. The practice of short selling can, however, apply only to articles or goods that are legally fungible or substitutable such as grain, corn, or shares of stock. The practice of short selling in the grain or security markets, for instance, not only is legally permissible but is welcomed as a stabilizing trading influence by necessitating the placing of purchase orders, to fill short selling commitments, when market activity normally might be low or even panicky. Since real estate as a commodity is nonfungible or non-substitutable it is not subject to the market-stabilizing practice of short selling. Lack of centralized control as well as absence of short selling causes wide price fluctuations in real estate transactions as well as "sticky" market operations that may lead to a "freeze" or suspension of real estate sales and related market activities.

Poor adjustment of market supply and demand. Although fixity in real estate location, as stated above, prevents equalization of supply and demand on a regional or national level, it is the durability of real estate that causes maladjustments in supply and demand on a local market level. Land itself is indestructible and physically will stand forever. Improvements, if properly maintained, will last a hundred years or more. Thus, where demand suddenly falls, for any reason, inability to adjust (withdraw) supply will cause real estate to become a "drug" on the market. An over-supply of real estate creates a "buyer's market" which readily results in lower purchase price offerings and keen competitive trade practices.

On the other hand, a sudden increase in demand for real estate is also difficult to meet. The housing problem caused by shifting of population due to defense or war efforts is an illustration in kind. It takes weeks or even months to construct a single home; construction conditions must be favorable for the entire building industry to supply in excess of one and one-half million dwelling units during a given year. Even at an anticipated favorable rate of home construction, averaging one and one-half million starts per year, it would require thirty-five years just to replace the nation's housing stock. Based on conservative estimates, another ten years of construction time are required to provide replacement for housing destroyed in interim years by wear and tear, action of the elements, and circumstances causing functional and economic obsolescence. The time required to bring the forces of supply and demand into reasonable balance, as well as the uncertainty of keeping these price-determining forces in equilibrium, makes real estate market transactions a calculated business venture. The risks involved are reflected in higher interest rates, especially those applicable to the equity part of a real estate investment.

Kinds of real estate markets

Although reference was made in general to real estate market characteristics, in practice market operations are classified according to type of property traded. The kinds of real estate markets recognized as specialized fields of operation include the following:

1. Residential
2. Commercial
3. Industrial
4. Farm
5. Special purpose properties

Each of these broad fields of market operations is further subdivided into smaller and more specialized market areas as follows:

Residential Market—(1) urban, (2) suburban, and (3) rural housing
Commercial Market—(1) office buildings, (2) store properties, (3) loft
buildings, (4) theaters, (5) garages, and (6) hotels and motels
Industrial Market—(1) factories, (2) utilities, and (3) mining
Farm Market—(1) timberland, (2) pastureland, (3) ranches, (4) orchards,
and (5) open farmland (for produce, tobacco, cotton, and so on)
Special Purpose Properties—(1) cemeteries, (2) churches, (3) clubs, (4)
golf courses, (5) parks, and (6) public properties (buildings, highways,
streets, and the like)

Each of these specialized areas of the real estate market is further classified as to rights of ownership or use. Thus, it is in order to speak of (1) a
rental market involving transfer of space and (2) an *equity* market involving transfer of real estate ownership. The interrelation and function of
these markets will be discussed in the chapters on real estate selling, management, and valuation.

ANALYSIS OF THE REAL ESTATE MARKET

Nature of real estate as an investment

As an investment, real estate requires large capital outlays. To be productive land must be combined with units of labor and capital. The improvements placed on land, generally, far exceed in dollar volume the market price or worth of vacant land. The improvements to land ratio may
vary from a low of 1 to 1 in the 100 percent business district, that is, one
dollar of improvements per dollar of vacant land value, to a ratio of 5 to
10 to 1 in residential and commercial land use, and 50 to 1 for land developed for industrial purposes.

The large expenditures required to put real estate into productive use
call for careful analysis of the nature of real estate as an investment. Capital outlays are made in anticipation of future returns from which the purchaser expects to recoup his dollar investments. Based on experience records, average residential or commercial improvements must yield a net
income extending over thirty to fifty years in order that required amortization payments necessary to write off the building investment are met. Even
if gross income—income before deduction of operating expenses, including
taxes, maintenance, and so forth—is used as a market guide, an average of
eight to ten years gross income must be aggregated for invested capital to
"turn over" once. Such slow capital turnover calls for great care in the
analysis of the real estate market particularly in forecasting the certainty,
quantity, and quality of future property rights to income.

Forces influencing real estate supply and demand

The real estate market is sensitive to changes in the balance of economic,
political, and social forces that influence the supply and demand for real
estate. Among the more important influences that must be considered in
an analysis of the real estate market are the following:

1. Changes in number of population and family composition
2. Wage levels, employment opportunities, and stability of income
3. Personal savings, supply of mortgage funds, and interest rates
4. Rent levels, vacancies, and rent control
5. Taxation and land use control
6. Supply of land, cost of land, labor, and building materials
7. Changes in the arts and building obsolescence

Changes in number of population and family composition. Most real estate transactions involve the transfer of space or ownership in residential realty. This is understandable since shelter or housing constitutes one of the basic human needs—next to food and clothing. The demand for shelter varies of course with changes in population and in family composition. The basic forces that contribute to a demand for housing arise from:

1. Increase in population
2. Migration of population
3. Changes in family formation
4. Aging and changes in family requirements

Since the year 1900, U.S. population has increased at an average rate of 1.8 million persons per year. Although this growth was due in a large measure to immigration during the years 1900 to 1930, internal growth resulting from an extraordinary number of marriages and an increased birth rate in the years following World Wars I and II are principally accountable for the continued population growth during the past two decades. This growth of population supports a demand for approximately six hundred thousand new dwelling units per year. The market for residential real estate is further affected by the unusual mobility of population and the resultant migration from rural to urban centers, and more recently from urban to suburban areas. America is facetiously called a nation on wheels, but the real estate market offers statistics to support the validity of this statement. Rental space is subject to high tenant turnover and, in addition, approximately 8 percent of the total housing supply clears annually through the real estate market.

Changes in family formation have further caused an increase in housing demand. Based on census data, an average of 490 persons were reported per hundred families in 1890. In 1970 the number of persons per hundred families declined to 320.[1] This represents a decrease of 170 persons per hundred families over a span of eighty years. To state it differently, whereas 490 persons caused a demand for 100 dwelling units in 1890, the same number of persons required 153 units in 1970. Thus housing demand has increased 53 percent due to changes in family size. This continuing trend, caused to a large extent by the preference of affluent single persons as well as widows and widowers to occupy independent dwelling units, in addition to housing requirements attributable to internal migration and "undou-

---

[1] U.S. Department of Commerce, Bureau of the Census, Series P–25, No. 449, August 18, 1970.

PERCENT DISTRIBUTION OF THE
FOR THE YEAR 1940 AND
BY AGE

1940

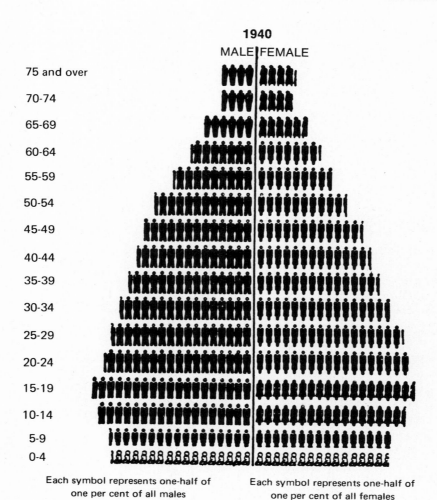

MALE | FEMALE

75 and over

70-74

65-69

60-64

55-59

50-54

45-49

40-44

35-39

30-34

25-29

20-24

15-19

10-14

5-9

0-4

Each symbol represents one-half of   Each symbol represents one-half of
one per cent of all males   one per cent of all females

bling" of families, creates an annual market demand estimated at 350,000
dwelling units. The aggregate estimated demand for housing from all
causes, exclusive of replacements, currently totals 950,000 dwelling units
per year. If replacements are added, 1,600,000 dwelling units must be constructed annually to keep pace with American family housing needs.

A factor of increasing significance in an analysis of the real estate market is the noticeable change in the age composition of the U.S. population.
People live longer and are better cared for through pension and social se-

POPULATION OF THE UNITED STATES
FORECAST FOR THE YEAR 2000
AND SEX

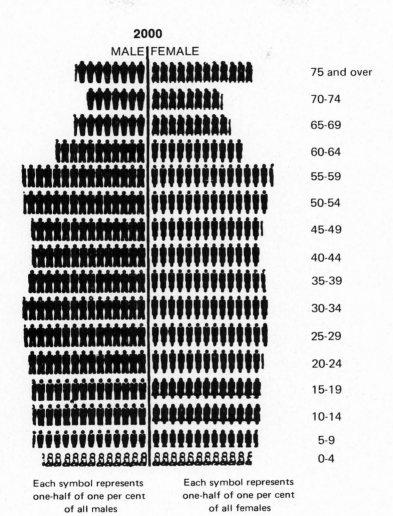

2000

MALE｜FEMALE

	75 and over
	70-74
	65-69
	60-64
	55-59
	50-54
	45-49
	40-44
	35-39
	30-34
	25-29
	20-24
	15-19
	10-14
	5-9
	0-4

Each symbol represents   Each symbol represents
one-half of one per cent   one-half of one per cent
      of all males   of all females

curity plans than ever before. These aging people demand independent
dwelling units in increasing number and seek retirement in areas where
mild climate keeps housing and clothing costs at a minimum. As a result,
during the past decade states such as California, Arizona, New Mexico, and
Florida experienced extraordinary population gains and great activity in
real estate market transactions. Because of the importance of age composition as a factor influencing the real estate market Chart 1, showing the estimated distribution of total population by age and sex for the year 2000 as

compared with the year 1940, was prepared from special reports of the Bureau of the Census. An inspection of this chart discloses that whereas only 20.2 percent of total population was fifty years old or over in 1940, 33.0 percent is expected to exceed that age in the year 2000.

Wage levels, employment opportunities, and stability of income. The real estate market is sensitive to changes in wage levels, employment opportunities, and stability of income. Rental payments and housing costs are closely geared to ability to pay. In fact, there are definite "rules of thumb" accepted by mortgage lenders and federal housing agencies under which total housing costs should not exceed 20 to 30 percent of the wage earner's income. Homes, too, can now be purchased on time-payment plans, as can other consumer goods, and payments are made out of income on a monthly basis. The introduction of the amortization mortgage which made home purchases possible "on time" has in fact revolutionized the residential real estate market and, since World War II, proven a bonanza to the house-building industry. During the decade 1940 to 1950 and in spite of wartime restrictions, home ownership increased from 43.6 percent of total occupied dwelling units to 55.0 percent. Since the year 1950, home ownership has increased at the rate of 0.7 percent per year reaching 61.0 percent in 1960. During the decade 1960 to 1970 the rate of increase in home ownership, due to the construction of large apartment complexes, has slowed to 0.2 percent per year reaching a high of 64.4 percent in 1970. A maximum ratio of 70 percent owner occupancy is estimated for the year 2000.

Personal savings, supply of mortgage funds, and interest rates. Higher wage and salary payments are significantly reflected in the increase of total disposable personal income which—after correction for changes in purchasing power—rose from $155 billion in 1929 to $614 billion in 1970. Concurrently, estimated savings of individuals rose in excess of 600 percent during the same period. These personal savings and investments by insurance companies have provided a great reservoir of mortgage funds that have sustained the home-building boom since World War II. The mortgage loan insurance and guarantee policies underwritten by the Federal Housing Administration and the Veterans Administration have proven still more important.

Mortgage credit policy may be called the barometer of the residential real estate market. A tightening or liberalization of mortgage lending policy has a direct and immediate influence on home construction and real estate market activity. Most homes are bought on credit. Terms, therefore, are an important part of a purchase transaction and often influence the transaction price. Real estate brokers are well aware of the role that terms play in bringing about a sale. It is not uncommon, therefore, to see new homes advertised for *XX* dollars of down payment and *YY* dollars of payment per month, without reference to the total transaction price. To most buyers who enter the market with small equity down payments, price undoubtedly means *size of monthly payments*. With uninsured (conventional) mortgage payments on single residential homes now extending over twenty-five- and thirty-year periods and Federal Housing and Veterans Administration underwritten mortgage loans extending over thirty-five and forty years, the home ownership market for real estate will in fact revert to a rental market with government acting as the benevolent landlord.

Rent levels, vacancies, and rent control. Rental activity, particularly in metropolitan areas, still forms an important part of the total real estate market. There are still approximately 22 million dwelling units that are renter occupied, and the owners of these units are much concerned in securing a fair return *on*, and adequate return *of*, their investment. The rental market is highly competitive; in areas not subject to rent control, rent levels are in direct relation to costs of housing and contractual service requirements. If rents are set too high in relation to servicing costs, tenants will economize on space and vacancies will result. Since housing supply, as noted above, cannot be withdrawn from the market, competition to maintain full occupancy will force prices into line. In the analysis of the real estate market, a study of prevailing vacancy ratios to total rental supply should prove of interest. Ratios exceeding 3 to 5 percent are indicative of either an oversupply in rental space or overpricing. In either case, downward adjustments in rents are necessary to stimulate demand. The importance of vacancy ratios as a measure of the economic health of rental housing has caused real estate boards in the larger communities to maintain occupancy records as an index of real estate market activity and guide to broker members.

During periods of economic stress, when war or defense efforts necessitate sudden shifts of population, housing supply in affected areas proves inadequate and competitive bidding for available housing units causes rents to rise unduly. To protect renters from possible exploitation, rent control laws are enacted to maintain price stability. Such laws, though justified when enacted during periods of emergency, work great injustice to the owners, particularly when unreasonably invoked or kept in force beyond the period of economic need. A more detailed discussion of the social, political, and economic impact of rent control on the market for real estate is presented in Chapter 27.

Taxation and land use controls. Taxation is one of the more important forces that influence the supply and demand for real estate. This force may be positive or negative and is often used as a governmental tool to compel or deter real estate development or to direct employment of land for particular uses. In many urban areas, particularly those of high population concentration, vacant land is assessed and taxed in excess of its contribution to overall real estate market value in order to stimulate its use and thus indirectly discourage the holding of vacant urban land for speculative purposes. The wisdom of using the power of taxation for legislative purposes will be discussed in succeeding chapters. It should be stressed, however, that as a market force, taxation policy affects importantly the supply and demand for real estate.

In states where homestead laws are operative, and where owner occupants are given tax exemptions up to certain limits of the assessed value of their property, the burden of municipal costs is shifted largely to owners of business and tenant-occupied properties. Such tax policy is directly designed to encourage home ownership and the use of land for residential owner occupancy. Homestead laws have proven popular with states that seek to develop land with the aid of migrant settlers. As a marketing device, the law is also popular with real estate brokers, builders, and suppliers of home furnishings.

Other land use controls, whether of private or public nature, also affect real estate market operations. Controls, generally, are designed to direct real estate use and development in the interest of the community at large and to protect the investment of real estate owners from exploitation or misuse of neighboring lands.

Supply of land, cost of land, labor, and building materials. The availability of land and the cost of land, labor, and building materials affect the supply side of the real estate market. Though physically abundant, land that is economically usable is often in short supply. Improvements in the form of access roads, drainage facilities, water, and other community utilities must be added to "raw" land before it ordinarily can be subdivided and offered for sale through marketing channels. Since such improvements are costly and can be successfully carried out only with community sanction and on a relatively large scale, a scarcity of economic land often occurs. Scarcity of building sites in turn causes upward pricing of real estate holdings to a point where community development and real estate market activities may be adversely affected. On the other hand, speculative optimism, unchecked by community foresight and planning, may cause economic land to be produced in quantities too great to be absorbed by prevailing demand, creating an oversupply which may depress the market for real estate for many months or even years.

Cost of labor and building materials also affects importantly the market supply of real estate. Where labor and material prices rise faster than the "lagging" prices of existing real estate improvements, new construction activity will be slowed until demand prices and costs of improvement again attain an equilibrium. This "spurt and coast" cycle of building activity is particularly evident during and immediately following periods of war or defense emergencies.

Changes in the arts and building obsolescence. More buildings are torn down than fall down. This destruction of often physically sound improvements is caused by changes in the arts and by building obsolescence. Rapid advance in building design and methods of construction have sparked the demand for modern homes that offer greater conveniences, hence greater amenities of living. Improvements in home heating, lighting, insulation, soundproofing, air conditioning, and interior design have brought about an active demand for home modernization and replacement that is estimated to sustain a high level of real estate market activities for many years to come. Based on surveys of the Federal Housing Agency, more than six hundred thousand dwelling units, or 40 percent of anticipated new construction, will be required each year to meet replacement demands caused by physical deterioration, changes in the arts, and building obsolescence.

The real estate cycle

Crystal ball gazing to foretell future events is a favorite American pastime. This practice in the field of business is more formally known as *economic forecasting*. Business necessitates forecasting, for the merchant today must stock up to meet the anticipated demand for tomorrow. It is understandable, therefore, that businessmen in general take a keen interest in scientific methods that may foreshadow the course of future events. Today most of the larger business firms rely on services of skilled analysts who are thoroughly trained in the field of economics. As a result, statistical services are made available, commercially, by many specialized consulting firms.

Since the causes of yesterday or yesteryear may result in the effects anticipated for tomorrow, a study of past business events is generally accepted as basic to scientific forecasting of business trends. The Cleveland Trust Company has made studies of general business activities covering a period of more than one hundred years and has computed relative trends in relation to a norm of business activity. These studies reveal a rhythmic change from major booms to major business depressions interspersed by minor periods of prosperity and minor business recessions. The regularity of the periodic business swings from boom to bust has led to the belief in the existence of a business cycle which, subject to minor changes and disturbances, will inevitably repeat its swings. In retrospect, the pendular movements of business activity from optimism to overoptimism, to caution, to pessimism, and to panic appear as a logical sequence and are traceable to violations of economic laws of supply and demand and to lack of central business control. In recent years, the application of economic checks and balances under federal government controls has counteracted cyclical economic behavior, and doubt is now expressed whether under continued maintenance of such controls, economic history will repeat itself.

This doubt is supported by the fact that the business boom that commenced in 1940 has extended over a period more than twice as long as any prior business upswing since 1850. Undoubtedly governmental policies of "easy" money, price controls, and price inflation have kept the current boom "in business." Whether such policies or governmental efforts to control business operation can effectively continue, however, is open to reasonable doubt.

Relation of real estate cycle to business cycle

Real estate activity, too, has experienced cyclical swings which have reoccurred with rhythmic regularity. Based on a study by Roy Wenzlick and Company, real estate booms and depressions, though varying in intensity, have followed at intervals of fifteen to twenty years. This real estate cycle study indicates a definite relationship between real estate and general business activity, the principal difference being the greater peak intensity of real estate booms and depressions and the longer years, that is, the span of the cycle. As a rule, the downward swing of the real estate cycle precedes that of the general business recession and lags behind the period of general business recovery. The greater intensity of real estate booms and depressions, as well as the longer life of the cycle span, is a direct effect of the inflexible and peculiar economic characteristics of real estate that influence its supply and demand as noted above. Once an oversupply of housing saturates the real estate market, economic inability to adjust the supply to active demand creates abnormal vacancy ratios and competitive pricing conditions upon which real estate depressions have fed in the past.

The real estate cycle is, in fact, a composite of the general business and housing or construction cycles. The former operates on the demand side, positively or negatively through increased or decreased overall employment wage levels, supply of mortgage funds, interest rates, and personal savings. The latter, on the supply side, reacts to population changes, family formation (excess of marriages over divorces and family dissolution through deaths), vacancy ratios, and cost of land and housing supplies in relation to prevailing and anticipated rental levels.

Irrespective of the validity of the cycle theory, a study of real estate economic market behavior and the causes that influence its supply and demand is deemed essential as a guide to those who serve the market in a business capacity or who seek sound real estate investment opportunities. For those who enter the real estate market, a knowledge of the social, economic, and political forces that affect real estate as a commodity and of the legal requirements which govern the transfer of real estate and limit its ownership and use is an essential and basic prerequisite.

READING AND STUDY REFERENCES

1. BROWN, ROBERT K., *Essentials of Real Estate*, Chapter 6. Englewood Cliffs, N.J.: Prentice-Hall, Inc., 1970.

2. *Fact Book 1969*, United States Savings and Loan League, pp. 7–52. Chicago, 1970.

3. HUSBAND, WILLIAM H., and FRANK RAY ANDERSON, *Real Estate*, Chapter 12. Homewood, Ill.: Richard D. Irwin, Inc., 1960.

4. MARTIN, PRESTON, *Real Estate Principles and Practices*, Chapter 21. New York: The Macmillan Company, 1959.

5. RATCLIFF, RICHARD U., *Real Estate Analysis*, Chapter 10. New York: McGraw-Hill Book Company, 1961.

6. RING, ALFRED A., *Questions and Problems in Real Estate Principles and Practices* (rev. ed.), Chapter 3. Englewood Cliffs, N.J.: Prentice-Hall, Inc., 1972.

7. UNGER, MAURICE A., *Real Estate* (4th ed.), Chapter 2. Cincinnati: South-Western Publishing Co., 1969.

4

REAL ESTATE OWNERSHIP
AND INTERESTS

The concept of ownership embraces the rights of:

1. Possession
2. Control
3. Enjoyment
4. Disposition

Ownership is either absolute or limited. Historically, ownership of real property is based on possession, for it was reasoned that in the vast majority of cases the true owner was in possession. Occupation and normal use spell possession, and possession is acquired through physical control and domination. Hence, possession is a question of fact. Such possession and control result in the enjoyment of the benefits of the use of land for shelter and cultivation and include the right to alienate or transfer these rights to others, subject to certain limitations and restrictions imposed by the state, by law, or created by contract.

Development of property rights

Undoubtedly personality and its right of ownership were recognized far earlier than any rights in land. At first man lived by hunting, fishing, and foraging for fruits and berries. His home life was simple. He had no particular use for the land. A few crude weapons, some rough clothing, and several cooking utensils served his purposes. He lived in a cave or hut and moved from place to place as game or climate led him.

Later, man domesticated animals and began the wandering life that water and pasturage for his flocks dictated. Not until he reached the stage of development in which he was head of a large family or clan did he begin to have settled places of abode. As his numbers increased, as the need for hunting and ranging the flocks farther afield arose, and as the number of very young and very old people in the tribe grew larger, actual settlements became necessary. These had to be so located as to afford maximum protection by a minimum number of warriors. Hence we find London in a swamp and Paris on an island in the Seine. Here in our own country, aborigines lived in cliffs and mesas.

Still later agriculture began. Land was cleared close to villages. Crops were conveniently near and were a more satisfactory source of food than were flocks and herds. At first this land was owned by the village in communal proprietorship and allotted each year. As time went on, the farmer as a class developed.

Now it is simple to trace the development of property rights. What one has worked to produce, he wishes to keep. The harder he has worked, the more he values it; and what he values he wants recognized as his. Naturally personal property rights came into being first; realty then had no value. But later, when agriculture began, the man who had laboriously cleared the land, grubbed out stumps and underbrush, and cultivated the soil wanted his possession respected and assured to him. So did property rights in land come about.

Feudal and allodial systems

Much of what has just been written pertains to almost prehistoric conditions. Since those times, two well-defined but very different types of land ownership have developed. Historically they are interesting and well worth fuller examination than the scope of this book permits. The feudal system conceived the absolute ownership of all land to be in the king or sovereign, the subject having merely a feud or right to use the land in return for services. The allodial system, on the other hand, recognized the principle that land might be owned by an individual, subject to no proprietary control of the sovereign. Both of these systems existed in England. When the United States was settled, the theory of the allodial system was the one upon which our law of real property was based. The allodial system is the result of the breakdown of the feudal system, which left its mark on our theory of real property ownership. This is evidenced by such heritages as the right of the state to impose taxes, to exercise its police power, and its right to escheat.

Governmental limitations on ownership

The allodial system, although free of the "services" and "duties" of the feudal system, did, nevertheless, impose certain political rather than proprietary obligations on the landowner. The latter had to repair bridges, roads, and fortresses. In this country, landowners have duties and ines-capable limitations on ownership, which are enforced for the mutual wel-fare of the community, such as:

1. Police power of the government
2. Eminent domain
3. Right of taxation
4. Escheat to the state

Police power. The police power is a sovereign power inherent in state government and exercised or delegated by it to the village, city, county, or other governing agency to restrict the use of realty in order to protect the well-being of its citizens. Under police power, the rights in property, its use, and occupation may be restricted—without compensation whatsoever —when government deems such restrictions necessary in the interest of the welfare, morals, or safety of its citizens. It is to this power that citizens take recourse for city planning and zoning as well as for building, urban, and subdivision control. Regulations of rent control authorities, building, fire, and health departments are exercises of the police power and are in fact limitations upon the "use" of land.

Eminent domain. The right of eminent domain is the power inherent in the governmental body to "take" an owner's land, by due process of law, when the necessity arises. Only two requirements must be met: the use must be public, and just compensation must be paid to the owner. Whether or not the owner wants to surrender his land makes no difference, nor can he set his own price. His desires are not consulted; but a fair valuation, fixed by expert appraisers or by due process of law, is paid him. Land is obtained for streets, parks, public buildings, and other public or social pur-poses through the exercise of this power.

Right of taxation. Under the right of taxation, the state levies taxes for its support and for the maintenance of all its varied branches that protect and benefit its citizens. It is fair that citizens should pay for the protection and benefit they receive. Land, because of its permanence and accessibility, is a convenient article to tax and is usually the basis for local taxation. If such taxes, when levied, are not paid in due course, the owners may lose their land as the result of tax law enforcement.

Escheat. Under the allodial system, escheat does not limit land owner-ship, but rather provides for the reversion or escheat of land to the state where an owner of land dies leaving no heirs and not disposing of the land by will. This, however, seldom happens, for generally, difficult as it may sometimes be, heirs can be found. Since it is not possible to conceive of land becoming unowned, that is, owned by no one, the law of escheat to the state provides a logical solution.

Contractual limitations on ownership

Contractual limitations on ownership are affected by:

1. Deed restrictions—limiting by covenant the use of the property described therein either perpetually or for a limited time.

2. Easements—in favor of others over the property, such as rights of ingress and egress. Such easements are created in deeds or other indentures and in contracts, such as agreements giving the right to remove top soil, cut timber, mine subsurface minerals, and similar rights.
3. Leases—giving tenants or lessees the right to use premises for certain periods of time, for stated purposes at agreed-upon periodic rental payments.
4. Mortgages—imposing liens on the ownership. The use of land as security for indebtedness, for example, makes the owner's title subject to such encumbrance and creates certain obligations on the part of the owner limiting his ownership.

Involuntary limitations on ownership

Rights of possession, control, enjoyment, and disposition of realty are further limited and often imperiled by involuntary liens imposed by law. Such liens, which may be specific or general in character arise out of lawful claims to have certain debts paid out of the debtor's property, usually by means of sale. Specific liens are those that encumber directly a given parcel of real estate and usually one specifically benefited or made subject to the lien as condition for the debt. General liens, as a rule, arise out of unsecured debts or obligations of the owner and affect all the property of the debtor, both personal and real. A detailed discussion of liens will be presented in Chapter 16.

Protection of property rights

The owner should guard his ownership by not allowing others to acquire rights therein by trespass, for such rights may become permanent; for example, squatters rights, prescriptive rights to maintain walls, fences, roads, pipes, conduits, and so forth. In order to protect one's rights against such trespassers, resort should be had to the courts to eject or restrain such trespassers before sufficient time has elapsed for them legally to perpetuate their invasion of the owner's ownership of property. In deserving cases, the courts will not only oust such trespassers but will award damages to the owner for any losses arising therefrom.

How ownership passes

The ownership of property may be transferred by descent, by will, by voluntary or involuntary alienation; all of which methods are fully discussed in Chapter 7.

In the transfer of property, great care must be taken to ascertain the property rights to be conveyed as well as the obligations which ownership imposes. Since covenants, leases, restrictions, mortgages, liens, taxes, and realty-use agreements attach to the land and remain in force for the duration of the interest, the principals involved in a transfer of realty are well advised to call on competent professional aid in the determination of their respective rights and duties. Debts and charges to be assumed must be fixed and disclosed, and appropriate monetary adjustment should be made for accrued and prepaid items to date of property transfer or settlement.

Property

In its legal conception, property is the right to possess, use, and dispose of a thing. Technically, therefore, property is not the thing itself but the right to, or interest in, it. In practice, however, the thing itself is also termed property.

Realty and personalty

Again from the practical viewpoint, property is of three kinds: realty, personalty, and mixed. Realty may be defined as "the land, buildings thereon, and anything permanently affixed to the land and/or the buildings." Personalty, on the other hand, is anything that does not fit the definition of realty. For example, a watch, chairs, rugs, and cultivated flowers are personalty; whereas trees, buildings, furnaces, and plumbing, as well as the land to which they are affixed, are usually realty. Mixed property is of little importance, being such as may be alternately or interchangeably realty or personalty. A key in the door, for example, is an integral part of the building, hence realty; but the same key found in the street is merely personalty. For practical purposes, realty is often, though incorrectly, termed *real* property, and personalty *personal* property.

Real property and personal property

Considering these terms in their legal aspect, as indicating the interest in a thing rather than the thing itself, we find that there may be both real property and personal property interests in realty. From a technical, legal viewpoint, real property is any interest in realty that is measured as to duration by a life, or lives, or by a longer span. Any other interest in realty is personalty. The actual length of time is no criterion; the life may be only a few months or years, yet one who is entitled to use and enjoy realty during that period has a real property right therein. If one's right be under a lease for ninety-nine years (longer than the normal life), his interest is personal property.

Real estate

For all commercial purposes the term *real estate* has two distinct meanings. First, it is the article dealt in, and in this sense it includes realty and all interests therein, whether legally they are real or personal property. Second, it is the name of the business engaged in by those who conduct commercial transactions in real estate.

Fixtures

We know that realty includes not only the land and buildings thereon but also anything definitely or permanently affixed to the land and/or buildings. The latter group is known as *real fixtures* and, like the land, is included in a sale or covered by a mortgage unless specially excepted. There are also fixtures known as *chattel fixtures*, which are things personalty by nature annexed to or used with land but retaining their original character of personalty. Chattel fixtures are not included in the sale or mortgage of land unless by special agreement.

Whether an article is a fixture depends mainly on the intention of the person who placed it. The following criteria applied to each case will aid in reaching a decision:

1. *The reasonably presumable intent of the person placing the article.*
The owner's statements to neighbors may show whether or not he intended
the article to become a fixture; or a conditional sales agreement may expressly state that the article is to remain personalty until fully paid for. So,
too, the courts will rule that if the article is usually intended to become a
fixture, a person cannot claim a contrary intention and so violate the ordinary reasonable presumption.

2. *The method of annexation.* Generally if the article is specially adapted
for use where placed, and if to remove it would leave the building or land
incomplete, it is a fixture. The annexation may be actual, such as lighting,
plumbing, and heating equipment, or constructive, such as awnings, screens,
and blinds, which may or may not be in place.

3. *The relation of the parties.* Often the relation between the parties is
such that the ordinary presumable intention is negatived. For example, a
permanent owner may be presumed to be permanently annexing the article.
Although a tenant is ordinarily bound to leave articles fastened to the building, nevertheless, if he has leased the property for business, it is a general
rule that his trade fixtures, such as shelves, counters, and showcases, do not
become fixtures in the legal sense. But such equipment must be removed
before the lease expires, and a renewal that fails to state that the equipment is to be the tenant's property may deprive the tenant of ownership.

Estates and chattel interests

Rights in realty that amount to real property in the legal sense (extending in duration one or more lives, or in perpetuity) are termed "estates";
those that are personal property are known as "chattel interests." There
may be a combination of several estates and chattel interests in the same
piece of realty. The principal chattel interests are leaseholds (Chapter 10)
and liens (Chapter 16). The most common estates are fee simple, fees determinable and upon condition, life estates and remainders, dower, curtesy,
tenancy in common, joint tenancy, and tenancy by the entirety.

Fee simple. Fee, fee simple, and fee simple absolute, all having the same
meaning, may be defined as "the largest possible estate in real property."
The owner of this estate may use it and dispose of it during his lifetime or
by his will as he desires. If he does not make any such disposition, the real
property automatically passes at his death to his heirs or distributees without any future limitation other than the limitations mentioned before,
which, it must be remembered, affect all real property. The instrument creating the estate contains usually the words ". . . to A and his heirs and
assigns forever . . ." Most realty is held in fee simple, and the term "ownership" ordinarily indicates such a right. A fee simple is, therefore, the subject of the usual commercial transactions in the sale of realty. All other
estates in real property are less than the fee simple and some part of it.
When gathered together, they make a complete fee. This splitting up of the
fee is usually in terms of quantity or time.

Fee upon condition and fee determinable. In both these estates the holder has a fee simple except that there is a limitation that may take his rights from him and give them to another. Both give the holder all the benefits of full fee ownership subject to the happening of a future contingency that ends his rights if it occurs. The distinction between the two is that if the contingency occurs in a determinable fee the ownership will automatically revert to the grantor, while in the event the contingency is a condition subsequent the ownership may be brought to an end by reentry. An illustration of these restricted fees or estate titles is as follows: If Brown deeds to Green for as long as the latter refrains from smoking, the fee is determinable if only by Green's life-span which constitutes the maximum length of years over which this restriction is operative. Where property is deeded for as long as the use is for religious or educational purposes by a church or university, the fee is upon condition and could go on and on eternally. These forms of holding are now seldom used because they involve technical legal phraseology; their purpose in most cases may be more satisfactorily accomplished by means of either a "living" or a "testamentary" trust, as explained below.

Life estates and remainders. Very common, simple examples of "fee splitting" are life estates and remainders. A man gives land to A for his life, and at A's death it is to go to B. A, who is known as the life tenant, takes a life estate; that is, the full right in the property for life; and B takes a remainder, which is the right to receive and use the property at A's death. When A dies, the fee is reunited in B, who is then the owner of a fee simple in the land. The life interest may be measured by the life tenant's own life or by that of any other person. The remainder may be so created that the remainderman cannot be known until the termination of the life estate. If he can be determined, the remainder is vested; if not, it is contingent. Let us take, for example, a gift to A for life, with the remainder to B. Since B's right to succeed is fixed, his possession merely being suspended until A's death, he has a vested remainder. But suppose the gift were to A and his children after death, and that if A left no children, then B should take it. Here B's remainder is a contingent one, because it cannot be determined whether he will ever receive the property until A's death, and he then will receive nothing if A leaves children.

In a life estate, the remainderman may receive a life estate or a fee simple. In most states, statutory law provides that the remainderman must be living, or born within twenty-one years after the death of some person or persons who were in being at the time of conveyance. If the remainderman is not living when he is to receive the estate, then the title will return to the grantor or his heirs, and they are said to hold a reversion in fee.

The life tenant has certain rights and duties. The owner of a "fee" estate may let the property fall into disrepair or disuse, but the life tenant must think of the remainderman. Hence, though he is entitled to the income and use of the land, he is obliged to keep the property in fair repair and pay the usual, normal carrying charges, including taxes. He must also pay the interest on any mortgage on the land. If he erects any buildings on the land, they usually become the property of the remainderman. Naturally, since the life tenant's rights cease at death, he can give no rights extending beyond that event. His deed would convey a right of possession ending then, and if he were to make a mortgage, the lien would then expire.

Dower and curtesy

Dower is the estate for life given by law to a wife in all real property owned by her husband at any time during marriage. The requirements for dower are (1) a valid marriage, (2) ownership of real property by husband, and (3) his death. The interest attaches as soon as the property is acquired or the marriage takes place and cannot be cut off without the wife's consent. For this purpose, she usually joins with him in the deed when property is transferred by mutual consent. Upon his death her dower interest entitles her to a life estate in one-third of the real property as a means of support after her husband's death.

Curtesy is the interest given by law to a husband in real property owned by his wife. It is established by (1) a valid marriage and birth of a child, (2) sole ownership by the wife at her death, (3) her death, and (4) no disposition of the property by her will. This interest does not attach until the wife's death, and she may defeat it by deed in her lifetime or by her will, in either case without her husband's consent. If the curtesy right exists, it entitles the husband to all the net income as long as he lives.

As a rule the surviving husband or wife seeks to avoid the lengthy process of handling property in which his or her respective claims are limited. Usually, therefore, their rights are admeasured and a lump sum equivalent to their future rights of dower or curtesy (as the case may be) is calculated. When the remainderman pays that amount to the widow or widower, she or he should execute a release and the property may then be sold free of the claim.

During the husband's lifetime, the wife's dower rights are legally "inchoate." Until his death, the wife cannot sell, assign, transfer, or cancel this right except by release to a purchaser, which she generally does by joining in her husband's deed. On the other hand, the husband cannot circumvent the dower right, and any purchaser who acquires title to real property from the husband, in states where dower is effective, without search as to the existence and release of dower rights may acquire a "clouded" title. Dower rights become "consummate" upon the husband's death, and the widow may thereafter dispose of her dower interests in any way she chooses, provided she elects dower rather than accept the will or a child's portion if her husband died intestate.

Both dower and curtesy are a survival of ancient common law and have outlived their usefulness. They were entirely abolished in England in 1925 and are now the law in only twenty-two states. Nearly all states have modified dower and curtesy rights as originally conceived, by statutory enactment, and seldom are these rights identical, in statutory provision, in any two states.

Most states have substituted other and fairer rights in their place. Some states give the surviving spouse the benefit of "community property," a larger life estate or a fee simple interest varying from one-fourth to one-half in the land and a like interest in personal property owned at death.

To illustrate the application of dower and curtesy, as modified, two representative state provisions may prove of interest. In New York, the surviving husband or wife has the right to accept the provisions of the will of the deceased spouse or to elect to take the share to which the survivor would have been entitled if the deceased spouse had died intestate. This new law has been in effect since 1930 and as a result there is no need for both parties to join in the deeds unless they are joint owners. The wife, however, must join in the deed to cut off her dower if she married before September 1, 1930, and if the husband acquired the property before that time. Curtesy was abolished entirely if the wife died after August 31, 1930.

Under the law in Florida, the widow takes a life estate in the homestead and one-third fee simple estate in all other realty, also title to one-third of the personalty owned by the husband at the time of his death. The dower is free from liability for the debt of the husband and free from all costs of administration. The dower's right extends to all real property owned during the marriage by the husband that has been conveyed by the husband without release of dower by the wife. Dower does not become complete until the widow elects to take dower which she must do by signing a written paper in the office of the county judge within nine months after first publication of notice to creditors.

Though dower and curtesy have largely been abolished, the substitutes for them still require in most states that both spouses join in the deeds. Divorce, when legally sanctioned and recognized under state law, terminates interests granted under dower, curtesy, or other rights substituted in their place. By court order property rights of the divorced parties are allocated by decree and property interests, thereafter, are individually controlled as if the marriage had never existed. It is of interest to note, however, that in a few states[1] dower or curtesy is cut off only for the spouse who by court order is declared at fault in the divorce proceeding.

Community property

In eight states—Washington, Idaho, California, Arizona, New Mexico, Texas, Nevada, and Louisiana—dower and curtesy do not exist. In their stead, the joint interest of husband and wife and the rights of a spouse in the property of his or her mate are known as "community property."

The rules regarding community property are not uniform throughout the states that recognize that form of ownership. Briefly, a community property interest prevails between husband and wife in all real and personal property held in the name of either unless the law and instrument of conveyance specifically reserve the property as the separate property of either. Under the community property laws of most states, the wife is automati-

---

[1]Illinois, Massachusetts, Oregon, Rhode Island, and West Virginia.

cally entitled to one-half of the real and personal property, or income, of the husband and the husband is entitled to the same share in the property of his wife.

The sharing of income between husband and wife gave taxpayers in the higher income brackets who resided in states that legally recognized the community property law a federal income tax advantage. By congressional action effective in 1946, this advantage was neutralized when joint return privileges for federal income tax purposes were extended uniformly to all U.S. taxpayers.

A proposed constitutional amendment giving women equal rights in all social, political, and economic matters as currently enjoyed by their male counterparts will negate existing and so-called protective state laws that were intended to safeguard the interests of the *weaker* sex. It is reasonable to assume that adoption of the women's equal rights constitutional amendment will cause abandonment of remaining dower and curtesy laws in affected states and encourage enactment of statutory provisions similar to those now in effect in the community property states as explained above.

Homestead

In many states, the law permits a "homestead exemption." This exemption is not of common law origin, and its details vary in the several states. It usually has two purposes: (1) to exempt the home from debt and (2) to provide the widow (sometimes the widower) with a home for life. In most states the value and area of the exempt homestead are limited. It usually must be occupied as the family home, and a written declaration of homestead must be filed. It is then free from general claims for debts except those that are a lien on the property, such as taxes and mortgages.

As a rule, homestead exists in favor of a head of a family, residing thereon, and may cover a maximum of 160 acres of land if outside or ½ acre if located within an incorporated city or town. A homestead right generally is not lost by a divorce if there are minor children which the husband is bound to support, provided the husband and wife do not abandon the homestead. Homesteads in a few states are exempt from taxes up to a stated amount of assessed value. It is not necessary that the owner be the head of a family in order to be entitled to this exemption.

Homestead lands necessitate that both husband and wife voluntarily execute and sign the deed of transfer of homesite property, as well as any mortgage instrument that encumbers the homestead title and gives priority of property claim to the lender. In many states the legal instrument used to release or waive homestead rights must be acknowledged before a notary or an authorized officer of the court to be valid.

Trusts

It may be well to discuss quite briefly the important subject of trusts as they relate to interests in realty. Most men, in considering plans for the future, follow the policy of providing an income and the use of the family home for their widows, with remainder to the children at her death. The trust is quite similar in purpose to the life estate and remainder, which

came into use many years ago, long before trusts were known. The granting of life estates to assure protection for a survivor has persisted until
comparatively recent times, but it is not always desirable. For one thing, a
life estate places the burden of managing the property on the widow, and
often she does not have the ability required. Besides, she naturally tends
to think of the property as her own and handles it as she desires, regardless
of other interests. A trust in the husband's will can remedy this situation.
The trustee appointed is versed in real estate matters, knows how to manage real estate, and will see that the widow is provided for and that the
property is reasonably well taken care of for the children. A trust is especially necessary if the realty is income producing, although in the case of
a small home, it may scarcely be worth the effort.

Trusts created for the convenience and benefit of the surviving spouse
and children may be established by will or may be placed in effect during
the lifetime of the owner. The former is known as a *testamentary trust*, under which the trustee administers the property as directed by provision of
the will during the lifetime of the surviving spouse and at her death distributes the trust property to the children then living. The *living trust* is
effective during the owner's lifetime with trust benefit accruing to the principal during his life and to his spouse after his death. Trust property as in
the case of the testamentary trust is distributed among the surviving children at the widow's death. The assets of a living trust are, as a rule, not
subject to the provisions of a probate, the disposition of trust assets being
governed by the trust agreement.

A trust wisely drawn and effectively administered has manifold advantages: First, *protection*. There is assurance that the assets and the income
will be available when the need arises without guardianship or court actions
of any kind in the event of the owner's death or incapacity. Second, *continuity*. There is no interruption in the flow of income in the event of the
husband's death. The wife, as a rule, is familiar with the people who administer the trust and can turn to them for financial advice and counsel.
Third, *tax savings*. Estate taxes can be minimized by giving the spouse the
opportunity to claim marital tax deductions. This is accomplished by giving the wife a general power of appointment over one-half of the trust assets during her lifetime and by will. Double taxation, too, can be avoided
where the trustee may employ under the trust agreement as much as necessary out of the trust assets, not subject to the wife's control, for her maintenance and support. Thus a second tax on the distributed assets is avoided
in the estate of the wife upon her subsequent death. Fourth, *convenience
and flexibility*. During the lifetime of the husband the trust is completely
flexible. Changes may be made as unforeseen circumstances warrant, and
trust administration instructions may be altered as convenience dictates.
The establishment of real estate trusts as an investment device to avoid
dual taxation, as under corporate ownership, will be briefly outlined below:

Number of owners. Realty may be owned by one or more persons. If it is owned by one person only, his title is said to be *sole*. If there are two or more owners, their rights are *tenancy in common, joint tenancy*, or *tenancy by the entirety*. Each of these has certain important distinctions that should be noted.

Tenancy in common. The ownership of realty by two or more persons, each of whom has an undivided interest, is called tenancy in common. Upon the death of one, ownership passes to the heirs or to whoever is designated under the will of the deceased. The law expresses this principle by stating that there is no survivorship in a tenancy in common—that is, the surviving owner or owners do not become owners of the interest of the one who has died. This of course seems to be fair and reasonable and is the relationship presumed to be intended unless the instrument creating the ownership specifies to the contrary. It is this interest that is taken by two or more heirs inheriting the property of a deceased person or by two or more devisees under a will.

The owners in common may have equal shares, or the interests may differ in amount. They are entitled to share in the income and are obligated to contribute to the charges according to their shares. They may all join to sell the property, or one may sell his interest if he desires, in which case the purchaser becomes a tenant in common with the others. If one wishes the property sold and the others do not, he may bring an action for partition, in which event the property is sold at auction and each owner is paid his share of the proceeds.

Joint tenancy. In joint tenancy the undivided interest of the two or more owners is *with survivorship*—that is, if one dies his share or interest passes to the remaining owners. This form of ownership used to be favored by the law many years ago, but now the courts will recognize a joint tenancy only when the instrument makes it clear that survivorship is intended—by the use of such appropriate words as "to the grantees, their survivor, survivor's heirs and assigns." For practical purposes it is nearly the same as a tenancy in common, with but two exceptions. (1) If one joint tenant sells his interest, the purchaser becomes a tenant in common with the remaining owner or owners. (2) Even in those states having dower, a joint tenant may convey his interest free of his wife's dower. In practice, however, attorneys recommend that a wife join in the signing of a deed where real estate interests, no matter how ordered, are sold or transferred by a husband. For a joint tenancy to stand up under court contest, it must be proved that the joint owners have equal interests and have acquired title by a single deed, at the same moment of time, and that possession is identical and undivided. A breach of any of these prerequisites creates a common rather than a joint tenancy in some states.

Tenancy by entirety. In most states validity is given to the rights under the common law, wherein a husband and wife are joined together as one person; consequently, when they take title to land together, each becomes the owner of the entire property. This estate is spoken of as a tenancy by the entirety. They may take title to a piece of property as joint tenants or as tenants in common, but the presumption is that unless the instrument indicates to the contrary, a conveyance to them as husband and wife is intended to create a tenancy by the entirety. Such a conveyance to two unmarried people would be a tenancy in common. As tenants by the entirety, neither can convey the property or force a partition during the lifetime of the other. If either one dies, the entire property is owned by the survivor. This form of ownership is very useful in connection with the purchase of a home by a husband and wife, since it makes certain that the survivor will continue to own the home regardless of whether a will is drawn, or even if the will is contested successfully.

Condominium ownership

The divided ownership of units of horizontal space that in the aggregate comprise a single parcel of property dates back to an ancient Roman concept of land tenure. This concept, which has been of little practical significance in the Western world, burst into sudden prominence when President Kennedy on June 30, 1961, signed the Housing Act of 1961, under which the Federal Housing Administration was authorized through Section 234 to issue mortgage insurance for individually owned units in multifamily structures. To implement this law most states have enacted enabling legislation, known as "Horizontal Property Acts," under which condominium ownership is prescribed as well as legally protected. As a rule, legislation requires the separate assessment and taxation of each space unit and its common interests and estops the assessor from treating any part of the common element of a structure as a separate parcel for taxation purposes. As a rule, too, statutes bar the placement of mechanic's or other liens on the common elements of a structure held jointly by two or more condominium owners.

Under FHA regulation 26 (b) of Section 234, a multifamily structure to be offered under condominium ownership must first be committed to a plan of apartment ownership by a recorded declaration or similar "public deed" that has been approved by the FHA commissioner prior to its execution. This document, referred to as a declaration, must include the following six basic items:

1. A description of the land and the multifamily structure, describing their respective areas
2. The number and descriptions of family units expressing their measurements, locations, rooms, main entrance doors, and immediate places with which they communicate, and any other data necessary in order to identify each readily
3. Description of the common areas and facilities
4. A clear expression of the purpose for which the multifamily structure and each of the family units are destined
5. Compliance with the requirement that basic value shall not exceed the FHA appraised value of the multifamily structure and each family unit, and according to these values, the percentage appertaining to each owner in the expense and profits of, and the rights in, the common areas and facilities

6. Everything relative to the administration of the property by an association or a cooperative of owners

Other provisions essential to assure quiet title and protective (joint) ownership include the following:

1. Restrictions limiting use of space for residential purposes and occupancy by a single family
2. A covenant granting an undivided percentage share of the common elements (halls and stairs of ingress and egress, etc.) to each condominium owner
3. A statement that the common elements cannot be separately mortgaged or severed in ownership from the individually owned space units
4. Regulation concerning maintenance of each apartment unit without interference or disturbance of other owner occupants
5. A stipulation concerning maintenance and use of the common structural elements and regulation concerning majority action in case of major catastrophe, fire, general wear, tear, actions of the elements, or functional or economic obsolescence that requires rebuilding or destruction of the building improvements
6. A clear statement of regulation concerning general management pro rata support of operating expenses, and means and ways by which bylaws and declarations of agreement can be amended by majority action

Under condominium co-ownership, each purchaser of an apartment receives an exclusive right to use, occupy, mortgage, and dispose of his particular apartment, plus an undivided interest in the areas and fixtures that serve all tenant owners in common. Each deed is subject to identical covenants and restrictions governing the repair and maintenance of the building. Although condominium ownership gives greater flexibility to the fee owner in matters concerning financing and sale of his individual apartment as a space unit, and offers tax advantages identical to those enjoyed by owners of single-family structures, this method of ownership, as under a stock cooperative venture, requires formation of a central administrative body to act on behalf of the condominium owners in matters that concern the common operations of the multiunit structure as an integral whole. Thus all condominium co-owners are obligated to share the expenses of operation and maintenance, which are levied either as rent or as monthly assessments to each according to his share or value of ownership. Owners, too, are bound to observe recorded rules and regulations governing use and occupancy of both individually owned premises and those held in common. Although the condominium owner cannot be ousted or dispossessed (as can a defaulting tenant) for infraction of bylaws or regulations, he is nevertheless subject to court actions resulting from filing of liens against his fee interest or those sought to compel compliance with terms of the declaration of ownership. Judging by the keen interest shown by the National Association of Home Builders in condominium legislation and by the significant number of high-rise apartments completed and under construction under proposed condominium ownership, the future of this new form of property ownership seems bright indeed.

Cooperative ownership

The cooperative form of mutual ownership differs from a condominium entity in that the ownership of the entire property (land and improvements) is acquired by a corporation. The corporation as a rule finances the purchase by placing a mortgage on the property for up to 70 or 80 percent of its value and obtaining the balance by the sale of equity shares in the corporation to the cooperative tenant owners. Each owner-occupant in effect holds a proprietary lease subject to liens, debts, and obligations incurred by the corporation. The lease terms stipulate the payment of rent to the corporation to cover pro rata shares of the amounts necessary to meet mortgage debt, maintenance expenditures, property taxes, and building-related expenditures such as hazard insurance and sinking fund (replacement) reserves. Since under condominium ownership each family unit is separately mortgaged and insured, a default in payment by one does not affect the ownership control of other owner-occupants. Under cooperative title ownership, the mortgage and the insurance are placed by the corporation on the entire property, and a default in payment by the corporation due to default in payment by some cooperative tenants affects occupancy and title to property of all cooperative participants.

Uniform partnership

In all but two states a Uniform Partnership Act has been written into law. Under this statutory provision a partnership is legally declared an *entity* and can own real estate in the name of the partnership. However, in most agreements presently in effect, a partnership is still interpreted as an association of individuals rather than a distinct entity. In other words, the partnership name is merely a convenient designation of a group rather than the title of a separate legal organization. A transfer of title to realty made to a partnership should be made to the individuals composing the partnership. If it is made to the partnership name, the individual persons nevertheless become the owners of the property. To the extent that the property was purchased with partnership assets, the realty should be considered as an asset of the partnership; and even though it is not purchased with the partnership assets, it should be borne in mind that all the assets of a joint partner are liable to partnership debts. We find a speedily decreasing use of the partnership for business purposes and consequently very little real partnership realty. Even when a business does operate as a partnership, it usually arranges to purchase realty, if it is necessary to the business, under some corporate name or in the name of one or more of the individual partners.

Real estate operators and investors occasionally buy real estate as partners or as a syndicate. As a matter of fact, what they are doing is creating either a relationship of joint tenancy or a tenancy in common, and they should bear this in mind when title is conveyed to them.

Corporation realty

A corporation is a separate legal entity and has such powers as its charter or certificate of incorporation gives it, subject to such additional rights and obligations as are imposed by law. If its charter or purposes specifically or implicitly will permit the ownership of real estate, the corporation may make such a purchase; and such real estate, like the other assets of the corporation, is under the management and control of the officers and directors. The stock of the corporation is personalty, even though all of the assets of the corporation may happen to be realty. In most states, stock corporations meet with very few impediments in receiving and transferring real estate; but some of the states require a stock corporation to obtain a certificate of consent of a certain percentage of the stockholders before it can negotiate a mortgage. Nonstock corporations are subject to more rigid regulations. Some of them cannot make the purchase of real estate without a court order, and in most states they can neither sell nor mortgage their real estate without a special application to the court for leave to do so. It is for this reason that nonstock operations, if they find it desirable to own real estate, often form separate stock corporations to take title.

Syndicate realty

A group of individuals or corporations, or both, may, by agreement, form a combination for the purpose of trading in real estate. The agreement creating such combination is known as a *syndicate agreement* and is executed by all the parties who are to participate in the venture.

Syndicates are used generally in transactions involving extensive and costly real estate holdings too large perhaps for any one individual or corporation to handle. They are also used when the members want to limit their individual investment or wish to have the advantage of the judgment of other associates in the project.

The syndicate agreement . . .

1. Sets forth the type and location of the real estate owned or to be acquired by the syndicate.
2. Designates a syndicate manager, fixes his compensation, and specifies his powers and duties.
3. Indicates the respective interests of the syndicate members.
4. Provides for contributions to be made from time to time to carry out the syndicate's operations and fixes limitations on capital to be used.
5. Fixes duration of the syndicate and provides for withdrawal of syndicate members on certain terms.

Syndicates are taxed by federal and by some state authorities on a partnership basis—that is, the respective members' interests in syndicate profits are taxable against the members whether such profits are actually distributed or not.

Investment trusts

With enactment of new trust law provisions applicable to ownership and disposition of real property in January 1961, real estate investors by the thousands have purchased trust shares in newly formed investment trusts throughout the country. Under provision of the new trust laws and regulations governing same adopted by the Internal Revenue Service on April 24, 1962, real estate investment trusts that meet regulatory standards are now able to avoid corporate income taxes, provided the trust distributes 90 percent or more of annual earnings to its shareholders. Elimination of corporate income taxes thus avoids double taxation and, in effect, could double net income to trust shareowners.

The concept of the new trust law is similar to the provisions applicable to regulated investment companies such as mutual funds. To qualify as a real estate investment trust, a trust must meet the following more important requirements:

1. At least 75 percent of the trust's assets must be in real property.
2. Not more than 25 percent of the value of a trust's total assets may be represented by securities.
3. There must be at least one hundred beneficiaries (trust shareholders), and 50 percent or more of the trust cannot be owned by five or fewer individuals.
4. Income from assets that are held for less than four years cannot exceed 30 percent of total earnings.
5. At least 75 percent of the trust's gross income must be derived from real property earnings.
6. An additional 15 percent of gross income must come from either real estate or investment sources.
7. Ninety percent or more of earnings must be distributed to shareholders.
8. Trust may not hold real property primarily for sale in the ordinary course of business. This restriction, for all practical purposes, excludes land development companies from trust law exemption benefits.

In its present form, the investment trust is not likely to replace the limited partnership or syndicate, since the latter generally do not meet the one-hundred-beneficiary requirement of the 1961 trust law. Unincorporated advantages of partnership and syndicates will continue to favor the formation of those forms of ownership for small investment undertakings.

READING AND STUDY REFERENCES

1. BROWN, ROBERT K., *Real Estate Economics*, Chapter 2. Boston: Houghton Mifflin Company, 1965.
2. FRIEDMAN, EDITH J., *Real Estate Encyclopedia*, Chapter 20. Englewood Cliffs, N.J.: Prentice-Hall, Inc., 1960.
3. HEBARD, EDNA L., and GERALD S. MEISEL, *Principles of Real Estate Law*, Chapters 1, 4, and 7. New York: Simmons-Boardman Publishing Corporation, 1964.
4. HUSBAND, WILLIAM H., and FRANK RAY ANDERSON, *Real Estate*, Chapters 1, 4, and 5. Homewood, Ill.: Richard D. Irwin, Inc., 1960.
5. KRATOVIL, ROBERT, *Real Estate Law*, Chapters 3, 16, 17, 18, and 34. Englewood Cliffs, N.J.: Prentice-Hall, Inc., 1969.

6. LUSK, HAROLD F., *Law of the Real Estate Business*, Chapters 5 and 6. Homewood, Ill.: Richard D. Irwin, Inc., 1965.

7. RING, ALFRED A., *Questions and Problems in Real Estate Principles and Practices* (rev. ed.), Chapter 4. Englewood Cliffs, N.J.: Prentice-Hall, Inc., 1972.

5

CONTRACTS

Documents used in the transfer of ownership or interests in realty are professionally known as "instruments." There are a great many instruments in use with the aid of which the purchase, sale, exchange, leasing, financing, control, use, and ownership of realty is established and generally recorded to minimize possible disputes and settle claims. These instruments vary not only because of different purposes that created their need but also because of differences in state, county, or municipal laws or customs that govern the disposition of rights and interests in realty. No one book can possibly contain all the real estate instruments now in use throughout the United States, but the basic requisites and principles underlying each of the more important instruments can effectively be presented as a guide to successful real estate transactions.

One of the most important and most widely used real estate instruments is the real estate *contract*. Sales, purchases, and exchanges of realty are continually being made and engage the interest and attention of owners, purchasers, and brokers. These transactions usually are entered upon voluntarily and almost without exception are initiated by a contract embodying the terms of the agreement. Since the contract governs the performance of agreed-upon terms, it is essential that the owner who is about to sell, the prospective purchaser, and the broker who is protecting the interest of one or both parties to the transaction have a working knowledge of the contract in terms of its purpose and its effect upon the signing parties.

Purpose of contract

The contract seeks to describe fully the premises referred to, and to set forth the price and terms together with the obligations of the respective parties. Its purpose is to provide time to verify ownership, title conditions, and accuracy of statements and conditions affecting the transfer of the property, and to permit, in advance of title closing, preparation of essentials making the closing merely a mechanical process carrying out the agreement of the parties.

It is possible, of course, to arrange for transfer of a property without the medium of a formal contract. The owner could deliver title directly by deed in exchange for cash or other considerations. In practice, however, such direct property transfers are most uncommon and fraught with many pitfalls. Time is essential to ascertain the quantity and quality of the owner's interests in a property. Thus, if A transfers to B by *warranty deed* (see Chapter 9, page 152) ownership of the house in which he lives and it later develops that A was merely a tenant, B, in fact, acquired a lawsuit against A. As far as the property is concerned, B's rights are no greater than those A possessed which in this instance may be nothing.

Definition

A contract for the sale or exchange of real estate must contain the elements of any legal contract. Legally, a contract is a deliberate agreement between competent parties, upon legal consideration, to do or abstain from doing some legal act.

Essentials of a valid real estate contract

The five essentials of a valid real estate contract are:

1. Competent parties
2. Offer and acceptance
3. Consideration
4. Legality of object
5. The contract must be in writing and signed (if real property is involved)

Competent parties. Naturally there must be at least two parties to a contract; a man could not make an enforceable contract with himself. The parties must meet on the same mental plane—an idiot or an insane person, not knowing the nature of his act or what he signs, cannot make a binding contract. A delusion upon one subject may, however, not incapacitate him, since he may be thoroughly intelligent as to other things. The parties must meet on the same legal plane; an infant cannot be bound by his contract. He may sell his realty, receive and spend the price paid him, then disaffirm his contract, and a court will restore his property to him.

The question of competency, from a practical viewpoint, concerns more particularly the legal capacity to sell of executors, trustees, and persons acting under a power of attorney. Those persons have only such rights and privileges as may be given them by the instruments appointing them. Care should be taken to have them produce such instruments for examination by the buyer's counsel before a contract is entered upon with them. It may be that they are restricted as to price, terms, time within which to act, or in some other way that would prevent their fulfillment of the contract.

A corporation that is about to sell real estate authorizes its president or some other officer, by resolution or bylaw, to execute the contract. Ordinarily, the purchaser does not insist upon seeing the original or a certified copy of such bylaw or resolution but assumes the fact that the officer has authority to execute the contract since he is in possession of the corporate seal, which he impresses upon the contract. There is no reason, however, why inquiry concerning the officer's authority should not be made, particularly if the purchaser is paying a considerable deposit on the signing of the contract. Where the sellers are co-owners (joint tenants, tenants in common, or copartners), it is essential that the purchaser insist that all the owners sign the contract. In states where the seller's wife must join in the deed to release her dower, there is a curious situation. In some such states it is customary to have her join in the contract, so that she can be forced to sign the deed; in others she is seldom asked to sign the contract, it being assumed that she will voluntarily sign the deed. Of course, if both husband and wife own the property, they should both sign the contract.

Offer and acceptance. The entire purpose of a real estate contract is to bind the buyer and seller to do something at a future time. We do not make written contracts to buy things that we pay for and take away with us. But a real estate deal is different. The seller says he owns the property, that his title is good and marketable, and that it is subject only to certain liens and encumbrances. None of these things can be verified by examining the property. The buyer must have the title searched. He does not want to go to this expense unless he knows he has a deal; nor does the seller wish to remove his property from the market unless he has a deposit and a commitment that binds the purchaser.

To safeguard the interests of both parties, a written contract is drawn. Each promises to do certain specific things in the future: the seller to give possession and title; the buyer to pay the price in accordance with specified terms. The offer and acceptance of contract terms must relate, of course, to a specific property. No contract is created unless there is a *meeting of the minds*. A mutual mistake will void the agreement.

Consideration. The promise of one party to the contract must be supported by an undertaking of the other. Each must obligate himself. Each must put some consideration into the agreement. A mere promise, even if made in writing, would not be binding upon its maker. A, seeing his good friend B, says to him, "B, I will give you my house tomorrow." B cannot enforce the delivery of the house. But if A offers to give B the house if B ceases to use tobacco for one week, then there is a mutual obligation or consideration, and if B performs his promise, he can enforce delivery of the house to him. In real estate contracts the seller usually promises to sell and convey realty, and the purchaser accepts the offer and creates the mutual obligation by agreeing to pay a certain price for the realty. A more extended discussion of the adequacy of various kinds of considerations will be found in the chapter on deeds.

Legality of object. An agreement, to be an enforceable contract, must contemplate the attainment of an object not expressly forbidden by law or contrary to public policy. For example, an agreement for the sale of realty to be used expressly for an illegal purpose is unenforceable, for its object is contrary to law. An agreement by which A, a confirmed woman hater, promises B a house upon B's promise never to marry is against public policy, for it discourages marriage and is therefore unenforceable.

Necessity of writing. The contract for the sale of real property is expressly required by law to be in writing and signed by the party who is to be bound by it. In many states the contract, by recent laws, may also be signed by an agent, provided the agent has written authority from his principal in whose name he is acting. This rule is the old *statute of frauds* in its present form, which is intended to prevent fraudulent proof of a fictitious oral contract depriving the owner of valuable realty. For commercial reasons, a written contract is practically a necessity in a real estate transaction. There are usually many terms and provisions agreed upon, and it would be impracticable to attempt to carry them all in one's memory. Even aside from the opportunity for fraud, natural forgetfulness would give rise to innumerable disputes.

The writing may be upon any lasting substance, made with anything from stylus to paintbrush, and in any language that can be translated into English. Care must be taken, however, to see that all the provisions are embodied in the contract, for after it is signed nothing can be added to it except by consent of all parties. Anything left out of the written contract, even though agreed upon in the discussion leading to the contract, is unenforceable. Care should also be taken to see that the various provisions state explicitly what is intended. No explanation can later be given to change the meaning of a provision that on its face appears clear. The words put into the instrument may mean something entirely different from what was intended; yet, if the error does not appear on reading the contract, no explanation can be given.

Receipts and binders

In conducting the negotiations leading up to the sale, the broker often finds that when he has the deal nearly ready for agreement, he cannot at once bring the parties together for the drawing of a contract. Yet he must somehow "hold it together" until that can be done. He may take a small deposit from the buyer, for which he gives a receipt. This receipt must be carefully drawn so as to comply with the statute of frauds. The law does not require special technical words, but it does demand written words that clearly express the essential terms and the intention of the parties.

Most real estate men use a form of receipt that is a binder as well. It is prepared in duplicate; one part of the instrument is signed as a receipt, and the other is signed by the prospective buyer, so that he is making a binding offer in writing, subject to the seller's acceptance. When the seller does accept this offer in writing, the two papers, the receipt and the acceptance, together constitute an agreement to enter into a written contract even if no formal contract is ever drawn up. The following is a satisfactory form for use:

SALES DEPOSIT RECEIPT

Date ....19........

Received from ....

of ....

the sum of .... Dollars

as deposit on the purchase of ....

.... (City, State)

on the following terms and conditions:

TERMS:

    Price .... Dollars

    Mortgage: ....

Remarks:

CONDITIONS:

    Contract to be signed at the office of .... Co.

    at ....M. on .... 19........

    This deposit is to apply on the amount of .... Dollars

    which is to be paid on contract, leaving a balance of .... Dollars

    payable on closing of title.

    Taxes, mortgage interest, rents and insurance premiums to be apportioned.

Rights of tenants as follows: ....

Title to close at .... on .... 19........

IMPORTANT:

This deposit accepted subject to seller's approval. If seller disapproves, the deposit is to be refunded. If the seller approves and purchaser fails to sign the contract as above stated he agrees to pay ....

Co. a sum equivalent to the usual brokerage commission.

I hereby accept the terms and conditions above.

Commission due and payable on signing of contracts.

.... CO.

Associate Broker

.... Seller

Purchaser
(Please read this receipt and take copy.)

Options

Occasionally a buyer is not sure he wants to buy, but he is willing to pay something to the owner for the right to buy. The owner may be willing to hold his property off the market in return for a consideration. Such an agreement, to be binding, must also be in writing. It should, of course, limit the time for its exercise and should also, to be legal, specify the essential details of the sale if the option is exercised. The option itself may embody all the terms of sale. However, a proposed contract of sale may be attached to the option. This is desirable so that none of the details may be omitted. The following is a good form:

OPTION CONTRACT

Option to purchase agreement made ...., 19...., between ...., residing at ...., first party, and ...., residing at ...., second party,

WITNESSETH:

In consideration of the sum of .... dollars paid by second party to the first party, the receipt whereof is hereby acknowledged, the first party hereby grants, bargains, and sells to the second party, ... heirs, executors, administrators, successors, and assigns, the exclusive option to purchase the real property known as .... (street number) in the .... more particularly described in the form of agreement hereto annexed, and made a part hereof.

This agreement is upon the following terms and conditions:

1. This option and all rights and privileges thereunder shall expire on ...., 19......., at .... o'clock .... M.

2. This option shall be exercised by the second party by written notice signed by him, and sent by registered mail to the address of first party as above set forth within the above time limit.

3. The total purchase price shall be .... dollars to be paid by second party if this option is exercised as provided in the annexed form of agreement; and the sum paid for this option shall be credited on account of the cash payment to be made on closing title as provided in said form of agreement.

4. Should the second party not exercise this option as herein provided for, the said sum of .... dollars shall be retained by the first party, free of any claim of the second party, and neither shall have any further claims against the other.

5. Should this option be exercised as herein provided, it is agreed that the parties hereto shall, respectively, as seller and purchaser, perform the obligations stated in the annexed form of agreement to be performed by the seller and purchaser therein named.

6. The second party shall have the right to assign this option, and if so assigned by him any and all acts to be performed by him hereunder may be performed by any assignee, whether such assignment be made before or after the exercise of this option.

[It is often desirable where a purchase money note and mortgage is provided for, that the option agreement provide that "in the event of such assignment, second party shall become a party to the note to secure which the purchase money mortgage mentioned in the annexed form of agreement is made."

The sentence quoted above may be added as a sentence in the sixth paragraph.]

IN WITNESS WHEREOF, first party has signed and sealed this instrument, the day and year first above written.

.... (L.S.)

IN THE PRESENCE OF:

....

(Acknowledgment)

Formal contract of sale

Even though a preliminary receipt or binder may be used, it is customary to enter into a formal contract of sale. Many forms are in use, and no special wording is compulsory. In many communities custom dictates the use of specially prepared and printed contract forms. Often, too, the formal contract is entered into directly without the preliminary receipt or binder agreement noted above. The contract form presented below is representative of those in general use.

CONTRACT FOR SALE OF REAL ESTATE

Agreement, made and dated .... 19......., between
.... residing at ....
hereinafter described as the seller and ....
residing at ...., hereinafter
described as the purchaser.

Witnesseth, that the seller agrees to sell and convey, and the purchaser agrees to purchase all that lot or parcel of land, with the buildings and improvements thereon and described as follows:

....

....

....

....

The price is .... dollars payable as follows:
.... Dollars, on the signing of this contract, the receipt of which is acknowledged.
.... Dollars, in cash on the delivery of the deed as hereinafter provided.
.... Dollars, by taking title and assuming a mortgage now a lien on said premises in that amount, bearing interest at the rate of .... percent per annum, the principal being due and payable as follows:

....

.... Dollars, by the purchaser executing and delivering to the seller the purchaser's money note and mortgage on the above premises in that amount payable in .... installments of $............... each or more at the option of the owner of the premises, together with interest at the rate of .... percent per annum payable with said installments, until ...., when the unpaid balance shall be due and payable.

Said note and mortgage shall be drawn by the attorney for the seller at the expense of the purchaser and shall contain clauses usually employed by the .... Company, together with a clause making it subordinate to the lien of the present first mortgage of $..............., any extensions or renewals thereof or any new first mortgage not exceeding $............... that may be placed thereon in lieu of the present first mortgage.

The following are to be apportioned as of the date of closing:

1. Rents and interest on mortgages
2. Insurance premiums on existing policies other than liability and compensation insurance
3. Taxes and water rates for the calendar year
4. Fuel on premises

Said premises are sold subject to building restrictions and zoning ordinances and restrictions of record and subject to ....

The seller shall give and the purchaser shall accept a merchantable title such as (name of title company or counsel) will approve and insure. Said title to be subject only to customary exceptions. In the event the title shall not be found merchantable and acceptable, due to title defects, the seller agrees to use diligence to clear the title and shall have .... days to do so. If after .... days the title has not been cleared the party holding the deposit made hereunder and all monies that may have been paid to him under this contract shall return such monies to the buyer together with reasonable title expense and thereupon all parties shall be released from all obligations arising out of this contract agreement.

All fixtures and articles of personal property attached or appurtenant to or used in the operation of said premises are represented to be owned by the seller, free from all liens and encumbrances except as herein stated, and are included in this sale.

If there be a mortgage on the premises and such mortgage has been reduced by payments on account of the principal thereof, then the seller agrees to deliver to the purchaser at the time of delivery of the deed a proper certificate executed and acknowledged by the holder of such mortgage and in form for recording, certifying as to the amount of the unpaid principal sum of such mortgage and rate of interest thereon, and the seller shall pay the fees for recording such certificate.

The deed shall be in proper statutory short form for record, shall contain the usual full covenants and warranty, and shall be duly executed and acknowledged by the seller, at the seller's expense, so as to convey to the purchaser the fee simple of the said premises, free of all encumbrances except as herein stated.

All sums paid on account of this contract, and the reasonable expense of the examinations of the title to said premises are hereby made liens thereon, but such liens shall not continue after default by the purchaser under this contract.

The deed shall be delivered upon the receipt of said payments at the office of ...., at .... o'clock, on ...., 19....... The risk of loss or damage to said premises by fire or other hazards until the delivery of the deed is assumed by the seller.

If the buyer fails to perform the covenants herein contained within the time specified, and the seller elects not to require a specific performance thereof, or sue for damages, the aforesaid deposit made by the buyer shall be retained as liquidated damages.

The parties agree that .... brought about this sale, and the seller agrees to pay the commission at the rates established or adopted by the Board of Real Estate Brokers in the locality where the property is situated.

The stipulations aforesaid are to apply to and bind the heirs, executors, administrators, successors, and assigns of the respective parties.

WITNESS the signatures and seals of the above parties.

Witnesses:

....

....

.... (L.S.)

.... (L.S.)

.... (L.S.)

.... (L.S.)

Divisions of contract

An examination of the form shows that the contract falls into eight general divisions:

1. Statement of parties
2. Agreement to sell and buy
3. Description of property
4. Financial statement
5. Miscellaneous provisions
6. Kind, form, and execution of deed
7. Closing date and place
8. Signatures

Although it is not necessary to use the form set forth, or any other particular form, the contract should contain the first four, the sixth, and the eighth divisions. If no closing date and place are fixed, a reasonable time is presumed to be intended, sufficiently far in advance to enable the seller and purchaser to prepare to complete the transaction. Although the miscellaneous provisions are not absolutely vital, their absence from the contract may give rise to dispute and inconvenience. Experience shows the advisability of using a printed form, filling in the blanks.

The contract is usually prepared in duplicate so that each party may retain a copy. In opening, the first words are "Agreement, made and dated . . . 19 . . ." The word "agreement" is not necessary. If the writing contains the necessary elements, it is a contract whether so labeled or not. Dating the instrument is convenient as a memorandum of the fact, however, and is the usual practice.

Statement of parties

Following the date, the words "between . . . ., hereinafter described as the seller, and . . . ., hereinafter described as the purchaser," indicate the place for insertion of the names of the seller and purchaser. The names of both should be correctly written and for convenience should be followed by the address of each, since it is usually necessary to have the address of each party for use in preparing the instruments later required to consummate the contract.

Each of the parties approaches the bargain from a different viewpoint. The seller is about to undertake to deliver his realty at a future date upon payment of an agreed price. Until the closing of title, he obligates himself not to seek other sale, although he has only a small part of the price in the form of a deposit. The purchaser, on his part, is about to pay a deposit to secure the property, will incur additional expense in examination of the title, and will abandon further search for a location. Each of the parties, therefore, is interested in the financial capacity and good faith of the other.

The seller wishes to be sure his purchaser can and will fulfill the contract, particularly if the market is falling, for if the purchaser later defaults, the seller will very probably sustain a loss. If the market is rising, the danger is much less, for, in case of the purchaser's later failure to complete the contract, the seller has an opportunity to sell at a higher price. Of course, the seller may protect himself to some extent by requiring a larger deposit when he has any doubt as to his purchaser's good faith or knows him to be a "dummy," and also to cover the broker's commission.

The purchaser should satisfy himself that the person recited as seller owns and has a right to sell the property. A seller who is an executor, trustee, attorney-in-fact, or agent should show the instrument appointing him and giving him power and authority to sell. If the seller does not produce proof of his ownership and authority to sell, it is often advisable to deposit the initial payment, which would in ordinary course be delivered on signing the contract by the purchaser to the seller, with some third person agreed upon to hold it in escrow until the seller produces such evidence. In most jurisdictions it is customary for the real estate broker to hold the deposit in his business trust account until the date of closing or to recommend an attorney as the escrow agent and for drawing the documents essential to the closing of the deal. Occasionally the seller has not title but has contracted to buy from the owner and is now undertaking to sell before he has taken title. In such a case the purchaser must consider the third person before he signs a contract. He will best protect himself by paying only a small deposit and having the contract provide for a definite closing date without right of adjournment.

"Witnesseth," the word following the names of the parties, means nothing legally or practically and might just as well be left out. Many years ago it had a meaning, and it survives only because it has always been used.

Agreement to sell and buy

"That the seller agrees to sell and convey." These words are the seller's promise. He promises not only to transfer his rights but also to deliver the necessary instrument (deed) to transfer his title. "And the purchaser agrees to purchase" creates the mutual obligation by the purchaser's acceptance of the seller's offer, thus completing the consideration that supports the contract.

Description of property

"All that lot or parcel of land, with the buildings and improvements thereon" are the formal opening words of the description of the property. "All" indicates that the contract is intended to cover every particle of the land described in detail following. "With the buildings and improvements thereon," although not legally necessary, should always be included to contradict any presumption of an intent to except from the sale any of the structures on the land.

Next follows the specific description of the realty. The description is the most important as well as the most difficult part of the contract. Although it is not necessary to describe the realty in as much detail in the contract as in the deed, nevertheless, legal rights are being created by the contract and it is of importance that a proper description be included.

1. By street number of house
2. By lot number on a map
3. By metes and bounds
4. By monuments
5. By rectangular (or government) survey

The nature, importance, and use of these property descriptions are detailed and explained in the following chapter on land surveying and property descriptions.

Limitations and restrictions

It is of utmost importance that the purchaser bear in mind that the seller is bound to give a good and marketable title free of all encumbrances except those stated in the contract. Customarily these are set forth after the description. Tenancies are most common. If not mentioned, the buyer is entitled to an empty house. The seller is protected by merely stating that the sale is subject to tenants' rights, but the buyer should insist on the inclusion of details of space, duration, rent, deposits, and options. A survey may show some encroachment. Buildings often encroach on the street, so often that a clause covering the situation may be printed after the financial statement in the form. The seller is safe if the contract states merely, "subject to any state of facts an accurate survey may show." This, however, is dangerous for the buyer, who should see a survey if the seller has one, or else substantially the following words should be added: "Provided such survey does not show the title to be unmarketable." Many properties are subject to restrictions and limitations such as setbacks, type and cost of buildings, easements for party walls, driveways, street railways, and public utility poles and equipment. These must all be recited, since the mere mention is enough to protect the seller. A satisfactory clause, which may be amplified, is, "subject to covenants, consents, restrictions, and easements, of record or existing, which are not violated by the present buildings or present use." Zoning restrictions are usual in a great many communities. They, too, are encumbrances in the eyes of the law and should be stated. In the form on page 72, mention of them is made just below the financial statement. A more general form of this clause might read, "subject to zoning restrictions, regulations, or ordinances of any municipal, town, village, or other governmental authority."

Installment assessments

In many places assessments, particularly if substantial in amount, are made payable in periodic installments either by law or by application of the property owner. There should be a clear understanding between buyer and seller if there are any such assessments. If the buyer wishes to protect himself, he may insist on the following clause, under which the seller is required to pay the future installments:

If at the time of the delivery of the deed the premises or any part thereof shall be or shall have been affected by an assessment or assessments which are or may become payable in annual installments, of which the first installment is then a charge or lien, or has been paid, then for the purposes of this contract all the unpaid installments of any such assessment, including those which are to become due and payable after the delivery of the deed, shall be deemed to be due and payable and to be liens upon the premises affected thereby and shall be paid and discharged by the seller, upon the delivery of the deed.

Financial statement

Next upon the form (page 71) appears, "The price is . . . . . ." These words open the financial statement, wherein are set forth all the provisions with respect to amount and terms of payment of the purchase price. Following the opening words, the financial considerations are divided into:

1. Deposit on contract
2. Cash on closing
3. Existing mortgages
4. Purchase money mortgages

It is not necessary that every contract contain all four divisions of the total price. There is nearly always provision for a deposit in signing the contract and for cash on the closing. Sometimes no provision for a purchase money mortgage is made, it being agreed that the purchaser shall pay all cash over the existing encumbrances. Or, it may be that there is no encumbrance on the property and that the purchaser is to pay all cash, in which event only the first two divisions will be present. In addition, in some states bonds rather than notes are used to evidence the mortgage debt in which case the wording of the contract is changed accordingly.

Deposit on contract. The deposit is the amount paid by the purchaser to the seller as earnest money. Its amount varies, being usually from 5 to 10 percent of the price. This deposit is forfeited to the seller if the purchaser defaults in carrying out the contract. Its amount is, therefore, always an important question to be agreed upon by the parties and is regulated by various considerations. Their confidence in each other may reduce it. A long time between the date of the contract and the date agreed on for the closing of title should increase it, for during this period the property is really the purchaser's and the seller cannot seek other sale for it. The deposit should be large enough to compensate the seller for any commission that he must pay on the sale and to make it worthwhile for the purchaser to complete his contract even if he repents his bargain. The purchaser, having nothing until delivery of the deed, naturally wants to make as small a deposit as possible. The payment of the deposit is acknowledged in the contract; no separate receipt is necessary. Payment of the deposit is generally by check and is not usually certified. Title does not pass, and if the check should be unpaid, the contract could be voided by the seller. However, if the seller is making a very good bargain and does not wish to lose the sale, he may insist upon receiving the deposit in cash or by certified check.

Cash on closing. The cash on closing is the amount to be paid to the seller upon delivery of the deed: ". . . dollars in cash on the delivery of the deed as hereinafter provided." Some forms provide for payment either in cash or by certified check. The seller may insist that the contract provide for payment in cash; then, if he wishes, he may take a certified check on the closing. Since the deed and possession of the property are to be delivered on the closing, nothing less than cash or a certified check should be taken by the seller. The amount of cash to be paid on the closing of title naturally will be the difference between the total price and the deposit, if there is no provision for existing encumbrances or purchase money mortgages. If there are such, the closing payment is the difference between the total price and the sum of the other items.

Existing mortgage. Many improved properties in the built-up districts are mortgaged for part of their value. These mortgages usually remain on the property even though it is sold. A contract for sale, therefore, often involves in the financial statement an existing mortgage. The mortgage is always accompanied by a bond or a note, under the terms of which bond or note the original borrower or some subsequent owner, who has secured an extension of its time of payment, has undertaken to pay the amount of the loan that the mortgage was given to secure. The purchaser may take the realty *subject* to this mortgage, or he may *assume* its payment. In either event, to prevent foreclosure of the mortgage, he must pay the interest, taxes, or amortization, if required by agreement or statute. If, however, he merely buys subject to the mortgage, he undertakes no personal obligation to pay the loan, whereas if he assumes the mortgage he becomes personally liable for the loan, and should the property under foreclosure not bring enough to pay the mortgage, interest, and expenses, he would be personally liable for the deficiency. For obvious reasons, the purchaser usually endeavors to have the contract provide that he take the property subject to the mortgage. In actual experience the purchaser generally assumes the mortgage.

The purchaser, in order to know what he is buying, should always secure a detailed statement of the terms of the existing mortgage, particularly the principal amount, the amount due at time of closing, the interest rate, the name of the mortgagee, the interest payment dates, and the dates and amounts of amortization payments. If the existing mortgage is not being amortized, then it is important to know when the principal of the mortgage falls due. The purchaser must know when he may be compelled to pay or renew the mortgage. Possibly he cannot pay it and has reason to believe he could not procure a new loan for as great an amount. He wants to have time to prepare. He might not buy at all if the mortgage were to become due very soon. If, on the other hand, he thinks the mortgage is low and that he could procure a larger loan, then he wants it to become due shortly. If, in any way, the seller has any control over or option in respect to the mortgage or any of its terms, the purchaser should see that the contract makes proper provision to protect his desires or requirements.

Purchase money mortgage. The purpose of a purchase money mortgage is to take the place of cash for part of the price. The purchaser may not have sufficient cash to pay the full price over the existing mortgage, and the seller may be willing to leave part of the price as a loan to the purchaser. In order that the seller may have some security for the loan, the purchaser makes the loan a lien upon the property. The purchaser gives his bond or note for the amount agreed upon and a purchase money mortgage pledging the property as security. No general rule can be made as to a safe amount to leave on purchase money mortgage. However, in any event the seller should always see that he receives more than enough cash to pay the cost of foreclosing the mortgage and more than enough to cover any depreciation in the property, accrued interest, and unpaid taxes.

As to the purchase money mortgage, the contract should specify the date and manner of payment of the principal sum, the interest rate, and interest payment dates. The seller should require an appropriate form of bond or note and mortgage that, in its incidental provisions, will give him full protection, particularly with reference to default in the existing mortgage. For this reason also, the contract should provide that the bond or note and mortgage be prepared by the seller's attorney. Since the purchase money mortgage is taken by the seller as an accommodation to the purchaser, it is customary to provide that the purchaser shall pay all expenses in connection with it, including the cost of drawing the instruments, the recording fees, the mortgage tax (if any), and the internal revenue stamps on the bond or note (if any). The purchaser should always seek a provision that the purchase money mortgage shall be and shall remain subordinate to the present existing mortgage or any mortgage to secure a similar amount in event of payment thereof. The form of contract shown on page 71 gives a satisfactory wording for this clause, so set up that by crossing out unnecessary words and filling in the blanks the form may fit either a straight or an installment mortgage.

Miscellaneous provisions

The balance of the contract (except for closing date and place, which in this form is near the end) consists of a number of short paragraphs known as *miscellaneous clauses*. These appear in varying order, depending on the form used. For convenience they will be considered in the order they take in the form on page 72.

Apportionments

It is customary to arrange, as far as possible, for the seller's interest to cease and the purchaser's to commence on the day the title is closed and the deed delivered. Actually, however, it is impracticable to do this. For example, if title is to be closed in the middle of the month and the rents are due and payable the first of each month, it would be cumbersome for the seller to collect just half the month's rent from the tenants and then for the purchaser to collect the second half after he has taken title. Hence the provision for adjustments for this and similar items in the contract. Of course, the matter of adjustments and those items to be adjusted, or apportioned (the words are used synonymously), will depend upon the practice in the community where the property is located. It is now becoming the custom to apportion nearly every item that arises.

As to rents, although the seller may have collected rents over a period extending beyond the date of transfer, he must pay or allow to the purchaser the fair proportion of the rents then paid but which will be earned after the transfer. Likewise, the interest on the existing mortgage, if there be one, has been accruing since the last interest date, and on the next interest date the amount of interest for the full period will be payable. The seller allows to the purchaser the portion of the interest that has accumulated up to the date of closing title.

Insurance policies are paid for in advance for a period of one year, and in some instances longer. Of course, the seller may cancel his policies and the purchaser may secure new ones, but the surrender value is less than the proportion of the premium for the remaining period; therefore, the seller usually seeks to have the purchaser take over the present policy and pay the seller the proportion of the premium for the time remaining until expiration. As to fire insurance, the purchaser, if very careful, may stipulate a maximum amount of insurance that he will take, thus avoiding purchasing more insurance than he needs. It will be noted in the form reproduced on page 72 that there is a provision exempting liability and compensation insurance from apportionment. This is done because liability insurance is nontransferable in some instances, and most of the companies refuse to permit any transfer of compensation insurance. Therefore, the seller usually must cancel these two types of insurance after the closing of title and receive simply the return premium.

It is customary to adjust real estate taxes. Depending on the law of the county or community, real estate taxes are levied for definite periods and made payable at designated times as fixed by law. The apportionment generally involves the fiscal period to which the taxes, whether due or prepaid, are applicable. The seller would pay the proportion of taxes due from the commencement of the period up to the date of closing the title. To illustrate: Suppose taxes are levied for the fiscal period July 1 to June 30 and are payable in equal shares on October 1 and April 1. If title closes June 1, and the contract makes no mention of the adjustment of taxes, the seller must pay the half due April 1, although that covers the period to June 30. If the contract provided for tax adjustments, the purchaser would have to pay for the month of June, or one-sixth of the amount that was due on April 1.

Where water consumption charges are considered a lien against the property, if unpaid, it is customary to provide for apportionment. Generally a reading is taken of the water meter as close as convenient to the date of title transfer. Where meters are not installed, adjustment of "flat" charges is made for the pro rata period on the basis of previous bills and the average consumption indicated by them. Similar adjustments may apply for gas and electric light charges depending on community custom or law. It is customary also to adjust fuel, if any, at the time of closing by the measurement of the amount of oil or coal on the premises at the current price.

Property restrictions

Title is generally conveyed subject to record restrictions and the contract should note this fact. As a rule, reference is made that "said premises are sold subject to building and zoning restrictions, and encroachments or rights-of-way of record." Where deed restrictions are applicable, a notation to this effect should also be made.

Approval clause

The approval clause binds the purchaser to accept a title such as the named company or counsel would approve. To safeguard against acceptance of a defective title, it is important that the purchaser make certain that the title company or counsel named are trustworthy and of good repute.

In a number of southern and midwestern states it is customary for the seller to furnish an up-to-date abstract of title. This abstract contains the chain of title to the property together with all pertinent data of public record that affect or limit ownership. This abstract is generally reviewed by the purchaser's attorney to make certain that the title is free from defects and readily merchantable. The purchaser often presents the abstract directly to a title company for title check and guarantee. In those states where custom requires the seller to furnish an abstract of title, the approval clause may be altered to read as follows:

The seller is to furnish a complete abstract of title brought down to date and showing a merchantable title of record, subject only to ordinary exceptions customary, but in the event the title shall not be found merchantable of record, seller agrees to use diligence to make the said title merchantable of record and shall have .... days to do so. If, after .... days, the said title has not been made merchantable of record, the party holding the deposit made hereunder and all monies that may have been paid to him under this contract shall return all such monies to the buyer, and thereupon all parties shall be released from all obligations hereunder, or upon the request of the buyer, the seller shall deliver the title in its then existing condition.

Personal property

Many articles used in a building, such as shades and lighting or cooking fixtures, are almost a part of it, yet legally the question of whether or not they were included in the sale might give rise to a dispute, if not specifically mentioned. A great deal of trouble also may be occasioned when the owner, without any explanation, turns over to the purchaser articles for which he has not yet paid and to which he has no title, such as stoves, refrigerators, and so forth. To prevent quibbling and to compel the seller to state his ownership positively, the contract reads: "All personal property appurtenant to or used in the operation of said premises is represented to be owned by the seller and is included in this sale."

Street rights

The contract may also contain a specific declaration by the seller that he intends his sale of the premises described in the contract to include, and that he will convey also, whatever rights or title he may have to the center line of an adjoining street. The principal value of such right or title is that should the municipality ever take title to the street, an award would be payable to the owner. The award might be considerable, and the purchaser should always see that the contract contains this agreement. Further, to accomplish this purpose the same paragraph assigns and obligates the seller to assign to the purchaser any award already made.

Form of deed

"The deed shall be in proper statutory form for record. . . ." This is most important. At no place in the contract up to this point has the seller stated any particular form of deed he would deliver. He may give any kind of deed that is sufficient to pass title. He must under this clause use the form prescribed by law. It is short, contains no useless verbiage, and is therefore more satisfactory and cheaper to record. The form of contract under discussion further provides that the deed shall contain the usual covenants and warranties by which the seller guarantees to the purchaser the title and the rights conveyed by the deed. These covenants are very valuable to the purchaser. A discussion of them will be found in Chapter 9, "Deeds." It is usual, though not compulsory, for the seller to agree to give such a deed. Occasionally the seller will give no covenants, which means the contract must then be altered to state that fact. The purchaser in such cases should seek advice as to whether or not he may safely take the form of deed that the seller desires to give.

Where state law requires that the deed contain a "lien law trust clause," the contract should provide for such a covenant to be given by the seller. The purpose of this trust clause is, where applicable, to require the seller to apply the proceeds of the sale first to the payment of all claims against the property that may be made the subject of a lien before the seller uses the proceeds for any other purpose.

Deposit money a lien

By law, the deposit paid by the purchaser is a lien upon the property. So that there may be no doubt, it is customary to stipulate expressly that not only the deposit but also the reasonable expense of examination of title shall be liens upon the property. And it is only fair, for the seller's protection, that the contract further provide that they shall not continue to be liens after default by the purchaser.

Closing date and place

Several lines below the financial statement appears a paragraph beginning, "The deed shall be delivered upon the receipt of said payments at the office of .... at .... 19........." The blanks should be filled with the place and time at which title is to be closed. The place of closing should be agreed upon; there is no governing custom. Usually the office of the attorney representing either party, a title company, or the broker's office is selected. If no time is set, a reasonable time is assumed to be intended. For convenience a date and an hour are ordinarily set. Unless the contract specifies that time is "of the essence," either party is entitled to an adjournment for a reasonable time.

Loss in case of fire

Equitably, the premises belong to the purchaser from the time the contract is made. The purchaser, however, is not in possession and presumably expects to receive the property in substantially the same condition as when he signed the contract. Should there be a fire loss, it might be questionable who should bear the loss. To avoid this uncertainty, the contract form as set out on page 72 expressly states, "The risk of loss or damage to said premises by fire or other hazards until the delivery of the deed is assumed by the seller." The law of some states places this burden on the seller even though the contract does not specifically cover this point. Still other states provide that unless the contract makes some provision as to fire loss, the purchaser is freed of his contract if the loss is substantial but must take title with an allowance for a minor fire loss.

Purchasers who are very careful in the preparation of contracts will very often have the above-mentioned clause further state the amount of fire insurance that shall be carried by the seller, so that there may be assurance that if a fire occurs there will be sufficient insurance to make good the entire building loss.

In some areas or time periods when housing is in short supply, a purchaser may wish to make certain that the premises are delivered, at time of closing, in substantially the condition in which they were found on the date of signing the contract. To assure that the purchaser will not be compelled to take delivery of a fire-, storm-, or riot-ravaged property, a clause can stipulate that damages from the above contingencies incurred during the contract-to-closing period and exceeding in amount two, three, or more thousand dollars shall make the contract, at the option of the buyer, null and void, and monies deposited or held in escrow toward the purchase of the property shall be refunded.

Other contract clauses

Occasionally circumstances necessitate the inclusion of other contract clauses to cover special circumstances or contingent conditions. The need for such special clauses may arise as follows:

Contract contingent upon purchaser's ability to secure mortgage on acceptable terms. Suppose a veteran who is eligible for benefits under the GI Bill of Rights wishes to contract for the purchase of a property. He knows that the purchase contract must be approved by the Loan Guarantee Division of the Veterans Administration and that even if so approved he must obtain mortgage funds at the amount, rate, and for amortization periods that suit his needs. Under such circumstances, he should provide in his purchase contract a clause to cover this contingency. This clause may be as follows:

This contract and all rights and obligations hereunder are contingent on the purchaser securing a first mortgage for not less than $............... with interest at not in excess of .... per centum per annum, amortizing over not less than .... years.

Purchaser undertakes to proceed expeditiously to obtain such mortgage loan and to pay all the expenses thereof and apply the net proceeds thereof on this contract. Seller shall have the right to seek said mortgage loan on purchaser's behalf, if the purchaser fails to secure an acceptance of said mortgage within .... days from the date hereof, in which event purchaser agrees to cooperate fully and execute any and all appropriate papers and agrees to pay all usual expenses of such mortgage loan. Should a commitment for said loan not be obtained as aforesaid, then purchaser may cancel this contract.

The above right of cancellation shall cease upon the issuance of said mortgage commitment or commitments after said period of time but prior to actual cancellation of this contract. In the event said commitment is subject to Veterans Administration approval, then this contract shall also be subject to Veterans Administration approval. If the Veterans Administration shall not approve said loan, then either party may cancel this contract in which event the seller shall return to the purchaser the money paid hereunder and upon said payment to the purchaser this contract shall be null and void. Purchaser represents that he is an honorably discharged veteran of the armed services of the U.S.A. and entitled to the benefits under the GI Bill of Rights.

The clause making the purchase of the property contingent upon the buyer's ability to secure a specified mortgage sum of money at a reasonable rate of interest, for a specified term of years and subject to conventional amortization provisions is of course advisable in all instances where loan money must be found that will enable the purchaser, be he a veteran or not, to complete the purchase transaction on stated financial terms.

Seller's ability to comply with contract terms—other than those offering title—is questionable. Where there is doubt that the seller is able to comply with the contract terms, such as delivering the premises ready for occupancy by purchaser at time of closing, for instance, the purchaser may wisely include a clause to read as follows:

It is understood and agreed that should the seller be unable to comply with the terms of this contract, the purchaser may elect to reject title, in which event, the seller shall refund the amount of the deposit to the purchaser, together with the costs of the title examination at net title insurance company rates, and there shall be no further liability between them.

Premises to be delivered in present condition. To avoid possible misunderstanding as to responsibility for attending to required repairs, or other questionable conditions of the premises noticed by the purchaser subsequent to signing of contract, the seller may wish to protect himself by including the following clause:

It is understood and agreed that the seller makes and has made no representations or warranties to the purchaser, or his agents, with respect to the physical condition of the property, except as otherwise provided herein; and that the seller will deliver said premises at closing in its present condition, reasonable wear and tear excepted. The purchaser represents that he had inspected the premises and knows the condition thereof and is purchasing said premises "AS IS."

Broker's commission clause. In most states, the broker becomes entitled to his commission as soon as he has carried out his assignment of securing a ready, able, and willing buyer who agrees in writing to purchase the property on the seller's terms. The omission of the broker's commission clause does not affect the broker's rights to compensation. The object of the clause is to avoid possible controversy as to which broker was the procuring cause of the sale and to fix the amount of the commission, which generally is based on custom or specific agreement between broker and seller.

In some states, it is deemed that the broker has not done his job until the buyer takes title. Sometimes, too, the seller insists that the commission shall be due and payable only upon title closing. Under such circumstances it is best to include in the contract a special clause to be signed by the broker. This clause may be as follows:

The broker agrees, as a consideration for the seller entering into this contract upon the terms herein stated, that the broker shall be considered as having earned a commission only if, as, and when title shall close; which said commission shall be payable out of the proceeds of sale at that time, and that no commission shall be due or payable by the seller unless and until such closing of title regardless of the cause of failure of the title to close; and that commission, if payable, shall be at the rates in force at the date of this contract. The broker's agreement hereto is evidenced by his signature below.

....

Broker

Binding on heirs and executors. The parties, having made a contract, and both desiring that it be consummated, agree, for the purpose of avoiding anything that might prevent its completion, that "the stipulations herein are to apply to and bind the heirs, executors, administrators, successors, and assigns of the respective parties." If the seller dies, his heirs or executors taking title must carry out the contract in his stead and convey. In like manner, if the purchaser dies, his executors or administrators shall pay as provided in the contract. Any person taking title from the seller, knowing of the contract, may be compelled to convey. Should the purchaser assign his contract and the assignee fail to carry out the provisions, the seller may look to the purchaser and compel his performance of the contract terms. The purchaser's only protection when he assigns his contract is to request a written promise of performance from his assignee.

Execution of the contract

The law requires the contract to be signed by the party to be bound or by his agent authorized in writing. The duplicate copies are customarily each signed by both parties. Signing may be by subscribing one's name, or if the parties are unable to write, by marking. Any mark made with the intention that it constitute signing is sufficient. Mere signing makes a valid contract. The seal, acknowledgment, and witnesses are not necessary.

It is advantageous to seal the instrument. It raises in some states a presumption that the person who has affixed his seal received a consideration and places the burden of disproving it upon him, should he desire to defeat the contract. Another advantage of sealing the contract is that, when it is sealed, the obligations of the parties are kept alive by law for a greater length of time, the statute of limitations on sealed instruments being longer than on instruments not under seal. In most states the statute of limitations provides that sealed instruments are enforceable over twenty years, whereas instruments not under seal are limited generally to a maximum period of three to five years. The seal, however, has not the advantage of restricting the obligation to the one signing the contract. An undisclosed principal may, notwithstanding the seal, be held. The legal effect of seal is further discussed in Chapter 9, "Deeds."

Witnessing the instrument accomplishes little. It is convenient as a memorandum of the fact that the witness was present and saw the parties sign.

No instrument can be recorded unless it is acknowledged or proved. Although contracts are not usually recorded, nevertheless in exceptional cases, if fraud is suspected, great harm may be avoided if the contract is placed on record and public notice of its terms so given. For the same reason it is very often wise to have the contract acknowledged. The parties acknowledge their execution of the instrument before an officer to whom they are known to be the persons executing the instrument and who is empowered by law to take acknowledgments. The officer then signs a certificate of acknowledgment upon the instrument. If the parties either cannot or will not acknowledge the instrument, the fact may be proved by the witness, who swears before the proper officer that he was present and saw the parties sign the instrument and that he knew them to be the persons described in the paper. The officer then signs a certificate of these facts on the instrument, and it can be recorded.

Nonperformance of contracts

Usually contracts of sale are fully carried out, but it is necessary to have some understanding of the rights and liabilities that may be invoked by breach of contract. The default may be, obviously, by either party.

If the seller fails to carry out the contract, his failure may arise from either of two causes, unwillingness or inability, each of which gives the purchaser different remedies. The seller may be able to fulfill the contract but may unreasonably refuse to do so. In such case the purchaser may pursue any of three courses. (1) He may recover the amount of his deposit with interest and the reasonable expense he has incurred in examination of the title. (2) He may, if the seller still has title to the property, bring an action to compel the seller specifically to perform the contract. If he is successful in his action, the seller must carry out the terms of the contract, or he may be jailed until he does so. (3) The purchaser may, if he wishes, or if the seller has disposed of the property, sue for the loss of his bargain, in which case he may recover as his damages the difference between the value of the property and what he agreed by his contract to pay for it. Should the value be less than the price, this remedy is ineffectual, of course.

The seller may, however, be quite willing to carry out the contract, but he may be compelled to default by his inability to give the title he has promised. His title may not be clear; there may be other people who have some interest in it. In such a case, if the seller acted in good faith, knowing nothing of the defect, the purchaser may recover only the amount of his deposit, interest, and title examination expenses. But if the seller, knowing of the flaw in his title, permitted the purchaser to act to his detriment in entering into the contract, then the purchaser may recover for the loss of his bargain the difference between the value of the property and the selling price.

In signing the contract, the purchaser, having only himself to consider and not having to deliver title to property, which may without his knowledge have some defect, does not receive as much consideration as the seller. He should not undertake the obligation of the contract unless he sees his way clear to perform his part. Should he default, his seller may (1) forfeit the deposit and cancel the contract, or (2) bring an action against the purchaser for specific performance, or (3) sue for his damages—the difference between the value of the property and the price the purchaser agreed to pay, this relief being appropriate naturally only if the price exceeds the property's value. Generally a clause providing for forfeiture of the deposit as liquidated damages is inserted in the contract as a safeguard against the purchaser's nonperformance.

Escrow contracts

Without becoming involved in legal technicalities, an escrow contract may be described briefly as a three-party agreement among the seller, the buyer, and the escrow holder. Such a contract is used in many localities for real estate sales. Some of its advantages are the following:

1. The seller receives no money until his title is searched and found marketable.

2. The seller knows that, if the title is found to be marketable, he is certain to be paid and the contract will be carried out.

3. Neither buyer nor seller need be present at the closing of title.

Briefly, the escrow contract states all the terms of the sale to be performed by seller and buyer. The escrow holder is usually an attorney, a bank, or a title institution. Sometimes, at the signing of the contract, the buyer's cash and the seller's deed and the various other papers that are to be delivered by each are all turned over to the escrow holder, who, when the title search has been completed, makes the adjustments, records the title instruments, and remits the amount due to the seller. Other escrow contracts may provide for initial payment of the deposit only and for the seller and buyer to deliver later the papers and moneys needed to consummate the transaction.

Installment or land contracts

In some instances, particularly in the sale of vacant lots, it is found that the purchaser has not sufficient cash to pay a deposit and, within the usual period, take title and pay the balance—or the purchase may not seem desirable on those terms. Yet he would be willing and able to pay the price in installments. In such cases it is usual to have the financial clause provide for times and amounts of installments at stated intervals, and the payments to be applied first to interest on the purchase price, then to payment of charges, such as taxes as they accrue, and finally to payment of the unpaid balance of purchase price. Under such a contract it is usually agreed that the deed shall not be delivered until a certain amount has been paid upon the price. The usual custom is for the purchaser to give a purchase money mortgage for the balance of the price, the mortgage to be paid in such manner as may be agreed upon. For the seller's protection the contract should also provide that, in event of a default in payment by the purchaser, the contract be canceled and all sums paid by the purchaser be deemed rent for the period from the time he took possession up to the default. In some areas this type of agreement is also known as a *contract for deed*.

Contracts for exchange of real estate

Occasionally, a situation arises where the purchaser, in lieu of cash or as a part payment, offers some real estate of his own which he wishes to dispose of and which the seller is willing to accept. In such instances the contract for exchange is used. This contract is similar in many respects to the contract of sale, except that the consideration is paid wholly or partly in property instead of cash. The instrument is dated and contains the names of the parties the same as the contract of sale, except that for convenience they are termed "party of the first part" and "party of the second part." Usually the person who pays the least cash is designated as the first party. Following the names of the parties are set forth the agreed value of the first party's realty, its description, and the encumbrances subject to which it is sold. Then follows a similar statement with reference to the second party's property. As in the contract of sale, the description and enumeration of encumbrances should be full and accurate.

Since the properties are being exchanged, and no cash, or only a small amount, is passed, the parties may set any value they wish upon the properties to be exchanged. They may agree on any values as long as such agreed values do not affect the cash difference to be paid. However, such values should be reasonably close to true value since the question of "capital gain or loss" may be checked by the income tax authorities. For example: the first party owns X, which it is agreed is worth $25,000 and which he is to convey subject to a $15,000 mortgage. The second party owns Y, agreed to be worth $20,000, which he will convey subject to a $14,000 mortgage. In this case the first party's equity or value over the encumbrance is $10,000, and that of the second party is $6,000, the difference being $4,000, which the second party will pay. A part of the difference may be paid on the signing of the contract, but quite often no payment is made until the closing of title.

Historically, most exchanges developed because neither party could find a cash buyer. In recent years, however, because of the increased tax burdens, many alert real estate brokers, using the term *trades* rather than *exchanges*, are working out deals and earning commissions by securing an exchange for the owner who would like to sell but who can ill afford to because the increased value of his property would, on a sale, result in an excessive "capital gain" tax liability. By a trade such a seller receives under terms of the transaction what he believes is a more advantageous parcel of real estate without incurring the liability of a present tax. Thus, a cash sale with its resultant capital gain tax is postponed until sales conditions and tax liabilities appear more favorable from the seller's point of view.

Property exchanges, too, are deemed advisable where one party in the exchange transaction seeks a new and more favorable basis for depreciation (tax) allowance in order to increase the net cash flow after income taxes. For example, Mr. Brown purchased a property that was worth $20,000 fifteen years ago. At the time of the purchase the building was valued at $10,000. The building, for income tax purposes, was 100 percent depreciated to date. The property now is estimated to have a value of $100,000, and the owner pays income taxes on the net earnings from the property in the amount of $8,000. To better his investment position, Mr. Brown exchanges his property for one worth $150,000, assuming a purchase money mortgage for the difference in the exchange value of the two properties. The new property is composed of $100,000 worth of land and $50,000 worth of depreciable improvements. The basis of the new property after acquisition is now $60,000 (the $50,000 difference in price plus the $10,000 remaining bases on the land). By this exchange, Mr. Brown accomplished two investment objectives:

1. He postponed a large capital gain tax which he would have incurred in an outright cash sale ($100,000 less base of $10,000 equals a capital gain of $90,000).
2. He established a new depreciation basis of $50,000 that enables him to increase his net cash income flow by $2,500 where the rate of depreciation is calculated at 5 percent per annum under straight line depreciation over a remaining economic life period of twenty years.

Other reasons for property exchange transactions that motivate parties may include the following:

1. Continuity of income is assured while one or both parties are looking for a suitable property to replace the one to be sold.
2. One can build up an estate by exchanging for continually more valuable

properties without tax gain penalty that would be incurred in cash sale transactions.

3. Brokers can take advantage of additional client motivations to serve their specialized needs while earning commissions from each party to the exchange.

READING AND STUDY REFERENCES

1. BROWN, ROBERT K., *Real Estate Economics*, Chapter 7. Boston: Houghton Mifflin Company, 1965.

2. HEBARD, EDNA L., and GERALD S. MEISEL, *Principles of Real Estate Law*, Chapter 10, New York: Simmons-Boardman Publishing Corporation, 1964.

3. HUSBAND, WILLIAM H., and FRANK RAY ANDERSON, *Real Estate*, Chapter 9. Homewood, Ill.: Richard D. Irwin, Inc., 1960.

4. KRATOVIL, ROBERT, *Real Estate Law*, Chapter 11. Englewood Cliffs, N.J.: Prentice-Hall, Inc., 1969.

5. LUSK, HAROLD F., *Law of the Real Estate Business*, Chapter 12. Homewood, Ill.: Richard D. Irwin, Inc., 1965.

6. RING, ALFRED A., *Questions and Problems in Real Estate Principles and Practices* (rev. ed.), Chapter 5. Englewood Cliffs, N.J.: Prentice-Hall, Inc., 1972.

7. UNGER, MAURICE A., *Real Estate* (4th ed.), Chapter 4. Cincinnati: South-Western Publishing Co., 1969.

6

LAND SURVEYING
AND PROPERTY DESCRIPTIONS

Necessity for land survey

To transfer title to real property from one individual or estate to another, it is essential that a positive identification be made of the parcel of land involved. Failure to do so may lead to disputes as to the amount of realty conveyed and to court action for setting aside by *rescission*[1] the original agreement and transfer for lack of a "meeting of mind" as provided under the statute of fraud.

History of land surveying

Since land constitutes the major source of wealth in the United States, interest in the extent and amount of this wealth has always been of paramount concern to property owners and lawmakers. Official land surveys date back to 1785 when public lands north of the Ohio River were recorded under the direction of the geographer of the United States. Subsequent acts of Congress gave weight to the importance of land records by establishment in 1812 of the General Land Office as a branch of the Treasury Department. The land office was transferred in 1849 to the Depart-

---

[1]The act of rescinding or annulling, thereby restoring to another party in a contract what one has received from him.

ment of the Interior and by act of Congress in 1946 was given the important status as Bureau of Land Management.

As land transfers became more frequent, and positive identification of land holdings more important, the art of land surveying became specialized. At first, land identification and measurements were made or supervised by lawyers who were generally called upon to write formal and legally acceptable land descriptions. Later, men who specialized in the use of transit and land measure instruments were given official status by the various states as "land surveyors." Although civil engineers, as a rule, are technically qualified to make land surveys, most states require demonstration of technical and educational competency by examination and licensing of individuals who hold themselves out as public land surveyors.

Purpose of land survey

Land, characteristically, is nonhomogeneous at least as far as geographic location is concerned. It is possible, therefore, to give definite and indisputable identification of any and all parcels of land irrespective of whether same is under separate or single ownership. Although the principal purpose of land surveying is to identify any given landed property, the need for land surveying is fourfold as follows:

1. The necessity to secure accurate boundary data essential in the writing of a legal description.
2. The establishment of a definite quantity of area measurement in acres, square miles, or square feet units within a designated legally described tract of land.
3. To reestablish boundaries that have become obliterated or lost by actions of nature or man or both. Resurveys, too, become necessary due to changes in magnetic bearing, use of inaccurate instruments in the original survey, or errors in calculation or judgment by field surveyors.
4. To split a tract of land into separate units of ownership or to subdivide a large tract into smaller units for development and sale.

Whatever the purpose of the survey, the resultant land description should contain the following: (1) a definite point of beginning, (2) definite tract or parcel corners, (3) specific length and directions of the sides of the property, and (4) the area in accepted units of measure contained within the described boundaries.

Kinds of land descriptions

Broadly speaking, land descriptions may be classified into those applicable to incorporated or urban areas and those used in sparsely settled or rural areas. In most urban areas provision is made for the establishment of "control points" for land measurement purposes, and subdivision regulations, as a rule, provide for orderly plotting of blocks and lots in community subdivisions before such are officially accepted for county record filing purposes.

Legal description in urban areas

Land identifications most frequently used for real property in urban areas include, as noted in the chapter on contracts, the following descriptions: (1) by street number of house, (2) by tract subdivision, and (3) by metes and bounds.

Street number of a house. This is the weakest form of all the possible descriptions. Although sufficient to identify a property for contract of sale or lease purposes, this mode of description should never be used in a deed or mortgage and never to describe a vacant lot or plot.

Tract subdivision. Quite often the owner of a tract of vacant land decides to subdivide it into homesites. This in various parts of the country is spoken of as a "subdivision," or a "development," or selling from a "map" or "tract." The owner of such a tract provides for the necessary land survey, the cutting through of designated streets, the naming and numbering of blocks and lots, and the preparation of a required tract map which is filed in the proper county office.

The map shows the various blocks and lots, numbered for convenience of identification, and usually bears a subdivision title, the owner's and surveyor's names, the date of survey, and the date of approval by community or county officials. The following is a simple illustration of a fairly small tract that the owner has decided to sell in lots.

**Map of land at Mineola, Nassau Co., N.Y.   Property of James Smith.
Surveyed by John Jones, C. E.   Dated April 1, 1970.**

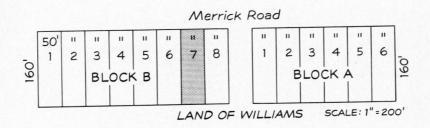

The simplest manner of describing a lot upon this map would be, "All that certain lot, piece, or parcel of land, known upon a map of land at Mineola, Nassau County, N.Y., the property of James Smith, John Jones, surveyor, April 1, 1970; as and by the lot number 7 in Block B." Such a description fully identifies the lot, and reference to the map on file will always show the exact location of the lot. The surveyor, in making such a survey, uses some permanent landmark upon the plot so that all lots may be physically located by measuring from it.

Metes and bounds. A description by metes and bounds is usually found in the cities. Metes (measures) and bounds (direction) make possible a description of such accuracy as is requisite in locations where land is of considerable value and boundaries must be definitely fixed. Suppose upon the following diagram the realty to be sold is the lot X. A description of this lot would read, "Beginning at a point on the southerly side of Kent Street, 100 feet easterly from the corner formed by the intersection of the southerly side of Kent Street and the easterly side of Broadway; thence southerly parallel to the easterly side of Broadway, 100 feet; thence easterly parallel to the southerly side of Kent Street, 20 feet; thence northerly parallel to the easterly side of Broadway 100 feet to the southerly side of Kent Street, and thence westerly along the southerly side of Kent Street, 20 feet to the point or place of beginning." That gives an exact description, each side being meted and bounded—that is, measured in feet and direction indicated. It is most important in such a description that the point of beginning be

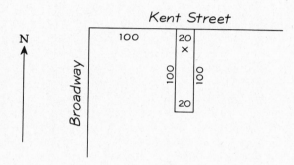

carefully identified to avoid uncertainty of location. The entire description is worthless if there is an error in the starting point.

The property just described is what is known as a *regular lot*; the front and rear dimensions are the same, also the sides, and the angles formed are right angles or nearly so. Many times it is necessary to draw a description of an *irregular lot*, such, for example, as the southerly triangular lot shown in the following diagram.

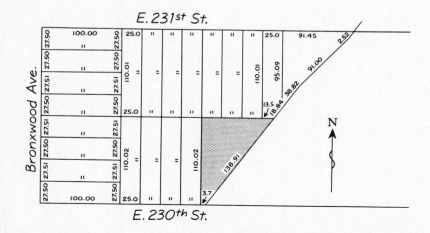

A description of this irregular lot would read as follows:

Beginning at a point on the northerly side of East 230th Street, 200 feet easterly from the corner formed by the intersection of the easterly side of Bronxwood Avenue and the northerly side of East 230th Street; running thence northerly and parallel to the easterly side of Bronxwood Avenue, 110 and 2/100 feet; thence easterly parallel to the northerly side of East 230th Street, 88 and 50/100 feet; thence southwesterly, 138 and 91/100 feet to a point on the northerly side of East 230th Street, which point is 3 and 70/100 feet easterly from the point or place of beginning; and thence westerly along the northerly side of East 230th Street, 3 and 70/100 feet to the point or place of beginning. All as per official records of Plat Book "C" of Denver, Colorado.

In both the foregoing illustrations of metes and bounds descriptions, the directions have been given largely by reference to the fronting or an intersecting street. That type of reference is natural in any place where blocks are laid out, for the lots fit into the block and usually side lines are parallel to the intersecting streets. Consequently, there is no need to give the exact compass bearing of each course or lot line. When, however, the land to be described is in an area with few intersecting streets and no regular lot layout, the description should give the bearing in minutes, degrees, and seconds of each course. The following is a diagram of such a plot.

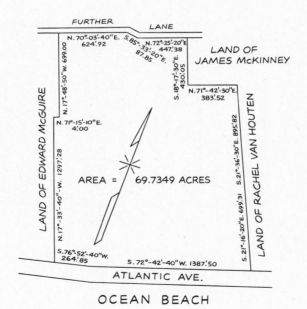

A description of this land would read as follows:

All that tract or parcel of land situate in the Town of East Hampton, County of Suffolk and State of New York, bounded and described as follows: BEGINNING at the junction of the westerly line of land of James McKinney and the southerly side of Further Lane, and running thence along the land of said James McKinney, south 18 degrees 17 minutes 30 seconds east 430 and 5/100 feet; thence along the land of said James McKinney north 71 degrees 42 minutes 30 seconds east, 383 and 52/100 feet to land of Rachel Van Houten; thence along the land of said Rachel Van Houten south 21 degrees 36 minutes 30 seconds east 895 and 82/100 feet to a point; thence still along the land of Rachel Van Houten south 21 degrees 16 minutes 20 seconds east 699 and 31/100 feet to the proposed Atlantic Avenue Highway, thence along said Atlantic Avenue south 72 degrees 42 minutes 40 seconds west 1387 and 50/100 feet; thence continuing along said Atlantic Avenue south 76 degrees 52 minutes 40 seconds west 264 and 85/100 feet to land of Edward J. McGuire; thence along the lands of said Edward J. McGuire north 17 degrees 33 minutes 40 seconds west 1297 and 28/100 feet, thence north 71 degrees 15 minutes 10 seconds east 4 feet; thence continuing along the land of said Edward J. McGuire north 17 degrees 48 minutes 50 seconds west 699 feet to Further Lane Highway; thence along said Further Lane Highway north 70 degrees 3 minutes 40 seconds east 624 and 92/100 feet; thence continuing along said Further Lane Highway south 85 degrees 33 minutes 20 seconds east 87 and 85/100 feet; thence continuing along said Further Lane Highway north 72 degrees 25 minutes 20 seconds east 447 and 38/100 feet to the point or place of beginning.

Containing by actual measurement as per survey dated April 10, 1971, of Nathan F. Tiffany 69.7349 acres. Atlantic Beach, New Jersey.

Because of the technical competency required to derive directional bearings north, south, east, and west with accuracy to minutes and seconds of degrees, metes and bounds descriptions should be prepared only by registered land surveyors. In metes and bounds descriptions as shown in the following circular diagram, the bearings or course of a line of direction is the angle that line makes from the central point of a departure parallel

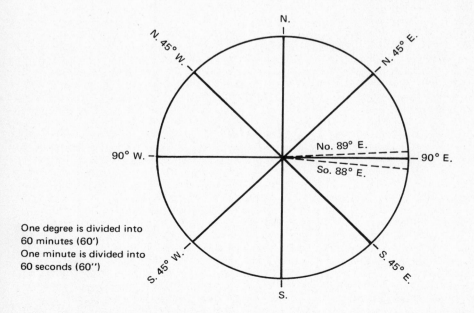

One degree is divided into
60 minutes (60')
One minute is divided into
60 seconds (60")

with a meridian. As shown in the diagram below, the bearing of any line cannot exceed 90 degrees. A line running almost due east might have a bearing of "north" 89 degrees east. If this same line were rotated three degrees in a clockwise direction, its bearing would become "south" 88 degrees east.

Bearings may be measured and described either from the magnetic north and south (in which case they are called *magnetic bearings*) or from a true astronomic meridian north and south (in which case they are called *true bearings*). The bearings of a given line as expressed under the two systems will differ by the amount of the magnetic declination for that date and locality.

Land description in rur-urban or farm areas

Outside the populous districts it is customary to describe land either by "monuments" or by "rectangular (or government) survey" methods. These methods of land descriptions are illustrated and described as follows:

Monuments. Where land is not so valuable or when the expense of a survey to determine exactly the distances and directions of the property lines would be out of proportion to the value of the land, a description by monuments may be warranted. There are occasions, too, when the buyer and seller are not so keenly concerned with the exact area; they are thinking in terms of a piece of land that both know and have gone over, and they are thinking of it as it stands, and not of its exact size. If a buyer likes a certain farm, with its woodlot and various fields, and if he gets all of it as its boundaries run, he is satisfied—whether it contains somewhat more or less than its supposed acreage.

Under the circumstances, it is usual to describe such a tract by identifying its boundaries as fully as possible without exact measurements or directions.

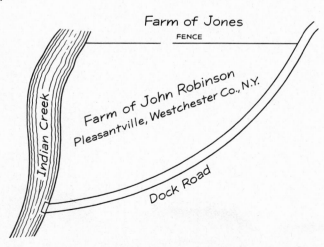

The farm as illustrated may be described without mention of metes or bounds as follows:

The farm of John Robinson at Pleasantville, Westchester County, N.Y., bounded and described as follows: Beginning at the dock on Indian Creek at the foot of Dock Road; thence along Dock Road to the point where said road is met by the fence dividing the farms of [the seller] and Jones, thence along said fence to the side of Indian Creek, and thence along said Indian Creek to the Dock, the point of beginning.

Monuments may be tangible or intangible. If tangible, they are either natural or artificial. Rivers, lakes, streams, trees, rocks, springs, and the like, are natural. Fences, walls, houses, canals, streets, stakes, and posts are artificial. The center line of a block is an example of an intangible monument. Since all monuments are susceptible of destruction, removal, or shifting, they should be used only where necessary, and then every available identifying fact should be stated; for instance, not merely "a tree" but "an old oak tree." Thus even after it has become a stump it may still be identified from other trees.

Rectangular or government survey. Recognizing the weakness of metes and bounds and monuments descriptions particularly in rural areas, the federal government adopted on April 26, 1785, the rectangular survey. This system currently applies to thirty states including Alaska. It does not apply to the original thirteen states, the other New England and Atlantic Coast States (except Florida), or to West Virginia, Kentucky, Tennessee, and Texas. This method of land description is relatively simple and enables land to be described in brief symbols and words.

This system is based on surveying lines running north and south, called meridians, and east and west, called base lines. These are established through the area to be surveyed, and each is given a name and number by the land office in Washington, D.C. A map showing the location of the several prime meridians and their base lines in the United States is shown below. To minimize errors in measurement caused by the curvature of the earth and the consequent converging of meridian lines as they extend north and south of the equator, the surveyors divided the area between intersections into squares, or *quadrangles*, twenty-four miles on each side. These quadrangles, formed to reestablish a distance of twenty-four miles at succeeding standard lines drawn parallel to the base line—north and south—were further subdivided into sixteen areas each measuring six miles by six miles, called *townships*. The townships containing an area of thirty-six square miles were again subdivided into *sections*, each a square mile containing 640 acres, and the sections were then divided into halves, quarters, or smaller subdivisions as the need called for to describe individual land holdings.

To identify the exact location of a given thirty-six-square-mile area, the rows east and west and parallel to the baseline were numbered as townships[2] 1, 2, and so forth, north or south, of a given base line. The rows

---

[2]The term *township* as used here should not be mistaken for a "political" or governmental area designated as a township. The latter may comprise an area smaller or many times larger than thirty-six square miles.

MAP OF PRIME MERIDIANS AND THEIR BASE LINES
WITHIN THE UNITED STATES

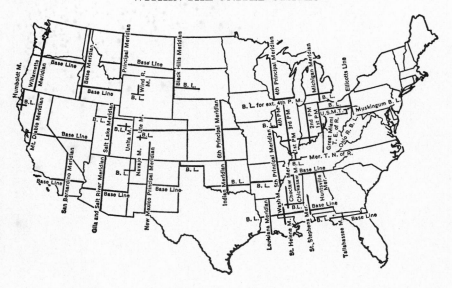

north and south parallel to the meridians are called ranges and were numbered 1, 2, and so forth, east or west of a principal or guide meridian. The numbering system is illustrated by the following diagram.

Sections are identified by number as indicated on the following diagram:

**Section 12, Township 3 North,
Range 2 East of Principal Meridian
in King County, Texas**

6	5	4	3	2	1
7	8	9	10	11	12
18	17	16	15	14	13
19	20	21	22	23	24
30	29	28	27	26	25
31	32	33	34	35	36

6 MILES

6 MILES

Owing to the spherical shape of the earth, the meridians converge as one goes north—the north side of a township is approximately fifty feet shorter than the south side. To correct this error, as previously noted, the government established certain principal meridians and others, called guide meridians, which are changed at each parallel to make allowances for the earth's curvature. This problem really concerns only the surveyor and is mentioned only so that the reader may not be confused in studying the diagram.

In describing a section, it is customary to state first the number of the section, then the township and range: "Section 12, Township 3 North, Range 2 East of the principal (named) meridian." It may be abbreviated: "Sect. 12 T. 3 N. Rge 2 E, ... County, State of ...."

The description of a part of a section is simple. For example, the plot A on the diagram below is, "West ½ of Southwest ¼, Sec. 12." The same diagram indicates the description of other parts of the section.

The excellent chart that follows was prepared by the Chicago Title and Trust Company. It contains much data of help to the conveyancer.

Each section, as shown, contains 640 acres. To calculate the area where the description indicates that only a part of a section is to be conveyed, one need merely multiply the fractions as described and multiply the sum total by 640 acres. In the diagram shown above the top northwest corner of the section is described as follows: N.W. ¼ of the N.W. ¼ of the N.W. ¼ of Section 12. Multiplying ¼ × ¼ × ¼ × 640 acres $= \dfrac{640}{64}$, or 10 acres, as is indicated in the illustration.

Use of terms "more or less." The seller should use care to undertake to

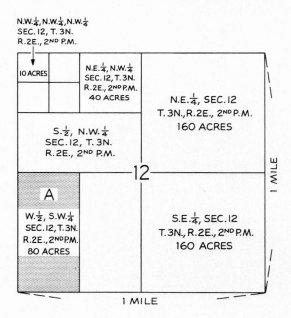

N.W.¼, N.W.¼, N.W.¼
SEC. 12, T. 3N.
R.2E., 2ND P.M.

10 ACRES

N.E.¼, N.W.¼
SEC. 12, T. 3N.
R.2E., 2ND P.M.
40 ACRES

N.E.¼, SEC. 12
T. 3N., R.2E., 2ND P.M.
160 ACRES

S.½, N.W.¼
SEC. 12, T. 3N.
R.2E., 2ND P.M.

—12—

A

W.½, S.W.¼
SEC.12, T.3N.
R.2E., 2ND P.M.
80 ACRES

S.E.¼, SEC. 12
T. 3N., R.2E., 2ND P.M.
160 ACRES

1 MILE

1 MILE

convey only what he owns. As a general rule he should use the same description as was used when he bought the property.

If he has reason to believe that he has not as much depth or width of land as his deed calls for, he may then use the words "more or less." "More or less" is a question of reasonableness. Sometimes a variance of a few inches is unreasonable, as in the width of a city lot, whereas a foot might not be unreasonable in the depth of the same lot. If the variance is reasonable, the seller can give good title under a description using the words "more or less." The purchaser, if "more or less" is used, will often have the contract provide minimum dimensions or area, less than which he will not take. If a house is standing on the lot, a small variance makes little difference, for the building will remain and produce rent, whether the description indicates slightly wider or narrower dimensions than the lot actually possesses.

Description of improved property

A purchaser offering to buy improved property is always presumed to be intending to purchase three things: (1) the land, (2) the structure, capable of occupancy and rentable, and (3) the right to maintain it. If the building stands in from the lines on all sides, there is no difficulty; but in cities, a building is often constructed to fill the entire width of the lot.

If the building exactly fills the lot, not encroaching on either side, the seller may use any description that accurately describes the land; the building will pass with a description of the land. The purchaser may, if he wishes to be sure he is signing a contract for the house he has in mind,

A SECTION OF LAND—640 ACRES

	80 rods	10 chains	330 ft	
A rod is 16½ feet.			5 acres	5 acres
A chain is 66 feet or 4 rods.		20 acres	5 chs	20 rds
A mile is 320 rods, 80 chains or 5,280 feet.				
A square rod is 272¼ square feet.			40 rods	10 acres 660 feet
An acre contains 43,560 square feet.				
An acre contains 160 square rods.	80 acres	660 feet	10 chains	
An acre is about 208¾ feet square.				
An acre is 8 rods wide by 20 rods long,				
or any two numbers (of rods)		40 acres		80 rods
whose product is 160.				
25×125 feet equals .0717 of an acre.				

CENTER | 20 chains | 1,320 feet

Sectional Map of a Township with adjoining Sections. | OF SECTION

36	31	32	33	34	35	36	31
1	6	5	4	3	2	1	6
12	7	8	9	10	11	12	7
13	18	17	16	15	14	13	18
24	19	20	21	22	23	24	19
25	30	29	28	27	26	25	30
36	31	32	33	34	35	36	31
1	6	5	4	3	2	1	6

160 acres

40 chains, 160 rods or 2,640 feet

have inserted after the description the words "known as and by the house number ...., ... Street."

Suppose, however, that the building not only fills the entire lot but also encroaches on the lot alongside. If the encroachment is not in excess of a few inches, and if the building has been standing for many years, an easement has probably arisen permitting the building to remain. In such case a description by street number would be improper, for the seller does not own and cannot convey the building and all the land upon which it stands. He should use a description that describes the land he owns as if it were a vacant lot. The building and easement will follow with the land so described. The seller is protected, for he is undertaking to give only what he has, and the purchaser gets what he intended to buy. In practice it is usually better for the seller to frankly disclose the actual situation to the buyer, who then may take the title subject to the encroachment.

Occasionally the building on the lot alongside encroaches on the seller's land, so that the seller has possession of less than that called for by his deed. How shall he then sell safely? He may use a description, taking in only so much land as is actually in his possession, diminishing his width dimensions as much as necessary. He may use the description called for by his own deed, using "more or less" following the width dimensions. Or, he may describe merely by house number. Under any of those descriptions he can give what he contracts to convey. To be certain of the exact location of the improvements in relation to land boundaries, the purchaser should obtain a survey prepared by a professional engineer or a licensed land surveyor.

READING AND STUDY REFERENCES

1. DAVIS, RAYMOND E., and FRANCIS S. FOOTE, *Surveying—Theory and Practice*, Chapters 22 and 23. New York: McGraw-Hill Book Company, 1953.

2. HEBARD, EDNA L., and GERALD S. MEISEL, *Principles of Real Estate Law*, Chapter 9. New York: Simmons-Boardman Publishing Corporation, 1964.

3. KRATOVIL, ROBERT, *Real Estate Law*, Chapter 5. Englewood Cliffs, N.J.: Prentice-Hall, Inc., 1969.

4. LUSK, HAROLD F., *Law of the Real Estate Business*, pp. 127–35. Homewood, Ill.: Richard D. Irwin, Inc., 1965.

5. RATCLIFF, RICHARD U., *Real Estate Analysis*, Chapter 3. New York: McGraw-Hill Book Company, 1961.

6. RAYNER, WILLIAM H., and MILTON O. SCHMIDT, *Elementary Surveying*, Chapter 16. New York: D. Van Nostrand Co., Inc. 1955.

7. RING, ALFRED A., *Questions and Problems in Real Estate Principles and Practices* (rev. ed.), Chapter 6. Englewood Cliffs, N.J.: Prentice-Hall, Inc., 1972.

7

TRANSFER OF TITLE

Historical significance

Title to realty is a legal concept which confers upon the rightful holder a lawful claim to all the requisites or elements that constitute ownership. Title legally conferred sanctions not only exclusive possession to an owner but also recourse to legal power to defend his title holdings.

Historically, and prior to the development of the legal concept of ownership, title to realty was solely evidenced by possession and the physical power to defend it. Title in fact during the early history of mankind was chiefly acquired by *conquest* (might was right) or by more peaceful means of *discovery* in the name of powerful and sovereign empires or nations. Whole continents, including America, were thus acquired by discovery and exploration. Since the development of the concept of land ownership and under the allodial system, sources of title in the United States are traceable to grant by foreign power (prior to the Revolution) and grant by state or federal government. From person to person, of course, acquisition of title may be traced by (1) will, (2) descent, (3) voluntary alienation, and (4) involuntary alienation. These methods of title transfer will be discussed more fully in the pages following.

Early methods of transferring title

Probably the earliest transfers of title were accomplished by the stronger taking possession from the weaker. This system was unjust, and as society developed, protection was given to the owner in preserving his possession. Under the feudal system the sovereign or king owned all the land. He parceled out the land to his lords, each of whom in turn subdivided his portion among his retainers. This subdivision went on indefinitely. No one had any title save the king. Each had only a "feud" or right to possess the land during the pleasure of his overlord. The tenant was bound to give his superior aid and fealty, and the superior was bound to protect the tenant. The tenant could not even give up his possession or transfer it without his overlord's consent. The evils of this system finally resulted in laws that made it possible for a tenant to sell his holding and substitute another in his place.

The early method by which a transfer of realty was accomplished was the mere delivery of possession. A man who had been in possession of land for many years, and whose claim to it had never been questioned, was presumed to be its owner. No one could contradict his claim of title. This presumption is the foundation of our present law of "title by adverse possession." If such an owner desired to sell, he simply delivered to the purchaser a clod of earth from the land, in the presence of witnesses, saying at the time some appropriate words such as, "I put you in possession of this land." This procedure was as nearly an actual delivery as the subject matter of the sale would permit.

The statute of frauds

Transfers by delivery only necessarily gave rise to many disputes. There being no written record of the transaction, false statements permitted gross frauds. Possession was forcibly taken and held. As a result, the *statute of frauds* was eventually adopted, which prevented fraud by declaring that no transfer should be enforceable unless in writing. From this statute flows the present system of transferring title by means of written instruments: the deed, mortgage, lease, and so forth. The statute of frauds in substance has been enacted into the law of each state.

Present methods of transferring title

The term *title* must be considered as including not only the full fee simple but any other interest in real property. Under strict legal rules, title to real property can be transferred in only two ways, either by operation of law, or by purchase or gift. Transfer by operation of law takes place only by escheat or when the title passes to the heirs of an owner who dies leaving no will. Every other transfer is considered a purchase or gift.

For all practical purposes, however, title to realty may be transferred in any of the following ways:

1. By descent
2. By will
3. By voluntary alienation
4. By involuntary alienation

Title by descent. One who dies leaving no will is said to have died intestate. Such property as he may have owned at his death passes to his heirs by operation of law. The rights and priorities of the persons entitled to share in his estate are fixed by law in the several states. Those to whom the real property passes are called heirs, and those who take the personal property are called next of kin. In most states the distinction between heirs and next of kin has been abolished, and those who inherit real or personal property are called "distributees." The rights of the surviving spouse are always protected, whether by dower or "intestate share." The real property immediately becomes subject to the widow's rights, if there be a widow. If the deceased owner leaves children, the realty is divided among them in equal shares, provided all are living. Should any of the owner's children be dead, leaving children, such children divide equally the share their parent would have taken if living. If, for example, the deceased had four children, A, B, C, and D, and if A, B, and C survived him but D predeceased him, leaving two children who were living at the death of their grandparent, then A, B, and C each would receive one-fourth and the two grandchildren each one-eighth of the property. If there are no children or issue of deceased children, the property goes to the parents of the deceased and his collateral relatives—that is, brothers and sisters and their descendants—in accordance with the law of the state in which the property is situated.

Title by will. During his lifetime an owner may dispose of his property by deed, mortgage, lease, and so forth. He may also make disposition of it to take effect at his death. This is usually accomplished by will (as it is legally termed, "last will and testament"). The owner making the will is known as the *testator*, and when he is dead he is said to have died *testate*. The will must be executed with certain formalities, required by law. Upon the testator's death, it is offered for probate to an appropriate court, which, if the will is regular and no valid objection is raised, admits it to probate, and a public record is made of it. Although many laymen attempt to draw wills, this practice is exceedingly dangerous. Any error in form or manner of execution may invalidate the will, and usually such errors are not discovered until the will is offered for probate, when it is too late for the testator to remedy the mistake.

A gift of real property is a *devise*, and the recipient is a *devisee*. A gift of personal property is a *bequest*, or *legacy*, and the recipient is a *legatee*. These terms are often erroneously used interchangeably, and sometimes grave troubles arise from such carelessness. As has been said, the will cannot cut off the rights of the surviving spouse. Consequently, it is usual for the testator to make some provision for the spouse, stating that it is "in lieu of statutory rights." Even such a provision is binding only in case the spouse fails within a certain legal time to elect to take the statutory rights instead.

A will should and usually does appoint an *executor*, who is empowered to carry out its terms and provisions. In most states, unless the will gives him rights and duties with reference to the realty, he has no interest in the real property unless it is needed to pay debts. It passes to the devisees immediately upon the testator's death. The executor's duties are only to collect the personal property, pay debts and legacies, and account to the court.

Title by voluntary alienation. Alienation may be defined for practical purposes as the transfer of the owner's interest and title by the owner to another. Voluntary alienation may be by gift or sale, and is the normal commercial real estate transaction. It may be a deed or gift of a home by a parent to his daughter upon her marriage, or the sale of realty under a contract consummated by the delivery of a deed. Mortgages and leases are both instances of voluntary alienation.

Title by involuntary alienation. Involuntary alienation is a transfer of the title without the owner's volition. Tax sales and public sales in actions to enforce liens are instances of involuntary alienation. The property of the intestate leaving no heirs, which passes to the state by escheat, is a transfer of title of this class. An unusual example is the loss of the land, under certain circumstances, through erosion, or washing away. And of the same nature is accretion, or the increase of an owner's land through the action of currents depositing soil adjacent to his land. His area is increased by no voluntary action of his.

Another example of involuntary alienation is title by *adverse possession*. This situation arises where the record owner of the property has failed to keep possession and the property has been seized adversely by another. The conditions for a title by adverse possession differ in the various states, but in general are as follows:

1. The possession of the claimant must be open and notorious.
2. The possession must be hostile to, and to the exclusion of, the true owner.
3. The possession must be under a claim or color of title.
4. The possession must continue uninterruptedly for a period required by law.

This statutory period varies in the different states. Naturally it is set to extend long enough so that the record owner, if at all interested, pays some attention. In some states it is as long as twenty years. In other states the statutory period is as short as five years where adverse possession is under "color of title" and where possessor pays taxes.

If the claimant can prove all of the above conditions, he has a good title to the property, and all the rights of the record owner cease. It is, however, exceedingly dangerous to purchase property from one whose sole claim of ownership is based on adverse possession because, whereas a title running through a chain of deeds is perpetuated on the records, a title by adverse possession depends for its validity upon the four conditions listed above, no proof of which appears on record. Consequently, if the person or persons who know the facts concerning the adverse possession die, it is no longer possible to prove the elements.

No one should acquire title from an adverse possessor except upon competent legal advice, for there is no more highly technical subject in real estate law. The purported owner may merely be a squatter on the land, or title to the realty described may be subject to questionable legal determination because of natural or artificial land accretion or erosion.

Squatters. A squatter is one who settles on land without any claim of title or legal right to do so. Squatters cannot obtain title by adverse possession, for such title can be perfected only where there is some color or claim of title. Color of title must be based on a written instrument, although such written instrument may be defective. Yet in many states a "claim" of title may be held sufficient under certain circumstances to ripen into good title.

Title by accretion. Title by accretion is acquired by an owner of land to additional soil attaching to his property by the gradual and imperceptible operation of natural causes. Such accretion is quite common where properties front on oceans or rivers. Accretion by artificial means, through pumping and soil filling, is also common where river or bay areas are sufficiently valuable to warrant the necessary expenditures.

Loss of title by erosion. Erosion is the loss of land resulting from a gradual eating away of the soil by natural causes, such as when the sea gradually encroaches on abutting land. The upland owner is divested of title to land so lost by erosion.

Protection of title

As landed property became more valuable and ownership of real estate more diverse, it became increasingly important to provide safeguards to protect the true owner from loss of title by claim, error, or fraud. With cooperative aid of public and private agencies, transfer of title by the rightful and true owner and continued, though absentee, ownership were safeguarded by one or more of the following methods of title assurance: (1) recording acts and examination of title, (2) title insurance by private companies, (3) land title registration by public agencies in accordance with legislative enactments.

Recording of conveyances

Possession of property is notice to the world that the possessor claims or has some interest in the property. An owner in possession under a valid deed may be discovered to the actual knowledge of anyone who goes to the property. However, it is not always practicable for the owner actually to be in possession. He may own many buildings, or the structure may be an office or factory building or vacant land. One might go to the premises many times and not find the owner. Some method of *constructive* notice of ownership had to be devised as a substitute for *actual* knowledge, to protect the owner by relieving him of the necessity of remaining constantly in possession and to protect persons who, desiring to deal with the property, would wish to ascertain the real owner. Otherwise A, an owner, might sell his land to B, giving him a deed; and if B did not take possession, A might turn about and sell it to C. Or he might give a mortgage to D to secure a loan after he had sold to B. To prevent such frauds, recording acts have been enacted in all states. These provide that all instruments affecting real property may, when properly proved, be recorded in a certain public office in the county where the property is located. All such instruments are copied on the records and indexed. When so recorded, they are notice to the world with exactly the same effect as if the owner were actually in possession.

Constructive notice is just as good as actual notice. Consequently, one dealing with real estate is bound by all recorded instruments. Suppose A sells a piece of land to B and B fails to record his deed; A then sells it again to C, who knows nothing of the prior sale to B, and records his deed before B's deed is recorded. Under the theory of notice, C's right to the property is ahead of B's because B was not in possession and the records at the time C bought the property showed title in A. B should have protected himself by recording his deed as soon as he received it. Constructive notice is, however, no better than actual knowledge. If C, in the case above, had known of B's purchase, he could not obtain any right superior to B by recording his deed first.

Proof of execution

No instrument may be recorded unless proved as required by the law of the state. Proof varies in the several states. Some require a subscribing witness; others an acknowledgment; others both. The following are the officials who are authorized to take acknowledgments: notaries public, commissioners of deeds, justices of the peace, judges of courts of record, mayors of cities, ambassadors and ministers residing abroad, consular agents, and commissioners of deeds appointed by the governors of states to take acknowledgments in other states. Each of these officials has definite limits of authority. He cannot act outside the area of his authority. Within his area of authority he may take an acknowledgment of an instrument to be recorded elsewhere. When he does this, the instrument cannot be recorded elsewhere without a certificate attached from the clerk of the court of the county or city in which the official is qualified to act, stating that the official is qualified to take acknowledgments of instruments intended to be recorded in that state, that the signature of the official is known to the clerk, and that the signature affixed to the certificate of acknowledgment is genuine.

Examination of records

It is readily seen that one who contemplates a real estate transaction not only must inspect the realty involved but also must procure a thorough examination of the records to ascertain the owner and the condition of the title and all instruments concerning which the law presumes everyone to have notice. The examination reveals the entire history of the title from the earliest record to the present time and shows the chain of deeds, wills, and actions by which the property has passed from owner to owner, as well as mortgages, leases, restrictive and other agreements, and instruments encumbering or affecting the title or use of the property. The examiner first *abstracts* all the instruments conveying the title; that is, he makes a separate digest of each. This gives him what is known as a chain of title. He may find his chain very simple, consisting perhaps of a grant from the state to A and successive deeds from A to B, B to C, C to D, D to E, and E to F, F being the present owner. Usually, however, someone in the chain has died owning the property. In that event he may find deeds from A to B and B to C and no deed from C, although F claims ownership. The probability is that C died owning the property. In that case his will (if he left one) was probated and is on record in the court. If he left no will, it is usually found that an administrator of his personal property had been appointed, and the papers on file for that purpose state the names of his heirs. The examiner accordingly turns to the records of deaths and wills to fill the gap and finds the will or record of death of C. This supplies him with the names of C's devisees or heirs, and he then resumes his search by locating the deed from them to D, and so continues his chain. The chain is often broken by some legal action, such as foreclosure. Some person in the chain may have mortgaged the property so that the chain of title stops in D. A search of the records of legal actions shows that D was cut off in a foreclosure suit. Examination of the judgment in the action reveals the name of the official who sold and gave a deed of the property. Search against him will show his deed, and the chain is resumed. After the chain of title is completed, separate search is made against each owner for the period he owned the property to ascertain what encumbrances he may have placed upon the property.

The examiner's completed works is an *abstract of title*. In many states the abstract passes with each sale of the property, being kept up to date by the addition of a memorandum of each new transfer. It is deemed so valuable that in some states it is customary to provide in the contract of sale that the seller shall deliver the abstract of title at or before the delivery of the deed.

The title examiner

The law of real property is complicated and technical. The average person dealing in real estate has no knowledge of these rules, nor has he time to examine the title. He usually employs counsel or a conveyancer to do this work for him—someone who is familiar with the records, their location, indexes, and, more important, the law applicable to the various situations in the title which the examination might reveal. The responsibility of the examiner to his employer should be noted. He does not guarantee the result of his search. He simply asserts (1) that he has sufficient knowledge and experience to be a competent examiner of titles and (2) that he will use his knowledge honestly and diligently in accordance with the appropriate rules of law. His report of title is only his opinion, backed, to be sure, by his legal training and a careful scrutiny of the records. The records are copies of instruments; he is not responsible if the signature on some deed in the chain later proves to be a forgery. C may have died intestate owning the property. X and Y thereafter conveyed the property by deed, reciting that they were the only heirs of C. Z may thereafter claim to have been an heir as well. The examiner is not to blame. He may pass upon some situation in the title in accordance with the law as then in force. Later a court may reverse the decision upon which the examiner based his opinion. For none of these things is the examiner liable, yet his employer may lose large sums as a result.

As the records in the county and other offices grow in size and complexity, it is safe to have searches made only by someone familiar with them. Specialists in this field of work are at every county seat. Customs and the volume of work will regulate their type and methods of conducting business. To a large extent in the rural counties and even in the cities, a great deal of title searching is done by lawyers or conveyancers. In some places the searching is customarily done by men who make a specialty of making up abstracts and who supply them to lawyers on order. The lawyer then reads the abstract and certifies the title.

In more active counties, abstract companies do this work. Every abstract company has a force of employees, duplicate and often additional records, maps, and surveys, and supplies complete and accurate abstracts.

Title insurance

No system of title searching is perfect. As previously indicated, errors may creep in, or forgeries and other things that cannot be guarded against may cause loss. To remedy this situation, title insurance has come into use in the larger cities. It is a direct growth of the abstract company. Many of these companies, years ago, devised the idea of insuring not only their abstracts but going a step beyond, and for an additional fee, reading and insuring the title as well.

Like all other insurance, title insurance is a distribution of loss among all insured. Title companies are organizations authorized by law to examine and insure titles. They charge a fee or premium for their service. The amount of the premium is usually based upon the value of the property and covers not only the expense of the examination and abstract, but also an additional amount that is placed in a general fund to cover the losses insured against. The company makes a careful examination of the title. If it is satisfied that there are no apparent defects in the title, it insures against any loss. Should there later be a loss, by reason of forgery or any other defect arising prior to the insurance, the title company pays the loss. This, in brief, is the theory of title insurance.

In seeking title insurance, the person about to acquire the title or some interest in the real property first applies to the title company. He agrees to pay a certain fee for examination of the title. The title company on its part obligates itself to make an examination of the title and to insure against undiscovered defects. It does not, however, agree to insure against defects and encumbrances that may appear from the examination.

After the examination is completed, the applicant should therefore insist on being given a *report of title*, which is a statement setting forth a description of the property, the name of the record owner, and a detailed list of all objections to the title, that is, encumbrances and defects found upon the records. The reason for having this report is simple: it enables the applicant to know the exact condition of the title. If he is a purchaser, his contract stipulates that he shall take title subject to certain encumbrances. The report sets forth all the encumbrances found on the records. The purchaser demands that the seller dispose of all those not agreed upon in the contract, before delivering a deed. If the applicant has agreed to make a mortgage loan, he insists that the owner render his title free and clear before the loan is made.

After the objections not agreed upon have been removed, the title is closed and the instruments passing title are delivered and recorded. The title company now prepares to issue its policy of the title insurance. There may, of course, still be encumbrances on the property which have been agreed upon. For example, the transaction may be a sale of the property subject to one or more mortgages. The policy should be carefully examined to see that the property is properly insured without any exceptions other than those agreed upon.

Title insurance policy

The usual form of title insurance policy contains four parts:

1. Agreement of insurance
2. A schedule describing the subject matter of insurance
3. A schedule of exceptions
4. Conditions of the policy

The agreement of insurance usually reads as follows:

[The company] in consideration of the payment of its charges for the examination of this title to it paid doth hereby insure and covenant that it will keep harmless and indemnify .... (hereafter termed the assured) and all other persons to whom this policy may be transferred with the assent of this company, testified by the signature of the proper officer of this company, endorsed on this policy, against all loss or damage not exceeding .... dollars which the said assured shall sustain by reason of defects, or unmarketability of the title of the assured to the estate, mortgage, or interest described in Schedule A hereto annexed, or because of liens or encumbrances charging the same at the date of this policy. *Excepting* judgments against the assured and estates, defects, objections, liens, or encumbrances created by the act or with the privity of the assured, or mentioned in Schedule B or excepted by the conditions of this policy hereto annexed and hereby incorporated into this contract, *the loss* and the amount to be ascertained in the manner provided in the annexed conditions and to be payable upon compliance by the assured with the stipulations of said conditions and not otherwise.

This agreement is dated and executed by the proper officers of the company under its corporate seal.

The company's charge is a fixed rate based usually on the amount of insurance named. Unlike other insurance, it is a flat fee, paid but once. Customarily the company insists that the property be insured for at least its full value. The insured also should want the property insured for its full value, since the company is in no case obligated to pay more than the amount set forth in the policy. The insured may, if he contemplates improving the property, have his title insured for a sum greater than its value at the time of transfer. The date of the policy is very important. The company insures only against loss to the insured arising from some defect at or prior to the date of the policy. The insured should insist that the policy be dated at or after the time title is closed. Because the policy is issued under seal, the time to sue upon it does not begin to run until a loss is sustained. The statute of limitations may be twenty years. The loss might not occur until fifteen years after the policy was issued. In such cases the right to sue on the policy would not expire until thirty-five years after the date of the policy.

The schedule describing the subject matter of insurance usually follows the agreement of insurance. It is divided into three parts. First it states the estate or title of the insured. Next comes a brief description of the instrument under which the insured acquired his estate or interest. Third is a description of the premises covered by the policy. This description should be sufficiently detailed so that the property may be easily identified. The policy covers not only the land but all buildings and fixtures thereon. It does not cover personalty. The insured should see to it that the description is clear.

The schedule of exceptions is virtually the most important part of the policy. It sets forth a detailed list of all encumbrances and defects against which the company does not insure. No loss arising from any of these exceptions is covered by the policy. The insured should insist that only such encumbrances as he has agreed to shall be inserted in the schedule. Much trouble has arisen on this point, and many companies insist, before the closing of title, that the insured consent in writing to such objections to the title as have not been removed. Nearly all companies refuse to insure against the rights of tenants and persons in possession of the property; therefore those rights usually appear in the schedule. All encumbering facts shown by a survey are excepted, or if there be no survey, the policy will except "any state of facts an accurate survey may show."

The last part of the policy is a statement of the conditions of the policy. These conditions are seldom read but are very important. They specify the terms of the company's liability and the relations between the company and the insured. First it is stipulated that the company will, at its own cost, defend the insured in all actions founded on a claim of title or encumbrance prior to the date of the policy and thereby insured against. This stipulation not only assures the insured against loss but saves him the inconvenience and expense of litigation.

Should the insured contract to sell the property and the purchaser reject the title for some defect not excepted in the policy, the company reserves the option of either paying the loss or maintaining at its own expense an action to test the validity of the defect. In such a case the company is not liable under the policy until the termination of the litigation.

If the policy is issued to a mortgagee, the company's responsibility arises only in the event that the mortgage, upon foreclosure, is adjudged to be a lien upon the property of an inferior quality to that described in the policy, or in the event that the purchaser at the foreclosure sale is relieved by the court of completing his purchase by reason of some defect not excepted in the policy.

The conditions of the policy also provide for arbitration, in certain cases, of disputes as to the validity of objections to the title insured. The policy covers the insured even after he has sold the property, should he be sued upon the covenants in his deed.

The policy is not transferable, except that if it insures a mortgagee and he sells the mortgage, his rights under the policy may be passed to his assignee. But even the company's consent must be obtained.

Should there be a loss under the policy, the company, having settled the claim, acquires all the rights and claims of the insured against any other person who is responsible for the loss. This right is based upon the legal doctrine of subrogation. The title company may be able to collect all or part of the loss from the person who caused the loss.

In any case, if the company has paid a loss totaling the amount of the policy, it reserves the right to take over the property from the insured at a fair valuation. There is a very good reason for this provision. In some instances the title is defective but can, with time and effort, be cured. The company in such cases pays the fair value to the insured, receiving a deed from him. It then owns the property and at its pleasure can take such action as may be necessary to remove the defects in the title.

Encroachments on others

The building on the lot may cover more land than is within the lot lines. The municipality either owns the street or has an easement to use the street for public purposes. In either event no one has a right to encroach upon it, except by legal permission. Such an encroachment by a permanent structure may render the title unmarketable. Likewise, if the building encroaches upon a neighbor's land without his consent, the neighbor may be able either to recover damages for the encroachment or to compel the removal of so much of the building as encroaches on his land. A purchaser could not be compelled to accept a title under such conditions. The survey should indicate party walls, and it should also be examined with reference to any restriction upon the property and as to whether or not such restrictions are violated by the building. The effect of such conditions could be determined only by one familiar with the law applicable in each case.

Encroachments by others

The entire building may stand upon the proper lot, and a neighbor's building may encroach. The title to the portion of the lot that is not encroached upon is marketable, but it may be doubtful whether or not the encroachment affects the marketability of the lot as a whole. This is a question not so much of law as of commercial utility, and the courts consider it to be the latter. If the court finds that the encroachment does not substantially lessen the value and extent of the property, it will compel a purchaser to accept it. If the encroachment does substantially lessen the value and extent of the land, the purchaser may refuse to take it, or he may take it and be given an allowance for the land lost by the encroachment.

Use of title policy

Of course, the insured seldom needs to resort to his policy to recover a loss, but he should always refer to it in subsequent transactions with reference to the property. It tells him at once just what property he owns and what are the encumbrances on it. If he later enters into a contract to sell the property, he should use the description in the policy and undertake to give a title subject to just those encumbrances stated as exceptions in the policy.

Land title and registration

Throughout the history of title recording, means and ways have been sought to make transfer of real property as simple and safe as the transfer of other property, doing away, if possible, with the repeated search and examination of titles. The search for some permanent form of title registration is still prompted by the tedious and often difficult and cumbersome method by which title changes and, in addition, by the ever-present fear that ownership in farm or home, despite title insurance, may be invalidated by court order because of faulty or illegal property transfer somewhere in the chain of title grantors. Although the development and perfection of title insurance has speeded the search and transfer of title, particularly in urban areas, the necessity to reestablish and recheck the chain of ownership and title encumbrances every time a sale takes place still impedes the use of realty as a readily transferable, liquid asset or form of investment.

Under present operation of the recording acts, deeds and other instruments affecting rights or property in realty are placed on public record. These records are generally maintained in the office of the registrar by the clerk of the county in which the property is located. They are notice to the world as to constructive ownership in realty, and an examination of all recorded instruments affecting the property in question is necessary to determine the validity and condition of title. In early days, far fewer instruments were on record; it was therefore possible to examine a title with fair speed and consequent reasonable time and expense. Now, the more active counties have such voluminous records that the operation is slow, time consuming, and expensive, and, in addition, this condition is becoming worse as time passes and more and more instruments are recorded. Yet, theoretically, it is necessary for each title examination to go back and study the records from the earliest recorded instruments. To overcome the increasing burden of tracing the title back to the date of conquest by war or revolution or to the date of original gift or sale by a sovereign ruler, some states —Illinois, Indiana, Iowa, Massachusetts, Michigan, Wisconsin, and others—have established by statute a maximum period of time varying from thirty to fifty years beyond which an otherwise valid title need not be searched to prove ownership good and marketable. These laws do not estop an individual, however, who claims an interest in the property arising from events antidating the statute of title limitation from filing an affidavit of claim and from recording such claim for all to know and heed. Obvious interests that are evident by physical inspection, such as easements or party walls, need not be recorded to be protected in these states against title search statutes of limitations. In most states, however, there is still no legal date that can be fixed beyond which there is no need of going back to search a title. The lack of such a basic date, in brief, is the problem faced by title searchers.

In actual practice, title and abstract companies usually "assume title good at some fairly early date." There is nevertheless an irritating duplication of work on successive title examinations. And some meticulous attorneys are not satisfied unless the examination is carried back to the earliest date, as witness the following story:

In a legal transaction involving transfer of property in New Orleans, a firm of New York lawyers retained a New Orleans attorney to search the title and perform other related duties. The New Orleans attorney sent his findings, back to the year 1803. The New York lawyers examined his opinion and wrote again to the New Orleans lawyer, saying in effect that the opinion rendered by him was all very well, as far as it went, but that title to the property prior to 1803 had not been satisfactorily answered.

The New Orleans attorney replied to the New York firm as follows:

I acknowledge your letter inquiring as to the state of the title of the Canal Street property prior to the year 1803.
Please be advised that in the year 1803 the United States of America acquired the territory of Louisiana from the Republic of France by purchase. The Republic of France acquired title from the Spanish Crown by conquest. The Spanish Crown had originally acquired title by virtue of the discoveries of one Christopher Columbus, sailor, who had been duly authorized to embark upon the voyage of discovery by Isabella, Queen of Spain. Isabella, before granting such authority, had obtained the sanction of His Holiness, the Pope; the Pope is the Vicar on Earth of Jesus Christ; Jesus Christ is the Son and Heir Apparent of God. God made Louisiana.

A number of suggestions have been made to remedy this date situation. All of them hinge on some method of registering title and stem from the system first suggested by Sir Robert Torrens of Australia.

Origin of the Torrens system

Sir Robert Torrens was a businessman who had been a collector of customs in charge of shipping. In this position he became familiar with a law under which ships were registered. The registry showed the name or names of the owners of every vessel and all liens and encumbrances against it, and it revealed briefly and simply the condition of the title. Later Torrens became registrar-general of South Australia. His experience with shipping led him to believe that the principle of registration of titles could be applied to land as well. In 1857 he introduced a bill providing for the registration of land titles. This bill became a law in South Australia the next year. The idea spread rapidly. British Honduras in Central America passed a Land Registering Act the same year. Queensland, Tasmania, and Victoria followed in 1861, New South Wales in 1862, New Zealand in 1870, Western Australia in 1874, and Fiji in 1876. Other British colonies have since adopted the system.

The system in England

Although at first the idea of a system of land title registration spread rapidly, the speed was not maintained. A Land Registry Act, known as the *Lord Westbury Act*, was passed in 1862. The law was a failure and was repealed in 1875. Only 411 titles were registered during those years. The Act of 1875, which repealed this law, simplified the system and corrected many of the mistakes of the old law. It failed, however, to provide an assurance fund out of which losses could be paid. Compensation for loss to the injured through error or otherwise was lacking, and this defect was a serious one. Under a new act in 1897, an assurance fund was provided, the national treasury making good any deficiency. Registration became compulsory in the County of London by the same act. The records show that 3,825 titles were registered in England and Wales in the twenty years from 1875 to 1895 and that in the following ten years 91,284 titles were registered in London alone.

England evidently did not get a workable Torrens system until nearly forty years after South Australia had one. The system, however, had to struggle against conditions peculiar to English land ownership. The law of entail[1] prevailed, and many English freeholds were inalienable. The owner in possession had only a life interest. Great landed estates existed, and a large proportion of the land was in the hands of comparatively few persons. England was jealous of its customs and the lawyers were opposed to changes. However, in spite of many handicaps, the Torrens system seems to have been successfully adopted.

The system in the United States

The Torrens system has had only a fair amount of success in this country. The first act in the United States was passed in Illinois in 1895. It was declared unconstitutional by the supreme court of that state but was amended in 1897 so as to remove the constitutional objections. It was further amended in 1907. Massachusetts passed a Torrens law in 1898, which has been considered successful. Amendments to this law were made in 1899, 1900, 1902, and 1905. There was an Ohio act in 1896 which, however, did not meet a judicial test and was repealed in 1898. It was reen-

---

[1]The law of entail was a device used to prevent the divesting of land from a family's estate. Under this law, land could only be deeded or willed to heirs of the body, i.e., direct descendants. If an owner died without leaving direct heirs, the land reverted to the grantor or other person named in the deed. Because of this law of "fee tail" property so restricted was virtually unmarketable, since the land so entailed could be reclaimed upon failure of issue in the direct line of inheritance of the original grantee.

acted in 1912, a constitutional amendment receiving popular approval. New York enacted a Torrens law in 1908 which, as someone has said, "did not even begin." It was also described as being the worst registration law in the world. An amendment in 1910 did not help it, but rather insured its failure. Important amendments were made to the law in 1916 and 1918. These amendments were designed to correct the defects in the previous law and to make the system more workable and popular. Opinions regarding the present law differ, but it is an undeniable fact that land title registration is not popular in New York.

The following states have Torrens system laws: California, Illinois, Massachusetts, Oregon, Minnesota, Colorado, Washington, New York, North Carolina, Ohio, Virginia, Georgia, Utah, and South Dakota. From present indications, the law is evidently of no practical use in a number of these states. Massachusetts, however, has a law quite different in many respects from the other states, and indications are that it is meeting with success. Reports from Cook County, Illinois, show that many titles are being registered under the Torrens act. Hawaii also has a working Torrens system law. Those who favor the Torrens system assert that only in the last-mentioned places and under the federal laws of the Philippine Islands, Hawaii, Guam, and Puerto Rico is there a true enactment of the system.

Definition of the Torrens system

The system has been defined by Sir Robert Torrens himself as follows:

The person or persons in whom singly or collectively the fee simple is vested, either in law or in equity, may apply to have the land placed on the register of titles. The applications are submitted for examination to a barrister and to a conveyancer, who are styled "examiners of titles." These gentlemen report to the register: First: Whether the description of land is definite and clear. Second: Is the applicant in undisputed possession of the property? Third: Does he appear in equity and justice rightfully entitled thereto? Fourth: Does he produce such evidence of title as leads to the conclusion that no other person is in position to succeed against him in an action for ejectment?

The *procedure for registration* of titles under the Torrens system is:

1. Owner of fee title files an application with court having jurisdiction under statute of state in which property is situated, setting forth prescribed information as to property involved and abutting property.

2. Application is referred to official title examiners, who report results of such examination to court.

3. Notice is then given to all parties who appear from such examination to be interested in the property. Such notice is also published in a newspaper for period prescribed in statute.

4. If title is approved by examiners and no adverse claims have been established after such notice, the court issues directions to the recording officer to register the title and issue certificate of registration of title.

5. Certificate of registration of title sets forth the nature of applicant's title, *i.e.*, fee simple or otherwise, as well as the encumbrances affecting the title if any. Such certificate is issued in duplicate—one to register of title

and the other to applicant. The registrar records the certificate in registration book.

6. Transfer of registered title is effected by usual form of conveyance accompanied by seller's certificate of title. The form of conveyance and such certificate are then delivered to register, who cancels seller's certificate and issues new certificate to purchaser.

7. When certificate of registration is issued, good title in registered owner is deemed conclusive subject to certain exceptions prescribed by statute.

8. Generally, a fund is created out of fees paid for registration for compensating persons deprived of interests in registered property. Once property is registered, it cannot be set aside or overcome against the registered owner, except for fraud. Claimants who establish interests in such property after registration must, therefore, look to the fund for due compensation after judicial determination of the extent of damages suffered. If the indemnity or assurance fund is insufficient to pay the claim, claimant must wait until the fund reaches the amount necessary to justify payment. Payments are made on claims in order of their filing.

9. Registered property may not be withdrawn from registration except for justifiable cause, and then only on court order.

Judicial determination of validity of registered title

Since title once registered establishes irrevocable ownership in the registrant, except for fraud, great care is taken in the initial registration to assure that the title applicant is the true owner. Each applicant for title registration under the Torrens system thus initiates a judicial proceeding under which the court sets public hearings to legally establish and "quiet" the title. At such hearing, all persons claiming an interest are heard and their rights adjudicated. The official title examiner reports his findings and, on the basis of the due process hearings, the court orders the property registered in the name of the true owner, subject of course to liens or encumbrances reported by the title examiner and those established as a result of trial and court order. Judicial determination of title—as of all lower court orders—is subject to appeal and may be invalidated within statutory period of limitation upon proof of fraud. If someone later proves to have just claim against the property, he is paid out of an insurance (assurance) fund which is maintained by fees charged for registration.

Arguments in favor of the Torrens system

It would be desirable to have a system of registration that accurately determines the ownership of a piece of land and all liens and claims upon it, records or registers these facts, and issues a certificate of registration to the owner, the title registered being absolutely conclusive and indefeasible and the results being obtained speedily and cheaply. These objectives are what the Torrens system is designed to accomplish. Some of its advantages, as suggested by those who favor the system, may be summarized as follows:

1. The title to the property is searched once and for all. Duplication of searches is eliminated. It is not necessary to go behind the registry to effect transfers after the first registration.

2. Transfers, after the initial registration, can be speedily accomplished. Transactions relating to registered titles can be accomplished in a day. The original registration, however, usually takes a longer time than a title company examination.

3. Registration makes the title irrevocable except for fraud. There is no need for title insurance other than that provided by the registration system. Under the system of title insurance, the title company's liability is limited to the amount of the policy and may not fully protect the owner if there is an increase of value in consequence of improvements, or for any other cause.

4. The speed and safety with which dealings with registered titles can be accomplished should make land titles more marketable and realty consequently a more liquid asset. There is no evidence anywhere to show that experience with the law in any place has proved this to be so.

5. The expense of transferring titles to realty and of securing mortgages on it is reduced. This advantage applies more to transfers and mortgages of titles already registered than to the initial registration, although some state that registration in the first instance is cheaper than title examination and insurance.

Objections to the Torrens system

The following is a statement of some objections that have been advanced by opponents of the system in the United States:

1. There can be no true Torrens system in this country because any law making a registered title indefeasible violates the constitutional guarantee that no one shall be deprived of property without due process of law. Some person or persons, possibly infants, having rights in the property may, through error or oversight, not be named in the action to register the title and may not receive notice of it. It is asserted that the omnibus designation, "all other persons, etc.," does not remedy this defect and that as to these persons there has not been due process of law. It must be remembered, however, that anyone so injured will be compensated from the assurance fund, but it is true, nevertheless, that he is deprived of his rights in the property itself.

2. Under the provisions of the law, the initial registration is by means of a judicial proceeding resulting in an order or judgment of a court, but the law permits the transfer of a registered title to be made by a registrar or other public official without notice to anyone. This provision is upon the assumption that the transfer is merely the performance of a ministerial act. The question has been raised whether such an official, not being clothed with any judicial authority, is not in reality performing a judicial function in interpreting an instrument and passing upon its sufficiency. The registration of the title in the name of the new owner is conclusive and binding

upon all the world. Of course, one would not be allowed to profit by his fraud, if a forgery or other fraud had been committed, but the registered title may again be transferred, and one taking it in good faith would have an indefeasible title. In cases of this kind, again, injured parties must look to the assurance fund; they cannot recover their property.

3. Property cannot be removed from the system, once the title has been registered, except by permission of the court. No matter what may be the desires of the owner, his property is in a particular class and must stay there forever except by permission of the court. The system prevents the sale and mortgaging of the property to those who will not deal with a registered title.

4. Upon the death of an owner of registered property, a petition must be made to the court for an order directing registration of the title in the heirs and devisees. This is a proceeding involving some legal expense and is in addition to the proceedings on the estate in the surrogate's court. Property not under the provisions of the registration act passes at death directly to the heirs and devisees. Under the Torrens law they do not get title until, as a result of the court's order, it is registered in their names. Although additional expense for the new registration may be small, it is avoided when the title is insured by a title company instead of being registered. The title policy protects not only the insured but also his heirs and devisees, and there is no expense except the initial premium. Registered property, is, of course, like other property, subject to the lien of decedent's debts.

5. Title registration is neither easy nor speedy. It takes the form of an action at law. Not only is the title examined (in nearly the same manner as in a title company examination), but, in addition, legal proceedings must be conducted. Notices must be given, published, and posted on the land, and delays are caused by the successive steps in the court proceedings. After all, the registration is not complete and conclusive until a certain period has elapsed (thirty days after final order in New York). Does this indicate that the system has both ease and speed? Surely not on the initial registration. The answer, of course, is that *subsequent* transfers can be accomplished in a simple manner and without delay. This may be true, but what owner wishes to undertake to have his title registered? If his title is marketable, he can sell it just as readily (perhaps more so) unregistered as registered. Registration would cost him something and would add nothing to the value of the property. If the title is bad, it cannot be registered. There may be a few *questions* as to title that could be remedied by an action under the Torrens law, but the same thing could be accomplished by an action under other provisions of the law.

6. The initial registration is not cheap. There are the fees for the examination of the title to be paid; the expense of publication of the notice, filing fees, and other incidental expenses, the contribution to the assurance fund, and then the services of one's own attorney must also be paid for.

7. In a number of states, including New York, the county is not behind the assurance fund; that is to say, recovery of compensation for damages is limited to the amount in the fund, although future contributions may pay the claim in full in time. Efforts have been made to amend the law so as to make the county liable for claims in full regardless of the amount in the assurance fund. The attorney general of New York State rendered an opinion that such an amendment would be unconstitutional, referring to the section of the state constitution that prohibits any county, city, town, or village from incurring indebtedness except for county, city, town, or village purposes. It is, therefore, an objection to the registration of a title, or to the bringing of land forever under the registration law, that those who may be deprived of rights in the land by error or omission or misconception may not be able to recover compensation except after an indefinite period. If the system once gets under way and the assurance fund grows in size, this objection will be minimized.

8. It may be difficult to obtain a mortgage on a Torrens title because the mortgagee may be deprived of the security of the real estate if the encumbrance is omitted from the registration certificate issued on a subsequent transfer of title. An innocent transferee of such title certificate obtains an indefeasible title free of such mortgage encumbrance. The mortgagee must therefore resort to the assurance fund for compensation resulting from such omission and is thus deprived of the security on which his loan was originally predicated.

Conclusion

Most real estate owners and dealers are alive and receptive to good ideas, but they are not using the Torrens system. Although there are defects in the system of title examination and insurance, it evidently possesses more attractions than does the one advocated by Torrens law adherents. Perhaps this preference is due partly to the fact that title insurance has reached a high development in the larger communities and partly to the fact that a model land title registration law has not yet been enacted. Most title examiners realize that some method must be devised to avoid the inconveniences of the present system of examining and ascertaining the validity of land titles. The remedy may be merely a simplification of the present system or the enactment of an ideal registration law. Certainly in most states there is little public demand for such a law. The sentiment in favor of one may increase, and it is quite possible that the future will see in general use throughout the country a title registration law, probably basically patterned on the Torrens system, with modifications to remove its present objections.

READING AND STUDY REFERENCES

1. FRIEDMAN, EDITH J., *Real Estate Encyclopedia*, Chapters 22 and 23. Englewood Cliffs, N.J.: Prentice-Hall, Inc., 1960.

2. HEBARD, EDNA L., and GERALD S. MEISEL, *Principles of Real Estate Law*, Chapters 8 and 14. New York: Simmons-Boardman Publishing Corporation, 1964.

3. HUSBAND, WILLIAM H., and FRANK RAY ANDERSON, *Real Estate,* Chapters 4 and 5. Homewood, Ill.: Richard D. Irwin, Inc., 1960.

4. KRATOVIL, ROBERT, *Real Estate Law*, Chapters 6, 9, and 14. Englewood Cliffs, N.J.: Prentice-Hall, Inc., 1969.

5. LUSK, HAROLD F., *Law of the Real Estate Business*, Chapters 8, 9, 10, and 11. Homewood, Ill.: Richard D. Irwin, Inc., 1965.

6. RING, ALFRED A., *Questions and Problems in Real Estate Principles and Practices* (rev. ed.), Chapter 7. Englewood Cliffs, N.J.: Prentice-Hall, Inc., 1972.

7. UNGER, MAURICE A., *Real Estate* (4th ed.), Chapter 5. Cincinnati: South-Western Publishing Co., 1969.

8

MORTGAGE INSTRUMENTS

In most real estate transactions, a buyer finances the major portion of the purchase price by borrowing and pledging the real estate involved as security (collateral) to assure the repayment of the purchase loan with interest over a specific period of time, generally ten to thirty years. The promissory note and the mortgage are the two instruments by which a loan on realty is secured. A bond is used in some states instead of a note. The note (or bond) is the evidence of indebtedness and promise to repay; the mortgage is the pledge of specific realty as collateral or security. The note or bond in effect creates a *personal* liability which attaches to the borrower and which is enforceable in case of breach no matter where the debtor may take up residence.

Evidence of debt

In all cases in which a mortgage is given to secure a debt, it may truly be said that the debt is the life of the mortgage. If the debt is unenforceable for any reason, so is the mortgage. Since a note is generally used to evidence the debt, it might be well here to enumerate the essential elements of a valid mortgage note:

1. A writing
2. An obligor (borrower) with contractual capacity

123

3. An obligee (lender or nominee) with contractual capacity
4. A promise or covenant by obligor to pay a specific sum
5. Terms of payment
6. Default clause, including mortgage covenants by reference
7. Proper execution
8. Voluntary delivery, and acceptance

In some states a bond is given by the borrower as evidence of the debt. Most states, however, use a note worded substantially as follows:

After date, for value received .... hereinafter designated as the obligor, promise to pay to the order of ....
hereinafter designated as the obligee the sum of .... dollars, lawful money of the United States [which sum said obligor do hereby ....
covenant to pay to said obligee, ... or assigns (on the ....
day of ...., nineteen hundred and ...., with interest thereon, to be computed from the .... day of ....,
19........, at the rate of .... per centum per annum and to be paid on the .... day of .... next ensuing the date hereof, and ....thereafter)].

AND IT IS HEREBY EXPRESSLY AGREED THAT the whole of the said principal sum shall become due at the option of said obligee after default in the payment of interest for .... days, or after default in the payment of any installment of principal for .... days, or after default in the payment of any tax, water rate, or assessment for .... days after notice and demand. All of the covenants and agreements made by the said obligor in the mortgage covering premises therein described and collateral hereto are hereby made part of this instrument.

Signed and sealed this .... day of ...., 19 ....

.... L.S.

IN THE PRESENCE OF

....

....

(Acknowledgment)

An examination of the form reveals that the note consists of three divisions:

1. An acknowledgment of indebtedness
2. A promise to pay
3. Provision for default

Acknowledgment of indebtedness

By insertion of the borrower's name and his designation as the obligor, the debt is acknowledged. Although it is not necessary to add his place of residence, it is often done for identification.

The borrower is designated as the obligor, since he gives his obligation. He acknowledges himself indebted to the lender, the person who receives the obligation, known as the obligee. Often there are several borrowers. Since the lender wants the fullest security, it is customary in such event to insert the words "jointly and severally" following the names of the borrowers. By such an obligation the lender may collect from any one or all of the borrowers. Each of them makes himself liable to pay the entire indebtedness. Of course, they may have any arrangement they wish among themselves for apportionment of the debt, but no burden is placed on the lender to collect proportionately from them.

Following the designation of the obligee is stated the amount of the indebtedness: "................... dollars, lawful money of the United States." That is the usual form, and calls for any sort of legal tender of the United States.

Promise to pay

The language so far has been entirely a recital of indebtedness. Now the obligor states the terms of his promise to pay: "Which sum said obligor does hereby .... covenant to pay." If more than one borrower, "jointly and severally" should be inserted in the blank space. The promise is made to the obligee, and since the note is personal property, to the executors, administrators, or assigns of the obligee, if an individual; or, "its successor and assigns" if a corporation. Next is set forth the date on which the principal shall be payable: "on the .... day of ....
................, nineteen hundred ...." Under these terms the borrower cannot pay the note until the due date.

Usually, the lender is reluctant to give a prepayment privilege; he wants to know that his money is invested for the full period and that he will not suddenly have his money returned and be compelled to seek another investment. On the other hand, the borrower should insist on incorporating a full prepayment privilege into the note and mortgage because its omission may at a later date interfere with a sale of the property or prevent the owner from refinancing. When the lender is willing to grant such a privilege, it is customary and fair to provide that notice of such intention be given a certain length of time in advance and that additional interest be paid for a certain period of time. Very often it is stipulated that such a privilege shall not be operative during the first two or three years of the loan. The following are typical prepayment clauses, which would be inserted just before the default clause:

1. At any time during the term hereof, the obligor shall have the privilege to pay the entire unpaid principal upon giving thirty (30) days' written notice to the obligee of the intention so to do and payment of sixty (60) days' additional interest beyond the date of such prepayment.
2. During the first three (3) years from date hereof and upon thirty (30) days' written notice to the obligee of the intention to do so, the obligor shall have the privilege to pay the entire amount of unpaid principal, provided payment of additional interest is made for a period of sixty (60) days beyond the date of such prepayment. After the initial period of three (3) years subsequent to date of this indebtedness, obligors reserve the right to prepay any amount at any time without penalty provided thirty (30) days' notice of such prepayments is given in writing to the obligee.

Following the due date appears the interest clause: "with interest thereon, to be computed from the .... day of ....,19......, at the rate of .... per centum per annum, and to be paid on the

.... day of .... next ensuing the date hereof, and .... thereafter." The appropriate dates should be inserted in the blank spaces. The date of the note is the date from which interest is usually computed. The interest is not paid in advance. Interest may be payable at any agreed interval, monthly, quarterly, semiannually, or annually. Generally it is payable monthly and usually accords with the date of the note. For example, if the note were dated September 14, the interest would become payable October 14 next ensuing, and so forth. This is not a fixed rule. Many investors, particularly banks, desire interest payments to come in on certain dates and to that end have their notes provide that the first interest payment be due on the first of their interest dates following the making of the loan, and monthly thereafter.

Interest payment due for a portion of a month, or other interest period, is, as a rule, paid in advance and at time of the mortgage closing. The rate of interest is agreed upon by the borrower and lender and inserted in this clause.

Although a definite date is fixed for repayment of the amount loaned, few term mortgage loans are paid when due. Unless the property has depreciated in value, the loan is usually allowed to remain. Often the date of payment is extended by a formal instrument known as an *extension agreement* (see Chapter 11), which designates a new date of payment in the future and may make any agreed changes in the interest rate or other terms of the note or bond.

Many forms leave the entire interest clause blank. In using such a form, care must be taken to insert all the requisites: due date of principal, date from which interest runs, its rate, and dates of payment. Care should be taken also not to use a form of interest clause providing for payment of interest at a specified rate "until the full amount of principal and interest is paid." Such a clause prevents the lender from increasing the interest rate, even after the date due, except by express agreement.

Repayment in installments

Instruments of indebtedness, such as those that have been discussed, by their terms make the principal payable in its entirety at a specified time. It may be agreed that the principal shall be payable in installments at designated intervals. Such an arrangement may provide for periodical payments of fixed amounts of principal in addition to interest or may call for regular, uniform payments to include both interest and principal.

The following clause inserted in the note in place of the clause in parentheses on page 124 will make the mortgage debt repayable in installments:

In installments as follows: $................ on the .... day of .... 19........, and a like sum quarterly thereafter on the .... days of ...., and .... in each year until the full amount of principal is paid, together with interest thereon from the date hereof and on the unpaid balance from time to time, at the rate of .... per centum per annum, payable quarterly, with each installment of principal.

Simple changes in the wording will permit the use of this form for monthly or semiannual installments. It is usual, for facility in bookkeeping, to provide for interest payments at the same time that each installment of principal becomes due, but this is not necessary. In fact, on large mortgages it is customary to spread payments so that taxes, installments of principal, and interest will become due at reasonable intervals. Interest may be made payable at any intervals stipulated.

If the borrower desires the option of paying more than the fixed installment of principal on any due date, this may be provided for by inserting the words "or more" following the amount of the agreed installment. The lender, however, often does not wish to receive some odd amount of payment, although he is willing to permit the borrower to increase his payment. Moreover, such an option would permit total prepayment without penalty. He therefore should have the note provide that the extra payment be a certain amount or a multiple thereof, such as $500 or $1,000, $1,500, $2,000, and so on. The borrower, on his part, may have agreed to pay installments of $500 or more in the amount of $250 or a multiple thereof. Suppose he pays $1,000 on a certain due date; if no other provision has been inserted in the note, he is bound to pay the usual installment on the next due date. He may not be able to do so and so become in default, although he had really paid the installment in advance. He may guard against this situation by having it stipulated in the note that extra payments are made "in anticipation." The clause should then read substantially: "........................ dollars or more, in the amount of .... dollars or a multiple thereof, in anticipation, on the .... day of ....," and so on.

The type of amortization that is generally used in connection with home loan financing is known as the *level* payment plan. This plan provides for a fixed amount payable periodically to include both interest and an installment of principal. The following wording should be substituted for that in brackets on page 124 when monthly or quarterly installments, including principal and interest, are desired:

.... with interest at the rate of .... per centum per annum, which sum .... said obligor   do   hereby .... covenant to pay to said obligee, or assigns, to be paid in the following manner:
($) Dollars on the first day of ...., 19........ and a like sum of .... ($) Dollars ⎰ quarterly-annually
⎱ on the first day of each succeeding

month ⎰ thereafter until the .... day of ...., 19.....,

when the balance of said principal sum and interest shall become due and payable. Each of said payments when received by the obligee shall be applied: FIRST to the payment of interest at the rate of .... per centum per annum, computed from the .... day of ...., 19 .... on the unpaid balance of the principal sum hereof and, SECONDLY towards the reduction and payment of the principal sum hereof.

During the early years of the mortgage only a comparatively small part of each payment would go toward principal. For example, during the first year at 8 percent interest, a $10,000 mortgage loan to be amortized over three hundred months (twenty-five years) would require payments of $77.19 per month, or $926.28 for the year. Of this amount only $131.10, or approximately 14 percent of the total payments made, applies to a reduction of the mortgage loan. The balance of $795.18 goes toward payment of interest due at the rate of 8 percent per annum on the remaining monthly mortgage debt balances. But each year as the balance of principal decreases, there is less interest, and the amount applicable to reduce the principal increases. Since plans for mortgage payments of this nature and variations of it are so widely used, there are included in the Appendix (pages 575–90) tables showing monthly and other periodic mortgage payments at various interest rates, the amount of principal balance remaining at various times, and the amount of principal and interest that comprise each payment.

Default clause

The property pledged as security might be sufficient at the time the loan is made; yet if a large amount of unpaid interest accumulates, the security may not be sufficient to cover both principal and interest. So likewise the owner may permit taxes and assessments to go unpaid. These liens are ahead of the mortgage and would consequently depreciate the security. To prevent the happening of these contingencies, the default clause is inserted. Under the terms of this clause, the total amount becomes immediately due if the interest is not paid within a specific number of days after it becomes due or if taxes or assessments remain unpaid for a certain number of days after they become due. If the principal of the loan is payable in installments, there should be provision for default in such payments. It is usual to make the grace period thirty days as to interest when payable semiannually, ten or fifteen days when payable monthly or quarterly. The tax period is usually fixed at thirty days, occasionally sixty days—and this will ordinarily not be shortened even if interest is payable monthly. Of course, on second mortgages, the grace period for both interest and taxes is made much shorter. The grace clause protects the lender, who can thereby check any wastage of his security within a short period. Should any default occur, he can foreclose the mortgage at the end of the stated grace period.

The mortgage given with the note contains, in addition to the default clause, many other provisions for the protection of the lender. These are incorporated under the last sentence in the note, which begins, "All of the covenants ...." Occasionally the insurance clause is inserted in the note, by the terms of which the borrower agrees to keep the property insured against fire for the benefit of the lender. The property is security for the loan. If it burns down, the security loses most of its value. Fire insurance protects against this. Should there be a fire loss, the insurance is payable to the lender to the extent of his loan and interest.

Some forms omit any reference to specific clauses of the mortgage, substituting, for a detailed default clause, the following:

AND IT IS HEREBY EXPRESSLY AGREED that the whole of said principal sum shall become due after default in any of the covenants and agreements made by the said obligor   or any mortgagor   in the mortgage covering premises therein described and collateral hereto, all of which covenants and agreements are hereby made part of this instrument.

Execution

The note or bond should be executed in the same manner as a deed. It must be signed. It need not be witnessed or acknowledged, since it is not usually recorded. The better practice, however, is to have the signature both witnessed and acknowledged. Although it need not be sealed, it is advisable to have it so, for the time limit in some states within which suit can be brought upon a sealed instrument is longer than upon one not under seal.

Enforcement

Customarily, if amortization, interest, or taxes are not paid, the lender seeks relief by foreclosing the mortgage upon the land, since by so doing he not only can enforce the mortgage against the security but may ask for judgment upon the note in case the amount realized upon the sale of the realty is not sufficient to satisfy his claim. However, the note is an instrument for the payment of money, and nothing prevents the lender from suing upon the note without regard to the mortgage. If a judgment in such action does not enable the lender to collect his claim, he may then, upon permission of the court, sue to enforce the mortgage by foreclosure.

Usury

In nearly all states a maximum rate of interest is fixed by law. For the lender to collect more than that rate is usury. When a usurious loan is made, in some states the lender may collect only the maximum legal rate of interest; in others he loses all interest; in still others the penalty is loss of the entire amount loaned and interest. In most states, however, a corporation is not permitted by law to plead the defense of usury. If, therefore, the borrower is a corporation, the lender may exact any rate of interest the borrower agrees to pay. This inability of corporations to seek relief in the usury laws has resulted in innumerable corporations coming into existence to operate in realty; lenders feel more secure in loaning to them, especially if a fee or commission is charged for making the loan.

Money for mortgage loans is purely a commercial commodity. Its value depends on whether or not it is plentiful. When money is plentiful, the interest rate is low; when scarce, high. This is not a matter that can be regulated by law; it is purely economic. The usury laws do not protect the borrower; in fact, they usually harm him, for when money is valuable the lender will see that he gets a fair return, and since that may exceed the maximum allowed by law, the lender fixes the interest rate in the note at the maximum allowed by law and collects the difference as a fee or discount for lending. This custom of charging a discount or bonus may subject the lender to the possibility of losing the amount of his loan or of engaging counsel to defend a claim of usury, and he naturally charges an additional amount for taking the risk. Consequently, if the legal maximum were 6 percent and if 8 percent would give the lender a fair return, he collects not only 6 percent but sufficient extra as a safeguard. This amount is paid by the borrower. The usury laws, therefore, actually add to his burden.

The matter of usury presents a peculiar economic problem, one that should be given careful study. All borrowings fall into one or the other of two classes—necessity or voluntary. In the voluntary loan the borrower does not have to get the money. He accepts the loan if its amount suits him and pays whatever is the fair charge for the money, depending on the security, length of loan, interest rate, and the supply of mortgage money. As to this type of borrowing, there should be no usury laws. Their only result is, as indicated above, actually to increase the cost. The necessity borrower, on the other hand, presents a very different picture. He often has little or no security to offer, but he must get the money (possibly he is borrowing for medical care for wife or child). He may be at the mercy of an unscrupulous lender who does not charge what the loan is fairly worth but takes advantage of the borrower's distress and charges most extortionately. The laws aimed at such outrages are necessary and should be strengthened; but it is indeed unfortunate that the laws curbing loan sharks actually operate to increase the cost of voluntary real estate mortgage transactions.

The mortgage

In ancient times, the borrower deeded his property outright as security to the lender, who thereafter was its legal owner. In case of any default he took possession. All the borrower retained was an equitable right to be given back his property if he fully satisfied the loan and interest. He had merely an "equity of redemption." In some states, known as *title* states, this system is still used, except that until a default occurs the borrower retains possession of the property. This instrument is a pledge and has been so recognized from earliest times. It is called a mortgage or dead pledge to distinguish it from a live pledge, which means the article is held in the actual possession of the lender until redeemed.

In most states, known as *lien* states, a mortgage is not an actual transfer for title, but only creates a lien under which in case of default the lender may proceed to collect from the property. Since the mortgage is not a transfer of title, it is personal property. As such it may be passed by assignment, and upon the lender's death goes, not to his heirs as is the case with real property, but to his executors or administrators. Since a mortgage is merely a lien, there may be a first, second, third, or as many mortgages on the property as its owner can procure, each being subject or subordinate to all prior mortgages.

Elements of a valid mortgage

A mortgage is a security device and need not be of any prescribed form. In title states, it usually takes the form of a deed of conveyance with a defeasance clause. In lien states, a form is used wherein there is merely a mortgaging clause that "the mortgagor hereby mortgages to the mortgagee." In still other states, the usual form employed is the deed of trust that conveys the legal title to a trustee with a power of sale in the event of a default. Upon payment, the deed of trust becomes void. In most states the form named second above is used. This type of mortgage is found to include the following elements:

1. A writing
2. A mortgagor with contractual capacity
3. A mortgagee
4. An interest in real property that may be mortgaged
5. Purpose (secure payment of a debt or obligation)
6. Mortgaging clause
7. Description of premises
8. Mortgagor's statutory covenants
9. Proper execution
10. Voluntary delivery and acceptance

Notwithstanding the fact that the writing fails to qualify as a valid legal mortgage because of some defect in form or the like, it may still be good as an equitable mortgage. A deed, absolute in form and given as security for a debt, is an example.

MORTGAGE CONTRACT

THIS MORTGAGE, made the .... day of ...., nineteen hundred and
.... BETWEEN ...., the mortgagor, and
................................, the mortgagee.
WITNESSETH, that to secure the payment of an indebtedness in the sum of
.... dollars, lawful money of the United States, to be paid on the ....
day of ...., nineteen hundred and ...., with interest
thereon to be computed from ...., at the rate of ....
per centum per annum, and to be paid .... according to a certain
note or obligation bearing even date herewith, the mortgagor hereby mortgages
to the mortgagee, ...
....
....
....

together with all fixtures and articles of personal property, now or hereafter attached to, or used in connection with the premises, all of which are covered by this mortgage.
And the Mortgagor covenants with the Mortgagee as follows:
1. That the mortgagor will pay the indebtedness as hereinbefore provided.
2. That the mortgagor will keep the buildings on the premises insured against loss by fire for the benefit of the mortgagee; that he will assign and deliver the policies to the mortgagee; and that he will reimburse the mortgagee for any premiums paid for insurance made by the mortgagee on the mortgagor's default in so insuring the buildings or in so assigning and delivering the policies.
3. That no building on the premises shall be removed or demolished without the consent of the mortgagee.
4. That the whole of said principal sum and interest shall become due at the option of the mortgagee: after default in the payment of any installment of

principal or of interest for .... days; or after default in the payment of any tax, water rate or assessment for .... days after notice and demand; or after default after notice and demand either in assigning and delivering the policies insuring the buildings against loss by fire or in reimbursing the mortgagee for premiums paid on such insurance, as hereinbefore provided; or after default upon request in furnishing a statement of the amount due on the mortgage and whether any offsets or defenses exist against the mortgage debt, as hereinafter provided.

5. That the holder of this mortgage, in any action to foreclose it, shall be entitled to the appointment of a receiver.

6. That the mortgagor will pay all taxes, assessments, or water rates, and in default thereof, the mortgagee may pay the same.

7. That the mortgagor within .... days upon request in person or within .... days upon request by mail will furnish a written statement duly acknowledged of the amount due on this mortgage and whether any offsets or written defenses exist against the mortgage debt.

8. That notice and demand or request may be in writing and may be served in person or by mail.

9. That the mortgagor warrants the title to the premises.

10. That the whole of said principal sum shall become due at the option of the mortgagee after default for 60 days after notice and demand, in the payment of any installment of any assessment for local improvements heretofore or hereafter laid, which is or may become payable in annual installments and which has affected, now affects or hereafter may affect the said premises, notwithstanding that such installment be not due and payable at the time of such notice and demand.

11. That the whole of said principal sum shall become due at the option of the mortgagee, if the buildings on said premises are not maintained in reasonably good repair or upon the failure of any owner of said premises to comply with the requirements of any department of the State, County or City within three months after an order making such requirement has been issued by any said State, County or City Department.

12. That the whole of said principal sum shall immediately become due at the option of the mortgagee if the mortgagor shall assign the rents or any part of the rents of the mortgaged premises without first obtaining the written consent of the mortgagee to such an assignment, or upon the actual or threatened demolition or removal of any building erected, or to be erected upon said premises.

13. That if any improvements, repairs, or alterations have been commenced and have not been completed at least four months before the making of this loan, the mortgagor will receive the advances secured by this mortgage and will hold the right to receive such advances as a trust fund to be applied first for the purpose of paying the cost of improvement, and that he will apply the same first to the payment of the cost of improvement before using any part of the total of the same for any other purpose.

IN WITNESS WHEREOF, this mortgage has been duly executed by the mortgagor.

.... L.S.

.... L.S.

In presence of:

....

....

(Acknowledgment)

Identification of parties and instrument

The opening words, "This mortgage," merely identify the instrument as such. In many states the form commences with "This indenture." Next appears the date—not a requisite, but convenient and customary. The parties are then named, the borrower first, followed by the lender, just as in the note. After each name, however, the party's residence must be added. In this form they are designated mortgagor and mortgagee, respectively. Often they are stated to be the "party of the first part" and the "party of the second part." Although a mortgage is personal property, it nevertheless conditionally transfers a right to have the property sold to satisfy the debt evidenced by the note. Consequently, in the states that recognize dower or other marital real property rights, it may be necessary to have the spouse join in order to surrender dower or other claims. Of course, dower or other rights have no application in case the mortgage is given to secure a part of the purchase money. "Witnesseth" is no more important here than in a deed.

Statement of the obligation

"That to secure the payment of an indebtedness .... according to a certain note or obligation bearing even date herewith." In these words the obligation of the note is stated. Care should be exercised to state the indebtedness, its terms of interest, amortization, and so on, and date of repayment exactly the same in both the note and the mortgage. Any variation may later create trouble. The form given has the interest clause partially printed. Should the note provide for installment principal payments, the wording may easily be altered to suit the requirement.

The note is not usually recorded, but the mortgage should be. Many parties to mortgage transactions do not wish the terms of the loan to become known to anyone examining the records. It has therefore become quite common to omit a specific statement of the terms of the obligation in the mortgage. If such secrecy is desired, this provision in the mortgage may be made to read "that to secure the payment of an indebtedness in the sum of .... dollars [stating the principal sum secured to be paid], together with the interest thereon according to a certain note or obligation ...." This wording is not improper any more than it is wrong for the man who discounts his paper at a bank to fail to publish to the world the terms upon which he secures credit.

The pledge

As security for the performance of the obligation just stated, "the mortgagor hereby mortgages to the mortgagee" the realty pledged as security. Here should be set forth a description of the property. It should be described with just as much particularity as in a deed. By legal construction the quoted words at the beginning of this paragraph mean substantially that the mortgagor conditionally transfers a right in the property to the mortgagee of such nature that, if the loan is not paid in accordance with the bond, the property may be sold to satisfy the claim. In many states the mortgage actually states that the borrower "grants and releases" the property to the mortgagee. Where such a form is used, the description is followed by a *defeasance clause*, which states that if the loan and interest are paid in due course, the rights of the lender are defeated and his interest in the property ceases.

The form of mortgage illustrated contains, following the description, what is spoken of as the *personal property clause*. Much of the equipment (electric refrigerators, shades, blinds, screens, and so forth) in even a one- or two-family house now is on the border line between realty and personalty, and it is important that the mortgage cover it as well as the land and the building. In apartment buildings the lobby and hall furnishings are often worth quite a large sum of money. The personal property clause in the mortgage makes all such things part of the security. In the event of foreclosure, they are included in the sale.

Covenants and clauses

Following the description appear the covenants made by the mortgagor. In the form illustrated on pages 131–32 there are thirteen. Others may be added to suit special situations.

By the first covenant the mortgagor agrees to pay the indebtedness, and to do so as provided in the mortgage. The covenant implies also that if any default arises in carrying out the terms of the obligation, the lender may have the property sold to satisfy his claim in due legal course by means of an action in foreclosure.

The second covenant binds the mortgagor to keep the mortgaged premises insured against loss by fire, at all times until the debt is fully paid, in an amount not exceeding 100 percent of the insurable value in a company approved by the mortgagee. The mortgagor must turn over to the holder of the mortgage the policy endorsed with the standard mortgage clause. Failure to do so entitles the mortgagee to procure such a policy and charge the premium to the mortgagor. The proceeds of a fire loss may be retained by the mortgagee and applied in reduction of the indebtedness or paid over to the mortgagor for the repair of the mortgaged premises. For a fuller discussion of the problems relating to fire insurance, see Chapter 22, "Insurance."

The third covenant prohibits the removal or demolition of any building on the pledged property, thereby preventing any lowering of the value of the security. If the land is worth $2,000 and the building $8,000, together they are sufficient security for a mortgage loan of $6,000. But if the building is removed, the pledge is entirely inadequate. Should the borrower attempt any such act, he may be enjoined by court order at the instance of the lender, who may also forthwith call the loan and commence foreclosure.

The fourth covenant permits the holder of the mortgage, at his option, to accelerate the due date of the entire principal in any of the following cases:

1. A default in the payment of interest or a principal installment for the period of grace provided
2. An unpaid tax, water rate, assessment, or annual installment thereof for the period of grace provided after notice and demand
3. A default, after notice and demand, in turning over the fire insurance policy or in reimbursing mortgagee for premium on such insurance
4. A failure to furnish requested estoppel certificate after lapse of the period of time provided therefor

This *acceleration clause*, as it is commonly called, is fair and does not constitute a forfeiture or a penalty in the eyes of the law.

The fifth covenant is known as the *receiver clause*. An action to foreclose the mortgage takes several months. During this time the owner is collecting the rents, thereby getting all the benefits from the property, and, knowing that he will soon lose it, he neglects to expend anything in keeping up the property. With the receiver clause, the mortgagee can prevent this injustice by applying for the appointment of a receiver. The receiver steps into the owner's shoes, collects the rents, and pays the carrying charges from the time of his appointment until the sale of the property in the action. Whatever net profit he has at the termination of his duties is an additional fund from which the mortgagee may satisfy his claim.

The sixth covenant is an agreement on the mortgagor's part to pay all taxes, assessments, and water rates. If they are not paid, the mortgagee may call a default under the fourth covenant. But this covenant goes further than that. It permits the mortgagee to pay them, if the mortgagor fails to do so, and add the amount of such payments to the amounts of principal and interest due him.

By the seventh covenant the mortgagor obligates himself to give, within a certain time (usually fixed at five days upon request in person or ten days upon request by mail), a written statement duly acknowledged of the amount due and whether any offsets or defenses exist against the mortgage debt. Such a statement is known as an *estoppel certificate*. Its purpose is readily explainable. If the holder of the mortgage desires to sell it, he is entitled by this covenant to place in his assignee's hands a statement by the owner of the land of how much is owing on the mortgage. The purchaser is thereby assured that no claim of payment or reduction can be made later by the debtor and that there are no offsets or defenses existing against his mortgage debt.

The eighth covenant specifies that the notice provided in the various covenants may be served either personally or by mail. Without this clause it would be necessary to secure personal service on the owner, a thing that is often very difficult to accomplish, particularly if the owner desires to evade service. A notice deposited in a regularly maintained mail receptacle, postpaid, and properly addressed, is presumed to have been received by the addressee.

The ninth covenant is similar to the covenant of warranty in a deed. It is a guarantee by the mortgagor that he has good title to the property described in the mortgage.

Special clauses

Following the nine foregoing covenants, it is usual to insert a number of special clauses. Some of these are used so often that they appear in the printed forms. Others are seldom used and are typewritten in the form when needed.

Clauses ten through thirteen, as they appear in the form on page 132, may be briefly explained as follows:

The tenth clause, as its wording indicates, provides for the situation in which an owner may, if permitted by law, have changed a lump-sum assessment for street or other improvements into an installment assessment payable over a period of years. Ordinarily a mortgagee is not greatly concerned by this change. In most instances it does not seriously affect the security for his loan. This clause, however, does give him the right to insist that any such assessment be paid and removes the right from the owner of the property to extend the time and payment arbitrarily and without the mortgagee's consent. A mortgagee might wish to use this clause if, for instance, a number of assessments were probably going to be levied against the property and he wished each one to be taken care of in full as it was levied.

The eleventh clause is applicable principally in large cities, and especially in connection with old and obsolete improvements. The problem of modernizing and bringing up to date some of the older buildings is always present, and in many cities the municipality itself is stepping in and forcing, by various means, the modernization of a number of dwelling houses. For this purpose the law in some places permits the municipality to vacate a building or, in some cases, do the necessary work itself and make the cost a first lien against the property, even ahead of the mortgage. The purpose of this clause is not only to obligate the owner to maintain the property in good condition but also, in the event of a default on his part in doing that, to permit the mortgagee to step in and do the work before the municipality has either made the building tenantless or undertaken to do the work itself.

The twelfth clause is quite important. The latter part of it, which permits the calling of the mortgage in the event of the actual or threatened demolition or removal of any building, is legally unnecessary because the holder of the mortgage, even in the absence of such a provision, has an absolute right to invoke the aid of a court to restrain the depletion of the security for his claim. The earlier part of the clause, having to do with an assignment of the rents, is important because the decisions in some jurisdictions seem to make a distinction between the rents and the property. The land and building may be mortgaged to one person, but the rents may be either mortgaged or assigned to someone else, who may be entitled to collect them until such time as the holder of the mortgage on land and building has foreclosed and title is transferred as a result of the foreclosure.

The thirteenth clause is specifically required in those states that invoked a lien law and, as its wording indicates, is simply an obligation on the part of the owner to use the funds received on the loan to pay for work done on the property before he diverts such funds to any other use.

Other clauses

Sometimes it is deemed expedient to include a clause known as the *Brundage clause*. Mortgages are personal property in the hands of their owner and as such are subject to tax. A lender, in considering the desirability of an investment, takes into consideration not only the interest return but also any taxes which may reduce that return. If the tax should rise materially, the mortgage would yield a lower net return. The mortgagee may protect himself by making it possible for him to call in his mortgage in the event of any taxation levied against the holder of the mortgage. The clause first came into use quite a number of years ago in New York at a time when there was agitation to place a tax on mortgages. It may be wise to use the clause in view of the possibility that federal or other taxes subsequently may be levied against mortgages.

A *sale in one parcel* clause is needed in a mortgage that covers more than one lot. For instance, a mortgage might cover four adjoining lots. Should the holder of the mortgage, by reason of a default, foreclose on the property, he must offer the lots for sale one at a time, and only so many lots are sold as will bring the amount necessary to meet his mortgage claim. In addition, if the mortgagor has sold any of the lots before the foreclosure, the mortgagee is met with the rule that the lots must be sold in the action "in the inverse order of alienation." That means that he must first sell such of them as are still owned by the mortgagor, then the rest by selling the last one sold first, and so on, back to the first lot sold by the mortgagor. Should a sale of the lots separately not bring enough to pay the mortgagee's claim, he may offer them for sale in bulk, taking whichever offer brings the highest bid. It is inconvenient to do this; many properties are of more value in one piece. Hence the clause permitting sale in one parcel is ordinarily used unless the property mortgaged is a single lot.

An owner's rent clause is necessary in those states where decisions have held that a receiver appointed in the event of a foreclosure is entitled to enforce only those contracts that the owner had. Obviously the receiver would be entitled to force tenants to pay rent under their leases, but equally obviously the owner has no contract with himself to pay himself rent, and, in New York and some other states, it has been held that the receiver has no right to enforce payment of rent from an owner, whether the owner occupies all or part of the premises. With this explanation, the clause becomes clear in that it makes a specific contract whereby the owner, in the event of a default and the appointment of a receiver, agrees to pay a fair rent to the receiver.

Clauses in junior mortgages

Junior mortgages (those subject to others superior in lien) usually contain two appropriate clauses.

Default in prior mortgage clause. This clause is for the protection of the mortgagee and provides that if the mortgagor defaults in payment of interest, principal, or taxes on any prior mortgage, such interest, principal, or taxes may be paid by the mortgagee and added to the amount of his loan, and that he may forthwith declare a default and proceed to foreclose. This is a very important matter to the junior mortgagee. Should the prior mortgage be foreclosed, he may be compelled either to abandon his lien or else to purchase the property and replace the prior mortgage. This clause permits him to prevent a default in the prior mortgage while he forecloses his own mortgage.

Subordination clause. The other clause usually found in junior mortgages is the *subordination clause*, which is designed for the protection of the mortgagor. When the junior mortgagee made his loan, he was willing to take as security the property already subject to a mortgage or mortgages to secure a certain sum or sums. There should be no reason why his mortgage should not continue in the same subordinate position. But without any provision to cover the situation, the junior mortgagee's mortgage would automatically become a first lien upon payment of the prior mortgage claims. Hence it is customary to insert a clause by which the junior mortgagee's position is fixed. The following is a satisfactory form:

This mortgage shall be and remain subordinate to the present first mortgage or any renewal thereof, or in event of its payment, to any new mortgage provided the excess (if any) of said mortgage over the amount of the present first mortgage be applied in reduction of the principal of this mortgage.

Remedies of mortgagee

In the event of failure of the owner to pay the loan when due, the mortgagee should decide whether he wishes to continue the loan or withdraw. If the mortgage is not excessive, the mortgagee may be willing to let it stand, in which event he may let it run open, or extend it with or without modification of its terms. If, however, the mortgagee either wishes to get his money for other uses or feels that the mortgage is excessive (and certainly if there has been an interest or other default), he should select and pursue one of the following remedies:

1. Management agreement
2. Mortgagee in possession
3. Foreclosure by advertisement
4. Legal foreclosure

Management agreement. In many instances the mortgagee does not wish to foreclose. If he believes the default is the result of poor management by the owner, he may persuade the owner to designate a real estate agent satisfactory to the mortgagee to step in, operate the property, and turn over to the mortgagee all net income after payment of operating expenses. These payments would be applied by the mortgagee to liquidate arrears of taxes and interest. No particular form of agreement is necessary to put this arrangement into effect; usually it is done simply by a letter from the owner to the agent, in some form like the following:

[Address to agent.]

The undersigned hereby appoints you its agent for the management of property [insert description].

You are instructed to remit monthly to the [mortagee] all the net income from said property after paying the operating expenses, to be applied on account of interest or installments that are or may become due on the first mortgage and on taxes, water charges, or assessments that may have become a lien on the premises. You are also to furnish the [mortgagee] with a duplicate monthly statement of your receipts and disbursements.

No leases or extraordinary repairs or alterations are to be made without the approval of ourselves and the [mortgagee].

It is our understanding that your charges are to be .... percent of the gross collections. Please confirm this arrangement.

Very truly yours,

....

(Signed by owner)

Mortgagee in possession. Another quite frequent remedy is known as *mortgagee in possession, under an assignment of rents.* This method can be used only with the owner's consent. The mortgagee is then operating the property, but he has no greater title than he had under the mortgage. His rights are to collect the rents, pay expenses, and apply any balance to reduction of the mortgage debt. When the default has been cured, the mortgagee must step out and return possession to the owner. This remedy, which has been recognized from early times, has many disadvantages. The mortgagee must carefully watch every item of income and expense and render an account when called upon. It is usual to have an agreement signed between the owner and mortgagee, fixing specifically the rights and obligations of each. This is known as an *assignment of rents.*

Foreclosure by advertisement. By statute in many states the mortgagee may foreclose his mortgage by exercising the right given him in the mortgage to sell the property to pay the indebtedness. The method is not a proceeding in a court but consists of giving notice to the owner, if he can be found, and advertising a public sale of the property; hence its name, *foreclosure by advertisement.* It has one great fault: it does not place the purchaser at the sale in possession of the property. The owner may refuse to surrender possession. The purchaser is then able to get possession only by means of a tedious, expensive action in ejectment. For this reason, although apparently the most direct remedy, foreclosure by advertisement is seldom used unless the mortgagee is in possession at the time of the sale.

Legal foreclosure. The usual remedy is a *foreclosure by action at law.* A legal action is commenced in which the owner of the property, the maker of the note or bond, and all other persons who have any interest in the property subordinate to the mortgagee are made parties defendant. Of course, prior lienors should not be made parties; their claims cannot be affected. At the time of commencing the action, a notice of the action should be filed in the office of the clerk of the county in which the property is located. This *notice of pendency,* or *lis pendens* as it is often erroneously termed, is a warning to everyone that the action has been started and that the defendant's rights are being attacked. Anyone acquiring the rights of any defendant thereafter assumes them with presumed knowledge of the action.

The complaint describes the note or bond and mortgage, states that the interests of the defendants are subordinate to the mortgagee, that a default has occurred, and that a certain sum and interest are due the mortgagee. It then asks for a judgment directing the sale of the property free of the interests of all the defendants, that the mortgagee be paid his claim and expenses from the proceeds of the sale, and that, if the sale does not realize enough for that purpose, a judgment for deficiency be given against the maker of the note or bond.

A copy of the summons and complaint must be served on each of the defendants. They are given a certain time in which to set up formally any claim they may have contrary to the allegations of the mortgagee's complaint. Should any of the defendants make answer to the complaint, the issue must be tried out.

If no answer is made, or if the issue raised by answer has been found in favor of the mortgagee, he proceeds to judgment. The amount due him is ascertained and a formal judgment is entered in his favor directing the sale of the property by the referee or master designated or by the sheriff. All defendants who have appeared in the action are given notice of the sale, which must also be advertised as the law requires. Any person may bid at the sale, which is held at public auction in a public place. If the property is a plot consisting of more than one lot, and if there is no clause in the mortgage permitting the sale in one parcel, each lot must be offered for sale separately.

The sale of the property may or may not bring enough to pay the mortgagee's expenses and his claim. He should protect himself by seeing to it that either the bid of an outsider is sufficient to cover him or that he is the highest bidder. In this way, if the property does not bring enough to satisfy his claim, he gets the property, and if more than enough is realized, he does not care what becomes of the property. The amount bid is paid to the officer conducting the sale, who first pays the expenses of sale and the expenses of the action. Then he pays the mortgagee's claim, or as much of it as the balance will pay. If he has more than sufficient to satisfy the mortgagee's claim, he retains the surplus and deposits it in the custody of the court.

He then files a report of his proceedings with the court. If his report shows that he did not realize enough to pay the mortgagee's claim, he specifies the amount of the deficiency, and the mortgagee may enter a judgment against the maker of the bond in that amount. Should there be a surplus, the referee must specify its amount. Any person who has had a valid claim against the property cut off in the foreclosure may commence a "surplus money proceeding," in which the rights and order of priority of all claimants are ascertained and the surplus divided, as far as it will go, to those entitled, in order of their priority.

The purchaser at the sale, upon paying the amount of his bid, receives a deed of the property from the officer who conducted the sale. This deed entitles him to possession of the property, and he may have the aid of the court in removing from possession anyone who was made a party to the action. It is for this reason that all tenants and persons in possession of the mortgaged property are made defendants, even though they have no leases or recorded claim to the property.

Foreclosure practice varies widely in the different states. In some, foreclosure by advertisement works quite satisfactorily under the law. In others, notably New York and Illinois, foreclosure by legal action is slow and very expensive. Practically, although the rights of owner and other interested parties should be protected, the inconvenience and large expense of foreclosure in many states retards the free flow of mortgage money. Every support should be given those groups seeking simpler, less expensive, and uniform foreclosure laws.

READING AND STUDY REFERENCES

1. BROWN, ROBERT K., *Real Estate Economics*, Chapter 8. Boston: Houghton Mifflin Company, 1965.
2. BRYANT, WILLIS R., *Mortgage Lending: Fundamentals and Practices*, Chapter 7. New York: McGraw-Hill Book Company, 1956.
3. HEBARD, EDNA L., and GERALD S. MEISEL, *Principles of Real Estate Law*, Chapter 12. New York: Simmons-Boardman Publishing Corporation, 1964.
4. HUSBAND, WILLIAM H., and FRANK RAY ANDERSON, *Real Estate,* Chapter 7. Homewood, Ill.: Richard D. Irwin, Inc., 1960.
5. KRATOVIL, ROBERT, *Real Estate Law*, Chapter 20. Englewood Cliffs, N.J.: Prentice-Hall, Inc., 1969.
6. LUSK, HAROLD F., *Law of the Real Estate Business*, Chapter 15. Homewood, Ill.: Richard D. Irwin, Inc., 1965.
7. RING, ALFRED A., *Questions and Problems in Real Estate Principles and Practices* (rev. ed.), Chapter 8. Englewood Cliffs, N.J.: Prentice-Hall, Inc., 1972.
8. UNGER, MAURICE A., *Real Estate* (4th ed.), Chapter 6. Cincinnati: South-Western Publishing Co., 1969.

9

DEEDS

Definition

A deed is a written agreement in proper legal form which conveys title to, or an interest in, realty. The deed is the instrument by which the transfer of realty is effected. Upon proper delivery and acceptance, the deed supersedes the contract for sale previously signed by the seller and purchaser. To state it differently, the contract for purchase and sale merges in the deed which, when properly signed and delivered, evidences the change in title, or transfer of an interest in the realty.

Purpose of deeds

Every contract of sale or of exchange, and the terms of sale in an auction agreement, provide for the final closing of the transaction by delivery of a deed. In the early days of history, title was transferred in the presence of witnesses by token delivery of the property. When a sale was to be consummated, the buyer and the seller would go with various witnesses to the land to be transferred, and the seller would make a symbolic delivery of possession; that is, he would dig a clod of earth from the ground and hand it to the purchaser with appropriate words stating that he was thereby delivering possession to him. If it was winter and the ground was frozen, he would break a twig from a tree and hand that to the purchaser. This method of transferring title was unsatisfactory because its proof depended upon the memory of men and the honesty of the parties and their witnesses. It was quite possible for the seller to return later on, when the purchaser was temporarily away from the land, resume possession, and, with the aid of purchased forgetfulness of the witnesses, make it difficult or impossible for the purchaser to prove the transfer. As a result there developed the use of a written instrument signed by the seller, which ultimately developed into the present form of deed.

Essentials of a valid deed

As already noted, a deed of conveyance must be in writing in order to comply with the statute of frauds. This does not mean that a certain prescribed form must be used. The wording is immaterial as long as the intent to convey is expressed. However, there are certain requisites that must be met regardless of the language employed. They may be stated as follows:

1. Names of parties as grantor and grantee
2. Consideration
3. Granting and habendum clauses
4. Designation of quantity of present interest transferred
5. Description of premises
6. Proper execution
7. Voluntary delivery, and acceptance to pass title

In addition to these requisites a deed, to be valid, must be from a party competent to convey to one capable of receiving the grant or title of the property. Delivery of the deed must also be intentional and voluntary and need not necessarily be a physical or direct delivery. Moreover, in some states (mortgage lien states) a deed absolute on its face may be declared a mortgage if given to secure an indebtedness.

To be operative as a deed, the written instrument must convey a present interest in land. If it postpones the passing of title until the grantor's death, the deed as such is invalid. It may be effective as a will, depending on whether or not it meets the requirements for a valid testamentary document. Also, a deed delivered to the grantee after the grantor's death does not operate to pass title.

In considering questions involving the validity and construction of deeds with respect to the title, it is the law of the state in which the property is located that governs.

Types of deeds

The various types of deeds may be divided into statutory and nonstatutory deeds. In most states the statutes set forth a very short form of deed in which all of the covenants or warranties mentioned are implied as though they were written in full. Although the use of statutory form of deed is not mandatory, it is recommended that this form be used, particularly in counties where the recording officer has the right to charge an additional fee for the recording of longer forms. Commonly used statutory deeds are named as follows:

1. Bargain-and-Sale Deed (with or without covenant against grantor's acts)
2. Full Covenant and Warranty Deed
3. Grant Deed
4. Quitclaim Deed
5. Executor's Deed
6. Referee's Deed in Foreclosure
7. Referee's Deed in Partition

The nonstatutory forms include the following:

1. Administrator's Deed
2. Guardian's Deed
3. Committee's Deed
4. Cession Deed
5. Deed of Trust
6. Deed of Confirmation (Correction Deed)
7. Deed of Surrender
8. Deed of Release

Forms of deeds

Deeds vary in content and form depending on the nature of the title interest to be conveyed, and the purposes to be served. Variations in deed forms are also caused by differences in state laws or statutory provisions that govern the transfer of title in realty. Despite these variations in form, the essentials of a valid deed are substantially the same in all states. A simple statutory bargain-and-sale deed which meets the requirements of most states is presented below:

FEE SIMPLE—BARGAIN-AND-SALE DEED

THIS INDENTURE, made the .... day of .... nineteen hundred
and ...., between .... part   of the first part
and .... part   of the second part,
WITNESSETH, that the part   of the first part, in consideration of ....
Dollars, lawful money of the United States, paid by the part   of the second
part, do   hereby grant and release unto the part   of the second part,
.... and assigns forever,
ALL ....
together with the appurtenances and all the estate and rights of the part   of
the first part in and to said premises,
TO HAVE AND TO HOLD the premises herein granted unto the part   of
the second part, ... and assigns forever.
IN WITNESS WHEREOF, the part   of the first part ha   hereunto set
     hand   and seal   the day and year first above written.
IN PRESENCE OF

.... (L.S.)
....

(Acknowledgment)

The opening words are "This Indenture." They have no significance now. The instrument would be effectual without them. They survive from ancient days, when the documents were written in duplicate on the same sheet and then torn apart, each party keeping a piece (indenture). Genuineness was proved if the torn edge of one fitted the other.

These words are followed by the date. As in contracts, it is not necessary that the deed be dated. It is convenient as a memorandum of signing, however, and in the absence of proof to the contrary is presumed to be the date of delivery of the instrument. Hence deeds are usually dated.

Next are set forth the names of the seller and the purchaser, in that order. Each name should, for identification, be followed by the address of the party. Some states require that the purchaser's address be designated in detail as to street and number. In the deed under discussion, the seller is designated "party of the first part" and the purchaser "party of the second part." They may also be termed, respectively, "grantor" and "grantee." If the seller is married, this must be considered. In the states still recognizing dower, the wife must release her dower interest—usually accomplished by reciting her name in the deed at this point and having her sign the deed. In states not recognizing dower, other marital interests may require both spouses to join in the deed upon a sale by either. The status of the parties should be definitely indicated by appropriate words; for example, "John Jones and Mary Jones, his wife." "Witnesseth" has no present-day meaning and could be omitted without affecting the validity of the instrument.

Consideration

The statement of the consideration (that which is given to the seller in return for the deed) comes next. There are several classes of considerations. Since they may differently affect the title conveyed and the rights of the purchaser, an examination of each will be helpful. For general purposes, considerations are divided into three classes: good, valuable, and illegal. Good considerations and valuable considerations give very different rights to the purchaser and must not be confused. A valuable consideration is the giving of money or money's worth by the purchaser at the time the deed is delivered. It need not be exactly equal to the value of the property, but it should bear some fair relation to the property's value and have some present value. The usual commercial sale of realty for cash, or part cash and part purchase money mortgage, or an exchange at a fair price, exemplifies a valuable consideration. A good consideration, on the other hand, is one not measurable in terms of money or money's worth, or one that is measurable in terms of money or money's worth but does not pass at the time of the sale. For example, if A gives his son B his farm by reason of natural love and affection, this consideration is not measurable in terms of money. Or, if A, who has been for several years indebted to B in the sum of five thousand dollars, gives B a deed of his farm when B cancels the indebtedness, the consideration is not a transfer of present value between the parties.

The distinction between these two classes of considerations will readily be understood if one bears in mind the principle that, equitably, a man is trustee of his property for the benefit of his creditors. If he has no debts, or if he will be left, even after the conveyance, with ample property to pay his debts, he may give away his property or sell it for any price, and no one may object. But if he has creditors, he is not permitted, even unintentionally, to cheat them by disposing of his property without substituting in its place something of value received for it. A good consideration is sufficient to support a deed between seller and purchaser, but it is in fraud, possibly unintended, of creditors of the seller, and they may be able to set the deed aside. A deed delivered for a valuable consideration, which leaves in the seller's hands something of value, is good as against the world. The creditors are in just as good a position as before the conveyance; one form of asset merely has been substituted for another. Courts guard the rights of creditors very jealously; one creditor may not secure an unfair preference over the others. It is for that reason that the deed to the creditor B (in the paragraph above) would be set aside. He should not receive any special advantage. Also, if the seller has debts, careful scrutiny should be given any sale in which the price is far less than the value of the property. At the instance of creditors, a court may set aside the deed if convinced that the debtor has parted with his property for an inadequate consideration.

From the foregoing it might appear that every time one bought a piece of property he would be obligated to inquire into the kind and amount of consideration paid for the property by the previous owners. Fortunately, the recording laws simplify the situation. These laws provide that any creditor feeling himself aggrieved must bring an action to establish his claim and that in bringing that action he must file a notice of its pendency in the recording office. Therefore, a purchaser is usually entitled to rely on the fact that previous transfers have been supported by valuable consideration, unless he finds some action pending when he examines the title. He cannot rely on the general assumption, however, if the seller in one of the previous deeds has been a fiduciary; in that event the deed or other recorded instrument must show a full consideration. Another exception applies to the present purchaser: he cannot protect himself against his own acts merely by recording the deed, and if he purchases the property and gives in exchange therefor merely a good consideration, he is liable to suit to set aside the tranfer to him as being in fraud of creditors.

An illegal consideration may be defined as "anything that the law prohibits." It really is a misnomer since, being illegal, it is not a consideration in the eyes of the law. If the purchaser promises, in return for the deed, that he will operate the premises conveyed for an unlawful purpose, the consideration is illegal and the deed void.

Expression of consideration

Some consideration should always be stated in a deed. This shifts the burden of proving lack of consideration to anyone attacking the deed. To be sure in some jurisdictions the seal at the end of the instrument imports consideration and performs the same service, but it might inadvertently be omitted. The amount stated need not be the actual price paid. This differs from a contract of sale in which the *promise* to pay a given consideration must be accurately stated. Failure to specify the agreed-upon consideration in a contract may prove costly to the seller or purchaser, since under the Parol Evidence Rule of law a written contract cannot be modified by oral or other evidence. The Parol Evidence Rule, however, applies only to *promises* and not to *recitations* of prior agreements. The payment of consideration as recited in a deed, therefore, cannot be disputed for purposes of defeating the deed. This legal rule, in effect, maintains the stability of deeds of record.

Whenever the parties to a transaction desire secrecy as to the actual consideration involved, the amount stated in the deed need merely be a nominal sum such as "ten dollars" or "one hundred dollars." There is, however, one important exception to this rule. When the seller is a fiduciary, the purchaser should always insist either that the deed state the full, actual consideration or that the seller give a declaration, signed and acknowledged, in a form that can be recorded, setting forth the actual amount received. This is done because the fiduciary is not selling his own property and is bound, therefore, to sell only for a fair price, and the purchaser might subsequently be called upon to prove that fact.

Granting clause

Following the recital of the consideration in the form, the words "do hereby grant and release unto the party of the second part .... and assigns forever" constitute what is known as the *granting clause*. It is by this clause that the interest or title is transferred, and care must be taken to see that this clause is properly worded. If, for example, the interest to be given by the grantor to the grantee is an estate in fee simple, the words "to the party of the second part, his heirs or assigns forever" should be used; or, for a life estate, "to the party of the second part, for and during his lifetime and thereafter to [naming the person who shall then receive it]." Any instrument under consideration is always construed against its maker, and the grantor is presumed to intend to grant a fee simple estate unless he expressly limits it either in this clause or in the habendum clause. This rule has one exception: it is presumed that a grantor who has an individual estate as well as a representative right to sell intends to convey all his individual right, but only such representative rights as he expressly states.

Description

Any description that unquestionably identifies the property is sufficient for the deed. It is not usual to use street number descriptions, it being desirable to designate the property with more particularity. A description by street number is appropriate in a contract, since the contract is normally consummated within a short time. A deed, on the other hand, remains a permanent record and becomes a part of the chain of title. Consequently the description used should, if possible, be one that may be identified with reasonable ease many years later. It is for this reason that the use of street numbers, which may change as buildings are altered or demolished, and of monuments, such as fences, trees, and stones, which may be removed, is inadvisable.

The various forms of descriptions have been fully discussed in Chapter

6. There are, however, certain precautions that should be observed in drawing the description for a deed. The form of description should never, except upon expert advice, be changed. Much trouble has resulted from failure to observe this rule. The seller should always use the same description as that in the deed by which he took title. If for any reason a change in the form of description is made, it is best to follow the description with a statement that the premises described are the same as those conveyed to the seller by his grantor, naming him, by a certain deed, reciting its date and the date and place of record. In fact, since errors sometimes occur, this statement is not out of place in any deed. Any error in the description is thus corrected by reference to the former deed.

As said before, any description is good that unquestionably identifies the property. If, however, the description is so indefinite that it is impossible to fix the property intended to be conveyed, the deed is void for uncertainty. If, for example, a deed conveys "any one of ten lots," it cannot be told what lot is intended to be conveyed, and no amount of explanation would point to any particular lot as the one intended.

An ambiguity in the description will not necessarily make the deed void. Ambiguities may be *patent* or *latent*. If patent, that is, if the ambiguity appears upon the face of the instrument, resort may be had to evidence outside the instrument to discover what was the intent of the parties. For instance, the description may be of "the most easterly two of my lots on the south side of *X* Street." As it reads, this description is very ambiguous; yet it can be easily ascertained, by an examination of the public records, just where the grantor's lots are and which two are the most easterly. The patent ambiguity may be caused by an inconsistency in the elements of the description. Such would be a description by metes and bounds of a house on *X* Street followed by a recital that it is the property known as 125 *Y* Street. Here is a clear inconsistency, yet the ambiguity appears on the face of the deed and the deed is good if explanatory evidence indicating the property intended can be procured.

As to latent ambiguities, the rule is quite different. These do not appear upon the face of the instrument, the description being apparently definite and clear. The parties may have intended to transfer *X*, but by error a description of *Y* was put in the deed. On its face the deed shows no ambiguity whatever. Such a deed may be reformed by an action brought to correct it, or the grantee may compel the grantor to give a correct deed. However, it must be borne in mind that those who come after are entitled to rely upon instruments that have been recorded. If the deed is ambiguous on its face, anyone examining the records becomes aware of it and can guard against it. But if the deed appears clear, then the public is entitled to rely on it even though it may be quite contrary to the intentions of the parties to it. Consequently, if anyone has acted in reliance upon such a deed and would be put to a loss by the parties changing the deed or explaining it, then it must stand without change or explanation of any kind.

Appurtenances

Following the description is a recital: ". . . with the appurtenances and all the estate and rights of the party of the first part in and to said premises." By "appurtenances" is meant all those rights that go with the land, although not necessarily within the area described. The easement to keep a wall standing on the next lot, a right-of-way to the highway, and spring and drainage rights are examples of appurtenances. The right to the appurtenances goes with the property by law, so that there is really no need for this clause in the deed.

Habendum

The next clause, the habendum, commencing "To have and to hold . . . ," describe the estate granted to the grantee. It should be consistent with the granting clause. Any variation in the statement of the estate granted in this and the granting clause is dangerous. The safest course is always to have the granting and the habendum clauses read exactly alike.

If the property is being sold subject to encumbrances, it is usual to set them forth following the habendum clause. The grantor is assumed to be conveying free and clear of all encumbrances except those specifically mentioned. Hence a careful enumeration should be made of each encumbrance preceded by the words "subject to"; for example, "subject to a mortgage now a lien on said premises to secure the payment of $10,000.00; to the rights of present tenants as monthly tenants; and to all covenants and restrictions of record."

Often, particularly when an owner of a large plot is selling vacant lots for building purposes, he wants to restrict them for the benefit of the entire plot. He may believe that the property will be more valuable if houses of only certain types are erected. This purpose is usually accomplished by means of "restrictive covenants," which are inserted in the deed at this place.

Testimony clause

In the form of deed now under discussion, the bargain-and-sale form, the final provision beginning with the words "In witness whereof . . . ." is the testimony clause. This paragraph is a purely formal recitation of the fact that the grantor has signed and sealed the deed. It could just as well be left out as long as the signing is actually done.

Signature

The party or parties of the first part, who are transferring the title, must sign the deed. They usually do this as in executing a contract, by affixing their signatures, or marks, if they cannot write. It is customary for such a mark to be a cross and for someone present to write the grantor's name as an identification around the cross, thus:

Since a corporation has no hands and is not any physical person, it must act through designated agents—its officers. They have such powers as are given them by the governing body of the corporation, its board of directors, or its trustees if it is a business corporation. The different municipal corpo-

$$\text{John}\left(\overset{\text{his}}{\underset{\text{mark}}{\times}}\right)\text{Brown}$$

rations, including cities, villages, towns, and school districts, have governing boards under various names, each of which authorizes execution by
some proper official. A corporation executes an instrument by affixing its
seal. The form of the corporate seal is usually definitely fixed, the corporation always using the same form. Business corporations generally adopt
a form consisting of two concentric circles between which appear the corporate name, the name of the state in which they are incorporated, and
occasionally the year of organization.

It is customary for the officer directed to execute an instrument to sign
the name of the corporation and then his own name and title. Often another officer signs in attestation. Most important, however, is the corporate
seal, which the authorized officer impresses either upon the instrument itself or upon a wafer, which is then pasted on the instrument.

Seal

Historically, an instrument under seal was called a *deed*. The seal was
essential—more so than the grantor's signature—to the validity of a deed.
Sealing, formerly, was accomplished by an impression made upon wax. In
the few states in which the placing of a seal is still a legal requirement, the
individual grantor signifies his intention to seal by pasting a paper wafer
after his signature, by adding the letters *L.S.* (*locus sigilli*, "place of the
seal"), or in some other way indicating intention to seal.

Except as a means of authentication, the legal effect of the seal has been
abolished in most states. The seal on deeds no longer is accepted as conclusive evidence of consideration, nor does it extend, except in a few eastern states, the statute of limitations. Nevertheless, the use of the seal still
continues. Many states require a corporate deed to be under seal, even
though an individual deed need not be. Irrespective of statutory requirements, however, it is good practice to have the corporate seal affixed as
evidence that execution of the instrument was duly authorized.

In states where the deed is to be executed under seal, it is good practice
to incorporate this intention by inclusion of a clause that attests to this fact:
"In witness whereof this instrument has been duly signed and sealed by the
parties named above. . . ."

Witness

Some states require one or more witnesses; others none. Even though
not required, someone usually signs as a witness. A witness is convenient as
evidence of the signing, or to prove the execution in the event that the
signer fails to acknowledge his execution of the deed.

Acknowledgment

Although a deed is valid in most states without acknowledgment, it is
good practice to secure acknowledgment because, as a general rule, an in-

strument cannot be recorded unless the signature is proved before some public officer, usually a notary public, or attested to by subscribing witnesses. The manner of acknowledgment by an individual is explained fully in Chapter 5, "Contracts." A corporation cannot, of course, acknowledge its signature, yet the seal must be proved. This is done by the officer who affixed the seal. He is sworn by an officer authorized to take acknowledgments and on oath states his residence, his official title in the corporation, that he affixed the seal, that the seal affixed is the corporate seal, and that he acted by order of the governing board of the corporation. The officer taking the acknowledgment then certifies these facts on the deed and signs it, stating his title.

Quitclaim deed

The bargain-and-sale deed discussed above transfers full title to the property. It uses the words "grant and release" in the granting clause. Under the law, the use of these words places in the deed an implied covenant on the part of the grantor that he has possession of the property and substantial title. Hence, the bargain-and-sale deed or some variation of it, with one or more covenants, is used in consummating a sale. Sometimes a person or persons, other than the buyer or the seller, appear to have some vague though legitimate claim upon the property. Such a claim constitutes a "cloud on the title." At other times a person who really has an interest in the property, for instance, a wife entitled to dower, has never been in possession of the property. In such cases it is often desirable to have such persons release any interest they may have in the property. They should not sign a bargain-and-sale deed, because they cannot warrant that they have any substantial title or possession. Therefore, it is customary to use what is known as the *quitclaim deed*, which is very similar in its wording to a bargain-and-sale deed except that instead of the words "grant and release" in the granting clause, it uses the words "remise, release, and quitclaim." By the use of these words, the person signing the deed does not, by implication or otherwise, warrant possession or any right of title whatever. Such a deed will pass any title the signer may have, but it does not tie him to any warranty.

Bargain-and-sale deed with covenants

Every purchaser of property should and usually does examine the records to make sure that the seller's title is marketable. The records may show satisfactory title in the seller, yet there may be many flaws that the records do not indicate. There may be some misstatements in the deeds. For example, in the prior chain of title, there may be a deed from A, B, and C, stating that they are the only children of a former owner; yet there may be other children who have a right. This is just one of numerous possible defects in the title that cannot be discovered from an examination of the records but that may come to light after the purchaser has taken title. The bargain-and-sale deed, discussed in this chapter, may not satisfactorily cover such a situation. It is therefore customary to ask the seller, who is being paid a fair price for the property, not only to give possession and transfer title but also to make various covenants, inserting them in the deed, under which he gives guarantee to the purchaser.

Covenant against grantor's acts

Grantors who are fiduciaries, such as executors and trustees, have no interest in the property or the proceeds of its sale except as representatives of others. They do not wish to assume any future obligations; in fact, in a reasonably short time they will account to the court and want to be discharged of further obligations to the estate. Hence they customarily are willing to covenant only that they "have not done or suffered anything whereby the said premises have been encumbered in any way whatever." This is known as the covenant against grantor's acts and, as it states, is merely a declaration that the grantor has himself done nothing to harm the title. This covenant, if broken by the grantor, is considered to be broken at the time of delivery of the deed, not at any later time. In other words, "it does not run with the land." No subsequent purchaser of the land benefits by it except insofar as the time to sue for its breach is by law usually fairly long and the subsequent purchaser may become entitled to sue on the covenant by reason of covenants in later deeds.

Full covenant and warranty deed

The usual form of contract of sale, when the seller is acting for himself individually, provides that the seller shall give a deed containing the full covenants and warranties. These give the purchaser every possible future guarantee. The form of the full covenant and warranty deed varies substantially among the states. A cursory inspection of these deed forms may disclose only three or four specific covenants, but close examination reveals that there are actually five, regardless of how they may be grouped or consolidated. These covenants are generally implied in the statutory deed, or where enumerated are inserted, as a rule, between the habendum and testimony clauses as follows:

1. Seizin
2. Quiet enjoyment
3. Encumbrance
4. Further assurance
5. Warranty forever

The purpose of these covenants is to create a continuing future obligation upon the grantor. As to all or any of them, the purchaser may know of a breach at the time he takes title, yet his rights are not affected. It will be noted that the covenants naturally fall into two classes: the first and third covenants relate to the past; the second, fourth, and fifth to the future. The first and third do not run with the land; the others do.

Seizin. "That the said [grantor] is seized of the said premises and has good right to convey the same." Under this covenant the grantor guarantees that he owns and is in possession of the property, and that he has good right to sell it. The covenant relates to the time of the transfer and naturally, if broken at all, is broken at the time of delivery of the deed. Any right of action under it commences to run from that time. The purchaser may recover from the seller, in case of breach of this covenant, whatever his expense may be up to the amount he paid for the property.

Quiet enjoyment. "That the party of the second part shall quietly enjoy the said premises." By this covenant the seller guarantees that the purchaser shall not be disturbed in his possession of the property. It relates to possession and not to the title. To make the seller liable for a breach, it is necessary to show that the purchaser has actually been dispossessed. Mere threats and claims of outsiders of some rights in the property do not constitute a breach of this covenant.

Encumbrance. "That the said premises are free from encumbrances." Since this covenant guarantees against encumbrances, it is most important that any encumbrance subject to which the property is sold be stated in the deed. This may be done at any place, usually after the description or the habendum clause or following this covenant. If this covenant is broken, the purchaser may recover from the seller his expense in paying off any encumbrance that may have been a lien when he bought the property. Like seizin, this covenant limits any recovery to the price paid and is broken, if at all, at the time of delivery of the deed.

Each of the remaining covenants binds the seller to future obligations. No right of action may be in existence at the time of the sale, and therefore the covenant itself and not the cause of action runs with the land.

Further assurance. "That the party of the first part will execute or procure any further necessary assurance of the title to said premises." The seller undertakes to procure and deliver any instrument other than the deed which subsequent events show to be requisite to make the title good.

Warranty forever. "That said (grantor) will forever warrant the title to said premises." This covenant is an absolute guarantee by the seller to the purchaser of title and possession of the premises. It is the most important of the covenants. If it is broken, the purchaser may recover his damages up to the value of the property at the time of sale.

The effect of covenants

The five covenants discussed do not by any means guarantee a marketable title to the purchaser. The purchaser may have much actual trouble with his title and possession, although no covenant is broken. There may be some person or persons making claims to rights in the property. If, however, the purchaser is not actually put out of possession, he has in most states no redress; neither the covenant of warranty nor that against encumbrances has been broken. Many technical defects in a chain of title or possession may not be sufficient to permit ousting the purchaser or to constitute a breach of any covenant, but may, nevertheless, be a cloud on the title.

The purchaser, under such circumstances, may have what is known as a *good title*. Others cannot put him out of possession, because others cannot eject him unless they first prove that they have title to the property. But, on the other hand, the purchaser will find serious difficulties when he comes to sell, because the courts uniformly say that a purchaser cannot be compelled to take title unless the title tendered to him is a *marketable title*, and a marketable title is one that is so reasonably clear on examination that the purchaser is not being placed in the position of buying, as the courts often put it, "a lawsuit." No court will compel him to take a title that has such apparent defects as to indicate definitely that there is a reasonable doubt; the title must be clear on the records.

Trust law provision

In some states the law requires that all deeds contain a provision seeking to protect the rights of persons having claims against the property (mechanic's liens arising out of unpaid charges for services or materials used in improving the property. This clause, where required, generally reads as follows:

The grantor covenants that he will receive the consideration for this conveyance and will hold the right to receive such consideration as a trust fund to be applied first for the purpose of paying the cost of improvement and that the grantor will apply the same first to the payment of the cost of the improvement before using any part of the total of the same for any other purpose.

The purpose of this clause is apparent. The grantor obligates himself to see to it that the proceeds of the sale, before being used by him for any other purpose, are applied toward the payment of any charges remaining unpaid for services or materials in improving the property.

Grant deed

In some states (California, for example) where warranty deeds are rarely used, a statutory grant deed is substituted in its stead. A grant deed warrants that the grantor has not already conveyed to any other person and that the estate conveyed is free from encumbrances made or suffered by the grantor or any person claiming under him, including taxes, assessments, and all liens. The grant includes rights-of-way and building restrictions. The grantor's warranty covers encumbrances made during his possession of the property but no other. It conveys further any title to the property that the seller may later acquire. Where applicable, these warranties carried by a grant deed are usually not expressed in the average deed form. They are called *implied warranties* and under the law are effective in a grant deed whether expressed or not.

Executor's deed

The purpose of this type of deed is to convey the title to a decedent's realty. When the will contains no power of sale, the executor must obtain court authorization. The deed must recite the full consideration paid for the property, except where given in distribution of the decedent's estate, and in that case it should contain an appropriate recital to that effect. It contains only the covenant against grantor's acts. All executors must join in the execution of such a deed.

Referee's deed in foreclosure

This is a deed in which the grantor is an officer of the court appointed in an action to foreclose the mortgage on the owner's property. It is given to the purchaser on the sale pursuant to the foreclosure judgment and, at best, conveys only such title as the mortgagor had at the time the mortgage was made. The judgment may provide that the mortgaged premises be sold by or under the direction of the county sheriff, instead of a referee, and that he execute a deed to the purchaser. Aside from the usual requisites, the deed should recite the basis upon which the conveyance is founded. It must also recite the price bid by the purchaser at the sale and contain appropriate recitals as to the encumbrances subject to which the property was sold. It is made without covenants.

Referee's deed in partition

This form of deed is used to convey the title to real property sold pursuant to the judgment in a partition action. It parallels in form and content the referee's deed in foreclosure.

Administrator's deed

This type of deed is used in conveying the real property of an intestate when authorized by the court. It is executed by the administrator and should recite the proceeding under which he is directed to sell.

Guardian's deed

This fiduciary form of deed is the one used to convey the interest of an infant in real property. Inasmuch as the permission of the court must be obtained by a guardian in order to sell and convey the property of his ward, appropriate recitals with respect thereto should be made. As in all fiduciary forms of deed, the full consideration must be recited. The deed should contain the trust clause and a covenant against grantor's and infant's acts.

Committee's deed

Given the case of infants, idiots, and lunatics who are without capacity to make a valid conveyance, the committee appointed for a person of unsound mind must obtain authority from the court to sell and convey the incompetent's real property. This form of deed has as its purpose the accomplishment of such a transfer. In form it is like the guardian's deed.

Cession deed

This form of deed is used to convey the street rights of the abutting owner to a municipality. A form of quitclaim deed may be used containing a recital as to the purpose for which it is given.

Deed of trust

Generally, this form of deed has the purpose of transferring the legal title to a piece of real property by the owner thereof to some individual or corporation as trustee for the benefit of another and/or the grantor himself. In effect, the trust deed is not a true deed, as it is not given primarily to convey title from one to another.

In some states, a deed of trust is used to secure an indebtedness, just as a mortgage is used in others. As such the trust deed provides that specific property be made security for the payment of a debt by the performance of an obligation without the necessity of a change of possession. There are three parties to a trust deed, borrower (*trustor*), lender (*beneficiary*), and a third party called a *trustee*, to whom legal title of the property is conveyed. The theory is that he shall hold it in trust for the beneficiary and has the power to sell the property if the trustor does not fulfill his obligations as recited in the instrument. A trustor signing the trust deed retains what is called an equitable title; that is, he enjoys the right of possession and can do with the property whatever he pleases so long as he does not jeopardize the interest of the lender, who is called the beneficiary. Under a trust deed, the holder of the legal title, the trustee, has no other interest in the property until such time as there is a default made on the terms of the trust deed.

Deed of confirmation

When a deed contains an error with respect to the description, names of the parties, execution, and so forth, a deed of confirmation is necessary to correct the defect. For this purpose a quitclaim deed is generally used with a clause inserted stating the reason for which it is given. Such a deed is often called a *correction deed*.

Deed of surrender

This nonstatutory form of deed is used to convey an estate for years or a life estate in a piece of real property to the remainderman or holder of a reversionary interest, as the case may be. Following the recital of consideration and intention to extinguish the life estate comes the granting clause, usually worded: "does hereby grant, bargain, sell, surrender, and yield up to the party of the second part and . . . assigns forever." After the description should be added, "and all the estate, right, title, interest, term, property, claim, and demand whatsoever, of the party of the first part, of, in, or to the said premises and every part thereof." It is customary to insert a covenant against grantor's acts, but otherwise this deed is without covenant. A quitclaim deed might be used just as effectively, and is more often used to accomplish the same result.

Deed of release

This form varies with the purpose for which it is given. It is used to release the premises described therein from the lien of a mortgage, a dower interest, a remainder interest, or a reverter for the breach of a condition subsequent. It is most frequently used in connection with mortgages. Very often a mortgage covers more than one parcel and provides that the mortgagee shall clear the title to each parcel for an agreed sum. When the mortgagor pays the consideration, the mortgagee executes a release, and that discharges the parcel from the lien of the mortgage. A satisfaction piece should be used if the mortgage affects only one parcel or only one parcel remains to be released. A release is recorded in the conveyance books. In many states this instrument is known as a *release of mortgage*.

Taxation

Prior to January 1, 1968, United States revenue stamps were required on all deeds, individual and corporate, at the rate of fifty-five cents for each five hundred dollars or fraction thereof. If the property was being conveyed subject to an existing mortgage, the amount due thereon was deducted from the purchase price and the amount of stamps necessary was computed on the remainder. A purchase money mortgage did not reduce the amount on which the stamps were calculated. For instance, if the price was $20,000, made up of an existing mortgage of $5,000, a purchase money mortgage of $8,000, and cash in the amount of $7,000, the stamps were calculated on $15,000. Though discontinued as a U.S. revenue stamp tax, many states have enacted legislation under which a surtax identical in amount and procedure is levied on all deeds of conveyance.

In some jurisdictions, a documentary state tax is imposed additionally on all deeds and conveyances. In Florida, for instance, the tax is thirty cents for each one hundred dollars of consideration. This tax is payable on the full value and must be paid regardless, whether the buyer agrees to pay an outstanding mortgage or takes the property subject to it. This tax is not payable on deeds given because of love and affection, or in dividing property between joint owners except where money is received in the exchange of properties. Some states nevertheless levy a minimum state documentary tax as well as a minimum surtax on quitclaim deeds and other conveyances even though no monetary consideration is involved.

READING AND STUDY REFERENCES

1. FRIEDMAN, EDITH J., *Real Estate Encyclopedia*, Chapter 21. Englewood Cliffs, N.J.: Prentice-Hall, 1960.
2. HEBARD, EDNA L., and GERALD S. MEISEL, *Principles of Real Estate Law*, Chapters 9 and 11. New York: Simmons-Boardman Publishing Corporation, 1964.
3. HUSBAND, WILLIAM H., and FRANK RAY ANDERSON, *Real Estate*, Chapter 6. Homewood, Ill.: Richard D. Irwin, Inc., 1960.
4. KRATOVIL, ROBERT, *Real Estate Law*, Chapter 7. Englewood Cliffs, N.J.: Prentice-Hall, Inc., 1969.
5. LUSK, HAROLD F., *Law of the Real Estate Business*, Chapter 8. Homewood, Ill.: Richard D. Irwin, Inc., 1965.
6. RING, ALFRED A., *Questions and Problems in Real Estate Principles and Practices* (rev. ed.), Chapter 9. Englewood Cliffs, N.J.: Prentice-Hall, Inc., 1972.

10

LEASES

Landlord and tenant

Individuals or corporations often acquire real property for income-producing purposes, or they may find it profitable to permit others at times to hire it at a stipulated periodic fee, or *rental*. In either instance, the owner and the user of the property enter into an agreement which establishes the *landlord and tenant* relationship. The landlord is, of course, the one who is letting the property; the party who hires it and agrees to pay the rent is referred to as the tenant. The landlord is usually but not necessarily the owner of the property; he may himself be the tenant of the owner, letting the premises to his own subtenants. This latter type of agreement establishes an estate, legally known as a *sandwich leasehold*, for years. In effect, the original tenant is now sandwiched in between the user of the property, or "top" lessee, and the owner of the leased fee—the landlord.

Leases

The agreement under which the tenant hires the property from the landlord is known as the *lease*, that is, the agreement under which the tenant goes into possession, specifying how long possession shall continue and the amount that shall be paid the landlord for the use of the property. The time for which the tenant may hold possession is known as the *term*. The

amount reserved to the landlord is known as *rent*. A lease may be merely
an oral agreement under which the property is let for a short term, or it
may be a lengthy document containing many special provisions and covenants.

Essentials of a valid lease
No particular wording or form of agreement is required by statute in
in order that a writing constitute a valid lease. The intention of the parties is the important thing. It is sufficient in law if the intention is expressed
to transfer from one to another possession of certain real property for a
determinate length of time. Substance, and not form, is what counts. A contract is not a lease merely because it is denominated as such. In order that
an instrument create the relationship of landlord and tenant, it is essential
that there be the following:

1. A lessor and lessee with contractual capacity
2. Agreement to let and take
3. A sufficient description of premises
4. Term
5. Consideration
6. An execution such as required by statute
7. A delivery and acceptance

Although a covenant or promise to pay rent is almost always included
in a letting agreement, the absence of such a covenant or promise to pay
rent does not affect the validity of a lease. Likewise, failure to fix the duration of the term does not affect the validity of a lease. The rent and term
provisions are, nevertheless, extremely important and should not be omitted unless there is a good reason for keeping these facts a secret. Even
then, careful consideration should be given to the possible legal consequences that may result from such action. If no definite term is stated, the
lease will be legally insufficient to create a tenancy for years, and a tenancy
at will or a periodic tenancy (month to month) will result. It should also
be remembered that a lease, as is the case with a deed or mortgage, does
not become effective until it is intentionally delivered to the lessee or his
duly authorized agent.

Types of leases
Broadly speaking, leases are classified as either short-term or long-term
in duration. This division, based on length of time and terms of use, is
rather arbitrary. Generally, however, leases extending over ten or more
years may appropriately be referred to as long-term leases. Such leases, as
a rule, are lengthy documents containing many special provisions and
landlord-tenant covenants.

Lease agreements are further subclassified as to type, depending on the
methods used to determine the amount of periodic rent payments. The
most frequently used types of leases are the following:

1. Flat, straight, or fixed rental leases
2. Step-up, or graduated rental, leases

3. Reappraisal leases
4. Percentage-of-gross-sales leases
5. Escalated or index leases
6. Net and net-net leases

The flat, or straight, lease is one in which the rental is a fixed sum paid periodically throughout the entire lease term. This type of lease, which at one time enjoyed wide use and popularity, has come—at least for long-term leasing—into gradual disuse. The reason, no doubt, is the steadily declining purchasing power of the dollar. Whereas in selling a property the owner can reinvest his equity in another type of property, in a lease his payments are due over a series of future years, and—where rentals are fixed in amount—a declining dollar value deprives the property, or fee, owner of a fair return in proportion to the value of his property as measured in terms of constant dollars. As a consequence, the use of the flat, or straight, lease is, in practice, restricted to short-term month-to-month leases or, at maximum, yearly leases unless clauses provide for escalation of rental payments as market conditions or changes in indexes, as explained below, necessitate.

The step-up, or graduated rental, lease is intended to give the land user an opportunity to lighten his operating expense burdens during the early, formative years of his business enterprise and to give the landlord an opportunity to participate in future business growth through successively higher rental payments. Such lease agreements must be cautiously evaluated, as excessive rents historically have proven a prime cause of business failure and the resultant bankruptcy.

The reappraisal lease, which establishes rentals as a percentage of property value at fixed intervals of three to five years, is rarely used today. This type of lease has proven expensive to maintain and has been the cause of lengthy litigation where value agreements were difficult to arbitrate because of divergent professional estimates and opinions.

The percentage-of-gross-sales lease has gained steadily in popularity and, for short-term commercial leasing, is used most frequently at present. Under this lease, the tenant agrees to pay a stipulated percentage of his gross sales from goods and services sold on the premises. Generally, leases of this kind provide for a minimum rental ranging from 40 to 80 percent of amounts considered fair in relation to property value. Percentage rentals may range from as low as 2 percent of gross sales for department stores or supermarkets to as high as 75 percent for parking lot operation. Tables for typical percentage rental payments are available through the Institute of Property Management, Chicago, Illinois, and through Prentice-Hall, Inc.[1]

Percentage leases, as a rule, should be drafted by experienced attorneys and should be entered only with responsible tenants who, on the basis of past performance, have earned a high credit rating. Since the lessor's share

[1]Stanley L. McMichael, *Leases: Percentage, Short and Long Term*, 5th ed. Englewood Cliffs, N.J.: Prentice-Hall, Inc., 1959, pp. 46–47.

of rental income is directly related to the business success flowing from tenants' operations, lease clauses should govern details of effective store operation and provide for modes of accounting and periodic auditing of business sales and gross receipts. The landlord, on the other hand, should covenant to maintain the property in prime operating condition and to exclude competitors from neighboring properties that are under his ownership or control.

Escalated or index leases have come into vogue in recent years as a result of high and continuous inflation that erodes the purchasing power of the rental dollar. Such leases either provide for rental adjustment in direct proportion to increases in taxes, insurance, and operating costs or provide for rental increments in proportion to cost-of-living or wholesale price indexes as periodically published by the U.S. Department of Commerce.

Net or net-net leases are generally of long term (ten years or longer) duration. Where the lease requires the tenant to pay all operating costs, including real estate taxes and insurance, the rental agreement is known as a *net* lease. Where in addition to the above-named normal operating costs the tenant further agrees to meet mortgage interest and principal payments, the lease is designated as net-net. Such net-net leases are deemed suitable for large office, commercial, and industrial properties and are preferred by investment trusts and more recently by offshore investment funds which acquire real estate under purchase and leaseback agreements.

Rent

Rent has been defined as a "definite periodic return for the use of property." It may be payable in money, or it may be payable in the produce of the land. The amount of rent need not be definitely fixed in advance, but it must be capable of being made definite at some time. For example, leases may be made with the rent fixed as a certain share of the crop to be raised on the land; when the crop is harvested, the amount of rent is known. Store property is sometimes leased with a provision that the landlord shall receive a fixed sum of rent, plus a percentage of the tenant's gross receipts above an agreed amount. Such leases are called *percentage leases*. The additional sum is part of the rent, the total rent being determined when the results of the tenant's business are known.

The amount of rent to be paid may be uniform throughout the life of the lease. Such leases are called *straight* or *fixed rental leases*. Or the rental may be graduated upward, as in the so-called graduated rental lease. Another type of lease, based upon the manner of payment of rent, is the *reappraisal lease*, which provides that the rent for the first term is either fixed or graduated; the tenant is then given the option of renewal for additional terms at an annual rental, payable monthly, which is to be a certain fixed percentage of the value of the property. Rental payments may also be of a stipulated base amount which periodically is subject to escalation in accordance with cost-of-living index scales.

Rent must also be periodical, that is, payable at regular recurring intervals—so much payable in one sum for the term, or so much each week, month, or year of the term.

It is dangerous to give possession of property without establishing a tenancy. A purchaser of real estate who enters into possession of the property he is buying under a contract of sale and before delivery of the deed is not a tenant unless he is made so by express agreement. Because of the delay and expense of an eviction action of a "nontenant," which must clear through a superior court, it is advisable to establish the nominal relationship of landlord and tenant in such cases. This is accomplished by a letting agreement between the parties in which the term and rental are specified. The agreement may be a separate instrument but is often contained as a special clause in the contract of sale.

Janitors are employees and often receive the use of an apartment as part of their wages. It is usually advisable to have the employee sign an agreement for the use of the apartment at a nominal rental. If he is ever discharged, the letting agreement can be terminated and possession of the apartment secured if necessary through a simple dispossess proceeding.

Term of lease

There is no legal limitation upon the term of a lease. It may be for one day, or it may be for 999 years. Regardless of the length of the term, the right of the tenant to use the leased premises is *personal* property and his holding is a *leasehold*. The right of an owner to receive rent and to resume possession at the end of the lease is *real* property.

Oral and written leases

Under the statute of frauds in most states, leases for more than one year must be in writing and subscribed by the party to be charged. It follows then that leases for terms up to one year may be oral.[2] With regard to written leases, it is important that the agreement clearly express all of the terms of the lease, as the writing will be controlling when claims arise regarding possible oral understandings of matters concerned with the letting of the property. Leases for three or more years in duration are recordable in most states. It is good practice to record long-term leases in order to protect the interests of innocent parties and to give constructive notice of the agreed terms that affect the possession and use of the property.

Possession of real property is actual notice of the occupant's claim upon it, and for this reason the recording of a lease is not always important. Failure to find a lease on record is not conclusive evidence that the tenant's lease is a short one. Many tenants fail to record their leases through carelessness, through a desire to avoid the expense and inconvenience of doing so, or to avoid revealing their rents and terms. However, when the lease is for a fairly long term, it is advisable to record the lease so that, if later lost, a copy can be had from the records, and any possible claim of failure of public notice can be avoided.

---

[2]An oral lease for one year to commence at a future date is also valid in most jurisdictions.

From the standpoint of the term of the lease, tenancies may be classified as definite or indefinite. Definite tenancies may be for a day, several days, a week, several weeks, a month, several months, a year, or several years. The most common definite tenancies are the monthly tenancy, the tenancy for several months, for one year, or for several years. The most common indefinite tenancies are the month-to-month, at will, and by sufferance.

Monthly tenancies. A monthly tenancy is a letting made for one month only. If at the end of the month, the tenant holds over and pays rent and the landlord accepts it, there is by implication a renewal of the letting for another month, and so on from month to month as an indefinite tenancy. The rule as to termination of such tenancy varies among the different states. In some jurisdictions, a notice of at least fifteen days must be given by the landlord or the tenant of the intention to terminate the agreement. In others, notice for a full month period is legally mandatory. In still others, the provisions of the statute are solely for the benefit of the tenant. Where this is the case, the landlord is required to give the tenant due and advance notice of his election to terminate the agreement; the tenant, however, is not required to give any notice to the landlord of his intention to vacate the premises.

Tenancy for term of year or years. More important than the monthly tenancy are those for a definite term of a year or longer. The necessity for having such agreements in writing is governed by the statutes of the state in which the property is located.

The tenancy for a year ends without notice on the last day of the term of the lease. If the tenant continues in possession, he is a holdover. The landlord can dispossess him as such, or he can elect to hold him for a further period of one year. The landlord may, however, enter into a specific agreement with the tenant that if his possession continues, it is as a month-to-month tenancy. In the absence of an agreement of this kind, the acceptance of rent by the landlord from a holdover is usually construed as a renewal of the lease by the landlord for one year, regardless of the number of years in the term of the original lease.

Indefinite tenancies. Tenancies of this type are of uncertain duration, and, until properly terminated, they continue indefinitely by the rental period as the case may be. They may arise in any one of three ways: (1) by express agreement of the parties, (2) by the tenant's holding over and paying rent in accordance with the terms of an expired lease, or (3) by the tenant's entering and paying rent under the terms of a void lease for years. In order to bring such tenancies to an end, notice of termination must be given by the party desiring to conclude the tenancy.

Tenancies at will. A tenancy at will is one in which the owner of a piece of property makes a general letting thereof to a person terminable at the volition of either party. It may arise by implication as well as by express agreement. Sometimes it results from the landlord's permitting the tenant to enter into possession for an indefinite period without reserving any rent. The reservation of rent, however, will not prevent the creation of a tenancy at will, provided it is agreed that the tenancy may be terminated without cause by either party at any time. When rent is payable once a month, this type of tenancy is usually spoken of as a *month-to-month* letting. It will be noted that the essentials of this simplest of all types of tenancy are as follows:

1. The existence of the relationship of landlord and tenant
2. The indefiniteness of the term
3. The right of either party to terminate at will

The common-law rule is that the termination of a tenancy at will may be effected by either the tenant or the landlord at any time without notice. However, this rule has been changed in several states by statute or judicial decision, and notice of termination is required. For example, by statute in New Jersey, Massachusetts, Florida, and other states, both the tenant and the landlord must give notice, whereas in some, including New York, California, and Indiana, the obligation is not reciprocal and rests solely on the landlord. In New York, the statute requires the landlord to serve upon the tenant a written notice of thirty days in the manner therein prescribed.

Tenancy by (or at) sufferance. A tenancy by sufferance arises when a lawful letting or permission has ended and the tenant continues in possession wrongfully. Such a person has only a naked possession and, in the true sense, is not a tenant. At common law, he is not entitled to any notice to quit. In practice, however, several states have enacted statutory provision under which the owner is obliged to give notice for a period equal to that where possession is held under a tenancy at will. Apparently, the legislatures enacting such statutes ignored the fact that a tenant at will holds rightfully whereas a tenant by sufferance holds wrongfully. However, the courts have corrected this legislative error by applying the doctrine of *laches*. One court put it thus:

The notice is clearly necessary only in case there is such a tenancy at will or by sufferance as needs to be terminated. Such a tenancy is not created within the meaning of the statute by the tenant simply holding over his term without the assent of his landlord. To entitle the tenant who holds over a definite term to notice, the holding over must be continued for such a length of time after the expiration of the term, and under such circumstances as to authorize the implication of assent on the part of the landlord to such continuance. In such case the tenancy existing by the implied assent of the landlord ought to be terminated before the tenant can be removed, and hence the tenant is a tenant by sufferance within the meaning of the statute and cannot be removed by summary proceedings or action of ejection without the previous notice to quit.

Long-term leases

As the name implies, long-term leases are for a relatively long period of time, although the time varies according to the type of property leased. For example, three years or more would be considered a long-term apartment lease, whereas ten years or more might be considered a long-term store lease, and twenty-one years or more would be considered a long-term ground lease. Many long-term leases and, particularly, long-term ground leases are net rental leases. A net rental lease is one in which the tenant pays taxes, assessments, all operating expenses, and a net rental figure to the landlord.

Ground leases

A ground lease is one made for the rental of a parcel of unimproved land for a term of years. The agreement usually contains the provision that a building shall be erected on the land by the tenant. It frequently contains a further provision regarding the disposition of the building at the end of the term. The building, although erected at the expense of the tenant, legally becomes real property and is, therefore, unless otherwise provided, the property of the landlord, subject, however, to the tenant's right of possession for the term of the lease. So that the tenant can get back the cost of the building, the lease must provide that the landlord, at the expiration of the term, shall pay the tenant all or part of the cost or appraised value of the building, or in the absence of such a provision, the term of the lease or the renewal privileges must give the tenant sufficient time to amortize the entire cost of the building during the period of his occupancy. Ground rent is often computed on the basis of a certain percentage of the value of the land. The tenant pays all taxes and other charges, the landlord's rent being net. So that the landlord may obtain the benefit of an increasing land value, it may be provided that with each renewal of the lease a reappraisal of the land be made and the rent increased proportionately. It may be provided that, at the end of a term, the landlord may either pay the tenant for the building or renew the lease at his option. No set rules govern leases of this kind; each bargain is consummated upon negotiations by the parties concerned. The provisions mentioned above are merely suggestive of what may be agreed upon.

The problem of the tenant erecting a building on leased ground is either to use it for himself or to sublet it to tenants, his own rent or the rent he obtains from subtenants being sufficient to make the operation profitable. He must make the building rent cover the following items:

1. The ground rent payable to the owner
2. Taxes of all kinds, and assessments for local improvements
3. Premiums on policies of insurance against fire, liability, workmen's compensation, and plate glass; and charges for water, heat, light, and power
4. Labor and repairs, including all charges for upkeep, maintenance, and service to tenants
5. Interest on capital invested, that is, on the amount expended in erection of the building
6. An amount sufficient to amortize the cost of the building during the term of the lease or by the end of the last renewal of the lease
7. A sufficient amount over and above all the foregoing charges to compensate the operator for his services and the risk involved in the enterprise

In the process of computing the rent expected to be realized from the building, provision must be made for vacancies and losses through bad debts.

Termination of leases

Leases may be terminated by any one of the following events:

1. Expiration of term of lease
2. Surrender and acceptance, either express or implied
3. Breach of conditions of the lease
4. Constructive eviction of the tenant
5. Actual eviction of the tenant
6. Exercise of right of eminent domain
7. Destruction of property
8. Bankruptcy of lessee
9. Foreclosure of mortgage

It has been noted that leases for several years end on the last day of their term without notice and that monthly tenancies and tenancies at will are self-renewing or continuing until notice of termination has been given. Prior to the end of the term of a lease, the tenant may offer to surrender possession of the premises to the landlord, and if such offer is accepted, the lease is terminated. This may be done orally even though the lease be written, for the act of the landlord in taking possession shows that the obligations under the lease have ended. If a lease has been recorded, it is advisable to have the surrender agreement reduced to writing, signed, acknowledged, and recorded.

The surrender of a lease and the acceptance of the surrender may be implied by the acts of the parties. The mere quitting or abandonment of the premises by the tenant and reentry by the landlord, even though nothing be said, may be construed to be such an implication. To avoid the danger of the landlord's accepting a surrender against his will or intention, it is advisable to have the lease so drawn that the landlord may, to protect the property, reenter as the agent of the tenant.

A breach of conditions may terminate the lease. The conditions of a lease may be divided into two classes, those for which the landlord can dispossess the tenant by summary proceedings and those for which he cannot bring summary proceedings.

Summary or dispossess proceedings can be brought only for the following reasons:

1. Nonpayment of rent
2. Holding over at the end of the term
3. Unlawful use of the premises
4. Nonpayment of taxes, assessments, or other charges when under the terms of the lease the tenant undertook to pay them
5. If the tenant in certain cases takes the benefit of an insolvent act or is adjudged a bankrupt

For breach of other conditions of a lease, possession can be obtained only by means of a lengthy and expensive ejectment action. An important lease, however, properly drawn, contains provisions that bring every condition and covenant into the class for which summary dispossess may be obtained. Such leases provide that additional charges, such as taxes, insurance premiums, water, expenses of repairs and alterations, and, in fact, anything for which settlement is made in money and for which the tenant is liable, may be paid by the landlord, and that the sum so paid shall become additional rent. They also provide that the term is conditioned upon performance of the covenants and limitations on the part of the tenant, and this provision gives the landlord the right to notify the tenant that he elects to end the term of the lease at a fixed time. In other words, there is a "conditional limitation" on the term. Failure of the tenant to pay the charges that have become additional rent, or the holding over of the tenant after termination under the landlord's option, permits the landlord to obtain possession through the ordinary dispossess proceeding.

An eviction may be either actual or constructive. It is an actual eviction if the tenant is ousted from the demised premises, in whole or in part, either by act of the landlord or by paramount title. Constructive eviction occurs when the leased premises have become in such a physical condition, owing to some act or omission of the landlord, that the tenant is unable to occupy them for the purpose intended. No claim of constructive eviction will be allowed unless the tenant actually removes from the premises while the condition exists. If he so removes and can prove his case, the lease is terminated. He may also be able to recover damages for the landlord's breach of the covenant of quiet enjoyment.

There may be constructive eviction from a portion of the premises only, but the tenant can take advantage of the fact that a lease is an entire contract and remove from the entire premises, or he can retain possession of the remainder and refuse to pay rent until restored to possession of the entire premises.

The tenant's contention of constructive eviction must rest upon some act or omission of the landlord by which the tenant was deprived of the use of the property for the purpose or in the manner contemplated by the lease. The erection by the landlord of a building on adjoining property as a result of which the tenant's light was diminished would not be constructive eviction, but the storage of materials on the sidewalk in front of the tenant's premises for a period of time might interfere with his use of the premises to such an extent that constructive eviction could be proved. Failure of the landlord to furnish steam heat or other facility contemplated by the lease usually amounts to constructive eviction.

When leased property is taken for public purposes under the right of eminent domain, leases on it terminate. The tenant is given an opportunity to prove the value of the unexpired term of his lease in the proceeding under which the property is taken and may receive an award for it.

Although under the common law the destruction of a building by fire or otherwise would not terminate a lease or relieve the tenant of his liability to pay rent, nearly all of the states have passed laws that provide that in case of the destruction of the entire property, the tenant may remove immediately after the destruction, and the lease is thereupon terminated.

Frequently it is expressly provided in the lease that it shall terminate in the event of the bankruptcy of the tenant or lessee. In such instance the bankruptcy works as a forfeiture that the court will enforce. However, if the lease does not provide that the term thereof shall come to an end upon the bankruptcy of the lessee, the question of termination depends upon the action of the trustee in bankruptcy. Rejection by him constitutes a breach of the lease and brings it to an end. The lessor may then assert a claim for future rents, which are provable and dischargeable in the bankruptcy proceeding. In cases in which the trustee accepts the lease as an asset of the bankrupt, it is of course not terminated. The foreclosure of a mortgage or other lien will terminate a leasehold estate, provided the lease is subsequent or subordinate to the lien being foreclosed and the lessee is made a party thereto and properly served with a copy of the summons and complaint.

Dispossess proceedings

The right to recover possession from a tenant through the summary proceeding known as *dispossess* is one given by statute and is not a common-law right. The action is brought in courts of minor jurisdiction, that is to say, courts of justices of the peace in country districts and city or municipal courts in cities. A petition is prepared reciting the tenancy, setting forth the cause of action, and praying the court for a warrant of dispossess. The tenant must be notified, either personally or through some member of his family, or by posting of notice on the leased premises. There is a return day on which the tenant may appear and answer. The court may not grant the petition; it may give judgment to the tenant. If the tenant does not answer, or if the court decides against him, judgment is given to the landlord and a warrant of dispossess is issued immediately. As a matter of compassion, the court may stay the warrant for a short time, and in a case of distress, such as serious illness in the tenant's family, there can be little objection to a reasonable delay. The tenant who does not peaceably remove after the warrant has been issued may, with his belongings, be forcibly removed by a marshal or other public official.

The right to dispossess was greatly restricted during and following the periods of World Wars I and II, and that right is still suspended or abridged in areas where rent control laws are effective. In the enactment of emergency rent laws, the federal or state legislatures felt that it was necessary to protect tenants against eviction by landlords whose sole desire was to increase their income by raising rents. In case of emergency, it was deemed, too, that public interests supersede those of the owners of the buildings. A more detailed discussion of rent control laws and their social and economic consequences will be presented in Chapter 27.

Form of lease

The usual parts of a lease describe or state the premises, term, amount of rent and manner of payment, and the covenants and conditions agreed upon. The agreement is made between two or more parties known as *lessor* and *lessee* (or landlord and tenant). Written leases usually are dated and signed by both parties. Seals, witnessing, and acknowledgments are sometimes added. The number of lease forms in general use vary from the short monthly letting agreement to the lengthy agreement drawn to contain provisions for an important long-term lease. No single form will fit every case —a lease must be drawn to express the intended agreement between landlord and tenant.

Covenants by tenant

All important leases contain certain covenants, that is, definite agreements made by the tenant and binding upon him. They may appear to make the lease a one-sided agreement, but such is not the case. The tenant is renting the landlord's property, but he does not have to rent it, and the landlord does not have to let it to him. The landlord can, therefore, in making the rental, state exactly the terms and conditions upon which he permits the tenant to use his property. The landlord grants the only thing he has to give the tenant, that is, quiet and peaceful possession for the term of the lease. The tenant, on the other hand, agrees to pay the rent, to use the property in the manner specified in the lease, and to comply with the conditions laid down by the landlord in the lease. When leases are made for a long period of years, the covenants become of great importance. Leases, it will be seen, frequently run long beyond the prospective lifetime of the landlord. The rights of all future owners and mortgagees of the property are affected by the terms and conditions of the lease. Although it is important for the tenant to read carefully the covenants in the lease he is asked to sign, the landlord should also carefully consider what covenants the lease must contain in order to protect himself, his heirs and assigns, for the entire term of the lease.

Some leases contain a privilege for a renewal or renewals for one or more periods. Provision is usually made in any agreement for renewal as to how the rent for the additional periods shall be determined. To do otherwise would be unfair to the owners and would detract from the value of the property.

Repairs

The general rule is that neither party to a lease is required to make repairs, but the tenant is required to surrender the premises at the expiration of the term in as good a condition as they were in at the commencement of the lease, reasonable wear and tear and damage by the elements excepted. Occasionally the lease provides that the landlord shall make certain repairs only. There is no legal requirement that the landlord make the ordinary repairs for the upkeep of the property, except that the building must be kept tenantable. If a building becomes untenantable, the tenant may remove on the ground that he has been constructively evicted. Destruction of the building usually terminates the lease, neither party being obligated to rebuild unless the lease provides otherwise.

Improvements

All improvements become the property of the landlord when made. It is proper in some cases to provide that some or all improvements may be removed at or prior to the expiration of the lease. Fixtures and machinery installed by the tenant are usually considered personal property and are removable when the tenant removes. The lease usually provides that no alterations to the building shall be made without the consent of the landlord.

Liens

The tenant may make repairs, alterations, or improvements to the premises with the consent of the landlord. The landlord should guard against the contingency of the tenant's neglecting to pay for the work so performed, and the consequent filing of mechanic's liens by those who did the work. The law permits the mechanics and materialmen under such circumstances to enforce their liens against the landlord's property, although they may not be able to hold the landlord personally liable. Where work of this kind is contemplated, the lease should provide that if such a lien is filed the landlord may pay it and add it to the next installment of rent falling due under the lease. This may result in a dispossess of the tenant for nonpayment of rent, unless he reimburses the landlord for the amount he has paid to free his property from the lien.

The landlord may demand further protection from liens by requiring that the tenant deposit cash or file a bond as a guarantee that the cost of the repair or construction work will be paid. This requirement is of especial importance in leases that provide that the tenant is to make any extensive repairs, alterations, or improvements.

Security furnished by tenant

A landlord, when making an important lease, may properly require the tenant to furnish security for the performance of the terms of the lease. This security may be in the form of cash or negotiable securities, or it may be in the form of a bond executed by personal sureties or a surety company. There is no rule as to the amount of the security, but it is usually in proportion to the amount of rent reserved by the lease. The security may be a sum equal to the rent for one month or several months, or even a year or more. It is often agreed that the tenant shall receive interest at a certain rate on cash security deposited by him.

Unless a security deposit clearly appears to have been intended by the parties as liquidated damages, the lessor may retain only so much thereof as equals the amount of damages suffered by him. In cases in which the lessor desires the deposit to constitute liquidated damages and the lessee is agreeable thereto, care should be taken that the amount provided for is not excessive. If the deposit is disproportionate to the damages, the security provision may be held invalid as being in the nature of a penalty.

A transfer of the property by the lessor does not of itself carry with it the security deposit. The same also holds true in the case of an assignment by the lessee of his term. The lessor's covenant to return the deposit to the lessee is personal. Generally, the lessor remains personally liable to his lessee for the deposit, notwithstanding the fact that he turns it over to the transferee of the reversion. Of course this liability may be otherwise stipulated in the lease.

Additional charges paid by tenant

The lease may provide not only that the tenant shall pay the landlord an agreed rental but also that he shall pay some or all of the expenses and carrying charges of the property. In cases where the tenant pays all expenses and charges, the rent paid to the landlord is said to be a *net rental.* The landlord's income from the rent of the property is net to him, and the tenant meets all charges in connection with the property. These charges may includes taxes, assessments, water rates, and fire and plate glass insurance premiums. Interest on mortgages is not usually included among the charges to be paid by a tenant. In instances, however, where the tenant agrees to meet both mortgage interest and amortization payments, the lease is classified as *net-net.*

It should be a part of the agreement that the landlord may pay any or all of such charges that the tenant fails to pay and that any charge so paid becomes additional rent payable with the next installment of rent under the lease.

Sale and leaseback

In recent years more and more businesses and corporate entities have found it profitable to sell their real estate holdings and thus free additional capital for expansion of their business operations, and to lease back the properties, thus sold, under custom-designed long-term leases. Institutional investors, but principally nationally known insurance companies, have found real estate occupied on a long-term basis by reliable tenants who enjoy a high credit rating an excellent and secure investment. As a consequence, sale and leaseback transactions have increased significantly. At the time of sale and leaseback closing, the parties to the transaction in effect exchange instruments. The seller, generally a business corporation, deeds the realty to the buyer, an insurance company or like investor, and the buyer in turn leases the property to the seller under mutually agreed-upon terms.

Such long-term leases as a rule extend for twenty or thirty years with option to renew for like or lesser succeeding periods. The lease terms usually require the tenant to pay all operating expenses, including taxes and insurance, thus yielding a net return or cash flow to the buyer-lessor that yields a return in excess of that obtainable from a like sum invested in high-grade corporate bonds or government securities.

The sale and leaseback transactions have proved mutually advantageous. The lessee, or seller, in effect has obtained 100 percent financing and has realized cash far in excess of that obtainable under conventional mortgage financing. Further, the seller-lessee now enjoys significant income tax advantages, since the entire rent becomes tax deductible as a cost of business operations. Such deductions are considerably larger than the sum total of owners' deductions allowable for interest on mortgage debt, real estate taxes, and permissible deductions for depreciation on building improvements.

Fire clause

The long form of lease generally provides that the tenant shall give the landlord immediate notice of any fire. It is then the landlord's duty to repair the damage as speedily as possible. If the tenant remains in possession, the rent continues regardless of the fire; but if the damage is such that the tenant is compelled to remove, the rent ceases until such time as the property is restored to its former condition. In cases of total destruction of the property by fire, the lease is terminated; rent is paid up to the date of the fire, and thereafter the liability of the parties ceases. It is advisable to include a fire clause in the lease so that in the event of fire the rights of the parties are clearly defined. In some states the law provides that a fire that renders the premises untenantable terminates the lease. If there is no such provision of law, or if the law provides the contrary, the lease of the premises continues regardless of any damage by fire.

Assignment, subletting, and mortgaging of lease

The tenant's rights under a lease, being personal property, are assignable unless the lease itself contains a covenant forbidding an assignment. A landlord often makes a lease relying on the financial stability of the tenant. The tenant is personally acceptable to him, and therefore it is often his desire to prevent an assignment of the lease to another person. A landlord may in any event consent to a proposed assignment if he wishes to do so.

It has been a rule that once a lease has been assigned, with the landlord's express or implied consent or ratification, it is thereafter freely assignable. To prevent this assumption, it is well to provide that the landlord's failure to insist upon a strict performance of the terms and conditions of the lease shall not be a waiver of his rights as to any future breach of the conditions. The lease should also provide that an assignment (even with landlord's consent) shall not relieve the original lessee of his liability to pay rent, except that he shall be credited with any rent collected by the landlord from the assignee.

The usual rule regarding assignments is that the original lessee can be held personally for the rent called for by the lease even though he has assigned it and the assignee is in possession. Of course, the owner of the property may waive this right by express or implied agreement, but unless such agreement can be shown, the liability continues. In order to retain possession, the assignee of the lease would, of course, have to pay rent and comply with the other terms of the lease. His failure to pay the rent would permit the landlord to dispossess him. If the landlord wishes to sue for the rent due him, his suit against the assignee will be to recover rent based on use and occupation, unless the assignee has made some binding agreement to pay the rent called for by the lease. Rent based on use and occupation may be the same rent that the lease calls for, but not necessarily so.

A subletting is a letting of premises by a tenant to an undertenant. It may be for all or part of the premises, for the whole term or for part of it. Many leases provide that there shall be no subletting without the consent of the lessor. This covenant is valuable if the landlord wishes to control the character of the occupancy.

The tenant may mortgage the lease; that is, the leasehold (the tenant's rights under the lease) may be given as security for money borrowed by him, unless the lease restricts him from so doing. In most states, a mortgage on a lease is a conveyance coming under the provisions of the recording act and is, therefore, recorded in the same manner as a mortgage on real property, and not as a chattel mortgage. In some jurisdictions it is considered to be a chattel mortgage. In the absence of a statute or legal decision in any particular state, it may be considered advisable to file it both ways.

Use of the premises

Unless the lease contains a restriction, the tenant may use the premises in any legal manner. In his use of the premises he may not, however, interfere with occupants of other parts of the building. Illegal use would permit an action for dispossession by the landlord, and a lease specifically made for an illegal purpose would not be enforceable by either party. The purpose for which the premises are to be used is often stated in the lease; for example, "private dwelling," "boardinghouse," "retail drugstore," and so on. In this connection, where it is desired to limit the use of the property to some specified purpose, it is well to have the lease state that the premises shall be used for the purpose mentioned, *and for no other*. It was held, where the lease simply stated that the tenant was to use the premises for a certain trade, that he could use it for other trades. The lease may contain a covenant that the premises may not be used for any purpose that is extra hazardous, objectionable, or detrimental to the neighborhood, or similarly undesirable.

Compliance with orders of governmental authorities

Under the police power of the state, laws have been enacted governing and controlling the use, occupancy, and condition of real property. These laws are enforced through various departments and bureaus. It is appropriate to provide in certain leases that the tenant will, at his own expense, comply with the orders issued by these authorities. The importance of such a provision in a lease depends on the use for which the premises are leased to the tenant and the extent to which control passes to the tenant. In the case of a factory building leased to one tenant, for example, it should usually be a condition that elevators, stairways, and fire escapes be kept in a safe condition and that the provisions of the labor department, health department, fire department, and building department be complied with by the tenant.

Guarantors and sureties

The landlord may require and the tenant may give a guarantee by a third party of the faithful performance of the terms of the lease by the tenant. The agreement of guarantee must be in writing and signed by the guarantor and may be a separate instrument, but it is often endorsed upon the lease. The guarantee may also be in the form of a bond executed by personal sureties or a surety company.

Tenant liable after reentry

It is frequently desirable to include in a lease provisions to the effect that if a tenant is dispossessed by summary proceedings, or if the tenant abandons the property and the landlord reenters and takes possession, the landlord has the option of holding the tenant liable for the rent until the end of the term of the lease. The landlord may relet the premises as the agent of the tenant, and in such event he credits the tenant with the amount he collects from the person to whom the property is relet. A clause of this kind prevents absolute termination of the lease by a summary proceeding or the landlord's reentry.

Right of redemption

In some states the law provides that, if a tenant is dispossessed when more than five years of his lease are unexpired, the tenant has a right to come in at any time after the dispossess and pay up all arrears, and again obtain possession of the property. That is to say, he has a right of redemption. In the long form of lease, the tenant as a rule specifically waives this right of redemption. The advantage of such a clause is that it enables the landlord to be rid of a tenant who does not meet his obligations promptly, and then to obtain another tenant without fear of the first tenant's coming in and claiming the right of redemption.

Tenant to indemnify landlord for damages

It is proper to provide in a lease that the tenant shall hold the landlord harmless from all claims for damages to both person and property of every kind and nature. This clause tends to relieve the landlord of claims that may be made because of accidents to persons having access to the property or passing on the street adjacent thereto.

The responsibility for injuries received upon the premises often falls upon either the landlord or the tenant. The general rule is that he who has the custody and control of that part of the premises where the accident occurs is liable to damages for the injuries resulting. Consequently the tenant of an entire building, having control and possession of the entire building, is responsible for any injury caused by a negligent condition of the building. As to apartment houses or other buildings in which there are several tenants, each tenant usually has custody and control of his own apartment or space in the building, whereas the landlord retains the custody and control of those parts of the building that are used in common by the tenants: namely, the roof, halls, stairways, and entrance. In such a building, therefore, the tenants are responsible only for injuries arising from negligence in their apartments, whereas the landlord is liable for injuries sustained upon roof, halls, stairways, or entry. It must be borne in mind, of course, that neither the landlord nor the tenant is liable for an injury caused by a negligent condition existing in the building unless he either actually knew or should have known of the condition. Also, neither the landlord nor the tenant is responsible for an accident unless it was caused by negligence on the part of either of them. In most states an exception to the above rules exists under which the landlord may be responsible for some accidents in a building even if a tenant has possession and control of the entire building. Such would be an injury arising from a negligent condition that existed at the time the landlord leased the property to the tenant. For example, a tenant is in possession and control of a one-family dwelling house. The stair carpet installed by the tenant becomes worn and causes a visitor to trip, fall, and injure himself. In that case the tenant is responsible for the damages sustained. Suppose, however, that the staircase was so erected as to be very steep and the treads very narrow so that it would be dangerous to anyone going up or down the stairs. In that event a person falling upon the stairs would have a claim against the landlord rather than the tenant. In other words, if there is some inherent defect in the property at the time of the creation of the lease, the landlord is liable for any injury caused by that inherent defect. Also, if the landlord rents the property for either a dangerous or an illegal purpose, he is then liable for damages.

In certain cases both the landlord and the tenant are liable for damages, as when the landlord creates a nuisance and the tenant continues it.

In one recorded case, the landlord of a building installed a sink without an overflow pipe. The tenant allowed the water to overflow from the sink, with the result that the property of a tenant in a lower apartment was damaged. The injured party was allowed to hold both the landlord and the tenant for damages.

Leases subordinate to mortgages

A lease of property is subject to mortgages and other liens upon the property of record when the lease is made; that is, such liens would be superior to the rights of the tenant. When the lease is made, the tenant usually takes possession of the property. He may also record his lease. Either would give notice to persons thereafter dealing with the property of the rights of the tenant, and a mortgage made after the lease would therefore be subordinate to the lease. It would seem to be important, therefore, that tenants who propose to erect a building or spend money in considerable amounts on the property should inquire into existing mortgages. It is also important for mortgagees to find out about existing leases. Leases may be an advantage to the property rather than a disadvantage, the amount of rent and length of time called for by the lease being the determining factors. A case is on record where a bank loaned $82,000 on a piece of property, ignoring the rights of the people in possession. The mortgage was afterwards foreclosed, and it was then found that the property was occupied by tenants having a ten-year lease with an option of a further renewal of ten years at an annual rental of $6,000. It is evident that a rent of

$6,000 was entirely inadequate for a property costing a mortgagee in excess of $82,000, and the lease was especially disadvantageous in that it had a long time to run at the low rental.

Leases often provide that they shall be subordinate to mortgages up to a certain amount, and this provision may permit the landlord to increase existing mortgages up to the agreed amount. The provision of the lease should be that the tenant will execute necessary agreements to effect such subordination.

Covenants by landlord

The covenant in the lease specifically made by a landlord is that of quiet enjoyment. There are implied covenants of possession and sometimes fitness for use. There is usually no warranty, as to the lease of a whole house, of habitability or suitability. However, if a landlord leases an apartment in a house, or an office in an office building, there is an implied covenant that the portions of the building used by all of the tenants are fit for the use for which they are intended. The implied covenant of possession is that the tenant can hold possession against everyone, including the landlord. The landlord is usually allowed, under the terms of the lease, the right to show the property to another tenant or to a purchaser for a short period before the expiration of the lease, and the lease also usually gives him the right to enter and make necessary repairs or comply with the requirements of governmental authorities. The important point for the tenant is that it is incumbent upon the landlord to accord him possession for the term of the lease, subject only to its conditions.

READING AND STUDY REFERENCES

1. BLISS, HOWARD L. and CHARLES H. SILL, *Real Estate Management*, Chapter 28. Englewood Cliffs, N.J.: Prentice-Hall, Inc., 1953.
2. FRIEDMAN, EDITH J., *Real Estate Encyclopedia,* Chapter 31. Englewood Cliffs, N.J.: Prentice-Hall, Inc., 1960.
3. HEBARD, EDNA L., and GERALD S. MEISEL, *Principles of Real Estate Law*, Chapter 13. New York: Simmons-Boardman Publishing Corporation, 1964.
4. HUSBAND, WILLIAM H., and FRANK RAY ANDERSON, *Real Estate*, Chapter 10. Homewood, Ill.: Richard D. Irwin, Inc., 1960.
5. KRATOVIL, ROBERT, *Real Estate Law*, Chapter 30. Englewood Cliffs, N.J.: Prentice-Hall, Inc., 1969.
6. LUSK, HAROLD F., *Law of the Real Estate Business*, Chapter 18. Homewood, Ill.: Richard D. Irwin, Inc., 1965.
7. RATCLIFF, RICHARD U., *Real Estate Analysis*, Chapter 9. New York: McGraw-Hill Book Company, 1961.
8. RING, ALFRED A., *Questions and Problems in Real Estate Principles and Practices* (rev. ed.), Chapter 10. Englewood Cliffs, N.J.: Prentice-Hall, Inc., 1972.
9. UNGER, MAURICE A., *Real Estate* (4th. ed.), Chapter 7. Cincinnati: South-Western Publishing Co., 1969.

11

OTHER REAL ESTATE
INSTRUMENTS

The real estate broker, and in fact anyone engaging in activity in real estate, must be reasonably familiar with the various documents and papers that are used. Some, such as contracts, deeds, mortgage instruments, and leases, require lengthy study and hence are made the subject of separate chapters. There are a number of other instruments, however, which are used quite often and with which everyone concerned with real estate should be fairly well acquainted; these can be discussed together. The purpose of this chapter is, therefore, to take up and discuss the functions and use of the following:

1. Satisfaction of mortgage
2. Extension of mortgage
3. Assignment of mortgage
4. Release of mortgage
5. Subordination of mortgage
6. Certificate of reduction of mortgage
7. Estoppel certificates
8. Mortgage share participation agreements
9. Party wall agreement
10. Beam right agreement
11. Agreements creating driveway easements
12. Power of attorney

13. Affidavit of title
14. Bill of sale
15. Restriction agreement
16. Affidavit of heirship
17. Consolidation agreement
18. Spreading agreement
19. Collateral bond
20. Boundary line agreement

Satisfaction of mortgage

The word *satisfaction* when used legally means receipt, and the expression *satisfaction piece* simply means a formal written receipt. Thus *satisfaction of lien*, *satisfaction of judgment*, and *satisfaction of mortgage* are each names of a particular type of formal acknowledgment of payment. When a mortgage is paid off, the property owner should insist on having the original mortgage and bond or note returned to him. If he has these, it is of course impossible for anyone to substantiate a claim on the mortgage. A very important point to be borne in mind, however, is that mortgages are nearly always recorded and that the mere payment of the amount of the mortgage debt and the surrender of the bond or note and mortgage by the mortgagee to the property owner do not change the fact of the records in the recording office where the mortgage was originally filed. It is therefore very important that some procedure be followed that will not only close the door against a suit on the note or bond and mortgage but secure the cancellation of the mortgage of record. For this purpose the mortgagee, upon receiving payment, should be required to sign a formal receipt or satisfaction piece, which is then recorded. The recording officer, upon receiving it, marks the mortgage on his records as being canceled or satisfied. In that way the lien of the mortgage is removed and the mortgage no longer continues to affect the property in any way.

The satisfaction piece recites a detailed description of the mortgage, giving its date, amount, and the date and place where it was recorded, as well as the names of the parties to the mortgage. If the bond or note and mortgage have been assigned, the satisfaction piece should recite the details of each assignment. If any assignments have not been recorded, they should be recorded, so that there is a clear chain of ownership of the mortgage from the original lender down to the person executing the satisfaction piece. The instrument should further state that the mortgage debt has been paid and that the mortgage may be discharged on the records. When this satisfaction piece is filed and the necessary fees paid, it is customary to stamp or write across the face of the mortgage as copied in the recording books a statement to the effect that the mortgage has been "canceled or satisfied by satisfaction piece filed on [the date when filed]."

Much trouble is constantly arising through the failure of property owners to record the satisfaction piece of a mortgage when they pay it off. They seem to feel that, since they have repossessed the bond or note and the mortgage, nothing concerns them any longer. Often they destroy the mortgage instruments. This gives rise to considerable difficulty when, possibly, many years later, they seek to sell the property and then discover that, although the mortgage has long since been paid off, it is still "open on the record" and constitutes a flaw or cloud on the title. The only safe procedure is for the owner to record the satisfaction piece as soon as he receives it. In some places it is required that the original mortgage be recorded with the satisfaction piece, as an additional check against forgery. One of the most prolific sources of forgeries in connection with real estate has been the filing of a forged satisfaction of mortgage by someone who has decided to turn criminal and who then, posing as the owner, negotiates a new mortgage loan, keeping the holder of the old mortgage quiescent by continuing regular payments on the mortgage. There have been instances of criminals doing this thirty or forty times before being discovered. Requiring the filing of the original mortgage with the satisfaction piece is at least something of a safeguard.

The satisfaction piece should, of course, be signed by the present holder of the mortgage. His signature must be formally proved, either by acknowledgment made by himself or by the deposition of a subscribing witness. If the mortgage is held by several people, each one must sign the satisfaction piece. If it is held by executors, it is customary to endeavor to secure the signatures of all, although legally any one of the executors may satisfy a mortgage if the original holder was the testator. If a mortgage is held by trustees, each of them should be required to sign. If a mortgage is held by a guardian for an infant, signature by the guardian is sufficient until such time as the ward becomes of age. Then it is advisable to have the satisfaction piece executed by both the guardian and the ward.

In some jurisdictions, the county clerk will arrange, upon request by the rightful holder of the mortgage, for direct cancellation of the mortgage on the county records. Where this is permissible, the mortgagee presents the original mortgage to the recording clerk who will stamp the record mortgage page and the original mortgage instruments as follows:

For and in consideration of the full payment of the sum of money secured to be paid by this mortgage, I hereby cancel and discharge the same from record. This .... day of .... 19......
Attested ....
       Clerk of .... Court
       ....
       Mortgagee

This direct cancellation procedure, for which a nominal charge is made, obviates the necessity to prepare a satisfaction of mortgage instrument and thus saves related acknowledgment and recording fees.

Extension of mortgage

A mortgage always states a certain time when the principal shall be paid. It may be payable on demand, in which event the holder of the mortgage may require its payment at any time, or it may be payable at some date in the future—either in installments or in full at some set time, possibly three to five years after the loan is made. After the due date has passed, if the mortgage is not paid, a situation arises in which the lender may demand payment at any time, possibly to the great inconvenience of the property owner, who may have difficulty in refinancing on sudden call. So, also, the lender may be inconvenienced by having his investment suddenly paid off when he finds it inopportune to get a new investment. This inconvenience is very likely to arise, because the lender naturally will demand his money when mortgage money is scarce and interest rates high and he wishes the funds for some other form of investment, or because real estate at the time is unattractive. Thus, in either case it is difficult for the property owner to secure other financing except at considerable expense. On the other hand, if the property owner pays off the mortgage, he will probably do so at a time when money is plentiful and interest rates are low, and the lender will find himself unable to secure any other investment at so attractive an interest rate. It is therefore advantageous on the mortgagor and the mortgagee alike not to let the mortgage run open or past due.

Many mortgages are so arranged, at the time they are first placed on the property, that they continue during a considerable part of the useful life of the building. Such are the mortgages that amortize themselves at from 3 to 5 percent per year and consequently run twenty or more years. As to these mortgages, there is no concern over their becoming past due. They do not become past due until finally paid off.

It is important, however, that mortgages running without any reduction provisions be extended periodically. Many investors do not wish their mortgages to be reduced. They feel they are safe and desire the fixed income arising from a mortgage running for a period of three to five years without reduction in principal and consequent change in the amount of interest coming in. When this is the case, the holder of the mortgage, shortly prior to its due date, should inspect and reappraise the property and decide whether he wishes the mortgage to continue for the same amount or wishes it reduced and, if so, to what extent. It is then a matter of negotiation between the property owner and the mortgagee as to the amount of the mortgage to be extended, the period of time, and the interest rate. Naturally, if the holder of the mortgage desires the mortgage reduced below an amount that the property owner feels he can secure elsewhere, a new mortgage will be arranged; but if the parties agree, a written agreement should embody terms of the extension.

Such an extension agreement is dated. The first party is the holder of the mortgage; the second is the owner of the property. There follows a brief description of the mortgage giving sufficient facts to identify it, such as its date, amount, parties, date of record, the office in which recorded, and a statement of the book or *liber* and page of record. The instrument states the date to which payment has been extended, the interest rate, and the times when interest shall be paid. If any arrangement is made for amortization, that fact also will be stated. There should also be stated the present amount or balance of principal and the date to which interest has been paid. In this way any possible dispute between the parties as to past payments is settled. Following in the form are a number of clauses that conform in a general way to the clauses appearing in a mortgage. It may be noted that by the use of an extension agreement old mortgages that omit clauses which have since become important may be cured of this deficiency and, wherever the mortgage is extended, the extension agreement should be looked upon not as a perfunctory paper but as one of only slightly less importance than the original mortgage instruments that underlie the extension agreement.

Under the extension agreement, the present property owner agrees to pay the mortgage debt and the interest. This makes him the primary debtor, and in some instances, when the property owner wishes to avoid this responsibility, he may prefer to let the mortgage run open rather than become liable for a deficiency in the event of foreclosure. It is also the general impression that the making of an extension agreement releases from liability the person liable on the note or bond; but this is not true in most states. The law governing is a phase of the law or suretyship. Applied to extension agreements, it works as follows: on an open or past-due mortgage, and up to the time the mortgage is extended, the holder of the mortgage can enforce payment at any time, and even though the property passes into the hands of a third party, the original bondsman can demand that the mortgage be collected and force the holder of the mortgage to foreclose. If the original bondsman fails to do this, he permits himself to continue liable and risks having the property decline in value; but (and this is the important thing) the minute the holder of the mortgage by a written extension agreement puts it out of his means to enforce collection, he releases the old bondsman to the extent of any value the property may lose, after the extension agreement is made. Quite possibly at the time the extension agreement was made, the property was worth more than enough to satisfy the mortgage. It would therefore be unfair to hold the old bondsman for any loss that might thereafter accrue by reason of subsequent shrinkage in the value of the property.

The extension agreement is prepared in duplicate, and both copies are executed by both parties. Usually extension agreements are not recorded, but since the agreements may need to be offered in evidence of foreclosure, it is generally customary to have the signatures of the parties proved either by acknowledgment or by deposition of a subscribing witness.

Assignment of mortgage

A bond or note and mortgage are personal property, and hence their ownership may be transferred by mere delivery. It is not necessary, technically, to have any instrument executed for the purpose of transferring the mortgage instruments. However, it is always customary to use what is known as an *assignment of mortgage*. The use of such a written instrument accomplishes two purposes: (1) it may be recorded, so that the records show the transfer of ownership; (2) it negates any possibility that possession by the transferee is the result of fraud or theft. The instrument is always dated, although often at the end. The assignor, naturally, is the person transferring the note and mortgage. Sometimes he is called the party of the first part. The transferee is the assignee, or party of the second part. The consideration stated may be nominal, unless the transfer is made by or to a fiduciary, when the full consideration should be stated. Next follows a description of the mortgage assigned, which normally consists of a statement of the date of the mortgage, the names of the parties, the amount of the mortgage, and the date, place, book or *liber*, and page of recording. The instrument technically also assigns the bond or note, because in legal theory the bond or note is the principal indebtedness and the mortgage merely the security. It is customary to include in an assignment what is spoken of as *the covenant*, a paragraph that recites the amount of unpaid principal, the interest rate, and the date to which interest has been paid. It should always be the purpose of the transferee to have this clause used, for it is at least to some extent an assurance that he is not purchasing a mortgage that actually represents less than the amount he has been told. To be sure, the covenant is binding only on the assignor, and usually the assignee will insist on a written statement or estoppel certificate from the property owner as well.

In many cases in which a mortgage is being assigned at the instance of the owner of the property, the assignor insists on using a *no recourse clause*. This is a short paragraph that says, substantially, "This assignment is given and received upon the express understanding that no recourse whatever shall ever be had to the assignor, his or its heirs, assigns, successors, or personal representatives." The effect of this clause is to transfer the bond or note and mortgage without any obligation on the part of the assignor. It is nearly always used by banks, trust companies, and fiduciaries.

The assignment must be signed by the assignor, but the assignor's wife or husband need not join. If the mortgage is held by more than one person, all should sign, even if they are executors and trustees, although technically, in many states, if the mortgage was part of the testator's estate, the assignment may be executed by just one of the executors. If a mortgage is held by the guardian of an infant or a committee for an incompetent, an assignment should be executed by the guardian or the committee. If the infant has reached his majority, however, the assignment should be executed by the former infant also.

Since the assignment should be recorded, its execution must be duly attested by proof of the signature of the assignor either by acknowledgment or by deposition of the subscribing witness.

Release of mortgage

The meaning of the term *release of mortgage* varies in some of the states. When a mortgage is paid off, in some states the instrument given to evidence that fact is spoken of as a release of mortgage, and where that is the case, its form and functions are the same as has been discussed earlier in this chapter under *satisfaction of mortgage*. Release of mortgage, as used here, refers to what might technically be called *release of part of mortgaged premises*. In other words, the instrument now under discussion is used for the purpose of removing from the lien of the mortgage a part of the real estate pledged by the mortgage as security for the bond or note.

The situation requiring the use of this instrument arises generally in connection with what are termed *blanket mortgages*; that is, mortgages that cover a large, usually vacant tract of land. At the time the mortgage loan is negotiated, the tract may have been subdivided into lots, and in some instances no subdivision may as yet have been made; but in any event there will come a time when the land is ripe for sale in "retail" lots, and the property owner is then faced with the problem of transferring title to the lots as he sells them free and clear of the lien of the mortgage. Seldom does he wish to pay off the entire amount before selling the lots; usually he is financially unable to do so. More often than not he intends to pay out of the price of each lot a fair amount toward reduction of the mortgage, so that it may remain on the balance of the lots for the lessened amount.

If the tract owner expects to sell the lots reasonably soon after placing the mortgage, he usually seeks an agreement with the holder of the mortgage, which is either embodied in a separate instrument or included as a schedule in the mortgage itself. The agreement designates the lots and specifies the amount that must be paid to release each one. It also states the charge for preparation of releases and usually that no releases may be had if there are delinquencies of any sort under the mortgage. Experience indicates the wisdom of having such an agreement. The mortgagee naturally wishes to protect his mortgage and, unless some previous agreement has been made, it is quite possible that he may insist on being paid more than a fair amount for the earlier lots as they are released. This may place an embarrassing financial burden on the subdivider or developer. As the lots are released, the release price for each should be somewhat more than the pro rata of the mortgage loan on each lot, usually 125 percent. Such a price is reasonable in view of the fact that the most desirable lots usually are the first sold. Also, it must be realized that as lots are sold the tract is being broken up. The preparation of such a schedule or agreement made at the time the mortgage is placed, or before the developer or subdivider starts his selling campaign, obviates any disputes.

When the time does come for lots to be released, the instrument accomplishing that purpose is spoken of as the release of mortgage. This instrument recites the holder of the mortgage as the party of the first part and the owner of the land as the party of the second part. There follows a reference to the mortgage, giving the names of the parties and date and where recorded, so that it may be identified. Next appears a recital of the consideration paid for the release, which naturally reduces the amount of the mortgage, and a description of that part of the mortgaged premises that is released. The instrument ends with words confirming the fact of the release and that the portion so released is free and clear of the mortgage debt, but stating that the remaining premises are still a pledge to secure the balance of the mortgage. The party of the first part executes the release, and the property owner or lot buyer should immediately record the release so that the county records may show that this particular part of the mortgaged property is no longer subject to the mortgage.

Subordination of mortgage

Mortgages normally have priority according to the order in which they are recorded; that is, if two mortgages are recorded against a piece of property, the first or prior mortgage is the one that was first recorded. Occasionally it is desired to change this order of priority, and that can be accomplished by means of a subordination agreement. Usually this will occur when a piece of property is already mortgaged and it is desired to obtain a new first mortgage, the holder of the present mortgage agreeing that his mortgage shall become a second mortgage. For instance, often a lot is sold to a builder for part cash, with the rest a purchase money mortgage taken back by the seller. An agreement is made at the time of the sale that the builder may obtain a first mortgage for the purpose of erecting a building on the lot, and the lot owner agrees to subordinate all or part of his purchase money mortgage to the new mortgage. This is not an extraordinary arrangement; many owners of lots do prefer, in order to sell them, to take back a mortgage behind a first mortgage on an improved, income-producing piece of property rather than to continue to own unimproved, non-income-producing land or to have a mortgage on such land.

The subordination agreement is sometimes made between two parties and sometimes between three. In a two-part agreement, the owner of the mortgage to be subordinated is the party of the first part and the new mortgagee the party of the second part. As is usual in real estate agreements, the instrument opens with a statement of the names of the parties; then comes a brief reference to the property, followed by a statement that the party of the first part is the owner of the existing mortgage, the particulars of which are fully stated. Next is a statement that the present owner of the property is about to make a mortgage to the party of the second part covering the premises to secure a stated amount. When the agreement is in three parts, there will also be a statement that the third party is the owner of the premises involved. The instrument recites the consideration of the subordination, which normally is that the new lender will not make the loan unless the present mortgage is subordinated. Then follows the declaration by the party of the first part to the effect that the mortgage held by him is and shall continue to be subject and subordinate in lien to the new mortgage. This agreement is usually prepared in duplicate, and the new lender, after it has been executed by all parties, will record one copy either at or before the time that he records his mortgage. In this way the new mortgage, even though recorded after the existing one, becomes a first lien, and the existing mortgage a subordinate lien.

Certificate of reduction of mortgage

When a mortgage loan is negotiated, the mortgage states the amount of the lien. As the mortgage is reduced in amount, nothing normally appears of record to show the reduction of the mortgage. Occasionally it is desirable, or possibly even necessary, to have the records show the reduction. This is accomplished by a certificate of reduction of mortgage. The most usual circumstances under which this instrument is needed arise when a purchaser is buying a piece of property subject to an existing mortgage that is represented by the seller as having been reduced. The purchaser naturally should have some definite and distinct proof of that reduction. Most contracts of sale contain a provision for the seller to obtain and deliver such a certificate on the closing of title. The certificate is executed by the holder of the mortgage. It describes the mortgage fully, so that there may be no question as to the mortgage referred to. It further recites that the person executing the certificate is the holder of the mortgage. The certificate then goes on to state the exact balance of principal, the current interest rate, and the date to which interest has been paid. If the terms of the mortgage have been changed, it may further recite at what future date the mortgage is due and the details of any agreement for its payment in installments. Usually the certificate further states that it is made by the holder of the mortgage, who knows that the property is being sold and that the purchaser relies on the statement in the certificate in paying for the property. This statement constitutes what is called in law an *estoppel certificate*, by which the holder of the mortgage, having given such a certificate upon which the purchaser of the property relied, is thereafter *estopped*, or legally prevented from urging that the balance of the mortgage and other terms are different from those stated in the certificate. The certificate, naturally, must be signed by the holder of the mortgage. Usually he acknowledges it; this must be done if it is to be recorded. Occasionally he simply verifies it, that is, swears to its truth before a notary public or other officer authorized to take affidavits.

Estoppel certificate

In the preceding paragraph concerning the certificate of reduction of mortgage, the use of the word *estoppel* was explained. There are various certificates of this nature, but all of them have the same basic purpose; namely, to provide a written statement signed by one, which, when acted upon by another, cannot be denied. In the previous illustration in connection with the reduction of a mortgage, the certificate was obtained from the holder of a mortgage for the benefit of a person purchasing the property. There are other instances in which estoppel certificates may be sought. For example, assume that M holds a mortgage on a piece of property. He desires to sell it to P. P, naturally, has been told by M that a certain amount of principal on the mortgage is unpaid, and that it bears interest at a certain rate, which interest has been paid to a stated time. That is all right as far as it goes, but suppose that P pays for and takes an assignment of the mortgage and then finds, when he sends out his first interest notice, that the owner of the property insists that the mortgage is a lien for a lesser amount, that the interest rate is lower, or that the interest has been paid to a later date. This makes a very embarrassing situation for P which may result in loss. To avoid controversy, P, before taking the assignment, should insist that M obtain an estoppel certificate from the owner.

Then, too, if there is a second mortgage on the property, P, if he is wise, will insist on an estoppel certificate from the holder of that mortgage to prevent him later, possibly in the event of foreclosure, from insisting and perhaps proving that the prior mortgage is a lien for a lesser amount than P has been told.

Mortgage share (participation) agreements

Mortgages are not always held by one person, whether an individual or a corporate entity, but sometimes in shares by a number of persons. The shares are arranged in many different ways, as indicated in the chapter on real estate financing. Very often, however, the situation involves just two or three people. If, at the time the mortgage loan comes into existence, several contribute the amount of the loan, the mortgage may be made to all of them, naming them, specifying the share of each one, and stating whether those shares are equal in all respects or have some order of priority. If, however, the mortgage loan is split up after it comes into existence, and in some instances if the amount is subscribed by several at the time of the loan, it is advisable to have a written agreement specifying the amount and order of the various shares. This is accomplished by what is known as a *share ownership*, or participation agreement. Such an agreement not only fixes the amount of the share of each person interested in the mortgage but also specifies the priority among them, if any, and the method of collection and distribution of interest and principal as it is paid. The share ownership agreement also provides for the management and operation of the mortgage with particular reference to foreclosure.

When each of the parties holds an interest and there is no priority among any of them, there seldom is need of any agreement, because in nearly every instance the mortgage or the assignment of the mortgage shows the interests of the various parties. The share ownership agreement is ordinarily used only when there is a senior and a junior share. The senior usually holds the mortgage papers and appears on the records as being the holder of the mortgage. He normally insists on this to protect his superior rights. The very purpose of the agreement is that the holder of the junior share should have a document to evidence his rights. The wording of the agreement makes the senior shareholder substantially a first mortgagee and the junior shareholder a second mortgagee, except that the senior has the right in his own discretion to take whatever steps he may see fit in the enforcement of the mortgage. The agreement provides that he shall collect the interest and the installments of principal and that he shall apply payments of interest first toward interest on his share and installments of principal to the reduction of his share until it is paid off.

The instrument is usually prepared in duplicate and executed by both parties. Either may record it. Generally the senior shareholder does not record his copy of the agreement, since he appears of record to own the mortgage in its entirety, but the junior shareholder very often does so, so that the records may show his interest in the mortgage. Either of these shares may be assigned as a mortgage held by one person, except that the assignment instrument describes a share, and not the entire mortgage, as being assigned.

Party wall agreement

Where buildings are erected solidly attached, it is often arranged to have but one wall between them, so as to save the additional space and the greater expense of two independent walls. Such a wall is known as a *party wall* and, theoretically at least, stands so that its middle is on the dividing line of the two lots and so that each building uses the wall. In actual practice, most party walls come into existence without any agreement whatever. The owner of two lots erects a building on each lot and builds a single wall dividing the two buildings. This becomes a party wall the instant he sells one or both of the lots, and its status as a party wall continues until both buildings are removed. Should one of the buildings be destroyed by fire or taken down for any reason, the owner of that lot would have the right to erect another building still using the wall. Of course, the two owners might terminate the status of the wall as a party wall by agreement between them.

Party walls may also be created by agreement. Occasionally two men owning adjoining lots each decide to build, and they agree that a single wall, to have the status of a party wall, shall be erected between the buildings. Quite often the party wall agreement comes into existence because a building has already been erected on one lot and the other lot is vacant. When the erection of a building on the vacant lot is proposed, a survey may show that the wall of the erected building stands partly over on the vacant lot. To avoid litigation and obtain satisfactory practical results, a party wall agreement is made, under which the new building will use the existing wall. It is executed in duplicate by the adjoining owners and should be recorded.

Beam right agreement

Occasionally the wall of the existing building is sufficiently heavy to be used as a party wall but does not encroach at all on the next lot. Consequently, when the owner of the next lot is about to build, he has no means of forcing the use of the wall. In order to avoid the expense of erecting a separate wall, however, he may negotiate an arrangement whereby he will be permitted to use the wall as a joint wall, and set his beams into it. Of course, he has to pay for this right, and the amount, although a matter of negotiation, will be somewhat near the cost of erecting a separate wall. The joint wall so created is not correctly called a party wall because it does not stand on the dividing line, and normally the owner of the existing building does not wish to surrender any rights to any land that he owns. The form should be prepared in duplicate and signed by both owners, the signatures properly proved, and recorded.

Agreements creating driveway easements

Easements arise in various ways, and the subject is quite a voluminous one from the legal point of view. From the practical real estate aspect, the most important easements are those that have to do with driveways, particularly driveways for automobiles. Such easements may arise in several ways.

Suppose, for example, that a builder erects a row of semidetached dwellings. He does not wish to waste land by having a separate seven- or eight-foot driveway running from the street to the rear of each lot but plans to have a driveway between buildings, half of it on one lot and half on the other. This driveway would run back to the rear of the lots, where it would fan out to two garages, one on each lot. To create the easement necessary for this purpose, the owner does not need to file any special instrument; he brings the easement into existence simply by reciting it in each deed.

Suppose that two lots stand on the north side of a certain street and the easement is to be created between them. When the easterly lot is sold, there would be added to the deed a description worded substantially as follows:

. . . together with an easement in the most easterly four feet of the premises adjoining on the west for ingress and egress of pleasure automobiles only to a garage erected or to be erected in the rear of the premises herein described, and subject to an easement over the most westerly four feet of the premises herein described for a similar easement in favor of the premises immediately adjoining on the west.

A similar recital with the necessary alterations in wording inserted in the deed when the west lot is sold would bring this easement into existence as between the purchasers of the two lots.

If, however, the easement is to be created after the lots have been sold, or if the builder desires to create the easement at the very outset of his building operation or to create a driveway easement in the nature of a roadway through the middle of the block, or something of that sort, a more formal instrument is used. If the builder creates it himself, the instrument will be in the nature of a certificate. If it is brought into existence by the several owners of land affected or benefited, it will be joined in by all of them. A study of the form will indicate that great care must be observed in describing the premises covered by the easement, the nature of the easement, and whom it benefits. It is always advisable, if the easement is for an alleyway or something of that sort, that some method be provided for allotting and collecting the expenses of maintenance and upkeep.

Power of attorney

The word *attorney* originally had the meaning of *agent*. The word is now in ordinary thought associated entirely with lawyers; yet there are, in fact, other types of attorneys. Pension attorneys, for example, are very often not lawyers. There are also patent attorneys and a type of agent known as an *attorney-in-fact*, who acts under a *power of attorney*. That is the name of the instrument giving him his authority. Many agencies are created orally or by informal instrument, but some acts, particularly the handling of certain phases of real estate, cannot be performed by an agent unless his status and power are definitely established by the written instrument known as a power of attorney. Such would be the execution of a mortgage, its extension, assignment, or satisfaction, and the execution of a deed. All of these acts, if not performed by the principal in interest himself, can be performed only by his agent when acting under a formal power of attorney. Note that this instrument names first the principal and then the agent, who is designated as an attorney-in-fact. If the instrument refers to real estate, it should be drawn precisely so as to describe correctly the real estate involved and the specific authority delegated to the attorney. Wherever in real estate dealings an agent is so acting, those who deal with him must take care to examine the power of attorney to make sure that the act is authorized, and in every instance some proof should be obtained that the principal is still living, for under the law the power of attorney ceases the instant the principal dies. Wherever real estate instruments are delivered by an attorney-in-fact, the power of attorney should be a matter of record. Consequently, the attorney-in-fact should see to it that the instrument is properly signed by the principal and that it is proved by subscribing witness deposition, or acknowledged, and recorded.

Affidavit of title

Upon the closing of title, the purchaser has had the records examined, has inspected the property, and quite probably has secured a survey. Suppose he finds that the title seems to be in one X, and that this man, or someone purporting to be X, has signed the contract of sale and now appears and offers a deed signed by himself. It is customary to have him execute an *affidavit of title*, which establishes the identity of the person signing the deed as the same X who appears from the records to be the owner of the property. It is also his statement under oath that he has not created any liens or encumbrances on the property that may not appear of record and, further, that during all the time he has owned the property, he has never heard of any claim of title, lien, or encumbrance made by anyone. All of these are important matters, and it is for this reason that in nearly every case an affidavit of title is required of the seller. It is further necessary, occasionally, to prove special facts, such as, for instance, that X and Y, executing the deed, are actually husband and wife, if that is a necessary element of the transfer. Also, if there are judgments against the name X, or a similar name, the affidavit should state specifically that those judgments are not against X but are against some other person of similar name.

The affidavit of title is signed by the seller and verified, that is, sworn to by him before an officer authorized to take oaths. It is not recorded, but should be carefully kept by the purchaser with his other title papers.

Bill of sale

Technically, a transfer of real estate should not involve a bill of sale in any way. This instrument is used when a writing evidencing the transfer of personalty is desired. A bill of sale would be used in the sale of a boat or an automobile. Occasionally, however, in a real estate transfer, some articles on the premises that are personalty, which normally might be removed by the seller before closing title, have been included in the sale. To be sure, the seller might merely move from the premises and leave them. In that case, when the purchaser took possession, they would be construed as having been delivered to him, and title would be his. But the purchaser may desire something to evidence this transfer, and in that case a bill of sale will be used. This instrument is often resorted to when the owner of a store sells the property to the purchaser together with store fixtures and equipment.

Restriction agreement

Several property owners may agree to impose certain restrictions upon their respective properties for the benefit of their group and all subsequent owners of the properties involved. These agreements usually impose setback restrictions or limit the number of families that may occupy dwellings, restrict property against objectionable uses, and sometimes prescribe type of construction. Such agreements should be signed not only by the owners but also by existing mortgagees who might otherwise cancel the agreement by foreclosure. A common owner may impose similar restrictions on all property owned by him by a written declaration joined in by mortgagees if any. Such agreements and declarations should be recorded.

Affidavit of heirship

This affidavit sets forth the heirs or distributees of a decedent who died intestate. It is taken as proof of the passing of title to real estate to certain individuals. It is used on title or mortgage closings to establish sufficiency of signatories to instruments involved in transaction. Such affidavits should indicate that such heirs or distributees are over twenty-one and thus competent to sell or mortgage property.

Consolidation agreement

By this agreement, two or more mortgages may be consolidated into one single lien and the terms of payment and interest may be stated and made applicable to the combined mortgages. This agreement is signed by the owner of the property involved and the holder of the mortgages involved. It is recorded on the mortgage records.

Spreading agreement

Such an agreement spreads the lien of a mortgage over property other than that already covered by the mortgage. It is signed by the owner of the property and the holder of the mortgage. Spreading agreements are usually resorted to when a mortgagee requires additional security as a condition to continuing the investment. Such agreements are also filed on the mortgage records.

Collateral bond

This type of bond is signed by a party other than the primary bondsman. The primary bondsman is the mortgagor of the real estate. A collateral bondsman is required usually when the mortgagee wishes to strengthen the security of his loan. The collateral bondsman may be resorted to in the event the primary bondsman fails to make good on his obligation.

Boundary line agreement

Boundary lines between different properties may become uncertain because monuments used to describe them have been obliterated. In such instances, the owners involved may agree on fixed boundary lines, evidencing such agreement by an instrument drawn in recordable form and recorded in the conveyancing records. Consent of existing mortgagees should be included in such instruments.

READING AND STUDY REFERENCES

1. BROWN, ROBERT K., *Real Estate Economics*, Chapter 7. Boston: Houghton Mifflin Company, 1965.
2. HEBARD, EDNA L., and GERALD S. MEISEL, *Principles of Real Estate Law*, Chapter 12. New York: Simmons-Boardman Publishing Corporation, 1964.
3. KRATOVIL, ROBERT, *Real Estate Law*, Chapters 4 and 16. Englewood Cliffs, N.J.: Prentice-Hall, Inc., 1969.
4. RING, ALFRED A., *Questions and Problems in Real Estate Principles and Practices* (rev. ed.), Chapter 11. Englewood Cliffs, N.J.: Prentice-Hall, Inc., 1972.
5. UNGER, MAURICE A., *Real Estate* (4th ed.), Chapter 8. Cincinnati: South-Western Publishing Co., 1969.

12

TITLE CLOSING

Preliminary requirements

In the contract for sale of real estate, a clause generally provides for title closing and delivery of the deed at a designated office on a certain day and hour. The date of title closing, as a rule, is four to six weeks removed from date of contract to provide ample time for the buyer and seller to fulfill the preliminary contract requirements incident to the transfer of title. Where time of performance is not specified in a contract, the law in most states will uphold that closing must proceed within a "reasonable" time. What span of time is deemed reasonable will depend upon the circumstances of each case. The condition of the market, the known wishes and necessities of the parties, the fluctuations of values, and many other factors may enter into a determination of a reasonable time. On the other hand, the parties to the contract may deem punctual performance within a given time as one of the essential requirements to the forming of a binding contract. In such instances "time is of the essence," and where so stated it means that each party to the contract must carry out his part of the contract *on time* in order to claim the benefits of his rights under the agreement.

192

Many details must be attended to prior to the actual closing. The closing itself usually requires the presence of a number of people, and unless advance preparations are made, delays and adjournment may result, with consequent irritating loss of time. There is considerable nervous stress on those involved in the closing; this is an additional reason why everything possible should be attended to beforehand, so that at the closing itself the parties may have a minimum of details to consider. The closing of title is the final step in the consummation of the contract and must be carried out in exact accord with the contract provisions. For that reason it is essential that a copy of the contract be brought to the closing. For a complete listing of all instruments and documents that may be required by the seller and the buyer at time of closing, see Appendix pages 517–18.

The title search

In practice, many of the details incident to title closing are attended to in advance to forestall possible delay at the time set for delivery of the deed. The most important requirement on the purchaser's part is to have the title searched. He will make arrangements for this as soon as the contract is signed. If he engages an attorney or conveyancer to do the entire work, that man immediately starts his examination of the public records. If an abstract company is to do the work, the order must be placed at once, the same as with a title insuring company. Whichever method the purchaser may choose to ascertain the condition of the title, the work requires a considerable period of time and should be started immediately. After the search is completed, the purchaser receives a report of title that shows the conditions revealed, and these conditions may determine the subsequent steps taken by the purchaser.

Survey

The report of title indicates only the conditions as shown by the public recording offices. The purchaser should, in nearly every instance, have the property surveyed, and since it takes a number of days to have the survey completed, this matter should not be put off until the last minute. The survey should be ordered from a civil engineer and surveyor who is well acquainted with the neighborhood where the property is situated. Otherwise, there is the danger of surveys being made of neighboring properties by other men yielding different results. If the survey is promptly ordered, it can be turned over to the title searcher and examined by him in connection with the title. In this way not only will the survey be obtained but it will be available for the examining counsel or title company in connection with its work. Occasionally conditions shown by the survey have an important bearing on the examination of the title itself.

Before the survey is ordered, in connection with a mortgage loan, it should be ascertained what surveyor or surveyors are acceptable to the lender; so, too, when a title company is examining the title, a surveyor should be selected who is acceptable to the company. It is wise also to ascertain if a survey of fairly recent date has already been made; sometimes expense may be saved by using this survey, if physical conditions have not materially changed.

Inspection

After the purchaser has arranged for the title search and for a survey, a third very important step that he should take in preparation for the title closing is the inspection of the property. Most real estate men understand the practical importance of an inspection. They call at the property and verify such matters as the names of tenants, space occupied, rents, length of lease, and deposits of security. These naturally come into the financial picture, and the main purpose of an inspection is to see that, as a practical matter, the income of the property is as represented in the contract. There is, however, an additional important purpose: to make sure that no one occupying or in possession of any part of the premises has or claims any rights of ownership or encumbrance on the premises. The law is clear that possession gives notice just as strongly as a recorded instrument. There have been cases of purchasers moving into houses and not recording their deeds. Their rights are just as well protected under these circumstances as if the deeds had been recorded. The inspection, therefore, should always include the questioning of all the occupants so as to make sure that they are simply tenants or employees of the seller. This inspection should be completed in advance of the date of closing.

Riparian rights

Where land borders a body of water such as a lake, river, ocean, or bay, the water is considered an integral and component part of the land. The owner of such land, provided he has *riparian rights*, is entitled to have access to and use of the shore and waters as well as to have the water contiguous to the land. Riparian rights generally include rights to the use of water for construction of piers, boathouses, fishing, and other purposes. The use of water is limited under common law only to the extent of specifying that such use may not injure or interfere with another person's riparian rights or prior claim to the subject water.

Where the body of water is in effect, or potentially classified as navigable, the use of water must not interfere with public rights, and construction of piers or boathouses extending into the waters requires permits and approval by both the Army Corps of Engineers and the county authorities. Land rights, too, extend only to the water's edge in case of tidewater and to the bank in case of a navigable river. In case of nonnavigable waters, riparian rights typically extend to the middle of the lake, brook, or similar body of water unless limited to a point extending into the submerged area as specified in the legal description in the deed of title.

Since it is legally permissible for a title owner to separate or reserve riparian rights when the land is sold, the new owner, at time of purchase, should make certain as to the legal status and his control, if any, over permissible riparian rights. Such rights further extend over land and buildup on the owner's shore by accretion (where sand or land is washed ashore), and by the same token deprive an owner of land destroyed by erosion or land severed by a change in the course of a stream or by change in the contour of a body of water.

Report of title

As long as possible before the date set for the closing, the report of title should be received. The purchaser is now in a position to know the results of the title search, the survey, and the inspection. He is equipped with all information concerning the property that he has contracted to buy. The report of title certifies the name of the owner, who naturally will be the seller; the legal description of the property; and the status of taxes and all liens and encumbrances affecting the property or the owner. The encumbrances and objections to title, if any, require immediate attention, so that they may be disposed of and the title closed without the necessity of an adjournment, and the report should be given careful scrutiny immediately upon its receipt so that steps may be taken to this end.

Encumbrances subject to which the purchaser takes title

The report of title furnished by the examining counsel or the title company often sets forth several encumbrances, and it is provided in the contract that some of these shall remain upon the property. They should be carefully scrutinized to see that they are not other or more extensive than the contract provides. If the report of title shows a mortgage, care should be taken to see that the amount unpaid on the mortgage, its due date, amortization amounts and periods, interest rate, and interest payment dates are in accordance with the terms of the contract. If the contract provides for a different amount or terms of the mortgage, the purchaser should insist upon the delivery to him of a written statement from the holder of the mortgage, executed and proved so that it may be recorded, stating that the amount or terms of the mortgage have been changed and are now as the contract specifies. If such a statement is not delivered, the purchaser is entitled to an opportunity to make inquiry of the holder of the mortgage.

The purchaser is interested in the property in one of three ways: for investment, for his own use, or for demolition to make room for a new structure. In any case the rights of the tenants are of great importance. If the property is bought as an investment, it is necessary to know what the rent return is. If it is acquired for the purchaser's own use or demolition, the length of the tenants' terms of occupancy will determine how soon possession may be obtained or the building torn down. For these reasons all existing leases should be carefully examined to see that they are exactly as provided for in the contract as to amount of rent, date it is payable, expiration of tenancy, and all other details. The purchaser should detect any provisions in the leases for renewal, rebate of rent, special repair, or other unusual clauses.

All restrictive or other covenants shown upon the report of title should be examined carefully. They might be of such nature as to affect materially the use of the property. If a survey has been obtained by the purchaser, he should check it to see if the building violates any restrictive covenants that are upon the property. The survey will also show any physical conditions of the structures that may affect the title. Any covenants or survey variations not agreed upon in the contract may be waived by the purchaser if he deems them unimportant. If, however, they materially lessen the value of the property, the purchaser is justified in refusing to take title.

Encumbrances to be removed

All encumbrances shown upon the report of title, other than those waived by the purchaser or those listed in the contract, must be removed. This removal is the seller's duty. He must deliver a title free and clear of all encumbrances except such as are, by the contract, specifically excepted. Customarily the purchaser, as soon as he receives his report of title, notifies the seller of all encumbrances that must be removed. The seller should come to the closing prepared to remove all such encumbrances. If there is a mortgage that has to be satisfied, he should have the holder present with a satisfaction piece ready for delivery. The same arrangement may be made with regard to a judgment that is a lien. Often, for convenience, the mortgagee or holder of the judgment gives a statement of the amount due him, and the purchaser or his attorney holds out that amount from the price, going to him after the closing, paying the amount stated, and receiving the satisfaction piece. If a title company representative is closing the title, it is customary for him to hold the money for this purpose and secure the satisfaction piece. Very often the property is subject to the lien of unpaid taxes. It is usual then for the purchaser or his representative to hold out an amount sufficient to pay them. They are later paid by him, and any surplus is returned to the seller.

Instruments to be delivered

The contract provides for the delivery of certain instruments. If property is sold, there is a deed, and often a bond or note and purchase money mortgage. These should be carefully examined to see that they are in accord with the contract. The deed must convey the proper estate, must adequately describe the property, and must be in the form provided in the contract. The bond or note and mortgage must be for the agreed amount and upon the terms set forth in the contract. Those instruments should then be signed, acknowledged, and rechecked to see that the execution is proper. It is usual also to have the seller execute what is known as an *affidavit of title*, by which he swears that he owns the property and states how long he has owned it, that no one has made any claim to it, that his title has never been questioned, that there are no liens upon it except such as are specifically mentioned, and that there are no judgments against him.

When title passes

Legal title to property passes when the instrument of conveyance is delivered, which is not necessarily on the date of execution. The instrument may have been signed long before the day of delivery, but no title is passed until delivery. In the absence of proof to the contrary, however, the law presumes an instrument to have been delivered on the day it was executed. In spite of this legal presumption, a strong practical presumption has developed in recent years that a deed is recorded promptly after delivery and title closing. Hence it is desirable that, if convenient, the deed be dated within a few days prior to the title closing to forestall any demand for proof that the seller was still living on the date of closing title. To make a legal delivery, the grantor must have been legally competent, not only at the time of execution but also at the time of delivery; that is, he must have been of legal age and of sufficient understanding to make a contract. The delivery must be voluntary and intentional. An owner having executed a deed of his property might retain it forever and no title would pass. If the deed were stolen from him, the thief would obtain no rights under it. A deed recorded after the grantor's death is always open to question, upon the suspicion that it may not have been delivered by the grantor.

Delivery in escrow

Occasionally it is convenient to make a conditional delivery of the deed. For example, if the seller is not ready at the closing to submit proof that he has paid a certain lien upon the property, and if it would be inconvenient to call all the parties together again, the deed may be delivered *in escrow* to a third person, who acts as agent for both seller and purchaser and who is authorized to deliver the deed upon receiving proof of payment of the lien. The terms of the agreement under which the delivery is made should be very carefully drawn, should specify exactly the conditions to be met before final delivery, and should be signed by the seller and purchaser.

From the moment, however, that the instrument is legally delivered, the grantor's rights cease and the purchaser becomes from that instant entitled to all rights conveyed by the instrument.

In a *contract for deed* or land installment contract, months or years may elapse between the date that the contract is signed and delivery of the deed. Under such circumstances it is deemed equitable to arrange for a third and neutral party to collect payments and to assure that contract terms are carried out as agreed upon. In some states, "escrow companies" specialize in such services. Commercial banks and financial institutions often arrange for delivery in escrow to protect security of loans or to accommodate their depositors. Attorneys frequently serve as escrow agents when one or both parties live out of town or find it inconvenient to attend the closing personally. Whether title is closed by escrow or conventionally with buyer and seller in attendance, the details of closing, including adjustment of income and charges, are basically not affected. In an escrow arrangement, of course, money, deeds, and other instruments to be exchanged and delivered by the escrow holder are well prepared in advance and held in trust for such purposes by the fiduciary agent.

Types of title closing

The procedure at time of title closing and the adjustment and allocation of closing costs vary with the kind and character of the interests affected and subject to which the transfer or exchange of title is to be effected.

While all types of title closing have much in common, each has sufficient special features that warrant independent and detailed consideration. The principal types of title closing, detailed below, may be classified as follows:

1. Conventional sale, subject to an existing mortgage
2. Property exchanges
3. Mortgage loans
4. Leasehold sale
5. Combination sale and new mortgage financing

Conventional sale, subject to an existing mortgage. Most title transfers involve the purchase and sale of "old" buildings. As a rule the seller has owned the property for some time and in most cases his interest is subject to an existing mortgage. Where this is true, the title closing procedure is simpler than when a new home and mortgage is involved and where, as will be indicated below, many additional closing details need to be considered.

Upon the closing of title, the seller's rights cease, and the purchaser at once becomes entitled to every interest in the property. Since it is not practicable for the seller to settle and pay all his accounts respecting the property, it is much more convenient to adjust between seller and buyer such items as rents, insurance premiums, taxes, and mortgage interests. The contract usually provides for an adjustment of these items and may include others. Customarily the adjustment is made as of the date of closing title, but the contract may set another date.

The adjustments are made in the form of a purchaser's debit and credit account; the debit column contains all the items for which the seller is entitled to credit, and the credit column all items for which the purchaser is entitled to credit. Let us take an example.

Suppose a property is being sold for $30,000. Of this amount $1,500 is to be paid on signing the contract, and $6,000 on closing. The purchaser takes title and assumes an existing mortgage of $12,500 with interest at 7 percent per annum payable semiannually, the last interest having come due and having been paid two months before the closing of title. The balance of the price is to be paid by a note and purchase money mortgage for $10,000. The property is rented to a tenant who pays $300 per month rent in advance and whose rent was due and paid on the first of the month in which title is closed on the fifteenth. There is a fire insurance policy upon the property which was paid for the current year two months prior to the closing of the title. The premium was $72.

In this case the first debit to the purchaser or credit to the seller is the total selling price, $30,000. The next debit entry is for unexpired insurance. The policy was paid for in advance by the seller and has at the time of closing ten months to run. If the seller should cancel the policy, he would receive a refund from the insurance company of less than the unexpired value computed on a pro rata basis. Hence the contract provision for an adjustment of this item. Since the premium is at the rate of $6 per month, the seller is entitled to a credit of $60 for the unexpired term of the policy. Another credit to which the seller is sometimes entitled arises in case of a postponement of the closing at the purchaser's request. In such events the postponement is often conditioned upon the purchaser's paying interest on the purchase price from the original date set for closing. The amount of interest is then placed in the column of seller's credits.

The purchaser's first credit is the amount paid on signing the contract, $1,500. Next he receives credit for the amount of the existing mortgage, $12,500. Two months' interest on the mortgage has accrued up to the date of closing, and since the interest is payable semiannually, there will be a full six months of interest due four months after closing, which the purchaser, being then the owner, will have to pay. So he deducts the seller's share of the interest from the purchase price by crediting himself with $145.83, which is one-third of $437.50, the interest for six months. The note and purchase money mortgage for $10,000 that is given for part of the price entitles the purchaser to a credit for that amount. The final credit he receives has to do with the rent. The tenant has paid the seller $300 rent for the month. Since title is closed, in the middle of the month, the seller should turn over to the purchaser one-half of this amount. This is accomplished by the purchaser, who takes a credit for $150.

The adjustment as finally computed would appear as follows:

	Credit to Purchaser	Debit to Purchaser
Total price		$30,000.00
Paid on contract	$ 1,500.00	
Existing mortgage	12,500.00	
Interest at 7 percent for two months	145.83	
Purchase money mortgage	10,000.00	
Insurance adjustment		60.00
Rent for one-half month	150.00	
Total credit to purchaser	$24,295.83	
Total debit to purchaser		$30,060.00
		24,295.83
Balance due from purchaser		$ 5,764.17

The purchaser, therefore, after the adjustments are made, owes and must pay to complete the transaction the sum of $5,764.17. It is probable that the contract in the case above provides that the purchaser shall pay for drawing the note and purchase money mortgage and for the recording fee, recording or intangible tax (if any), and documentary stamps on the note.[1] The purchaser will be required to pay an additional sum to cover these items. Should any taxes be a lien upon the property, the purchaser, since he wants to be sure they are paid, usually deducts their amount from the balance he owes and pays them himself. In the same way the purchaser

---

[1]In some jurisdictions custom calls for payments of the intangible tax and the recording of the mortgage by the seller. In any case provisions of the contract are binding as to disposition of these expenditures caused by the purchase mortgage indebtedness.

would deduct an amount sufficient to cover any mortgage or judgment that is to be satisfied.

It is customary to compute time upon a basis of a 360-day year and 30-day month, unless a considerable sum is involved, in which case often the exact number of days is used. In counting the number of days in a certain period, the first day is excluded and the last day added. For example, to compute interest for a period of days, the amount due for one month is divided by 30 and multiplied by the number of days. The period from February 1 to March 15 would be one month and fourteen days. Interest, unless otherwise specified, is at the maximum legal rate.

It is usual to incorporate the statement of adjustments into a *statement of closing of title*, which contains, in addition to the memorandum of adjustments, a notation of the date and place of closing, the names of those present, and the details of all instruments delivered. It is valuable for future reference in the event of a dispute. When the title is examined by a title company and closed by its representative, he usually prepares the closing statement.

Closing title on exchanges. Exchanges occur less frequently than sales, and most real estate men approach their closing rather diffidently, probably for two reasons: (1) they are less familiar with them, and (2) they are somewhat more involved. The procedure would be much simpler if an exchange were considered in the light of two sales. For example:

Suppose that A, the owner of No. 1 First Street, and B, the owner of No. 2 Second Street, have agreed to exchange properties. If this transaction is considered as two separate sales—A sells his First Street property to B and B sells his Second Street property to A—it is easier to avoid confusion. Prior to the closing, each of the parties should follow the procedure that has been outlined in the case of a sale, except that, since both A and B are sellers, each should make the seller's preparations as to his property and make the buyer's preparations as to the property he is receiving from the other. The encumbrances on the respective properties should be disposed of exactly as in the manner of a sale, and all other details should be handled in the same way.

At the time of closing of title, both A and B are prepared with a completed search and report of title inspection and survey of the property that each of them is to receive. Each will execute the deed necessary to effect the exchange. The adjustments are most easily made in the form of two individual, separate sales transactions. In this way no confusion will arise as to where the credit should rest for the various mortgages, taxes, rents, and other items affecting each property. It is then a simple matter to bring the two totals together and work out the final amount payable by one to the other.

Closing mortgage loans. A mortgage loan is not initiated by any formal contract in the usual course. Ordinarily the property owner or a broker negotiates the loan with the lender, and the lender, having made an inspection and appraisal of the property, offers to make a loan for a certain amount and states the terms. If the owner and the lender can agree on the terms and amount of the loan, the owner is usually called upon to sign an application for the loan whereby he makes himself responsible for the payment of the expenses that will be incurred in the examination of the title, preparation of instruments, and recording fees. The searcher is then engaged, usually by the lender, although sometimes the arrangement calls for the owner to have the search made and reported to the lender. If the report of title shows satisfactory conditions, the lender sets a date for closing the mortgage loan, which is usually at the lender's office. The note and mortgage and other papers that may be required are executed and the adjustments are made. On a loan the adjustments are fairly simple. There is just one credit to the borrower, and that is the amount of the loan. There is then set up in a column the cost of the title examination, recording and other fees, survey expenses, and a charge for the preparation of instruments. The total of these items is deducted from the amount of the loan, and the balance is the net amount paid to the borrower. In many cases, however, there are some liens or encumbrances on the property that must be removed by the borrower. If, for instance, there are taxes, it is quite usual for the lender to procure tax bills with penalty interest, if any, calculated to the date of closing, deduct the amount necessary to cover them, pay them directly to the tax office, and return the receipted bills, when received, to the borrower. If a small mortgage on the property is to be paid off, the most convenient way to settle it is for the borrower to arrange with the holder of the mortgage to be present at the closing with a satisfaction piece and the mortgage papers. The lender then deducts from the amount due the borrower a sum sufficient to cover the mortgage, the cost of the satisfaction piece, and the cost of recording it, and in that way the mortgage is disposed of.

If there is an existing mortgage for the same or larger amount than the new loan, the lender may take over the mortgage by assignment, thus saving the borrower the mortgage tax that is payable in some states on the recording of a new mortgage. The assigned mortgage may then be extended by formal extension to meet the terms of the loan commitment given by the lender. The mortgagor also signs an owner's estoppel certificate indicating the principal sum of the mortgage so assigned and the date to which interest is paid, as well as the rate of interest applicable thereto. If the new mortgage is made by a corporation, the mortgagor must have executed a stockholders' consent signed by the holders of more than two-thirds of the outstanding capital stock, a certificate by the secretary indicating a resolution of the board of directors authorizing the officers to make the mortgage on behalf of the corporation, and a declaration by the president or vice-president and the secretary or assistant secretary certifying that the holders of more than two-thirds of the capital stock consented to the borrowing of the money by the corporation. This last instrument is recorded in the office of the county clerk or register with the mortgage.

Closing title on leaseholds. Occasionally the transaction is not a sale, or an exchange, or a mortgage loan, but a sale of a leasehold. The situation may be, for example, as follows:

A holds a lease for ten years at a net rental of $12,000 per year on an apartment house. Each month he pays the owner of the property $1,000 and pays all the operating expenses as they come due. A sees an opportunity to sell this lease to advantage. B receives the proposition, investigates the property, and deems the purchase of the unexpired term of the lease a good buy. He undertakes to pay A $2,500 for an assignment of the lease, and a contract is drawn for that purpose. Such a contract is very similar to a sales contract except that naturally the subject matter of the transaction is not the fee ownership of the property but is simply the leasehold interest. B should have the title examined just as if he were buying the fee. He may possibly want a survey, although that is not likely, but he certainly should carefully inspect the property. The seller should be prepared to give an assignment of lease instead of a deed. At the closing of title, not only will the instrument be delivered but the adjustments will be set up very much as though a sale were taking place. That is, the price of $2,500 will appear just as it does in an ordinary sale. If $1,000 of this price was paid at the time the contract was signed, A receives a credit of $2,500 and B a credit of $1,000, the amount paid on the contract. A will then receive credit, if any is due him, for the rent that he has paid the owner, and B will receive a credit for any rents due to him from the actual tenants in the building. Other items such as insurance, taxes, and interest on mortgage will be credited the same as in a sale.

Combination sale and new mortgage financing. In instances where a transaction involves both a sale and a mortgage financing for a substantial part of the total sales price, as is the usual situation where the home buyer is purchasing a newly constructed home, he must be prepared to meet at time of closing many additional costs and settlement payments. These payments, which are exclusive of the sales price obligations specified in the contract, aggregate between 3 and 5 percent of the purchase price of a twenty-thousand- to thirty-thousand-dollar home. These expenditures vary, of course, with location and customary service charges. Few purchasers are aware of the large and additional cash outlays required of them and as a result great financial hardship results especially where the buyers have relied on necessary cash down payments only and now are called upon to meet substantial settlement payments over and above the necessary cash to cover the purchaser's equity in the property.

Title insurance usually constitutes the largest closing cost item. This is a one-time expenditure and the insurance is effective for the life of the loan where the policy is issued in favor of the lender. For an additional fee (as a rule considerably less than the payment for the initial coverage), the insurance policy may be extended to cover the fee owner as explained more fully in Chapter 7. Since the policy issued in favor of the mortgage lender also protects indirectly the borrower or purchaser, the issuance of an additional title policy in favor of the purchaser is the exception rather than the rule. Insurance costs vary with the amount of protection required. Insurance rates, however, are generally uniform for given areas and are readily quoted or published by leading title companies.

The next largest item of closing costs is the *mortgage service charge*. This payment, in essence, is a mortgage brokerage fee to cover the expenses incurred in placing the purchase money mortgage with a lending firm. Under Veterans Administration regulation, the 1 percent blanket mortgage service fee must also cover any or all of the following:

1. Lender's appraisals
2. Lender's inspections, except in construction loan cases
3. Loan closing or settlement
4. Preparing loan papers or conveyancing
5. Attorney's services, other than for title work
6. Photographs
7. Postage and other mailing charges, stationery, and other overhead costs
8. Amortization schedules, pass books, and membership or entrance fees
9. Escrow fees or charges
10. Notary fees
11. Commitment fees of Federal National Mortgage Association, and preparation and recording of assignment of mortgage to that association
12. Trustees' fees or charges
13. Loan application or processing fees
14. Any other fees, charges, commissions, or expenses except:
    a. Fee of Veterans Administration appraiser and of compliance inspectors designated by Veterans Administration
    b. Recording fees and taxes paid to public officials
    c. Credit report
    d. That portion of the taxes, assessments, and other similar items for the current year chargeable to the borrower; and his initial deposit (lump-sum payment) for tax and insurance account
    e. Hazard insurance
    f. Survey
    g. Title examination
    h. Title insurance

Under the FHA-insured loan provisions, the 1 percent service charge covers all reasonable closing cost items incurred by the lender with the exception of the lender's appraisal fee and the attorney's or closing fee. A 2 percent service charge is generally applied by lenders making conventional loans. Where the seller agrees to accept the purchase money mortgage, this charge may be limited to attorney's fees for drawing the instruments and for loan closing or settlement charges.

At the time of closing, lenders require that the purchaser (mortgagor) arrange for *hazard insurance* on the property in an amount sufficient, at least, to protect the loan. This insurance is to protect the insured against loss by fire, windstorm, and other specified hazards. The cost of this insurance varies with the type of construction and the location factors, and with the special terms of the insurance contract. It is customary at the time of closing to pay the premium for one year. This is a continuing expense of property ownership which has to be met for an advance period through a prepayment at the time of loan closing. If an escrow account is set up to take care of the succeeding yearly insurance payments, then at the time of settlement the purchaser pays into an escrow account an amount sufficient to cover one-twelfth of the premium for the following year. Each month thereafter the purchaser pays an equal amount into the escrow account so that the accumulated sum will meet such premiums as they fall due. Under the escrow-account arrangement, the payments to the insurance company are made directly out of this fund.

The *property survey*, as previously mentioned, should be undertaken by a licensed land surveyor. Such a survey shows lot lines, dimensions, and the location of improvements with reference to lot lines. The costs for such surveys range from $50 to $100 for residential lots and are customarily borne by the purchaser.

The *closing fee* in the settlement of a Veterans Administration-financed property cannot be charged as a separate item when the 1 percent mortgage service charge is made. As previously noted, the blanket mortgage service charge of 1 percent is inclusive of this service. Generally, however, in connection with FHA or conventional loans, where the services of an attorney are called for to assist in the closing of the purchase loan and related transactions, a fee ranging from $50 to $100 or more, depending on the nature of services rendered, is charged the purchaser.

Where the purchase mortgage funds are supplied by third parties or where the mortgage loan is guaranteed or insured by federal agencies, an *appraisal report* is mandatory, as a rule, and the cost for same is charged to the purchaser. This report is normally prepared by appraisers who are either independent agents or who are officers or employees of the lending or insuring agents. The appraisal fee generally varies with the distance to be traveled and the type of appraisal required. For a residential property, the appraisal fee averages from $35 to $50.

Another charge generally accounted for at time of title closing is *prepaid interest*. When a new mortgage is negotiated to cover part of the purchase price, prepaid interest is customarily charged from date of settlement to the beginning of the following month. This makes it unnecessary to bill interest for periods of less than one month's time. Where outstanding mortgages are involved, an adjustment is made between the seller and the buyer, each bearing the respective obligation—the seller to date of closing and the buyer from that day hence. Where interest on an existing mortgage has accrued, an appropriate credit will be given the buyer for interest charges due to date of settlement. Interest payments during the life of the mortgage are a continuing expense of home ownership. When the mortgage loan is insured by the Federal Housing Administration, an additional one-half of 1 percent is added to the interest costs to cover FHA insurance. This payment, as is the case with other types of insurance, is payable monthly in advance. An escrow account is created by the lending institution to which the purchaser contributes on a monthly basis in the same manner as was described for hazard insurance payments.

Since real property taxes, if unpaid, constitute a lien prior to the mortgage lien, provision usually is made at time of closing to provide for their prepayment in an amount sufficient to allow the lender or mortgage service agent to meet the tax payments as they fall due. Taxes are another continuing expense of home ownership. As a rule, the estimated real property tax for the year is prorated on a monthly basis and added to the payments due each month for the mortgage interest, principal, and hazard insurance. In addition to this procedure of setting up an escrow account out of which taxes may be paid, payments are made to cover tax adjustments pursuant to contract agreements reached between buyer and seller.

There are a number of "other costs" or miscellaneous charges which the buyer must be prepared to meet at the time of title closing. These may include any or all of the following:

1. Tax on mortgage and on bond or note. A mortgage is classified as personal property and most states levy a documentary stamp tax on the promissory note, an intangible tax on the amount of the mortgage debt, and a fee for recording the mortgage document. These fees and charges must be paid to the collector before the real estate mortgage may be recorded. Some states place the entire tax on the bond or note incorporated in the mortgage. The total mortgage and bond or note taxes average about $3 to $5 per $1,000 of mortgage debt in most states.
2. Most lending agencies require a credit report showing outstanding debts of the borrower, if any, and his credit relationship with various people and organizations with whom he has had financial dealings. The charge for this report is small and varies from the average credit report from $10 to $25 depending on location and custom.
3. Recording fees for deeds, mortgages, assignments, and mortgage satisfactions are customarily paid by the purchaser as part of title closing costs. These recording fees vary with length of the instrument and recording fee customs. A charge of $2.50 to $3.50 per record page may be expected as typical in most jurisdictions.
4. Stamps on deeds required by state law are generally paid for by the seller and thus do not as a rule appear in the buyer's closing statement. However, where the purchaser under terms of the contract agreed to meet these charges the costs involved are as follows: A surtax (formerly federal stamp tax)[2] is charged in most states at the rate of fifty-five cents per five hundred dollars or fraction thereof exclusive of the value of existing (old) mortgage obligations which are transferred to the purchaser as part of the purchase agreement. State documentary stamps, where applicable, average twenty to thirty cents per hundred dollars of consideration stated, or fraction thereof.

In addition to the various costs and settlement charges enumerated above, adjustments are made for accrued or prepaid rentals where tenants

---

[2]President Johnson, in 1965, signed into law the excise tax reduction bill repealing the federal documentary stamp tax on real estate transfers, effective January 1968.

occupy the premises. The buyer, too, in addition to miscellaneous settlement costs must be prepared to meet the cash balance due under terms of the purchase contract agreement.

Adjustments and closing statements

It is generally deemed good practice to prepare at time of closing a buyer's and a seller's statement showing the credits and debits incurred by each and the balances due.

Suppose, to take an example, a property legally described as Lot 15, Block 8, Mimosa View, as recorded in Plat Book "C," page 122, of the public records of Alachua County, Florida, is sold by A. B. Conrad to S. W. Swan, purchaser, for $30,000 subject to terms as follows: $2,000 upon signing of contract, this deposit to be held in escrow pending title closing. The buyer agreed to assume an existing mortgage of $10,000, payable in installments of $120 per month covering 7 percent interest and amortization on debt balances, to give Conrad a $15,000 purchase money mortgage lien payable monthly at 7.5 percent per annum over a period of twenty-five years and $3,000 cash upon closing. The property is unoccupied, so there will be no rent adjustment. There is a homeowner's hazard insurance policy which was prepaid for one year in the amount of $96 four months prior to title closing. The intangible tax on the new mortgage is $30, and documentary stamps on the note, $22.50. Title insurance to be paid by purchaser is $280. Cost of mortgage and note preparation is $25. Credit report is $10. Recording fees for deed and mortgage are $7. State documentary stamps and surtax charges are $90 and $22 respectively. County taxes for the calendar year are $450 and city taxes for the same period $350. Attorney's closing fees of $80 are shared by buyer and seller. Closing date is October 15. On the basis of these facts, typical buyer's, seller's, and broker's résumé closing statements would appear as follows:

BUYER'S CLOSING STATEMENT

Date: October 15, 19—
Seller: A. B. Conrad
Purchaser: S. W. Swan

Property: Lot 15, Block 8, Mimosa View, as recorded in Plat Book "C," page 122, of public records of Alachua County, Florida.

	Charges	Credits
Total purchase price	$30,000.00	
Paid on contract		$ 2,000.00
First mortgage (assumed)		10,000.00
Purchase mortgage		15,000.00
Proration and adjustments:		
Insurance—unexpired	64.00	
County taxes to Oct. 15		356.25
City taxes to Oct. 15		277.07
Interest on 1st mortgage		29.17
Prepaid interest 2nd mortgage (½ month)	46.88	
Total	$30,110.88	$27,662.49
Amount to close		2,448.39

BUYER'S CLOSING STATEMENT

(Continued)

Add expenses paid by broker:

Preparing second mortgage and note	25.00
Recording fees for mortgage and deed	7.00
Intangible tax on mortgage	30.00
Documentary stamps on note	22.50
Title insurance	280.00
Attorney's fees	40.00
Credit report	10.00
Total expenses	414.50
Balance due from buyer	$ 2,862.89

We hereby agree to the correctness of the foregoing statement
and acknowledge receipt of a copy of same.

_____

_____

SELLER'S CLOSING STATEMENT

Seller: A. B. Conrad
   Property: Lot 15, Block 8, Mimosa View, as recorded in Plat Book "C," page 122, of public records of Alachua County, Florida.

Date: October 15, 19—
Purchaser: S. W. Swan

	Charges	Credits
Total purchase price		$30,000.00
First mortgage (assumed)	$10,000.00	
Purchase mortgage	15,000.00	
Proration and adjustments		
Insurance—unexpired		64.00
County taxes to Oct. 15	356.25	
City taxes to Oct. 15	277.07	
½ month interest on $10,000	29.17	
Prepaid interest on $15,000		46.88
Total	$25,662.49	$30,110.88
Balance due seller	4,448.39	
Less expenses:		
State documentary stamps	90.00	
State surtax	22.00	
Attorney's fee	40.00	
Brokerage commission	1,800.00	
Total expenses	$ 1,952.00	
Balance due seller	$ 2,496.39	

We hereby agree to the correctness of the foregoing statement
and acknowledge receipt of a copy of same and the balance of
payment as shown.

_____

_____

BROKER'S RESUME STATEMENT

	Credits	Charges
Deposit from buyer	$ 2,000.00	
Check from buyer	2,862.89	
To buyer's expenses		$ 414.50
To seller's expenses		152.00
Brokerage fee		1,800.00
Check to seller		2,496.39
Total	$ 4,862.89	$ 4,862.89

In the above statements, the charges to the buyer constitute credits to the seller and conversely on the latter's statements, credits to the buyer are recorded as charges to the seller. The first debit to the buyer (credit to seller) is the total selling price of $30,000. Next is shown a credit to the buyer for down payment of $2,000. In most states, this amount is retained in escrow by the real estate broker and thus is not recorded as a debit to the seller but is due seller at time of closing. The existing and new purchase money mortgages of $10,000 and $15,000 respectively are shown as credits to the buyer and debits to the seller. The prorated charges are allocated as follows:

1. A credit to the seller and debit to the buyer for unexpired insurance for eight months at $8 or $64.
2. County and city taxes, a seller's charge for nine and one-half months and a credit to the buyer. The prorated amounts are $356.25 and $277.07.
3. A half-month interest accrued on the first mortgage, or $29.17, due the buyer and hence a credit to him and a charge to the seller. To make mortgage payments fall due on the first of each month, the buyer is charged with interest for a half month on the new mortgage in the amount of $46.88 (one twenty-fourth of $1,125.)

Deductions are made from the balance due the seller, as shown on the statement, for expenses incurred by the broker covering the preparation of the deed, attorney fees, and the brokerage commission of 6 percent on the selling price. Likewise, to the amount due from the buyer at closing are added broker's expenditures, covering preparations of mortgage instruments, outlays for documentary stamps, intangible taxes, title insurance, and so forth, as shown on the buyer's closing statement. The broker's résumé statement itemizes all moneys received and paid out in connection with the property transaction, verifying that the broker's only compensation for time and efforts expended since first showing the property is the real estate commission which in this case amounted to $1,800.

Rejection of title

Ordinarily titles are good and marketable, and contracts are not usually entered into either for sale or for exchange, or for the sale of a lease if the title appears at all doubtful. Nor does an applicant for a mortgage loan usually subject himself to the expense of a search if he has any suspicion that his title may be unmarketable. Unfortunately, however, an examination of title occasionally shows a title to be bad. In case of a sale or exchange, the party affected is entitled to reject a title after due opportunity has been given to dispose of the objection or defect, and in any event is entitled to the return of any deposit paid on the signing of the contract, together with interest at the legal rate from the time of payment of the deposit. He is also entitled to be compensated for such reasonable expenses as he may have incurred in the examination of the title. No recovery may be had beyond the expenses, in the event of defective title, on a mortgage loan, but in the event of a sale of the fee or leasehold, or in the event of an exchange, damages for the lost profit on the transaction may be collected if the seller was guilty of a fraud or if he should have known that his title was defective.

READING AND STUDY REFERENCES

1. FRIEDMAN, EDITH J., *Real Estate Encyclopedia*, pp. 458–61. Englewood Cliffs, N.J.: Prentice-Hall, Inc., 1960.
2. HEBARD, EDNA L., and GERALD S. MEISEL, *Principles of Real Estate Law*, Chapter 15. New York: Simmons-Boardman Publishing Corporation, 1964.
3. HUSBAND, WILLIAM H., and FRANK RAY ANDERSON, *Real Estate*, Chapter 5. Homewood, Ill.: Richard D. Irwin, Inc., 1960.
4. LUSK, HAROLD F., *Law of the Real Estate Business*, Chapter 13. Homewood Ill.: Richard D. Irwin, Inc. 1965.
5. RING, ALFRED A., *Questions and Problems in Real Estate Principles and Practices* (rev. ed.), Chapter 12. Englewood Cliffs, N.J.: Prentice-Hall, Inc., 1972.
6. UNGER, MAURICE A., *Real Estate* (4th ed.), Chapter 22. Cincinnati: South-Western Publishing Co., 1969.

13

REAL ESTATE FINANCING

Importance of real estate credit financing

Real estate as an income-producing asset is characterized by a *slow* capital turnover. By this is meant that even under favorable circumstances many years are required before the aggregate annual gross income derived from a property equals or returns the total capital investment. On the average for most residential, apartment house, and commercial real property, five to ten years are required for the capital to "turn over" once. This may be compared with personal or corporate assets represented by merchandise inventory, both hardware and software, which "turns over" weekly, monthly, or at least several times during a given year. A street peddler may conceivably replenish his wares several times a day and thus generate an income that far exceeds the total capital required to carry on his business operations. The risk involved in projecting estimates of productivity far into the future calls for expert analysis of real estate as an investment medium and as a basis for credit financing.

The large capital outlay necessary to finance the acquisition of realty appears even more significant when comparison is made between the total capital outlay and the anticipated *net* rather than *gross* operating income of real property. As will be more fully discussed in Chapter 21, "Property

Management," the greater share of real estate gross income is required to meet expenditures for property taxes, maintenance, hazard insurance, and other related operating charges, leaving, as a rule, 40 percent or less of gross income to cover costs of ownership. In other words, only the minor part of total income is available to meet required provisions for recapture "of" the capital over the useful life-span of the property, and also a fair interest return (commensurate with risk involved) "on" the capital ventured by the owner. When based on *net* income, twenty or more years may be required before capital return equals the capital investment. Based on net income that can safely be set aside for amortization of capital, the economic life of real estate improvements must extend for thirty to fifty years or even longer in order that the buyer may recoup his invested capital.

The large amount of capital necessary in relation to the small annual net return which becomes available for capital retirement or replacement keeps ownership of real estate out of reach of the average buyer unless credit aid from others or from private or public lending agencies can be secured. Indeed only a fraction of the huge output of the building industry could be marketed each year if 100 percent cash purchases were made the rule rather than the exception. Because of the investment characteristics of real estate and the inability of the average buyer, even after many years of saving, to amass the necessary full purchase price of a home or business property, real estate credit financing is not only a widespread practice but a necessary and all-important function of the real estate business.

Extent of mortgage financing

Durability and fixity of location make real estate an ideal medium for credit extension and hence mortgage lending and financing. Although the practice of mortgage lending dates back to biblical days (see Nehemiah 5:1–7), extensive use of credit as a major source of real estate financing did not become popular until the beginning of the twentieth century. In fact, mortgage debt financing in the years prior to World War I was considered a necessary evil and those who made use of this mode of credit— for whatever reason—were anxious to discharge the debt as soon as possible.

During the last three decades, a significant change has taken place in the use of credit as a mode of finance and in the acceptance of the real estate mortgage as an appropriate means to further a desirable end—widespread home ownership. The shift of emphasis from saving to credit financing in the acquisition of homes and real property has, in effect, wrought a financial revolution. *Income* rather than *capital* now serves as the important criterion and guide in the determination of one's ability to own and pay.

The ever-increasing use and importance of mortgage debt financing can best be visualized by reference to mortgage debt statistics reported by the board of governors of the Federal Reserve System. In the twenty-year span from 1950 to 1970 outstanding mortgage debt on one- to four-family houses increased from $45.2 to $282.5 billion. During the last three years of the above period alone, mortgage indebtedness increased at an annual rate of $12.2 billion. Based on the last census data, 66.8 percent of all single-family homes are mortgaged and 89 percent of homes acquired since 1970 involve use of some mortgage credit.

Trading on the equity

Apart from the necessity to borrow funds, probably the greatest justification for incurring indebtedness is to be found in the principle of trading on the equity. In conformity with this principle, it is economically advisable to borrow funds when the use of such funds brings a higher rate of return than the rate, or cost, of borrowing. To illustrate: Assume that property costing $100,000 brings in a gross rental of $17,000 per annum and that it is free and clear of encumbrances. If the taxes, repairs, and other expenses and provision for depreciation amount to $9,000 annually, the net income is $8,000, or 8 percent on the owner's investment. Now suppose the owner mortgages the property for $70,000 at 7 percent per annum. The interest amounting to $4,900 would reduce the net income to $3,100 per annum, but since the owner's equity investment is now only $30,000, his rate of return is $10\frac{1}{3}$ percent per annum. It can be taken as a rule, therefore, that when mortgage money can be borrowed at a rate less than the rate of net return on the property unmortgaged, borrowing raises the rate of return on the owner's equity investment.

Trading on the equity, as illustrated above, is sound provided the amount borrowed is in reasonable relationship to the amount invested and the ability of the debtor to meet the fixed and generally long-term obligations. In fact, trading on the equity does not increase the earnings of the borrower but rather compensates him for the additional risks assumed in securing the safety of borrowed funds and in underwriting the priority of interest and amortization payments to which the lender, under the financing agreement, has a legal claim.

Economic basis for mortgage financing

Borrowing against future income or for purposes of putting land into productive use is often an economic necessity. Care, however, must be taken to assure that the project to be financed is well conceived and that reliance to meet the loan obligations is placed not only on the income-producing power of the property but also on the financial integrity and ability of the borrower. The *personal* factors in mortgage lending have rightfully merited greater emphasis in recent years. Success of mortgage lending in the final analysis depends on the intent of the borrower and his sincerity of purpose to carry out the mortgage terms. It is true that many lenders consider the property as final security in terms of foreclosure, but such remedy is often a costly "cure" and an admission that the symptoms of mortgage failure were present to begin with and that the capacity or intent of the borrower was not analyzed with care.

When property is unimproved, or inadequately improved, borrowing to erect a suitable improvement is invariably an advantage. An annual loss or a very small annual return may be turned into an annual income commensurate with the value of the property. The land may be valuable, but it will yield its economic rent only when improved with a building, and it is often a financial advantage to obtain a mortgage loan to pay all or part of the cost of such building. Suppose that a parcel of unimproved land is worth $100,000. The taxes amount to $2,000, and the loss of interest on the money invested in the land is 7 percent, or $7,000, a total annual loss of $9,000 to the owner. To save this loss the owner puts up a building costing $200,000, and he borrows all of this amount on a mortgage at 7 percent. The land and building together produce a rent income of $45,000, and the taxes, repairs, depreciation, and other charges are $22,000, leaving a net rental of $23,000. Out of the net rental, $14,000 is paid as interest on the money borrowed, leaving $9,000 for the owner, being 9 percent on his investment which is still $100,000. He has, therefore, stopped his loss and now has an income of $9,000. It is probable that in cases of this kind the amount of depreciation of the building would be represented by a corresponding annual payment to reduce the amount of the mortgage. No careful mortgagee would allow the building to depreciate and permit the mortgage to remain for its full amount. It is possible that the annual payments on the mortgage would be much more than the depreciation, and if so it would mean that the owner was constantly increasing his equity by a further investment.

The advantages of borrowing to buy a home are generally not measurable in monetary terms. The home is one of the most essential parts of family life, and the returns that flow from home ownership are rightfully classified as "psychic income" or amenities. It is there that the family head strives to provide shelter for his dependents on a basis as free and independent as possible. For this reason, the utopia of home ownership would include freedom from mortgage or other household debts. Still, the advantages of home ownership to the American way of life are deemed of such great importance that home purchase plans, largely mortgage financed, and often government approved, guaranteed, or insured, are accepted as a national policy.

Kinds of mortgages

Broadly speaking, the instruments used for real property debt financing may be classified into two principal kinds: *term* and *amortization* mortgages. Both kinds serve the purpose of securing a debt which the borrower under separate bond or note promises to discharge together with interest by the end of a stipulated period of time, usually measured in number of years. It is the method of principal debt repayment that differentiates these two kinds of mortgages. Under the term mortgage, the debt is payable in full at the end of the specified term, whereas under the amortization mortgage, the principal is repaid in installments, usually monthly, over extended periods of years. A more detailed discussion of each kind of mortgage follows:

Term mortgages. Whenever a mortgage debt agreement calls for the repayment of the principal sum, in full, at the end of a designated period of time, the unamortized debt remains outstanding for a *term* of months or years. To differentiate the debt status of term mortgages, they are further subclassified into (1) straight, (2) closed, and (3) open-term mortgages.

Most mortgages prior to 1933 were nonamortizing or *straight*; such mortgages were generally placed for a term of three to five years with interest payable quarterly or semiannually. These straight term mortgages were generally renewed for subsequent three or five year terms or refinanced if payment was demanded. Inability to budget the repayment of the total mortgage debt during the comparative short term caused financial grief to many homeowners when mortgage refinancing was sought in a period of depression or during times when mortgage funds were difficult to obtain. During the financial crisis from 1933 to 1935, the government through the Home Owners Loan Corporation, a temporary relief agency, refinanced over a million term mortgages on an amortizing basis under which principal and interest payments were due monthly over periods up to fifteen years. Since that time the success and general acceptance of the amortizing payment practice has caused the issuance of term mortgages to be the exception rather than the rule in mortgage lending.

Term mortgages that upon maturity, or due date, were not extended were said to be past due or *open* mortgages. Such open mortgages were payable on demand at the request of the mortgagee and conversely the mortgagor could pay off an open mortgage any time such payments met his convenience. In practice, open mortgages proved financially hazardous because the mortgagee could and generally did call for payments—under threat of foreclosure—when mortgage funds were scarce and mortgage interests high. The mortgagor on the other hand, had the opportunity to refinance the debt when mortgage funds were plentiful and interest rates low. Under such circumstances the lender, of course, was at a disadvantage. Because of such hazards it is most unlikely today that an informed lender or borrower would take the chance of allowing a term mortgage to remain open.

Technically the classification *closed* mortgage applies to any unexpired mortgage that is not in default. In the mortgage market, the designation *closed* mortgage is applied to term mortgages under which the mortgagee has advanced the maximum loan agreed upon. Thus where a $10,000 mortgage loan is to be paid in fixed installments of $2,000 each during various stages of house construction, the mortgage is said to be *closed* when the last payment is made and the mortgage has reached the $10,000 debt limit agreed upon.

Amortizing mortgages. Nearly all mortgage loans currently made include some provisions for periodic amortization of the mortgage principal. This kind of mortgage and method of mortgage debt reductions, although introduced during the early history of savings and loan institutions as a service to members, was not popularized until after the depression of 1929, when government participation in the mortgage lending field developed a trend toward this kind of mortgage. The amortization mortgage offers advantages to both lender and borrower. The desirable features of this mode of debt financing include the following:

1. Periodic reduction of the mortgage debt over long periods of time ranging from ten to thirty years depending on loan company policy and government insured or loan guarantee provisions
2. Interest rates averaging 7 to 8 percent, which are applicable only to remaining balances of mortgage debt
3. Monthly payments of interest and principal (like rent) which under the budget plan may include escrow amounts covering taxes, hazard insurance, water charges, and assessments, if any

To the lender, the amortizing mortgage assures a constant or even improving loan-to-value ratio, since in most instances the mortgage principal payments equal or exceed normal and anticipated property value losses due to wear, tear, and obsolescence. For the borrower, the amortizing mortgage removes the fear of inability to meet repayment or replacement of a large maturing debt sometime in the future. This mortgage plan enables the owner to liquidate his debt gradually, to build up his equity, and to travel steadily and surely toward his goal of 100 percent, mortgage-free ownership. Amortizing mortgages are issued under two types of payment plans: (1) the level, or constant, mortgage payment plan and (2) the straight principal reduction plan.

The level, or constant, mortgage plan may be illustrated as follows: Assume that Mr. Jones is married, is thirty years of age, and is employed at a salary of $15,000 a year. He locates a desirable one-family home for which he must pay $30,000. He has saved enough to invest $10,000 toward the purchase price. He has to borrow $20,000. He finds he can obtain such a mortgage with interest at 7.5 percent and amortization by which he will repay the entire $20,000 loan in twenty-five years. The monthly payments under the constant mortgage plan are $147.80 or $1,-773.60 a year. After five years he will have reduced the mortgage to $18,345.40, at the end of ten years to $15,941.60, at the end of fifteen years to $12,448.00, and at the end of twenty years to $6,107.80. At the end of twenty-five years, when Mr. Jones is fifty-five years of age, he will own his home free and clear and have reduced his shelter rent payments by $147.80 a month. The total mortgage payments over three hundred monthly periods aggregated $44,340. This means Mr. Jones will pay $24,-340 in interest, the remainder being principal. Under term mortgage financing, Mr. Jones would probably have paid no amortization and at the end of twenty-five years would still owe $20,000 and would have paid $37,500 in interest, or a total of $57,500 if the mortgage were then satisfied. Under the constant mortgage plan, the monthly payments do not change in total. The periodic amount is allocated to interest and principal on a varying basis (see Appendix, page 575). As the mortgage debt is reduced, the interest portion of the constant payment decreases, and the amount applicable to amortization increases accordingly. This type of mortgage plan is popular with most borrowers, including owners of income property, and is quite commonly used. FHA and GI mortgages are of this type.

Another type of mortgage amortization is known as the straight principal reduction plan. Under this plan, the borrower pays a fixed periodic installment of amortization and pays interest on the reducing balance so that his total periodic payment of interest and amortization varies downward over the term. If Mr. Jones had chosen this plan, his first monthly payment would be $191.67[1] as compared with $147.80 under the constant plan as noted above. The straight principal reduction plan has the advantage of enabling the borrower to calculate readily how much he has paid on the principal, but it also has the disadvantage that during the early period of the mortgage plan, the amortization amount is large and makes the borrower's combined interest and principal payments greater, and this at the time when he is generally least able to carry the additional financial burden. For this reason, the constant payment method has become generally preferred.

Types of mortgages

To the investor, builder, or homeowner, many kinds of mortgages are available. The purpose of each mortgage, to be sure, is to secure payment of an obligation, but each mortgage differs in some particular respect to meet the needs of the borrower, the terms of the lender, or the conditions imposed by mortgage market operations. The name of each type of mortgage is usually derived from the special conditions or distinguishing features that it possesses. Each type of mortgage, too, may be issued as a term or amortization loan depending on duration of the debt, lending policy, or governmental regulations. The best known and most commonly used mortgages are listed and briefly explained below:

1. Construction or building loan mortgage
2. Package mortgage
3. Open-end mortgage
4. Blanket mortgage
5. Purchase money mortgage
6. FHA insured mortgage
7. GI guaranteed mortgage
8. Conventional mortgage
9. Trust deed mortgage
10. Participation mortgage

Construction or building loan mortgage. Since mortgage loans, as a rule, are made only on improved properties, builders and potential homeowners

---

[1]This amount is derived as follows:
Principal repayment—$20,000 ÷ 300 months   = $ 66.67
Interest payment, first month—$20,000 × .00625 =   125.00
     Total payment for first month   = $191.67

in need of interim construction funds arrange with lenders for "stopgap" financing for a period of three to six months or until the completion of the proposed structure in accordance with building plans and detailed specifications. The building or construction loan mortgage is distinct in that the amount of the loan is not fully paid to the borrower at the time of mortgage closing. The purpose of this type of mortgage, as the name implies, is to aid an owner or his builder in financing the erection of a building. To provide for the distribution of mortgage funds at intervals of construction, an agreement known as a building loan contract is incorporated in the mortgage or recorded as a separate instrument in addition to the mortgage. This agreement between the lender and the borrower provides in substance that the borrower shall erect a certain building—as described by plans and specifications—on the land legally identified and that the lender shall loan, upon the security of such land and building, a specified amount to be repaid upon completion of the building. The agreement further provides that the amount of the loan shall be advanced to the borrower in installments as the building progresses, stating either that the amount and times of advances are to be at the lender's discretion or in certain amounts at fixed periods in the course of construction.

The payment of interest specified in the building loan agreement, depending on custom and amount of construction loan, is payable either on the entire amount of the loan from date of agreement or on only the amounts of the installments from the date of the advance. The former method of interest payment is supported by the theory that the lender is setting aside the amount agreed upon as of the time the mortgage is signed, even though the money is actually paid out as the work progresses. Loan advances as a rule are made at predetermined building stages, after inspection by the lender's representative and certification of satisfactory progress of construction. It is often provided that the loan shall continue until a definite period after completion. This enables the builder to sell his property more readily and provides needed time for the buyer to convert the construction loan into a permanent loan or to refinance the mortgage when necessary.

Package mortgage. To convert a house into a home designed for modern ways of living, many types of fixtures and equipment are deemed essential. Heating, cooling, and ventilating systems have for many years been classified as realty, and their reasonable value in most states is permitted to be included in the estimate of total value upon which the mortgage loan is based. The eligibility of other types of equipment to be classed as real estate under the law of fixtures is still questionable in many jurisdictions.

Under the principle of the package mortgage, all types of equipment may be classified as realty and included in the mortgage loan, provided: (1) it is the expressed intent of the parties that the article be realty; (2) the equipment is paid for with the mortgage money; (3) it is appropriate for use in the home; and (4) there is some degree of actual annexation. Based on this interpretation, the Federal Housing Administration district office in Chicago permits inclusion of the following types of household equipment for mortgage insurance purposes: refrigerators, ranges, automatic laundry equipment, automatic ironers, automatic dryers, automatic dishwashers, and garbage disposal units. All Federal Housing Administration and Veterans Loan offices now accept one or more of the equipment mortgages, provided such financing is at the request and mutual consent of borrower and lender.

Although many lenders still object to acceptance of package mortgages on the ground that the equipment will wear out before the loan is substantially reduced, most of the larger lending institutions have voiced favorable experience with this type of mortgage lending. It is said that the package mortgage reduces the number of delinquent loans by strengthening the credit position of the homeowner, whose total monthly payments on his debts are reduced during the early years as compared with payments under the old practice where equipment costs were concentrated in a short period of two or three years at high commercial rates. By spreading out these equipment payments over the entire life of the low-interest mortgage, the homeowner is in a better position to meet any emergency that may arise during the early and crucial stages of home ownership.

Open-end mortgages. The need to secure funds for additions or major repairs to a home in the years subsequent to the original purchase financing has long posed a problem to the owner. To add a fireplace, extra room, garage, or to replace a roof or other major structure, it is generally necessary to borrow funds either over a short term and at high cost or by costly refinancing of the existing mortgage debt. Under the open-end mortgage, it is possible for an owner to secure additional advances from the lender up to, but not exceeding, the original amount of the existing amortizing mortgage. These advances can now be secured at little extra cost. It is now possible to secure title insurance on the additional advance anywhere in the United States for $7.50 per $1,000.00 (minimum charge $10.00) on the strength of a simple home-owner's affidavit in which he testifies that he has not encumbered the property or caused a lien to be placed on it since the issuance of the original mortgage agreement. The nominal cost is an all-inclusive charge with no extras for title search, abstract of title, closing charges, or attorney's fees. The title service is further offered on all titles, whether previously insured by the company sponsoring this plan or not. Undoubtedly title companies generally will extend similar services thus broadening the trend toward modern and more flexible mortgage financing.

The open-end mortgage, too, strengthens the investment portfolio of the lending companies. Prime loans can thus be restored in principal amounts to profitable investment margins, and loans made for property improvement purposes as a rule advantageously increase the value of the credit security upon which the loan is based. Borrowers, too, benefit from lower overall interest rates and longer loan periods on funds thus obtained.

These benefits are especially apparent when comparison is made with interest and service charges required for improvement loans made over one- to five-year periods, even when issued under the insured "discount" loan plan available under Title I of the Federal Housing Administration Act. The saving, of course, is due to the fact that interest payments are computed on "reducing" debt balance, under the open-end mortgage plan. whereas the "discount" loans require interest payments on the entire loan and no interest credit is given for principal payments made periodically during the life of the short-term debt.

Blanket mortgage. When a mortgage covers several houses or a number of lots it is referred to as a *blanket mortgage.* An operator may have bought a tract of land, subdivided it into lots, and placed a mortgage on the whole. If his plan is to sell the lots to individual purchasers, it becomes necessary to free each lot from the blanket mortgage. The most convenient manner in which this end may be accomplished is by means of a *release schedule* clause inserted in the mortgage. By this schedule, a release price is placed on each lot. When this amount is paid to the holder of the mortgage, he executes an instrument that releases the lot from the mortgage. Of course, even if such a clause were not in the mortgage, the operator could arrange for a release, but it would be a matter for negotiation as to the amount to be paid each time a lot was sold. The schedule in the mortgage saves all this inconvenience and makes it possible for the operator to know in advance just what he must pay to release each lot. It is customary to set the release price on each lot slightly higher than the fair proportion of the loan for that lot, for the reason that the better lots are usually sold first, and also that after each lot is released, the balance better secures the remaining mortgage loan.

Purchase money mortgage. In many sales of realty the purchaser does not wish to pay the full price in cash. Under such circumstances it is stipulated in the contract between the parties that the purchaser shall give to the seller his bond (or note) and a mortgage on the property to secure part of the price. This is known as a *purchase money mortgage.* Such a mortgage becomes a lien contemporaneous with the passing of title. It is prior to any lien against the purchaser. In cases where dower still exists and where the purchaser is married, it is a lien ahead of his wife's rights; consequently, the wife in most states need not join in a purchase money mortgage. In order that there will be no doubt of its status, it is customary to insert in the mortgage, following a description, what is known as a *purchase money clause*, reading substantially as follows:

This mortgage being a purchase money mortgage is given and intended to be recorded simultaneously with a deed, this day executed and delivered by the mortgagee to the mortgagor, this mortgage being given to secure a portion of the purchase price in said deed expressed.

Any mortgage given as part of the purchase price, whether the loan is made by the seller, another individual, or lending institution, is classified as a purchase money mortgage and is thus prior to any purchaser's liens that are in existence at the time of sale.

FHA insured mortgage. The Federal Housing Administration was created in 1934 by act of Congress to encourage the construction and ownership of homes, especially those in the lower price ranges. Under this act, borrowers may obtain loans up to 97 percent of the value of newly constructed low-value homes that meet the requirements of the administrator. These loans on residential properties may be made on terms up to forty years. The Federal Housing Administration does not lend money. It insures loans made according to its regulations by approved lenders. For such insurance, the borrower pays a premium of 0.5 percent per annum on average debt balances outstanding during the year. Since its inception, the Federal Housing Administration mortgage has proved highly advantageous to both the borrower and the lender. Millions of people who might otherwise never have owned their homes have been enabled to do so on a basis that has proved very sound. The favorable interest rates and long term for repayment enable people of moderate incomes to acquire desirable homes within their means on a basis that assures freedom from mortgage debt within a definite period of time. Specifically, under the Federal Housing Act as amended, individuals are able to borrow up to 97 percent of the value of proposed or existing homes approved for mortgage lending purposes by the regional office of the Federal Housing Administration. FHA mortgage loans cannot exceed 97 percent of the first $15,000 of appraised value plus 90 percent of the next $10,000, and 80 percent of the excess over $20,000.[2] The maximum mortgage loan is $33,000 for one-family dwellings, $35,750 for two- and three-family dwellings, and $41,250 for four-family dwellings.

The rate of interest under FHA regulation is currently 8 percent plus 0.5 percent of the average annual outstanding loan to cover mortgage insurance premiums. FHA maximum loan and percentage ratios are subject to change by administrative and congressional action. Frequent changes have been made to adjust loan and interest ratios to housing needs and to the supply and demand of mortgage funds.

The requirements of the Federal Housing Administration as to construction and location of the property are high and are based upon very sound principles. In addition to the liberal terms obtainable by the borrower, he also has assurance that the construction of his home has met the minimum standards of experts. This is a very important feature, and it safeguards the interests of the home buyer. Federal Housing Administration mortgage fi-

---

[2]Different loan-to-value ratios apply for dwellings not approved for insurance prior to the beginning of construction which were completed within one year before the application for insurance. The borrower, too, must be the owner and occupant, otherwise the mortgage cannot exceed 85 percent of the amount that an owner-occupant can obtain. The current loan-to-value ratio for dwellings not approved for insurance is 90 percent of the first $25,000 of appraised value plus 80 percent of the excess over $25,000.

nancing is obtainable through most lending institutions. To obtain such a loan, the prospective borrower must file his application with an eligible institution. The institution then deals with the Federal Housing Administration, making the transaction a simple one insofar as the borrower is concerned. Should the required mortgage be on proposed construction, the borrower must furnish complete plans and specifications. The lending institution supplies the Federal Housing Administration with complete data, and the loan is then considered from the standpoint of physical security as well as the borrower's ability. Should it be found acceptable in all respects, a commitment is issued by the FHA which enables the lender to bring the transaction to a conclusion.

"GI" guaranteed mortgage. Under the Servicemen's Readjustment Act of 1944, as amended, the "Korea" GI Bill of July 1952, and the Veterans Housing Act of 1970, eligible veterans and unremarried widows of veterans who died in the service or from service-connected causes may obtain guaranteed loans for the purchase or construction of a home. Although the Veterans Administration administers the provisions of the act, it does not, as a rule, lend any money.[3] As in FHA insured mortgages, the loans are made by banks and other qualified mortgage lenders. The Veterans Administration merely guarantees the payment of a part of the loan and pays the lender any loss sustained, in case of default, up to the amount of the guarantee.

The maximum guaranty credit for any one veteran is 60 percent of a loan on the reasonable value of a veteran's home, with a top guarantee of $12,500. This guarantee need not be used immediately or in any single transaction. Termination dates set for application of GI mortgage loans have been eliminated under the Veterans Housing Act of 1970. This new law further reinstates and extends indefinitely all unused VA entitlement of World War II or Korean conflict veterans. For veterans who served after January 31, 1955, the 1970 act extends "until used" unexpired and not yet accrued entitlement. Provisions of this law as applicable to purchase of mobile homes will be discussed in Chapter 28, "Real Estate and the Mobile Home."

The GI loans are written for terms up to forty years, and the interest rate may not exceed legal limits set by the Veterans Administration. No special mortgage forms are required other than those used in the state in which the property is situated. The mortgage, however, must provide that the veteran shall have the privilege of repaying the indebtedness in whole or in part without payment of a penalty. To be eligible for a Veterans Ad-

---

[3]Since July 19, 1950, and subject to periodic congressional renewal, the VA has been authorized to make direct loans to veterans in areas where private capital at approved rates of interest for GI home financing is not available. These direct loans are limited to a maximum amount of $21,000 each except that this amount may be increased to $25,000 in high-cost areas. Although over 84 percent of the nation's 3,076 counties are certified as eligible for direct loans, the amount so guaranteed and administered averaged less than $200 million per annum during recent years.

ministration guaranteed loan, a veteran borrower must have had at least ninety (90) days of active service during the official war periods or have been disabled in the service during the war. The veteran must also have been discharged under conditions other than dishonorable. Only improvements that meet VA minimum construction standards are subject to mortgage loan guaranty.

Conventional mortgage. A mortgage that is not FHA insured or GI guaranteed is generally referred to as a *conventional mortgage.* Such mortgages are, as a rule, made at lower loan-to-value ratios than those that are government insured or guaranteed. Conventional mortgages, too, are subject to institutional regulations, as is more fully described in Chapter 14.

To make conventional loans more competitive with high loan-to-value financing authorized under government-sponsored mortgage programs, a new concept in home financing was introduced and placed into operation in February 1957, by the Mortgage Guaranty Insurance Corporation of Milwaukee, Wisconsin. Under provisions of this insured lending program, home purchasers can obtain conventional mortgage loans up to 90 percent of appraised property value, at going (prevailing) rates of interest and at insurance costs less than half those charged under the FHA mortgage lending system. To illustrate: Mr. Birch, who is steadily employed and earns $15,000 annually, has an opportunity to purchase a new home which the federal savings and loan association in his hometown appraised at $30,000. For personal reasons, Mr. Birch wishes to invest only $3,000 cash and thus seeks a 90 percent conventional mortgage loan of $27,000. Since under federal savings and loan regulations loans in excess of 80 percent of value cannot be offered without additional security as guarantee of debt payment in case of default, Mr. Birch is informed that under Mortgage Guaranty Insurance Corporation (M.G.I.C.) provisions a guarantee of the top 20 percent of the requested loan is offered which enables the savings and loan association to lend the full 90 percent mortgage at costs as follows:

1. A one-time insurance charge of 2 percent, or $540, to be paid at time of mortgage closing, or
2. An initial charge of one-half of 1 percent of the mortgage loan at time of closing, that is, $135 plus a $20 appraisal fee and one-fourth of 1 percent annually of remaining mortgage balances until the outstanding mortgage debt is reduced to 75 percent of property value. The annual charges are accrued monthly together with regular principal and interest payments. This latter charge arrangement is generally preferred.

In consideration of either of the above payments M.G.I.C. guarantees, at its option, either to take possession of a foreclosed property and pay the insured mortgagee the outstanding debt, including defaulted interest and foreclosure costs, or to pay 20 percent of this amount without taking possession of the property. In most cases M.G.I.C. chooses the latter alternative, thus avoiding the problems associated with maintenance and resale of the property.

In looking at the mortgages offered to it for insurance, M.G.I.C. considers both the property and the mortgagor but tends to place more emphasis on the latter. It insures first mortgages on one- to four-family homes, and currently about 99 percent of those were owner occupied at the time of insurance. Except for a special program which is used only rarely, the maximum loan is limited to 90 percent of market value and is limited in amount by state or federal rules controlling mortgage lending institutions. Although it insures mortgages on older homes, M.G.I.C. requires especially careful appraisal of both the house and the neighborhood and may require modernization of facilities within the house. Special practices apply to other types of property whose value may drop sharply. Because of its recognition of the essential role of credit reporting in determination of risk, M.G.I.C. has established a program to improve the quality of such reports and thus lower the level of risk undertaken by both itself and its approved lending institutions. In checking on a mortgagor, M.G.I.C. pays particular attention not only to the level and stability of his income and to his housing cost-income ratio, which should not exceed 25 percent, but also to other long-term commitments for monthly payments, which should not exceed 33 to 35 percent of income in total.[4]

The success of the Mortgage Guaranty Insurance Corporation, the nation's oldest and largest insurer of residential mortgage loans, can be gauged by the fact that M.G.I.C. reached the $5 billion mark of insurance in force within a span of thirteen years of operation. This form of insurance is currently available in forty-nine states and the District of Columbia.[5] As of October 1970, M.G.I.C. reported to the author the following statistics: average loan-to-value ratio, 86.1 percent; average appraisal, $23,914; average sale price, $23,864; average age of property, 12.7 years; and average interest rate, 8.53 percent.

Another program of insured home financing, dubbed "Piggyback," has been launched by Lumbermen's Investment Corporation of Austin, Texas, with the cooperation of M.G.I.C. This nationwide new loan program is intended to lower housing costs by saving home buyers the expense of second mortgage financing where conventional mortgages up to 90 percent of home value are not readily available.

Under this new plan, the amount of money over what an institutional investor can legally lend (usually 75 percent) is advanced by a separate corporation up to 90 percent of the value of a single-family owner-occupied residential property. The amount of the loan is advanced in two portions: 83⅓ percent by an institutional investor (such as an insurance

[4]For a full study of the Mortgage Guaranty Insurance Corporation, see the report by the Institute of Environmental Studies, University of Pennsylvania, December 1967, *The Private Insurance of Home Mortgages—Summary and Conclusions*.

[5]Fifty-five hundred mortgage lending firms throughout the country are currently authorized to originate M.G.I.C. insured loans. Underwriting offices are located in Milwaukee, Atlanta, Philadelphia, Los Angeles, and Hawaii.

company) and 16⅔ percent by Mortgage Finance Corporation, a subsidiary of Lumbermen's Investment Corporation. An agreement between the co-investors gives the institutional lender a priority of interest in the first lien on the property. M.F.C.'s investment is backed by a declaration of equity. It is given a priority in the proceeds of an M.G.I.C. mortgage loan insurance policy. There is no second lien.

According to C. W. Smith, senior vice-president of M.G.I.C. and developer of the "Piggyback" concept, the success of the new split-loan technique involves three factors:

1. The use of private mortgage loan insurance rather than a junior lien on the property to protect the secondary investor.
2. The fact that 80 to 90 percent loans commonly command an interest rate 0.25 percent per year higher than loans of 75 percent of value or less and that this differential will adequately compensate both the primary and secondary investors.
3. Second mortgage lenders normally charge very high rates of interest because of the junior nature of their securities. M.F.C., however, will be protected by M.G.I.C.'s coverage which will be prime security against loss.

The Milwaukee-based mortgage guaranty insurance company has successfully served since 1962 as the private enterprise counterpart of the Federal Housing Administration (FHA) insured loan program. Under terms of the private insurance program, institutions can now lend in excess of legally permitted loan amounts up to 90 percent of appraised home value. The excess loan amount is insured against loss caused by loan delinquency and subsequent foreclosure at public auction. The cost of this insurance to the borrower does not exceed 0.5 percent of outstanding loan balances.

Trust deed mortgage. In addition to the regular mortgage, there is in common use in many states a device called a *trust deed mortgage.* It consists of an instrument that conveys to a person (usually to a third person —trustee) a trust to hold the property as security for the payment of a debt to the lender. Essentially the purpose of the transaction is the same as a mortgage. The principal difference lies in the method of enforcement in case of default. The trustee, under the law, is merely carrying out the expressed will of the parties according to mortgage trust deed terms. In practice, the creditor by this means is freed from the requirements of ordinary foreclosure, frequently obtaining a speedier and more efficient method to bring about a sale. The borrower, too, in many states where this practice of mortgage lending is followed, is not entitled to the usual right of redemption from foreclosure sales. There is a tendency for legislatures and courts to abolish the differences between the two mortgage forms where the trust deed method of financing is customary. Often, when the amount of the loan is so large that no single person is willing to advance it, a trust mortgage is used. In a loan of millions of dollars upon a group of buildings, for example, the mortgage is made to a trustee. Instead of a single bond (or note), many are issued, and one or more bonds go to each person advancing a part of the loan, depending upon the denomination of the bonds. The trustee acts as such for the benefit of the bondholders. The mortgage contains, in addition to the usual clauses, various provisions concerning the rights and duties of the trustee and of the bondholders.

Participation mortgage. A participation mortgage is one in which two or more persons own a share. These persons do not own the entire mortgage jointly, but each owns a specified interest in it. A mortgage may be made to a trustee, who will issue a certificate of ownership to each person having an interest in it. As payments of interest and principal are made, each participant receives his pro rata share. An arrangement of this kind usually means that each ownership in the mortgage is coordinate. In some participation mortgages the ownerships are not coordinate, but one ranks ahead of another. An owner may wish to secure a mortgage of a certain amount, but on application to a lender may find the lender willing to give a smaller amount. Someone else, however, might wish to take the difference subject to the first lender's amount, so that the mortgage is made for the total amount and is usually made to the first or largest lender, and the securities are placed in his possession. An agreement is made between the two lenders, called a *participation agreement*, or *ownership agreement*, in which the mortgage is described and in which it is set forth that one party owns the mortgage to the extent of a certain amount of principal and interest only and that the other party owns the rest of the mortgage debt, but that the ownership of the first party is superior to that of the second party, as though one held a first mortgage for his share and the other a second mortgage for the remainder. The share of one lender in a participation mortgage of this kind is called a *prior, or senior, participation*, and that of the other lender a *subordinate, or junior, participation*.

Mortgage pattern variations

For sake of clarity, the various types of mortgages have been described as if each were independent of the other. In practice, however, the features of the various types of mortgages may be combined to form a mortgage pattern that will best serve the purpose of the loan and the requirements of the borrower. A package mortgage may thus be open-end and issued as a conventional loan, or it may be FHA insured or GI guaranteed. A purchase money mortgage may likewise be any one or more of the various types of mortgages described above. The purchaser in quest of a loan should carefully study the features of each type of mortgage. The lender, in turn, should suggest the mortgage pattern most suitable under the circumstances, considering both the qualifications of the borrower and his probable future income and budgetary needs.

Second mortgages

The second mortgage was commonly used in real estate financing prior to the depression of the early thirties. At that time most lenders would not loan more than two-thirds of value, and it was necessary for buyers to seek additional credit. This was usually provided by a second mortgage taken back by the seller of the property or by a third person. It was usually made for a short term and provided for amortization. When the depression came and real estate values dropped, the security behind such mortgages rapidly disappeared. In addition, holders of first mortgages, who had not previously required much, if any, amortization, became aware of its necessity and made demands upon the borrower that were difficult or impossible for him to meet. The resulting loss of property through foreclosures amply evidences the fact that this was not a sound means of financing in most instances. Very few such mortgages are now made in connection with acquisitions of single-family residences. Lenders are usually able to meet the requirements of borrowers by means of one mortgage on a long-term amortizing basis, repayment of which is geared to the financial ability of individual borrowers.

Equity financing

Since the mortgage is the underlying, and usually the major part of the financing, it has been first discussed. The complete job, however, has not been done—the equity must be financed, else there can be no purchase. It must now be considered, therefore, how that part of the cost between the mortgage and the price is to be obtained. This is a matter for the purchasing owner to arrange.

Chapter 4 presents in some detail various types and kinds of ownership and interests—mainly from the viewpoint of title. Now they must be considered as they relate to financing.

Individual financing

The purchasing owner usually obtains his equity financing from his own funds, often from savings he has accumulated. This situation is specially the case with the home buyer. He does not want others sharing his ownership, possibly interfering. The amount of money is not large enough to require or justify any group ownership. And, in addition, most lenders require individual ownership of the home. Consequently, on small operations and homes especially, the individual saves until he can finance the equity in the home he wishes to purchase.

Group financing

In investment or speculative operations, the prospective purchaser will often, when he has neither sufficient funds nor inclination to carry the whole burden, interest others, who, by a mutual contribution plan, will share the equity financing. The specific methods will vary to suit the circumstances of the case. The following are the most usual.

Partnership

Many purchases are shared by just a few associates—generally not more than two or three. They may, and often do, speak of themselves as partners. Actually they are not, but are simply joint venturers. Each contributes his agreed share of the necessary equity financing fund—for purchase and, possibly, alterations or other physical work. Title is usually taken in the names of all, though sometimes one will become owner for the benefit of all. Their rights, obligations, and shares are agreed upon, ordinarily by a separate contract. Technically, they become joint tenants or tenants in common. This method has the objection that death of any of the owners may cause delay, taxation, and other inconveniences. Hence, it is normally used only when the term of ownership is expected to be fairly short. Nor is it used when a large sum is involved, since the individuals do not wish to become personally liable on any mortgage financing.

Corporation

A real estate corporation may be organized with the property in question as the principal asset. The organizer of the corporation can then issue stock for the purpose of raising funds necessary for the purchase. This method is simple and inexpensive. Death of any stockholder creates no problem, since the corporation's life goes right on. Any mortgage obligations are executed by the corporation, so that no stockholder becomes personally liable. Yet each shares in any profit in accordance with his stock holding.

Tenant ownership corporations

Tenant, or *cooperative* ownership is an expression denoting multiple ownership with profits and losses shared by the respective owners. It has come into general use to describe apartment buildings taken over by a group of families, to be owned, occupied, and operated by them for their mutual benefit and profit. Briefly, it is ownership by an occupying group: a highly restricted community of homes under one roof. It differs from single-home ownership in the sense that the tenant-owner does not have the same degree of responsibility toward his home as the individual home-owner does. This type of ownership is customarily under a corporate setup, each tenant-owner being a stockholder and holding his apartment under a proprietary lease. Cooperative, or tenant, ownership differs from syndicate ownership essentially in the sense that it is not speculative for profit and that it anticipates permanent home ownership.

To facilitate cooperative home ownership, the Federal Housing Act under Title II, Section 213, provides for cooperative housing insurance. This form of federal mortgage insurance is designed to help nonprofit membership corporations or trusts to construct or purchase housing for their members at a saving.

A cooperative housing project generally is a multifamily management-type structure known as a garden apartment or elevator-type building. The structure, as a rule, is managed for the cooperative owners by a managing agent who is compensated on a salary or commission basis. Members of the cooperative unit venture acquire ownership of the apartment dwelling unit and have the privilege of using or selling the premises subject only to cooperative restrictions imposed to protect the quality of the cooperative investment and the general amenities of ownership. Each owner-occupant pays in addition to his initial equity interest a monthly charge (rent) as his proportionate share to cover mortgage amortization, interest, taxes, hazard insurance, and operating costs, including use of common utilities and managerial expenses.

Sponsors of cooperative housing—builders, property managers, or interested groups of families—who seek financing under the Federal Mortgage Insurance Act apply through an "approved mortgagee" for loan processing. The cooperative nonprofit trust agreement is submitted to the Federal Housing Administration, together with schedules showing proposed rents, charges, capital structure, rate of return, and methods of operation. If approved, the maximum insurable mortgage is $20 million for a private mortgagor and $25 million for a public (city, state, or public institution) mortgagor.

Specific mortgage loan limitations are based on the following:

1. *Management-type projects.* For garden-type buildings not to exceed an amount of $9,900 per family unit without a bedroom; $13,750 with one bedroom; $16,500 with two bedrooms; $20,350 with three bedrooms; and $23,100 with four or more bedrooms. For elevator-type buildings, limits of loans are increased per family unit as follows: $11,500 without a bedroom; $16,500 with one bedroom; $19,800 with two bedrooms; $24,750 with two and three bedrooms; and $28,050 with four or more bedrooms.

   Total mortgage loans are limited to 90 percent of the estimated replacement cost of the property when the physical improvements are completed and where construction falls under Section 207 for multifamily rental units up to $5 million. Under Section 213 covering cooperative housing, the loan limit is 97 percent of replacement cost new.

2. *Sales-type projects.* The maximum insurable mortgage for sales-type, speculative, cooperative housing, is $12.5 million and cannot exceed the greater of the following amounts: (1) A sum equal to the total amount of the individual mortgages which are insurable if each apartment owner were to own his home separately or (2) a sum equal to the maximum amount for which a similar management-type project would be insurable as outlined above for garden-type buildings.

In high-cost areas the insurable amounts per family unit may be increased up to 45 percent. For allowable increase permitted in any particular area, the local Federal Housing Authority office should be consulted. Maximum mortgage maturity at approved rates of interest may extend up to forty years from the date amortization begins.

Cooperative ownership of apartment dwelling units has increased significantly in larger urban areas and has proved a successful compromise between ownership of individual dwelling units and the attendant responsibilities and renting of apartment units managed under the profit motive of landlord ownership.

Condominium financing

As discussed in Chapter 4, pages 59–60, individual financing of horizontal space units in multistory apartments is authorized under special enabling legislation passed in most states and the District of Columbia. Where condominium financing is sought under Section 234 of the FHA Housing Act of 1965, the declaration or plan of ownership as well as 80 percent of the units offered to specific purchasers must be approved by the FHA before sales or offers to sell can be processed.

Individual owner-occupied condominium units may be mortgaged up to a maximum of $33,000. Lending amounts are computed as follows: 97 percent of the first $15,000 of appraised value, plus 90 percent of the next $10,000 and 80 percent of the excess over $25,000. Loans to a nonoccupant cannot exceed 85 percent of the amount an occupant-mortgagor can get. Interest rates vary with economic conditions and limits set by the Federal Housing Administration. Allowable interest rates reached a high of 8.5 percent during 1970.

Under conventional financing, it is deemed desirable to submit the condominium declaration, the contract of sale, and the description of plan to the lender's counsel for approval prior to publication or recording of documents. It is also advantageous to select and recommend a single lender who is familiar with the entire project in order to facilitate and expedite closing of title to and mortgages on the individual units. Some builders and developers of multiple-unit apartment structures deem it wise to consider the feasibility of alternate permanent financing in case condominium units do not attract purchasers as anticipated. Such standby financing would prevent a costly delay when ownership plans are changed to meet shifting housing demands or investment market conditions.

Syndicate ownership

The syndicate is a joint venture whereby two or more persons pool contributions with which they purchase, hold, and dispose of real estate through the agency of a manager or other representative. It is a method for operating or speculating in real estate. It enables numerous persons each to take a small share in a project with the result that should there be a loss, the loss is distributed among the group without resulting in serious financial embarrassment to any one member. The syndicate is simple to create and easy to terminate. The members of a syndicate are not primarily interested in long-term ownership, but in quick turnover with resultant profit, so that the funds derived therefrom may be used for other similar enterprises.

Sale and leaseback

A method of real estate financing which has gained wide popularity particularly with owners of large industrial or commercial properties is the sale and leaseback transaction. Under this method of financing the owner, in return for full value, conveys title to his property by deed to a real estate investor or an institutional lender—generally an insurance company—and leases back the property for a long term.

Under provisions of the lease the former owner becomes the lessee and agrees to pay a net rent as well as all operating expenses, including taxes, insurance, maintenance, and essential replacements.

The sale and leaseback transaction has many advantages as a mode of real estate financing:

1. The seller (user of realty) obtains the full cash value of the property which, as a rule, is twice the amount that could be obtained under mortgage financing and this without the burdensome provisions of mortgage debt clauses and the possible threat of foreclosure in case of nonpayment of interest and/or principal.
2. The seller is able to reinvest the cash in his business enterprise in which as a "specialist" he has greater skill to increase net operating earnings. The sale, too, increases flexibility of capital investment and mobility of the enterprise in case expansion or relocation becomes necessary.
3. The seller, often, secures substantial tax advantages. If the sale yields a price less than book value of the property the loss can be reflected in income tax reporting. Then, too, the entire amount paid for rent becomes a business expense, whereas under mortgage borrowing only the interest portion of the debt and accrued depreciation are tax deductible items.

The purchaser, also, gains advantages which make the sale and leaseback transaction financially profitable to him:

1. Since the lessee assumes all operating expenses and burden of management, the net income (rent) provides a rate of return, generally, more favorable than that obtainable under a mortgage debt in investment.
2. Equity ownership provides an excellent hedge against inflation. If the property enhances in value during its investment life, it is the investor who will benefit in the long run.

The advantages to buyer and seller under a sale and leaseback transaction as outlined above are not all-inclusive but are sufficiently substantial to make consideration of this type of real estate financing worthy of serious and profitable consideration.

READING AND STUDY REFERENCES

1. BRYANT, WILLIS R., *Mortgage Lending: Fundamentals and Practices*, Chapters 1 and 2. New York: McGraw-Hill Book Company, 1956.
2. FISHER, ERNEST M., *Urban Real Estate Markets: Characteristics and Financing*, Chapter 2. National Bureau of Economic Research, 1951.
3. HUSBAND, WILLIAM H., and FRANK RAY ANDERSON, *Real Estate*, Chapters 22 and 23. Homewood, Ill.: Richard D. Irwin, Inc., 1950.
4. LUSK, HAROLD F., *Law of the Real Estate Business*, Chapter 4. Homewood, Ill.: Richard D. Irwin, Inc., 1965.
5. MCMICHAEL, STANLEY L., and PAUL T. O'KEEFE, *How to Finance Real Estate* (2nd ed.), Chapter 1. Englewood Cliffs, N.J.: Prentice-Hall, Inc., 1953.
6. RATCLIFF, RICHARD U., *Real Estate Analysis*, Chapter 7. New York: McGraw-Hill Book Company, 1961.
7. *Real Estate Guide*, a real estate service published by Prentice-Hall, Inc., Englewood Cliffs, N.J. See section 12, "Federal Aids to Financing."
8. RING, ALFRED A., *Questions and Problems in Real Estate Principles and Practices* (rev. ed.), Chapter 13. Englewood Cliffs, N.J.: Prentice-Hall, Inc., 1972.
9. UNGER, MAURICE A., *Real Estate* (4th ed.), Chapter 14. Cincinnati: South-Western Publishing Co., 1969.

14

REAL ESTATE INVESTMENT

The nature and character of real estate investments

In a capitalistic society the vast majority of citizens are motivated by a desire to achieve during their working life-span a high degree of financial independence. Such independence is generally enhanced through the economic process of *savings and investment*. By investment is meant the commitment of savings or funds with a view to safeguarding the capital while earning a fair return commensurate with the nature, character, and risk of the savings or investment venture.

In judging the nature and quality of savings or investment opportunities a prudent individual should consider the following as guidelines:

1. Required quantity and safety of initial capital outlay
2. Quantity and quality (safety) of periodic or annual income
3. Degree of inflationary protection
4. Liquidity of invested capital
5. Capital appreciation
6. Income tax shelter

Required quantity and safety of initial capital outlay

Excluding the purchases of real estate for family shelter purposes, in which case residential properties may be purchased with federal government insured or guaranteed mortgage loans up to 100 percent of a property's appraised market value, the acquisition of real property for investment usually requires large outlays of venture capital. Until recent years the purchase of investment real estate was largely limited to wealthy individual buyers and more often to realty corporations and institutional buyers such as insurance companies and banking firms. The small investors, as a rule, were attracted to the stock, produce, and security markets where the initial outlay both in number and in value per share, or other unit of measure, could be suited to the limited buying power of the individual.

Since 1960 when Congress enacted special tax treatment for real estate trusts, as was noted in Chapter 4, real estate as an investment has become competitive with corporate stocks, bonds, and related securities. As reported in the December 1970 issue of *The Mortgage Banker*, seventy-six major real estate trusts have been formed within a decade with total assets exceeding $3.7 billion. Now real estate trust securities in excess of $1 billion per year are anticipated to be offered and sold through stock exchange facilities in the 1970–80 period. As a result of such magnitude of public offerings and under controls over investments exercised by the Security and Exchange Commission, the quality of the real estate investment medium will further be enhanced in years to come.

Quantity and quality (safety) of periodic or annual income

Real estate, because of its fixity and durability extending over an economic life of forty to sixty years, forms an excellent long-term investment medium. Where apartment structures and office buildings, shopping centers, warehouses, and other commercial and industrial developments are professionally planned in accordance with feasibility studies prepared by experts, both the quantity and the quality of periodic income, under competent property management, is deemed economically superior to income derived from other forms of monetary investments provided, however, that liquidity of the invested capital is not a prime consideration.

To illustrate current techniques of investment analysis under which the profitableness of a capital venture can be tested, the author is making use of a professionally prepared feasibility study which supports the proposed construction of a moderate-rise 170-unit apartment project in a rapidly growing, urban community. The financial section of this study has, with permission of the project developer,[1] been made available for use in this publication. Table 14-1 details the project costs which aggregate the sum of $4,300,000. Table 14-2 shows anticipated operating income and expenditures under typical management and at an anticipated occupancy ratio of 95 percent. Table 14-3 presents an analysis of the projected "cash flow" (cash remaining after all expenditures and outlays, including mortgage principal and interest payments, have been met. This and the succeeding tables project operations over a ten-year period from 1972 to

---

[1] Major Construction Corporation, Tampa, Florida; W. Robert Little, president.

TABLE 14–1
PROJECT COSTS
GLEN SPRINGS APARTMENT PROJECT

Land		$ 200,000
Land development—utilities, etc.		200,000
Improvements:		
Building costs:		
Apartment space	264,140 sq. ft. @ $9.50	2,509,000
Balconies and corridors	49,560 sq. ft. @ $4.00	198,000
Stairs—open	5,880 sq. ft. @ $5.00	29,000
Elevator shafts	29,054 sq. ft. @ $0.50	15,000
Elevators	10 sq. ft. @ $13,000	130,000
Appliances, stove, etc.	170 sq. ft. @ $1,000	170,000
Carpet and draperies		134,000
Recreational facilities		84,000
Contractor's fee		150,000
Architectural services		65,000
Total improvement costs		$3,484,000
Financing and legal costs:		
Mortgage fees		90,000
Construction loan interest		135,000
Taxes during construction		4,000
Risk insurance		4,000
Title and recording		10,000
Miscellaneous—legal		15,000
Total finance costs		$ 258,000
Developer's fee		$ 150,000
Contingencies—1%		$ 40,000
Total project costs		$4,332,000
Rounded to		$4,300,000

1981 inclusive. Table 14-4 presents an interesting breakdown of operating and replacement costs as scheduled to be incurred year by year over a ten-year span under typical but competent management. Table 14-5 projects the amount of tax-sheltered cash income accruing year by year to equity investors who sponsor this apartment project.

As will be noted in Table 14-3, this apartment investment venture projects a net return ranging from a low of 21.2 percent during the initial year of operation to a high of 33.2 percent during the tenth year of project life. The average rate of equity return for the ten-year period of operation is 29.0 percent. Such high annual returns are typical of prudently planned real estate investment projects and account for the recent growth and popularity of investment trusts and syndicates, as well as for the trend in equity sharing and equity income participation by all major insurance companies that offer mortgage loans to real estate developers.

Degree of inflationary protection

Except for a selected number of "growth" stocks, few investment mediums have equaled the inflationary protection offered by urban land holdings and their capital improvements. This has been especially evident during the steep inflationary period that began in 1964 and reached a climax at the rate of 6 percent per year during the three-year period from 1967 to

TABLE 14–2
INCOME AND OPERATING EXPENSE STATEMENT
GLEN SPRINGS APARTMENT PROJECT

Income:

60—1-bedroom, 1½-bath apts. @ $290		$ 17,400
77—2-bedroom, 2½-bath apts. @ 360		27,720
33—3-bedroom, 2½-bath apts. @ 425		14,025
170 Apartment units		$ 59,145
$59,145 per month times 12		709,740
Less 5% vacancy and collection loss		35,487
Effective gross income		$674,253

Operating expenses:

Management—5%	$ 33,700	
R.E. taxes	60,000	
Selling and advertising	3,000	
Resident manager	10,560	
Janitor and yardmen	15,600	
Workmen's comp., social security	2,350	
Hazard insurance	4,500	
Utilities	16,200	
Elevator	3,600	
Decorating and repairs	16,800	
Replacement reserve	25,000	
Other expenditures—pool, etc.	1,800	
Total operating expense		$193,110
Net operating income before debt service		$481,143

1970. Whereas most capital assets lost in terms of purchasing power of their dollar value, adequately improved realty, especially apartments, shopping centers, and selected commercial properties, have increased in terms of constant dollars as a result of rapidly increasing costs of construction and rising cost of money as reflected in interest rates that reached statutory usury levels in all fifty states. In the absence of rent and price control, real property, like a ship upon the ocean waters, floats above its purchasing power-constant dollar line irrespective of depth or rise in the level of prices. It is this ability to hold its purchasing power integrity that has in recent years popularized the demand for shares of real estate trusts and syndicates.

Liquidity of invested capital

Despite the ready availability of real estate syndicate and real estate trust shares on national stock exchanges, the relative nonliquidity of real estate as a form of capital continues to be the economic Achilles' heel of this mode of property investment. Inability to adjust readily to economic market demands has caused real properties and especially urban lands to reach phenomenal "boom" levels of inflated value and conversely deep and lasting economic depressions for which real estate has gained a "bearish" reputation. Where, however, a well-informed investor balances his investment portfolio so as to weather impending and generally short-range economic fluctuations, the relative nonliquidity of real estate should prove no handicap in garnering the long-term capital benefits that are forecast, both

TABLE 14-3
ANALYSIS OF ESTIMATED CASH FLOW (thousands of dollars)
GLEN SPRINGS APARTMENT PROJECT

Year	Gross[1] Income	Operating[2] Expenses	Replacement Reserve	Land Rent	Operating Income	Debt[3] Service	Return to Investors (Cash Flow)	Percentage Return
1972	665	168	2	53	442	315	127	21.2
1973	685	172	2	54	457	315	142	23.7
1974	706	177	2	54	473	316	157	26.2
1975	727	183	15	55	474	317	157	26.2
1976	749	188	15	55	491	317	174	29.0
1977	771	193	16	55	507	318	189	31.5
1978	794	199	27	56	512	318	194	32.3
1979	818	205	32	56	525	319	206	34.3
1980	843	211	61	57	514	320	194	32.3
1981	868	217	74	57	520	320	200	33.2
Totals and Average %	7,626	1,913	246	552	4,915	3,175	1,740	29.0

[1]Rent increases projected upward at 3 percent per year (conservative estimate).
[2]See ten-year expense projection—Table 14-4.
[3]Increase in debt service based on mortgagor's participation of 10 percent in increased gross rental income

TABLE 14-4

TEN-YEAR OPERATING EXPENSE SCHEDULE (thousands of dollars)
GLEN SPRINGS APARTMENT PROJECT

Expenses	1972	1973	1974	1975	1976	1977	1978	1979	1980	1981
Taxes	60.0	60.9	61.8	62.7	63.7	64.6	65.6	66.6	67.6	68.7
Management fee	33.3	34.3	35.3	36.9	37.5	38.4	39.7	40.9	42.2	43.4
Resident manager	3.0	3.2	3.4	3.7	4.0	4.3	4.6	4.9	5.2	5.5
(Incl. apartment)	10.6	10.9	11.4	11.8	12.3	12.8	13.3	13.8	14.4	14.9
Janitors, yardmen	15.6	16.5	17.5	18.6	19.7	20.8	22.1	23.4	24.8	26.3
Insurance and taxes	2.4	2.4	2.5	2.5	2.6	2.6	2.7	2.7	2.8	2.8
Fire and EC	4.5	4.5	4.5	4.8	4.8	4.8	5.1	5.1	5.1	5.5
Utilities:										
Electric	3.6	3.6	3.6	3.6	3.6	3.6	3.6	3.6	3.6	3.6
Water, sewage, trash	12.0	12.2	12.4	12.7	12.9	13.1	13.4	13.6	13.9	14.2
Telephone	.6	.6	.6	.6	.6	.6	.6	.6	.6	.6
Pool maintenance	.6	.6	.6	.6	.6	.6	.6	.6	.6	.6
Grounds expense	1.2	1.2	1.3	1.4	1.5	1.5	1.6	1.7	1.8	1.9
Elevator service	3.6	3.8	4.0	4.2	4.4	4.6	4.8	5.0	5.2	5.5
Decorate and repair	16.8	17.5	18.2	18.9	19.7	20.4	21.3	22.1	23.0	23.9
	167.8	172.2	177.1	183.0	187.9	192.7	199.0	204.6	210.8	217.4
Replacement reserve										
Draperies (life 5 yrs.)	.3	.3	.4	13.0	13.6	14.2	.4	.5	15.6	16.4
Carpet (life 6 yrs.)	1.0	1.1	1.2	1.3	1.4	1.6	26.3	27.6	29.0	30.4
Appliances (life 12 yrs.)	—	—	—	—	—	—	—	2.5	15.8	26.6
Recreation equip.	.3	.3	.3	.3	.3	.3	.3	1.0	1.0	1.0
	1.6	1.7	1.9	14.6	15.3	16.1	27.0	31.6	61.4	74.4

TABLE 14-5

ANALYSIS OF CASH FLOW AND TAX LIABILITY DURING INITIAL TEN YEARS OF OPERATION (thousands of dollars)

GLEN SPRINGS APARTMENT PROJECT

	1972	1973	1974	1975	1976	1977	1978	1979	1980	1981
Gross income	665	685	760	727	749	771	794	818	843	868
Operating expense	170	174	179	198	203	208	226	237	272	291
Operating income	495	511	527	529	546	563	568	581	571	577
Less—Land rent	53	54	54	55	55	55	56	56	57	57
Mtge. interest	285	283	280	277	274	272	269	267	264	262
Income—before depreciation	157	174	193	197	217	236	243	258	250	258
Depreciation— 200% declining balance (Cost of $3,900)	156	150	144	138	132	127	122	117	112	108
Taxable income	1	24	49	59	85	109	121	141	138	150
Tax-free income	156	150	144	138	132	127	122	117	112	108

as to adequacy of net return and capital safety, by real estate research analysts and leading economic forecasters.

Capital appreciation

Dr. Homer Hoyt's extensive three-year study *One Hundred Years of Land Values in Chicago*, published by the University of Chicago Press in 1933, and subsequent studies by this author and by Dr. H. B. Dorau during his career as chairman of the Department of Real Estate at New York University, have revealed a remarkable close relationship in the rise of land values as compared with the percentage growth of population. Although these research findings have proved of great interest to the body of real estate investors, land economists have not been astounded by these anticipated revelations. As Will Rogers, the well-remembered lecturer and humorist, used to say when referring to real estate land acquisitions: "They just don't make that stuff any more." Since *people* make value, not stone, brick, steel, or mortar, it should not be astounding to find that the pressure of increasing population should cause real estate values to keep a concomitant level of rising values. Capital appreciation, too, is caused by the "plowing back" of the so-called population-induced "unearned" value increments. To illustrate, since the conclusion of World War II, values of unimproved lands in suburban areas of expanding urban centers such as New York City, Los Angeles, California, and Miami, Florida, have doubled every five years in geometric progression. That is, a tract of land worth $2,000 per acre on the outskirts of town in 1950 sold for $4,000 per acre in 1955, for $8,000 in 1960, $16,000 in 1965, and at the rate of $32,000 when carved into building lots in 1970. This geometric growth indicates a compound interest (plowed under) increment—after taxes—at the rate of 12.5 percent per year. Whereas such income is derived from deposits of savings or security investments yielding such a high rate would be subject to income taxes at normal corporate or individual tax rates—even if not withdrawn—the income realized through increment in land values is subject only to capital gain taxes at one-half or less than the regular income tax rates applied to ordinary income. This opportunity to convert annual income into capital gain for tax purposes further enhances the status of real estate as a medium for capital investment.

Income tax shelters

Perhaps the most compelling reason for the upsurge in real estate investment activity is to be found in the opportunity offered to obtain tax-sheltered income. The secret to the financial wizardry under which an investor "may have his cake and eat it too" is *leverage*. Leverage as used in the financial world is merely a sophisticated term of recent origin applied to the long-existing practice of trading on the equity, as more fully explained in the preceding chapter. The practice of leverage merely entails the use of other people's money (O.P.M.) to make more money with what one already has. The greater the amount of borrowed money (percentage of loan) in relation to cost or value of the property, the greater the leverage and as a rule the higher the yield on the equity portion of the investment venture.

Leverage, however, is merely a financial device to maximize the *cash flow* which a property under prudent management yields to its equity owners. By cash flow is simply meant the dollars left after all expenditures essential to property operation, including reserves for replacement of short-lived fixtures as well as payments of mortgage principal and interest, are met. What interests the sophisticated investor is not whether the venture produces a taxable net income but rather the amount and relative size of the cash flow and the extent to which this cash flow is tax free or *tax sheltered*.

Perhaps the operations of leverage and the significance of cash flow can best be illustrated by reference to the financial data sheets for the Glen Springs Apartment Project as set forth in Tables 14-1 to 14-5 inclusive. As will be noted in Table 14-1, the apartment project is estimated at $4.3 million, of which $400,000 represents land value. The sponsoring insurance company agreed to purchase the land at its value of $400,000 and to lease it back for a period of sixty years at a rate approximating 12.5 percent of land value. The insurance company further agreed to place a first mortgage loan of $3.3 million at 8⅝ percent for a loan period of twenty-seven years. The constant annual loan payment is $94.45 per thousand dollars of loan, or $315,000 for the mortgage loan of $3.3 million. The remaining equity of $600,000 is supplied by the developers.

Table 14-3 shows the analysis of estimated gross income, operating expenses, and rent, debt service payments, and remaining cash flow over the ten-year period 1972 through 1981. Based on a modest upward rental adjustment of 3 percent per year and operating expenditures as detailed in Table 14-4, the cash flow varies from a minimum of $127,000, or 21.2 percent return on equity investment of $600,000 during the initial year of operation, to $200,000, or a return of 33.2 percent in the year 1981. The average equity rate of return over the ten-year period is 29 percent. The success of the project is based on a projected rate of occupancy of not less than 95 percent average per year. The scarcity of residential housing in the community makes this level of occupancy a certainty.

The amount of tax shelter that this project offers to equity investors in this venture is detailed in Table 14-5. Reference to this table and Table 14–3 will disclose the tax-sheltered annual cash flow over a ten year period as shown on the following page.

As tax-sheltered cash flow diminishes and reaches zero when mortgage amortization and allowable depreciation are equal, equity owners sell or exchange the project property for another. Generally the sale realizes a capital gain to its owners, at least to the extent that book depreciation (depreciation deducted in amounts of dollars) exceeds market depreciation

Year	Cash Flow	Taxable Income	Tax-Sheltered Cash Flow
1972	$ 127,000	$ 1,000	$126,000
1973	142,000	24,000	118,000
1974	157,000	49,000	108,000
1975	157,000	59,000	98,000
1976	174,000	85,000	89,000
1977	189,000	109,000	80,000
1978	194,000	121,000	73,000
1979	206,000	141,000	65,000
1980	194,000	138,000	56,000
1981	200,000	150,000	50,000
Total 10-year period	$1,740,000	$877,000	$863,000

(depreciation as a fact). The new owners then reestablish a purchase value tax base and are in a position to reap their share of tax-sheltered income, although at a reduced rate of depreciation applicable under law to "old," or existing properties.

Other points of interest in connection with the above illustrated method of project financing are the following:

1. The purchase and leaseback of the underlying land at a market rate of interest generally applicable to junior mortgages, but lower than the rate of return anticipated to be earned by the equity investment, in effect does constitute a second mortgage. This further increases the leverage factor and contributes to an increased amount of cash flow per dollar of invested venture (equity) capital. It is of interest to note that the land purchase-leaseback operation allows the deduction of the entire rental payments as a cost of operation. As for the developers, land value is in effect being amortized or for tax purposes depreciated.

2. As a safeguard against the financial ravages of inflation, lending companies, as a condition precedent to the placement of a mortgage loan, currently insist on a part of the equity "action" or, in financial nomenclature, on an inflation "kicker." This is accomplished by having one or more of the following made a part of the lending agreement:

   a. A stipulated percentage part of the cash flow
   b. A stipulated percentage of "overage" rentals collected in excess of a specified gross income
   c. Direct participation in equity (venture) financing (through a wholly owned subsidiary realty corporation)
   d. No provision for repurchase or reversion of the leased land, thus becoming the "fee owner" of the property at the expiration of the fifty- to sixty-year lease agreement
   e. Tying mortgage interest rates to a ratio relationship with the prime rate of interest charged by major commercial banks or providing for mortgage rate adjustment in accordance with a specified cost-of-living or price index

Since all major mortgage lending firms by tacit agreement at present require some form of inflation protection, the practice of mortgage lending at fixed rates of interest, which were available prior to 1965, is now outdated, and for practical purposes nonexistent.

Mortgage lending project requirements

The preliminary requirement for attracting an interest in project participation by either equity or mortgage lending investors is the submission by the developer of a narrative report, better known as a *feasibility study*. This study in effect "sells" the project and demonstrates both the economic need and the profitability of the proposed undertaking. This feasibility study generally contains statistical data, community and project information, economic market forecasts, and conclusions that fall into the following categories:

1. Project proposal
2. Community data and economic trends
3. Neighborhood and project site data
4. Project development and construction details
5. Financial requirements, and operating income, expenditures, and cash flow analysis

The project proposal section of the feasibility report essentially serves as a letter of transmittal. An overall view of the general market area is sketched, and stress is laid on either increased or neglected demand (possibly both) for residential or commercial space which the project is intended to supply. The developer and equity participants are named, and biographical information concerning them is given to establish the extent of professional capability, financial integrity, community standing, and reputation of project sponsors. This report section also contains a summary of total financial requirements and a proposal of the methods by which the project is to be "packaged."

The community data and economic trends section of the report is deemed essential because mortgage and often equity investors are headquartered or domiciled in distant cities and need to be informed by means of words and pictures as to the nature of the socioeconomic environment in which the project is to be situated. Investors are interested in the economic base that supports or sustains economic life, the soundness and stability of this base, and the anticipated economic prospects over the investment life of the proposed project. Next in importance are the number, quality, and composition of the population. Available census data for the area are generally quoted, and comparative growth is analyzed in relation to that of the region, the state, and the nation as a whole. Of further interest is historical employment data, for at least the past decade, as to number by job categories and percentage charges both plus and minus over the period under study for the community compared with these job categories for the state and the nation.

Neighborhood and site data are next in order for discussion and analysis. It is helpful to submit an area photograph from which the relative position of the site, the neighborhood, and surrounding street and traffic patterns can qualitatively be studied. A word picture concerning geographic and existing neighborhood service facilities should be drawn. Items such as elevation, drainage, soil characteristics, trees and vegetation, road patterns, service utilities, nearness of churches, schools, and shopping facilities are important in judging the merits of the venture proposal. Site and soil characteristics as well as street and traffic floor patterns are especially important where the improvements are to be high rise or densely populated.

Project development and construction details should include a floor and site plan of the proposed improvements and a description of specification details that cover the quality of design and construction features. Items of general interest for an apartment project include the following: number of bedrooms and bathrooms, size of living room, number of square feet of enclosed living area, heating, air conditioning, washer, dryer, disposal, dishwasher, stove, refrigerator, telephone, TV outlets, wall-to-wall carpet, and other features. Where the project includes recreational facilities information should be given concerning the number and location of such facilities. Last, but by no means of least importance, are access roads, driveways, and tenant and guest parking facilities.

The financial section of the report should contain the projected rent roll and where possible a rent schedule comparison with like projects in support of the feasibility of the proposed undertaking. Schedules normally included in this section of the project study are similar to those shown in Tables 14-1 to 14-5 inclusive.

Real estate investment securities

The opportunity for mortgage investors to realize high interest yields and to participate in inflation generated equity returns has popularized real estate as a mode of investment and has led to a significant increase in real estate syndication and the formation of hundreds of real estate trusts. The latter were in great demand after the passage of the Real Estate Investment Trust Act that became law on January 1, 1961. Under provision of this act, REITs were exempted from taxes at corporate rates on net income distributed to their shareholders where the trust complied with provisions of the trust law and regulations governing same adopted by the Internal Revenue Service on April 24, 1962 (see Chapter 4, page 63).

The big lure of syndication—which involves the breaking up of large single investments into small pieces—is the ability of the syndicator to provide small investors, generally under limited partnership arrangements, with tax-sheltered income and highly leveraged capital gains. Syndicates, too, are as a rule less tightly regulated, especially those engaged solely in intrastate operations and thus exempt from Securities and Exchange Commission registration. The popularity of syndicates was and continues to be enhanced by promotional seminars held under the auspices of professional syndicators. These seminars are designed to tout the investment advantages of real estate as compared with corporate stocks, bonds, and like securities. The most active market for syndicate operations continues to be in the Golden West where extraordinary population growth has kept real estate values rising. In California alone hundreds of sizable syndicating companies are in existence, and almost every good-sized real estate concern in that state has taken an interest in this profitable form of diversified investment ownership.

Real estate trusts, during the last decade, have grown to be giant investment corporations, and hundreds of such trusts are traded currently on major stock exchanges. The provisions of the 1970 Housing Act will further broaden and strengthen investment trust opportunities. To illustrate, the new mortgage-backed security program, authorized for operation by Ginnie Mae (see Chapter 15 for explanation of Ginnie Mae and Fannie Mae) will make available high-yielding securities backed by pools of FHA and VA mortgages that bear the full faith and credit of the United States government. The medium for capital investment will take the form of two types of securities:

1. The *bond-type security* will be backed by pools of mortgages held as collateral. These securities will yield, until repayment on date of maturity, an interest rate that varied in 1970 from 7.5 to 8.5 percent return, paid semiannually.

2. The *pass-through security* differs from the bond-type security in that interest and principal from the pooled mortgages are paid and "passed through" each month to investors. Investors are guaranteed a minimum yield on these securities whether or not there are delinquencies on the underlying mortgages, since the latter are insured or guaranteed as to principal by the United States government.

Investments of this nature, issued by private investment corporations but subsidized by government agencies, are also aimed at tapping the resources of huge unused pension funds. In turn the proceeds from these securities are hopefully expected to provide the financial stimulus under which the housing industry is to be spurred on to fulfill the goal of supplying 2.5 million housing units per year during the decade ahead.

READING AND STUDY REFERENCES

1. ELLWOOD, L. W., "Influence of the Available Mortgage on Value," *The Appraisal Journal* (October 1949), pp. 446–53.
2. HAYES, SAMUEL L., and HARLAN, LEONARD M., "Real Estate as a Corporate Investment," *The Appraisal Journal* (July 1968), pp. 361–82.
3. KAHN, SANDERS A., CASE, FREDERICK E., and SCHIMMEL, ALFRED, *Real Estate Appraisal and Investment*, Chapters 24, 25 and 26. New York: The Ronald Press Company, 1963.
4. RATCLIFF, RICHARD U., *Real Estate Analysis*, Chapter 6. New York: McGraw-Hill Book Company, 1961.
5. RING, ALFRED A., *Questions and Problems in Real Estate Principles and Practices* (rev. ed.), Chapter 14. Englewood Cliffs, N.J.: Prentice-Hall, Inc., 1972.
6. RING, ALFRED A., *The Valuation of Real Estate* (2nd ed.), Chapter 21. Englewood Cliffs, N.J.: Prentice-Hall, Inc., 1970.

7. SOELBERG, PEER, and STEFANICK, NORBERT, "Impact of the Proposed Tax Reform Bill on Real Estate Investments," *The Appraisal Journal* (April 1970), pp. 188–211.

8. SPRING, CHARLES E., "Imaginative Financing Needed More Than Ever," *Real Estate Today*, III, No. 4 (October 1940), 7–12.

9. WENDT, PAUL F., and CERF, ALAN R., *Real Estate Investment Analysis and Taxation*, Chapters 1, 5, 6, and 7. New York: McGraw-Hill Book Company, 1968.

15

THE MORTGAGE MARKET

Kinds of mortgage markets

Broadly speaking, mortgage markets are classified as *primary markets* and *secondary markets*. The primary market is made up of lenders who supply funds directly to borrowers, bear the risks associated with long-term financing, and who, as a rule, hold the mortgage until the debt obligation is discharged. The secondary market is composed of lenders who seek an outlet (employment) for their funds, but who are neither equipped nor willing to originate or service the mortgage debts. These lenders merely buy mortgages as long-term or temporary investments in competition with other types of securities, such as government or corporate bonds. Agencies that purchase mortgages for resale or lend against them as a collateral security are also active in the secondary market as will be more fully explained below. Primary and secondary market operations are not as clear-cut as the above explanation would lead one to believe. Many lenders act in a dual capacity, as primary market lenders to the limit of their own funds for investment and as originators, service agents, and assignors of mortgages for which they find a profitable demand in the secondary mortgage market.

The role of lenders

An adequate supply of funds at reasonable rates of interest is largely responsible for the significant growth in the total housing supply that took place after World War II. Although home mortgage credit, to an ever-increasing extent, is underwritten (insured) or guaranteed by governmental agencies, nearly all direct financing is supplied by private lenders.

The sources for credit are many. Each source has it peculiarities which may be caused by state or federal laws, or by internal organizational rules of the lending institutions which forbid mortgage lending in excess of certain amounts or in certain geographical areas. Private sources of credit are supplied by two principal lending groups: (1) individual lenders and (2) institutional lenders.

Individual lenders

Individual (private) lenders formerly accounted for the largest part of funds outstanding on mortgage loans. Although at the present time individual lenders account for less than one-ninth of the total mortgage debt, they still are important as a source of prime mortgage funds and are by far the largest source for junior mortgage loans. Funds supplied by individual lenders include those loaned by trustees of individual trusts, estates, endowment, pension, or corporate funds and those made available by fraternal and similar nonprofit organizations who seek investment outlets for their surplus funds.

As a rule, the individual lender cannot compete with the institutions in securing prime mortgage loans. Because of the benefits arising from large scale operations, institutions can supply funds at lower costs and hence lower interest rates than those that the individual can afford to offer. It is true that the lending requirements of the institutions are more stringent than those that govern the individual, but institutions, on the other hand, are less apt to be compelled to take advantage of a borrower's adverse condition during times of economic stress.

Institutional lenders

Increasing interest by state and federal agencies in home construction and liberalization of home mortgage lending policies have sparked institutional lenders to assume a leading role in home mortgage financing. The institutions whose lending practices and policies exert the greatest influence on the mortgage market include the following:

1. Savings and loan associations
2. Life insurance companies
3. Commercial banks
4. Mutual savings banks
5. Mortgage companies

The changing pattern in the percentage distribution of the total mortgage debt on one- to four-family nonfarm homes among the principal mortgage lenders from the end of 1950 to the end of 1968 is depicted in Chart 15-1. The total dollar debt on nonfarm homes, including multifamily properties, exceeded $300 billion in 1970.

CHART 15-1

MORTGAGE LOANS OUTSTANDING ON ONE- TO FOUR-FAMILY NONFARM HOMES, BY TYPE OF LENDER, YEAR-END 1950 AND 1968.[1]

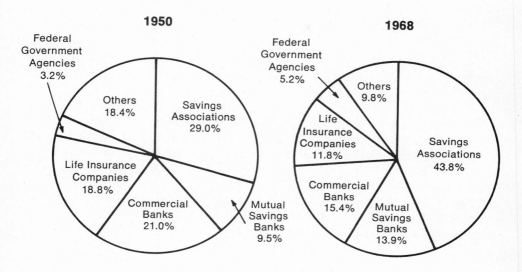

Source: Federal Home Loan Bank Board.

Since all lending institutions are subject to rules and regulations that govern the use of their funds for mortgage loan purposes, a summary of the practices and procedures that are peculiar to each may prove of interest.

Savings and loan associations. Among institutional lenders, savings and loan associations account for the greatest share of the home loan mortgage market. Although savings and loan associations have been active for over one hundred years, regulations that govern their loan activities on a regional and national scale did not go into effect until 1932 when Congress created the Federal Home Loan Bank System. Today all federally chartered savings and loan associations, and most state chartered associations that can qualify, are members of the Federal Home Loan Bank System and subject to its supervision. Membership in the FHLB permits borrowing by the association from a district home loan bank whenever funds are needed to pay off the share accounts of withdrawing members or to finance additional mortgage loans.

Most savings and loan associations, too, if qualified, have joined the Federal Savings and Loan Insurance Corporation (authorized by Congress in 1934) under which membership deposits are federally insured up to

---

[1]"The Savings & Loan Fact Book," United States Savings & Loan League (Washington, D. C., 1969), p. 38.

$20,000. This insurance, together with uniform lending policy and accounting supervision, has greatly increased public confidence in savings and loan institutions and brought about a considerable increase in their total assets and outstanding mortgage loans.

Under FHLB regulations, savings and loan associations may make home mortgage loans, other than FHA and GI loans, up to 90 percent of the appraised value of the home offered as security, provided the loan is to be amortized on a monthly basis over a period of thirty years or less and provided the loan does not exceed $35,000. Loans up to $45,000 are permissible provided the loan-to-value ratio on conventional loans does not exceed 80 percent. "Second" mortgage liens under FHLB regulations are permissible. Conventional loans, too, are restricted to an area of one hundred miles from the home office. However, participation purchases in conventional loans secured by other savings and loan associations may be made beyond the hundred-mile limit provided participation ownership does not exceed 50 percent in any one mortgage and the aggregate of all participation mortgages does not exceed 20 percent of association assets. This enables the channeling of funds from areas of low housing and mortgage demand to areas of high demand. Loans in excess of $45,000 and beyond the hundred-mile limit may be made on homes and on income-producing property, provided such loans do not exceed one of the following: one-half of 1 percent of associations' total outstanding loans, $250,000, or limits imposed by state regulations. Straight loans (unamortized) may be made for periods not exceeding five years provided the loan does not exceed 50 percent of appraised value. If the loan period is three years, the loan-to-value ratio of unamortized loans may be increased to 60 percent. Unamortized loans for periods up to one and a half years may be made up to 80 percent of appraised value.

Veterans Administration guaranteed loans can be purchased by savings and loan associations without restriction to the hundred-mile loan limits, provided the guarantee is applicable to at least 20 percent of the mortgage loan. FHA loans may be made up to a distance of one hundred miles from the home office and may be purchased on homes beyond this limit provided the mortgage is serviced by an insured association in an area in which the security is located. All loans in excess of $45,000, those on business properties, and those located beyond the hundred-mile home office limit (Veterans Administration and FHA included) cannot exceed 20 percent of total assets, this limit being set by FHLB loan regulations. Within this 20 percent asset rule, too, fall loans for property improvements. Such loans cannot be made for more than five years and are limited to $5,000 with a maturity not exceeding eight years.

Life insurance companies. Prior to 1965, life insurance companies ranked next to savings and loan associations in importance. Since 1965, and undoubtedly because of continued and deep inroads of inflation and the resultant erosion of the purchasing power of the dollar as shown in

CHART 15-2

DECLINE IN THE PURCHASING POWER OF THE DOLLAR

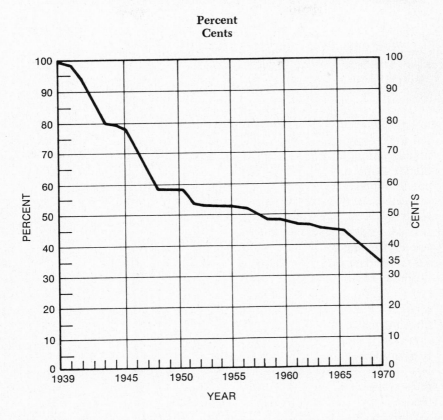

Percent
Cents

Chart 15-2, insurance companies have steadily, if not wholly in some instances, withdrawn from mortgage lending on individual residences. As noted with real estate investments, life insurance companies are currently interested not only in exacting the maximum possible interest return on their mortgage loans but also in seeking a part of the equity (action) returns and especially that share of increasing gross or net income ascribable to inflationary causes. In the overall field of mortgage financing, including multifamily residential structures (see Chart 15-3), life insurance companies rank first among the institutional lenders. The long-term nature of life insurance company assets, and the ability of actuaries to forecast the dollar amounts required in cash annually, make real estate mortgages, particularly amortizing mortgages, ideally suited as an investment medium for life insurance company funds. The increasing importance of life insurance companies as investors in real estate mortgages can best be judged by the volume of their mortgagee holdings which increased from approximately $6

CHART 15-3

MULTIFAMILY RESIDENTIAL LOANS OUTSTANDING
BY TYPE OF LENDER, YEAR-END 1968

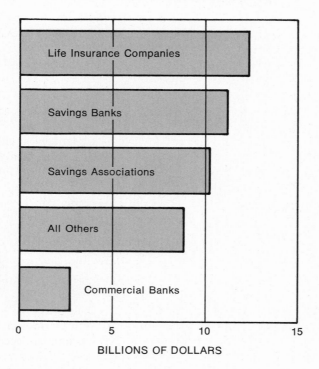

BILLIONS OF DOLLARS

Source: Federal Reserve Board.

billion in 1940 to $16 billion in 1950, $42 billion in 1960, and to $70 billion in 1968. This represents an increase in mortgage loan investment of 1,067 percent in the twenty-eight year span. All indications point to a continued growth of life insurance companies' assets and a further significant expansion of their mortgage loan investments.

Most of the larger insurance companies have expanded their mortgage loan operations on a national scale. Some of the insurance companies have tied their mortgage loans to life insurance plans (at low interest charges), but most others seek mortgage loan investments as an outlet for surplus funds at interest rates averaging 8 to 9 percent. These loans are made either through branch insurance offices located in the various states or through loan correspondent brokers who process the loan applications and generally service these mortgage loans at a rate averaging one-half of 1 percent of the mortgage debt balance. Relaxation of state insurance company regulations, which permit a greater number of insurance companies to invest in out-of-state securities, caused insurance companies to play an important role in secondary mortgage market operations also. Insurance companies generally lend up to two-thirds of the appraised value of the security and over periods not exceeding thirty years, provided loans are amortized. FHA and GI mortgages are accepted at government regulated loan-to-value ratios and at the legal rate of interest where such prove profitable to the lending companies.

Commercial banks. Mortgage lending policies of commercial banks differ widely, depending on the size of bank operations and community financial needs. In active and growing communities, commercial banks find it more profitable to seek and meet the short-term financial needs of local business firms. Commercial banks, too, as compared with other institutional lenders, are required by law to maintain their assets on a relatively liquid basis to meet withdrawal requests by their depositors. All national banks and most state banks cannot make loans in excess of 75 percent of their time or savings deposits, or of their combined capital and surplus,[2] whichever is the greater. Loans generally are restricted to 70 percent of the appraised value of improved real estate, and loan maturity cannot exceed ten years unless at least 40 percent of the loan is repaid in that time. Amortized loans may be made up to 80 percent of appraised value and may extend over twenty-five years provided the loan is fully amortized over the loan period. FHA insured and GI guaranteed loans are accepted at government allowed loan-to-value ratios and loan periods, provided bank operations make the extension of such loans feasible and profitable.

As a rule commercial banks are principally concerned with the financial needs and welfare of the local community. Greater emphasis, too, is placed on the integrity and financial condition of the borrower to assure loan repayment without recourse to foreclosure, which may impair community goodwill and adversely affect the bank's public relations. Although commercial banks among all lending institutions control the largest percentage of total U.S. savings, their role in mortgage lending, in relation to their total assets, will remain a secondary function. It is essential that commercial banks maintain a high degree of liquidity to meet withdrawal requests of their depositors and to finance the short-term commercial needs of the community.

Mutual savings banks. The influence of mutual savings banks in the field of mortgage financing is felt principally in the seventeen northeastern states in which these banks are organized. The majority of mutual savings banks are located in New York and Massachusetts where approximately 75 percent of total savings bank assets are concentrated. Mutual savings banks by law (except in Delaware and Maryland) are restricted to invest-

---

[2]Government or state insured or guaranteed loans are not subject to loan-deposit ratio limitations as stated above.

ing their funds in home states or adjoining states. Since 1950, however, all savings banks have been freed of the geographical loan restrictions in regard to purchase of FHA insured and GI guaranteed mortgage loans.

Since mutual savings banks are primarily organized to promote and encourage thrift, savings deposits generally are less subject to withdrawal and are thus well suited for mortgage loan investment. Historically, savings banks preferred unamortized (term) mortgages of three to five years duration which, in practice, however, were almost automatically renewed for additional three- to five-year periods, or in some instances allowed to continue unextended. The depression of 1930–35 caused great mortgage investment losses to the savings banks, and since that time amortization of mortgage loans is the rule rather than the exception. In most states where savings banks operate, laws restrict loans to 66⅔ to 80 percent of appraised value of the improved real estate, although in a few states conventional loans may be made up to 90' percent of value under certain conditions and restrictions. Loans generally are amortized over periods not exceeding twenty-five years.

Mortgage companies. The liberalization of investment laws permitting insurance companies and banks in one state to acquire mortgage loans made in other states (particularly if such mortgages are FHA insured or GI guaranteed) created a need for financial middlemen who would initiate mortgage loans and service them for the investing companies. Many real estate firms found their related business operations well suited to fill this financial brokerage service and entered the mortgage lending field as independent mortgage companies or as loan correspondents for life insurance firms, banks, or other institutional investors.

In many states, the operations of mortgage firms reached sizable proportions, especially in areas of the South and West where dependence on out-of-state funds is greatest. A mortgage market study of the Jacksonville, Florida, area conducted by the Bureau of Economic and Business Research at the University of Florida indicates that two out of three recorded mortgages in principal amounts of $5,000 to $20,000 were initiated by real estate firms and brokers. The principal role of these lenders is to provide funds for brief loan periods only. Assignment records indicate that the mortgages initiated by these brokerage firms are sold directly within a month or two to buyers in the secondary market.

Mortgage companies generally retain the right to service the mortgages that they initiate. A servicing fee of one-half of 1 percent of the outstanding debt balances is generally paid by the investment purchaser to the servicing firm. Thus, an outstanding mortgage balance of $10,000 yields $50 per annum, and this sum must cover not only the ledger and filing costs but also the mailing of monthly statements, follow-up correspondence, costs due to delinquent payments, and general overhead and office management expenses. Only by servicing a great volume of mortgages can mortgage loan service operations prove profitable. This fact results in competition for large "blocks" of mortgages in newly created subdivisions by those who combine the mortgage brokerage and mortgage servicing operations.

Probably the most dominant policy of these mortgage companies is to deal in mortgages that are most readily salable in the secondary market. As a result, these "temporary" lenders prefer government insured or government guaranteed mortgages, and conventional or uninsured mortgages for which they have advance purchase commitments. Generally mortgage companies restrict their conventional loans to selected residential and business risks, and to loans in price ranges most suitable to the needs of investment firms that comprise the secondary mortgage market.

The secondary mortgage market

Ever since the Great Depression in the early thirties, attempts have been made to stimulate housing and general construction activity by endowing mortgage securities with a reasonable degree of liquidity. The success of the Federal Reserve System—since 1913—in providing relative liquidity for commercial banking, and of the Home Loan Bank System—since 1932 —in providing relative liquidity for home investment loans processed by supervised savings and loan associations, encouraged proponents who sought similar mortgage reserve credit facilities through privately owned or government operated national mortgage banks. The need for reserve credit mortgage banks and the feasibility of successfully operating them have long been recognized by both government agencies and private associations who have sought to stimulate the lagging housing industry and to further the goal of constructing 25 million housing units during the 1970–80 decade. Those who successfully supported the establishment of both government-operated and privately owned but government-regulated mortgage credit banking and mortgage security exchange facilities have for many years stressed the economic need for greater liquidity of mortgage debt financing. The expressed aim of mortgage bankers and building-related industries too has been for nearly two decades to bring about the establishment of a market mechanism by which mortgage-backed bonds and notes could actively be traded in the same manner as other stock and bond securities. In support of their contention, proponents of the government-regulated secondary mortgage markets have pointed to the highly successful and stable mortgage banks that operate in other countries. The housing acts and succeeding events that brought about the establishment and development of secondary mortgage markets for government insured or guaranteed (FHA and GI) mortgages and those issued by private (conventional) banking and mortgage lending institutions will be briefly outlined and explained below.

The Federal National Mortgage Association

The first government efforts to create a secondary mortgage market which would stimulate construction and provide a market for the government insured FHA mortgages occurred in 1935 with the organization of the Reconstruction Finance Corporation Mortgage Company. Up to 1938, cumulative purchases of the RFC mortgage company were less than $80 million; operations were suspended in 1938 and the portfolio was liquidated after organization of the Federal National Mortgage Association.

Real estate by its very nature represents long-term capital investment and therefore mortgages placed on real estate as security are deemed equally nonliquid in character. Nevertheless, experience of highly successful and stable mortgage banks in other countries shows that a considerable degree of liquidity, hence marketability, can be obtained for the mortgage as an instrument of real estate financing. In view of the successful operation of European mortgage markets, Congress passed legislation, contained in Title III of the National Housing Act of 1934, under which the Federal Housing Administration was authorized to charter "national mortgage associations." Upon application, charters could be granted to private individuals or government agencies. These associations were to have the power to make or purchase certain insured or uninsured mortgages and to obtain operating funds by sale of their own notes or bonds. Since no private organization availed itself of this opportunity up to 1938, the RFC was ordered by President Roosevelt on February 7, 1938, to organize and supervise the first national mortgage association, later called the Federal National Mortgage Association, or better known as FNMA (Fannie Mae).

The announced objectives of the first national mortgage associations were three:

1. The provisions of a market for the new FHA Title II 90 percent mortgages
2. The making of loans on large-scale rental projects under Section 207 of the National Housing Act
3. The issuance of obligations of the association for purchase by individuals and institutional investors

Although the circumstances surrounding the origin of FNMA might indicate an intent to establish a permanent secondary market, it is clear in retrospect that the agency was organized as an emergency measure, the objective being to provide liquidity for government insured mortgage loans insured at high loan-to-value ratios and at relatively low rates of interest. The association in effect was to provide money for the stimulation of new construction by purchasing mortgage obligations insured up to 100 percent of loan value by another government agency. Thus the government was to occupy the dual position of insurer and lender.

More than 12 percent of all Title II loans insured by the FHA in 1938 and 1939 were purchased during the same period by FNMA. Thereafter purchases dwindled because of war economy and the cessation of new construction. By the end of 1945 only $7.4 million remained in FNMA's portfolio of aggregate purchases of $271.5 million. Mortgage purchase activity of the association remained at a low level until reorganization in 1948 under revised Title III of the National Housing Act. Under the new Title III, the association was given the power to purchase FHA loans insured under certain other sections of the Housing Act and loans guaranteed by the Veterans Administration under Sections 501, 502, and 505A of the Servicemen's Readjustment Act. Supervision of FNMA was transferred from the RFC to the Housing and Home Finance Agency in 1950, in a move designed to place all home loan activities under the direction of a single agency.

The principal criticisms levied at the policies and functions of the Federal National Mortgage Association as constituted up to 1968 may be summarized as follows:

1. Only government guaranteed and insured mortgages were eligible for purchase by FNMA, thus no liquidity whatsoever was provided for conventional mortgage securities.
2. Emphasis was on new construction and current mortgage lending. Both volume of purchases and timing of operations appeared motivated by political rather than economic considerations.
3. Most FNMA purchase activities seemed concentrated in those states where inadequate local laws made availability of mortgage funds from private and out-of-state sources too risky and thus too costly. In fact, government indirect lending at below market rates of interest in areas where economic risks normally dictate a higher interest rate constitutes a veiled subsidy which discourages rather than promotes the flow of private mortgage funds. FNMA's inability to market its huge portfolio of veterans loans, at par, as well as the lack of private funds at government "pegged" interest rates was offered, by critics, as proof of the harmful effects of the mortgage interest subsidy practice.
4. The Federal National Mortgage Association encouraged unwise lending by its failure to regulate the quality of loans and was hampered by its lack of power to reject mortgage offerings in areas where economic conditions, or antiquated laws, made mortgage loans a questionable or marginal undertaking.

Those who sought the establishment of national mortgage banks on a more permanent basis suggested that steps be taken to correct the basic weaknesses of FNMA by:

1. Broadening its activities to cover all types of mortgage loans.
2. Transferring jurisdiction to a permanent board as independent in operation as the Federal Reserve Board was intended to be.
3. Bringing mortgage operations more nearly in line with a unified national monetary policy, one guided by economic rather than political consideration.
4. Being permitted to buy and sell loans at a discount when credit conditions indicated that such purchases were in the interest of national credit policy.

To partially meet these criticisms, but principally to provide stimulus for the lagging housing industry, the Federal National Mortgage Association, under the Housing Act of 1968, was partitioned into separate and distinct corporations. One corporation continues to be called the Federal National Mortgage Association (Fannie Mae) but is now operated as a private corporation whose stock is privately held, though operations are regulated by the secretary of the Department of Housing and Urban Development. To broaden FNMA's secondary mortgage market operations, especially in the private (conventional) sector of mortgage lending, Congress under the 1970 Housing Act which President Nixon signed into law on July 24, 1970, provided the mechanism for a secondary market in "conventional" mortgages. The Emergency Home Finance Act of 1970 also allows the Federal Home Loan Bank Board to buy and sell both government-backed and conventional mortgages. For this purpose the FHLBB has created a separate corporation, the Federal Home Loan Mortgage Corporation, to operate its secondary mortgage market. Aims and procedures that will guide the operations of these government-backed secondary mortgage markets are as follows:

1. Development of standardized mortgage deed of trust and note forms that will be operative in most states.
2. Encouragement of legislation to change archaic usury and other statutes that hinder mortgage lending and impede the free flow of mortgage funds among states.
3. Conventional mortgages will be purchased in approved minimum and maximum amounts under a free market auction similar to, but conducted separately from, auctions held for purchase of government-backed (FHA and GI) mortgages.
4. The conventional auction will be conducted by telephone. To qualify, mortgage sellers will be required by FNMA to pay a participation or offering fee of one-hundredth of 1 percent of the amount of the offer. The fee will be nonrefundable. The seller will also be required, upon acceptance of the offer, to pay a nonrefundable commitment fee (good for a six-month commitment period) in the amount of three-quarters of 1 percent of the commitment amount.
5. Upon acceptance of the offer the seller must subscribe to FNMA common stock in an amount equal to a specified percentage, generally one-half of 1 percent. Upon delivery of the mortgages the seller must subscribe for an additional amount of common stock equal to one-half of 1 percent of the remaining balances of such mortgages. Servicers of FNMA mortgages, unless specifically authorized otherwise, must at all times offer sufficient shares of FNMA common stock equal to a specified percentage (currently 1 percent) of the total of the unpaid balances on all of the mortgages being serviced for FNMA.
6. The selling price of conventional mortgage loans will be adjusted to realize a given yield under the Free Market System auction. If the specified mortgage rate of interest is at or above the yield, the mortgage will be purchased at par, otherwise the purchase price will be adjusted downward to produce the bid yield and on the basis of a thirty-year mortgage to be paid off in twelve years regardless of actual terms of the loan.
7. As with FHA and GI mortgages, the conventional loans must be made to mortgagors and on properties that meet standardized credit, construction, and location standards.
8. Mortgages (conventional as well as government-backed loans) are intended to be held by FNMA until amortized as scheduled, thus providing a supply of *new* money for the home industry in addition and above the amounts that are normally generated from traditional (private) sources.

9. FNMA is authorized to buy mortgages up to a twenty-five to one debt to capital ratio. To succeed as investor owned secondary market corporations, FNMA and FHLMC must earn an overall yield on outstanding capital that will provide a profitable return to its capital investors.

Government National Mortgage Association

On the division of the Federal Mortgage Association in 1968 into two parts, the second part became known as the Government National Mortgage Association, or, for short, Ginnie Mae. GNMA as a government agency remains a division of the Department of Housing and Urban Development. It is a corporation without capital stock and is designed to handle the special assistance, management, and related financial functions of the pre-1968 FNMA, which functions remain essentially unchanged.

Ginnie Mae and Fannie Mae will also work "in tandem" for the purchase of mortgages for lower-income families. Under these working arrangements Ginnie Mae can commit itself to low-yield mortgages—at par —and then sell these mortgages to Fannie Mae at the current market rate with Ginnie Mae absorbing the price differential. Ginnie Mae's securities which are backed by pools of FHA and VA mortgages are underwritten, of course, by the full faith and credit of the United States government.

Other secondary market facilities

Standardization of mortgage loan practices brought about by Federal Housing Administration mortgage insurance regulations has, in the judgment of leading investors, given liquidity to FHA mortgages equal in many respects to that ascribed to corporate and government bonds. To illustrate, a field survey disclosed that the FHA "mortgage package" is now sold in the marketplace and transferred from mortgagee to mortgagee by means of a simple assignment placed on record at the point of inception of the mortgages.

The survey in question covered sixty mortgages which were on properties located in Hillsborough and Pinellas counties, Florida. These mortgages were processed by a commercial bank, sold, and assigned in a block or "package" to a local federal savings and loan association. These mortgages in turn were bought by another commercial bank in Florida and resold by them to a savings bank in New York State. This New York institution may in turn sell the same mortgages at nominal recording fees.

The high degree of negotiability of these mortgages and their popularity among investors are probably ascribable to the following:

1. Standardization of the product
2. Evidence of the security included in the "package" (note or bond and mortgage instrument)
3. The insurance of the mortgage and its scheduled payments by the FHA
4. The insurance of the genuineness of the title to property as evidenced by the title insurance policy which runs to the original mortgagee, its successors, and "assigns"

This survey demonstrates that FHA insured mortgages can now be traded readily as long as there is a balance due. Thus, in a direct way, real estate mortgages do compete with corporate, municipal and government bonds as an investment medium. With similar standardization and guaranty of quality of indebtedness to be injected into placement of "conventional" mortgage loans as made possible under the Housing Act of 1970 and regulations of the secondary mortgage corporations as detailed above, the relative liquidity of prime real estate loans promises to become, at long last, a reality.

The FHA home mortgage plan which made the trading in "package" or group mortgages possible may be summarized as follows:

1. The setting up of standards for home construction and sounder development of neighborhoods
2. More systematic inspection and appraisal of homes for mortgage lending purposes
3. Elimination of high financing costs by standardizing fees and by eliminating second mortgages and recurring renewal fees
4. Lower interest rates
5. Gradual repayment of mortgages through amortization
6. Greater protection to the lender through mutual mortgage insurance

Safety in mortgage lending

As has already been noted, a mortgage is a direct lien on the property covered. If the loan is not paid, the property may be sold and the proceeds applied to pay it. From the point of view of safety, the mortgage should be a *first* lien, that is, it should be prior to all other claims against the property. It is true that there are mortgages that are not first liens; they may be second mortgages or third mortgages. Usually, however, no mortgage but a first mortgage can be considered a safe investment. As an illustration, assume that a parcel of improved city realty is appraised at $25,000 and that the owner secures a first mortgage of $15,000. The property can depreciate in value about 40 percent before there is danger of loss to the holder of the mortgage. Suppose the owner places on the property a second mortgage of $5,000. If the property depreciates only 20 percent, the equity has disappeared and the holder of the second mortgage is in danger of loss. This risk is increased if the owner neglects to pay taxes and assessments and interest on the two mortgages. In the event of foreclosure, the sum of the liens may exceed the value of the property, and unless recovery can be had on the bond or note, the second mortgagee may lose part of his investment.

Dwellings, apartment houses, stores, and office buildings are classed as properties of stable values and are based on a fair appraisal; loans on them should be secure. Factories and garages are not always salable or rentable, and it is not usually wise to make too full a loan on them; the percentage of value loaned should be less. Theaters and churches are special buildings; some investors will not loan upon them at all, and others loan only a small percentage of their value. In the case of special buildings, and in fact with all property, the safety of the loan is increased if the *land* value is a large proportion of the total value. Some lenders favor loans when the land value alone equals or exceeds the amount of the loan.

Mortgage loans are sometimes made on unimproved and unproductive land. There is danger in doing this, as such land produces no income and is frequently difficult to sell. Of course, a choice plot in a large city may be an exception to this rule, but it certainly applies to land in suburban sections. Farmland of good quality is not usually unproductive land, but the loan should be based on its value as farmland and not as potential building lots.

Mortgage lending procedure

The first step in the lending process is the filing of an application by a prospective borrower. At this point, the lender should obtain information from the borrower as to the amount of the loan required, the rate of interest desired, the proposed terms of repayment, and the purpose for which the loan is secured. Should the borrower require a lower rate of interest than the institution's policy permits, no further time need be spent in processing the loan application. The same would be true with respect to the requirements of the borrower as to amortization or term. The question of use of the loan is important. It is one thing if the borrower wants the loan to pay part of the purchase price of a piece of property that he intends to put to some sound use, or to repair or rehabilitate property that he owns, or to refinance existing debts against the property; it is quite another if he desires to raise money on property that he owns for some highly speculative enterprise that may bring about his financial downfall.

The lender should obtain information also as to the financial means of the prospective borrower, including his occupation and income, his age, his existing financial obligations, and his assets, including bank accounts, stocks and bonds, and so forth. This information enables the lender to determine the financial ability of the borrower and his worth as a bondsman. It is not profitable for lenders to have to foreclose mortgages to get back the money they lend. Profitable mortgage investment requires the repayment of interest and amortization on a regular basis over the term of the loan. If a buyer is financially weak, there is danger that he will not be able to meet these requirements. The question of the borrower's credit is therefore very important.

If the mortgage appears acceptable to the lender on the basis of the application, he must then proceed to appraise carefully the property offered as security. The question of appraisal is covered in detail in another chapter. For the purpose of this chapter, it is sufficient to say that great care must be exercised in determining the worth of the physical security as well as the future of the neighborhood in which it is located. An owner may have an excellent building in a neighborhood that has a very poor future outlook. The condition of surrounding properties and the trend of an area can adversely affect a given property even though it be excellent itself. In addition, the lender should proceed to appraise the financial ability of the borrower. It would not be sound business policy to take the borrower's statement of his means at its face value. Certainly, the lender would not, without inspection and appraisal, take the borrower's word that he owned an excellent building at a given location which was in a certain state of physical repair and which produced an income of a given amount. Hence a credit investigation is made either by the lender himself or by one of the many credit agencies that operate for this purpose.

Having inspected the property and determined its value, and having weighed and established the financial capacity of the borrower, the lender is then in a position to determine how much he can safely advance and upon what terms he can advance it. It is unlikely, with respect to any loan, that the highest standards of the lender will be met from the standpoint of *all* of the factors involved. It may be that the borrower's circumstances are excellent and that the property is a good one, but that there is some likelihood of neighborhood decline beyond average. This being the case, the lender may decide to require a more rapid rate of amortization. In another case it may be found that although the borrower's credit is not as strong as it might be, the property itself and its surroundings are beyond average, or the desired amount of loan is sufficiently low to offset this particular weakness.

Where the borrower desires to avail himself of mortgage terms authorized under FHA insured or GI guaranteed loan provisions, and the lender is able and willing to make the loan under the specified terms and rates of interest, special application forms provided by the federal agencies must be submitted, together with required filing fees for independent check and loan approval by the FHA or VA, whichever is involved. Both agencies make detailed and careful field checks, applying ratings to all the physical property, the site, the location, the ability of the mortgagor to shoulder the financial obligation, and the mortgage pattern wherein all factors bearing on the quality of the loan are correlated. Based on the results of the agency's investigation, the institutional lender is authorized to process or reject the loan application; if the former, the maximum amount of the loan, the interest rate, and the loan period subject to which the federal agency commits itself to insure or guarantee the loan are considered. Should the amount of the loan and loan terms that the lending institution is able or authorized to offer be acceptable, the next step involves the closing of the loan.

Truth-in-lending laws. Prior to closing and during the negotiations for the placement of the mortgage loan, it is important that the mortgage lender (creditor) act in full compliance with the truth-in-lending law. This law became effective on July 1, 1969, and was enacted to protect purchasers or occupants of homes who pledge their real property as security for the indebtedness. Since this is a "consumer" law, the provisions of this statute do not apply to business, industrial, or commercial transactions.

Essentially the law provides for "disclosure" of the "true annual interest rate" on the loan. Thus where finance, mortgage, brokerage, or placement charges are discounted and are subtracted from the face of the loan or added in the form of higher periodic payments over the loan period, the borrower must be informed fully as to the effect of such charges on the actual, or true, rate of interest that the mortgage loan must bear. To illustrate, if a lending institution charges a two-point (2 percent) mortgage placement fee and subtracts this charge from the face of the loan, the effect of such a charge is to increase the true rate of interest. Let us assume that the loan request is for $10,000 and the "nominal," or coupon, rate of interest is 7½ percent. If the loan is to be repaid monthly over twenty-five years, the periodic payment including interest and principal is $73.90. However, if the service charge of 2 percent, or $200, is subtracted and the net loan amount is thus $9,800 instead of $10,000, the true interest rate is 7¾ percent and not 7½ percent as stated on the face of the note or mortgage. In cases involving improvement loans where interest at a stipulated rate is charged on the original amount of the loan rather than on the remaining periodic balances of the amortized loan, the "true" interest could readily be double the "stated" rate where the loan extends over a period of three years or more.

Disclosure requirements under the truth-in-lending law are as follows:

1. All mortgages must state the "true," or effective, annual interest rate on the loan.
2. All mortgages—except first mortgages made for construction or purchase of a home—must state the total dollar amount of interest to be paid over the loan period.
3. Amounts of default, delinquency, or similar charges must be disclosed.
4. Property encumbered as security for the debt must be described in detail.
5. Amounts charged, or penalties imposed, for prepayment of indebtedness must be explained.
6. All finance charges must be itemized.
7. A borrower must have the right—generally within three days—to cancel any credit transaction and to request repayment of deposits, earnest money, etc., without penalty. This right of *rescission* of the loan contract does not extend to purchase money mortgages or those contracted for the financing of new home construction.

Failure to comply with the truth-in-lending law subjects the lender to civil penalties ranging from a minimum of one hundred dollars to a maximum of one thousand dollars plus court costs and attorneys' fees, if the debtor wins the lawsuit. The debtor, however, even if he wins an award in court, must still repay the mortgage debt, including the agreed-upon finance charges. The following items on first and junior mortgages, however, need not be included in figuring the finance charges:

a. Costs of abstract or title insurance
b. Fees for preparation of documents
c. Escrow payments for taxes, insurance, etc.
d. Notarization fees, appraisal fees, and credit report charges

Closing of the loan

In placing funds in a first mortgage, the lender should satisfy himself that the mortgage is a valid lien; that is, that it is made and executed by the owner or owners of the fee simple, that they have a legal right to mortgage the property, that all other rights have been released or subordinated, and that it is superior to all other liens on the property. It is usually necessary to see that there are no encroachments or other defects affecting the marketability of the title and that no restrictions have been violated or adversely affect its value. These things can be determined only upon an examination of title by a competent attorney or a title company, or by a certificate of registration under the Torrens law. An accurate survey should always be obtained with the examination of title.

After these investigations have been completed, the loan is then "closed." At the time of closing, which follows the procedure described in Chapter 12, the borrower signs two instruments. One is a mortgage that pledges the property to the lender for the amount of the loan, the other is a bond or note by which the borrower personally promises payment of the loan and interest as specified in the repayment clause of the mortgage instrument. The bond or note and mortgage are vital documents and are discussed at length in Chapter 8. One of the important provisions of the mortgage should be that the borrower will at all times maintain adequate fire and hazard insurance. The amount of the fire insurance should be equal to the replacement value of any physical improvements upon the property. The mortgage states further the specific terms of the agreement under which the money is advanced and defines the rights and remedies of both parties. It is necessary that the mortgage be recorded in the official records of the county in which the property is located. Failure to do this may create serious complications.

Setting up the loan for supervision

Adequate records are essential to the proper handling of mortgage investments. There are six basic records that should be set up when the loan is made. The creation of these records serves to put the mortgage on the lender's books. They are:

1. Mortgage card
2. Tax card
3. Mortgage document file
4. General correspondence file
5. Inspection and appraisal form
6. Insurance record

Mortgage card. The mortgage card is the accounting record of the amount loaned and the terms upon which it is loaned including interest and amortization. It should include the number assigned to the particular investment, the location of the property, the owner's name and mailing address, the rate of interest and amortization, the maturity date, the due dates of payments, and the original amount of the mortgage as well as its balance as reduced from time to time. Some lenders may include additional information on this record, but the data described above are those generally and basically used. Periodic bills for amounts due are prepared from this record and sent to the borrower.

Tax card. This record should contain the particular number designating the loan, and the location of the property by diagram description and by the technical method of designating the real estate used by the taxing authority. Usually properties are designated according to tax maps, or, in thickly populated localities, by a particular section, block, and lot number. This card is used for periodic searches of the tax records for determining whether the borrower has paid taxes levied against the property. Such taxes are a lien prior to the mortgage, and the lender must therefore be concerned with their prompt payment.

Mortgage document file. This file should contain the original documents used in creating the loan. These usually include the note and the mortgage, a survey of the property, and the title search, as well as the lender's original approval of the mortgage. The importance of this record is apparent. It contains the basic written agreement between the borrower and the lender, and its possession is essential in establishing the claims of the lender should default occur or controversy arise.

Correspondence file. At the inception of the loan this file would contain little more than the original application of the loan and whatever correspondence or memoranda may have developed in connection with negotiations and ultimate closing. It is in this file that all subsequent correspondence, memoranda, copies of credit reports, and so on, are placed in chronological order so that they are available for reference and study should the need arise at any future date.

Inspection and appraisal form. This form is one that is not set up at the time the loan is placed on the lender's books, since it was previously developed in connection with the consideration of the application and the final decision of the lender as to the loan that is finally made. This record provides specific data as to the type of property, location, value of land and building, neighborhood trend, rental income, and a multitude of other important items of information bearing upon the property itself. It is basic and essential to future supervision of any particular investment. The results of subsequent appraisals and inspections are noted on this form.

Insurance record. Insurance is an essential requirement of any mortgage loan on improved real estate. It is most important that the lender have a record of the insurance carried on the property and of the expiration date of such insurance so that he may undertake to assure himself that it is continued in force. This record usually contains, in addition to the loan number and location of the property, information as to the name of the insurance company and agent, policy numbers, and their amounts and expiration dates.

Supervision of the loan

The value of real estate is not a permanent or static condition. Many forces come into play that either adversely or beneficially affect value. Examples of adverse forces would be obsolescence, lack of adequate maintenance, and neighborhood changes as a result of influx of undesirable elements. The lender has no assurance therefore that the quality of his security will remain the same during the life of the loan. The factors that constitute sound borrower's credit may also change. In a period of depression, owners' incomes may decline or cease. Death of a wage earner may cause financial embarrassment. Beyond the question of financial ability, the owner's attitude toward a piece of property may change detrimentally. Should the neighborhood become less desirable with the passing of time, his original pride in his home may cease, and as a result he may not maintain it to the same extent that he would have otherwise. These are a few of the factors that make necessary diligent, constant, and well-informed attention to every loan. The remainder of this chapter will be devoted to a discussion of the procedures and policies that should strictly be adhered to throughout the life of a mortgage.

Adequate controls providing for billing, tax searches, reinspection and appraisal, and renewal of insurance must be established. In addition, a control must be set up that will bring to the attention of the supervisor the expiration of particular loans, so that proper consideration may be given to the lender's policy with respect to renewal or termination at maturity. The above are the routine periodic functions that should be performed with respect to each loan. The fact that they are routine is no justification for an assumption that they are not important. They are as important to the administration of the mortgage portfolio as breathing is to sustain life.

So long as the borrower pays his obligations promptly and subsequent inspection and appraisal of the property indicate a satisfactory situation as to physical condition, neighborhood trend, and value, the investment may be considered satisfactory and no further action need be taken with respect to it. This will not always be the case. There will be instances in which the borrower fails to pay taxes, interest, or amortization as due, and there will be other instances in which reinspection and reappraisal will indicate a condition that affects the security of the loan and for which a remedy must be sought.

Default must be cured by either an immediate payment or an acceptable arrangement for its liquidation over a period of time. When default occurs, the supervisor is placed in the position of a physician, who is required to treat the illness of a patient. The skill with which he handles this condition will, to a large degree, be the determining factor in restoring the investment to good health. Many loans that appear hopelessly delinquent are revived and caught up simply by a friendly, intelligent, and cooperative gesture on the part of the supervisor. A large part of the success of the mortgage-handling policy of a lender depends on the methods employed.

The first thing a physician must do in determining proper treatment in a given case is to obtain all the data relative to it. This he does by consulting the patient's previous record and obtaining all possible current information from him. The same method is applicable to the treatment of mortgage defaults. It is only after the supervisor has completely familiarized himself with a given case that he can determine and recommend specific action. The attitude of "pay or else" has long since proved itself to be a short-sighted and harmful policy. There are many cases in which the continuance of an honest mortgagor in ownership over a period of years on a basis that may be less than the strict terms of the mortgage is preferable to the immediate acquisition of the property and sale at a time when the market is such that loss is almost certain. This need not happen if the borrower is allowed an opportunity to get back on his feet on the basis of a program that will enable him to make good his obligation to the lender. Carefully trained, experienced, and well-informed supervision is essential to the proper handling of mortgage problems other than those of a routine clerical nature. The supervisor must know when to be firm and when to be flexible, as well as the limits of such flexibility as they apply to individual cases. His knowledge of a particular case is obtained from the records discussed previously in this chapter.

When reinspection and reappraisal indicate an adverse condition, immediate steps must be taken to cure it. Should the report indicate that value is declining because of neighborhood trend, the lender has no cause for action against the borrower, inasmuch as he does not control this condition. In such an instance, it is necessary for the lender to persuade the borrower to increase his amortization to an extent sufficient to bring the loan down to within a safe percentage of the reduced value. If the mortgage has not matured, the lender must depend entirely upon his persuasive powers or upon some concession in the interest rate in order to induce the borrower to meet his requirements. If the mortgage has matured, he can, of course, demand repayment of the loan in whole or in part as he sees fit. Should reinspection indicate that the owner is improperly maintaining the property, then the lender may proceed on the basis outlined above or he may make a demand for proper repairs in the event the mortgage gives him the right to do so.

Circumstances may indicate that fire insurance previously considered adequate should be increased. Again, this is a function that the lender must not overlook. Should a serious fire occur, lack of adequate insurance may impair the physical security. In New York State, the mortgagee has the right to apply the proceeds of an insurance loss in whole or in part to the reduction of the mortgage debt or to the borrower upon the satisfactory completion of adequate repairs of the damage.

When all reasonable efforts of the lender to cure default by means of negotiation fail, he has several alternatives. One of them is to acquire the property by foreclosure and to sell it. Another is to acquire the property by deed from the borrower. This is a less-expensive procedure than fore-closure, even though it may be necessary to give the borrower some pay-ment. It can be done only when a search indicates that good title can be acquired without foreclosure. If, in the lender's judgment, the financial con-dition of the bondsman justifies it, he can sue for the amount in default. This last right has been restricted by some states. Some mortgages provide that with respect to income-producing properties, the mortgagee shall have the right to enter upon the premises and to collect the rents either during foreclosure or until such time as the defaults are removed.

Servicing of the loan

Many lending institutions service not only loans to which their own funds are committed but also loans that were sold in the market to others, frequently out-of-state investors. Great care must be taken to maintain ac-curate and complete mortgage loan service records, for some secondary mortgage market investors retain the right—FNMA for instance—to trans-fer the servicing function of mortgages that they acquire to other institu-tions. Poorly maintained or incomplete mortgage file records may possibly cause embarrassing or even costly litigation.

Many lending institutions, particularly banks, seek to develop a large and active mortgage production and servicing department, not only because of the direct monetary benefits that result from large-scale operation but also because of the many indirect benefits that affect favorably the princi-pal or banking operations of the institution. For instance, valuable adver-tising benefits are secured from the millions of homeowners that are con-tacted periodically by the mortgage servicing department. Other benefits flow from the use of escrow funds and clearing balances in connection with the mortgage accounts, plus the goodwill and advertising value arising through dealings with materialmen, contractors, real estate and insurance offices, tax assessing and collection agencies, FHA field men, municipal authorities, chambers of commerce, and other agencies.

As borne out by experience and supported by experienced accountants and mortgage men, a bank or mortgage company can service from five hundred to seven hundred mortgage accounts by manual operation. At this point of mortgage service development it becomes necessary and economi-cal to mechanize. Posting up to five thousand or even seven thousand mortgage accounts can be handled adequately and economically by ma-chines similar to those manufactured by the Burroughs or National Cash Register companies. Servicing in excess of seven thousand accounts may necessitate conversion to even more mechanized posting such as the IBM punch card system or electronic computers developed by the International Business Machines Corporation. Conversions to mechanized mortgage loan servicing is a slow and expensive process, but experience has shown that substantial economies result as machines are utilized to their fullest advan-tage and as personnel are relieved of the slow manual routine details of processing payments.

Specific loan servicing functions may vary with the size of the mortgage banking institution or with organizational practices, but essentially a servicing department is composed of the following personnel: (1) cashier, (2) bookkeeper, (3) report clerk, (4) delinquency clerk, and (5) insurance clerk.

The *cashier* receives the mortgagor's remittance, pulls the cashier card, and journalizes the remittance. Payments are then deposited to a clearing account and the entries are balanced. The cashier card is then sent to the bookkeeper as authority and guide for further entries. Remittances that appear incorrect are sent to the delinquency clerk.

The *bookkeeper* receives the cashier cards and sorts them by names of mortgagees. He then posts the cashier card and simultaneously journalizes the breakdown of payment. Specifically, the bookkeeper posts escrow amounts, deposits escrow funds, deposits interest and principal to custodial account, and draws debt against the clearing accounts for total of above. Work is then balanced. The bookkeeper also mails receipts for mortgage payments upon request.

The *report clerk* receives the cashier card from the bookkeeper and prepares the report for mortgagees. He then computes service fees and summarizes the report. The report clerk then prepares the remittance check to each mortgagee and returns cashier card for filing.

The *delinquency clerk* sends the first delinquency notice to a mortgagor about the middle of the month showing the amount of late fee. A second notice, where necessary, is sent during the last week of the month. The delinquency clerk attends also to the following functions:

1. Handles all correspondence on insufficient or bad checks
2. Sends all delinquent cards to report clerk who prepares delinquency report, if required by mortgagee
3. Makes preliminary report to FHA and VA on mortgages subject to foreclosure
4. Handles all matters pertaining to foreclosures and acts as liaison between mortgagee and local attorney

The *insurance clerk* receives and checks all insurance policies, draws voucher for premium due, and forwards the policy or a certificate of insurance to mortgagee. He orders endorsements when required and maintains maturity tickler file. Generally, policy or renewal certificates are required by the clerk thirty days prior to expiration date. If not received, insurance coverage is ordered from local agent. The insurance clerk also handles all correspondence pertaining to insurance matters, claims for any loss, endorsement of mortgagee, and claim draft and affidavit of restoration of property.

Collateral duties performed by the above or by an administrative clerk include the following:

1. Prepare list ordering tax bills.
2. Check description on tax bills, draw voucher against escrow account, and remit.

3. Prepare statements for attorneys and real estate brokers in connection with proposed transfers.
4. Arrange for personal interviews with delinquent mortgagors.
5. Make periodic property inspections for mortgagees. (Some organizations —FNMA—require annual inspections, others once every two or three years.)
6. Analyze escrow accounts to determine adequacy of monthly payment for taxes and insurance.
7. Handle prepayments, payoffs, and matters involving refinancing.

In the servicing of mortgages, the lender must also keep in mind the rights of third parties, if any. For example, a mortgage insured by the FHA must be administered under the rules and regulations of the FHA if the insurance is to be kept in force. The same is true with respect to GI mortgage loans. A thorough knowledge of the obligations in this respect is essential to the proper supervision of such loans. When there are junior participants in a mortgage, the participation agreement describes the rights and obligations of the parties. These must be carefully observed, for failure to comply with them may result in serious complications and ultimate loss. It will be seen from the above that the origination, servicing, and supervision of mortgage investments are highly technical procedures that require adequate experience, constant diligence, and strict adherence to fundamentals.

READING AND STUDY REFERENCES

1. BROWN, ROBERT K., *Real Estate Economics*, Chapter 9. Boston: Houghton Mifflin Company, 1965.
2. BRYANT, WILLIS R., *Mortgage Lending: Fundamentals and Practices*, Chapters 10 and 11. New York: McGraw-Hill Book Company, 1956.
3. FISHER, ERNEST M., *Urban Real Estate Markets: Characteristics and Financing*, Chapter 6. National Bureau of Economic Research, 1951.
4. HEBARD, EDNA L., and GERALD S. MEISEL, *Principles of Real Estate Law*, Chapter 12. New York: Simmons-Boardman Publishing Corporation, 1964.
5. HUSBAND, WILLIAM H., and FRANK RAY ANDERSON, *Real Estate*, Chapter 24. Homewood, Ill.: Richard D. Irwin, Inc., 1960.
6. MARTIN, PRESTON, *Real Estate Principles and Practices*, Chapter 10. New York: The Macmillan Company, 1956.
7. MCMICHAEL, STANLEY L., and PAUL T. O'KEEFE, *How to Finance Real Estate* (2nd ed.), Chapter 1. Englewood Cliffs, N.J.: Prentice-Hall, Inc., 1953.
8. RATCLIFF, RICHARD U., *Real Estate Analysis*, Chapter 10. New York: McGraw-Hill Book Company, 1961.
9. RING, ALFRED A., *Questions and Problems in Real Estate Principles and Practices* (rev. ed.), Chapter 12. Englewood Cliffs, N.J.: Prentice-Hall, Inc., 1972.

16

LIENS

Lien defined

In addition to the estates and chattel interests already mentioned, various rights, known as *liens*, affect the possession and ownership of realty. A lien is the right given by law to a creditor to have a debt or charge satisfied out of the property belonging to his debtor. Liens may entitle the holder (lienor) to have the realty sold whether or not the owner desires it. A lien necessarily arises from the relation of debtor and creditor, and, although the creation of that relation may have been voluntary, the enforcement is wholly free from any question of the owner's volition.

Nature of lien

The right of a creditor to have his debt satisfied has its origin, under common law, in the use of personal property. In early times, liens generally were recognized after time, efforts, or goods had been expended by laborers, mechanics, or materialmen in the repairing or financing of another individual's personal property. The right to a lien, under common law, carried with it the right to "bond" or possess the personal property until the lien was satisfied. In fact, if possession of the property was surrendered, the lien was deemed discharged, or legally lost. Indeed, in such instances, possession was more than nine-tenths of the law.

The theory of possession was so strongly entrenched under common law that even the earliest and most obvious liens on real property—those supported by mortgage debts—were not recognized as liens, unless title and possession were transferred to the lienor or creditor. This mortgage lien theory, although modified as to possession and control, is still adhered to in the mortgage "title" states, where the use of the mortgage deed is mandatory.

The lien laws affecting real property, as practiced today, have their origin in statutory provisions enacted by each state in the Union. Under these laws, liens against real property, as described below, are enforceable in one form or another, even though possession, control, or title remains with the debtor, until physical and legal disposition of the property is made by the court.

Classification of liens

Liens are of two types: specific and general. A general lien affects all the property of the debtor. A specific lien affects only a certain piece or pieces of property.

The following liens are of the specific type:

1. Mortgages
2. Taxes, assessments, and water rates
3. Mechanic's liens
4. Vendee's liens
5. Vendor's liens
6. Surety bail bond liens
7. Attachments

General liens include:

1. Judgments (state and federal)
2. Decedent's debts
3. Inheritance tax liens (state and federal)
4. Corporation franchise tax liens

SPECIFIC LIENS

Lien of mortgage

A borrower of money or one owing a debt may, for the purpose of securing payment of the amount due the lender or creditor, execute an instrument known as a mortgage. This instrument purports to transfer to the creditor the title to specific real property. Since the transfer, from the point of view of the law in most states, is merely conditional, becoming null and void upon payment of the debt, the mortgage does no more than create a specific lien on the property. Because of the importance of mortgages in the real estate business, a separate chapter has been devoted to them.

Taxes, assessments, and water rates

Taxes, assessments, and water rates levied according to law become a specific lien on the real property affected thereby. If the charges are not paid, the taxing body may take such action to enforce them as will result in the sale of the property. A fuller description of liens of this character will be found in Chapter 17.

Mechanic's liens

The mechanic's lien is purely statutory, having no origin in common law or equity. It may be defined as a security claim given by statute to those who perform labor or furnish material in the improvement of real property. Predicated on the principle of unjust enrichment, laws have been enacted by the various state legislatures recognizing the claims of materialmen and laborers against the property to which they have added value. This right to a mechanic's lien is in addition to the right or action against the person who made the contract of employment or purchase. The lien is specific, as it affects only the property benefited and is governed by the provisions of the statute under which the right is obtained. The entire subject of mechanic's liens is highly technical; the laws vary materially in the different states; and everyone dealing with alterations or improvements to real estate should secure from an attorney in his own community legal advice as to his rights and obligations. A mechanic's lien is usually asserted through the filing of a notice of the claim with the county clerk. This notice must be under oath of the lienor or his agent and must set forth the claim in detail and substantially in form as follows:

CLAIM OF LIEN

STATE OF ....
COUNTY OF ....
Before me, the undersigned authority, personally appeared ...., who being duly sworn, says that he is the lienor herein [or (agent) (attorney) of the lienor herein] .... whose address is .... and that in pursuance of a contract with ...., lienor furnished labor, services, or materials consisting of .... on the following described real property in .... County, of .... State, owned by .... of a total value of $.............................. of which there remains unpaid $.............................. and furnished the first of the same on .... 19......, and the last of the same on .... 19......, and (if the lien is claimed by one not in privity—direct contact—with the owner) that the lienor served his notice of claim to owner on .... 19......, by ....
Sworn to and subscribed before me this .... day of ...., 19...... .
....
Notary Public
My Commission expires:

In many states, in order to perfect the right to a mechanic's lien claim, the statutory regulations provide for the recording of a notice of commencement of contract work with the clerk of records and for the posting of a certified copy thereof on the premises. Such notice identifies the parties involved, the property affected, and the work to be performed. Where such constructive notice is mandatory, work, that is, the improvements described, must be commenced within a stipulated time (generally thirty days), otherwise such notice is void and of no legal consequence.

To protect the owner from false claims by subcontractors with whom the owner is factually or legally not "in privity," statutory requirements make it mandatory for such lienors to serve a notice on the owner either before commencing the furnishing of services or delivery of materials or within a specified time (thirty to forty-five days in most jurisdictions). To further safeguard the owner against claims of liens, subsequent to meeting specified contract payments, the owner, as a rule, has the right to withhold the final payment (10 percent or more of the contract price) and to require the general contractor to furnish an affidavit stating that all subcontractors, laborers, and materialmen have been paid in full. The furnishing of such affidavit is generally a prerequisite to the institution of any suit to enforce a claim of lien. Unless enforced as noted below, liens expire after a lapse of one year, unless renewed for a further period by court order. The filing of the lien gives notice of it to all dealing with the property, and it is good against all except those whose rights are prior as shown by the public records. The lien is not affected by unrecorded instruments and takes precedence over a deed or mortgage given prior to, but not recorded until after, the filing of the lien.

The right to file a mechanic's lien is given not only to the contractor dealing directly with the owner of the property but also to the subcontractors. In Massachusetts, Pennsylvania, and several other states, the owner's property can be held for materials and labor supplied by a subcontractor in accordance with the provisions of the original contract. The law imposes upon the owner the obligation of seeing that the subcontractors are being paid by the general contractor, in order to avoid liens upon his property and additional costs for the work performed. In most states the law is that the subcontractor is entitled to a lien on the property by virtue of his subrogation to the rights of the contractor-in-chief. Subcontractors under this rule can hold the owner's property only for the amount due under the main contract—the one to which the owner is a party. If, however, the main contract calls for installment payments—that is, payments at certain periods or at certain stages of the work—and the owner anticipates these payments, he may be held by subcontractors for the amount so anticipated. They can rely on his making payments only according to schedule, and he deviates therefrom at his peril. Owners may also be held for payment of work done on their property with their consent and approval, either expressed or implied, even though the contract for the work was made by some other person, such as a tenant. The owner is not liable, however, for work done by a tenant without his knowledge or consent, nor is a remainderman usually liable for work done by a life tenant, and in such cases liens cannot be enforced against the owner's or remainderman's property.

In New York State, orders on payment (assignments of money due) are often encountered in connection with building loan mortgages. Although not creating a lien when filed, they nevertheless should not be ignored. Because a mechanic's lien, subsequently filed, might be superior to all advances made after the filing of the order, the lender is wise to insist that it first be satisfied and discharged of record.

Enforcement of mechanic's lien

A mechanic's lien is enforced by foreclosure. The foreclosure is a legal action against the owner and those whose claims against the property are inferior to the lienor's. A judgment of the court in favor of the lienor orders the sale of the property by an officer of the court, the payment into court of the moneys realized at such sale, a marshaling of those claims against the property that have been affected by the foreclosure, and a payment of the claims in their proper order.

Mechanic's liens may be filed by a contractor, subcontractor, laborer, or materialman. The notice of lien must be filed during progress of the work and the furnishing of the materials or within a specified period (generally within three months) after completion of the contract, final performance of the work, or final furnishing of materials.

The right to file a lien is an important one to mechanics and materialmen. They can ascertain the ownership of the property from the public records and can also find the amount of mortgages or other liens against it. This information assists them in determining whether or not to extend credit to the owner of the property. With due care, losses through bad debts can be reduced to a minimum. Some states give greater protection to mechanic's lien claimants than others. Most states, however, follow a middle road, favoring neither the mechanic's lien claimant nor the mortgagee. In states such as Illinois, Maine, and Massachusetts, where mechanic's liens are offered the greatest protection, objections may be raised on the grounds that such stringent laws discourage building operations, especially those of a speculative kind. New buildings are often financed by means of building loan mortgages. It is reasonable to assume that mortgagees will not be attracted to the building loan market should they find that the law protects the mechanic's lienor to the mortgagee's detriment.

The filing of mechanic's liens against a building in course of construction may or may not be an indication of the inability of the owner to meet his obligations, because frequently contractors and materialmen file liens for protection against the possibility that other claims may arise during the course of construction. The important thing for all persons interested in the operation is to get the building finished. It is then capable of producing an income and is more readily salable. Building loan mortgages are advanced from time to time during construction, and in some states (New York, for example) advances made by a mortgagee before mechanic's liens are filed are prior in lien to the claims of those who performed the work and furnished the materials. Cessation of work on the building often results in a foreclosure of the building loan mortgage and a consequent loss to the contractors.

Rights of lienors and others

The construction of a new building, or the making of any other improvement to real property, causes to arise certain legal rights and duties of the parties involved. The principal parties are the owner, the contractor, and the mortgagee. All of these rights and duties are clearly defined by the statutes of the several states and should be familiar to the parties or to those who act for them. The owner (or the one in possession, ordering the work, as in the case of work done for a tenant) must see that he lives up to the provisions of the contract, especially those concerning payments, and must take notice of subcontractor's claims when legally brought to his attention. He must ascertain the provisions of law regarding any money he receives from mortgages, some laws being very specific in disposing of his duty toward such moneys. The laws of several states provide that all moneys advanced to the owner are trust funds that will be used exclusively for the payment of contractors and materialmen. The contractor, that is, the one who does the work or furnishes the material, should safeguard his rights by complying with the statute should it be necessary to file a notice of his lien. He must also recognize the rights of other lienors and the duty, or advantage it may be to him, of acting in conjunction with them for the protection of all. The law may provide that the job may be taken over and finished by the lienors, in view of the advantage of such action to all in interest. Mortgagees must exercise care that all papers in connection with their loans are properly prepared and filed, that advances are made during the course of construction in accordance with the agreement for the loan, and that careful attention is given to all actual and constructive notices of mechanic's liens. One intent of a mechanic's lien law is to compel, as far as possible, the application of mortgage money to the payment of the cost of the improvement for which it was advanced.

Discharge of mechanic's lien

A mechanic's lien in most states may be discharged or become noneffective as follows:

1. By expiration, which occurs after the lapse of a certain period of time, generally one or two years after filing, unless an action to foreclose it or an action to foreclose a mortgage on the property has been begun within that period.

2. By payment, and by a certificate or satisfaction piece executed and acknowledged by the lienor and duly filed in the county clerk's office.

3. By an order of the court vacating or canceling the lien for neglect to prosecute it. This order may be obtained by service of notice by the owner on the lienor requiring the lienor to commence an action to foreclose the lien within a specified time, not less than thirty days. The claim of the lienor may be disputed by the owner, and he may take this course in order that the claim may be tried in court, or the lien canceled. If the court or-

der is obtained, the record of the lien will be marked "Discharged by Order of the Court."

4. By filing of a bond approved by the court. The bond may be that of two or more personal sureties or of a surety company. The record of the lien is marked "Discharged by Bond," the property is freed from the lien, and the lienor has recourse to the bond.

5. By deposit of money into court. Before an action is commenced on a lien, the amount claimed with interest to date of deposit may be deposited with the county clerk. After an action has been commenced, the amount deposited shall be such a sum as in the judgment of the court will cover the amount of any judgment that may be recovered in the action. The lien is marked "Discharged by Payment."

Vendee's lien

When the seller (vendor) defaults, the purchaser (vendee) has a lien for the money paid under the contract of sale. The lien also extends to sums spent by the purchaser in improving the premises but does not include the cost of title examination. For that reason this item is often made a lien by the terms of the contract. Being an equitable lien, it is enforceable by foreclosure.

Vendor's lien

This is also an equitable lien, one of the first to be recognized by most states. It arises when the seller conveys a piece of real property to the purchaser and does not receive the entire purchase price at that time. The seller has a lien for the unpaid balance. Foreclosure is the means of enforcing the lien, but such remedy is in addition to those that the seller may have at law.

Surety bail bond lien

In some states, a recognizance or undertaking in a criminal action or proceeding is a lien on the real property described in the affidavit of justification until discharged. In order to be effective against a mortgagor, judgment creditor, or purchaser, a notice of such lien must be filed with the recording officer of the county wherein the property is situated. The certificate of discharge must be executed by the attorney general or county district attorney and likewise filed with the recording officer.

Attachments

Another form of lien on real property is the attachment, which is a statutory privilege given to a plaintiff or complainant in the courts in an action for money damages before any judgment is procured. In some states every plaintiff in every action may file an attachment against the defendant's property. Most states, however, give the plaintiff this privilege only for specific cause: generally for the nonresidence of the defendant, or his removal, or threatened removal, of property from the state, or for his obtaining credit on the basis of a false financial statement made in writing. By filing an attachment, the plaintiff in the action virtually insures himself that there will be some property out of which the judgment could be paid if the action is successful.

In order to protect the defendant, the plaintiff obtaining the writ of attachment must file a bond in writing that if the defendant wins, the plaintiff will pay all costs and damages that the defendant may suffer because of the attachment.

An attachment is filed in almost the same way as a judgment lien and has substantially the same right of priority as the judgment. It lasts until the action has been disposed of. If the plaintiff wins, the lien of attachment is discharged. If the defendant against whom the attachment lien has been filed wishes to sell his property during the pendency of the action, he may file a bond equal in amount to the plaintiff's demand, plus costs. The county clerk would then mark the attachment lien "Discharged by Bond."

GENERAL LIENS

Judgments

A judgment is the determination of the rights of parties through an action at law. It may originate in either state or federal courts. Not all judgments are money judgments, but only those that give a money award are here considered. Judgment for the payment of money, when properly docketed, become general liens on all property of the debtor. The judgment docket is the book or register kept by the county clerk in which is entered a record of all judgments of which the clerk has been furnished with a transcript. The docket is arranged alphabetically according to debtors. When a search is made for liens against a property, it is important to examine the judgment docket to see if there are any judgments against those who now own, or for a certain time prior have owned, the property.

A judgment is enforced by execution and by the sale of any property of the debtor that may be found. Execution is a writ directed to the sheriff, the executive officer of the court. This writ authorizes him to seize the debtor's property and to sell so much of it as may be required to pay the judgment plus incidental expenses. The property may be real or personal. If there is real property apparently owned by the debtor, the sheriff, after legal advertising, offers to the highest bidder all of the debtor's right, title, and interest of, in, and to the property. This interest may be substantial or it may be nominal, or even nothing at all. The buyer at such a sale ascertains this at his own risk before making a bid. What is of interest to us in this discussion is the fact that the judgment is a lien on the debtor's real property and that such property may be sold against his will by an officer of the court.

Discharge of judgment

A judgment is a lien on property. This lien attaches in some states when the judgment is rendered, in others when recorded or docketed, and in still others upon issuance of the writ of execution. The lien attaches to all land held by the defendant and remains in effect for a statutory period of time, generally about ten years after the date when the judgment is perfected.

Under certain circumstances the lien may be renewed, but we seldom find this done. If the debtor pays a judgment, he is entitled to a formal receipt called a *satisfaction piece*. This satisfaction piece is filed with the county clerk, who, upon its receipt, marks "Satisfied" against the record of the judgment on the docket. Many judgments, after being obtained in a lower court, are reversed on appeal to a higher court. Pending the appeal the debtor may file a bond, approved by the court, in order to free his property from the lien of the judgment. The judgment in such a case is marked "Suspended on Appeal." Judgments obtained in any federal court, as a rule, must be docketed in the county wherein the real estate is situated in order to effectuate the lien of the judgment thereon.

Lien of decedent's debts

The real property of a decedent passes at his death to his devisees if he leaves a will, and to his heirs at law if he dies intestate. Title to the property vests in the devisees or heirs, subject to such liens as existed at the time of the decedent's death. The property is also subject to the lien of all just debts against the estate. The debts are paid, however, out of the personal property in the estate, using first that not specifically bequeathed, then that disposed of by legacies. If all the personal property has been used up and unpaid debts remain, the decedent's real property may be sold to pay them. It is important, in taking title to property from an estate or recently owned by a deceased person, and in making loans on such property, to obtain satisfactory proof of the payment of all debts of the decedent.

State estate tax

The estate tax, in some states called the *transfer* or *inheritance tax*, and sometimes known as a *succession tax*, is a tax levied by the state upon the right to inherit from, or to take under the will of, a deceased person. It is a tax usually not upon the estate, but on the recipients. The amount of the tax is, by law, made a lien upon the property of the estate, and, until paid, the realty is subject to it as an encumbrance, and clear title cannot be given. If the tax is not paid in due time, after the death of the deceased, the state may enforce its lien, which is a general lien, by selling enough of any of the assets of the inherited estate to pay the tax.

The amount of tax is usually found as follows. The value of the interest passing to each beneficiary is appraised. The tax is computed by taking a certain percentage of the appraised value. This percentage generally increases as the value of the bequest or inheritance increases. The beneficiaries are divided into classes, immediate kin being usually taxed at a lower rate than distant relatives, and distant relatives at a lower rate than nonrelatives. Relatives are also allowed certain exemptions, which are deducted from the value of their interests before computation of the tax. In some states the tax is based on the net amount of the estate regardless, to a great extent, of who the recipients may be.

Federal estate tax

The federal estate tax is imposed upon the transfer of the net estate of the decedents. It is laid upon the transfer of the entire net estate and not upon any particular legacy, devise, or distributive share. The relationship of the beneficiary has no bearing on the amount of the tax, and the transfer is taxable even though the property escheats to the state for lack of heirs. A resident of the United States is allowed a specific exemption. Credit may be taken against the federal estate tax for the amount of any estate, inheritance, legacy, or succession taxes actually paid to any state, territory, or the District of Columbia in respect to any property included in the estate. The rate of tax is progressive. The lien of this tax attaches to all property in the estate and continues for ten years.

Corporation franchise tax

In most states every corporation is taxed annually on its franchise, or right to do business in the state. There are various methods of computing the amount of the tax. It is usually based on the amount of capital, or capital stock, or net income of the corporation. The tax is a general lien on the property of the corporation and can be enforced against it.

Conditional bill of sale

There are certain encumbrances against real property that are not true liens. One of these is the conditional bill of sale. This is an agreement for the sale of articles of personal property that are to be used in the improvement of real property, under the terms of which title to the articles sold does not pass until the purchase price has been paid. The law in most states requires that the agreement be filed in the office of the county recording officer at or before the delivery of the goods to the premises if the rights of the vendor are to be superior to subsequent interests that may arise. If so filed, it is valid against the claims of later parties having an interest in the realty, even though the articles may be affixed to the realty. Articles that are frequently the subject of these agreements are gas and electric ranges, boilers, elevators, and lighting fixtures. The agreement remains as effective notice usually for one year only unless refiled.

Other encumbrances, not true liens

Other encumbrances against real property which, although not liens, must be considered, include easements, covenants and restrictions, governmental regulations, and proceedings for their enforcement.

Easements are rights of others to have certain uses of one's property. Some examples are party driveways, party walks, the right-of-way for ingress and egress over another's land, the right to maintain windows for light and air, and the right of drainage across another's property. Several easement agreements are discussed in Chapter 11. Easements are of two kinds: the easement appurtenant and the easement in gross.

Easement appurtenant is a right acquired by the owner of one parcel of land to use the adjacent land of another for a special purpose. This type of easement always requires two parcels of land owned by different persons. The property benefited by the easement is known as the *dominant* estate, the property that is subject to the easement is known as the *servient* estate. An easement appurtenant runs with the land and the benefits pass to subsequent grantees, whether mentioned in the deed or not.

Easement in gross is the right to use the land of another without the existence or necessity of an adjacent or dominant estate. An easement in gross is a *personal* right and does not run with the land. Illustrations are easements to place billboards, signs, or rights-of-way for private or public utility installations. The owner of an easement in gross need not, and as a rule does not, own adjacent property.

Easements are created as follows: (1) *Express grant.* A formal and written agreement is drawn between the parties or owners of land. This agreement is generally recorded. (2) *Implication or necessity.* Courts will support implied reservations or easements where the intent is clear or where the easement is strictly necessary to provide access to dominant land, to support adjoining buildings, partition walls, or for party driveways. (3) *Prescription.* This right or easement is acquired by open, exclusive, and continued use over a period of time, varying from ten to twenty years, depending on applicable statutory or common state law. Prescriptive rights cannot be acquired against property of the federal or state governments or against owners who are under any kind of legal disability, such as infants or insane persons.

Easements may be extinguished by express or implied release; also by merger of the dominant and servient properties, by nonuse over the statutory period (ten to twenty years), destruction of the servient tenement, wrongful or incompatible use, or where the purpose or necessity of the easement ceases to exist.

Restrictions may arise by any one of the following methods:

1. Covenant between two or more owners by agreement, which should be recorded
2. Statement at length in the deed of each property sold by a developer
3. Declaration of the developer by an instrument made and recorded by him before he sells any properties

The last method results in considerable saving in recording charges since in each deed there is simply a reference to the declaration, instead of lengthy and repetitive restatement of title restrictions. The first method usually develops between owners of adjoining properties who, after buying, find that some restrictive plans will be mutually advantageous. The second and third methods are conceived by the developer of a parcel as a part of his plan for cutting the land into lots, putting in improvements, and enforcing uniform development and use of all lots.

The effect of restrictions is to limit the use of the property and to provide that certain things may or may not be done with it, such as specifying the character, location, and use of buildings which may be erected or maintained. Their purpose is to protect the property and the neighborhood. Where, as is usual, the restrictions are similar for the entire development, they are known as *uniform restrictions*, and each owner has the legal right to secure their observance by his neighbors who are similarly restricted.

Government regulations restricting use of property are generally contained in zoning ordinances adopted by a county or a municipality. Such regulations aim to protect property values in the public interest by limiting the character, height, and location of buildings thereafter erected, and the uses to which they may be put.

Departmental violations

The building department, tenement house department, fire and health departments, and other governmental authorities regulate the use and occupancy of buildings. Although orders issued by these departments are not liens, they should be considered in dealing with real property. Disobedience to the orders may result in an action at law against the property, including a notice of pendency of action filed in the county clerk's office and the possibility of a penalty being imposed. When a notice of pendency of action is so filed, it is considered an encumbrance that should be removed by seller unless purchaser has agreed to take subject thereto. Seller does not have to remove violations not resulting in *lis pendens* unless the contract so provides.

Priority of liens

The usual rule as to priority of liens is that they rank in the order of their filing or recording in the office of the proper officials. A mortgage recorded yesterday has precedence over one recorded today, and both are prior in lien to a mechanic's lien that may be filed tomorrow, unless by its terms the mortgage is made subordinate thereto. In many states, however, there is no priority as among mechanic's lienors, even though the liens have been filed at various times during the course of construction. As to judgments, there is an exception to the rule of priority liens: a judgment is not good against the rights of those claiming under a deed or mortgage actually delivered prior to the date of docket of the judgment, even though the deed or mortgage has not been recorded. The reason for this exception is that the recording laws protect innocent purchasers and mortgagees for value, and such, it may be presumed, are those who hold the deeds and mortgages. They parted with value when the deed or mortgage was delivered to them, and they relied upon the record title in doing so. The same would be true of a purchaser who had a contract to buy but had not yet received his deed. The creditor who secures a judgment does so regardless of what a debtor may or may not own; he asserts an existing claim in an action at law, and when he secures his judgment it becomes a lien on what the debtor actually owns at that time. It must of course be recognized that deeds and mortgages given or contracts entered into to defraud creditors may be set aside and that reference is here made only to those given in good faith for value. It must also be noted that the lien of all taxes and assessments imposed by any governmental authority is superior to every other lien regardless of the date of the lien or its recording. Of course, the relative rank of any two or more liens can be changed by agreement between the holders of them. Such a change is often effected with respect to mortgages by means of an instrument known as a *subordination agreement* (see Chapter 11).

READING AND STUDY REFERENCES

1. HEBARD, EDNA L., and GERALD S. MEISEL, *Principles of Real Estate Law*, Chapter 5. New York: Simmons-Boardman Publishing Corporation, 1964.

2. HUSBAND, WILLIAM H., and FRANK RAY ANDERSON, *Real Estate*, Chapter 8. Homewood, Ill.: Richard D. Irwin, Inc., 1960.

3. KRATOVIL, ROBERT, *Real Estate Law*, Chapters 4 and 19. Englewood Cliffs, N.J.: Prentice-Hall, Inc., 1969.

4. LUSK, HAROLD F., *Law of the Real Estate Business*, Chapter 17. Homewood, Ill.: Richard D. Irwin, Inc., 1965.

5. RING, ALFRED A., *Questions and Problems in Real Estate Principles and Practices* (rev. ed.), Chapter 14. Englewood Cliffs, N.J.: Prentice-Hall, Inc., 1972.

6. UNGER, MAURICE A., *Real Estate* (4th ed.), Chapter 9. Cincinnati: South-Western Publishing Co., 1969.

17

TAXES
AND ASSESSMENTS

The right to tax

It was pointed out in Chapter 4 that ownership of property is subject to a number of important governmental limitations, among which a state's right to levy taxes for the support of government ranks first in significance. Since the power to tax in the hand of unwise government is tantamount to the power to destroy (property values), special safeguards are provided in the Constitution and by statutory law in the various states to protect the property owner against political exploitation and possible economic confiscation. However, contrary to common belief, the power to tax is not a "necessary evil," but rather, if wisely used, the most important source of revenue upon which the strength and support of government depends and without which an owner's rights may lack necessary protection and enforcement.

Basis for taxation

Since the costs of government (to safeguard health, welfare, law and morality) are recurring, annual property tax levies are imposed to defray the expense for state and community civic services. The equitable distribution of the cost of government is ever a problem. As a basis for taxation, two broad principles are accepted as guiding. One is the *benefit received* theory and the other the *ability to pay* theory. Under the former theory, taxes are imposed in proportion to benefits derived from governmental services. This theory, although fundamentally equitable, is not applicable in practice, since those often in greatest need of community aid and support are generally least blessed with possession of worldly (property) goods and hence unable to meet their share of the public expense. For this reason the principle "to each according to his needs and from each according to his ability to pay" is guiding and accounts for the widespread use of the *ad valorem* (according to value) tax system, especially on the community and county level.

Taxes may be levied upon both real and personal property. Once levied against real property, taxes become a lien and may be enforced by the sale of the property or some interest in it. There are, of course, other forms of taxation, such as the income or sales taxes which are not direct levies upon real property.

Tax exemption

Most states allow tax exemption in whole or in part on real estate owned by certain types of persons or corporations, such as:

Property of the United States
Property of the state
Property of municipality held for public use
Property purchased with proceeds of pension, bonus, or insurance up to certain limits
Property owned by religious corporations used for religious purposes
Property used for hospital, cemetery, or educational purposes

Some states grant property tax exemptions up to stated amounts of value for owner-occupied homes under statutory *homestead laws.* Many states, too, grant property tax relief where homes are owned and occupied by widows or disabled veterans. The nature of the use of property determines whether a piece of property is in fact exempt. Requirements of statute must be strictly complied with to gain tax exemption, for such exemptions are in derogation of sovereign authority and allowed only for the encouragement of the furtherance of the activities of a function deemed socially desirable.

Full or partial tax exemption for new single or multiple dwellings or remodeled or enlarged older dwellings is granted in many localities to induce the provision of additional dwelling accommodations during times of housing shortage. Such exemption is usually limited in time, as for instance ten years, and is also carefully restricted to secure maximum dwelling space rather than other types of building construction.

Various tax levies

In large cities there is usually one annual tax levy, which provides funds for all purposes for which the city raises money. In other localities there are various tax levies, which may be all or some of the following:

1. *State tax.* The expenses of the state government are met to a large extent

by special taxes such as income taxes, inheritance taxes, corporation taxes, stock transfer taxes, and automobile taxes. If these taxes do not provide the state with sufficient funds, a direct tax is levied in some states by counties, based upon the value of the taxable property in each county.

2. *County tax.* Each county of the state raises money by taxation for the expenses of the county government and its courts, penal institutions, hospitals, care of the poor, roads, and bridges.

3. *Town tax.* Local town government provides for its needs by taxation. Frequently state, county, township, and town taxes are levied and collected at the same time.

4. *School tax.* The school tax is often a separate levy by school districts for the purpose of maintaining the public schools. The appropriation for which the tax is levied is usually voted by the taxpaying residents of the district.

5. *Highway tax.* The highway tax is usually made by highway commissioners for the upkeep and repair of the roads within the district.

6. *City or village tax.* Incorporated cities and villages within a county provide for their recurring expenses by a separate and independent tax levy.

Determination of amount of tax

To ascertain the amount of tax against a particular piece of property, a tax rate must be determined. To arrive at the tax rate, two factors are used: the budget or amount of money to be raised, and the total valuation of taxable property within the district. The total amount to be raised by taxation divided by the total assessed valuation gives the rate, or millage, a *mill* being one-thousandth part of a unit of value—the dollar. The rate, or millage, applied to the value of a particular parcel of real estate gives the amount of taxes chargeable to it. For example, assume the budget to be $200,000,000, the assessed value of the property $8,000,000,000, and the amount derived from revenues other than taxes for real estate $50,-000,000. The tax rate would be determined by deducting $50,000,000 from $200,000,000 which would leave $150,000,000, which divided by $8,000,000,000 gives .01875, or 18.75 mills per $1, $1.875 per $100, and $18.75 per $1,000 of assessed valuation.

The budget

A budget is "a statement of probable revenue and expenditure and of financial proposals for the ensuing year as presented to or passed upon by a legislative body." It is customary, in the preparation of a budget, for each branch or department of the government to prepare in detail an estimate of the amount it requires for the period under consideration. This estimate and those of other departments are analyzed and amended, usually decreased, by the legislative body. After consideration of all estimates, the final figures are assembled, and the total of them represents the amount of money the political body appropriates for its use for the period. Usually there are revenues derived from sources other than taxation, and these, estimated as closely as possible, are deducted from the total of the budget. The remaining amount represents the sum that must be raised by taxation on property within the jurisdiction. In some states there is a tax on personal property. In others, since the enactment of income tax laws, so much personal property is exempt that the direct tax falls almost entirely upon real property.

Assessed valuations

Since the tax is apportioned to various properties in proportion to the value of each, it is necessary for the taxing body, acting through its representatives, to examine and appraise all taxable property equitably. Various methods of appraisal are used, some of which take the property at a fraction of real market value, such as one-half, two-thirds, or three-fourths. Others take the value to be the amount for which the property would sell at a forced sale, and again others use as a basis the full market value of the property.[1] Many large cities use the last method, which is generally coming to be recognized as the only one that is fair and equitable. Full market value has been defined as "the price that one who wishes to buy, but is not compelled to buy, would pay to a seller willing but not compelled to sell." Prices paid at auction sales, particularly forced sales, do not usually measure true market value, and neither do prices paid for property by those who have a need for that particular property only.

The assessor, in valuing property, frequently separates the values of land and buildings. The land is valued on the basis of the value of a standard or typical lot; that is, a lot of the unit of size usually marketed in the vicinity. If the assessor fairly determines the value of such a lot, he allocates to all similar lots the same value. It will of course be seen that in the valuation of lots in cities and villages each street, and in fact each block, must be considered separately. Main thoroughfares and business streets create values in excess of those on side streets and in residential districts. Corners, corner influences, plottage, and similar circumstances are taken into account in order that the assessor may make an equitable appraisement, one that is fair and just both to the taxpayer and to the community. In certain cities maps are published by the tax departments giving the front foot value of land in each block of the entire city.

The standard lot generally varies from 100 to 125 feet in depth, depending on prevailing subdivision practices. Lots of varying depth are appraised by rules that have been devised for the purpose. Under the 4–3–2–1 depth rule, and where a 100-foot depth is accepted as standard, variations from this standard cause an impact on lot value as detailed on the following page.

Other rules are known by the name of their sponsors who developed them from local income or market comparison data. Well-known rules are the Hoffman-Neil rule (New York City), Newark rule, Milwaukee rule,

---

[1]Full market value is generally estimated by analysis of comparable market sales and adjustment of sale prices for differences as to location, size, quality of construction, time of sale, and other pertinent data to reflect comparable value of the subject property.

Depth of lot in feet	equals	Percent of standard lot value
25		40
50		70
75		90
100		100
125		109
150		117
175		124
200		130

Somers rule, Cleveland rule, and Martin rule (Chicago). All rules, including the 4–3–2–1 rule, are interpolated to permit application for each foot of depth variation from the accepted "standard" lot.

Although all lots in a block may have the same value, the buildings may be different in both size and character. In the valuation of buildings, the tax assessor must consider whether they are new or old and whether they are or are not the proper improvement for the land. New buildings are usually worth their cost of production, and the assessment is computed on that basis. As the age of a building increases, allowance is made for depreciation. When the land value remains stationary and the building depreciates through age, the total valuation of land and building will tend to decrease from year to year. In many localities, land increases in value as time goes on, owing to its availability for a better building; that is to say, one producing a greater rental. The assessed valuation of the lot improved with an old building will increase, but the total of land and building will remain the same. In such cases the building is assessed, not at its cost less depreciation, but at *the amount it adds to the value of the land*. This condition may progress so that a once valuable building adds merely a nominal amount to the value of the land.

Assessors should always consider the rent a building is capable of producing. It has been stated as a principle that an improved parcel of real estate is never worth more than its capitalized rental value unless the value of the land alone exceeds this capitalized sum.

The cost of a building of a certain type can be determined to a fair degree of accuracy by means of certain factors derived from experience in actual building costs. These may be the cost per foot of the cubical contents of the building or the cost per square foot of floor space. The type of building is first considered—whether it is a loft, factory, nonfireproof walk-up apartment, elevator apartment, or office building. Then its size is ascertained. The proper unit is applied, and the result is the estimated replacement cost of the building. From this cost, allowance is made for accrued depreciation. The units of cost, whether on a square foot or cubic foot basis, are subject to revision, changing from time to time to meet varying conditions.

Assuming a homestead exemption of $5,000, a disabled veteran's exemption of $1,000, and tax millages for county, city, and school administration and operation totaling 38 mills, the taxes due on a $40,000-assessed residence would appear on tax records as follows:

Property of Taxpayer		
Value of land		$10,000
Value of building	$35,000	
Less depreciation	5,000	
Depreciated building value		$30,000
Total Property Value		$40,000
Less Homestead exemption	$ 5,000	
Veteran's exemption	1,000	
Total exemption		6,000
Taxable property—assessed value		$34,000

County rate = 19.4 mills
City rate = 8.6 mills
School rate = 10.0 mills
Total rate = 38.0 mills
Tax for 19— $34,000 × .038 = $1,292

Reduction of assessed valuation

The value assigned to real property by a tax official is merely the opinion of that official as to its value. The owner of the property may not agree with such opinion and may feel that his property has been assessed too high. It is his privilege to object to the assessment, and he is entitled to a hearing on his objections. In making a protest of this kind it is advisable to analyze the assessment as to land and building and see which is erroneous. Land may be assessed too high for one of two reasons: either a mistake has been made (in which case a correction is easily obtained), or the wrong unit of value has been applied. A change in the latter requires more care, for a reduction in the unit of value will affect the assessment on neighboring property also. A reduction in the assessed valuation of one lot usually results in a reduction of the value of adjoining lots also, often of all the lots in an entire block. Evidence of value may be offered by a taxpayer by way of information as to sales, mortgages, and so forth, and his contention may be supported by such evidence.

If the taxpayer's protest is based upon a claim of overassessment of the building, he has a fair chance of obtaining a reduction. Every building is considered separately, with the result that a reduction of assessed value of one does not necessarily mean that others must be reduced also. In making a claim of this kind, the owner may offer as evidence proof of the cost of the building, its rental, physical condition, sales price, mortgages, and so forth.

Certiorari

The action of the tax officials is subject to review by the court. If an owner believes that the assessed value of his property is too high and is unable to secure a reduction upon protest to the officials, he can appeal to the courts. This is a proceeding *a certiorari*; that is to say, it is a proceeding whereby the tax officials are required to produce their records and to certify to them to the court in order that the court may determine whether the officials have proceeded according to the principles of law by which they are bound. The court does not usually fix the assessed value, but it may criticize the administrative officers and give directions as to how they must proceed. It is, of course, also possible that the court will sustain the tax officials and find that they have proceeded according to law in fixing the assessed value, or it may direct the reduction of its assessed value.

Taxation practices

Each county and community generally follows a statutory tax calendar in accordance with which dates are set for the completion of the property assessment rolls, and for periods of three to six weeks during which the assessment rolls are open for public inspection. As a rule, notices of protest may be filed during the inspection period. Upon closing of the books, a board of review hears and considers protests made by property owners. Where relief is denied and the owner feels aggrieved he may then petition the court for a judicial review.

Taxes are assessed against the property in most communities by section or subdivision, block, and lot. By this method all outstanding liens for taxes (and also assessments for local improvements and water rates) can be readily ascertained. The system has many advantages over that of levying the assessment against the property by names of owners. Under the latter system, search must be made against the names of the owners for some time past to ascertain the existence of tax arrears.

Tax billing and collection

The procedure for tax billing and collection differs among the various states. Some states bill annually on a calendar year basis; others authorize separate billing by school, municipal, county, and sanitation tax authorities. Where separate tax billing is the practice, the tax burden is spread by statutory provision over budget years which may end in spring, summer, and fall. Thus school taxes may be billed in September, sanitation taxes in April, and county taxes in July.

In some states, taxes are due when billed and become a lien against the property that takes priority over all other private liens, including mortgages, that are on public records or pending under court action. Most states provide a grace period of thirty to ninety days during which taxes may be paid without penalty. Some states offer a 1 to 4 percent declining discount if taxes are paid during the first few months of billing. After the discount period, taxes are deemed due and payable, and penalties for late payment accrue in accordance with statutory law.

Assessments

Assessments are charges upon real property to pay all or part of the cost of a local improvement by which the property will be benefited. They do not recur regularly, as taxes do, and are not always apportioned according to the value of the property affected. For example, all lots fronting on a certain street are benefited by the paving of the street and are equally assessed for it, even though the corner lots may have a greater value than inside lots. Buildings are not considered in apportioning the assessment, it being assumed that the land receives all the benefit. Sometimes assessments are spread over a large area, the property nearest to the improvement being charged with a greater proportion of it than property more remote, the rate decreasing with the distance from the improvement. Only where local improvements are beneficial, that is, increase the value of the affected properties, will courts sanction the levying of special assessments. This is especially true where construction of express highways or other types of freeways limits access to and egress from the property of adjoining land owners. In a court case, some property owners in Miami Beach, Florida, challenged the right of the municipality to levy assessments for the widening of Indian Creek Drive in Miami Beach. The property owners contended that the widening of the drive from twenty-five to forty feet was carried forth to relieve congested traffic on another street and that as a result of the widening the affected street had turned into a noisy, heavily traversed thoroughfare for the use of the public generally and that the effect on property was to lessen the value and desirability of the sites for homes. The state supreme court in a four to three decision held for the property owners, reversing the Dade County Circuit Court which ruled in favor of the city. In the majority opinion, Justice Glen Terrell said: "Before the days of the automobile and creation of zoning ordinances, paving and widening of streets invariably conferred additional benefits to the abutting property. But this may be far from true at present. Commercial property is increased in value by widening and paving of streets . . . but who ever heard of making a traffic count to locate a home!"

How assessments are levied

Assessments must be levied according to law and, therefore, due notice must be given to the property owners in order that the proceedings be valid and the resulting charge on the property be an enforceable lien. The notice is usually given by advertisement.

There are two methods of procedure for laying assessments for local improvements: (1) a proceeding by authority of the courts and (2) an action taken by a board of assessors.

Assessments laid by authority of the courts

The proceeding under which land is taken for public purposes is called a *condemnation proceeding*. The property is said to be "condemned," and the proceeding is for the purpose of obtaining title to it and determining the amount to be paid the owners for the land taken. When the appropriation of the land for a public purpose benefits other land, part or all of the cost of the proceeding (including the damages paid to the owners of the land taken) is assessed upon the land benefited. The various parcels of land taken are called *damage parcels*, and the various parcels upon which the assessment is laid are called *benefit parcels*.

The proceeding may be in court or before commissioners appointed by the court. An opportunity to be heard is given to all owners whose property is affected. If the hearings are before commissioners, they must present a report for confirmation. The property owner may file objections to the report, and the courts will determine the merits of any such objections. Upon completion of the proceedings, the awards and assessments are fixed. The assessments are thereafter entered in an assessment book and become liens on the property affected, that is to say, upon the benefit parcels of the condemnation proceedings.

Examples of condemnation proceedings under which assessments are levied are those for opening and widening streets, and for acquiring land for public parks and playgrounds.

Assessments laid by local board

Many local improvements are made by public officials acting on the initiative of the property owners or their representatives. Such improvements include sewers, sidewalks, and the grading, curbing, and paving of streets. Notice of intention to do the work is given, and notice of the assessment levied to pay the cost is also given. Property owners may object to the assessment upon their property and may carry their objections to the courts.

Assessors are often limited, as to the amount of any assessment they may lay, to a fixed percentage of the value of the property assessed. This rule acts as a safeguard to the owner and may prevent actual confiscation of the property. In some cases it may, however, retard the improvement of suburban districts by preventing the performance of necessary work.

When assessments become liens

Assessments become liens when they are definitely known and fixed. In some cities they become liens by statute ten or more days after being confirmed and entered. By provision of law in some states, a large assessment (usually 3 to 5 percent or more of the assessed value of the property) may be divided into installments payable over a period of five to ten years or more. Interest is charged on the deferred installments at 6 to 8 percent per annum, and on due and unpaid assessments the interest rate is increased.

Enforcement of lien of taxes

There are several methods of enforcing the payment of taxes. The property on which taxes are unpaid may be sold at public auction. At such auction sale the property is struck down to the highest bidder. The sale, however, is subject to the right of the former owner to redeem the property from the sale by paying the amount of taxes, penalties, and interest within a certain time. Sometimes the sale takes the form of a lien against the property for a period of years. In most communities, the law permits the city to sell a lien on the property after taxes, assessments, or water rates have remained unpaid for a certain time. A list of all properties upon which there are arrears of taxes, assessments, or water rates is made up, and the date of sale is advertised. At such a sale the purchaser acquires not the property itself but a lien upon it. The bidding at the sale is by rates of interest; the person bidding the lowest rate of interest (which must not exceed a maximum rate set by law), becomes the owner of the lien. He then has what is virtually the same as a first mortgage on the property, which has, as a rule, two or three years to run and bears interest at the rate he bid at the sale. The interest is payable semiannually. If there is a default in the payment of interest or in the payment of subsequent taxes or assessments on the property, or if the principal is not paid off at maturity, the lien may be foreclosed by an action similar to an action for the foreclosure of a mortgage. By this method of enforcing the payment of taxes, assessments, and water rates, the city has been successful in obtaining the payment of the arrears. The only disadvantage that may be noticed about this method of enforcing payment of taxes is the fact that it has allowed certain people to purchase the tax liens, not for the purpose of making an investment at a fair rate of interest but rather for the purpose of making a profit through charges for legal services in connection with the foreclosure of the liens. In an action to foreclose the lien, the owner and all persons interested are made parties to the action and must be served. This procedure gives the owners notice and an opportunity to pay the liens, penalties, legal charges, and interest, and thus avoid actual sale of the property.

In some instances of titles that are defective, the tax lien foreclosure may be the most satisfactory method of clearing the title. Where such is the case, delinquencies will be deliberately allowed to accumulate; the tax lien will be bought in and foreclosed by an interested party who will become the owner on the foreclosure sale and thus secure the property with a clear, marketable title.[2]

Other municipal service liens

Many communities have found it advantageous to furnish their citizens with essential utilities such as water and/or electricity. Where such utilities are city owned and operated, service charges, as they are billed and entered upon the books of the respective municipal departments, become liens on the affected property. Where utility charges remain unpaid for a stipulated period of "grace," the municipality orders the department to "disconnect" the private service lines at utility distribution points and proceeds with enforcement of the lien.

In some communities it is customary to furnish water on a flat per annum charge, with rates varying with the size of the building or with number and size of the water service mains. To discourage waste, however, and to permit better utilization control, it is the preferred custom to install water meters and to base charges on the actual amount of water consumed at so much per cubic foot. Electricity at one time, too, was furnished on a "flat" per month or annum basis, but meters are now used almost universally for calculating service charges. Utility charges are generally adjusted

---

[2]Foreclosures of tax liens *in rem* (that is, against the property rather than the owner and lienors) are now protected by law in many jurisdictions. This procedure greatly simplifies the process and saves time and expense.

at the time of title closing and care is taken to free the property from all municipal liens that do, as is the case with taxes, assume priority over previously recorded private liens.

Federal taxes affecting real estate transactions

Federal taxes in recent years have greatly influenced the operations of income-producing real estate as well as the nature, character, and timing of real estate transactions. Significant new tax reform laws became effective in 1970. The impact of federal taxation on capital gains, ordinary (earned) income, tax preference income, and sale of homes by senior citizens will be summarized below.

The capital gain tax which is levied on the gain or profit derived from sale or exchange of capital assets, such as real estate, was and still is considered a limited tax intended to encourage investment in plant, housing, and similar capital facilities and to advance the level of economic well-being, that is, productivity as measured in dollar units of "gross national product" or output.

Until January 1, 1970, the capital gain tax derived from sale of real property held for investment for periods exceeding six months was computed in one of two ways: (1) by adding one-half the taxable gain to reportable income and then figuring the tax in the usual way in accordance with the applicable tax table, or (2) by figuring the tax without the capital gain and then adding 25 percent of the entire capital gain to that tax. The alternative that produced the lower tax was the one the taxpayer could select in filing his return.

The comprehensive tax reform law passed in 1969 brought about significant changes which, applicable as of January 1, 1972, are as follows:

1. The new *maximum* tax applicable to "earned" income has been reduced from 70 percent to a high of 50 percent. This means that earned income of less than $52,000 is taxed at graduated tax percentages of up to 50 percent. Earned income above $52,000 on a joint return subsequent to January 1, 1972 is taxed at a rate no higher than 50 percent.
2. Capital gain taxes have been increased from a maximum of 25 percent to 35 percent (a 40 percent increase). From January 1, 1972, on, income tax liability on capital gains is computed by adding 50 percent of such long-term gain to other income to derive the taxable income figure. Further, where earned income equals or exceeds the 50 percent tax bracket, capital gains are taxed at higher levels up to the new maximum of 35 percent of total capital gains, or 70 percent of one-half of the taxable gain, as shown in the example below.
3. A new 10 percent tax has been placed on "preference income" such as dividends, interest, accelerated (excess) depreciation, capital gains, and similar unearned income in excess of $30,000 plus the income tax on nonpreference income for the taxable year. For unearned income below $30,000 plus the tax liability, the preference income tax is not applicable.

To illustrate the computation of income tax liability under the new maximum tax law, let us assume the following: an earned income from real estate commission (or salary) of $102,000 and a capital gain of

$36,000 from sale of an investment. The income tax for married persons filing a joint return is then derived as follows:

1. Regular tax on earned income up to 50% bracket of $52,000 = $18,060
2. Excess of earned income over $52,000
   ($102,000 −$52,000), or $50,000 @ maximum rate of 50% = $25,000
3. Tax on full $120,000 which includes 50% of capital gain
   (see Internal Revenue tax table) $57,580*
4. Tax on earned $102,000 $46,420*

   Difference is tax on capital gain $11,160**
Total income tax liability $54,220

*Based on 70 percent tax table for married persons filing a joint return. Where combined earned and preference income (capital gain) exceed the 50 percent tax bracket, the tax due on preference income is derived as shown.
**Under old tax laws prior to 1970, the maximum tax on capital gain would have been 25 percent of $36,000, or $9,000.

Where a family member of a household has reached the age of sixty-five and where the property (residence) affected has been occupied for at least five of the eight years immediately preceding the sale, the qualified seller is allowed one tax-free sale in his lifetime provided the "adjusted" sale price is $20,000 or less. Where the adjusted sale price is more than $20,000, a pro rata part of the gain is tax-free, in the ratio that $20,000 bears to the actual adjusted sales price. To illustrate: Mr. Adler bought a home ten years ago for $15,000 and after reaching age sixty-five sells it for $33,000. He spent $1,000 on repairs and $2,000 on brokerage commissions. The adjusted sales price is $33,000 less $3,000, or $30,000. The allowable tax-free gain is the ratio that $20,000 bears to $30,000, or two-thirds times $15,000 capital gain, or $10,000. Only $5,000 of the total dollar profits is thus subject to capital gain taxation, and only one-half of $5,000, or $2,500, is added by Mr. Adler to other reportable income for income tax purposes. It is of interest to note that the senior citizen can make or revoke his election to benefit from this tax provision within three years of the date of the sale. This tax allowance privilege extends to owners of cooperative apartments and to owners of condominiums as well.

Where the homestead is sold and a new one is bought within a year, and the purchase price of the new home exceeds the price realized for the old one, the transaction need not be reported or an income tax paid on the profit, if any, realized at time of sale. Under provisions of the homestead tax postponement law, the "paper" profit realized in the exchange, though a factual and purchase transaction, merely necessitates bringing forward the profit by reducing the "cost basis" of the new home. Using the same illustration as applied above, let us assume that Mr. Adler, who realized a profit of $15,000 when selling his residence for $33,000, buys a condominium apartment for $45,000. For tax purposes the "cost basis" of the condominium is now $30,000 ($45,000 less $15,000), and a future sale of the condominium apartment for a price in excess of $30,000 is taxable as a capital gain, subject to tax benefits as noted above where the seller or owning member of the family is sixty-five years of age or older.

Postponing capital gain taxes

The increase in capital gain taxes from a maximum of 25 percent of total taxable gain to 35 percent, effective on sales made subsequent to January 1, 1972, makes the postponement of capital gain taxes, especially for those who fall into the upper-income tax brackets, even more advantageous than it was prior to 1972. Further, since income tax rates are progressive, that is, the "top" dollars of taxable income are taxed at increasingly higher rates than are the "bottom" dollars, it is good business practice to channel capital gains, and for that matter other sources of income, more evenly over future taxable years. Thus a capital gain of $100,000 that is processed at $20,000 per year over a period of five years may save between $10,000 and $20,000 in income tax payments (depending on the income tax bracket of the payer) when compared with tax payments due where the full capital gain is realized and taxable in a given year.

Under installment tax law regulations, the taxpayer may "elect" to report only the percentage of the entire sales price received in a given tax year, provided the amounts realized do not exceed 30 percent of the selling price. Where payments received in the year of the sale or in subsequent years exceed the 30 percent limit, the entire sale or balance due becomes taxable that year. It is important to realize that tax regulations include the following as part of the 30 percent payment limit:

1. Earnest money, option money, or down payments received in the year of the sale
2. Any such payments received in a preceding year, where the transaction is then closed in the following tax year
3. Any principal received through prepayment of the purchase money mortgage before the end of the year of sale or from sale of the mortgage in its entirety to another
4. The amount by which the purchase money mortgage or mortgage assumed by the buyer exceeds the cost basis of the seller

To avoid tax pitfalls, the taxpayer should make certain to stay below the 30 percent payment received regulations as stipulated above. Where the taxpayer elects to report under the installment tax sales provisions, he then accounts only for that portion of the entire price (below 30 percent) received during a taxable year and pays the capital gain tax applicable to that percentage of gain. This gain is generally figured at a much lower progressive income tax rate than would otherwise be possible.

READING AND STUDY REFERENCES

1. BLISS, HOWARD L., and CHARLES H. SILL, *Real Estate Management,* Chapter 28. Englewood Cliffs, N.J.: Prentice-Hall, Inc., 1953.

2. Brown, Robert K., *Real Estate Economics*, Chapter 17. Boston: Houghton Mifflin Company, 1965.

3. Husband, William H., and Frank Ray Anderson, *Real Estate*, Chapter 25. Homewood, Ill.: Richard D. Irwin, Inc., 1960.

4. Kratovil, Robert, *Real Estate Law*, Chapter 29. Englewood Cliffs, N.J.: Prentice-Hall, Inc., 1969.

5. Lasser, J. K., *Successful Tax Planning for Real Estate*. Larchmont, N.Y.: American Research Council, 1961.

6. Ring, Alfred A., *Questions and Problems in Real Estate Principles and Practices* (rev. ed.), Chapter 15. Englewood Cliffs, N.J.: Prentice-Hall, Inc., 1972.

18

REAL ESTATE BROKERAGE

Development of brokerage as a business and professional calling

Real estate brokerage as we know it today is a well-organized business and professional calling that came into being in the twentieth century and during the period historically referred to as the age of specialization. Prior to the development of the internal combustion and steam engines, that is, prior to modes of rapid transportation, population shift through emigration and immigration could generally be accounted for, as well as prepared for, at a leisurely pace.

Originally, friends, acquaintances, and relatives of those seeking to buy, sell, rent, or finance real estate (mostly homesteads) acted for one another. Business contacts were as a rule direct and personal between the parties to a transaction, and little help in the bargaining and negotiating stages of the deal was required. Mobility of population and enactment of civic (governmental) regulations, necessary to protect the health, welfare, and safety of those who settled in the developing urban communities, contributed to the complexity of real estate transactions; consequently, lawyers were called upon to guide transactions to their successful conclusion. At first lawyers not only drew up the required legal documents but also searched title, rendered opinion as to the marketability of title, held funds and documents in escrow, and closed transactions as agent for both parties. Often, too, lawyers negotiated and guided real estate deals through their various stages of completion.

The age of industrialization inevitably ushered in the age of specialization. Lawyers found their time fully occupied by strictly legal matters. Title searching became the province of abstract and title insurance companies, and real estate brokerage attracted specialists who found it profitable to act as agents, for a fee or commission, to serve the needs of real estate clients. Specialization has now reached a stage of refinement in professional know-how and service, where individuals and even entire organizations limit their operations to a single field such as investment brokerage, mortgage financing and servicing brokerage, industrial, commercial, residential, or farm brokerage, or management, consulting, valuation, subdividing, development, or mobile park planning and operation. At present real estate brokerage has reached a high degree of specialization and ranks first in both importance and volume of service in the entire field of real estate.

Law of agency

Every real estate man, whether employed to buy, sell, rent, lease, or appraise real property, is governed by the law of contracts—specifically, the phase of contract law known as the *law of agency*. The broker is an agent and, as such, represents another, called a principal, in dealing with third parties. He represents a principal who may be an owner or purchaser, lender or borrower, lessor or lessee. An agent under the law acts in a fiduciary capacity and is obligated to render faithful service similar in all respects to that imposed upon a trustee. As an agent, the broker owes a definite loyalty to his principal (client) and is prohibited by law from personally profiting by virtue of his agency, except to the extent of the agreed compensation or commission. A real estate broker is defined as one who negotiates between the buyer and seller of real estate, either finding a purchaser for one desirous to sell, or finding a seller for a buyer. He also manages estates, leases or lets property, collects rents, and negotiates loans on bonds and mortgages. He may also be defined as one who makes a bargain for another and receives a commission for doing so. The real estate broker is not a party, in the legal sense, in that he is not acting for himself. As a broker, he always represents someone else. Usually he conducts the negotiations, although in some cases he may merely act as a middleman in bringing the parties together.

Broker and salesman

Although some brokers conduct business without any associates or subordinates, nearly all active brokers have employees, who fall into two classes. One group consists of office employees—cashiers, clerks, stenographic help, and so on. The other group is composed of salesmen, who are actively engaged in conducting negotiations. The distinction between them and the broker is that, basically, the broker has the relationship with the principal. He is the one who has been engaged to sell the property, place the loan, or negotiate the lease. Some of this work he may actually handle himself; in fact, in many offices he actively participates in the more important transactions, but most of the actual work of brokerage is handled by his salesmen. They are responsible to the broker. The principal does not employ them and assumes no liability for their actions. The broker, though, as agent may, unless specifically estopped by his principal, delegate his powers to another. Discretionary agency powers in most states, however, cannot be delegated unless specifically authorized by the principal, by usage, or by imperative necessity. The legal distinction between the responsibility of the broker as an agent and that of his salesmen as employees is an important one.

Compensation

The compensation paid a real estate agent or broker is called a commission or brokerage. He is not paid a salary. Upon being engaged, he undertakes to work for a certain amount for completing the transaction, and his principal undertakes to pay him. The amount of this commission or brokerage is commensurate with the size of the transaction, that is, the amount of money involved. Usually a rate of commission is agreed upon or fixed by the custom of the business. Each transaction is paid for separately, and naturally the earnings of the broker are dependent upon his success in bringing about transactions.

The compensation of the salesman depends entirely on his arrangement with his employer, the broker. A novice may receive a small salary and a small share of any commissions earned by the broker as a result of the salesman's work. As he gains in experience and usefulness, his compensation changes. Ultimately he reaches a point at which his compensation is from 40 to 60 percent of the brokerage paid on his transactions, quite possibly with a drawing account against such earnings.

Especially during a period of real estate inactivity, some brokers pay salesmen a salary, with a reduced sales commission. This arrangement enables the employer to call upon the salesmen for assistance in the management of property and performance of other duties in connection with the operation of the office. The salesmen thus are assured of a steady income over lean periods, and the employer saves salary that would otherwise go to personnel employed in management and clerical work.

Sales brokerage

The broker engaged in selling must possess the highest qualities of salesmanship. He is dealing with a valuable commodity, and negotiations are often long and difficult. His office usually earns enough to cover overhead from commissions on property management and from insurance, but to make substantial earnings the broker must make sales. He must be familiar with the neighborhood in which he works and, of course, with every property that he undertakes to sell.

Lease brokerage

Although selling is the chief source of profit for the average broker, he is almost certain to transact some lease negotiations. Leasing smaller properties presents little difficulty, but leasing more valuable properties, particularly those with long-term leases, involves a multitude of details. Such lease transactions often present more difficulties than complicated sales. In the large cities many brokers make a specialty of negotiating leases. They are familiar with various businesses, trades, and industries. They know in detail the requirements of each type of business as to space, type of building, floor load, location, heat, power, and service. Although they usually do not disregard other types of business, their principal income arises from obtaining tenants for space or securing space for business firms desiring to locate in new quarters.

Mortgage brokerage

The mortgage loan broker must first of all obtain the application for a loan, and then find a lender with whom to place it. The application shows the amount of loan desired; the rate of interest the borrower is willing to pay; the number of years the mortgage is to run; the installments, if any, to be paid on the principal during the term; and the amount due at date of mortgage maturity. The application for a mortgage loan is generally supported by a report of value of the property which is offered as loan security. This valuation report is prepared, as a rule, by the mortgage broker or an independent appraiser and contains in addition to the estimate of current value photographs of the property and nearby structures, a floor plan, descriptions of the improvements on the property, income and operating cost data and terms of leases, if an income-producing property, and a location sketch showing placement of improvements in relation to site and street patterns. Increasing stress, in recent years, is placed on the financial ability, credit rating, and integrity of the borrower who will pledge his note or bond in connection with the loan. The broker customarily receives a commission of 1 percent of the amount of the mortgage loan if he is successful in placing it. It is best that closing and mortgage settlement payments due from the borrower, including the brokerage commissions, be stipulated in the mortgage loan agreement signed by the applicant.

Exchange brokerage

There are few brokers who specialize in exchanges only. Most brokers would much rather negotiate a sale than an exchange. It is difficult enough to convince a purchaser that an offered property is worth the price asked, and it is often still more difficult to convince each of the parties of the merits of the property to be exchanged. Nevertheless, most brokers realize that exchanges are certain to occur at times, and when a sale cannot be made, the alert broker always looks into the possibilities of an exchange. What ceases to be a possible source of one commission may be made to pay two.

The exchange of real property has been encouraged, too, in recent years by tax law provisions under which capital losses or capital gains are not recognized where property held for productive use in trade, business, or investment is exchanged for like kind of property similarly held for trade, business, or investment purposes. Under current tax laws it is thus advantageous to trade property where the owners seek to postpone payment of capital gain taxes until the property is disposed of in a taxable transaction, or where offsetting capital losses can profitably be postponed to later years.

Real estate brokers can render valuable services to their clients by considering their tax position and by suggesting tax-free property exchanges where such prove advantageous. To illustrate: Suppose a banking firm seeks to relocate in larger quarters. The present bank building was acquired at a cost of $40,000 fifty years ago, and this cost, for book account purposes, was allocated $10,000 to land and $30,000 to building. Although the building for tax purposes is now fully depreciated it still commands a market value of $20,000. The land value, too, has increased over the years to $30,000. If a "sale" takes place, the banking firm will realize a taxable capital gain in the amount of $40,000 ($50,000 sales value less $10,000 cost basis). Suppose further that the new property can be acquired at a cost of $60,000. By arranging for a property "exchange"—rather than a purchase and sale—the bank acquires a $60,000 property by exchanging its $10,000 book value property plus $10,000 cash. This exchange avoids the necessity for making an immediate cash outlay for taxes. The cost basis of the new property, of course, would be that of the old, plus current additional investment, or $20,000. Only when final disposition is made of this property is the capital gain subject to tax.

Exchange brokerage, because of operation of current tax laws, thus has taken on new and profitable significance. The alert broker who keeps abreast of these laws and who fits them advantageously to the property needs of his prospects can substantially enlarge his brokerage operations.

Since American families are exchanging homes with increasing frequency to suit their personal and vocational needs over the years, trade-in practices have become widespread in the more populated states throughout the nation.[1] It is estimated that households, on the average, are exchanged every five years and that the number of family homes retained for a lifetime and handed down to heirs and descendents is dwindling. Exchange practices developed in the field of real estate are essentially a take-off from practices that are commonplace in the fluid automobile market. Specifics about prevailing trade-in plans will be discussed in the following chapter on real estate marketing.

The broker's authority

In most states the broker's authority to negotiate a sale, exchange, or lease need not be in writing. In a few states, the statute provides that unless the broker has written authority he cannot recover any commission

---

[1] See *Real Estate Guide* (Englewood Cliffs, N.J., Prentice-Hall, Inc.), Secs. 1331–37, for details on "trade-ins."

for making a sale or an exchange. All states have a broker's license law that must be complied with so that the broker can collect his commission.

Ordinarily the broker is authorized to conduct only the negotiations. Unless he is merely a middleman, he has a certain amount of responsibility and actually represents his employer. His authority does not usually include the right to execute a contract of sale or purchase on behalf of his employer, but he may be given such right. Although authority to execute a real estate contract can be given by parole in some states, as a practical matter a broker should never, except under extraordinary circumstances, sign a contract unless he has written instructions in his office files. Although a broker may have signed a contract without any authority, the principal may, if he wishes, accept it and ratify the agent's act. A broker's authority to sign contracts may be inferred from circumstances or a course of dealing, or the contract may be ratified by the conduct of the principal.

Broker's license law

All states and the District of Columbia have enacted laws that govern the activities of real estate brokers. At one time, anyone who wished had a right to hold himself out as a real estate broker, solicit deals, conduct negotiations, give advice—even though his real business was another calling. Those who dealt with him would be guided by his opinion, statements, and suggestions, yet he might well be totally unfitted. In order to professionalize their calling and to protect the real estate business from unfair and unscrupulous competition, real estate brokers themselves petitioned their respective legislatures for licensing laws that would restrict real estate brokerage operation to those who could qualify by examination. Laws were urged to provide safeguards to protect the general public from incompetency and dishonesty in its dealings with unlicensed and unethical real estate brokers. Fundamentally, the purpose of all license laws for brokers is to assure the general public that the broker in the transaction knows his business. Under the license law, a person is prohibited from acting as a broker until he has first given satisfactory evidence to his state authorities that he is capable. Assuming a person is legally competent, and can prove himself to be a citizen of good character and a bona fide resident of the state for the required length of time, he may secure a license by taking an examination that covers:

1. The general law of real estate
2. The general law of brokerage (principal and agent)
3. The provisions of the license law itself

Of course, the applicant must also prove himself to be a citizen of good moral character.

It is true that in some states the real estate license law is largely a revenue measure, but in most the quality of the examination really requires a knowledge reasonably adequate so that none may secure a license who are unable properly to conduct a brokerage business. The state licensing authorities in the various states conduct examinations several times a year and will furnish all data upon application—even, in some states, indicating generally what subjects and laws should be made a matter of study. The officers of any local real estate board will gladly tell where to write for information.

It would not be practicable to attempt any detailed analysis of the laws of the different licensing states. However, the following are usual:

1. Before becoming eligible to take the broker's examination, it is necessary for the applicant, in a number of states, first to take a salesmen's license, work for a broker for a year (or more), then qualify to be a broker by another examination. The salesman's examination is fairly simple. Its real purpose is to force the applicant to serve an apprenticeship under a licensed broker.
2. There is an annual license fee, and no broker or salesman may ply his trade if he fails to qualify originally and pay his annual license fee.
3. Licenses must be prominently displayed.
4. No recovery of commission or compensation of any sort may be made if unlicensed.
5. It is a criminal offense to act as broker if unlicensed.
6. It is prohibited to "split commissions" with one acting as broker or salesman unless licensed to act in such capacity.

Educational requirements

In recent years the more populous states have enacted minimum educational requirements which broker applicants must satisfy before they are permitted to sit for the license examination. A number of states require one or two years' apprenticeship as a bona fide (full time) salesman employed by a licensed broker. In addition, some states require satisfactory completion of one or more courses in real estate principles and practices. Such prescribed courses may be completed at degree-granting schools or colleges or taken by extension or correspondence if approved by real estate commissions. The ever-growing necessity to protect the general public from unskilled and untrained real estate practitioners has led to legislative requests for more stringent license laws designed to raise the required level of education of brokers in order to make the service and brokerage aspects of the real estate business as professional as possible.

Private controls over brokers' activities

In addition to public regulation of real estate brokers and salesmen, an ever-increasing number of them are subjected to voluntary and private regulations when joining local boards of Realtors that are affiliated with the National Association of Real Estate Boards. Private controls, which are intended to supplement restrictions created by law, are exercised by compelling adherence to the Code of Ethics of the National Association of Real Estate Boards.[2] In principle, this stresses the golden rule: "Whatsoever ye would that men should do to you, do ye even so to them." Specifically, it provides a practical guide which governs:

[2]See Appendix pages 604–609 for complete statement of the Code of Ethics of the National Association of Real Estate Boards.

1. The professional relations of Realtors with one another
2. Their relations to their clients, i.e., principals who employ brokers
3. Their relations to their customers (buyers of listed property) and the general public

Whereas the public controls are created by law and are binding on all registered real estate brokers and salesmen, the Realtor's Code of Ethics is purely voluntary and is binding only on those registered brokers and salesmen who are members of the board of Realtors. The Code of Ethics, laudatory as it is, is not enforceable by the courts except where the code and the law unite in forbidding certain conduct. As a general rule, the Code of Ethics goes much further than the law in regulating and professionalizing the conduct of Realtors and their salesmen associates.

The broker may not act for both parties

The broker is usually the agent or representative of his principal. As such he owes it to his principal to give faithful, honest service. He should not allow personal considerations to interfere with his duty. "No man can serve two masters" is an age-old truth and applies to the real estate broker's relations with the principal to a transaction. A number of legal decisions hold that a broker, clothed with the slightest discretion, cannot secretly accept compensation from both parties. The interests of purchaser and seller are adverse, and it is inconsistent with the proper performance of his duty to one employer that he act for and accept reward from another. It is a breach of his implied contract with each. His acting for both without disclosing the fact constitutes a fraud and precludes the recovery of commission. It is the character of the employment that determines the matter, and where the broker is employed merely to bring the parties together, the terms having been arranged between the parties when they met, it is permissible for him to accept a commission from both even though he fails to notify them. Of course, in any case, the broker can accept a double commission with the knowledge and consent of the parties.

Sharing in profits

To act in the interests of his employer is clearly the duty of an agent. This means that on a real estate transaction the broker should get the best price and terms for his principal. It is highly improper for him to be at the same time a broker and a purchaser. He can, of course, purchase the property if he acts openly in so doing, and if the owner understands it and agrees to it, he may even receive a commission. The usual rule, however, is that an agent cannot buy from or sell to his principal while he acts as agent: A broker may be authorized to sell at a net price with the understanding that he shall receive as compensation all he can obtain above that figure. If he is merely employed to sell, however, and the owner names a price, he is in duty bound to do better if he is able, and he cannot pretend to sell at such a price when in reality he is getting more and has a secret interest in the profit thus obtained. In a specific court case a broker who had contracted to sell at a price of $17,000 advised his principal of the fact but later received an offer of $26,000 for the same property. He took an assignment of the first contract and then became the vendor under a second contract at the advanced price. He then had the seller deed directly to the second purchaser, received the $26,000, but accounted to the seller for only $17,000. The court held that the broker could not appropriate the difference between these amounts and that his principal was entitled to the benefits of the second sale.

The same rule applies to employees of the broker and also to officers of a corporation. A trustee cannot be interested in the subject of the trust. The interest of the principal must be his interest, and he can have no interest that, conflicting with those of his principal, can work injury to the latter.

Brokers must be employed

In order to recover commission for his services, the broker must have made a contract of employment with the one for whom he acts. As already noted, the contract need not be a written agreement except in states where the law requires it; but there must be employment, either express or implied, or the broker has no legal ground for his claim. Volunteers are not entitled to compensation, and a broker who performs a service without having it understood that he is to be paid for doing so may find himself classed as a volunteer.

A person who has merely inquired the owner's price for a piece of property and procured a buyer at that price is not entitled to a commission. If he were, an owner could scarcely quote a price to anyone without laying himself open to a claim from someone for commission when he sold his property. The courts generally agree that an owner cannot be enticed into a liability for commissions against his will.

It is, of course, more satisfactory if there is a written authorization stipulating the amount of the commission, for then the employment is easily proved. It is also a clear case of employment when the owner comes to the broker and lists his property with him. The owner, it is assumed, must know the broker expects to be paid a commission if he secures a customer. The amount of commission, in the absence of a definite agreement, would be such as was fixed by custom in the locality.

When commission is earned

A broker has earned his commission when he has accomplished that for which he was employed. If he was employed to sell, he must bring about a sale. He is not paid for making impressions, or for interesting people in the property, or for an unsuccessful effort. The rule that is supported by many judicial decisions is that the broker is entitled to commission when he produces a purchaser ready, willing, and able to purchase on the terms offered by the seller, or on terms that he is willing to accept. If a contract of sale has been signed, the broker has the best evidence of the success of his work, and a purchaser truly answering the description of ready, willing, and able would without question sign such a contract. The principal may capriciously change his mind and refuse to make a contract of sale with the broker's customer. He, of course, does not have to sell, but he is liable to the broker for commission. The broker has performed the service for which he was employed even though no actual sale resulted. He should, however, be prepared to prove that his customer answered the required description.

The broker may make a special arrangement with his principal whereby he limits himself to recovery of commission only in the event that a sale is actually consummated by delivery of the deed and payment of the purchase price. Such an arrangement, to be binding upon the broker, must be made prior to the time he has earned his commission. If made after rendering the service for which he was employed, it would probably not be enforceable by reason of lack of consideration. Any special agreement of this kind should contain a distinct provision that commission on the sale shall be due and payable only if and when the title passes to the purchaser. It should be remembered that the ordinary obligation of the broker is to bring the principals to an agreement so that there is "a meeting of the minds" as to the terms.

The procuring cause of a sale

It is an established rule that if an authorized broker is the "procuring cause" of a sale, he is entitled to his commission. He does not have to introduce the parties or bring them together personally. If through his efforts they get together and come to an agreement, he must be recognized.

Suppose a purchaser comes to the broker's office, is furnished by him with the information, and is sent to the property. If the purchaser then goes directly to the owner and a deal is made between them, even though the broker's name is not mentioned, the broker has an enforceable claim for commission. If a broker advertises property and receives and transmits an offer, even if the sale is finally consummated directly between owner and purchaser, the broker is entitled to commission.

General rules as to earning commission

In order to recover commissions, the broker must (1) show that he was employed, (2) be the procuring cause of the sale, (3) bring about the deal on the terms of his employer, (4) act in good faith, (5) produce an available purchaser who under the general rule is ready and willing to purchase and also legally able to do so, and (6) bring about a completed transaction. We have already seen that double employment or secret sharing in profits violates the requirement that the broker act in good faith. The purchaser brought by the broker must meet all of the terms as stated by the seller, unless the seller is willing to modify them. The broker must complete his work. He cannot abandon the negotiations and expect that if the parties, later and in good faith, get together and make a deal, he will be able to recover commission. The employer must give the broker a fair chance to complete the transaction once he commences it, but having done so he may refuse to negotiate further through him and may take up the matter directly or through another broker. Mere introduction of the parties by the broker or commencement of negotiations does not limit the owner forever to dealing with the purchaser through this broker.

Deferring or waiving commissions

In most states the broker engaged "to sell" has completed his work when he has brought the parties together and they have agreed on terms. He is entitled to this commission when his work is done. In some cases, in order to make a deal, an owner may modify his terms on condition that the commission be deferred or reduced. If this can be shown to be a consideration for the promise, the broker is bound by it. Another situation that often arises is that the buyer is willing to pay on the contract only a small deposit. In such a case the seller is unwilling to pay the broker until title closes for two reasons: First, he wants to be able to forfeit and retain the entire deposit if the buyer defaults; and second, if the broker is not yet paid, he will work harder to keep the buyer from "backing out." Hence, the seller, before agreeing to the terms, will make it a condition that the broker agree to defer payment of his commission until title closing.

Let it be repeated, however, that unless there is some agreement by the broker such as that above, or the very listing itself has stated that no commission is to be paid "unless and until title closes," the broker is entitled to his commission when he has procured a qualified buyer. The broker therefore hastens the signing of a contract, as the best evidence of agreement, and promptly presents his bill.

With increasing numbers of sales being "installment sales" that are intended to minimize as well as to defer payments of capital gain taxes, brokers, generally as a condition of employment, agree to receive commission payments in proportion to the amounts of principal cash payments made by the purchaser to the seller or his agent. Thus where the purchase agreement calls for 25 percent cash at time of closing and the balance in equal installments over a three-year period with interest on the purchase money mortgage debt at 8 percent on unpaid balances, the broker under commission agreement will receive only 25 percent of the total commission at time of closing and the balance in like installments over the following three years. The broker should make certain that the deferred commission agreement provides for interest payments on the commission balances due him at the same rate and in proportion to the amounts paid the seller under terms of the installment sales agreement. In practice deferred commission payments are the exception rather than the rule and where agreed upon rarely extend beyond a contract period of five years.

Who pays the commission?

It is the employer who is liable for the commission in every case. The employer of the broker is usually the owner of the property or the owner's representative. In some cases the purchaser employs the broker to obtain the property for him. The rule as to double employment has been noted. It is no violation of this rule for a purchaser to employ a broker to procure the property with the understanding that whatever commission he receives shall be paid by the seller. But in such a case the broker should advise the seller to that effect. Persons not owning the property, or those acting in a representative capacity, are personally liable for commission if they employ the broker to sell the property. It sometimes happens that a purchaser assumes, in the contract, the seller's obligation to pay the broker's commission. This agreement is good between vendor and vendee, but it has no effect upon the right of the broker to recover from his employer. A broker may usually employ subagents, but they must look to him for commissions.

Commissions on exchanges, loans, and rentals

The rules that apply to recovery of commission on sales apply also to exchanges. It is customary, however, for both parties to an exchange to pay a commission based on the value or price of their respective properties. A statement in the contract that each party shall pay the broker is sufficient notice to each that he is receiving commission from the other. The broker has no right to make a double commission secretly. It often happens that two or more brokers are interested in an exchange representing opposite sides, and they sometimes pool their commissions and take an equal division of them.

The broker is usually entitled to commission for procuring a mortgage loan only in the event of the loan's being actually made, or in case he had procured an acceptance of it and it failed to close through a defect in the title to the property or through a fault of the borrower. The reason for this is that there is rarely an enforceable agreement on the part of the lender to make a loan. The lender may agree to accept it, but this does not constitute a contract. In many jurisdictions the rule is that a broker has earned his commission when he produces a lender who is willing, ready, and able to make the loan on the terms offered.

The rule with regard to commissions for making leases is similar to that for procuring loans. The broker is not entitled to compensation unless a lease or a complete agreement on its terms is obtained. The broker would, however, be entitled to his commission if the owner tried to impose new and unreasonable terms upon a prospective tenant and the lease was not made for that reason. When a lease has been made, the broker is entitled to his full commission, and this is so regardless of the tenant's subsequent default unless, of course, the broker has made a binding agreement to the contrary.

Commission on percentage leases

Percentage leases are sometimes entered into with lessees of business property on the basis of a minimum rent, representing a certain percentage of the lessee's gross income from the business conducted by him on the leased premises. On this type of lease, the broker is paid a commission at the time it is signed, based on the minimum rental, and receives a further commission on the accrual of the additional rental computed on the percentage basis set forth in the lease. Such further commission is usually payable at the end of each year.

Commission on installment land contract

This type of contract is usually confined to the sale of vacant lots in a subdivision or lot development and provides that a purchaser shall pay for such lots in installments extending over a period of years. Brokers on this type of sale are usually paid in accordance with a written commission agreement calling for the payment of commission in installments equivalent to a percentage of the payments made on the purchase price.

Duty of principal to broker

The principal, having employed the broker, should give him a fair chance to accomplish his work. Many principals now avoid any question of unfairness by stating, at the time they employ the broker, that the property is being listed with other brokers. The principal cannot capriciously terminate the employment while the negotiations are being carried on; but if the broker has had a fair chance and failed, or has abandoned his efforts, the principal is free to treat with the same customer, either directly or through another broker, without liability to the first broker. An owner may employ several brokers to sell the property, and the first one who succeeds gets the reward. An owner may negotiate with purchasers himself and may sell without the help of any broker. An exclusive agency prevents the owner from employing other brokers but does not prevent a sale through his own efforts free from claim of commission unless the terms of the exclusive agency provide otherwise, as is the case where the principal agrees to and signs an "exclusive right to sell" contract. Exclusive listings, generally, are limited as to time of performance, the typical contract extending over periods from two to six months, depending on kind and type of property to be marketed.

Duty of broker to principal

It is the duty of the broker to act in the best interests of his employer and to obtain the best price and terms for him. He is bound not only to good faith but also to reasonable diligence, and to such skill as is ordinarily possessed by persons of common capacity engaged in the same business. He must follow instructions and not exceed his authority. He cannot refuse to reveal to his principal any information that may come to him relating to the transaction under consideration. Willful concealment of facts material to the interests of his employer amounts to fraud. The broker, however, is not obliged to violate a confidence, but he should make his position clear to his employer. If he knows that a prospective purchaser is not acting for himself but for someone else and he is in honor bound not to reveal the fact, he may withhold it, but he should advise his employer that he is dealing with an undisclosed principal.

Several cases have arisen in recent years which raise a legal point that should be noted. Ordinarily the law is that a broker, even if he accepts a listing, is not legally bound to make any effort to bring about a deal. He might get the listing and "go fast asleep." He is under no legal obligation if he makes no effort to sell for his principal, or to seek to buy, if that purpose was what he was engaged for. However, if he does go to work on the deal, and his principal relies on him to act diligently, then he will quit or become careless at his peril. In one case, the lower court held the broker liable, and although the verdict against him for his principal's loss was reversed on appeal, the reversal was on the facts, with the court affirming the legal principal that may be simply stated—if he goes to work, and his principal relies on him, he must work hard.

Statements made by a broker

A broker makes many statements in the course of negotiations that may be mere opinions or arguments or "sidewalk conversation." He may not, however, make misstatements of fact as to material matters, and a purchaser may disaffirm a contract induced by such misstatements. If the broker makes misrepresentations relying on information furnished by the owner, he is entitled to his commission even though the purchaser is relieved from the contract. Unauthorized misstatements made by the broker, with similar results, cause him to forfeit his rights, although if the fruit of the broker's work is accepted by the seller when the seller knows of such misstatements, the broker may recover commission.

Misrepresentations that relieve a purchaser from a contract must be as to some material fact, such as the size of the plot, the terms of leases, or the restrictive covenants. In one case it was shown that an owner made an unintentional misrepresentation of the size of the plot. The purchaser refused to sign the contract when the real dimensions became known, and the broker sued for commission. It was held that the broker was employed to sell a certain piece of property with which he was familiar, that the statement as to size by the owner was not a warranty, and that the broker could not recover a commission.

Termination of agency

The employment of the broker under an open listing is not usually for a definite time. It is revocable at will in good faith by either party or by mutual consent. If a reasonable period of time has elapsed and the object has not been performed, the agency may be considered at an end. It is also terminated by the death or insanity of either party, by bankruptcy, and by the destruction of the subject matter. If the transaction sought has been accomplished, either by the broker himself or by another broker, or by the principal, the employment has ceased.

Rates of commissions

The amount of commission due a broker on any transaction may be fixed by a definite agreement between the parties. In the absence of an agreement, custom prevails. The rates suggested by a real estate board are often evidence of the customs of the business in a particular locality.

READING AND STUDY REFERENCES

1. CASE, FREDERICK E., *Real Estate Brokerage*, Chapters 3 and 4. Englewood Cliffs, N.J.: Prentice-Hall, Inc., 1965.
2. HEBARD, EDNA L., and GERALD S. MEISEL, *Principles of Real Estate Law*, Chapters 16, 17, and 18. New York: Simmons-Boardman Publishing Corporation, 1964.
3. HUSBAND, WILLIAM H., and FRANK RAY ANDERSON, *Real Estate*, Chapter 17. Homewood, Ill.: Richard D. Irwin, Inc., 1960.
4. KRATOVIL, ROBERT, *Real Estate Law*, Chapter 10. Englewood Cliffs, N. J.: Prentice-Hall, Inc., 1969.
5. LUSK, HAROLD F., *Law of the Real Estate Business*, Chapter 15. Homewood, Ill.: Richard D. Irwin, Inc., 1965.
6. RATCLIFF, RICHARD U., *Real Estate Analysis*, Chapter 1. New York: McGraw-Hill Book Company, 1961.
7. RING, ALFRED A., *Questions and Problems in Real Estate Principles and Practices* (rev. ed.), Chapter 16. Englewood Cliffs, N.J.: Prentice-Hall, Inc., 1972.
8. UNGER, MAURICE A., *Real Estate* (4th ed.), Chapters 16 and 17. Cincinnati: South-Western Publishing Co., 1969.

19

REAL ESTATE MARKETING

The marketing of real estate, as practiced today by professionally trained and experienced real estate brokers and salesmen, is a development of the twentieth century. Prior to the existence of large scale urban centers (and to a large extent continuing today in suburban and rural areas) transactions involving real property were negotiated directly between the principals. With increasing urbanization and greater mobility of population, however, a need developed for skilled intermediaries who were able to expedite and facilitate the purchase and sale of real property. Men who could skillfully conduct real estate purchase and sale negotiations established offices and set themselves up as specialists in this field. This was the beginning of the brokerage business which, today, has advanced to the status of a semi-profession. The preceding chapter discussed the technical and legal aspects of brokerage. This chapter presents its practical phases—marketing.

At the outset it is important to emphasize that by legislative action, as well as by judicial decree, real estate as a commodity has become affected with a "public interest." By this is meant that real estate agents (brokers) in their business dealings on behalf of principals (clients) must, under penalty of law, consider their product (real estate) as "open" and for sale, lease, mortgage, and so forth, to all legally competent persons without discrimination because of the individual's race, color, religion, or national origin.

The open housing law

The open housing law governing the sale and rental of real estate by brokers, agents, or their employees was signed by President Johnson in April 1968 and became fully effective beginning January 1, 1970. Under this law, known as the Civil Rights Act, Title VIII, all housing sold or rented by real estate brokers and agents must comply with provisions of this important legislation. The only exemptions under this act apply to individual owners who sell without the aid of real estate agents and without discriminatory advertising, provided the seller does not own more than three homes or owns a multifamily dwelling of not more than four units, one of which he occupies. Because of the significance of this law and its provisions under which violation is considered a misdemeanor punishable by fines up to $1,000 or imprisonment up to one year, the full text of Public Law No. 90–284 is presented on pages 595–604 of the Appendix.

A decision of utmost importance to owners of real or personal property is the June 17, 1968, U.S. Supreme Court ruling upholding the constitutional validity of the Civil Rights Act of 1866 under which owners of property are barred from discriminating in the sale or rental of real or personal property to anyone on racial grounds. This landmark decision culminated a lawsuit brought by a Mr. Jones against Mayer Company, the builder of a community near St. Louis, Missouri, who had refused to sell him a home solely because he was a Negro. Jones's attorney centered his case around the almost forgotten Civil Rights Act of 1866. The district court dismissed the complaint and the court of appeals affirmed; however, the Supreme Court reversed, holding that the statute does cover discrimination on racial grounds and that the statute is constitutional under the Thirteenth Amendment to the Constitution.

This decision in effect voids the exemptions given individual property owners under the open housing law who sell their homes without assistance from real estate brokers. However, a person seeking protection under the reaffirmed Civil Rights Act of 1866 must bring his own action in which he cannot count on support from government agencies. Aside from an injunction ordering him to sell, where a lawsuit is successful, the property owner faces no penalty and there is no provision for damages as is the case under the open housing law.

Since the Supreme Court's decision goes, in part, beyond the intent of the 1968 open housing law, it is possible that Congress may enact legislation to limit the effect of the Supreme Court ruling in conformity with the recent will of Congress. Such action, however, in the light of the country's civil rights mood and current "liberal" developments, seems most unlikely.

The service functions of real estate marketing. Applied research in the fields of distribution and merchandising has yielded statistical proof that success in business operations is greater among firms that stress service and the consumer than among those that stress low profits, bargains, and competitive discounts. The twentieth-century slogans "The customer is king" and "The customer is always right," first and successfully applied by John Wanamaker, who lived to see his Philadelphia and New York City stores reach national prominence, have as a merchandising policy all but replaced the nineteenth-century concept of *caveat emptor*, "let the buyer beware." In real estate marketing, however, the shift toward consumer orientation is still in low gear. Most brokerage firms are still emphasizing the satisfaction of the seller and his ability to secure highest prices rather than filling customers' needs with sincerity of purpose and a true desire to help him buy. Perhaps it is because compensation for services rendered are paid by the seller that the notion is so strongly entrenched that interests of buyers and sellers are opposed. If, as demonstrated in Chapters 23 and 24 on property valuation and appraising, there can be only one market price that is fair to both buyer and seller, then the broker's efforts to bring about an exchange and closing on equitable financial terms represent a true professional service. Whether the buyer, the seller, or both pay for brokerage services, the quality and the ethical basis of the broker's efforts should be unaffected.

The broker's role in marketing

The principal reasons why sellers and buyers of real estate engage the services of a real estate broker are (1) the broker's reputation and ability to conclude transactions professionally and equitably, (2) his store of knowledge concerning the community and growth potentials of locations within neighborhoods, and (3) his skill and know-how in following through on matters affecting financing, insurance, taxation, accounting, and property management.

The real estate broker essentially renders a service. Although he deals with a commodity to be bought, sold, or traded, he has, as a broker, no financial interest in the property; and his compensation is not part of the profit that is added to the cost of the realty but rather a fee for professional services. Brokers, like lawyers and doctors, have organized into boards of Realtors to regulate their practice in accordance with ethical standards specified in the Realtors' Code of Ethics. The word "Realtor," used by an ever-increasing number of licensed real estate brokers, is the property of the National Association of Real Estate Boards and may be used only by legally qualified brokers who are members of a local board of Realtors affiliated with the national association. It cannot be too highly emphasized that "in union there is strength," and everyone engaged in the real estate business should be a member of his local board. In this way he not only keeps in touch with general developments in the field of real estate but is given better opportunities to cooperate with his fellow real estate men.

The real estate office

Real estate offices are of many kinds and sizes. A few specialize in certain distinct types of work. Most of them transact a general business. In the larger cities are found highly departmentalized offices, with separate departments each in charge of an executive and various subordinates. Some of the larger firms may have all the following departments:

1. Management	10. Drafting
2. Accounting	11. Cashier's
3. Collection	12. Stenographic
4. Insurance	13. Auditing
5. Legal or Closing	14. Mortgage
6. Purchasing	15. Brokerage
7. Leasing	16. Canvassing
8. Filing	17. Appraising
9. Lease custodian	18. Consulting

A number of these departments are in the management group covered in Chapter 21. Here and in the next chapter are discussed the departments engaged in selling, renting, and mortgage negotiations.

The sales organization

Each of these departments has it own functions, but basically all of them are engaged in selling ownership, equity, or space. The small office consists simply of the "chief" and one or more salesmen. The large office expands this organization. Naturally the ambition of every salesman is to work up to an executive position, and possibly to branch out ultimately into the operation of his own office. The executive must have the ability to obtain business. The salesman to a great extent carries through to a conclusion what he initiates. The broker is the producer; the other sales or office associates attend to the details. As time passes and business activities expand, more of the details must be passed along and a greater degree of reponsibility must be shifted to the office associates. No definite rules can be set down for the selection of junior salesmen. Usually, inexperienced but well-educated men are preferred because each office has its own policies and because it is easier to train a new man than one who has established fixed customs or sales habits. Young persons are usually deemed best because their learning capacity is more flexible and their ability to make working adjustments is more dependable. Men and women familiar with the community usually make good sales personnel. They know the town and its people and, as a rule, have a good circle of acquaintances.

Office layout

Obviously no one plan for office layout can be presented which will prove satisfactory to every office. Generally, office space on a street floor, where window displays can be used to attract passersby, is deemed most satisfactory. The office should be light and airy; the furniture clean and modern. The filing system should be up to date and records readily available. Index systems should be used that make all information in the office files easy to find. Fences, railings, and counters that appear to bar the customer from the office personnel should be avoided as much as possible.

The entire office should be well coordinated. There should be no wasted steps, the scheme of operation being such that the office will run smoothly. It should always be easy for a junior employee to get immediate help from one of the seniors when necessary.

Affiliation. The broker and his entire personnel should bear in mind that real estate is a profession. People do not have to go to the real estate office; they go there because they want to. Therefore, it should be the aim of everyone in the office to be known favorably throughout the community. The office should subscribe to all worthy charities. The executives should be members of welfare and other organizations and should take an active interest in them. One or more of the office executives should be on the boards of directors of the chamber of commerce and other civic organizations. As many as possible of the worthwhile clubs should be joined and frequently visited.

Salesmen's qualifications and selling guides

To be successful in selling real estate, the salesman must have certain qualifications, the first of which is good health. He should be neat in appearance, reasonably well dressed, conduct himself with great self-respect, and inspire the confidence of clients who rely on his services. He should be well informed, use tact and good judgment, and act with reasonable knowledge of, and in conformity with, the real property law and the laws of brokerage. The last is important in order to protect himself, the firm in whose name he is acting, and, last but not least, the principal whose property and interests are at stake.

The following points should prove to be as useful to future salesmen as they have been to salesmen in the past:

Analyze the property. Never offer anything without having thought it out clearly. Get it down on paper, because most people read better than they listen.

Never offer a property without having looked at it yourself. You cannot sell what you do not know, and you cannot know improved real estate without having thoroughly inspected it.

Always try to please the prospect. He does not have to deal with you, and he will not if you irritate him.

Talk to the prospect in his own language, and *never* talk down to him.

Remember that he will not buy unless he thinks it is to his own advantage, so you must convince him that there is some good reason why he may benefit by buying. Do not try to sell property unless you really believe that the prospect ought to buy it.

Never lie—and this maxim will stand no qualifying. Do not even misstate. Most prospects are on the lookout for misstatements, and the salesman is through the instant he is detected.

Never argue. You may prove you are right, but you will lose the sale.

Try to know every single thing about the property so that you can answer every question.

Get the prospect to the property, and do that as soon as possible. If there is more than one, get them all there. Do not handle them separately.

Concentrate on a few sales rather than put in a little work on many and close none.

Talk with discretion. Give your client ample opportunities to ask questions. Know when to stop; don't talk yourself out of a sale.

Use the telephone, but bear in mind that in most instances a personal interview is better.

Never fail to submit an offer. It is not your business to turn down an offer. Sometimes ridiculous offers are accepted. You cannot be absolutely sure of what your principal has in mind.

At all times be looking for business. It is surprising how many listings may be picked up while you are actually working on something else.

Bear in mind that your prospect is a busy man. Do not waste his time.

Do not worry about your competitors. You will get your share of the business if you go after it.

Never take anything for granted. Overconfidence has lost many a sale.

The sales process

Successful selling of real estate involves four essential steps: (1) listing, (2) prospecting, (3) negotiating, and (4) closing.

Listing. Listing is the general term that covers the various steps in obtaining authority to sell a piece of property. It goes without saying that no one can sell what he does not have. Therefore, just as a storekeeper must have a stock of goods on his shelves, so the real estate broker must have listings of property for sale. His first problem is to obtain listings. He cannot expect prospective buyers to call at his office, tell him their needs, and then wait for him to canvass the neighborhood desired for the right type of property. If the broker were to do so, the prospect would go meanwhile to some other broker who had been forehanded, and who would at once put him in touch with the type of property he wished and would make a sale.

It is important, therefore, for the broker to obtain listings immediately upon commencing business and at all times to keep adding to his listings to replace those he sells and those that are withdrawn or sold by other brokers. Listings are secured in various ways. A few of them come from owners who call at the office or write to the office asking that their property be listed for sale. By far the greater number of listings, however, are obtained by canvassing on the part of the broker and his salesmen, who solicit them. They should be doing this at all times when not otherwise engaged. In fact, even when working on a deal they should be watching for opportunities to get other listings. For example, a prospective buyer may want to purchase a property shown him, but to get available cash he may have to sell a property that he owns. At once the broker obtains the facts and sets out to sell this property; he may possibly earn two commissions, one on each sale. One very good way to secure listings is simply to ring doorbells and inquire of owners whether their buildings are for sale. One advantage of this method is that many listings of this type are fresh; that is, they have not been given to other brokers. Another way is by watching for all For Sale and To Let signs in the broker's neighborhood, locating the owner of each property so posted, and if possible obtaining from him authority to sell the property. Such listings are somewhat precarious in that other brokers are also working on them, but no broker can expect to have a very large number of exclusive listings. Newspapers are a splendid source. Every property advertised there is held by an owner who wishes to sell. He may be located and a listing obtained from him.

Whenever someone has bought a new home, there is a chance that his former home is on his hands and that he wishes to sell it. Every sale successfully consummated gives the broker an opportunity to request both buyer and seller to recommend him to their friends. Brokers occasionally advertise for listings. Neighborhood changes cause old residents to wish to move, and the watchful broker can go through the neighborhood offering to sell properties for such dissatisfied residents.

Listings must be carefully handled. Every particular must be obtained. Cards used for this purpose should contain space for an entry of the size of the lot, the size of the house, the type of house, the number of rooms, the age, the heating plant and its condition, the improvements on the house, whether owner occupied or rented, the amount of rent, when the existing mortgage or mortgages are due, and the interest rates and monthly mortgage charges. And also, the price of the property and the amount of cash required to effect the sale should be included.

It is very important at the outset to get the property properly listed. Most owners who want to sell have little idea of the market value of their property. They know what they paid for it and think of all the money they have spent for upkeep, and they usually consider that it is worth as much or more than the price they paid. They also have an idea that is best expressed by the statement they often use: "We can set a price and always come down from it." The result of that attitude is that the listing price is far higher than the property will ever bring. Many brokers simply list such property but make no effort to sell it until some months later, when they go back to the owner and see if he is willing to lower his price. But that is not a good way to negotiate sales. When the listing is originally obtained, the broker has a fair idea of what the property will bring in the current market. It is better not to list the property at all than to take the listing and then let it go to sleep. He should make every effort to persuade the owner to set a price at which a sale can be made. Of course a broker should not give the impression that he wishes an owner to throw his property away, but there is no use permitting an owner to list a property at $35,000 when, in all probability, it will not bring more than $25,000 in the current market. It would be far better to find out at once whether or not there was any possibility of making a deal by seeking to persuade the owner to set an asking price of, say, $30,000, from which, if need be, he could drop to meet a fair purchaser's offer.

Another error committed in many offices is the accumulation of a tremendous amount of dead listings. The office should make a point of keeping in touch with owners so that (1) the owner feels that efforts are being made to sell his property, and (2) if he sells it elsewhere, the broker learns of the sale and can remove the listing from his files. In some offices where no such care is taken as many as 80 percent of the listings are dead. This situation is discouraging to all the salesmen.

The files of listings should carefully be indexed, both as to geographic location and as to type. The extent of subdivisions of the index, of course, will depend on volume. The geographic division may divide the community into a few general districts, or it may be subdivided by blocks. The listing as to type may be simple—one-family, two-family, four-family, stores, garages, and so on; or it may be subgrouped further according to type of construction and price range.

Listings are classified into five general kinds: (1) net listings, (2) open listings, (3) exclusive agency listings, (4) exclusive right to sell listings, and (5) multiple (service) listings. Although open and net listings may arise out of an oral agreement between the broker and the seller, such unwritten contracts are difficult to enforce in case of controversy. It is highly desirable, therefore, that all listing contracts be in writing that sets forth clearly the nature of the agency and the manner of compensation due the broker. Strictly speaking, a "listing" is not a contract, or, at most, it may be classified as a unilateral contract which becomes an actual or bilateral contract upon performance by the broker. Lacking consideration—until performance—a unilateral contract is revocable by either party at any time prior to performance, even though a definite time is stipulated in the listing agreement. Nevertheless the principal owes certain duties to his agent, as was explained in the preceding chapter on brokerage.

The listing is the foundation and groundwork of the broker's business. Out of it arises his relation of trust and confidence with his principal and upon it he must base his rights for compensation. It is highly important, therefore, that any person engaging in the real estate business understand fully the rights and obligations underlying each of the listing contracts.

A *net listing* is a contract to sell or rent and obtain a minimum price for the owner. The broker, generally, adds his commission to the quoted net price. In some states, the broker cannot lawfully obtain a compensation greater than the usual and customary rate of compensation without the specific knowledge and consent of the owner. Because of the uncertainty of the agreed selling price, a net listing may give rise to a charge of fraud. Net listings, therefore, should be used with caution, and care should be taken to explain fully to the principal the pricing procedure to be used and the compensation which the broker will retain for services rendered.

Open listings are the simplest form of written or oral authorization and are commonly used in real estate practice. Under an open listing, the owner (principal) retains the right to list his property with other brokers. Where an open listing is given to more than one broker, the owner, provided he remains neutral as to the competing brokers, becomes indebted for compensation only to that broker who actually sells the property or finds a purchaser, as the case may be. If the owner himself sells the property, he is not obligated to pay a commission to any brokers holding "open listings." The sale of the property terminates the open listing and usually the owner need not notify the agents, since under the law effective in most states the sale cancels all outstanding listings in order to safeguard the owner against paying more than one commission.

An *exclusive agency listing* is a contract containing the words "exclusive agency." Under this form of listing contract, the commission is payable to the broker named in the contract. The purpose of the exclusive agency listing is to give the broker holding it an opportunity to apply his best efforts, unhampered by interference or competition from other brokers. Although in most states the exclusive agency listing binds the owner to pay the broker in the event of a sale by him or any other broker, the listing is not as broad in its scope and effect as most real estate men believe. This type of listing does not entitle the broker to a compensation where the property is sold by the owner to some prospect not procured by the broker. This listing is also revocable, unless a consideration was made. Further, the listing can be terminated if the broker has not performed. In that case, the owner's liability is limited by the value of services actually performed by the broker.

The *exclusive right to sell listing* is a contract in which the words "exclusive right" are used. This listing is similar in all respects to the exclusive agency listing except that under it a commission is due the broker named, whether the property is sold by the listing broker, or any other broker, or even by the owner within the time limit specified in the listing contract.

A form of exclusive right to sell listing which has been successfully adopted by some brokerage firms is known as *certified listing*. This mode of listing calls for the client to put down a deposit of fifty to seventy-five dollars to cover the cost of a detailed property brief and appraisal report which is prepared by a trained evaluator. The professional estimate of value serves as a basis for the selling (listing) price which is certified by the brokerage firm as accurately representing the fair market value of the property. If the seller-client agrees to an exclusive listing at this certified value, his deposit is credited toward the total commission due at time of sale. Where the seller deems the value estimate too low and declines to list his property at the certified price, he is furnished with a copy of the appraisal report, for which he paid in full with his initial deposit. When professionally applied, this mode of listing has induced buyer confidence and has generally strengthened the brokerage firm's public image. One brokerage firm that limits its operations to certified listings that are backed by the integrity and reputation of the firm's broker-owner has proven so successful that it employs the rather original advertising slogan, "List with us and start packing."

Prospective purchasers who are interested in a property listed as certified are supplied with a copy of the appraisal report to use as a guide during property inspection and for overnight study and general information. As a marketing aid, descriptive valuation reports have removed much of the mystery surrounding a transaction and appear to instill confidence in the buyer through an open and professional approach to selling as opposed to the more informal methods still widely used today.

Multiple listing is a name applied to an organized real estate sales service conducted by a group of brokers, usually members of a real estate board. These brokers combine their interests through the facilities of a central listing bureau. A standard "multiple listing" form is furnished by the bureau and must be used by all members. This form generally provides for an "exclusive right to sell" agreement between the seller and the member who acts as the bureau's representative. The listing agreement, when properly executed, is forwarded immediately by the initiating broker to the manager of the central bureau for sales processing. As a rule, the listing bureau arranges for an immediate appraisal of the property and forwards its value estimate together with a listing data form to all its members with the right to bring about a sale. Listings that in price exceed a specified percentage (5 to 10 percent) of the appraised value of the property are as a rule rejected by the listing bureau. The owner (seller), of course, is informed of the action and, in most instances, reduces his sales offering to within a price range deemed reasonable and acceptable. This procedure is intended to protect the purchasing public and, in addition, to build a reputation that merits the confidence of the buyer of real property.

Under the bylaws of a typical multiple listing bureau, sales commissions may be divided as follows:

1. Five to 10 percent of the gross commission goes to the listing bureau to cover operating expenses and general overhead.
2. Seventy to 80 percent of the remainder goes to the selling broker.
3. Twenty to 30 percent, i.e., the balance, goes to the listing member.

Assuming a $1,000 sales commission, and a distribution of 5–80–20 percent as noted above, the proceeds would be distributed as follows: $50 to the listing bureau, $760 (80 percent of $950) to the broker effecting the sale, and $190 (20 percent of $950) to the broker who initiated the listing.

There are numerous multiple listing services in operation today. During the past few years the number has grown rapidly, and in some states (California specifically), these listing bureaus have generally been successful, especially where the system is subject to strict membership control. The underlying principle of the multiple listing service is to secure wider distribution of the listing and to offer better, greater, and more uniform sales effort than is otherwise possible.

Prospecting. Having obtained listings, the broker's task is to sell the properties. He cannot make a sale until he has located someone who might be interested. That is called prospecting. To locate the prospect he can use various means. Nearly every real estate office has a file of properties wanted in addition to the listings of properties for sale. Every time an inquiry comes in for a type of property that the office cannot supply, a memorandum of that fact and the details of the location, type, and so on, of the property desired should be noted. Whenever a listing of property for sale comes into the office, a check should at once be made against the property-wanted file, and possibly a sale may be made in a short time.

A most likely source of prospects for any property is the tenants in the building. They do not want to move, but there is always the chance that the new owner may wish to occupy their space; so the broker or salesman should interview the tenant or tenants at once. This is particularly true of business property. If the tenant does not want to buy, the other storekeepers on the street should be canvassed. One of them may be persuaded to stop paying rent and become an owner.

Advertising is the largest source of prospects. Years ago it was thought that an advertisement should actually make a sale. Now, as far as real estate is concerned, the broker is satisfied if the advertisement puts him in touch with a prospect.

Newspapers often indicate a seller prospect also. The death notices, for example, reveal families that are broken up and whose homes must be sold. The records of business activities show distress sales opportunities. Records in the county clerk's and the surrogate's offices of pending partition actions and foreclosures, as well as applications to sell real estate for debts, are useful.

Personal contacts are important. The broker's friends know that he is skillful, and they are likely to refer prospects to him. The same is true of old customers if they know that he is reliable and industrious. The dates of lease expirations should be known whenever possible. Any such tenant may happen to want to buy rather than continue on lease. Some of the new arrivals in the community are transients, but others will want to lease or buy. Sometimes directories are useful. For example, a broker with a country estate near a golf club can often secure a prospect by means of a letter to the membership list. Occasionally a sale may be secured through marriage license records. New employees of the business houses in the community, particularly those from out of town, must live somewhere and may be referred to the broker.

Negotiating. Prospecting leads up to the negotiations. The first step in conducting negotiations starts with the initial contact with the prospect, which may be made in many ways. It may be the result of a telephone appointment, an unsolicited interview, or a response to an advertisement.

The broker or salesman is dealing with a valuable commodity, and there are often long and difficult negotiations. He must appraise and analyze the prospect at once and determine whether he is real or merely a "suspect." If he is not a real buyer, the salesman should not waste much time on him.

After the first interview, the salesman can usually determine whether or not the prospect is real. He may be merely a shopper. Possibly he has no intention of paying a fair price but is merely going from broker to broker expecting to stumble on some property that the owner wants to "throw away," or he may be merely a "looker" interested in a few free automobile rides, particularly in the pleasant seasons of the year. The quicker the salesman gets rid of this type of prospect the more time he will have to devote to bona fide prospects.

The broker must be a keen student of human nature and of the types of personality. The first contact is usually brief; in many instances the first impressions and analysis must be made in a few minutes. It is for this reason that the older and more experienced broker seems to have what to his salesmen appears to be a sixth sense, which is merely the ability to judge quickly and with a minimum of error the type of prospect before him.

Many prospects harbor an inner fear of real estate brokers and their representatives. This fear is a protective countermeasure to guard against the power of persuasion or salesmanship which may lead the prospect to a premature decision or cause him to be subjected to possible pitfalls of the trade. In reality, this fear is no longer warranted, or justified, by prevailing real estate practices. Most established brokers are conscious of the benefits arising from "satisfied" customers and community goodwill. Efforts thus are made not to *sell* the customer but to *guide* him in the purchase of what he wants or needs and can afford. The broker would be foolish who allowed a customer to contract to purchase a home "beyond his means" which could only result in the customer failing to be approved on his "credit rating" to qualify for a mortgage loan or, if he did take title, later being unable to carry the property and so losing it. This change in the philosophy of negotiating is beneficially reflected in the increasing number of services that the broker is called upon to render for the homeowner, as well as in the greater number of total real estate sales that clear through brokerage offices. Negotiating when carried forth in a spirit of *service* will not only win friends but aid in the building of a professional reputation that is essential to sound business growth and continued success.

The presentation. Having classified the prospect at the first contact, the salesman next presents the proposition. The presentation is to a large extent oral, but it must always be borne in mind that most people learn more by seeing than by hearing. Ordinarily the salesman should tell his story simply and truthfully, never dressing up the truth and never exaggerating. The salesman should use the prospect's language, for he is unfamiliar with real estate terms and may be buying a home for the first time. The prospect should be taken out to the property as soon as possible and shown the worst part of the house first. The salesman should always make it a point to familiarize himself thoroughly with the home before showing it to anyone. Thorough knowledge about the property inspires confidence in the viewer, whereas superficial or inaccurate statements may not only cost the sale but injure the reputation of the real estate firm. The wise salesman always goes into details, describing structural or property site weaknesses or faults in their true perspective but stressing with like honesty the good points, especially those that adapt themselves to the prospect's needs or wants.

It is wise always to have something in writing to give to the prospective buyer. This often takes the form of a *property brief*. The property brief may be simple or complicated. If the subject of the transaction is an apartment house or office building, it will take the form of a pamphlet of a number of pages including a description of the property, diagrams of the lot and of the building, floor plans, elevations, location of transit, and a detailed financial setup of the operating expenses and income. If it is a home, the property brief should give a diagram of the lot and of the house, photographs of the building, and a financial statement showing the operating expenses reduced to an average monthly carrying charge. Placing this in the hands of the prospect during the interview gives him something to look at that he will probably absorb more readily than the salesman's words and, in addition, something that he can take with him to study before making up his mind.

The temperament of the prospect will cause the salesman to fit the general scope of the presentation to the mold required by the prospect's type. In addition, as early as possible in the interview, the salesman should try to find out various facts about the prospect's business, his income, whether married and how long, the number and ages of his children, family income other than his own, interests outside his business, where and how he has previously lived, his church, and his club connections, if any. Obviously, the salesman with these facts in mind can more readily appeal to the prospect's situation. For example, if there are any children, "this is a safe, healthy place in which to bring them up." If they are of school age and the prospect is in the average income group, "the public schools are convenient and very good, and the trip to and from schools is safe."

Prospect's objections. Almost no sale is made without some objections and sales resistance. Objections may fall into three classes:

1. The prospect does not want to hear the salesman's story and is unwilling to give him an audience. The salesman must get by this objection or he will get nowhere. At once the salesman must determine whether this objection is frivolous or real. Most people do not like to be bothered. They may be busy, but there is no real reason why they should not listen to the salesman's proposal.

The best way to get around such a frivolous objection is to hurdle it, like the young salesman who finally, just before closing time, got in to see a business executive. When he was ushered into the office, the executive looked up at him sternly and said in an unfriendly voice, "I have refused to see seven salesmen today," to which the young salesman replied, "I know—I'm them." The prospect could not help thawing, and of course the story ends as it should, with the salesman making a sale.

If the objection is real, however, the salesman is wasting his time if he goes on. Not every prospect is going to buy, nor does everyone want to buy. Many times a man simply appears to be a prospect when actually he is not, and in that case the salesman's best course is to try to make a future appointment and depart.

2. The second objection is the desire not to spend money. Such people are usually sincere. The prospect considers the property too expensive, or says that he has not enough money to entertain the proposition, or that although he really is interested he would rather leave it alone for the present. The negotiations will collapse at this point unless the salesman can overcome such objections. One splendid way of doing that is to anticipate them and not let the prospect take a definite stand that he feels he must defend. The instant the salesman gets an inkling of this type of objection, he should work away from it and then, after a few minutes of conversation, approach that phase again. At this time it may be presented in such a way that the objection loses its force, if the prospect mentions it at all.

3. The third type of objection is the desire to avoid an immediate decision. The prospect thinks the offer is a fairly good one and that he may eventually accept it. He wants more time to think it over, to make comparisons with other property. The salesman sooner or later, with this type of prospect, is compelled to make a bold effort to force the prospect to a decision. Such an effort is always hazardous because most people feel that "there are better fish in the sea than have been caught." To tell a prospect flatly that the price is going up shortly nearly always results in his complete withdrawal and refusal to consider the deal further. However, if the same thought is conveyed to the prospect in a tactful way, he may very likely come to a favorable decision.

The closing. From the salesman's point of view, the closing is the particular stage of the negotiations at which the prospect finally agrees to purchase the property. Much has been written on this subject, but as far as the real estate man is concerned, no stereotyped rules of conduct can be laid down. Experience will teach him when to bring the matter to a head. In rare instances the psychological moment arrives at the first interview. The deal may be closed while salesman and prospect are standing in the living room of the home that the prospect is about to buy. More often, however, there are several interviews, but there comes a time when the salesman must frankly though tactfully bring the prospect to a decision. The trend of negotiations will usually indicate when the time is ripe. The seasoned real estate operator makes up his mind quickly. He notes the facts, verifies them, goes over the property carefully, and promptly makes his decision. The most difficult prospect is the one who has never bought a house before. He is timid, because this transaction is probably by far the biggest one that he has ever entered upon. He must be made to overcome his fears and make up his mind to make the purchase.

Classes of buyers

It would be a waste of time to offer a home to a wealthy man who lives in an apartment and has no desire for the cares of a home, but who wishes to invest his money in real estate. The builder, as a general rule, being engaged in the construction and sale of properties, is usually interested in vacant land that can be improved and sold at once. He is familiar with real estate, so that the salesman must deal in cold facts. The builder is not interested in generalities. He will not buy any particular plot at all unless he knows it is to his advantage to do so. The salesman, therefore, must be able to tell him the comparative prices of other properties, where mortgage financing can be obtained, where a ready market for the improved property can be found, what assessments are likely to be made for street improvements, and what public utilities are available. The salesman also should have a well worked out scheme for cutting up the property into lots suitable for the type of building that the prospect wants to erect. An apartment house builder, for example, would not be interested in a group of lots suitable only for medium-priced one-family houses.

The operator ordinarily is not much concerned with unimproved property, particularly if it must be held for a considerable time before it is ripe for improvement. He usually is interested in improved property, the price of which will permit him to resell at a profit.

This type of transaction appears to be much the same as mere speculation, but a distinction can be drawn between the two. The speculator is not concerned with value and never expects to do any work on the property before reselling it. He simply buys on the chance, which may or may not be supported by sound judgment, that he can sell for more than he pays. The operator, on the other hand, though not inclined to be a longtime holder, goes into a deal after the application of mature judgment. Usually he expects to do some work on the property: he may modernize the building so that higher rents can be obtained and operating costs lowered, or he may refinance the mortgage or mortgages on the property. In any event he believes that, as a result of the work he does on the property, he can interest an investor and sell the property for more than it cost him.

The investor believes in real estate as a thoroughly safe investment. He knows that even through a depression he will not lose his investment if he keeps the mortgage loan at a reasonable amount. He recognizes depreciation and intends to add each year to a fund to amortize the loss of value of the building. The type of property that the investor buys depends very often on his means as well as his previous experience. The locality may also influence his choice. In the smaller cities, one-family houses are attractive to investors, but in the large cities, where districts shift and the population changes, one-family houses are more attractive to occupying owners than to investors. If the investor's capital is large, he is likely to purchase apartment houses or office or loft buildings, from which the income is certain and steady. In any event the investor properly approached by the salesman must be assured of the safety of his capital and an adequate return on the amount he is asked to pay for the property.

Home buyers are numerically the largest group of real estate purchasers. Many brokers sell almost exclusively to them. The home buyer is often wary and is usually not a person of large means. The purchase of a home is probably the greatest single expenditure of his life. He offers strong sales resistance, yet he is the backbone of the real estate business, and the broker will be a signal failure unless he learns how to handle this type of buyer. The experienced broker selling homes knows that he is not dealing with mere bricks, mortar, or shingles, but with a purchaser's lifetime investment which must be spent wisely. The broker or salesman must realize, therefore, his sales responsibility and effectively but honestly present the benefits of home ownership to which the property under sale may make an important contribution. There should be no doubt in the salesman's mind that home ownership is a way of life that instills a feeling of belonging, strengthens family ties, and promotes sound civic development. The rapid growth of the United States during the past two decades from a nation of tenants to a nation of homeowners augurs well for continued success in real estate selling.

Public auction sales

An auction sale is a public sale to any person bidding the highest price for a property upon terms and conditions previously announced. The contract for sale, discussed in Chapter 5, facilitates the voluntary transfer of real property, generally privately negotiated. In a private sale, the seller deals with a *definite* purchaser, knowing in advance with whom the business transaction is to be concluded. An auction sale, on the other hand, is public, and anyone complying with the terms of the auction sale may become the purchaser. The owner does not even know, until the bidding has taken place, what price he is offered or will receive for his property.

Usually the seller can realize more for his property at private sale. He may, however, be compelled to sell at auction because the law requires the public sale of his property, because private purchasers do not appear, or because he thinks a public sale would bring a higher price. In the large cities there are regular auction rooms and licensed auctioneers, whose time and energy are devoted to auction sales. In the country districts the sale is usually held at some gathering place, such as the post office, the railway station, or the town hall, or on the property to be sold.

Auction sales are of two kinds—*involuntary* and *voluntary*. Because one differs from the other very materially in theory, purpose, and operation, they will be discussed separately.

Involuntary auction sales

The involuntary auction sale is brought about as the result of the enforcement of some lien upon the property. A lien, it will be recalled, entitles the holder, in the event of nonpayment, to satisfy the debt from the property. The lien may have originated in a voluntary act of the owner, such as borrowing on mortgage, but once the lien has come into being, its enforcement may be secured entirely without the owner's volition. If the owner has defaulted in payment, the law gives the lienor the right to have the property sold. From the proceeds of the sale the amount of the lien, interest, and all expenses are paid, and the balance, if any, belongs to the owner. A public auction sale, in theory of law, will bring the greatest price; therefore, all sales to enforce liens must be of that kind. The sale follows a legal action in which the lienor's right has been established.

The sale. If the lien is a judgment, the sale is usually conducted by the sheriff. Other liens usually are satisfied by a sale conducted by a referee appointed by and responsible to the court. The sheriff or referee may conduct the sale himself, but in cities it is customary to engage an auctioneer. Notice of the sale must be given strictly in accordance with the law. Failure to comply with every requirement may result in a sale's being set aside. The notice is given usually by advertising in the newspapers, and in the rural districts by posting a copy of the notice of sale in several prominent places.

The notice commences, as a rule, by naming the court of jurisdiction under power of which the sale is directed. Then follow the names of the plaintiff and defendant and their attorneys, if so represented. The notice may then read as follows:

Pursuant to judgment entered this .... day of .... 19........ I will sell at public auction at .... (place) .... on (month, day, and year) at 12 o'clock noon, through .... auctioneer; a parcel of land described as follows: ....

....

subject to any survey variations, building restrictions, violations of law, existing leases, and rights of tenants in possession, except such tenants and/or lessees as are parties defendant herein at the time of sale.

The approximate amount of the lien to satisfy which the above premises are to be sold is $..........................., with interest from ...., together with costs and allowances totaling $..........................., with interest from .... and expenses of the sale.
Dated .... 19........

Signed ....

Referee

In some places it is not required that the notice of sale contain a statement of the approximate amount of the lien that is to be discharged or satisfied by the auction sale.

Terms of sale. In any sale of real property there must be a written contract. In a private sale the contract is prepared and signed by the parties after their negotiations have led to an agreement. In an auction sale there is obviously no negotiation; the auctioneer offers the property, asks for bids, and sells to the highest bidder. So that the prospective bidders may know upon what they are bidding, terms of sale are prepared and read by the auctioneer before the property is offered. The terms of sale, usually prepared in duplicate, constitute the contract.

After the bids have been closed, the successful bidder signs a "memorandum of sale," one copy of which is kept by the officer selling, who in turn receives the deposit and after signing the receipt gives one copy to the purchaser. Each party then has the signed obligation of the other, and the subsequent course of the transaction is, in the main, similar to a private sale, except as the provisions in the terms of sale differ from the usual contract on a private sale.

Fraudulent bidding. The law prohibits any act by which the bidding upon property sold at involuntary auction is artificially limited or controlled. The property being sold is that of an unfortunate debtor. As much as possible must be realized from it, not only so that the lien may be paid but also so that, if possible, something remains for the owner. Full access and opportunity to bid must be given to all prospective bidders. No bidder is required to bid more for the property than he wishes. But the sale must be conducted in the usual manner, without undue haste, or failure to recognize any bidder.

The lienor at whose instance the property is being sold expects to be paid the amount of his claim out of the proceeds of sale. He therefore is justified in bidding for the property (if it is worth it) at least up to an amount sufficient to satisfy his claim. There is nothing improper in this, even though he cease bidding when that amount has been reached. Nor is it wrong for junior lienors to bid upon the property in an effort to protect themselves, nor for the owner to bid in an effort to have his property bring as much as possible. The mere fact that the successful bidder secured the property very cheaply would not be evidence of fraud.

The auctioneer and involuntary sales. In theory the function of the auctioneer should be to promote such a sale as will, by stimulation of interest, be a success. In involuntary sales he is under severe handicaps. The lienor, or plaintiff (the mortgage holder in a foreclosure, for instance) has no desire to spend more on the sale than the law requires, because he is permitted to charge and collect as a sale expense only the amount he would have laid out for the usual routine advertising. And if it is unlikely that an outsider will bid on the sale, there is no use running up the costs. Hence the auctioneer has a very slight opportunity to use his skill and is limited to what little he can do at the actual sale.

Voluntary auction sales

A voluntary auction sale is the free act of the owner. It differs in many important respects from the involuntary sale, in which an unfortunate owner is having his property taken from him and stands helplessly by while the lienor exercises his legal rights. In the voluntary auction, on the other hand, the sale is held because the owner believes that he can sell his property to better advantage by an auction sale than by a privately negotiated sale.

There are many reasons why an owner may prefer an auction sale to a private sale through brokers. Fiduciaries, such as executors and trustees, who are directed to sell for the best price obtainable, usually sell at auction. By so doing, they are fully protected from criticism. Even when they are not required to sell for the best price, they often sell at auction, believing that the auction gives everybody a chance and will produce the best price. Sometimes a property owner feels that the market is such that the only satisfactory way to sell his property is by engaging an auctioneer and taking advantage of the competitive spirit that an auction develops. Developers and subdividers often use voluntary auctions so that they can sell their lots all at one time and apply the money, which would otherwise be spent in a slow selling campaign through salesmen, to advertising publicity and conducting of the auction.

Types of voluntary auction sales. Not all voluntary auction sales are alike. The advertising, the publicity, and the method of conducting the sale depend on the type of property and other features.

If a large building or a plot is to be sold in one piece, the expense budget will include very little ordinary display advertising (billboards, posters, and so forth). The general public cannot handle so large and valuable a piece of property. The auctioneer will plan just enough newspaper and other advertising so that the general public may know of the sale, and he will devote his resources to the preparation of a very good descriptive booklet presenting, if the property is improved, detailed facts concerning its operation, expenditure, and income. His canvassers will solicit thoroughly a chosen list of people in the community who are or should be in the habit of buying that type of property. Many letters will be written, and even telegrams. An assiduous campaign will be carried on to secure appointments with likely buyers so that canvassers may present the details to prospective bidders.

If the sale involves a number of properties, say ten, fifteen, or more, each of average value, there will be strong emphasis on display and billboard advertising, because such properties are within the means of a large part of the buying public. In this type of campaign, it is not unusual to canvass persistently any particular list. The auctioneer relies on making everyone in the community aware of the sale; he knows that a large number of people will attend it and that the properties will be sold successfully. Of course, a circular will be prepared, giving a picture and a fairly brief description of each property, stating also such facts as its assessed value, the amount and terms of mortgage, and the operating expenses and income.

When a single small building or a single lot is considered for an auction, a peculiar problem is presented. In a small community full publicity can be given without the expenditure of too much money, but in a city it is almost impossible to get adequate publicity for the amount that may justifiably be expended in selling such a type of property. Auctioneers very often solve the problem by accumulating two or three buildings or lots, or possibly even more, in the same general locality and then selling them all at the same time. The advertising and publicity expenses for the sale of a number of properties will be about the same as for one property. When a number of properties are sold at one time the public, curiously enough, usually thinks they all belong to one owner, but the circular and other publicity can easily be arranged so as not to state so. Thus if there are five or ten properties, each owner can afford enough money so that the total sum that can be devoted to advertising and publicity is adequate. In fact, auctioneers often solicit the brokers in a particular neighborhood with the idea of building up a list of fifteen or twenty properties. A minimum price may be put on each piece so that the owner will not get too little for his property, and the auctioneer and the broker make some division of the sales charge. In this way the auctioneer obtains business, and the broker receives at least a small compensation on the sale of properties that may have been on his books for some time without his being able to move them.

Protective bidding. At the time of sale the owner may be unwilling to have the property sold for less than a certain sum; or, if the property is being sold by an executor to raise funds to pay creditors or beneficiaries, he may wish the property to bring enough to satisfy their claims. This situation gives rise to the question of proper protection. It is not improper for such creditors and beneficiaries to have the property bid up to cover them. The owner should not bid unless it has been announced by the auctioneer that the property will be protected up to a certain amount. The terms of sale, for the same purpose, may state that no bid of less than a certain amount will be accepted. "Boosting" with fictitious bids, by agents of the owner, for the purpose of inducing higher bids by others, is wrong and may result in the sale's being set aside by a court. Boosting hurts the reputation of auction sales and discourages honest bidders, and no wise auctioneer will permit it. If he detects it, he should at once withdraw the property from the sale.

Terms of sale. As soon as a property has been knocked down to a successful bidder, he immediately makes his deposit and signs the terms of sale. The terms of sale in a voluntary auction differ quite materially from those in an involuntary auction. In a voluntary sale, the owner may make such terms as he wants, although if he makes them too onerous, he will get no bids. Usually the owner has the terms of sale provide for adjustments and other matters of that nature as if the sale were a private one. Insurance, interest on mortgage, taxes, water, and other charges are apportioned. The purchaser pays his deposit usually to the auctioneer, and the auctioneer signs the receipt on the terms of sale. Later on, when title is closed and the deed delivered to the purchaser, the purchaser surrenders this receipt to the seller, who in turn returns it to the auctioneer upon receiving the amount of the deposit from him. The purchaser nearly always pays the auctioneer's charge for the knockdown. This charge is in addition to the price and varies according to where the sale is held and with the value of the property.

Successful auction sales

The public in general is inclined to feel that many auction sales are subject to suspicion. But this attitude is not a fair one. A great deal of land is brought into use by means of the auction, and the auctioneers perform an economic service in splitting up wholesale land into retail quantities. An auction cannot be successful unless both the auctioneer and the owner approach it in the proper way. They must realize that they are dealing with a tract of land that is about to pass into use and that it is entitled to reasonable consideration. A good auctioneer is not a leather-lunged man who makes wild and exaggerated statements. He is like any other salesman; he has a good commodity and he sells it. Mr. Joseph P. Day has given his opinion as to the formula for successful auction sales as follows:

The object of an auction sale is not alone to realize the greatest price but to show what a property would bring in a fair market, *properly advertised and promoted.* I emphasize "properly advertised and promoted" because an auction sale cannot be a success unless display advertising is used in proper mediums and personal promotion work is done. Promotion work has become an important factor in successful auctioning of property through attracting the largest number of people who might possibly be interested in the property being offered. A foreclosure sale very seldom attracts, even when advertised, as rarely do the parties in interest want to spend much money in advertising. A legal partition sale, when properly advertised and promoted, does attract a good audience.

Advertising of real estate at auction sale has stepped ahead in progress through using more mediums, getting up better booklets, style of literature, and having a house to house canvass in neighborhoods where the property is offered, through its promotion department, as well as more efficiency in getting up to date lists in connection with circularizing. The writer, in his more than a quarter of a century experience at auctioneering, has never used a brass band or given a free lunch, which was quite the custom before he came into the field. The soundness and attractiveness of the property being offered deserves a dignity that any other legitimate business should command.

READING AND STUDY REFERENCES

1. CASE, FREDERICK E., *Real Estate Brokerage*, Chapters 5, 6, and 7. Englewood Cliffs, N.J.: Prentice-Hall, Inc., 1965.
2. HUSBAND, WILLIAM H., and FRANK RAY ANDERSON, *Real Estate*, Chapter 11. Homewood, Ill.: Richard D. Irwin, Inc., 1960.
3. KRATOVIL, ROBERT, *Real Estate Law*, Chapter 12. Englewood Cliffs, N.J.: Prentice-Hall, Inc., 1969.
4. *Marketing Real Estate Successfully*, Chapters 5, 6, and 11. Chicago: National Institute of Real Estate Brokers, 1964.
5. MARTIN, PRESTON, *Real Estate Principles and Practices*, Chapter 8. New York: The Macmillan Company, 1959.
6. RING, ALFRED A., *Questions and Problems in Real Estate Principles and Practices* (rev. ed.), Chapter 17. Englewood Cliffs, N.J.: Prentice-Hall, Inc., 1972.
7. TECKEMEYER, EARL B., *Teckemeyer on Selling Real Estate*, Chapters 7–20. Englewood Cliffs, N.J.: Prentice-Hall, Inc., 1962.
8. UNGER, MAURICE A., *Real Estate* (4th ed.), Chapter 18. Cincinnati: South-Western Publishing Co., 1969.
9. WEIMER, ARTHUR M., and HOMER HOYT, *Real Estate* (5th ed.), Chapter 12. New York: The Ronald Press Company, 1966.

20

REAL ESTATE
ADVERTISING

The function of advertising

Anything that influences people favorably may be classed as advertising. This is a broad definition and covers a great variety of things. Ordinarily, advertising is thought of as being merely the use of the written, spoken, or printed word, but actually that is just one phase of advertising. The real estate man whose office may be viewed through attractive show windows in a good location is advertising. A good layout of the interior of his office is also advertising. The skill, neatness, dispatch, and coordination of his office force is still more advertising, and so are his manner of speech, his smile, his personality, and the actions and reactions of his personnel. It is very true that everything one does or says creates an impression, and every favorable impression so created is advertising. Therefore, the real estate man should constantly study his actions, his manner of speaking, and his methods of transacting business to see whether they impress favorably those with whom he comes in contact.

Methods of selling

Real estate transactions are brought about by direct personal sales efforts, by auctions or advertising, or by a combination of two or more of these. Occasionally a salesman may carry through the entire transaction unaided, but as a rule advertising efforts underlie successful selling. Auctions, for instance, are never held without some advertising, and many listings are secured as a result of a variety of advertising programs. To sum it up, it may be said that advertising is an essential aid to sound business development and plays an important part in promoting public confidence and goodwill upon which successful salesmanship depends.

Principles of advertising

Without making an extensive study of the general subject of advertising, the real estate man recognizes that the greater part of his advertising is something that the public absorbs through the eye. Newspapers, billboards, house signs, window displays, models—all these things produce a reaction as a result of being seen. The *first* principle of any such advertising is to catch the eye. No matter how good the property offered may be, no matter how much care may have been taken in preparation of the copy, or how important the message is, unless it catches the eye it will never be read. The first principle of advertising, thus, is to attract *attention*. Next, the advertisement must arouse *interest*. It must stir the reader's emotions or arouse his intellectual curiosity sufficiently to cause him to follow the advertisement from beginning to end. The copy, letter, or other advertising media must present more than mere statistics or commonplace expressions —it must be interesting and it must be human. The third principle of advertising is to arouse *desire*. It is poor advertising that leaves the reader without emotion. However, mere curiosity is not enough. The desire aroused must be strong enough to cause the reader to investigate further and to lead him to the next step, resulting in *action*. It is action that successful advertising seeks. Once contact has been brought about between the prospect and the broker, or his sales representative, salesmanship takes over where good advertising left off.

Classes of advertising

Real estate advertising falls into three general classes. The first may be designated as *general* advertising. This type of copy does not seek to sell or lease a specific piece of property or obtain a mortgage loan on a certain house. Its sole function is to place the advertiser's name and his business before the public. Very often advertising of this type in the smaller newspapers takes the form of "professional cards." Its purpose is simply to make people think of the real estate man's name when real estate comes to their minds. Occasionally general advertising is used with a little more definiteness to indicate some specific field or type of real estate in which the dealer is engaged. Examples of this would be a small box advertisement reading "JOHN JONES, real estate, factory sites," or "WILLIAM SMITH, real estate, mortgage financing." Advertisements of this type often appear in the real estate trade journals, where their function is largely to solicit cooperation with other brokers. Good examples of this are the advertisements of lists of brokers and appraisers appearing in nationally known real estate magazines. It is through such ads that brokers in one town seek out alert brokers in another when one of their prospects desires to reside there or to purchase property in that community for investment purposes.

The second type or form of advertising which creates goodwill and confidence in real estate as a profession is known as *institutional* advertising. In real estate, such advertising is carried out by the National Association of Real Estate Boards or by local real estate boards or groups who seek to inspire interest in a district, city, or mode of real estate transaction and to direct business to member firms. It seems reasonable to assume that the general public has greater confidence in an individual or firm governed by and holding to a code of ethics and business rules designed to protect its clients. Such advertising is often done by chambers of commerce, boards of trade, and civic associations, pointing out such matters as convenience of transit, low taxes, tax exemption or partial exemption within a community, or indicating industrial or agricultural opportunities in a certain locality. In this class also are the advertisements of groups of savings banks, indicating the desirability of opening and maintaining an account, or of an organization, government or private, for convenient financing of real estate purchasing or mortgages.

Specific advertising, the third type, advertises a particular article. It may be a classified ad, a display, or a reading notice, but in any event its purpose, whether large or small, no matter where placed or how arranged, is to sell a specific piece of real estate, to secure a mortgage loan on a definite property, or to lease a particular location. By far the greatest individual effort is expended in direct or specific advertising. It is by this form of publicity that the ingenuity and ability of the enterprising brokerage firm finds a creative outlet in drawing attention to the offering of a specific good or service.

Advertising rules

Experience with real estate advertising has led to the recognition of a number of truisms or rules which apply to so many of the media of advertising that they may well be considered before discussing the media themselves.

Symbols used as trademarks play an important role in attracting the reader's attention; every real estate man is urged to make use of this mode of identification. Symbols, however, must be designed with care. A flashy symbol, or one of colorful and unusual design, may attract attention but fail to associate the product or services offered with a *specific* real estate man. It is for this reason that symbols that partially incorporate a broker's name have proved so successful. Once a symbol or trademark has been adopted it should be used on letterheads and all advertising copy in order to popularize the broker's name and services. The symbol, it need be remembered, should arouse and strengthen the power of suggestion that motivates a prospect to select that particular broker as his agent in the real estate transaction. Many brokers use slogans in addition to, or as a substitute for, symbols. Some slogans have proven advantageous, but most of them have done more harm than good. In practice, slogans soon prove trite or juvenile in expression and, as a general rule, might better be omitted.

To attract the reader's eye every advertisement should display a good headline that caters to the prospect's wants or needs. Headlines such as "Why pay rent if you can own" or "Own a home, not rent receipts" will appeal to every tenant interested in the purchase of a home. Since rent money may in fact be applied toward the purchase of a home, headlines could call attention to this in a variety of ways, each intended to keep the desire for home ownership uppermost in the minds of interested prospects.

To attract and interest the reader, an advertisement should be simple and easy to read. The wording of the advertisement should be carefully chosen and, where possible, augmented by photographs or sketches that "tell a story." No essential facts should be omitted. The wants or needs of the reader must be kept in mind and the phraseology used should be suited to the level of thinking of the reader. Of course, every advertisement should be written for the purpose of leading the reader to further action.

Never permit an advertisement to run indefinitely. Standing copy is bad. Reiteration, of course, is essential, but the wise advertiser always varies the wording and the location of his advertisement. It is amazing how quickly the reading public notices repetition of an advertisement, and when that occurs the space is entirely wasted because the only reaction of the reader is the inference that the property is not salable.

Select a good position for your advertisement. Numerous rules have been laid down as to the page and quarter page that are most desirable. The best rule, however, is to observe the results of every advertisement and to let past performance be a guide as to the size and position of the ad and the day of the week on which to advertise. No general rules can be established because the size of the town and the type of newspaper available have an important bearing on the position and makeup of the advertisement.

The amount of space for an advertisement is often puzzling. Ordinarily a more valuable property is given more space than a less expensive one, but here again experience is the safest guide. Very often there is an element of apparent wastefulness in advertising which may arouse the reader's suspicion. This is particularly true of development advertising, where the advertiser frequently uses whole pages and extensive sketches without realizing that a large number of the readers get only the impression that since the bait is so attractive, the hook must be very sharp.

Every advertisement should be honest. This sounds axiomatic, but it is very true. Often an advertisement that almost condemns the property does more to sell it than an advertisement written in glowing terms. This has been discovered by many real estate men, and it is an interesting fact that specimens of such advertising are being reproduced from time to time in different real estate magazines.

Avoid color unless you can afford an expensive advertisement. Colors can be used satisfactorily only on high-grade paper. Color intensifies, attracts, and holds attention, but most brokers do not know how to combine colors so as to produce harmony. Therefore, if colors are to be used, an advertising specialist should be engaged.

Study your competitor's advertisements. If an advertisement interests you, try to determine what it is that makes it pull, and even if you find an advertisement that is utterly unattractive to you but is producing results for a competitor, try to find out why. Talk to some of his prospects, if the opportunity comes. Perhaps you are so close to the forest that you do not see the trees.

Always frame an advertisement from the buyer's point of view. You know all the reasons why the seller wants to sell, but that is not what makes a buyer show an interest. Before you sit down to prepare any copy, decide what type of prospect or person should want to buy it and write your message to him.

Always address your advertisement to some human interest or instinct. Every property has something that may be made the appeal motive. Decide what it is and write an advertisement around that central theme. As a result, the copy will present a comprehensive picture, instead of a garbled mixture of ideas. Here are some of the common appeals which the copy may develop:

Pride of ownership
Security
Saving impulse
Parental appeal
Prestige
Comfort instinct
Investment and speculation

In stressing "pride of ownership," appeal is made to classes of buyers who yearn for the satisfaction of owning a home or who would like to live among the more successful. Such ads should stress the spaciousness of the rooms, the restricted nature of the neighborhood, the beauty of the landscaped grounds, and the joy of the owner when showing this home to friends and visitors.

Emphasis on "security" has proved a most effective appeal in recent years. While progress in medical science and sanitation has lengthened average life, private and public old-age pension programs have strengthened the longing for security when retirement approaches. This appeal can reach an ever-widening market of buyers by sincere presentation of the safety that one derives from owning a haven for old age. Attention may be called, also, to peace of mind and permanence of occupancy as long as the owner desires.

Groups of buyers who are frugal-minded and to whom the "saving impulse" appeals can be successfully reached by pointing out prevailing low carrying charges (payable like rent) that lead to ownership of a home and not to a bundle of rent receipts. It is a fact that home ownership instills saving habits in mode of living and, of course, indirectly by periodic reduction of the mortgage purchase debt. The saving impulse appears instinctive in most people and this appeal, if honestly presented, will not only produce effective sales but result in long-term benefits through increased customer goodwill, upon which, in the final analysis, business success depends.

Attention, too, can be called to the windfall capital gains that accrue to real estate owners during years of abnormal monetary inflation. A home, like a ship upon the seas, will ride the rising crest of inflationary levels of prices and maintain its relative purchasing power as compared with other capital goods and services. This fact was driven home by an active developer who effectively advertised that residences built by his corporation "do not depreciate." To back up this claim his corporation offered to buy back any home purchased by an occupant and owned for a period of five years or more at the full price paid at the time of acquisition. With inflation causing an average loss of 4.5 percent per year during the 1965–70 period, it is no wonder that the builder reported "no takers" to his offer. Nevertheless this mode of advertising attracted attention and proved promotionally most effective.

Use of the "parental appeal" can be successfully made to young married couples and, of course, to families with school-age children who keep uppermost in mind the healthy family life and sound growth of their youngsters. Since, under current purchase practices, a home can be acquired on the "pay-as-you-live" plan, the parental appeal is among the strongest incentives that stimulate home buying. This appeal can be convincingly used by stressing such thoughts as: Here is a better place in which to bring up children; a home conducive to health and happiness for all the family; a place where happy childhood memories are instilled; a setting where good schools, good neighbors, and a clean and healthy environment contribute to sound character development and strong family ties.

Improved and higher standards of living have increased the number of home buyers who consciously seek public recognition or prestige. In advertising costlier homes and those in finer settings, effective use can be made of the "prestige" appeal. Who doesn't dream of a country home, or a city home, in a garden setting? There are those "well-to-do" who seek a home in an atmosphere of social elegance or in the vicinity of the town's outstanding personalities. In developing this appeal, reference should be made to fine architectural style, beautifully landscaped gardens, spacious living quarters, fireplaces in bedrooms and sitting rooms, and surrounding homes occupied by leading citizens.

A home as a place of rest and comfort, away from the busy everyday world, is gaining increasing appeal. Those who seek "comfort" in home life can be convincingly reached by highlighting selling points, such as enjoyable and restful living in a quiet atmosphere; nearness to transportation and other public and recreational conveniences; outdoor living; labor- and time-saving devices, playrooms, large living porches, guest room, extra bathrooms, and adequate storage and utility facilities.

For properties other than homes, the "investment" interests of the buyer generally prove guiding. The investment appeal can be successfully developed by presentation of factual data as to safety of investment, attractiveness of rate or amount of return, ease of ownership and managerial operation, adequacy of demand for space facilities, effect of growth of community on appreciation of the investment, adequacy of utility facilities, especially rail, water, and highway transportation, and available opportunities for financing and income employment. Where the investment opportunity offers special incentives for buyers of vision and quick action, the appeal should be broadened to attract buyers who are motivated by speculative capital rather than investment income gains.

Advertising agencies

Many real estate firms engage advertising agencies to handle their account. The use of agencies is successful in connection with large campaigns, such as a development or an auction of valuable properties. Ordinarily, however, its expense is far too great for the average parcel of real estate, so that the real estate man to a great extent prepares his own copy. In addition to analyzing and studying the results of his own advertisements and copy of his competitors, he will gain ideas from looking at the advertisements in the real estate magazines. He will, if he has time, do well to obtain and read some of the books written especially on the general subject of advertising.

Advertising media

The general field of advertising media may be divided into four general classes:

1. Publications, including newspapers and magazines
2. Out-of-doors, by means of billboards, car cards, and signs
3. Direct mail, including pamphlets and circular letters sent through the mails
4. Miscellaneous, including radio, television, motion pictures, blotters, calendars, and various kinds of cards and novelties

Since the average real estate man conducts his own advertising campaigns, including the writing of his own advertising copy, it may be well to look briefly at the different media.

Newspapers

The bulk of real estate advertising undoubtedly is done in local newspapers. Because their circulation is largely local, they are not very useful for broadcast advertising; but they get their message to the public quickly. Their life is short, usually only a few hours. However, it is necessary to analyze the results of all types of advertising for the curious results that are sometimes found. Although it is true that a newspaper advertisement ordinarily lives less than a day, it often happens that a month or more after a builder has advertised a certain type of house that he is building, a prospect comes walking into the office with a neat little bundle of advertising, which he has been clipping for a month or more. Having finally decided on the type of house he wants, the prospect has come to this particular builder because his plan, layout, and location suit him better than any of the others.

Three types of advertisements appear in the newspapers. The first is called *display*. The real estate man with a property that he wishes to sell prepares his copy and runs it in the real estate section for a day or two, buying as much space as he deems desirable and laying out his advertisement with the proper white space, capitals, headline, and argument. One of the greatest difficulties with this form of advertising is to know the amount of space to use. Brokers occasionally persuade owners to pay for the advertising, but generally the broker himself advertises on his own responsibility. Whatever he pays for the advertising lessens his net profit, and since he seldom has an exclusive listing, there is always the chance that he may not make a sale at all and the advertising expense will result in a net loss. He must therefore use skill and apply all the wisdom of his experience not only in the proper wording of the display advertising but in the amount of space that he uses. Here again it may be repeated that most brokers prepare their own copy, and, since public tastes change, they must be constantly on the alert to keep the copy attractive and interesting.

Another type of advertising, the *classified* ad, is used to a large extent for the sale of real estate. It is fairly inexpensive, for it takes up little room. It does not have the attractiveness of display advertising but nevertheless time has proved it a good means of reaching a specific person who is seeking a specific type of property. It is said that a person reading the classified ads is already half sold, for he is scanning the market to fill a need.

A survey to determine the effectiveness of the various methods of advertising that motivate home buyers was conducted by the Association of Newspaper Classified Advertising Managers and covered ten cities in all parts of the country. This survey disclosed the following interesting results:

1. Seventy-three percent of home buyers were motivated by newspaper advertisements.
2. Fifty-one percent of home buyers consulted real estate brokers.
3. Eight percent found the house through friends and neighbors.
4. Nine percent were motivated by Open House signs, billboards, and other advertising sources.

The growing use of classified ads as a means of selling to the general public requires some study of their makeup. Originally they came into use because they were inexpensive and were read only by bargain hunters. Hence they were cut down to a minimum of words. Currently advertisers have come to recognize the customer drawing power of the classified ad columns and include in it larger and more descriptive copy. Style of ad writing, too, should be studied, avoiding stereotyped words and phrases. "Charming," "bargain," "reasonable," "sacrifice," and "must be seen to be appreciated" are so worn out that these words leave little or no impression.

Classified advertising is "news" to the reader and should be written with care to prove worthwhile reading. If the ad is directed to a particular class of buyer, the copy should set forth the essentials that accurately describe the characteristics of the property, advantages of location, asking price, and terms of financing that would attract that type of buyer. A survey made by the National Institute of Real Estate Brokers revealed that a buyer's need is related to his situation in life. Thus a man with a family needs room, proximity to schools, work, and public transportation, and long-term mortgage financing. The retired couple, on the other hand, needs less room, accessibility to shopping, hospitals, and churches, and a short-term mortgage. The "status seeker" could be influenced by reference to prestige location, a swimming pool, a two-car garage, nearness to a country club, and architectural or estate features.

The third type of newspaper advertising is known as the *reading notice*. Every real estate man should endeavor to keep himself in the public eye. He is really a member of a semiprofession, at least to the extent that he has specialized knowledge of which the general public knows nothing. He should, even in the smallest community, build the reputation of "knowing real estate." To this end, whenever possible, he should write articles and have them published in the newspapers. In the larger communities the papers that carry real estate sections always want some articles of general interest around which to group their real estate advertisements. These articles, though often written up as interviews, in nine cases out of ten are prepared by real estate men for the purpose of drawing attention to themselves and some particular venture in which they are engaged. Although they give the impression of being general news stories dealing with real estate, nevertheless their particular virtue is that they give to the broker the appearance of special qualifications of expertness and in addition draw the public's attention to the particular line of real estate activity in which the broker-author is interested.

The selection of the proper newspaper and the proper issue of the newspaper in which to advertise is quite important. Of course, in some communities there is only one paper and the problem is easily solved, but many towns and cities have several newspapers, some of which are published in the morning and some in the afternoon. No definite rule can be given with regard to the issue to select. In some places all real estate advertising is carried in the morning papers, largely because the papers reach the homes about breakfast time when everyone interested in such advertising reads the papers and then goes out to answer the ads that appeal most. In such a community the evening paper reaches the public too late for any investigations to be made that day.

In the larger cities, on the other hand, the evening papers generally have their first edition out by noon or possibly earlier, with the result that a great deal of real estate advertising is carried in the evening papers. The buying public, engaged in its own affairs in the morning, buys papers at lunchtime and goes out to answer the ads in the early afternoon.

The day of the week on which to advertise is also a matter that only experience can settle. It has always been the practice to advertise heavily in the Sunday editions, in spite of the fact that Saturday has become largely a holiday. Apparently the principal reason that Sunday is the largest advertising day is that no advertiser wishes to find his name and his properties omitted from the large group in the Sunday section.

Then, too, in spite of Saturday's being so largely free from work, Sunday is still a large selling day, particularly for lots and newly constructed homes. The type of property has an important bearing on the day on which the advertisement is placed. Properties that appeal to investors, operators, and speculators may be advertised nearly every day of the week because such buyers are on the constant lookout for properties that may appeal to them. The advertising that must be concentrated at the end of the week is that of properties to be sold to what may be spoken of as the family trade, that is, properties in the nature of lots and medium to modest homes. The husband very often cannot take time off from his work during the week, with the result that he and his wife both look at the property on Sunday.

Magazines

In the periodical field, as far as real estate is concerned, there are two types: the general magazine and the trade magazine. Trade magazines include those of the local and other real estate boards, as well as such publications as may be issued by boards of trade, chambers of commerce, and other civic organizations. In magazines of this type, the real estate man usually inserts only general advertising. His purpose is more particular to call the attention of men in related professions to his name and address and to the fact that he is specializing in a particular phase of real estate, in some particular locality, or in a special activity such as management or mortgage lending.

General magazine advertising is very rarely used. Real estate is distinctly a geographic and local business. There are few firms whose activities spread beyond one city and its suburbs. Magazine advertising is usually confined to products that are used in a large area or throughout the entire country. The space is usually too expensive for an advertisement of a property whose ownership would appeal to readers located in a comparatively small area. Almost the only real estate advertising found in general magazines appears in those few whose readers might be interested in large country estates involving the expenditure of a very substantial amount of money.

Billboards and signs

Advertising by means of billboards is expensive, but lasting. It seldom pays in connection with a single piece of property unless the property is a large building or tract. Occasionally billboards are used for institutional advertising, presenting merely the broker's name, address, and business. Such billboards are often found on the main highways leading into a community, so that visitors who may be interested in purchasing or leasing in the town may be led to go to that broker's office.

A less expensive type of outdoor advertising is by means of posters and signs in railroad stations and bus terminals. These are often used because of their small expense and because the many people who are forced to wait for their trains and buses almost unconsciously read everything in sight. These signs are quite apt to become soiled in the course of time, and the broker who uses them should be careful to see that they are replaced periodically, so that they look neat and clean and do not give the impression, which the reader may get from a dirty sign, that the property itself is unattractive and the broker slipshod.

Signs advertising property for sale or to let are very widely used. They are simple and very effective. They need not tell very much of a story and are placed on the property to which they refer, so that they need not be descriptive. For instance, a For Sale sign in the middle of a vacant lot need not tell anything about the lot; the lot is there, in plain sight. Such a sign does not even give the dimensions of the lot unless the lot varies from the normal size. A To Let sign in a store window usually need not tell anything about the store because the passerby, if interested, can stop, look through the window, and decide then and there whether or not he is interested. The sign should simply indicate whether the property is for sale or to let and tell the reader where he may contact the broker, simply by giving the broker's name, address, and telephone number.

Brokers should avoid getting into a rut with their signs. Too many of them look alike. The alert broker will try for something to vary the monotony and thus catch the eye—possibly a border or a symbol. When possible they should be posted on the grounds rather than stuck on the house. The grass should be kept cut, and the grounds and house should look neat. Signs must be periodically inspected, renewed when soiled, and straightened up when they look neglected.

Car and bus cards

Most local and suburban transits carry advertising cards. An analysis will indicate that the great bulk of such advertising is of products that may be used anywhere and that very little of such space is devoted to real estate. However, a certain amount of real estate advertising can be very satisfactorily placed in cars and buses. Most of the riders are commuters and the real estate that may appeal to them will be sales of homes or rental property. Care should always be taken to analyze the type of people who use a particular line of cars or buses and to advertise only properties and apartments within their means and located either in an area served by that particular line or in another area that may be reached with equal convenience from the business or industrial center. For example, on a suburban train line connecting only high-class communities, it would be an utter waste of money to advertise modest homes that can be purchased with a small down payment and monthly installments "same as rent." On the other hand, such an advertisement might well be inserted in a line serving a modest neighborhood even though it advertised homes in a locality several miles away, provided there is an equally convenient and no more expensive means of transit to the advertised area.

Maps and pamphlets

In selling a single piece of property, it is seldom that a printed map or pamphlet is employed. To be sure, the broker or salesman may and probably will use a diagram, but it will be prepared in his office for the prospect when he appears; and although a property brief may be similarly prepared, it will not take the form of a printed pamphlet. Maps and pamphlets are ordinarily used when a number of properties are to be sold, either lots or homes in a development. In such a situation the seller can afford to include their cost in his advertising budget. His maps will be attractively prepared, and his pamphlet will be well written on good-quality paper. Never use a pamphlet or a map unless it is well prepared. The psychology of the prospect is always such that he judges the property from the means used to sell it. His first impression should not be one of cheapness, whether from a poor map, a mediocre pamphlet, or, for that matter, from a shoddily dressed salesman.

In the preparation of maps there is one point that many real estate men overlook. They know that the map must indicate all the lots, highways, and so forth, in the development or subdivision, but they fail to realize that the average buyer, looking at the map, does not know just where the property is situated. That fact may give rise to two bad impressions. In the first place, a prospect going out to find the property feels that he is diving off a springboard into unknown waters; and second, he has the feeling that the development must be "in back of beyond." It is always important to have the map show not only the development itself but also the main highways near it.

Circularization

A great deal of real estate selling is done by means of circular letters. This is a very important aspect of the business and care should be taken to observe a number of points. The first involves the careful selection of a prospect list. Although there are many companies throughout the country that sell lists of almost every type of prospect, such lists are of little use in the real estate business. The most satisfactory lists the broker can use are those he prepares himself. Names may be obtained from various sources. The telephone directories will give a general list. There are also various lists available of the members of churches, clubs, and civic associations, of civil service employees, and others. These, of course, should be used with selective care and with due regard to the type of property to be sold.

A real estate man who had just been appointed manager of a newly erected apartment house canvassed the district and, not without some difficulty, obtained the name of every tenant in all the comparable houses in the general area. The results of a letter to that list were highly successful. Every broker and salesman should also have a list of people he has dealt with, divided into types of buyers. A letter to such a list has the advantage of previous acquaintance, possibly even friendship. The people know him and are glad to hear from him, and perhaps may be in the market to buy.

The second problem in connection with circularization has to do with the type of material sent out. In the cities, where people receive a great deal of mail, such material gets scant attention, and the keynote of all circularization of this type is, "Make it short." The broker cannot do much more than stir interest, get a reply, and then finish the work through his salesmen. In the rural districts, on the other hand, not so much mail is received, and the local residents are quite willing to read even lengthy letters. It is for this reason that the circular letters used in farm colonization plans are apt to run from two to five pages in length. And these letters will be thoroughly read, although a letter of similar length written to a city dweller would get no reaction whatever on its way to the wastebasket.

The makeup of circularization material varies not only in length but in character. The farmer will read a long letter, single spaced, without anything to relieve what others would consider a monotonous makeup. The city dweller seems to be more fidgety. His attention jumps around. Not only must the letter addressed to him be shorter but the paragraphs should be broken up. Size of type must vary, diagrams and photographs must be reproduced, and some brokers even find the use of contrasting colors desirable. Of course, the broker must take care not to make up something so bizarre that it gets no results.

Aside from length and general appearance, circularization material must be well composed. Many brokers prepare a sequence of letters at the start of a campaign, each adding something to the preceding one. And yet, each letter must be complete and tell a story. Care should be taken that letters are simple, yet well expressed. It is essential that the broker use good English and that his appeal to the reader display good judgment. A well-written circular letter which quickly achieved the desired results is reproduced below:

Dear Mr. ———
Do you know the reason for all the hammering, sawing, painting, and decorating that has been going on in your neighborhood, at 426 S——— Street?

The whole house has been renovated from cellar to garret. A new heating plant, new radiators, new electric fixtures, and new wallpaper have made the house a thoroughly modern one.

This will interest you because it means that an improvement has been made in the neighborhood.

Furthermore, a modernized house like this one will attract the kind of buyers that you want as neighbors.

If you have a friend who is looking for a modern house in a good neighborhood, you will do yourself, him, and us a favor by telling him about this house.

Tell him also that it will be open for inspection on Tuesday evening, April 7. At this time he will have an opportunity to inspect the house from top to bottom, carefully and leisurely, and to decide whether or not it is the house he would like to own.

Better call him now—before you forget it.

Yours truly,

Miscellaneous advertising and use of novelties

In addition to the advertising media that have been discussed at some length, the real estate man may use a number of other devices that will keep his name and professional calling at public attention.

Ordinarily, *business stationery* is not thought of in an advertising sense. Nevertheless, stationery can be made very useful in creating a good impression. Writing paper should always be neat. The printed matter should be readable and reasonably conservative in its makeup. An effort should be made to avoid putting too much on the letterhead. For example, if the office handles insurance, it would probably be better to list only two or three kinds than to have a long list of twenty-five or thirty different types of insurance on the margin of the letterhead. The symbol used by the real estate man should always be a part of the letterhead, so that its general advertising value may be obtained. The broker must constantly use every available means of getting the public to know his symbol and to associate it with him.

The *business cards* should be conservative. If possible, every salesman should have his own. Nothing hurts a salesman so much as to have to present a business card that gives the impression that he is either a new employee or on trial, as indicated by the fact that his name is simply printed on an engraved card or is completely omitted from it.

Motion picture advertising is used to some extent in connection with real estate, almost entirely as a selling stimulus. This device must be handled and analyzed very carefully. Most real estate firms omit it entirely. The motion picture theatres have very little data on which to estimate the response to such advertising; consequently, their charges are more or less a matter of guess and may be entirely too high. Besides, the makeup of the audience is such that there are very likely only a few people in the theatre who are interested in the advertisement. Most of them feel that it is an intrusion on time for which they have paid; they came to see a movie, not advertising. If motion pictures are used at all, they must be very short and, if possible, should have some artistic appeal as well as show the property.

The *radio* is still an uncertain field of advertising as far as specific real estate is concerned. Time costs are very high compared with space costs in other forms of advertising. The message must be short, and since it is heard rather than seen, it does not make nearly so great an impression as a newspaper ad, a pamphlet, or a circular. Radio is useful in connection with the sale of a large number of buildings or lots. Developers were giving programs as early as 1922, and since then many stations from time to time have carried such advertising. For general advertising, the broker should seize every opportunity to get on the air, particularly if he can talk on some phase of real estate. Possibly he may be able to interest his local station in a series of broadcasts on subjects like "Repairs," "New Appliances," "What to Look For in a New Home," and other similar topics.

Television, although a more expensive mode of advertising than radio, has been successfully employed by real estate firms, particularly in the larger urban centers. Television broadcasts provide the opportunity to bring the model house directly into the homes of the television audience. Seeing the many home features which have increased the amenities of living in modern times is considerably more effective than describing them by spoken or written words. A number of real estate men now feature weekly television shows bringing to their viewers the "buy of the week," coupled with an informative discussion of why this home and others in similar settings are considered a sound investment. Where these television programs are sponsored and "acted" by sales personnel known to the home folks, the advertising effects are doubly effective and are known to have produced gratifying commercial results.

The builder of homes may make good use of *floodlighting*. Several such lights, advantageously placed, will so light up a building that the selling day is extended well into the night. With darkness all around, the flood-lighted home stands out and strikes the eye of the passerby, particularly the motorist. The appeal may be made even stronger by the use of variegated, kaleidoscopic lights, but blinkers should be avoided unless, possibly, the sequence is a short off and fairly long on.

The many *novelties* used in connection with real estate advertising take innumerable forms. Paperweights, thermometers, calendars, and other desk equipment are distributed by many brokers. They must be decorative and useful. Many of them are so drab and useless as to attract no attention and are simply thrown away. Some brokers distribute records and record books of various sorts; mortgage record books are distributed by real estate men engaged in placing and servicing mortgages for investment. The books are so set up that investors who have bought mortgages through them may readily keep informed as to interest payments and other items. Another type of record may be furnished to the investor owning real estate so that he may readily tabulate his income and expenses.

In advertising, the appeal to the eye is stronger than the appeal to the ear. This fact has been proved by many real estate men, not only in connection with attractive show windows but also in the development and use of models. Suppose, for instance, that a developer has a tract some ten miles out of the city. Some prospects will be glad to go to the development and look at it "on the ground," but a certain number must have the development brought to them, so to speak. For this purpose the developer may have in his office a large table, possibly the size of a billiard table, the surface of which is arranged to scale, showing the contours, roads, and so forth, of the development. It is made to simulate, as far as possible, the actual layout of the development. The surface is green to indicate grass; the roads are colored, so that they stand out; and the boundaries of the various lots are indicated by faint white lines. With such a model, the salesman can show the exact location of any lot and its relation to the others. As buildings are erected, an exact model of each building, garage, and garage driveway is placed on the model. If some particular lot appeals to the prospect, he can see just what neighboring buildings have been built and how they stand. Besides, the salesman has models of various types of houses and can lay out a house and grounds in a moment so that the prospect can get a bird's-eye view of just what his lot will look like with any of a dozen kinds of houses placed in any position on the lot. The use of this selling aid has secured very satisfactory results.

The developer can use various devices to center attention on his model home or the latest one finished. Quite likely he will have the building completely furnished, although in doing this he must avoid being drawn into advertising the furniture, draperies, and other household equipment. He also may obtain cooperation from the local public officials for an official opening, with a celebrity cutting the ribbon and opening the door. One developer even had the building wrapped in cellophane and a movie star pull the zipper that "opened the package"—his latest building.

READING AND STUDY REFERENCES

1. "Ads That Sell Homes Revive a City," *Editor and Publisher*, 97, March 21, 1964, 20.
2. CASE, FREDERICK E., *Real Estate Brokerage*, Chapter 9. Englewood Cliffs, N.J.: Prentice-Hall, Inc., 1965.
3. "Catching Up With the Times," *Printers Ink*, 283, May 5, 1962, 3.
4. *Practical Real Estate Management*, Volume 1, Chapters 21 and 24. Chicago: Institute of Real Estate Management, 1958.
5. "Real Estate Today," III, No. 4, 51–54, Chicago National Institute of Real Estate Brokers, 1970.
6. RING, ALFRED A., *Questions and Problems in Real Estate Principles and Practices* (rev. ed.), Chapter 18. Englewood Cliffs, N.J.: Prentice-Hall, Inc., 1972.
7. UNGER, MAURICE A., *Real Estate* (4th ed.), Chapter 19. Cincinnati: South-Western Publishing Co., 1969.

21

PROPERTY MANAGEMENT

During the past two decades, property management has developed into a highly specialized branch of the real estate business. As an *organized profession*, property management is of relatively recent origin, dating back to 1933 when the Institute of Real Estate Management was founded under the auspices of the National Association of Real Estate Boards. Specifically, property management is traceable to three interrelated causes which created a need for the property specialist: (1) urbanization, (2) technological development in building construction, and (3) absentee ownership.

Urbanization, with its attendant high concentration of population in selected and strategically located geographic areas, made the subdivision and leasing of large land holdings a profitable venture. Urbanization, too, increased the mobility of the tenant population and intensified the competitive adjustment of housing demand and supply. Knowledge of population trends, city growth, and neighborhood patterns became ever more important in forecasting and planning for the highest and best land use and in maintaining adequately the productivity of real estate investments. Population and city growth problems, together with the increasing complexity of the landlord-tenant legal, social, and economic relationship, established

348

the need for a property specialist who could effectively and profitably manage on behalf of the owner.

Technological development in building construction proved another cause for specialized and professional skill in property management. The development of steel, electricity, and the elevator made the construction of skyscraper office and apartment buildings possible. The servicing of these multistory buildings or huge garden-type apartment houses necessitated the hiring and supervising of large numbers of workers and technicians who could attend to the operation and maintenance of building equipment. Hiring and supervising of essential personnel, purchasing, storing, accounting, and legal requirements necessitated managerial skill and ingenuity which the average property owner no longer could profitably muster. Management of large structures under supervision of trained personnel is no longer the exception in the larger urban centers and increasingly is destined to be the general rule. Skillful property managers have demonstrated their ability to do all the owner would possibly do himself and often to do it better and more profitably.

A third and compelling cause which created a need for professional property management is *absentee ownership*. Real property, because of its durability and relative scarcity, has always proved attractive to investors. In the years following both world wars, inflationary economic practices have further enhanced the investment quality of real estate. High taxes and the feasibility of converting otherwise taxable income into capital gains has made ownership of real estate, under skilled management, a popular and profitable venture. Insurance companies and investment trusts, too, have found it profitable to balance their investment portfolios with equity ownership in real property. The popularity of the purchase-lease agreements under which ownership and management, but not occupancy or use, of large properties have changed attests to the fact that absentee ownership has proved economically worthwhile. Many of the largest and some of the most prominent and best-known buildings in the principal urban centers throughout the nation are currently under the competent care of real estate firms who specialize in property management.

The scope and objectives of property management

Property management may be said to be twofold in scope: (1) to maintain the investment (income) in the property and (2) to maintain the physical aspects of the property at a point of optimum efficiency and economy. The former covers administrative and executive functions in the fields of economics and finance, whereas the latter scope covers technological functions principally in the field of engineering. Athough each function in practice is administered by specially trained supervisors, all functions are economically interrelated and are subject to unified control under an overall executive plan.

Good property management begins before expenditures are made in the development of a site, or even before a property is acquired for investment purposes, the objective being to measure in advance of any financial commitments the greatest possible net return the property will yield under the highest and best land use and over the economic life of the structures and improvements. This net return must then be related to the investment in order to ascertain whether the *rate* of return is commensurate with the risk assumed in the financial venture. When the return *on* the investment is deemed adequate, that is, competitive with alternative forms of investment, and the return *of* the investment is sufficient to equal anticipated periodic accrued property depreciation, it is in order to advise the development or purchase of the property.

The tax position of the individual owner or corporation and the extent to which a property continues to provide adequate tax shelter to equity owners have become increasingly important in the managerial decision-making process. In all instances that involve taking advantage of accelerated depreciation tax allowances, an investment property, within ten years of ownership, may cease to provide meaningful tax shelter or, in fact, may yield insufficient cash flow to meet tax liabilities. When this investment position is reached and deemed critical, good management policy calls for an exchange or sale and purchase of like properties to reestablish a profitable tax basis for maintaining the cash investment flow at desired ownership levels.

Functions of management

Property management is often and erroneously confused with *rental agency*. The functions of the latter, as the term implies, are limited to the selection of tenants and to the periodic collection of rents. The owner, under rental agency, retains all rights and responsibilities connected with the maintenance and operation of the property, administers the policy-making decisions, and attends directly to the legal, social, and economic matters which ownership of property entails.

Under property management, the manager not only acts as administrator for the owner but assumes all executive functions necessary to carry out the objectives set by the owner. The manager in fact relieves the owner of all the labor and details involved in the operation and physical care of the property. The principal functions of management, generally, include the following:

1. Marketing of space, advertising, and securing desirable tenants at the best rates obtainable
2. Collection of rents
3. Physical care of the premises and attendance to tenant complaints
4. Purchases of supplies and equipment and expenditures for repairs
5. Hiring of employees and maintaining good public relations
6. Keeping proper accounts and rendering periodic reports

Organization of the management department

The management department of a brokerage firm is usually headed by a vice-president who may be an expert operating man or an individual who can bring in management business to the firm. He has under him residence managers or district managers, who are in charge of one or several buildings. These men are the contact men between the management and the tenants. The renting is done by the superintendents in each building, by the district managers, by the renting agents on the premises, or by the leasing department of the brokerage firm. The maintenance and repair work in all the buildings may be done by a maintenance organization, which is usually headed by a group of engineers. This work also may be let out on contract, except for the work that can be done by the superintendents and handymen.

When the owner of a large building decides to build up his own management organization, the usual procedure is first to select a competent building manager. The building manager then creates an organization consisting of a renting manager, an operating manager, service employees, and maintenance employees. Purchasing, collections, and accounting are handled by the treasurer, or by an assistant manager or office manager.

Marketing of space

The principal objectives of property management are to attain the greatest possible net return over the economic life span of the property and to protect the owner's capital investment at all times. To achieve these objectives, it is essential to market the available space effectively, at maximum possible rates, and keep vacancy losses to an irreducible minimum. The marketing of space is in essence a merchandising problem. The space-seeking tenant, as a rule, is familiar with the city, with the neighborhood in which the property is located, with prevailing rentals on a per room or per square foot basis, with availability of competitive space, and with the location advantages and disadvantages of the subject property. To secure the prospect as a tenant, the manager or his representative must be able to "sell" the space by matching the service opportunities that the property, under his management, has to offer with the specific needs and requirements that the prospect seeks to satisfy.

Merchandising of space, contrary to common belief, is more difficult than outright selling. In the latter case, when a property sale is consummated the broker is through with the deal and may turn to other properties he has to offer with renewed vigor and initiative. In merchandising space, the "sale" normally is for a limited period and periodically renewals must be renegotiated. The property manager is thus aware that his representatives must be truthful and the services offered superior in order that the tenant may remain "sold" as long as possible.

The first and perhaps most important step in the marketing of space is the establishment of a *rental schedule*. Although in theory the price of space should be based on operating costs, fixed charges, and a fair rate of return *on* the investment and *of* the investment (amortization) over the economic life of the property, in practice, rental prices are established by space supply and demand. Although in the long run rentals must be compensatory and meet fully operating costs and investment charges (if new space is to be forthcoming), in the short run, space values will fluctuate widely depending on forces affecting tenant space demand (purchasing power) in relation to the relatively inflexible space supply of apartment and commercial properties.

Rental schedules for the various units of space to be offered are most realistically established on a market comparison basis. This is effectively done by rating the subject property in relation to like properties in similar neighborhoods for which accurate rental data is available. The comparison approach, though simple in application, relies on sound judgment for effective use. Comparison is generally made with a number of typical space units, and price adjustments for the subject property are based on quantitative and qualitative differences. For example, in the pricing of an apartment unit, consideration should be given to the following: area of floor space, number of bathrooms, quality of construction, decorative features, floor location, type and quality of elevator service, nature and quality of janitorial services, reputation of building and characteristics of tenants, location of building in relation to public conveniences, and quality rating of neighborhood and neighborhood trends. Assuming that a standard unit in an ideal neighborhood rents for $250 per month and the comparative rating for the subject property, after due consideration of the factors enumerated above, is 90 percent, then the estimated fair rental is judged to be $225 per month. If a detailed comparison is made for each space unit with six or more selected and comparable units, a fairly accurate and competitive rental schedule can be established[1] and submitted for the owner's approval.

The next step in the marketing of space is the determination of the kind of tenants to be secured and the policy to be followed in advertising the types of units and services offered. Every effort should be made to attract qualified tenants who appear homogeneous in their family and living characteristics. Tenants react on each other and, as a whole, add or detract from the amenities of living and the congenial atmosphere that is conducive to pride of occupancy and a feeling of "belonging." Some buildings may be deemed best fitted for young couples with children, others may be best for older and retired people who cherish an atmosphere of quiet restfulness. The fact that an attempt is made to suit the facilities of the building to the housing needs and requirements of the tenant makes a favorable impression upon the prospect and generally contributes importantly to the development of tenant goodwill and to the furtherance of good public relations. If the rental schedule is properly prepared and the building space

[1]Students of management, and those seeking to perfect their judgment in rental schedule preparation, should study the rental formula developed by Leo J. Sheridan and William Karkow, two well-known Chicago building managers. Copies of the Sheridan-Karkow formula are available through the National Association of Building Owners and Managers, Chicago, Illinois.

effectively advertised, one out of every five eligible prospects calling at the property should as a rule become a building tenant.[2] If the ratio of tenants to prospects is greater or lesser, the space units may be underpriced or overpriced.

Collection of rents

The collection of rents need not pose a problem if the credit rating of each tenant, prior to his acceptance, is carefully checked and if the collection policy is clearly explained and firmly adhered to. In most communities with a population of ten thousand and over, credit bureaus have been established and it is possible to secure from them, at nominal cost, a credit record of the prospective tenant. Credit reports, as a rule, serve as an excellent safeguard against acceptance of tenants who have demonstrated financial instability. It is also wise policy to request references and to check with property owners from whom the applicant has rented in the immediate past. If the applicant, for instance, has not given proper "vacate" notice at his previous place of residence, or failed to pay his rent, the application should, of course, be rejected.

A firm collection policy is basic to successful management. At the outset, tenants should be impressed with the importance of making payments on time at the start of the rental period as specified in the lease agreement. Tenants may also be informed that the periodic statements are not sent and that it is their obligation to submit payments on the due date to the manager's office. In many cases, however, notices are sent. It is deemed good policy, for record purposes, to issue rental receipts even though payments are received by check. Such receipts permit uniform rental auditing and provide a ready reference for bookkeeping purposes.

A procedure for "follow-up" of past-due rentals should be rigidly and uniformly adhered to. A statement for past-due rents should be sent to delinquent tenants within five to ten days after the rental due date. This "due" notice may be followed with a "final" notice a week or ten days later.

If this notice is ignored or not satisfactorily acted upon, legal proceedings are then in order to obtain possession or to collect the unpaid rent.

Physical care of the property

Good property management demands a thorough knowledge of building service and maintenance requirements. Service is a "big" word. In the effective accomplishment of it, the interests of the owner and those of the tenants must be properly balanced. It is in the physical care of the property that the service interests of the owner and those of the tenants merge. The owner is interested that the manager give his structure constant care and attention in order that property investment may yield the highest possible net return over the life of the building. The tenants, on the other hand, are entitled to reasonable building service performance. The manager's

---

[2]See James C. Downs, Jr., *Principles of Real Estate Management*, "Merchandising Residential Space," Chapter VIII. Institute of Real Estate Management, 1967, Chicago, Illinois.

pride and concern about good service generally invites tenant cooperation and stimulates proper building use rather than abuse. Tenants, by and large, are reasonable in their demands, and complaints where voiced should be attended to promptly. No matter how small the request may be, good managerial policy calls for attending to it at once. Never should a request for service be ignored. Prompt action is essential in building goodwill not only with the tenants but also with the property owner whose interests are at stake.

At all times, the building should be kept clean and attractive. Inspection of the property should be made at regular intervals. It should be seen to that the janitor is on the job and carrying out his duties. Halls should be kept lighted and elevators running. Heating systems and building service utilities should be kept in proper order. Constant alert should be kept for possible defects around the property. Flaws and hazards should be checked for in sidewalks, stairs, flooring, roofing, wiring, plumbing, or anywhere inattention may cause an accident. The maintenance problems and repairs referred to above apply only to buildings that are rented to a number of tenants and where the landlord controls portions of the building. In some cases, the tenant agrees to attend to all repairs and consequently the owner is not liable for damages. The question of liability for damages is more fully discussed in the chapter on leases.

Purchases, wages, and expenditures for repairs

It is the manager's responsibility to supervise and authorize the prudent expenditure of money essential to the operation and maintenance of the building. Many expenditures are routine, such as the wages of employees and the bills for light, heat, power, and other recurring items. Even in meeting these expenditures, operational practices can be reviewed and economy practiced.

In meeting expenditures for repairs, the manager may refer all work to a general contractor who assumes all responsibility for carrying out the needed work, or the manager may purchase and stock required materials and hire skilled workers to attend to the repairs under his general supervision. The former practice is recommended when buildings under one management are small in size and number. With large buildings and extensive scope of managerial functions, the latter practice may prove more economical. Service, too, can be restored and repairs attended to more promptly where workers and technicians are subject to direct control. Where the latter practice of attending directly to repairs is followed, a repair voucher order should be issued for each job and an accurate record kept of labor and materials used. The owner is then billed for actual expenditures plus a nominal overhead service charge (5 to 10 percent) for job superintendence. The direct control of purchases, wages, and expenditures for repairs, provided the size and number of buildings managed warrant it, should prove more economical and more efficient in the maintenance and restoration of building service.

Hiring of employees

The success of property management depends to a great extent upon other people, that is, people upon whom the property manager must rely as employees or associates. It is therefore of utmost importance that the selection and training of personnel be given special care and consideration. Employees, although not vested with agency responsibility, indirectly represent the owner, and their conduct and serviceability affect public relations and tenant goodwill.

In selecting personnel, consideration should be given to the following:

1. Is the applicant technically qualified?
2. Is he sufficiently interested in his work to make it his life's task?
3. Is the compensation offered at least as high as that earned for similar work in the applicant's prior position?
4. Is the applicant congenial, emotionally adjusted, and worthy of becoming a member of the firm's "family"?
5. Does the applicant display interest which denotes possibility of growth with the firm?

These questions, of course, cannot be satisfactorily answered solely by the facts disclosed during the initial interview. A followup of the applicant's experience, personnel records, and direct interviews with prior employers may supply the needed information. The initial care and trouble assumed in the hiring of employees is repaid manifold in the economy that flows from the effective teamwork of competent and well-adjusted personnel. Proper personnel selection, too, reduces employee turnover and minimizes organizational inefficiency. The important fact should be kept in mind that it takes weeks and even months to effectively train an employee and that, as a consequence, changes in personnel will prove expensive. Initial care in hiring employees should receive the due attention that this important personnel function merits.

The careful selection of an employee should be followed with a well-thought-out and effective training program. The employee should be given an opportunity to meet his co-workers, to sense pride in his work, as well as to acquire a feeling of belonging to an organization that "cares." Where the executive, because of stress of work, is unable to instruct the new employee, a manual should be prepared in which the overall objectives of the organization are clearly stated. The manual should also set forth the conditions of employment, hours of work, holidays, sick leave, and vacation as well as complete instructions covering duties and responsibilities of the specific job to which the employee is assigned. Every employee, of course, should be informed that he is expected to give unstintingly of the time for which he is paid and that his work must prove worth his hire.

Keeping proper accounts and rendering periodic reports

One of the prime requirements of good management is the maintenance of an adequate system of accounts by means of which an orderly presentation of monthly activities, detailed as to income and expenditures, can be submitted to the owners. Accounting, although principally intended to provide statements of assets and liabilities and interim schedules of income and expenses, is also an important aid in providing a historical record of continuing property control and occupancy, as well as providing data useful in the determination of management policy. In selecting the appropriate accounting system, careful thought should be given to the type of forms and accounts best suited to the orderly and efficient operation of the property and to the types of records to be maintained for the reporting of required facts and figures.

Owner's statements, depending on size and number of properties managed, may be presented in summary or detailed (also known as *transcript*) form. Modern practice sanctions the detail reporting method. Under this method the owner is furnished a monthly statement which may contain property income and expense data as follows:

MONTHLY PROPERTY MANAGEMENT REPORT

Name of Building ....
Location ....
Statement for the Month of .... 19.......
And Accounts Receivable as of .... 19.......
Number of Units Rented ....
Number of Units Vacant ....

RENTAL INFORMATION AND RECEIPTS

Property	Name of Tenant	Rent per Month	Arrears	Amount Paid	Arrears at Close	Remarks

DISBURSEMENTS AND DISTRIBUTION

Work Done or Article Bought Contractor or Vendor	Capital or Cost	Payroll	Fuel	Water Gas Electricity	General Supplies	Insurance & Taxes	Maintenance & Repairs	Commissions	Total

Amount Collected $_____
Less Amount Disbursed $_____
Net Amount Deposited $_____

Where the manager is charged with the duty of maintaining social security and withholding tax records, and the filing of governmental reports, auxiliary accounting records should be kept and periodically submitted for the owner's check and approval. All funds received and those held for the owner's account should be deposited in a separate trust account and under no circumstances should such monies be deposited with the manager's personal or business funds.

Insurance

Although the brokerage and agency functions of insurance will be discussed at length in Chapter 22, it is important to stress here the property manager's responsibility to protect the owner against all major insurable risks. It is understandable for the owner to expect that the management firm will relieve him of every detail incident to the ownership of his property. As the owner's representative, the manager should be capable of determining and evaluating the risks involved and should make every effort to secure the best and most economical protection available in the insurance market.

Standard insurance coverage contracts which the manager should consider in the protection of his client's property include the following:

1. Standard fire insurance. This policy protects the insured against all direct losses or damages to real property by fire excepting those losses caused by perils or forces specifically excluded in the policy.
2. Extended coverage. The inclusion of extended coverage is a recommended practice. It provides for broader protection and includes risk compensation for losses due to perils of explosion, windstorm, hail, riot, civil disturbances, aircraft, vehicles, and other causes.
3. General liability. This policy insures the power against liability imposed by law for damages due to injuries caused to the persons or properties of others.
4. Workmen's compensation. This type of employee protection against injury is mandatory in most states and varies in accordance with state law.
5. Inland marine insurance is available to cover personal property losses and, more generally, damages to property that is mobile in nature.
6. Casualty insurance. This protects the insured against losses due to theft, burglary, plate glass breakage, elevator accident, steam boiler, machinery, and similar accident losses. Under this form of insurance, policies are also issued to cover a variety of accident and health injuries.
7. Rent insurance and consequential losses. This type of insurance is also referred to as *business interruptions insurance*. It compensates the owner for consequential losses incident to damage or destruction of the property.

It is the manager's responsibility, as agent for the owner, to keep accurate records of all insurance policies and to arrange for renewals well in advance of date of policy expiration. Care must be taken that insurance coverage is in proper relation to current property replacement costs and that dollar price changes due to increased construction costs or monetary inflation have been considered on or before the date of policy renewal. Good management, too, can assist in keeping fire insurance down to a minimum by eliminating fire hazards as much as possible. Sometimes the character of a tenant's business increases the insurance rate on the building. This fact should be recognized in setting the appropriate rent. Generally tenants agree to pay the additional premium caused by their mode of occupancy.

A study of insurance price schedules offered by competing companies may suggest ways of securing rate reductions. As a rule, liability insurance is carried so that any claim for damages is defended by the insurance company and loss, if any, is borne by them. Rent insurance is entirely optional with the owner. Many owners do not wish to carry it, being willing to assume the risk of a loss of rents in case of fire.

Choice of a manager

The choice of a manager naturally requires careful thought on the part of an owner. He wants the services of an agent who will produce the best results with the property. The results of the agent's work are shown not only by the size of the net income obtained but also by the condition of the property. The agent should have an accurate knowledge of conditions affecting rents, so that when space in the building is to be rented, a lease may be made for the owner on the best possible terms. If the owner or his agent does not know the market, valuable opportunities may be wasted. The knowledge the agent should possess comes only through experience and by his being in close touch with the requirements of tenants and the prices they are willing to pay for space. The agent needs to have trained assistants or associates to take care of each department of his business: collections, repairs, supplies, insurance, accounting, and so forth. An owner, then, will be careful to seek an agent who has the ability to give successful management and an organization known for its ability and efficiency in handling real property.

Management of cooperative apartments

Tax advantages accruing to owner-occupants as well as prestige connected with control over apartment space and over selection of neighboring tenants brought about profitable opportunities for professional management of cooperative apartments.

Contrary to general belief, cooperative ownership of multistory or garden-type apartments does not come about through spontaneous grouping and action of ownership-minded tenants, but rather through thoughtful and deliberate action of alert real estate brokers and managers who foresee the entrepreneurial opportunities resulting from organization, purchase, sale, and managerial operation of cooperative apartment enterprises.

With assistance of liberalized aid in mortgage loan financing offered to cooperative apartment owners under FHA and VA policies as explained in Chapter 13, real estate operators and builders have joined forces with real estate brokers and managers to popularize this form of cooperative real estate ownership. Through promotional advertising in connection with proposed construction, and direct solicitation of tenants in existing apartment buildings where cooperative ownership and management was deemed profitable, it proved advantageous to convince financially able renters of the significant gains accruing from co-ownership of apartment units. The real savings to be gained, aside from prestige of space control, are quite apparent. A renter, under income tax laws, cannot deduct any of the amount paid to the landlord as cost of shelter. As an owner, however, of his proportional share of the apartment building, he can subtract as an income deductible expense his pro rata contribution of the building's tax and interest payments on the mortgage debt. Although the co-owners' savings will vary with the amount of the mortgage debt, the real property tax burden, and the individual's income tax bracket, studies indicate an overall tax advantage from 15 to 20 percent of gross rent previously paid as a tenant of similar rental space. Other advantages of cooperative apartment ownership include freedom from arbitrary rent increases and landlord's whims and service neglects. Then, too, there is pride of ownership and a hedge against inflation in a rising rental market.

As in other forms of equity ownership there are pitfalls and disadvantages against which the purchaser of cooperative housing must guard. There is the possibility that failure of some tenant-owners to pay their share of mortgage or tax payments may cause action in foreclosure. In such a case since the mortgage constitutes a prior lien, the co-op equity may be materially reduced or even wiped out. If a receiver is appointed to administer the cooperative apartments, on request of creditors, the rental assessments may be increased to a point where savings which prompted the cooperative venture in the first place are largely eliminated. Before purchasing a cooperative apartment it is well, therefore, to investigate the extent of ownership of the seller, the financial status of the apartment corporation, the condition of the housing units, and the maintenance policy and assessment records under current building management.

Real estate men well versed in professional managerial practices are generally best fitted to plan and execute a cooperative building program. A property manager knows how to calculate accurately operating expenses, how to appraise property values, and how to direct building maintenance and operations to maximize benefits and minimize costs that are equitably shared by the corporate owners. Except for the fact that cooperative building management requires understanding of group relationships and that care must be exercised by the manager to avoid preferential treatment of individual needs that are in conflict with group interests or objectives, management practices and procedures applicable to cooperative apartment buildings are basically the same as those outlined for properties under single or corporate ownership.

Management of condominiums

The essential difference between cooperative and condominium ownership is that under the latter the purchaser holds *fee simple* title in the unit of space occupied by the apartment, whereas under cooperative ownership the purchaser holds only stock in the corporation that owns the building which in turn, by contract, agrees to assign occupancy rights subject to blanket restrictions covering all cooperative apartment occupants.

Condominium ownership is of recent origin and is steadily gaining in popularity. It promises greater flexibility to the owner-occupant in financing his purchase and in liquidating his debt without consulting other owners as he must do in a cooperative venture. Selling of the apartment unit space, too, is financially more flexible and less cumbersome than the disposition of shares of stock to a new apartment owner. Other advantages of condominium ownership include freedom of choice of an insurance agent, individual tax assessing, homestead tax exemption in some states, and freedom from foreclosure as a result of misfortune or negligence of others.

As with cooperative apartments, the common space units such as halls, stairways, service areas, walks, and grounds used for landscaping or recreation are shared by all condominium owners. Generally, joint agreements entered into by the condominium owners provide for the levying of assessments to cover costs of management, utilities, janitorial services, recreational facilities, and other related expenses arising from maintenance and repair of common spaces.

Since condominium ownership of space units is not restricted to residential buildings and can advantageously be applied to stores and offices, the opportunity is present for skilled property managers to widen the scope of their professional services.

Management contract

In the interest of sound owner-manager relationship, a detailed contract should be executed in which the rights, duties, responsibilities, and obligations of the owner and of the manager are clearly set forth. Standard contract forms have been prepared and are recommended for use by members of the Institute of Real Estate Management (Institute Form #P M–6). No special form, however, is required. Essentially, a management contract contains the following data:

1. Identification of the names of the parties to the contract
2. Complete description of the property to be managed
3. Term of contract, effective and termination dates
4. Compensation clause and agreement to reimburse agent if collections are insufficient to meet operating costs
5. Statement of authority of agent to assume charge of building employees, building operation, relations with tenants, and expenditures
6. Clause providing for agency accounting and submission of periodic statements

READING AND STUDY REFERENCES

1. BLISS, HOWARD L., and CHARLES H. SILL, *Real Estate Management*, Chapters 1, 2, 13, and 22. Englewood Cliffs, N.J.: Prentice-Hall, Inc., 1953.
2. DOWNS, JAMES C., *Principles of Real Estate Management*, Chapters 1 through 29. Chicago: Institute of Real Estate Management, 1967.
3. FRIEDMAN, EDITH J., *Real Estate Encyclopedia*, Chapters 25 and 26. Englewood Cliffs, N.J.: Prentice-Hall, Inc., 1960.

4. HUSBAND, WILLIAM H., and FRANK RAY ANDERSON, *Real Estate*, Chapter 18. Homewood, Ill.: Richard D. Irwin, Inc., 1960.
5. LUSK, HAROLD F., *Law of the Real Estate Business*, Chapter 3. Homewood Ill.: Richard D. Irwin, Inc., 1965.
6. RING, ALFRED A., *Questions and Problems in Real Estate Principles and Practices* (rev. ed.), Chapter 19. Englewood Cliffs, N.J.: Prentice-Hall, Inc., 1972.
7. UNGER, MAURICE A., *Real Estate* (4th ed.), Chapter 20. Cincinnati: South-Western Publishing Co., 1969.

22

PROPERTY
INSURANCE

The business of property insurance

The constant search for means to eliminate uncertainty and to shift the risks of ownership to agencies or companies best qualified to cope with them has caused the business of property insurance to develop into a highly important but complex and involved specialty. Because of its almost necessitous nature, insurance as a business is designated a *public calling* and the formation, operation, and solicitation of the insurance business are subject to stringent regulation under the laws of most states.

Because of the necessity for reliability and continuity in meeting hazard obligations, insurance as a business is carried on by corporations organized under special state laws. Generally, articles of incorporation and information regarding the scope of business, number and par value of shares, and other required data must be filed with the proper state official. Periodic reports and audits of operations are, as a rule, made additional requirements in order to protect the public interest.

The insurance business, almost in its entirety, is accounted for by two principal types of carriers:

1. Cooperative or mutual insurance organizations
2. Proprietary or stock companies

The cooperative or mutual organization is a nonprofit organization and operates for the benefit of its members. Insurance premiums are intended to cover losses of calculated risks and costs of general operation and business overhead. Surplus, if any, resulting from superior management or extra hazard control of the insured is returned as pro rata dividend at the end of the contract period. This form of cooperative insurance has proved economically successful in areas where the hazards are homogeneous and where unanimity of member interest permitted risk control and mutual cooperation. In the field of life insurance, the cooperative or mutual organizations have taken a leading role.

The proprietary insurance companies, or stock ownership enterprises, are known as *professional risk bearers.* This form of company is organized to apply business principles and practices to the field of insurance and to yield in return a profit to its owners or proprietors. This form of organization has proved not only competitive to the "mutual" companies in the field of life insurance but apparently better adapted to deal with heterogeneous hazards that commonly prevail in the field of property insurance. There is no one formula that permits calculation as to which type of carrier is best in a given area and for a given risk. Although price, that is, policy premium, is important, it is of secondary consideration. The all-important factor is the reputation and financial standing of the insurance firm. It is in the determination of the choice of the company, type, and adequacy of insurance that the average property owner seeks professional aid.

Functions and services of insurance agents and brokers

The very nature of the insurance business compels insurance companies to diversify their risks and to seek policyholders in far-flung areas as a safeguard against large-scale peril in a single region or community. The commonsense policy not to put all the risks in one "basket" necessitates insurance operations at great distances from office headquarters. Although many companies have established branch offices in the larger communities, the greater share of the insurance business is dependent on services of company agents or insurance brokers. Then, too, the characteristics of the business are such that insurance must be *sold*—it is rarely bought by individual businessmen or property owners. Generally, individuals give their insurance business to agents or brokers on the basis of professional confidence, or personal acquaintance, or friendship. The insurance companies' reliance on agents and brokers for the greater share of their business places the agents and brokers in a good bargaining position for policy terms on behalf of their clients and for compensatory commissions which the companies and not the policyholders pay.

Because of similarity of interests, and opportunities to meet insurance prospects, many agents and brokers associate their activities with those of real estate firms. Where successfully operated, however, the insurance business is a separate department placed in charge of a specialist who, in most states, must demonstrate his competency by qualifying for an insurance agent's or broker's license. Technically, there is an important distinction between the functions and services of insurance agents and brokers. Legally, the agent is the representative of the insurance company and owes it his loyalty. An agent, too, is generally charged with the responsibility for protecting his company's interests and should confine his operations to the insurance offerings of the company or companies that he represents. For his services the agent is compensated by payment of a commission on new insurance and on renewals of existing policies. In fact, the agent may be called a salesman for one or more insurance companies. His powers, as a rule, are limited to securing applications, delivering insurance policies, and collecting premiums. Acceptance of risks and settlement of losses are legally the sole responsibilities of the insurance companies and not those of their agents.

The insurance broker, on the other hand, is an independent operator and expert adviser who serves the interests of his clients always. The broker generally studies the insurance needs by inspecting his client's premises and then bargains with selected insurance carriers for the best terms and lowest rate obtainable. Often the broker will suggest improvements in the physical conditions of the property, such as the installation of a sprinkler system or the elimination of a hazard that may bring about a lower class rate and thus profitable savings in insurance premiums. The broker generally, because of his independence, is free to place his insurance business anywhere and prefers companies that he considers financially strong, prompt in settlement of losses, and otherwise competitive in rates and broker commission payments.

The need for property insurance

Virtually all structures erected upon the land are subject to the danger of partial damage or total destruction from various causes. Everyone dealing with real estate as owner, mortgagee, agent, or broker should be familiar with these dangers and the proper means of adequate protection against them—principally, by insurance. Insurance is the transference of the risk of loss from the insured to the insurance company. It is the substitution of certainty for uncertainty. By the payment of the premium to the insurance company, the company agrees to protect the insured against loss in accordance with the policy contract for the amount insured and for the period of time agreed upon.

Risks of ownership

Ownership of real estate entails a number of risks of financial loss that are foreseeable and also a number that are unforeseeable. An owner can protect himself against most of the foreseeable hazards by purchasing adequate and appropriate insurance. Unfortunately, however, until insurance companies, generally, write true all-risk coverage, which without qualification protects the insured against all hazards, it will be difficult, if not impossible, to enjoy complete freedom from unforeseeable risks. For example, several years ago an unforeseeable risk developed in liability insurance. It had been the belief that after title to real property had been conveyed, the former owner was not responsible for any accident that subsequently occurred. It was held by a court decision, however, that in certain instances a former owner was legally liable for injuries sustained on the premises after title had passed from his hands. This, then, prior to the court's decision, was an unforeseeable hazard not contemplated in the liability policy. Since the decision, however, the insurance companies have made it possible to secure protection against this contingency.

There are a considerable number of foreseeable hazards attached to ownership and maintenance of real estate. The first that comes to mind, of course, is the danger of *fire*, and close behind that is *public liability*, or, as it is also known, *bodily injury liability*. Other risks for which protection can be secured are *damage to plate glass, water damage, sprinkler leakage damage, leasehold loss* caused by cancellation of a lease because of fire, and *rent loss*, or the additional cost of renting other premises during the rehabilitation of the damaged premises. These are but a few of the more common hazards. There might be added the danger of loss from windstorm, tornado, hail, explosion, riot, civil commotion, strike, malicious damage and vandalism, and numerous others. Protection for any or all of the above can be obtained by purchase of policies covering the following:

1. Fire insurance
2. Fire insurance with extended coverage endorsements
3. Fire insurance with additional extended coverage
4. The "package" homeowners' policy
5. Business property general policy
6. Broad form business "umbrella" policy
7. The "parasol," or difference-in-conditions, all-risk property damage policy

Fire insurance

The fire insurance contract is a contract of indemnity. Its intention, if proper coverage is carried, is to indemnify the assured for monetary loss in such a manner that he will neither gain nor lose financially in the event of a fire loss. It endeavors to place the assured in the same relative position he was in prior to the loss.

Standard forms of policy are required by the different states and, though differing in some details, are all similar in basic provisions. These standard policies, as a rule, provide insurance coverage against all direct losses by fire and lightning. The contract generally recites certain uninsurable and excepted properties and mentions perils that are not included. The policy, too, provides for cancellation, at any time, by the insured and by the company after specified days of notice of cancellation.

When a loss occurs, the insured should immediately notify the insurance company of such loss and protect the property from further damage. He should then secure the estimate of several competent builders to ascertain the cost to repair the damage. One of the estimates should then be sent to the insurance company to be compared with the insurance company's estimate. If there are differences, the assured or his representative and the company adjuster discuss them with a view to reaching a compromise settlement. This settlement in the vast majority of cases is usually reached in a friendly fashion. If by any chance the differences are so great that the insured and the insurance company cannot reconcile them, then it is necessary for each to select an appraiser. The appraisers select an umpire, but in the event they cannot agree on an umpire, then, on the request of the insured or the insurance company, one may be selected by a judge of a court of record in the state in which the property covered is located. An award arrived at by the appraisers or by the appraisers and the umpire will then determine the amount of actual cash value and loss. An assured is permitted to make temporary repairs to prevent further damage, but he should not proceed with the complete restoration of the damaged premises until the loss has been adjusted, or at least until the insurance company grants him permission to commence the permanent repairs. The policy contract itself should show the amount insured, the rate and premium, the term, commencement, and expiration dates, and the name of the insured. From there on the policy is completed to suit the particular assured by the addition of the proper form (which states the details of location of property, type of building, and so on) and the necessary endorsements, clauses, riders, and warranties.

Fire policy forms with extended coverage and endorsements

In issuing a contract of fire insurance, it is necessary to determine the type of occupancy of the building in order to know which is the proper form to attach to the policy. Some of the more common forms in use today are the dwelling form, for private dwellings or apartment dwellings; the mercantile and dwelling or store and dwelling form, for use when there is a mercantile occupancy on the first or grade floor and dwelling apartments above; the mercantile form, for use in connection with buildings used solely for mercantile purposes; and the manufacturing form, for use in that type of risk. In addition to these, there are of course many other forms, some printed especially to suit certain individual properties or organizations. The form furnishes additional information showing how the insurance is distributed—that is, on one building or more, or over both building and contents, or solely on contents. The location of the insured property is shown; the type of material of which the building is constructed is specified in some forms, though not necessarily in all of them. If an average clause is used, it is filled in, and if there is a mortgagee, and loss if any is to be payable to him, he is mentioned in the proper place.

Endorsements not inconsistent with the provisions of the policy may be added throughout its life, modifying or extending the coverage. Some of the more common endorsements are those changing the ownership, increasing or decreasing the amount of the policy, and changing the rate or the mortgagee. The usual policy form provides that the loss payable under the policy shall be the actual cash value at the time of loss. This would, in most cases, be cost of replacement at the time of loss, less depreciation, although court decisions have, in a number of cases of disputed claims, brought in other factors to alter the value. Recently an endorsement has come into limited use (for an additional premium) which is quite desirable. It changes the measurement of loss payable under the policy to replacement cost with material of like kind and quality within a reasonable time after such loss, without deduction for depreciation, subject to certain limitations, one of which is that the damaged or destroyed property actually must be repaired, rebuilt, or replaced on the same site; otherwise the policy would not pay a loss beyond the actual cash value at the time of loss. The average or coinsurance clause is also changed by amending the words "actual cash value" to read "replacement costs, without deductions for depreciation." Extended coverage generally adds protection from perils of windstorm, hail, explosion, riot, civil commotion, aircraft, vehicle damage, and smoke. Additional coverage extends protection to ten or more named perils, including water damage from plumbing and heating systems, bursting of steam or hot water systems, vandalism, malicious mischief, vehicle damage of owned autos, freezing of plumbing, collapse, landslide, and glass breakage.

A special form policy is available for residential dwellings only. Rather than naming the various perils, this form stipulates that the policy covers against "all risks and physical damage." The most important exclusions, however, are wear and tear, earthquake, flood and wave wash, war, and nuclear reaction or contamination.

The homeowners' (package) insurance policy

The ever-increasing variety of risks for which homeowners seek protection and the competitive search by insurance companies to streamline insurance coverage and to broaden acceptance of insurance as "good business" caused the introduction in recent years of the Homeowners' Insurance (package) Policy. Under this form of insurance, homeowners are offered in one comprehensive policy protection usually offered under standard and extended coverage; the package policy insures household and personal property against theft, explosion, comprehensive liability, vandalism, collapse from all causes, and freezing and water damage. The widespread acceptance of this comprehensive homeowners' policy by the general public is no doubt due to (1) the savings effected by the special flat rate possible, as compared with cost of insurance under separate policies or "riders," and (2) the convenience and simplification resulting from a single all-purpose insurance policy.

Under circumstances where the homeowner owns his property free and clear from mortgage debt, he may select any kind or type of insurance—or none at all—as he deems best to serve his needs or convenience. Where the property, however, is subject to a mortgage debt, insurance as stipulated in the mortgage clause must be carried at the expense of the owner or mortgagor. Generally the terms of the mortgage require insurance protection only against fire and other hazards covered under "extended coverage" such as loss from windstorm, hail, explosion, riot, civil commotion, aircraft, vehicles, and smoke from confined (furnace) fires. Generally, too, the mortgage terms provide for prepaid insurance for one year in advance and for periodic (monthly) payments to an escrow account to meet the insurance premiums due for another year's period at time of policy expiration.

Where the property owner elects protection under the homeowners' (package) insurance policy, which in addition to coverage under extended coverage as listed above covers hazards arising from almost any conceivable damage to the home, it is important, where the property is subject to a mortgage, that the lender's approval be secured especially where periodic payments covering insurance are made to an escrow account set up for that purpose. Some lenders (mortgagees) may object to the added responsibility of collecting and paying premiums for insurance that has no direct bearing (such as coverage on personal property) on the value of the real property offered as collateral under the mortgage debt agreement. By prepayment of the homeowners' insurance policy and mortgagee's retention of one year's fire and extended coverage in the mortgagor's escrow account, most property owners can meet lenders' objections and thus benefit from the homeowners' (package) policy if they so desire.

Business property insurance

The wide variance among business properties, as to both construction and use of premises, makes it necessary to generalize about insurance practices. The exposure to loss that commercial properties are subject to may be classified as follows:

1. Building and improvement losses by direct damage of all kinds and causes
2. Loss of earnings as a result of direct damage to building
3. Loss or damage of building contents
4. Loss by public liability

Building and contents are generally protected with a broad policy covering fire and lightning and are frequently endorsed to give extended coverage for listed perils including vandalism, malicious mischief, and water and sprinkler damages.

Loss of earnings may be covered, as detailed below, through various forms of "business interruption" insurance to replace earnings lost while the business cannot operate as a result of an uninsured peril. Such policies could be broadened to include profit insurance and loss on inventory of completed goods.

As with home insurance, there are "package" policies for particular types of business risks such as motels, apartments, offices, and some types of retail stores. These policies are similar in approach to the homeowners' policy in that they combine a broad range of coverage in a single policy, usually at a savings over the cost of insurance for the individual perils named.

A recent development has been the introduction of two kinds of broad insurance policy:

1. The "umbrella" policy, which is a blanket liability insurance policy on an all-risk basis, written in amounts of $1 million or more and in excess of the basic (general) liability policies.
2. The "parasol," or difference-in-conditions, policy. This is an all-risk property damage policy to take care of any gaps in underlying coverage. This policy is usually written with provision for a sizable deductible amount for which the insured is liable (as he is, for example, in windstorm coverage).

Rates

Insurance is based on the law of averages. It would be difficult indeed to try to foretell, where many risks of the same nature are involved, how many would suffer loss in the period of one year and to what extent the loss would be. With ten or twenty thousand similar buildings, however, all with the same type risk and with proper statistics on hand, it would be easy to forecast with a great degree of accuracy the number of buildings that would suffer loss and the total extent of the damage to be expected. Knowing the total amount of the losses and the total value of the buildings, an insurance company could fairly easily calculate the rate per hundred dollars of value that should be used and, using that rate, could find the premium that should be charged each building, based on its value, in order to collect just sufficient funds to meet the expected loss. In actual practice, however, this rate would have to be increased to take care of the expense necessary to run an insurance company and to allow the company a fair profit from prudent underwriting.

There are a number of different types of rates, but the better-known ones are minimum, or class, rates and specific rates. Minimum rated risks take in whole groups of buildings of similar construction and hazard and give them the same rate. For instance, brick dwellings in a certain territory would all have the same rate, frame dwellings another. Many apartments of similar construction have the same rate as well as many store and dwelling properties. These rates are the lowest that can be had unless the rate for the entire class is lowered.

Other buildings such as mercantile and manufacturing buildings are specifically rated. That means a rate is promulgated by the use of a schedule to reflect the condition and occupancy of the building at the time it is inspected by the rating organization. Owners of properties that are specifically rated should always secure a schedule or "makeup" of their fire insurance rate. When this is received, it should be gone over thoroughly by an expert to make certain all the charges that go to make up the rate are in order. It may be that a hazardous tenant has left the building or that certain faults of management have been corrected since the rate was promulgated. If that is so, and it appears the rate is too high, a new rate should be applied for. The expert would also make a study of existing physical conditions to determine whether fire protection devices (such as sprinklers) or building alterations (such as fireproofing) would make a sufficient rate saving to justify the high cost of installation.

Coinsurance

When rates are figured for various risks, consideration must be given to the premium those rates will produce. The premiums produced are dependent on the amount of insurance purchased. Ordinarily, the greater the amount of insurance purchased, the lower the rate that is necessary to produce sufficient reserve to meet anticipated loss. Now it is a well-known fact that in territory that enjoys fire protection, most losses are partial, and yet there is always the danger in individual cases of total loss. Knowing that most losses are partial, a person might feel that it was unnecessary to carry more than a nominal amount of insurance. On a building worth $10,-000, such a person, therefore, might carry $2,000 insurance at a rate of $1 per hundred and a premium of $20. Another person, not knowing that most losses are partial, and desiring better protection, would insure for the full value, or $10,000, also at $1 per hundred, with a premium of $100. In the event of a $2,000 loss, if no coinsurance clause was in the policy, each would receive this amount, although the latter paid considerably more for his policy. It can be argued, of course, that the latter received a greater limit of protection; but inasmuch as most of the losses are partial, the danger of a total loss was not as great as the danger of a loss on the first few thousand at risk. Therefore, if the rate charged was the correct one for the first $2,000, it was excessive for the coverage over that amount. To equalize this distribution of the cost of insurance among policyholders and to penalize those going underinsured, the coinsurance or average clause was introduced and made a part of the policy. The clauses generally used are the 80, 90, or 100 percent average clauses. Of these, the 80 percent average clause is the one generally attached to the policy.

A great deal of misinformation has arisen with regard to these clauses. A number of people think that the insurance company will pay only 80 percent of any loss. Others feel that in the event of total loss, they would be able to collect 80 percent of the face amount of the policy. Both of these beliefs, of course, are wrong. The usual 80 percent coinsurance or average clause reads in part, "This company shall not be liable for a greater proportion of any loss or damage to the property described herein than the sum hereby insured bears to eighty percent (80%) of the actual cash value of said property at the time such loss shall happen, nor for more than the proportion that this policy bears to the total insurance thereon."

Various factors can enter into the determination of actual cash value, but under ordinary conditions it will be sufficient to consider actual cash value as replacement value, less depreciation. To illustrate the operation of the 80 percent average clause, consider the following example. A and B

both own buildings, the actual cash value of each being $10,000. A carries
$8,000 insurance, B carries $4,000 insurance. Both suffer a $2,000 loss:

	A's Company	B's Company
Actual cash value of building	$10,000	$10,000
Insurance required to be carried to meet requirements of the 80%		
Average clause (80% of $10,000)	8,000	8,000
Insurance actually carried	8,000	4,000
Actual loss	2,000	2,000

A should and did carry $8,000 insurance. His company, therefore, pays 8,000/
8,000 of the $2,000 loss, or $2,000.

B should carry $8,000 insurance but only carried $4,000. His company, therefore,
pays 4,000/8,000 of the $2,000 loss, or $1,000.

A carried the correct amount of insurance and therefore received the full
amount of his loss without any penalty of coinsurance. B carried only one-
half of the amount of insurance required by the average clause and therefore became a coinsurer with the insurance company for 50 percent of the
loss.

It should be remembered that if sufficient insurance is carried to meet
the requirement of the average clause, for all intents and purposes, in the
event of a loss the policy can be considered as written without any coinsurance feature and will pay dollar for dollar any loss up to its face amount.
The clause penalizes only when insufficient insurance is carried. It should
also be noted that the average clause does not limit the amount of insurance the owner is permitted to take out. He can insure for full value regardless of what clause is used. In unprotected territory, that is, territory
without benefits of fire protection, the average clause is usually not required
in the policy. The probable reason is that without fire protection almost
any fire would in all likelihood result in a total loss, and therefore it would
obviously not benefit the insurance companies to insist that large amounts
of insurance be carried. In states or jurisdictions where regulations provide
for "full" value insurance, the coinsurance concept is not applicable. Value
for insurance purposes is ascertained by the agent. The owner may request
higher coverage, but losses are limited to value as measured by cost of replacement less accrued depreciation based on age and conditions at time
of loss.

Plate glass insurance

Owners of buildings in which there is considerable plate glass are always
in danger of suffering financial loss through breakage or damage to the
glass from a multitude of causes. Plate glass insurance was devised to protect them against this type of loss. The Comprehensive Glass Policy agrees,
subject to certain conditions, to indemnify the assured for:

All damage to such glass, lettering and ornamentation, caused by: (a) the accidental breakage of such glass, except damage by fire, or enemy attack including any action taken by the military, naval or air forces of the United States in
resisting enemy attack; (b) acids or chemicals accidentally or maliciously ap-

plied thereto provided such glass, lettering or ornamentation so damaged is thereafter unfit for use for the purpose for which it was being used immediately preceding the occurrence of such damage.

The policy should describe the glass in detail and show its location in the building. If there is lettering or ornamentation on the glass, it should be described. The policy also should specify the number of plates and their height and width in inches.

In the event of loss, the company usually replaces the glass, lettering, or ornamentation, but has the option to pay for the same in money within the limits provided in the policy, if it so elects.

Rates are based on a number of factors, among which are kind of glass, location of glass in building, location of the building, and so forth.

Water damage insurance

The Water Damage Policy insures

. . . against all Direct Loss and Damage caused solely by the accidental discharge, leakage or overflow of water or steam from within the following source or sources: Plumbing Systems (not including any Sprinkler System), Plumbing Tanks (for the storage of water for the supply of the plumbing system), Heating System, Elevator Tanks and Cylinders, Stand Pipes for Fire Hose, Industrial or Domestic Appliances, Refrigerating Systems, Air Conditioning Systems, and Rain or Snow Admitted Directly to the Interior of the Building through Defective Roofs, Leaders or Spouting, or by Open or Defective Doors, Windows, Show Windows, Skylights, Transoms or Ventilators.

The policy undertakes to insure as above with certain exceptions and conditions that are specified in the policy. Except as provided differently in the policy, it covers "direct loss or damage caused by collapse or fall of a tank or tanks, or the component parts or supports thereof, which form a part of the plumbing system." The loss or damage so caused is considered to be incidental to and part of the damage caused by water. There are quite a number of hazards not covered by the policy. Seepage through building walls, floods, backing up of sewers or drains, the influx of tide, rising of surface waters, fire, or windstorm are some of the hazards for which the company is not liable. The insurance immediately ceases if the building or any material part of its falls except as a result of water damage. Certain property is uninsurable, such as accounts, bills, currency, deeds, and the like, and also buildings in process of construction or reconstruction, which are not yet entirely enclosed with permanent roof, and with all outside doors and windows permanently in place. There are a number of other hazards not covered unless an endorsement is attached to include the coverage. Among these are loss or damage "from repairs, alterations and/or extensions to the plumbing, heating or refrigerating systems, or buildings, except that ordinary minor repairs necessary to care and maintenance are permitted." The "breakage of or leakage from underground water supply mains or fire hydrants" and loss from "aircraft and/or aircraft equipment and/or objects falling or descending therefrom," all need to be endorsed on the policy to be included in the coverage. The insurance does not cover, unless endorsed thereon, loss or damage to a building that is vacant or unoccupied, unless it be a dwelling, in which event the insurance company will not be liable for any loss or damage caused by freezing, if the residence has been unoccupied or unheated for a period over forty-eight hours immediately preceding date of loss or damage, unless the water supply was shut off, and the water and other plumbing systems were drained during the unoccupancy. Unless endorsed thereon to the contrary, the policy does not cover property on which there is a chattel mortgage.

Sprinkler leakage insurance

The advent of sprinkler systems marked a great step forward in the never-ending fight against destructive fires. These systems when properly installed can save thousands of dollars for property owners by their prompt action in putting out fires before they become large and get out of control. They lessen considerably the danger of larger fire losses, but they do add a minor hazard of their own—that is, the danger of water leakage through some cause other than fire. When this occurs, considerable damage can be done to a building, as well as to its contents, unless the flow of water is shut off promptly. If the flow is not caused by fire, the fire policy itself would not cover, and therefore, to protect the property owner against this contingency, the insurance companies issue a Sprinkler Leakage Policy. Except as provided otherwise in the policy, this contract endeavors to insure against all direct loss and damage by sprinkler leakage to an amount stated in the contract. According to the policy, sprinkler leakage means the leakage or discharge of water or other substance from within the "Automatic Sprinkler System," resulting in loss or damage to the property insured. The automatic sprinkler system includes "Automatic Sprinkler heads, sprinkler pipes, valves, fittings, tanks, pumps and all private fire protection mains, connected with and/or constituting a part of the Automatic Sprinkler System." Unless added by endorsement, it does not include nonautomatic sprinkler systems, hydrants, stand pipes, or hose outlets connected to the automatic sprinkler system. Unless provided differently in the policy, it covers direct loss or damage caused by the collapse or fall of tanks or of their component parts or supports, which form a part of the automatic sprinkler system. Damage to the automatic sprinkler system itself is excluded, unless liability is specifically assumed for a stated amount. There are a considerable number of hazards not covered, many of which are also mentioned in the water damage policy referred to earlier. Loss by fire is excluded, but if a sprinkler head opens because of fire, the resultant water damage in connection with the extinguishing of the blaze would be properly covered by the fire insurance contract. Unless permitted by endorsement, the policy does not cover newly installed automatic sprinkler systems until they have been properly tested and any defects remedied.

Nor does it cover repairs, alterations, or extensions to the system beyond ordinary minor repairs. It does not apply to a building while it is vacant or unoccupied, or to property on which there is a chattel mortgage.

Leasehold insurance

A lessee of a building can suffer, under certain conditions, severe financial loss in consequence of the cancellation of his lease because of fire. A lessee may have made a long-term lease on favorable terms, and because of changing business conditions and neighborhood trends he may find that the actual rental value of the premises he occupies is considerably more than the actual rent he is paying under the terms of the lease. If then, because of a fire, the lessor, under a fire clause in the lease, cancels the lease, the lessee will suffer financial loss represented by the difference between the actual present day rental value of the premises and the amount paid under the lease. This figure, based on the entire time the lease has yet to run, plus any maintenance or operating charges paid by the insured, would roughly represent the insured's leasehold interest in the property. This can be insured by a Leasehold Interest Form attached to the standard fire insurance contract. Inasmuch as the insured's leasehold interest becomes less as each month passes, the policy provides that the amount insured shall be automatically reduced from month to month in accordance with a net leasehold interest table. In the event of loss, the company, instead of paying a certain specified sum each month, usually pays a lump sum, which mathematically is the "present worth," or the amount that, based on an agreed interest earning rate, would be equivalent at the present time to the payment of the amount due each month of that portion of the lease not yet expired.

Rent insurance

When a fire occurs, the owner not only suffers a loss based on the replacement value of the damaged portion of the premises but also may suffer a loss of rents or rental value. When a landlord rents a building to a tenant and desires to take out protection against *loss of rents* because of fire, he would take out rent insurance. On the other hand, when an owner suffers a fire loss in the premises in which he lives, he might suffer a *rental value loss*, that is, the rental value of the property if the owner desired to rent it. There are a number of rents and rental value forms in use. These are attached to the standard fire insurance policy. There are clauses based on the net annual rental value, clauses based on the time to rebuild, and clauses based on seasonal occupancy. Some are calculated on the entire building whether rented or vacant, others only on that portion of the building that is rented or occupied. The term *rental value* usually means the determined rental, less those charges and expenses that do not of necessity have to continue. The extent of the loss from the standpoint of time is usually computed from the date of the fire until the time when, with reasonable diligence and dispatch, the premises can again be rendered tenantable, even though the period extends beyond the termination of the policy.

Public liability

Insurance policies carried to cover public liability by owners, landlords, manufacturers, contractors, and tenants vary widely and are dependent on the type of property involved. Owners of property are at all times faced with the possibility of suits for actual or alleged bodily injury and property damage sustained by the public through negligence or alleged negligence. If such a suit is instituted, the property owner will be subjected to considerable expense to defend himself, even though the suit be groundless; and if, unhappily, judgment is rendered against him, it could very easily make him penniless and bankrupt. To protect owners and others against such misfortune, the insurance companies have devised a considerable number of liability insurance contracts to meet the requirements of their clients. A number of these contracts protect the assured against direct legal liability for the alleged negligent condition causing the accident. The Comprehensive Personal Liability Policy, and Owners', Landlords' and Tenants' Public Liability coverage, and Contractors' and Manufacturers' Public Liability coverage are policies covering direct legal liability. The Owners' and Contractors' Protective Public Liability Policy is an illustration of the protective type of liability policy covering against indirect liability. This policy, for instance, will protect the contractor against claims that may be brought against him for damage for which a subcontractor is directly responsible.

Most of the policies have two limits of liability, one for each person, and another for each accident in which more than one person is involved, but subject, however, to the limit for each person. Different types of policies have different agreements, but the general purpose in all of them is the same—namely, to protect the assured against suit even though groundless. The Owners', Landlords' and Tenants' Public Liability coverage agrees to pay on behalf of the insured all sums that the insured shall become obligated to pay by reason of the liability imposed upon him by law for damages, including damages for care and loss of services, because of the hazards defined in the special provisions of the policy. Defining the word *insured*, the policy states that "The unqualified word 'insured' includes the named insured and also includes any director, executive officer, stockholder, or partner thereof, if the named insured is a corporation or partnership, while acting within the scope of his duties as such."

When an accident occurs, written notice should be given to the company or any of its authorized agents as soon as possible. As a service to the company, it is good practice to go a step further and telephone the details of the accident as soon as possible after the occurrence. Speed sometimes helps a company in the adjustment of certain claims, and if it can have all the facts before it at the earliest possible moment, it can quickly decide on the best course to follow.

Owners or mortgagees interested in a large number of properties—properties that change hands frequently—can make special arrangements with the insurance carrier for automatic coverage on newly acquired properties and for the dating back for a certain period of time of the cancellation of liability for risks on which they no longer wish coverage to be carried. A master policy can be issued for such assureds and locations added or cancelled by endorsements, which are issued as necessary.

Workmen's compensation insurance

Workmen's compensation insurance is the outgrowth of the dissatisfaction with the law of master and servant, and former liability laws, under which it was frequently difficult for an employee successfully to recover damages from his employer for injuries sustained in the course of his employment. If he finally did receive judgment, it did not necessarily represent a true monetary relationship to the extent of the injury, and this disparity could work a hardship either on the employee, if the award was not sufficient, or on the employer, if it was unreasonably high. To overcome these weaknesses and to keep step with modern industrial progress, workmen's compensation insurance came into use, and it now applies to nearly all occupations. Two notable exceptions are farm laborers and domestic servants, but in these cases the employer can elect to bring them under the compensation law if he so desires. With certain types of employment, it is not necessary to bring the employees under the compensation law unless there are four or more workmen or operators regularly employed. The Standard Workmen's Compensation Policy agrees

To pay promptly to any person entitled thereto, under the Workmen's Compensation Law, and in the manner therein provided, the entire amount of any sum due and all installments as they become due,

1. To such person because of the obligation for compensation for any such injury imposed upon or accepted by this Employer under such of certain statutes, as may be applicable thereto, cited and described in an endorsement attached to this policy, each of which statutes is herein referred to as the Workmen's Compensation Law, and

2. For the benefit of such person, the proper cost of whatever medical, surgical, nurse or hospital services, medical or surgical apparatus or appliances and medicines, or, in the event of fatal injury, whatever funeral expenses are required by the provisions of such Workmen's Compensation Law.

All the provisions of the Workmen's Compensation Law, so far as they apply to compensation or other benefits for any personal injury or death covered by the policy, are read into and made a part of the contract. The policy also agrees "To indemnify this employer against loss by reason of the liability imposed upon him by law for damages on account of such injuries to such of said employees as are legally employed wherever such injuries may be sustained within the territorial limits of the United States of America or the Dominion of Canada."

Great caution should be observed by the employer to make certain that his employees are "legally employed." If, for instance, a minor who is under the legal age of employment is injured, the employer may find himself in a very serious predicament.

The insurance carrier has the right to inspect work places covered by the policy and to make suggestions for changes or improvements in an endeavor to reduce the number or severity of injuries during work.

The premium charged for the policy is based on the entire payroll of the employer. In most states the executive officers of corporations are considered to be employees and are included in the policy unless they specifically desire to be excluded from its benefits. The initial premium is based on the estimated payroll for the following year. At about the time the policy expires, the payroll is subject to an audit, and an additional premium is charged or a return premium allowed. The payments to be made under the contract in the event of injury are fixed by law. When certain serious injuries occur, payments are made in accordance with a schedule for the injury involved. When injuries of a minor nature are sustained necessitating the injured to remain away from work, approximately two-thirds of the injured employee's weekly salary is paid after a waiting period of a certain number of days. The reason for the waiting period, for which, incidentally, the employee receives payment if his disability continues beyond a specified period of time, and the payment of only a part of his normal weekly salary, is to discourage an employee from staying away from his work longer than is actually necessary.

It has been possible in this chapter to discuss briefly only a few of the many forms of insurance protection available to the owner of property. A property owner should very carefully analyze the risks he believes he is subject to, and he should consult his broker or agent, arranging for him to make a careful survey of insurance needs, and follow his recommendations for proper coverage. If this is intelligently done, and adequate insurance is carried to meet the hazards to which the owner is subject, he will have purchased, at comparatively small cost, security and protection against the possibility of sudden and severe financial loss.

READING AND STUDY REFERENCES

1. ATHEARN, JAMES L., *Risk and Insurance*, Chapters 5, 13, and 25. New York: Appleton-Century-Crofts, 1962.
2. KRATOVIL, ROBERT, *Real Estate Law*, Chapter 15. Englewood Cliffs, N.J.: Prentice-Hall, Inc., 1969.
3. RING, ALFRED A., *Questions and Problems in Real Estate Principles and Practices* (rev. ed.), Chapter 21. Englewood Cliffs, N.J.: Prentice-Hall, Inc., 1972.
4. RODDS, WILLIAM H., *Fire and Property Insurance*, Chapters 1, 2, 3, 11, and 23, Englewood Cliffs, N.J.: Prentice-Hall, Inc., 1956.
5. SNIDER, H. WAYNE, *Readings in Property and Casualty Insurance*, Chapter 39, 40, and 42. Homewood, Ill.: Richard D. Irwin, Inc., 1959.
6. UNGER, MAURICE A., *Real Estate* (4th ed.), Chapter 11. Cincinnati: South-Western Publishing Co., 1969.

23

PROPERTY VALUATION

Importance of value

In the successful operation of the various phases of the real estate business, a thorough and practical knowledge of the art of property valuation is essential. In fact, property valuation may rightfully be designated as the heart of all real estate activity. Whether buying, selling, investing, developing, lending, exchanging, renting, assessing, or acquiring property for public use, a working knowledge of sound valuation is essential to put land and its improvements to the highest, best, and hence most profitable use. It is important then, that all who are engaged in the real estate business know something about valuing real estate even though not all may qualify as expert appraisers.

Types of values

Although logic would dictate that only one type of value could possibly measure the economic significance that one or more individuals attach to a good or thing, common usage has put in vogue many measures and types of values, a few of which are listed below:

1. Economic value
2. Fair value
3. Real value
4. True value

5. Cash value
6. Capital value
7. Exchange value
8. Face value
9. Warranted value
10. Sales value
11. Book value
12. Stable value

13. Potential value
14. Sound value
15. Salvage value
16. Intrinsic value
17. Tax value
18. Use value
19. Rental value
20. Appraisal value

This listing of values by no means exhausts the many uses to which the term value is being put today. A complete enumeration would take pages of writing, particularly if the variations of political, social, and religious values were added to those used to define the importance of business and economic operations. Is it any wonder then that a learned U.S. Supreme Court justice once said that "value is a word of many meanings"? Undoubtedly the late Justice Brandeis had in mind the many uses of the term that prove puzzling to businessmen even to this day.

The question may now be asked, can there be that many types of value? Is there one value that fits the buyer, another the seller, a third the lender, and so forth? The answer is yes where value sought is subjective and where the estimate of value is to serve a special or limited purpose. To illustrate, value for fire insurance would differ in amount from value for a mortgage loan. In the former, emphasis is placed on the replacement cost of improvements that are subject to fire hazards regardless of the marketability or income-producing capacity of the subject property. Where the value estimate is to serve as a basis for mortgage loan determination, principal reliance must be placed on the earnings capacity of the property and on its marketability in case of default in mortgage payment. This illustration shows that a property can have different values for different persons where subjective, commercial, or special-use purposes must be considered and given due weight in the value estimate.

To prevent misinterpretation and error in acting on the basis of a value estimate, it is most important that the *purpose* of the value problem be clearly stated by the person requesting an appraisal study and that a definition of value be fully expressed in the appraisal report that is submitted to the client. Marketwise, however, at a given time and place there can be only *one* value, and that value is created by the multitude of people who affect the supply and demand of the good or thing that is traded. Each individual, of course, attaches his own scale of importance to a good or thing; this importance or scale of market preference is called individual or subjective value. It is the *market* balancing of the subjective values for a given good or thing at a given time and place—among buyers and sellers —that causes an equilibrium known as *objective* value. The existence of the many individual (subjective) values, as well as the fact that values do differ from time to time and from place to place, largely accounts for the origin of the many types of value and for the resulting value confusion that prove disturbing to professional and layman alike.

The meaning of value

It appears essential that further discussion of the topic of property valuation be based on a clear-cut definition of the term *value*. There are, of course, as many definitions as there are types of value. Omitting, however, the modifying prefix as shown in the listing of types of values above, the meaning of value can be expressed in two closely related definitions as follows:

1. Value is "the power of a good or thing (service) to command other goods or things in exchange."
2. Value is "the present worth of *future* rights to income."

The first definition can best be understood if the reader will visualize an exchange of goods or services that may take place in a "barter" economy. In such an economy, the *value* of a commodity can simply and directly be measured in relation to the quantity and quality of other commodities or services for which it is exchanged. For instance, so much fish for so much game, or so much corn for so much wheat.

The second definition may become clearer when consideration is given to the fact that most goods or services are acquired to yield the buyer satisfaction (utility) over one or more future service periods. Thus a home is purchased at a present worth of ———— thousand dollars in order to provide to the buyer anticipated amenities (psychic income derived from pleasure and prestige of ownership) and rental savings over the estimated economic life of the building. Where the future goods or services can be translated into money or money's worth, the *present worth*, or value, of such goods or services can be derived by "discounting" these future rights into a present sum or *present value*. This process of discounting will be demonstrated in the chapter on appraising.

With the use of money as a medium of exchange, the barter relationship of one good or service to another became more complex. In a dollar economy, thus, the introduction of prices became essential as a measure of the exchange power or value of one good or service to another. It is the introduction of money in the exchange of goods for dollars and dollars for goods that has caused the acceptance of the meaning of value as being synonymous with the term *exchange* or *market* value. As used by real estate men, market value is best defined under the "willing buyer, willing seller" concept as follows:

Market value is the warranted price expressed in terms of money that a property is estimated to bring, at a given time and place where buyers and sellers act without compulsion and with full knowledge of all the uses to which the property is adapted and for which it is capable of being used. The warranted price is further contingent on the seller's ability to convey title with all rights inherent in the property and with sufficient time for the transaction to mature normally under cash or cash equivalent terms of sale.

As this definition suggests, time of sale, terms of sale, relationship of the parties, knowledge concerning rights to be conveyed, present and potential uses for the property, time for the transaction to mature and close normally, and immediate transferability of good and marketable title all influence the estimate of a warranted price.

Value characteristics

For a good or service to have value, it must possess certain economic and legal characteristics, specifically the following: (1) utility, (2) scarcity, (3) demand, and (4) transferability.

Utility may be defined as the power of a good to render a service or fill a need. Utility must be present in order for a good or service to be of value. Utility, however, is only one of the characteristics or ingredients that make up value. Thus, where utility is present but demand or scarcity is absent, market value will not exist. For instance, water and air possess utility; yes, total utility, for both are essential to life itself. The value of neither air nor water, however, is measurable in terms of dollars, for each is abundant and free to all. To have market value, therefore, a useful good or service must be scarce. The influence of utility upon value, too, must be considered in relation to the size, shape, or form of the property, its geographic or space location, and its mobility and time availability. Variations in utility characteristics influence value; value differences, therefore, are caused by form, space, place, or time utility, as the case may be.

Scarcity is a relative term and must be considered in relation to demand and supply and the alternate uses, present or prospective, to which the good or service may be put. Thus Christmas trees may be scarce the day before Christmas and most abundant the week after. Value, too, will fluctuate accordingly. Gold and silver are relatively scarce, but their degree of scarcity, and hence value, can be affected by the discovery of new sources of supply or the introduction of a new metal offering equal or even greater utility. Everything else remaining equal, value differences will result with changes in the relative scarcity among market foods and service. Generally, the greater the scarcity, the more spirited becomes the competitive bidding for goods or services and the higher, as a rule, the transaction price or market value.

Demand is an economic concept that implies not only the presence of a "need" but the existence of monetary power to fill that need. Wishful thinking or necessity alone, no matter how strong, does not constitute demand; to bring about the latter, purchasing power must be available to satisfy the need or to back up the wished-for desire. Builders, developers, and investors in particular should keep the purchasing power aspects of demand in mind. Often large-scale housing developments are planned and carried out to fill a long-felt *need*, only to end in financial grief because of failure to consider accurately the effective buying power of the prospective purchaser or tenants. Hotels, amusement enterprises, and large commercial projects, too, have experienced a high rate of economic mortality chiefly because of failure to distinguish between need and demand and because of inability to measure accurately the effective purchasing power of their customers.

Research techniques enable a skilled appraiser to determine with accuracy the strength, depth, and direction of existing as well as potential demand for a given property at a given time and location. Market demand analysis is especially important in ascertaining the highest and best use to which land should be put. This type of valuation data research falls into the category of "feasibility studies," which should precede every important development project or large-scale financial undertaking.

Transferability is a legal concept that must be considered in the determination of property value. Even though the characteristics of utility, scarcity, and demand are present, if the good or thing cannot be transferred in whole or in part, market value cannot exist. The moon, for instance, has utility; it is scarce (there is only one), and there possibly might be a demand for it if ownership and use of it could be controlled. The lack of transferability, however, keeps the moon marketwise a free good. By transferability is not meant, necessarily, physical mobility but rather the possession and control of all the rights that constitute ownership of property. Ownership and transferability imply control of the "bundle of rights" which permits the possessor to (1) use the property, (2) sell it, (3) lease it, (4) give it away, or (5) refrain from utilizing any of these rights. In a value determination care must be taken to consider the degree of transferability and the extent to which this maximum possible bundle of rights has been impaired. Thus a property under faulty zoning or assessment or subject to a long-term uneconomic lease will reflect a lower value than a like property free from such legal and economic encumbrances. For a detailed discussion of ownership interest and public and private controls that affect property use and transferability, the reader is referred to Chapter 4.

Wealth versus property

All useful things owned by man are classified as *wealth*. An inventory of wealth would include all material and physical things controlled and owned by man. *Property*, on the other hand, is an "intangible" concept, being the right to own or possess wealth and to put it to legal use. Property, thus, is a legal right that expresses the relationship between owners and their possessions. In the economic sense, value is derived from ownerhip and control of the utility of a good or thing and not from the physical presence of land and the improvements thereon.

The legal concept of property

The use and ownership of wealth is, in essence, a legal right. In a capitalistic society these legal rights are recognized, classified, and enforced as *property laws*. When ownership of realty extends for periods of years, the rights of use and control are known as "personal" rights or personal property rights. When ownership extends for a lifetime or beyond, involving heirs or designated assignees the rights are designated real. Hence the terms *real property* and *real estate* have legal connotations. Although the appraiser is not held accountable for the validity or legality of title he must nevertheless specify the legal rights of ownership that underlie, or which he accepted as basic to, the value of a property.

The concept of highest and best use

Highest and best use is defined as "that possible and legal use or employment of land that will preserve its utility (usefulness) and yield a net income flow (rent) that forms, when capitalized at the proper rate of interest, the highest present value of the land." Although there may be a number of alternate uses to which a given property can logically be put, there can be only one use at a given time and place that forms the land's highest present value.

As previously stated, a determination of highest and best use involves knowledge of market supply and demand, present and potential, relative to the kind of utility that the land improvements make available. Knowledge of the equilibrium of supply and demand for land under different uses falls under the category of the *principle of balance* with which the specialist who is concerned with property value must be familiar.

Textbooks on property valuation[1] go into considerable detail to build a foundation for an understanding of the concept of highest and best use and the related principle of balance. For purposes of this writing, it suffices to point out that the effects of oversupply or undersupply, or overconsumption or underconsumption, or changes in the arts causing functional or economic obsolescence must be analyzed with care to measure the impact of such changes on the scale of value.

Value distinguished from price and cost

In the determination of market value of a property, care must be taken to differentiate value from price and cost. Value was defined as the "power of a good to command other goods in exchange." It was also pointed out that it is customary to measure the value or exchange power of goods in terms of money. With periodic fluctuations in the purchasing power of the dollar, important and inverse changes have taken place in the value-price relationship of property. Thus if the purchasing power of the dollar falls (as in the case of inflation), the price of a property (other things remaining equal) will rise. Conversely in periods of deflation prices will fall. In both instances, however, value—the power of a good to command other goods —may remain the same. The relationship of price to value can effectively be demonstrated by comparing the value-price ratio of a property with the value-price ratio of another commodity—coffee, for instance. For purposes of the following illustration it is assumed that prices due to inflation have increased 2.5 times and that no depreciation of any kind has affected the value of the property during the time under comparison.

Year 19—	*Price or Value of Property*	*Purchasing Power of Dollar in Terms of Coffee*
Ten years	$10,000	$ .40 per lb. × $10,000 = 25,000 lbs.
later	$25,000	$1.00 per lb. × $25,000 = 25,000 lbs.

---

[1]See Alfred A. Ring, *The Valuation of Real Estate* (Englewood Cliffs, N.J., Prentice-Hall, Inc., 1970).

In the above illustration it will be noted that the price of the property increased over a ten-year period from $10,000 to $25,000. This increase was due to inflation, that is, a fall in the purchasing power of the dollar. The relative price change has similarly affected the price of coffee from $.40 per pound to $1.00 per pound. Though prices for both commodities increased 150 percent, value—the power to command other goods in exchange—remained the same. The property as shown was exchangeable for 25,000 pounds of coffee in both periods under comparison and, though the dollar prices have increased two and one-half times, value, as a power to command, another good in this instance was unaffected.

Where property is held unencumbered by a mortgage, the change in the purchasing power of the dollar may have little or no influence on the value of the interest owned. Where interests in a property, however, are split between an equity and a mortgage holder, the change in the value relationship caused by monetary inflation or deflation may be significant. This may be demonstrated by using the same illustration employed above, but assuming a 60 percent mortgage and a 40 percent equity interest as follows:

Year	Price or Value of Property	Purchasing Power of Dollar in Terms of Coffee
19—	$10,000 Total	$ .40 per lb. × $10,000 = 25,000 lbs.
	6,000 Mortgage	.40 per lb. × 6,000 = 15,000 lbs.
	4,000 Equity	.40 per lb. × 4,000 = 10,000 lbs.
Ten years	$25,000 Total	$1.00 per lb. × $25,000 = 25,000 lbs.
later	6,000 Mortgage	1.00 per lb. × 6,000 = 6,000 lbs.
	19,000 Equity	1.00 per lb. × 19,000 = 19,000 lbs.

In this illustration, the value of the property, as a whole, has not changed. It commanded 25,000 pounds of coffee in 19— and the same amount ten years later. The value interests of the parties, however, were materially affected. Whereas the mortgagee could purchase, with his interest share, 15,000 pounds of coffee in 19—, his purchasing power (value) declined to 6,000 pounds or to 40 percent in the ten-year interval. The equity holder, on the other hand, benefited at the expense of the mortgagee. The value interest of the equity increased from 10,000 pounds of coffee to 19,000 pounds or nearly double that of ten years ago. Although in the evaluation of the entire property as shown no consideration need be given by the appraiser to a change in the purchasing power of the dollar, great care must be given to monetary changes where interests in a property are split between equity and mortgage owners.

Prices are also affected by terms and conditions subject to which the sale of the property is made. Suppose three houses similar in all respects are offered on the market on the following terms:

House A   All cash
House B   40 percent cash—60 percent purchase money
          Mortgage payable in equal installments over a ten-year period at 6 percent interest per annum

House C   10 percent cash—90 percent purchase money
Mortgage payable in equal installments over a twenty-year period
at 5 percent interest per annum

Assuming these houses to be equal in all respects it follows that their value should also be equal. However, prices reflecting the terms of the sale will differ. House A will sell at a price that equals value. House B will sell at dollar price reflecting value plus cost of securing the quoted mortgage terms. House C will bring a higher price still, reflecting higher cost of mortgage terms, and risk involved, as well as a price adjustment for the comparatively favorable amortization and rate of interest. Obviously to measure value accurately, price adjustments must be made for conditions and terms of each sale as compared with value found under an "all cash" transaction. Further, it must be made certain that the seller and buyer were fully informed and that the sale came about through "arm's length" bargaining and that the opportunity to buy was known and open to all. Where the buyer or seller is misinformed, or where the market is "black" or "gray," prices paid at the time of the transaction are doubtful as evidence of market value. To sum it up, before prices paid for a property can be accepted as evidence of value, consideration must be given to the effect on the price of one or more of the following: (1) the relationship of the parties —was the transaction based on "arm's length" bargaining?, (2) the terms of sale and "color" of the market, and (3) the effect of the passage of time since the date of sale and the impact, if any, of changes in the purchasing power of the dollar.

The relationship of cost to value is also subject to wide variance. There is a strong feeling in most people's minds that if a given property *costs* a given amount, then that amount or cost must be a measure of value. Such an assumption is greatly misleading. It is true that cost and value may be equal. This is the case when improvements (1) are new and (2) represent the highest and best use of the land (see Chapter 1 for a detailed discussion of highest and best use of land). As soon as a structure begins to age, cost and value, if only because of the impact of the forces of depreciation, move apart.

Cost is always a measure of a past sacrifice, of either labor or material, or both, and always represents a measure of *past* expenditures. In contradistinction, value is a measure of *future* rights to income or amenities which are anticipated as a result of ownership and utilization of a property. In practice, except as stated above, value and cost are rarely synonymous. The proverbial case of the hotel built in a desert is an illustration in kind. Costs, it should be remembered, even as a measure of past expenditures, in the light of current economic trends or construction practices may not be justified.

In normal times, when the supply and demand for land improvements and for building construction material is in equilibrium, cost is properly accepted as the ceiling of value, for no one conceivably would pay more for a building improvement than the cost to reproduce it. With constant changes in the building arts, in architectural design, in labor efficiency and material uses, original cost cannot serve well as an adequate measure of value. Even when cost as a measure of value is applied, it is *replacement* cost and not original cost that must be considered and then only after due allowance has been made for accrued depreciation. Attention is called to the fact that replacement cost rather than reproduction cost is referred to as a measure of property value. It is always the utilities and amenities of the building that the appraiser seeks to duplicate, and not merely a structure of given material that was built under labor construction practices perhaps long since outmoded.

What makes value?

At the outset it may be conceded that for all practical purposes a good or service has value only because people want it. Value, thus, is an "extrinsic" quality which is wholly created in the minds of people and which should not be conceived of as being "intrinsic" in the property itself. *People*, not stone, wood, or mortar, make value. Contrary to common belief, the principal forces that contribute to the making or breaking of property values must be sought in the environment or setting of the property rather than within the property itself. It is for this reason that in the valuation of property efforts must be made to see the "woods beyond the trees." It is to the social, economic, and political forces that operate within the nation, the region, the city, and the neighborhood that the appraiser must direct his attention for observation of the influences that make or break property values.

Forces influencing value

The average owner fails to understand why the informed broker or real estate appraiser should concern himself with national data in judging or estimating local property values. Those engaged in the real estate business, of course, know better. The federal government's direct participation in the field of housing, in mortgage loan guarantee and insurance underwriting, in mortgage interest rate control, in slum clearance and land rehabilitation, in housing research and rent control has had far-reaching influence in stimulating or retarding housing supply and in increasing and broadening the level of home ownership. Values of homes and all other types of real property are directly affected by governmental action or inaction in this important field of the national economy. Along with a study of political events and trends, the appraiser must keep a "weather eye" on the economic pulse of the nation. Population growth or decline, variation in the marriage rate, in birth and death rates, in national income, saving and spending, in monetary and fiscal policies—all can affect the value of property, depending on the direction and trend of economic action and the broad national objectives to be secured.

Assuming that the valuator is now aware of the impeding national political and economic trends, he must next concern himself with the relative economic health of the *region*. Value, as previously emphasized, is made by people, and unless the region is growing apace with the nation, property values, in general, will reflect the region's arrested growth. Where a region lacks diversity in economic activity, violent swings in realty values may result. In the determination of regional property value trends, consideration must be given to (1) income and employment opportunities, (2) tax differentials and state taxation practices, (3) climate, (4) industrial opportunities, (5) civic, social, and political conditions, (6) purchasing power of population based on bank clearings, savings, and investment, and (7) availability of credit and cost of money (interest rate).

Next, an analysis of the *city* is essential in order to study the urban forces that influence property values. A city may be conceived as a corporate entity offering cultural, social, and economic advantages to its residents. In this offering a city must compete with other cities near and far who vie for a share of the total urban market. The ability of a city to hold on to its present population and to continue to attract new residents acts as a stabilizing influence on property values. Like a business entity, a city as a whole must prosper if it is to continue soundly as a going concern. There, too, a study of per capita income, savings, employment, and production trends must be made. The more diversified the commercial and industrial activities, the more stabilized, as a rule, realty values will be.

In a study of residential property values, an analysis of the *neighborhood* is all-important. A neighborhood is the smallest geographic unit and is defined as "a single area in which the housing and population characteristics are qualitatively homogeneous." Mere size does not determine a neighborhood, although large size has the advantage of better protection from infiltration of inharmonious influences or detrimental property uses. As with the city as a whole, a neighborhood may be in the process of growth or decay. Few neighborhoods are able to maintain a high degree of quality or even stability for long. Buildings are subject to the forces of depreciation, and as a result of exterior obsolescence and changes in design and mode of living, the possible and often inevitable downward trend of neighborhood values must be carefully considered. In the analysis of a neighborhood, the following factors warrant study:

A. Topography and physical improvements
   (1) rolling or flat terrains, (2) features of natural beauty, (3) draining facilities and quality of soil, (4) condition and contour of roads, (5) transportation and availability of all essential public utilities, (6) quality and housing design, (7) proximity to schools, stores, and recreational facilities.
B. Nature and characteristics of population
   (1) living habits, (2) care of homes, (3) attitude toward government, (4) homogeneity of cultural interests, (5) percentage of homeowners.
C. Economic data
   (1) homogeneity of professional or business interests, (2) index of earnings and income stability, (3) frequency or property turnover and market price trends, (4) tax and assessment levels, (5) building mortality, (6) vacancies, (7) percentage of area development.

With national, regional, city, and neighborhood data forming a *general* value background and serving as a guide to the economic health of the area under study, the *specific* measures of value under the cost, market, and income approaches may now be applied to the site and its improvements.

The cost approach to value

Under the *cost* approach to property value, a detailed estimate is made of the dollar outlay necessary to replace the land and building improvements under current construction practices. Costs are generally and carefully arrived at by one of the following techniques: (1) the detailed inventory or *quantity-survey* method, (2) the modified engineering or *unit-in-place* method, or (3) the simplified *market comparison* method.

The *quantity-survey* method, as a rule, is used by experienced cost estimators in connection with pricing or construction "bidding" of multistory buildings and specialized commercial or industrial structures. Under this method a detailed estimate is made of the dollar outlay necessary to meet required labor, material, and equipment costs and charges. Every unit of labor from groundbreaking to final decorating and cleaning activity essential in the building process is itemized and costed. To this is added the unit prices times the called-for quantities of the various building material and equipment items. Under this method an accurate estimate requires the listing of total man-hours by skilled and unskilled classes of labor and a complete inventory of materials item by item, small and large, such as bags of cement, kegs of nails, board feet of types and kind of lumber, and type of equipment. To the summation of the costs of these labor and material items is then added a percentage to cover architectural fees and the builder's reasonable field and office overhead costs and profit. This costing method, if used with care by a trained estimator, produces accurate results. The application of this method, however, is time consuming and costly.

The *unit-in-place* method of cost estimating is simpler in application and less time consuming and is preferred by architects and builders in connection with costing of residential structures. Under this method only costs of structural units installed or in place as incurred by the contractor or to be charged by the various subcontractors are itemized and summarized. To illustrate, the number of cubic yards of concrete poured is multiplied by the unit cost in place. The same is done for number of square foot units of flooring, sheathing, roofing, plastering, and paneling. Cabinet work, plumbing, electrical work, and heating and air conditioning are similarly costed and added to arrive at a final total "in-place" structural cost. To this as in the quantity-survey method is added the architect's fees and a percentage to cover builder's overhead costs and profit. This costing method, if expertly applied, produces fairly accurate results, but it is still too time consuming and should be used only by experienced men thoroughly acquainted with operational details of the building industry.

The *comparative square foot or cubic foot* method is used almost exclusively by appraisers and by builders and architects when rough cost estimates must be had speedily. Under this method the applicable unit cost per square or cubic foot of a building is derived by dividing total building costs of similar structures recently completed by the volume of square or cubic feet contained within the exterior wall dimensions of the building's structural surfaces including attics, dormers, and basements and subfloor areas. Where the building to be costed is similar in size, design, quality, and quantity of construction of buildings completed within a three- to six-month period, the results obtained should prove quite accurate. The unit cost thus obtained is then multiplied by the total number of square or cubic foot space areas and to this is added a percentage for architect's fees, builder's overhead and profit.

The principal difficulty and lack of accuracy of the comparative costing method arises out of the fact that—except for large developments—no two buildings are exactly alike in method and quality of construction, and unless adjustments are made to reflect these differences the margin of possible error may prove too great to make the estimate reliable as a guide to building costs for proposed construction. To minimize errors and to perfect this costing method, square foot or cubic foot costs are calculated for a "standard" or "base" house of a given size, exclusive of land costs, and adjustments are then made for differences in size, perimeter, or shape of building, as well as for quality and quantity of features such as extra bathrooms, tiling, flooring, fittings, equipment, and other improvements. The application of the *modified* comparative method of cost estimating is further explained below.

Estimating the "standard" house. Since a comparison with anything in any field is best attained if a reliable standard of measure is available, a base house typical for a given geographic area is selected and priced under the quantity-survey or unit-in-place method by competent, reliable, and active builders. Generally specifications complying with FHA minimum property standards are set up and given to at least two, preferably three, community builders for detailed cost estimating. The several estimates are then analyzed, checked, and correlated into one composite estimate representative of local building costs for the selected base house. Suppose that a standard or "base" house approved for construction by the FHA in a given town contains one thousand square feet of building area and is being built by local contractors at a cost of $12,500. This fact then establishes a unit cost of $12.50 per square foot ($12,500 ÷ 1,000 sq. ft.) for residential construction subject to completion under established FHA building specifications and good workmanship.

Estimating the "subject" house. The next step under the cost approach to value is to adjust the unit cost of the base or standard house to reflect cost variations caused by size of the structure and by differences in quantity, quality, and number of fixtures (such as extra bathrooms) of the subject house. It stands to reason that building costs per square foot of construction will vary—other things remaining equal—with interior volume of space. This is due to the operation of the law of diminishing costs. Specifically, the initial and rather inflexible fixed costs of kitchen, bath, plumbing, and electric wiring are spread over more and more "empty" space units as the house is made of a larger design thus causing a decrease in the costs per unit of construction. Other adjustments are then made for extra perimeter walls, if any, caused by ranch-type or "wandering" exterior design and extras not contained in the base house.

To the cost of the main residence is then added the construction costs of other improvements such as carpets, porches, patios, storage areas. Last, but not least, the value of the land derived under the market comparison approach to value is then added plus land improvements such as landscaping, sprinkler systems, and walks and drives. Where the building and related improvements are old, allowance must be made for accrued depreciation resulting from (1) physical wear, tear, and actions of the elements, (2) functional obsolescence resulting from changes in the arts and design, and (3) economic obsolescence due to changes in demand for properties in the area under study. The cost approach to value as well as the means and ways of measuring depreciation will be illustrated in the following chapter on appraising.

The market approach to value

Under the market approach to property value, price data are gathered from transactions in similar properties that sold in recent times, which are comparable in condition and location to the property for which a judgment of value is to be formed. Where the market is active, the sales recent and similar in kind, the market approach, particularly for residential properties, yields satisfactory value results. The mechanics of the market approach are relatively simple and no great skill is required to master the method. The appraiser under this value approach secures price data for recent sales from either a financial news service or an abstract company, or directly from county deed records where a photostatic copy of the deed containing revenue stamps evidences each sale and the reported price at which the transaction was concluded. From the records, a dozen or more sales are noted and a field check is made to determine the comparability of each property and the extent to which, percentagewise, each property is better or worse than the subject property in respect to location, condition, and quality of neighborhood. Based on the field findings, each sales price is adjusted to what it would have been if the subject property had been the object of each sale. The weighted average, or correlated amount derived from analysis of all selected and comparable sales, represents a market index of value for the property in question. No further adjustment for depreciation is necessary under this procedure, as is the case under the cost approach to value, because the market price data already reflect the state of repair and the location characteristics of similar properties.

In the application of the market approach, caution must be exercised in accepting revenue stamps affixed to deeds as evidence of the transaction price. Buyers and sellers consider the property transfer proceeding as confidential and customarily do not stipulate in the deed the actual consideration that was paid for the property. It is true that the law requires that revenue stamps based on the exact transaction price be attached to the deed, but there are circumstances under which these stamps do not indicate the price for which the property exchanged. For instance:

1. A buyer may wish to give the impression that he paid an amount greater than the actual purchase price and for that reason affixes more revenue stamps than the law requires. There is no limit to the number or amount of stamps that may be purchased and the tax agent will gladly sell all the buyer wants. The attaching of excess stamps may be a device to have future buyers believe that the property is worth a great deal more than the "bargain" price at which it is offered to them.

2. Sellers who must deliver the deed at time of closing—with revenue stamps attached—may attempt, unlawfully, to save on this expenditure by purchasing fewer stamps than the sale price calls for. The county clerk from whom the revenue stamps are obtained does not question the transaction price quoted by the seller or the intent of the seller in obtaining more or fewer stamps than the law requires.

3. In some states documentary stamps need be affixed only in proportion to the actual cash consideration paid at the time of property sale. Thus if a property sells for a total consideration of $30,000, payable $10,000 in cash and $20,000 by an assumption of an existing mortgage, revenue stamps applicable only to the $10,000 cash payment need be purchased and attached to the deed of conveyance. Since the exact balance of outstanding mortgages is often not specifically stated in the deed, revenue stamps under such circumstances may be misleading as a measure of transaction price or value.

4. Many states do not have deed revenue stamp laws, and even where such laws are in force the requirements regarding the effects of existing mortgages differ. In some states only cash transactions need be considered, whereas in others state revenue stamps representing the full consideration must be attached to the deed.

5. In property exchanges, the interested parties may understate or overstate the transaction price for tax or other purposes that prove mutually advantageous.

Although in many jurisdictions revenue stamps do reflect fairly well the actual transaction price of the property, the possible exceptions noted above should be kept in mind when accepting deed revenue stamp data as evidence of market price or value.

The income approach to value

A third measure of value is known as the *income* approach to value. This approach or technique centers around the thesis that value is "the present worth of *future* rights to income." This approach, as the name implies, looks only to a property's future income or utility (amenities) as a basis for claims to present value. The application of this approach necessitates a determination of revenues that may reasonably be anticipated during the estimated economic life of the property. From the total gross revenues a deduction is then made for possible contingencies arising from vacancies and rental collection losses. The remaining balance is then referred to as *effective gross revenues* that the property will yield under competent management. An estimate of *net income*, net before interest and amortization charges, is then made by subtracting from the effective gross revenue the normal (stabilized) operating expenses that are incurred in the proper maintenance and utilization of the property. The net income, thus derived, is then capitalized (discounted) at a market rate of interest (capitalization rate) which reflects the quantity, certainty, and quality of the anticipated income "stream." The resultant capitalized amount represents the property's present worth or value. This valuation approach is particularly useful and important when there is an absence of market sales data or where conditions or changes in construction practices may make the reproduction of the existing facilities questionable.

The income approach, too, has weaknesses or pitfalls which arise out of the inherent difficulty to forecast with any high degree of accuracy the future income or future service life of a property. Another difficulty arises out of the great skill and judgment required to select with care and competence the appropriate rate of interest or capitalization that is applicable to the kind of income stream under consideration.

Gross revenue can be predicted with accuracy for only one or two years into the future. Thereafter, accuracy diminishes, but so does the weight that income of more distant years is accorded in the capitalization process. Income from leaseholds or other contractual agreements, as a rule, provides no problem in forecasting. The contractual payments are generally accepted at face value for the period of contract, giving allowance to certainty and quality of payments in the selection of the appropriate rate of capitalization.

The forecasting of income begins with a study of past income behavior. Not that the future is expected to be like the past, but rather that prevailing trends may be given due weight in estimating the anticipated earnings. In the study of past and current earnings, care should be taken to observe managerial skill and practices and accounting procedures. Only income derived under competent management should be accepted as capitalizable income. Income from superior or exceptional managerial efforts attaches to persons and not to the realty for which value is to be derived. Likewise, income from poorly managed properties must be adjusted upward to that expected under average, but competent and efficient management.

The capitalization rate—also known as the going rate of interest, cost of money, or market rate of interest—constitutes a ratio of income to value at which property is exchanging in the market. This ratio, or rate of capitalization, is generally accepted as a guide in the conversion of anticipated income into a sum of present value, especially where property is acquired for income or investment. There are a number of means by which the appropriate rate of capitalization can be checked in the market. Two of the most common methods used are (1) *the band of investment* method and (2) the *built-up* method.

Under the band of investment method, individual rates of interest applicable to "split" properties, such as first and second mortgages and equity investments, are weighted to arrive at the market rate of capitalization. To illustrate: Assuming that first mortgage loans are customarily made up to 65 percent of property value at 8 percent interest, that second mortgages can be secured for another 20 percent of the property value at 10 percent interest, and that the equity balance requires a return of 12 percent to be financially attractive to owners or investors, then the market rate of interest would be as follows:

Split Interest	Percent of Value	Split Rate		Weighted Rate
First mortgage	.65 times	8%	=	5.2%
Second mortgage	.20 times	10%	=	2.0%
Equity	.15 times	12%	=	1.8%
Total	1.00			9.0, or 9%

If the net income of a property—after provision for amortization (depreciation)—is $900 per annum, then the capitalized value of that income at 9 percent would be $900 divided by .09, or $10,000. The income of $900 would then be distributed as follows:

Split Interest	Value	Rate of Earning	Dollar Earnings
First mortgage (65%)	$ 6,500	8%	$520
Second mortgage (20%)	2,000	10%	200
Equity (15%)	1,500	12%	180
Total 100%	$10,000		$900

Under the built-up method, the rate of capitalization would be a composite of the following: (1) pure interest, i.e., interest that can be secured on government bonds; (2) rate of management, i.e., rate necessary to process and administer the investment; (3) rate for nonliquidity, i.e., rate necessary to compensate for relative inability to "cash in" the investment; and (4) rate of risk. The risk rate varies with type of investment. Thus a Veterans Administration guaranteed mortgage is relatively risk free. Non-insured mortgages, however, may cause losses to the investor or lender and such losses are reflected in the applicable rate of capitalization. Thus, the rate applicable to a first mortgage that is guaranteed by the Veterans Administration may be composed as follows:

Pure interest	6.50 percent
Management	.50 percent
Nonliquidity	1.00 percent
Risk	None
Total	8.00 percent

The rate of capitalization applicable to an equity property may be composed as follows:

Pure interest	6.50	percent
Management	.50	percent
Nonliquidity	1.00	percent
Risk (of loss)	1.00	percent
Total	9.00	percent

It is accepted practice to capitalize land income into perpetuity. That is, no allowance for depreciation or amortization is deemed necessary because of the characteristics of fixity and indestructibility of land. Improvements, however, have limited lives, and provision for amortization must be made. It is general practice to add a rate of amortization to the rate of capitalization. Thus, if a property is estimated to last fifty years, the amortization rate under the *straight line* depreciation method would be 2 percent per year. Assuming a capitalization rate of 9.0 percent, the "split" rate of capitalization—applicable to the improvements only—is 11.0 percent. If a *sinking fund* (Hoskold) method of depreciation is used, and assuming that the fund can earn 6 percent interest, then the amortization rate to be placed in the fund over the fifty-year period is .344 percent[2] and the "split" rate is 9.0 + .344, or 9.344 percent. The different rates derived under the straight line and the sinking fund depreciation methods are due to the assumption—not a realistic one—that provisions for amortization under the straight line method do not earn interest.

Under the *annuity* (Inwood) method of capitalization, depreciation is provided for at the same rate of interest as that applied to the investment income as a whole. Thus, where the rate on the investment is 9.0 percent, the amortization provision (over a fifty-year life span) is .1227 percent and the "split" rate applicable to the improvements is 9.0 plus .1227, or 9.1227 percent.

The higher the rate of capitalization when applied to a given income, the lower the resultant value. It may be for reasons of conservatism, therefore, that many appraisers prefer the straight line method for capitalization of depreciable improvements. The application of the annuity method, however, is gaining favor with leading appraisers and its use is recommended in modern appraisal practice.

Value correlation

Three separate and distinct techniques for measuring value, under the cost, market, and income methods, have been presented above. Each method may serve as an independent guide to a determination of property value. In practice, however, use is made whenever possible of all three methods or approaches to value to provide a check and countercheck on the accuracy of the value findings. Under normal conditions when supply and demand for properties is in equilibrium and when there are no restric-

---

[2]See Appendix, page 529, for amortization rates under "deposits needed to accumulate $1.00."

tions imposed on the availability of materials or the flow of investment funds, the three approaches to value should yield reasonably similar results. Should there be wide divergency in the separate value findings, then a recheck should be made for possible errors in the application of value data; if none are found, the cause for the value differences among the three approaches should be analyzed, explained, and given due weight in the final judgment or estimate of value of a property.

The art of analyzing and effectively weighing the findings under the cost, market, and income approaches to value is known as *correlation*. This term implies that careful consideration should be given to the relationship of the value results found under each approach and that a decision should be reached only after due study of the factors that cause the differences, if any, and after a weight has been assigned to each approach in accordance with its importance to the purpose that the valuation is to serve and the kind of property under study. In the valuation of a residential, owner-occupied property, for instance, the cost and market approach to value would carry more weight because the monetary income from a home is difficult to measure. Home ownership, in fact, yields a "psychic" income, called an *amenity*, to which a dollar sign cannot accurately be attached.

For commercial and investment properties, the income approach to value may carry principal weight, using the cost approach as a check to support the reasonableness of the value conclusions. The market approach cannot be applied with accuracy to this class of property because of the dissimilarity of the structural improvements and the importance of the location or site factors. On the other hand, in the valuation of vacant land or farmland, the cost approach may be wholly inadequate and reliance must be placed on the income and market data methods for a sound estimate of final value.

Conclusion

An attempt has been made to condense within the scope of this chapter the important principles and practices with the aid of which property value can be measured. Many books have been written on this subject and many schools of thought have influenced the development of current value theories.

Since no one chapter can possibly present an adequate coverage of all the important phases of the extensive field of property valuation, an effort has been made here to stress the importance of this specialized subject of study to related activities in the real estate business. Attention was called to the fact that many "types" of value are in current use and that care must be taken in defining the value terms, particularly where such may refer to individual or subjective values or to special types of cash outlays or investment expenditures. It is essential, for instance, to distinguish value from utility, price, and cost, and to realize the impact on each of these as
Forces influencing value need to be carefully observed. Property, though brought about by changes in the purchasing power of the dollar.

fixed and local in use and character, is subject to value forces that operate on a national, regional, city, and neighborhood basis. The impact of a war or a peace economy, population shifts, and changes in commercial or industrial trends or employment opportunities may have far-reaching influence on the value of a property.

Although only *one* market value can be recognized as guiding in a real estate transaction, data relative to cost, income, and market operations must be analyzed in the determination of a final estimate of value. Each of the value approaches or techniques may lend itself with greater accuracy to a specific type of property, but where possible all approaches should be employed to provide an effective check and countercheck on the final value judgment. The application of the value principles under each of the value approaches will be demonstrated in the following chapter on appraising.

READING AND STUDY REFERENCES

1. BROWN, ROBERT K., *Real Estate Economics*, Chapter 6. Boston: Houghton Mifflin Company, 1965.
2. HUSBAND, WILLIAM H., and FRANK RAY ANDERSON, *Real Estate*, Chapter 13. Homewood, Ill.: Richard D. Irwin, Inc., 1960.
3. RING, ALFRED A., *Questions and Problems in Real Estate Principles and Practices* (rev. ed.), Chapter 22. Englewood Cliffs, N.J.: Prentice-Hall, Inc., 1972.
4. ————, "The Labyrinth of Value," *The Appraisal Journal*, pp. 9–14. Chicago: American Institute of Real Estate Appraisers, January 1965.
5. ————, *Valuation of Real Estate*, Chapters 1, 2, 3, and 4. Englewood Cliffs, N.J.: Prentice-Hall, Inc., 1970.
6. *"The Appraisal of Real Estate,"* (5th ed.). Chicago: American Institute of Real Estate Appraisers, 1967.
7. UNGER, MAURICE A., *Real Estate* (4th ed.), Chapter 23. Cincinnati: South-Western Publishing Co., 1969.
8. WEIMER, ARTHUR M., and HOMER HOYT, *Real Estate* (5th ed.), Chapter 7. New York: The Ronald Press Company, 1966.

24

REAL ESTATE
APPRAISING

Appraising as a profession

Although the practice of real estate appraising predates the real estate business, having been applied by owners, operators, and investors since biblical days, appraising as an organized *profession* dates back only to 1932 when the American Institute of Real Estate Appraisers was founded. In 1935 another group of specialists organized the Society of Real Estate Appraisers. Both organizations are international in scope, with cooperating chapters in Europe and Canada; their representatives participate in international conferences that are held yearly in leading European cities. Since 1935, other appraisal societies have been organized on a state and national scale. Some of the smaller organizations have been founded to serve the local interests of their members; others which embrace valuation on a broader scale include in their membership those who are interested in technical appraising of industrial plant equipment and chattel fixtures.

The need for professional appraising became most apparent during the depression years following World War I. It was during that period, when great financial distress brought about a "flood" of mortgage foreclosures, that attention was called to the urgent need for real estate men who were professionally qualified to serve as expert appraisers in the valuation of property, especially where such was offered as collateral for mortgage loan investment purposes. It was to fill this need and to serve the impartial interests of banks, investment firms, and insurance companies that the American Institute of Real Estate Appraisers and later other appraising societies were organized.

Although real estate appraising has developed during the past forty years into the most specialized branch of the real estate business, relatively few practitioners have achieved true professional standing. This is because relatively few real estate firms or individuals devote their working time exclusively to real estate appraising. Most members of the two leading appraising organizations depend on other income which they derive from collateral interests in brokerage, investment, management, or mortgage financing fields of the real estate business. The collateral activities are by no means deemed a handicap, for the best known and most respected appraisers are those who have had a broad background in related real estate activities and whose judgments are tempered by wide and personal experience in all the varied phases of the real estate business. Having achieved, however, the experience and perception essential to the makeup of a qualified appraiser, professional status can be claimed only by those who devote their full time and specialized energies to activities that sharpen their value judgments, strengthen their value "know-how," and enhance the integrity and quality of their services to clients and to the general public.

Appraiser's qualifications

In the appraisal of real estate, ever greater stress is laid on an adequate selection and analysis of appraisal data upon which, in the final analysis, a sound conclusion of value largely rests. Appraisal data, however important it is in narrowing down the field of error, must be interpreted in the light of prevailing and prospective social, political, and economic conditions. The value conclusions reached, therefore, constitute at best an "estimate," the soundness of which largely depends on the quality of judgment possessed by the appraiser. The appraisal of real estate thus involves the stating of an "opinion" which should be backed, of course, by the experience and reputation of the evaluator. From this it becomes evident that the appraiser should be a man of sound judgment and of wide real estate experience, and one adequately trained in the fundamentals of property valuation principles and practices.

To perfect the practice of real estate appraising and to safeguard against incompetence by practitioners, appraisal societies are setting ever higher standards as a requisite for membership. For instance, to be eligible for membership in the American Institute of Real Estate Appraisers, and thus be privileged to use the coveted designation M.A.I. (Member American Institute) after his name, a candidate must be at least thirty years of age, must have a minimum of five years of appraisal experience, must have at least the equivalent of a high school education, must submit three acceptable narrative appraisal reports covering different classes of real estate property, and must pass two written examinations, each eight hours in duration, in order to demonstrate his ability to cope with valuation theory questions and case study problems. Even when meeting the above requirements, a candidate may still be short of the 120 points required for membership unless he has a college education with more than five years appraising practice and collateral business experience, and submits additional appraisal reports or requests additional examinations to satisfy the credit points set as a minimum by the admissions committee of the appraising institute. These stringent admission requirements account for the fact that the institute has fewer than five thousand M.A.I.'s as members. Many times more the number of professional appraisers now practicing are needed, however, if the demand for competent real property valuation services is to be met adequately. To this end, a comprehensive, nationwide educational program is sponsored by the American Institute of Real Estate Appraisers and the Society of Real Estate Appraisers in cooperation with leading universities and colleges throughout the nation.

Appraising tools

The tools of the real estate appraiser, in addition to his broad experience, mature judgment, and educational background, include maintenance of an efficient office and record filing system and possession of essential and up-to-date statistical valuation data which technically is known as the *appraisal plant*. Real estate appraising, despite the application of broad practices and principles, is still largely a *local* art and a geographically limited profession. This limitation in the range of area that appraisers can effectively serve is due to the peculiar characteristics of the commodity *realty* (See Chapter 1 for detailed discussion of the characteristics of land and realty) and the local or situs effect which environmental economic, political, and social forces exert on property values. It is true that appraisers may serve most anywhere as consultants in important value cases and that some appraisers are active in appraisal firms whose services are nationwide. In such instances, however, great reliance is placed on the availability of local value data and on the aid of resident appraisers or assistants who possess an intimate knowledge of local value trends and forces.

The accumulation of essential valuation data and the assembly of a useful appraisal plant are generally the outgrowth of many years of patient research and diligent application of the art[1] of real estate appraising. The most important data material which makes up the appraisal plant is contained in files that hold working sheet data and copies of completed valuation reports. It is over the years of active service as a real estate appraiser that a wealth of data is accumulated about numerous properties in a wide selection of streets, blocks, neighborhoods, sections, and areas of a city or

---

[1]The real estate appraiser employs scientific means in reaching his value conclusions. The application of judgment, however, at every step of the appraisal process holds appraising to the status of an art. Because of the importance of the judgment factor, real estate appraising should not and cannot be classified a science.

county within which the appraiser has chosen to practice his profession. It is to these files that reference is made for case history of given properties or income, price, occupancy, use, sale, or value trends in a particular area or section of the town. The proper maintenance of appraisal report data files, cross-referenced for ready use by subdivision, street, and client's name, has proved itself a most important tool in the hands of skilled appraisers.

An efficient appraisal plant should also provide ready access to most of the following:

1. An up-to-date and complete set of subdivision or city map records. In an active appraisal office, reference to such maps is almost a daily occurrence. Such maps permit a ready check of property location, dimension of lots, names and width of streets, and distances from points of street intersections or from other properties of interest. Such maps, too, permit record entry of dates of sale and price data and the noting of file numbers of sites for which appraisal data is available.
2. An up-to-date city or area zoning map. Zoning constitutes an important legal limitation on the use of real property; an appraiser must be on the constant alert for zoning trends and land use city patterns. Since it is the future uses and rights to income that influence present value, zoning laws and practices that do or may affect potential property uses must be followed with great care.
3. City or county maps showing existence of, and area served by, underground utilities. The value of a site may be materially affected by the presence or absence of sanitary and storm sewage systems, city water and gas mains, electric, telephone, and steam service, and proximity of fire hydrants and fire alarm-box systems. Since such services cannot always be verified by physical inspection of the site, reference to utility service maps may prove to be of great importance.
4. Maintenance of a sales transaction record showing by subdivision or street name dates of effected sales or current listings, indicated sales or asking prices, and reference to sources of information. Since the comparative approach to value in an active market and for homogeneous groups of properties may prove guiding, the availability and ready reference to a sales transaction record is a "must" in the development of an appraisal plant.
5. Availability of current community statistics, especially in reference to retail sales, bank clearances, savings deposits and withdrawals, employment, vacancies, number of utility service connections and disconnections, transportation routes and cost, insurance rates, rate of bankruptcy and mortgage foreclosures, building construction activity, deed and mortgage recordings, and any other statistical measure available in the area that may aid the appraiser in maintaining contact with the social, political, and economic "pulse" of the area in which he serves. Local statistics must, of course, be compared with those reported for the state, the region, and the nation to give relative measures of growth or decline in the value forces under study.
6. A library of professional books, journals, brochures, as well as publications and releases of selected governmental agencies. The library in a quantitative sense need not be too extensive, but qualitatively the appraiser should have within ready reach the best book writings in his field of specialization. These books are not merely helpful in maintaining

thought contact with authoritative writers but often contain helpful tables, forms, or demonstration reports that may offer time-saving devices which the appraiser may profitably incorporate in his practice. Reading acquaintance, and ready reference to professional journals, are, of course, a must. Articles of current interest, new concepts in appraising, court decisions that influence property rights and value are subjects that journal editors review for the benefit of their professional readers. Governmental agencies, too, make available a wealth of statistical and research information, particularly in the fields of construction, housing, and mortgage financing. Since most of the material is furnished without charge, an active file of latest governmental and statistical data should be kept as an integral part of the appraisal plant.

The appraisal process

With aid of his training, years of practical experience, and the tools of the profession as outlined above, the real estate appraiser in the evaluation of property generally follows an orderly and well-conceived plan of action known as the *appraisal process*. It is with the aid of this process that the appraiser seeks to reach a sound conclusion or estimate of value. This orderly plan of action—the appraisal process—involves the following steps and considerations:

1. Determine the appraisal problem.
2. Determine the purpose that the appraisal is to serve.
3. Secure a full and accurate description of the property to be appraised.
4. Make a preliminary estimate of the time, labor, and expense involved in the completion of the appraisal assignment and secure a written request for the appraisal services in which should be stated the fee agreed upon for services to be rendered.
5. Plan the appraisal, assign the work details, and assemble the essential appraisal data.
6. Make a study of the general economic, social, and political influences that bear upon value of the property to be appraised.
7. Analyze the appraisal data and reach a value conclusion under each of the following approaches to value: cost, market, and income.
8. Correlate the value findings.
9. Submit an appraisal report.

Because of the importance of the appraisal process in the accurate reporting of property value, a more detailed discussion of the various steps and considerations follows.

The first and important step in the appraisal process is to determine the appraisal *problem*. Some owners, buyers, or investors are not only interested in ascertaining an accurate estimate of value but also expect information regarding ownership or title interests, rights of tenants, property encroachments, claims of mortgagees and other lienors, conditions shown by accurate survey, tax liens, violations, and so forth. The appraiser should not accept the valuation assignment unless the client clearly understands the limits of the appraiser's professional responsibility and the area of study to which his specialized knowledge is confined. The appraiser, in essence, practices in the field of economics, for value in fact is the "heart" of economics. The appraiser should not hold himself out as a lawyer, architect, builder, engineer, surveyor, or title abstracter. If his client requests information in these specialized fields, authority should be secured to engage such qualified experts as the problem necessitates, arranging for independent compensation of the outside firms or individuals called upon for the specified service. Unless otherwise stated, the appraiser must assume (1) that the title is held in fee simple and that no legal claims, easements, restrictions, or other rights affect the title or use of the property except those stated to the appraiser by the applicant; (2) that the title and his valuation are subject to corrections which an accurate survey of the property may reveal; (3) that the sale of the property will be on a cash basis, since good or cumbersome financial arrangements do affect the price at which the property may sell in the market; and (4) that no responsibility can be taken by the appraiser for matters legal in character.

Some valuation problems, too, require special owner or tenant cooperation or aid from neighboring property owners or users. Where such is the case, the assignment must be accepted contingent upon the cooperation of the parties involved. Only when the problem is clearly defined and its limits known and understood should the appraiser proceed further and in line with the steps of the appraisal process.

Next, it is essential that the appraiser be provided with a clear statement as to the *purpose* that the appraisal is to serve. Even though only one value can exist for market purposes at a given time and place, different valuation purposes may warrant greater stress being laid on one or the other of the three value approaches, or the inclusion of special appraisal details in the final report of value. It can readily be seen that different interests are served if the valuation is for one or the other of the following purposes:

1. Purchase, sale, or exchange of property
2. Fire insurance or hazard underwriting
3. Valuation for utility rate determination
4. Investment or mortgage loan security
5. Inheritance, property tax, or assessments
6. Inventory or accrued depreciation

In each instance a different interest is served and different valuation details warrant emphasis and inclusion in the appraisal report. For instance, a report for fire insurance purposes would principally stress replacement costs as evidence of value, and the report would detail with great accuracy the construction features and material elements that make up the property improvements. For mortgage loan purposes, on the other hand, property income, its remaining economic life, and its ready marketability would receive major stress with replacement cost, less depreciation, merely serving as a ceiling of value beyond which lenders, as a rule, are restricted or unwilling to go.

To avoid possible misunderstanding or claims that the purpose of the appraisal influenced the value found, the professional appraiser should include not only a clear statement of the purpose that the appraisal is to serve but also a clear-cut definition of the term *value* as used in his report. Failure to do so may cause serious misunderstanding and, where warranted, even disciplinary action under the code of ethics to which all professional appraisers as members of their respective appraisal societies subscribe. The date of the appraisal, too, should be fixed and prominently stated. Values are subject to constant shifts because the laws of supply and demand operate in a dynamic society which does experience sudden and often unexpected changes. Then, too, value for specific purposes may have to be stated as of a given day in the past.

A full and accurate *description* of the property is next in order. Not only the exact limits of the area under appraisal must be known but the full legal property description must be cited to leave no doubt as to the precise location and identity of the realty covered in the valuation report. Although various kinds of property descriptions may be used, it is best to rely on one shown in the last deed of record. For a full discussion of kinds of property descriptions, reference should be made to Chapter 6 on land surveying and property descriptions.

Before proceeding with the valuation assignment, it is essential that the appraiser make a preliminary but careful estimate of the "time, labor, and expense" involved in the completion of the appraisal request. This preliminary estimate should serve as a guide in setting a fair appraisal fee commensurate with the responsibility and service requirements assumed. Many real estate boards recommend to broker members a percentage fee of their value findings. Where the recommended fee, for instance, is one-half of 1 percent of property value, the warranted appraisal fee on a twenty-thousand-dollar property would be one hundred dollars. This method of service fee determination, however, appears illogical and is subject to censure on ethical grounds. The temptations would indeed be great to boost value findings as a means to increase service fees. The code of ethics of the American Institute of Real Estate Appraisers specifically condemns this practice and stipulates that "it is unethical for an appraiser to accept an engagement to appraise a property if his employment or fee is contingent upon his reporting a predetermined or specified amount of value, or is otherwise contingent upon any finding to be reported." The rules further state: "It is unethical for an appraiser to accept any commission, favor, or emolument in connection with the appraising of a property other than a fair professional *fee* [italics supplied] for the responsibility entailed and the work and expense involved."[2]

Once the fair fee has been sanctioned, the client should be so informed. If the fee, as generally is the case, proves acceptable, the appraiser should request written confirmation of his professional assignment, and the fee should be stipulated in the letter of request or should be noted by the appraiser in his letter of acceptance. The fee seldom covers any appearance

---

[2] See Rules of Professional Conduct Article I ("Fees") and Article II ("Commissions and Favors"), American Institute of Real Estate Appraisers of the National Association of Real Estate Boards.

or testimony by the appraiser before any court, commission, or other body; to avoid later dispute, this should be clearly understood at the time of engagement and stated in the appraisal report itself.

Once the appraisal assignment and service fee are mutually agreed upon, steps are taken to "plan" the work details and to "assemble" the essential appraisal data. Much of the necessary general data pertaining to social, political, and economic influences on value are directly obtainable from office (appraisal plant) files or may be taken from previous appraisal reports in which the general value comments are deemed sufficiently recent and applicable to be of interest to the case at hand. General data bearing on value of the subject property, not available from the appraisal plant, should be secured whenever possible from "primary" sources. Data applicable to the site, the improvements, and the immediate environment must be obtained through personal inspection and through a detailed inventory of neighborhood, site, and improvement data that bear directly or indirectly on property values. Many forms have been devised by private firms and governmental agencies to aid the appraiser in this laborious task of gathering field data to insure that no important matter pertaining to the property is inadvertently omitted. A work form suited to residential properties and used by appraisers reporting to the Veterans Administration is here reproduced for illustrative purposes (pp. 406– 408).

Analysis of general appraisal data

Once the general and specific data applicable to the subject property are assembled and the property pictures, diagrams, sketches, and floor and plot plans are prepared or ordered to be drawn, the appraiser proceeds with an analysis of the data and extracts the conclusions to be deduced. Up to this point, the appraiser can rely upon assistance from his experienced associates or trusted office workers, but in the selection of the applicable data from the wealth of evidence collected and in the weighing of the evidence to reach his value conclusions, the appraiser must bear the sole responsibility. The first important analytical task involves a judgment as to how the general area influences pertaining to the neighborhood, the city, the region, and the nation affect the value of the specific site and property under study. Thus, the outbreak of a war or the maintenance of a defense or peace economy may affect differently the value of the subject property. The appraiser, of course, is not a prophet nor is he expected to be a crystal ball gazer, but he holds himself out as an analyst, as a professional specialist in the field of property values, and he is charged with the responsibility for weighing the possible alternatives, for judging the economic or value influences that each will exert, and for so informing his client. The client may or may not accept the value conclusions drawn by his appraiser, or modify them to suit his own judgment or premonitions, but the appraisal data, when properly and orderly presented and soundly and logically analyzed, inevitably should guide an informed reader to the same value conclusions as those reached by the professional appraiser.

The same careful analysis given to data on a national scale should be accorded to data affecting the region, city, and surrounding neighborhood. The growth or decay of the region, the competitive role of the city, its stage in economic development, the quality of government as expressed in civic services and benefits, the neighborhood rating, quality of location in relation to population trends, civic and cultural conveniences, all must be assigned due weights in the value rating of the property. There is no specific formula that aids the appraiser in this accomplishment. It is here that education, training, and long years of experience develop the keen judgment that distinguishes the real estate appraiser as a specialist in his field of operation.

Analysis of specific appraisal data

Specific data concerning the site and the property improvements are analyzed under the three approaches to value—cost, market, and income. Under the *cost* approach a determination is first made whether the improvements constitute the highest and best use of the land. If so, the appraiser proceeds with estimating the depreciated replacement cost of the existing building and inventoried fixtures. If the improvements do not constitute the highest and best land use, the cost approach must be applied with caution, since the structure would not be replaced or reproduced in its present use, type, or form. Assuming structural conditions under the highest and best use, the appraiser applies to the space volume of the structure, on either a square foot or a cubic foot basis depending on availability and accuracy of cost data, a unit cost multiple which he secures from national building cost services to which he may subscribe, or from local construction firms that furnish bids on request. Care must be taken by the appraiser to choose the appropriate basic cost factor that is applicable to the specific type of structure under appraisal, to adjust for variations caused by superior or inferior quality of construction, and to consider additional fixtures or decorating features, such as extra bathrooms, special flooring, and wall paneling, which, generally, may not be included in a "standard" structure of the class under study.

As a rule, little difficulty is encountered in estimating the replacement cost, "new," of a conventional-type structure. Difficulties arise, and often serious ones, in the accurate measurement of accrued depreciation from physical, functional, or economic causes. Because of the importance of depreciation as a "negative" value force and vital component of the cost approach to value, a summary presentation of depreciation measurements in appraisal practice will be discussed in a subsequent part of this chapter. To the depreciated replacement cost of the structure and the site improvements is then added the value of the land (found by market comparison or income capitalization, as shown below). The total thus derived represents the appraiser's estimate under the cost or summation approach to value.

A typical application of the cost approach to value in an appraisal of a residential structure is as follows:

VETERANS ADMINISTRATION
APPRAISAL REPORT

Form Approved
Budget Bureau No. 76-R231.13

CASE NUMBER

1. MAJOR STRUCTURES	A. CONSTRUCTION	B. TYPICAL CONDITION	C. BUILT-UP	D. AGE TYP. BLDG.	E. OWN. OCCUP.	F. VACANCY	G. ZONING	H. TRANSITION TO
NEIGHBORHOOD			%		%	%		
BLOCK			%		%	%		

2. STATUS OF PROPERTY

- A. PROPOSED
- B. PREVIOUSLY OCCUPIED — EXISTING, NOT PREVIOUSLY OCCUPIED
- C. EXISTING, PREVIOUSLY OCCUPIED
- D. IMPROVEM'TS, OR REPAIRS — ALTERATIONS,

3. CONSTRUCTION COMPLETED BEFORE DATE HEREOF

- A. WITHIN 12 CALENDAR MOS.
- B. MORE THAN 12 CALENDAR MOS.

4. TYPE OF PROPERTY

- HOME
- BUSINESS
- FARM

5. NAME AND ADDRESS OF FIRM OR PERSON MAKING REQUEST (Include No., Street or rural route, City or P.O., State and Zip Code)

6. PROPERTY ADDRESS (Include Zip Code)

7. NO. BLDGS.	8. NO. LIVING UNITS	9. LOT DIMENSIONS

10. UTILITIES

	PUBLIC	COMM.	INDIV.	11. TYPE OF STREET PAVING
WATER				
GAS				CURB
ELECT.				SIDEWALK
SANIT. SEWER				STORM SEWER

			CENT. AIR COND.
1/2 BATHS	REC. ROOM	CAR GARAGE	
LIVING RM.	STORAGE RM.	CAR CARPT.	TYPE OF HEATING & FUEL
DINING RM.	UTILITY RM.	BUILT-IN	
KITCHEN	RM.	ATTACHED	ROOFING DESCRIP.
FAMILY RM.	FIRE PLACE	DETACHED	

14. TITLE LIMITATIONS INCLUDING EASEMENTS, RESTRICTIONS, ENCROACHMENTS, ETC.

12. DESCRIPTION

			COMB. TYPES	CRAWL SPACE
DETACHED	WOOD SIDING	C. BLOCK	STORIES	YRS. EST. AGE
SEMI-DET.	WOOD SHINGLE	STONE	SPLIT LEVEL	NO. ROOMS
ROW	ALUM. SIDING	BRICK & BLOCK	% BASEMENT	BEDROOMS
FRAME	ASB. SHINGLE	STUCCO	SLAB	BATHS
	BRICK VENEER			

13. LEGAL DESCRIPTION

15. INTERIOR AND EXTERIOR REPAIRS (Show below ONLY repairs necessary to make property conform with applicable MPR's)

	$	$

TOTAL ESTIMATED COST INTERIOR AND EXTERIOR REPAIRS $

16. TRANSACTION OF COMPARABLE PROPERTIES

LOCATION	PRICE	DATE	STORY	S.F. AREA	RMS.	BED-RMS.	BATH	CONSTR.	GAR/CRPT	AGE/COND	FINANCING	EQ.	SUP.	INF.
												%	%	%
												%	%	%
												%	%	%

17. REMARKS (Describe: (a) Property comparability; (b) Detrimental influences; (c) Real estate market in community; (d) Highest and best use; (e) Explain depreciation; (f) Building lot, district, violations; (g) Comments on repairs; (h) Comments on any special assessments) (Use supplemental sheet if necessary.)

18. PROPERTY SHOWS EVIDENCE OF (Check)					
☐ TERMITE	☐ DRY ROT	☐ DAMPNESS	☐ SETTLE-MENT	☐ NO EVIDENCE	

19. ESTATE (Check)	
☐ A. FEE SIMPLE	☐ B. LEASE-HOLD

20. FUTURE ECONOMIC LIFE (Years)

22. DATA	DESCRIPTION	23. EQUIP.	CONDITION
ROOF			
FOUND.			
BSMT.			
FLOORS			
INT. WALLS			
BATH FINISH			
GUTTERS			

25. ANNUAL TAXES

GENERAL	SPECIAL	OTHER

24. OTHER IMPROVEMENTS	DESCRIPTION	DEPR. VALUE	MAIN	OTHER	DEPR. VALUE
		$			$
		TOTAL $			TOTAL $

21. CALCULATIONS

MAIN	CU. ☐	SQ. ☐ OTHER
RATE PER FT.		$
REPLMT. COST		$
PHYSICAL DEPR.		$
FUNCTIONAL		$
ECONOMIC		$
TOTAL DEPR.		$
DEPR. COST		$
TOTAL DEPR. COST OF IMPR.		$
OTHER IMPR. AND EQUIP.		$
LAND VALUE		$
TOTAL DEPR. COST OF PROP.		$

26. DOES PROPERTY CONFORM TO APPLICABLE MINIMUM PROPERTY REQUIREMENTS?

☐ YES ☐ NO *(If "No" explain in Item 17)*

27. ESTIMATE FAIR MONTHLY RENT TIMES RENT MULTIPLIER

$ _____ X _____ = $ _____

28. CORRELATION

A. COST APPROACH	B. CAPITALIZATION	C. MARKET APPROACH
$	$	$

29. I ESTIMATE "REASONABLE VALUE"

☐ "AS IS" ☐ "AS REPAIRED" ☐ "AS COMPLETED"

30. ESTIMATED REASONABLE VALUE
$

I HEREBY CERTIFY that (a) I have carefully viewed the property described in this report, INSIDE AND OUTSIDE, so far as it has been completed; that (b) it is the same property that is identified by description in my appraisal assignment; that (c) I HAVE NOT RECEIVED, HAVE NO AGREEMENT TO RECEIVE, NOR WILL I ACCEPT FROM ANY PARTY ANY GRATUITY OR EMOLUMENT OTHER THAN MY APPRAISAL FEE FOR MAKING THIS APPRAISAL; that (d) I have no interest, present or prospective in the applicant, seller, property, or mortgage.

31. SIGNATURE OF APPRAISER	32. DATE SIGNED

VA FORM OCT 1966 **26-1803**

VA FILE COPY 5

THE COST APPROACH TO VALUE

Derivation of adjusted cost per square foot of building.[3]

Cost per square foot of standard (1,000 sq. ft.) house	$ 12.00	
Adjusted for size 1,214 sq. ft. =		$11.40
Add for variations from standard house:[4]		

Item No.	Kind of Improvement	Extra Cost
1.	5-ply built-up roof	$ 100
2.	Extra bathroom	560
3.	Tile in 2 bathrooms	560
4.	Terrazzo flooring 1100 ft. @ .70	770
5.	Perimeter wall adjustment 6 ft. @ $14	84
6.	Sliding glass doors (2)	100
7.	Extra windows 5 @ $52	260
8.	Extra interior doors	88
9.	Garbage disposal	80
10.	Kitchen fan 10"	75
11.	Bathroom fan 8"	65
12.	64,000 B.T.U. Central Heating	975
13.	1000 watt bath wall heater	112
14.	Built-in bookcase	100
15.	Built-in vanity	80
16.	Double kitchen sink	38
17.	Insulation 2"	125
18.	Washing machine connections	125
19.	Wind wall 4 ft. @ $5	20
20.	Extra kitchen cabinets	50
	Total extras	$4,367

Extra costs per sq. ft. = $4,367 ÷ 1,214 sq. ft. =		$ 3.60
Adjusted building cost per square foot		$15.00

Replacement cost new of major land and building improvements:

Main house	1,214 sq. ft. @ $15.00 =	$18,210	
Carport	268 sq. ft. @ $ 4.25 =	1,139	
Patio	224 sq. ft. @ $ 2.00 =	448	
Entrance	24 sq. ft. @ $ 4.50 =	108	
Storage	119 sq ft. @ $ 4.75 =	565	
Total costs of improvements			$20,470
Cost of venetian blinds		150	
Value of land—by comparison		5,000	
Landscaping		350	
Walks and drive		150	5,650
Total value—via cost approach			$26,120
Rounded to			$26,100

The comparative method of building cost estimating as demonstrated above has proven an effective, speedy, and fairly accurate means for use

---

[3]For plans and specifications covering this building and land improvements, see Appendix pages 591–93.

[4]For deviations of cost factors, see Appendix pages 594–95.

by builders, architects and real estate appraisers. Where variations in ceiling heights or building practices necessitate cost quotations on a cubic foot rather than square foot basis, this cost method can be so converted by adding the third, or height, dimension and dividing total building costs by the cubic foot units contained in the base house.

It is important, of course, to keep building costs up to date. A revision or check of building cost variations should be made every three months to reflect changes in labor and material costs and building construction practices. Where gathering of local building costs proves burdensome recourse may be had to one of the many national building cost services and manuals that are available on a subscription basis from twenty to sixty dollars per annum. These cost manuals generally quote building costs for a variety of types of buildings in principal cities throughout the United States and furnish cost modifiers for other cities with a population of one hundred thousand and over. For smaller cities subscribers are invited to write to the editors for cost data applicable to a specific area or community.

Measures of depreciation

Where building improvements are old, overconstructed, underconstructed, or faultily constructed, allowance must be made for losses caused by accrued depreciation. Because of the importance of depreciation as a measure of "negative" value and the necessity to account for accrued depreciation accurately under the cost approach to value, detailed consideration will be given to the treatment of depreciation in appraisal practice. Depreciation was previously defined as a "loss in value due to any cause." To measure this loss in value most appraisers rely on one or the other of the following:

1. The theoretical method
2. The quantity-survey method

Under the *theoretical method* of measuring accrued depreciation, each property improvement is assumed to have an optimum total economic life. Although buildings of typical structural quality and design are deemed in practice to have identical life spans no matter where their location, economic building mortality studies and field experience prove otherwise. Structures in fast-growing communities and those in the larger urban centers are known to age faster, functionally and economically, than similar improvements located elsewhere. It is an established maxim that more buildings are "torn" down than "fall" down. Total economic life thus must be considered in relation to community size and growth, and in view of technological development in construction practices and building design. The determination of total economic structural life is thus a matter of appraisal judgment based on local building demand and space requirement needs.

The theoretical measures of depreciation are generally applied in proportion to *expired* economic life. This expired life, or effective building age, is derived as follows: (1) an estimate is made of the remaining number of years of economic life that reasonably can be ascribed to the building; and (2) this remaining economic life-in-years is then subtracted from the total economic building life expectancy that is assigned to a similar structure when new. The resultant effective age thus obtained is then used as a base for the measure of accrued depreciation. To illustrate: Assuming a building, when new, to have a total economic life of fifty years and at time of appraisal an estimated remaining life of thirty years, then the effective age used in the depreciation calculations is twenty years. Care must be taken not to confuse physical or chronological age with effective age. Two structures of identical design and structural age can differ materially in their effective age. One building may have been kept in better repair and maintenance and may have been affected adversely to a lesser degree by environmental or economic changes; it would therefore have less effective age than its sister building.

Using the effective age as a base, accrued depreciation is then determined under a number of measures, among which the *straight line* and the *sinking fund* depreciation methods are the two most commonly used. Under the straight line method, each year of economic age is given equal weight and no interest earnings are assumed on the depreciation provisions, nor is any discount weight given to the remoteness of the liability to replace the structure thirty, forty, or even fifty years from date of the appraisal.

Under the straight line method, assuming a total economic life of fifty years, each elapsed year would accrue depreciation at the rate of 2 percent per year. Given then an effective age of twenty years, the accrued depreciation is 20 $\times$ 2 percent, or a total of 40 percent. This percentage is then applied to the replacement cost, new, of the building for a final determination of the dollar value of accrued depreciation under the straight line method.

Under the sinking fund method of providing for accrued depreciation, it is assumed that the periodic provisions for depreciation can accumulate at compound interest over the total economic life of the structure to equal cost or value of the building. Assuming again an effective building age of twenty years and a sinking fund provision at 4 percent interest, the accrued depreciation would be derived as follows: Annual provision necessary to accumulate $1.00 over a period of fifty years at 4 percent equals $.00655. The accumulation factor, or amount of $1.00 per annum with compound interest at 4 percent at the end of a twenty-year period (effective age), is 29.78. The accumulation or depreciation per dollar of investment then equals .00655 $\times$ 29.78 = .19506, or 19.506 percent. This compares with 40 percent derived under the straight line method; the difference is due to the interest-earning capacity of the accrued depreciation under the sinking fund method. In practice the sinking fund method of depreciation is rarely used except in connection with public utility or similar type institutional properties. The straight line method, because of its simplicity and ease of computation, enjoys wide acceptance by leading appraisers.

Because of the practical difficulties of estimating with any degree of accuracy the total and remaining economic life of a structure, many appraisers adopt the engineering approach known as the *quantity-survey* (observed) method as a means of measuring accrued depreciation. Under this method, depreciation is recognized as being due to three distinct causes:

1. Physical depreciation caused by wear, tear, and actions of the elements
2. Functional obsolescence caused by changes in technology and building use and design
3. Economic obsolescence caused by environmental changes, principally in building or space demands

Physical depreciation and functional obsolescence in turn are deemed to be of two kinds: curable and incurable. Those losses in value that can be restored economically are deemed curable, others incurable. Economic obsolescence, because it is caused by outside forces over which the owner has no control, is always deemed—for practical purposes—incurable. An illustration of the application of the quantity-survey method for a twenty-year old (effective age) residence, follows:

Physical Deterioration
    Curable:

Sand, fill, and refinish floors	$ 125
Replace porch screening	175
Paint hall, kitchen, bath and bedrooms	325
	$ 625

    Incurable:
        Based on the *liability to replace*[5] at a capitalization rate of 9 percent, an effective age of 20 years, and a total economic life of 50 years, the incurable loss is 6.27 percent of $18,000 (see Appendix p. 573) $1,128

Functional Obsolescence
    Curable:

Relocate hot water heater from hallway to attic	$ 100
Replace outmoded light fixtures	185
	$ 285

    Incurable:
        Value loss due to sales resistance because of poor floor plan. This loss is judged to be equal to 5% of replacement cost new or $18,000 × .05 = $ 900

Economic Obsolescence
    Value loss due to proximity of highway to building improvements causing noise and posing traffic hazards to occupants. This loss is measured by multiplying the actual or estimated rental loss by the rent multiplier applicable, in the community, and allocating the amount of the total loss that is applicable to the improvements as follows:

---

[5]For full discussion of the *liability to replace* method of measuring incurable physical depreciation, see Alfred A. Ring, *The Valuation of Real Estate* (Englewood Cliffs, N.J.: Prentice-Hall, Inc., 1970), pp. 189–91.

Rental loss per month $15—times rental multiplier of
110 = $1,650. This represents the total loss to prop-
erty caused by economic conditions. The loss to the
building is derived by multiplying the total loss by the
ratio of the building to total property value. (80%
Building Value in this instance) or .80 × 1,650 = $1,320
    Total accrued depreciation $4,258

Assuming a replacement cost of $18,000, this method represents ac-
crued depreciation equal to 23.67 percent of building value. Because this
method necessitates detailed inspection in order to admeasure the separate
causes of value losses, the results obtained are deemed more accurate than
those obtained under the theoretical depreciation measures. The quantity-
survey method also permits judgment adjustments, if any, by the reader of
the report.

In practice, the amount or percent of accrued depreciation obtained
under the observed or quantity-survey method is, as a rule, checked by
one of the various theoretical methods that are customarily in use at the
subject location. Variations in the two estimates are then explained and
reasons for the divergence, if any, in the depreciation amounts are set forth
in the appraisal report.

THE MARKET APPROACH TO VALUE

The *market* or market-comparison approach lends itself well to the appraisal of land and to buildings, such as residences that exhibit a high degree of similarity and for which a ready market exists. In the determination
of land value under the market approach, sales of comparable sites are
analyzed and transaction prices are adjusted to a unit measure on a per
front foot, per square foot, or per acre basis as custom or usage dictates.
Where the front foot measure is used as a basis of value, price adjustment
is then made to compensate for lot depth that is greater or lesser than that
accepted as standard in the area under study. The adjusted (for nonstandard depths) unit or front foot price is then further modified to account for
differences arising from location, site improvements (utilities), and neighborhood factors to arrive at an adjusted unit price that is deemed representative of value that the subject land would bring if offered for sale.

Before illustrating the application of the land market-comparison approach to value, it is in order to explain briefly the application and logic
of rules developed to measure the influence on unit land values caused by
nonstandard lot depth. Since reason dictates and utility supports the fact
that the front of a lot is more valuable than its back portion, rules—supported by sales experience—came into use and are generally accepted,
especially by tax assessors, as measures of depth-value deviations.[6] Only
three of the many rules now in use will be referred to here.

---

[6]See page 286.

The first recognized rule for appraising lots of varying depth is credited to Judge Murray Hoffman, in 1866, and is generally known as the Hoffman Rule. Under this rule, the front half, or first 50 feet of a 100-foot-deep standard lot, is assumed to be worth two-thirds of its whole value. Similarly, it was assumed that the first 25 feet are worth two-thirds of the front 50 feet, and the front 12½ feet two-thirds of 25 feet, and so on. This rule applied only to lots of lesser depth than standard. To overcome this weakness another rule, known as the Davies rule, developed. This rule is based on a depth formula, $Y = \sqrt{1.45}\,(X + .0352 - .226)$,[7] and it can be applied to any depth under value comparison where the standard lot of 100 feet equals 100 percent of value.

Another rule which has grown popular with many appraisers because of its simplicity of application is known as the 4–3–2–1 Depth Rule. Under this rule, the standard lot is divided into four parts with the first equaling 40 percent of the value; the second 30 percent; the third 20 percent, and the fourth 10 percent of total value. As under the Hoffman Rule, to each part or quarter, where further depth divisions are made, the 4–3–2–1 prin-

COMPARATIVE DEPTH VALUE FOR NONSTANDARD LOTS

Depth in Feet	Percent of Value Under Rules Named		
	Hoffman	Davies	4–3–2–1
25	44.44	41.71	40
50	66.67	65.49	70
75	84.49	84.10	90
100	100.00	100.00	100
125		113.91	109
150		126.60	117
175		138.29	124
200		149.19	131

ciple applies. This rule originally applied only to lots of 100-foot depth or less. In recent years this rule has been modified to permit its application to lot depths exceeding standard depths. For each quarter depth (of standard) added, the value increase is deemed as follows: 9 percent for the first 25 feet of excess depth, 8 percent for the next, 7 percent for the next, and so on to 1 percent at which figure additional depths are deemed stabilized in value. The preceding table provides a relative comparison of the value influence of the three depth rules explained in this discussion.

With the aid of the depth tables, the application of the market-comparison approach in the determination of land value may now be demonstrated. It is assumed that recent land sales for six comparable lot locations were obtained from public deed transfer records. The sales price for four of these sales was checked with brokers, and the transactions were deemed acceptable for value comparison purposes.

---

[7]In this formula, Y equals the proportion of value of lot in question to value of the standard lot, and X equals the proportion of depth of lot in question to depth of standard lot.

The value analysis of comparable sales would then appear as follows:

LAND VALUE VIA MARKET APPROACH

Parcel Number:		1	2	3	4
Lot width and depth (standard depth = 100 feet)		100 x 110	140 x 143	130 x 120	130 x 120
Transaction price		$3,350	$4,250	$3,700	$3,700
Price per front foot		$33.50	$30.36	$28.46	$28.46
Adjustment depth factor (Davies Rule)		1,057	1.232	1.112	1.112
Market price—adjusted for depth		$31.69	$24.64	$25.59	$25.59
Quality Rating as to:	Subject Property Is:				
Location	Poorer		Poorer	Poorer	Poorer
Site facilities	Comparable		Better	Better	Better
Neighborhood	Comparable		Better	Better	Better
Market rating factor— percent		.95	1.40	1.35	1.35
Adjusted price (market price times rating factor)		$30.11	$34.50	$34.55	$34.55
Correlated value per front foot (based on appraiser's judgment of significance of each sale)		$34.00			
Value of subject property	75' x 100' =				$2,550
Rounded to					$2,500

In the application of the market approach for the property as a whole— land and improvements—the same rating technique as that used above is applied, except that the adjustment for lot depth is deleted and the comparison feature is expanded to give consideration to the type, age, and condition of the improvements. The actual market transaction prices are then modified as follows:

MARKET APPROACH TO VALUE BASED ON DIRECT COMPARISON OF SALE PROPERTIES

Sales Index No.:	1	2	3	4
Indicated price	$21,000	$22,500	$22,600	$20,500
Time adjustment	0	0	500	1,000
Price adjustment for time	21,000	22,500	23,100	21,500
Lot value difference	−500	500	0	−750
Adjusted price	20,500	23,000	23,100	20,750
Subject property rating in regard to:				
Construction:				
Type	Poorer	Poorer	Poorer	Same
Size	Poorer	Poorer	Better	Poorer
Features	Better	Poorer	Same	Better
Age	Better	Better	Poorer	Better
Condition	Better	Same	Better	Same
Subject property percent rating	1.10	1.00	.95	1.10
Adjusted value	$22,550	$23,000	$21,945	$22,825

INDEX SALES WEIGHTS AND MARKET CORRELATION

Index Sale	Adjusted Market Value	Weight of Sale*	Value Components
1	$22,550	.30	$ 6,765
2	23,000	.40	9,200
3	21,945	.20	4,389
4	22,825	.10	2,283
Correlated market value—total			$22,637
Rounded to			$22,600

*The weight of sale is based on the appraiser's judgment of the importance of each sale in the correlation of all. Thus recent sales, sales of like construction in similar neighborhoods, are given greater weight than older sales of less similar properties.

THE INCOME APPROACH TO VALUE

The *income* approach involves the discounting of future rights to income into a present sum or capital value. The application of the income approach requires a careful determination of the following:

1. The net income of the property—net before interest and amortization, but after deduction of all operating expenses
2. The remaining economic life expectancy of the property
3. The applicable risk rate of interest or rate of capitalization
4. The value of the land—if free and clear of the improvements
5. The replacement cost of the improvements provided they are new and represent the highest and best use of the land

The income approach to value, as a rule, is limited in application to property that is used primarily for income or investment purposes. It is not applicable with accuracy to the valuation of owner-occupied homes because the benefits or amenities derived by owners are difficult to measure in terms of dollars or even as hypothetical rental income. For apartment house, commercial, or industrial property, however, the income approach is applied under one of the following capitalization methods:

1. The land residual method
2. The building residual method
3. The property residual method

Which capitalization method to employ depends on circumstances as follows: Where the building improvements are new and represent the highest and best use of the land, the replacement cost of the improvements equal value, and under such conditions the land residual method is applicable. Under this method, as will be illustrated, the net income must first provide a return "on" and a return "of" (amortization) the building investment. The remaining net income is "residual" to the land; the capitalized value of this residual income is a measure of land value.

Where the building improvements are old and the land value can be secured with accuracy either by the market comparison approach or under the land residual approach (assuming existence of a hypothetical highest and best use structure), the building residual method of capitalization is applied. Under this method the net income first provides a fair return on the land investment; the balance of income is residual to the building and is capitalized over the remaining economic life of the improvements to form the building value.

Where neither the building is new nor the land value can be ascertained with a fair degree of accuracy, the appraiser employs the property residual method. Under this method the income is deemed applicable to the property (land and improvements) as a whole and is capitalized over the economic (income-producing) life of the property. To the capital sum thus derived is added the present value of the land "reversionary" interest. This method necessitates an estimate of the value of the land, ten, thirty, fifty, or more years in the future when its availability, free from present structural improvements, may be counted on. Since the discounting process, however, gives only fractional weight to future dollar interests, errors in land value estimates, particularly if in the distant future, carry relatively little weight in the capitalization of income under the property residual method.

To demonstrate the application of the income approach to value under each of the three residual methods of capitalization, the following assumptions are made:

As will be noted, the total value derived under each of the three residual approaches is identical. This is as it should be, since the assumptions made as to rate, life expectancy, and income have been kept the same. In practice, however, only one of the residual income approaches is applied, depending on the circumstances and conditions noted above.

In the capitalization of income the rate can be applied as illustrated above, or the "reciprocal" of that rate may be used as shown in "present worth" tables. Where the rate "on" the investment is the same as the rate "of" the investment (rate of amortization), the reciprocal table is known as the Inwood capitalization table. Where the return "of" is at a lesser (safe) rate, the reciprocal table is known as the Hoskold capitalization table. Which table to use depends on the investment opportunities in the area under study. Whenever a rate reciprocal table is used, the income to to be capitalized must be multiplied by the capitalization factor instead of divided by the combined rate as illustrated above. Thus an income of $9,400 capitalized at 9 percent over 20 years at a 9 percent rate of amortization equals $9,400 divided by .10995, or $85,800. Under the Inwood method of capitalization, the same value is derived by multiplying the income of $9,400 by 9.128 (Inwood factor 9 percent over 20 years), which equals $85,800. Inwood and Sinking Fund tables for selected rates of interest are shown in the Appendix under Growth of $1.00 per period, and Deposit Needed to Accumulate $1.00 respectively.

Strategic location values

Certain sites, because of their strategic location, acquire additional or special value. The most common illustrations are sites located at corners, key lots, and assembled lots that acquire plottage.

Corner lots, that is, those located at the intersection of two streets, are

1. Net income—before interest and amortization $ 13,000
2. Anticipated economic life of structure   20 years
3. Rate of capitalization   9%
4. Land value under highest and best use $ 40,000
5. Building value under highest and best use $ 85,800

Value under the land residual method:

Net operating income		$ 13,000
Income attributable to building:		
Building value (cost)	$ 85,800	
Return "on" the investment	.09	
Return "of" the investment	.01955	
(Amortization at 9% sinking fund		
over remaining life of 20 years)		
Total percentage return to building	.10955	
Required building income $85,800 × .10955 =		$ 9,400
Income residual to land		$ 3,600
Land income capitalized in perpetuity		
at 9% = $3,600 ÷ .09 =	$ 40,000	
Recapitulation:		
Building value—new	$ 85,800	
Land value	$ 40,000	
Total value	$125,800	

Value under the building residual method:

Net operating income		$ 13,000
Income attributable to land		
Land value under highest and best use		
$40,000 × .09 =		$ 3,600
Income residual to building		$ 9,400
Return "on" the investment	.09	
Return "of" the investment		
(Over 20 years at 9% sinking fund)	.01955	
Combined rate of capitalization	.10955	
Building value = $9,400 ÷ .10955 =		$ 85,800
Recapitulation:		
Land value	$ 40,000	
Building value	$ 85,800	
Total value	$125,800	

Value under the property residual method:

Net operating income		$ 13,000
Economic (income) life period—20 years		
Rate of capitalization:		
Return "on" the investment	.09	
Return "of" the investment		
(Over 20 years at 9% sinking fund)	.11955	
Combined rate of capitalization	.10955	
Capitalized value of net income:		
$13,000 ÷ .10955 =		$118,665
Reversionary land value	$40,000	
Present worth of $40,000 due 20 years hence:		
$40,000 × .1784 (Present worth of $1.00 at 9%) =		$ 7,135
Recapitulation:		
Property value—land and building—over 20 years =		$118,665
Present worth of land—discounted at 9%		$ 7,135
Total value		$125,800

worth more than ordinary inside lots. The amount of additional value given to a corner depends upon the importance of the intersecting side street, and the use for which the property is suitable. Generally, corner value influence is measured to a distance of one hundred feet with the value of the immediate corner location being greatest and then diminishing to the point of no corner value one hundred feet distance from the intersection. A corner value table developed for commercial property and proved by John A. Zangerle, of Cleveland, assigns corner value weights as follows:

Depth in feet measured from side street	Percent of side street lot value—added as corner value to lot facing main street
10	25
15	33
25	46
50	63
75	69
100	72

To illustrate:

For capitalization of income under the straight line method, the author developed a table of reciprocals (to permit multiplication of the income stream) known as the "Direct Ring Method of Capitalization Table" (See Appendix pps. 591–92).

Value of Lot *A*:

Main street, 50 feet × $1,000 =	$ 50,000
Corner value 100 feet × $500 × .63	
(63% for 50 ft. depth) =	31,500
Total Lot value	$ 81,500

Value of Lot *B*:

Main street, 50 feet × $1,000 =	$ 50,000
Corner value 100 feet × $500 × .09	
(72% for 100 feet, less 63% for first 50 feet) =	4,500
Total Lot value	$ 54,500
Value of Lots *A* and *B*	$136,000

Proof:

Main street 100 feet × $1,000 =	$100,000
Corner value 100 feet × $500 × .72	
(72% for 100 ft. depth) =	36,000
Total Lots *A* and *B*	$136,000

The reason why corner lots have added value may be summarized as follows:

1. Corner lots are usually more suitable for improvement with a building covering a larger proportion of the surface of the lot, and sometimes a building of a greater height, than are inside lots. When laws restrict the amount of land surface to be covered, corner lots are allowed a greater percentage than inside lots.
2. There is a greater amount of permanent air and light for corner buildings, especially in places where buildings are erected in attached rows.
3. There is a greater amount of window space for display of goods in corner stores, and corner stores are more conspicuous and attract trade more readily.
4. If both intersecting streets are important, the corner lot gets the benefit of fronting on both.
5. Passengers get on and off street cars and buses at corners, and subway stations are located there.
6. Additional light and air and a favorable position is incident to a corner even in residential districts.

Of course, space in buildings erected on corners means paying a larger rent (which means greater value), but the larger rent is a result of the advantages here enumerated.

Key lots. A key lot is one that has a special value because it is desirable or necessary for the proper utilization of adjoining land. Thus, two elements of value go to make up the total value of a key lot. One is its normal value, dependent on what use may be made of it as it stands alone, and the second is the additional value added because of the key position.

In addition to the normal type of key lot that is needed to utilize adjoining land adequately (such as a lot that, when purchased, will complete a square block of business property, or one that is needed for egress and ingress, and so forth), there are also lots that have a key value because, although not of shape or size to use, they represent a nuisance to the adjoining land in breaking up plottage. Such lots (often narrow strips or gores) arise usually as a result of careless descriptions in deeds and are sometimes very troublesome in assembling plottage.

There are many examples of owners of key lots who have tried to obtain prices in excess not only of normal value but of the value assigned to the lot by a potential purchaser because of its key position. In many such cases the potential purchaser has chosen to forgo the purchase of the key lot and has built around it, thus frequently impairing in large measure even the normal value of the property. The appraiser must use great caution to avoid being drawn into the pitfall of assigning too much value to the key.

Plottage and assemblage. These terms are frequently used rather loosely. The word *assemblage* is often used in referring to the acquisition of a group of adjacent lots to form *plottage.* More correctly, however, *assemblage* refers to the gathering together of two or more adjoining lots, to which added value may be ascribed because a building of greater size and capable of producing a larger net rental may be erected on the larger plot. In other words, the plot of two lots or more may be used or improved to greater advantage than the lots used singly. In some localities, the suitable improvement may be an apartment house; in others, it may be a loft building, office building, hotel, manufacturing plant, or special purpose building requiring a large amount of ground space. Assemblage is, therefore, of great value in such a locality.

The determination of its exact value is frequently a difficult matter. Generally speaking, the best way is to determine what would be the highest and best improvement for the land, calculate the probable net rents, and, using the principle of capitalization, determine the total value of the land and of its potential proper improvement. Then estimate what it would cost to build such an improvement, deduct from that the total, and the remainder will be the value of the land that has been assembled. A fair amount of this value should then be apportioned to each lot in the assemblage.

Value correlation

In following the procedure outlined in the appraisal process, a value estimate under each of the three approaches—cost, market, and income—is derived. These estimates must now be evaluated and in the appraiser's judgment correlated into a "final" estimate of value. Correlation does not imply, however, an averaging or mathematical weighing of the estimates secured under the independent value approaches. Where the estimates derived via the cost, market, and income approaches are relatively close together in their dollar value expressions, no special problem presents itself in correlating the findings and fixing the final estimate of value. It is where greatly divergent answers are secured under each of the three approaches that great skill and care must be taken in weighing the results and in determining the final estimate of value.

Whenever significant differences exist in the estimates derived under the three value approaches, the appraiser, as a first step, should review the data assembled under each approach and check the mathematical procedures that underlie the answer. Under the cost approach, for instance, a recheck should be made of the size of the structure and the volume of square or cubic feet reported. The cost factor, too, may be in error or inapplicable to the type and kind of structure under appraisal. More likely than not, the error may rest in the derivation of the amount of accrued depreciation. The economic age may have been misstated or an omission may have been made in the listing and weighing of the causes that account for total accrued depreciation. Under the market approach, judgment errors are easily committed. The transaction prices of the comparable properties may not reflect true property values or the properties selected may not represent real comparability. The judgment weights assigned may also warrant a careful recheck. The income approach is also fraught with appraising pitfalls. The revenue flow may be overstated or understated, allowance for vacancy and collection losses may have been omitted, operating expenses may not reflect operation under competent and efficient management, the remaining life of the property may be in error, and so may be the rate of capitalization, which especially warrants close inspection as to its appropriateness. The application of a rate of 8 percent instead of 9 percent may not appear serious to the uninformed, but the value results would differ one-eighth or one-ninth, or approximately 11 to 12.5 percent depending on which rate is the appropriate one.

If, after careful recheck of the various steps in each approach, significant differences still exist in the value estimates under each approach, then the appraiser must consider the results in the light of the problem and the purposes that the appraisal is to serve. Thus for mortgage loan purposes, the income-producing capacity of the property is all-important. For inheritance tax, condemnation, or sale purposes, the market data (provided the market is sufficiently active to prove guiding) should be given greatest stress. For fire insurance or protection against other hazards, the replacement cost may prove all-important. It is in the correlation of the value estimates that the experience, skill, and judgment of the appraiser can find no substitute. It is the human factor in the equation that causes real estate appraising to be a personal art rather than an objective science.

The appraisal report

The final step in the appraising process is the preparation of a comprehensive appraisal report. At one time an oral opinion or a letter of valuation sufficed. Such practices, however, are frowned upon today, and professional appraisers are advised to furnish their clients with a narrative appraisal report in which their value findings along with the contingent conditions upon which the appraisal is based are clearly set forth. No particular style of report is copyrighted, nor is any one form recommended. A good report, nevertheless, is one in which the data presented is so convincingly analyzed that the reader inevitably is led to the same value conclusions as those reached by the appraiser. As a rule the data should be sufficiently self-supporting to permit judgment adjustment by the reader or client, if he so chooses.

The following are deemed essential to a well-written and comprehensive appraisal report:

1. A letter of transmittal in which the value findings and the effective date of the appraisal are recorded. This letter, too, should state the number of pages contained in the report in order to forestall possible deletion of important pages or data by unauthorized persons.
2. A table of contents which permits quick reference to particular report material.
3. Two clear and preferably large (8″ × 10″) photographs showing front and side views of the property appraised.
4. A complete and accurate legal description.
5. A statement as to the purpose of the appraisal and definition of the term *value* as used by the appraiser.
6. A statement of highest and best use of the property, and whether the present improvements meet the test.
7. A summary statement of important conclusions, particularly those in which the report reader has a prime interest, to wit: taxes, assessments, operating income, operating expenses, and so forth.
8. An analysis of the general social, political, and economic influences on value, particularly in reference to the nation, the region, the city, and the neighborhood or environing area.
9. A factual presentation of site, building, and property data. An inventory should be presented of the important site utilities and building construction features.
10. An explanation of the appraisal process and the methods by which the value conclusions were derived.
11. An analysis of the cost approach to value followed by schedules showing unit cost deviations and depreciation calculations.
12. An analysis of the market approach to value. Separate comparative tables should be included showing sales considered in arriving at the market value of (1) the land and (2) the property as a unified whole.
13. An analysis of the income approach to value showing sources of revenue, allowances due to anticipated vacancies and collection losses, operating expenses, rates of capitalization and process employed in the discounting of the anticipated income into a present sum of value.
14. A correlation of the value estimates derived under the cost, market, and income approaches to value. The weight, if any, assigned to each approach or the methods of selection of one estimate in preference to another should be clearly set forth and explained.
15. A statement of limiting conditions in which the appraiser sets forth the areas—as in the fields of surveying, engineering, or law—in which he disclaims liability.
16. A certification of value in which the appraiser professionally warrants his findings and disclaims any personal interest in the property that could possibly influence his value findings.
17. A statement of qualifications of the appraiser, setting forth briefly his educational and professional background and experience that qualify him to render value opinions.
18. Addenda material containing some or all of the following: location sketch of the property, plot plan, floor plan, subdivision map, and city map on which markings indicate the subject property in relation to important business and civic centers. Also where deemed of interest, addi-

tional photographs of neighboring properties and street views, showing improvements, north, south, east, and west of the subject property.

READING AND STUDY REFERENCES

1. FRIEDMAN, EDITH J., *Real Estate Encyclopedia*, Chapter 33. Englewood Cliffs, N.J.: Prentice-Hall, Inc., 1960.

2. HUSBAND, WILLIAM H., and FRANK RAY ANDERSON, *Real Estate*, Chapter 14. Homewood, Ill.: Richard D. Irwin, Inc., 1960.

3. RATCLIFF, RICHARD U., "A Neoteric View of the Appraisal Functions," *The Appraisal Journal*, pp. 167–75. American Institute of Real Estate Appraisers, April 1965.

4. ———, *Real Estate Analysis*, Chapter 6. New York: McGraw-Hill Book Company, 1961.

5. RING, ALFRED A., *Questions and Problems in Real Estate Principles and Practices* (rev. ed.), Chapter 23. Englewood Cliffs, N.J.: Prentice-Hall, Inc., 1972.

6. ———, *Valuation of Real Estate*, Chapters 8, 9, 10, 13, 17, and 18. Englewood Cliffs, N.J.: Prentice-Hall, Inc., 1970.

7. "The Appraisal of Real Estate" (5th ed.). Chicago: American Institute of Real Estate Appraisers, 1967.

8. UNGER, MAURICE A., *Real Estate*, Chapter 23. Cincinnati: South-Western Publishing Co., 1969.

9. WEIMER, ARTHUR M., and HOMER HOYT, *Real Estate* (5th ed.), Chapter 8. New York: The Ronald Press Company, 1966.

25

SUBDIVIDING
AND DEVELOPING

Meaning

In practice, the terms subdividing and developing are used interchangeably. Professionally, however, the application of these terms differs significantly. There are owners, operators, and speculators, for instance, who are interested only in the less intricate business functions of acquiring tracts of land at wholesale and selling them—subdivided—at retail. There are others who are interested in going far beyond this initial stage of urbanization and who seek to assume business functions that involve the creation of an entire development and the building of "living" areas that will merge effectively with the surrounding civic and cultural environment.

Subdividing

Literally interpreted, subdividing merely means the "breaking-up" of one or more large tracts of land into smaller sites or plots, subject to community regulations, if any, governing the use of the land for which it may be offered for sale. Where subdividing is the owner's intent, he need not incur any additional expenses other than those incident to purchase and survey of the land, to place the markers or stakes at intended plot boundaries, and to submit a surveyor's *plat* of the proposed subdivision for city or county officials' approval. The plat, as a rule, contains information concerning (1) the subdivision name; (2) block, lot, and street designations and dimensions; and (3) proposed easements, rights-of-way, and land dedicated to public use. Once the plat is approved and signed by duly constituted municipal or county representatives, acceptance is made official by placing the plat on public records. It should be noted that the process of subdividing, as explained above, does not require any physical change in the land "per se." If the tract is in timber or pasture use it remains that way. The "paper" subdivision merely gives notice of intent to change the area to urban or suburban site utilization as noted on the plat of record. Actually, the land may remain for years to come in its *status quo*. Often the purpose of subdividing or platting is to establish a land use ahead of proposed zoning changes, or to give prospective home buyers, speculators, or developers notice that the land in question is deemed "ripe" for more intensive use and that such use has merited official sanction. The "paper" subdivision is frequently bought in its entirety for urban or suburban development as originally proposed, or it may be held for prospective higher and better uses. In the latter case, the tract of land may be replatted at any time such a change appears financially advantageous to the owner. The prime motive, of course, in any case, is to reap a financial reward from the undertaking.

Developing

Whenever land improvements are carried out in accordance with subdivision plans, and expenditures are being made to provide essential site facilities, the field actions are appropriately classified as *land developing*. The process of developing is ordinarily far more comprehensive in its scope than that of subdividing and requires, as will be shown, expenditures greatly in excess of those represented by the purchase price of the "raw" land. Developing, to be socially, politically, and economically successful, should be practiced only by the well informed, by men who are well acquainted with community space requirements, with population and real estate market trends, with community growth and growth patterns, and with the absorption rate at which building sites in newly formed subdivisions can profitably be sold. Generally, developers are men of long years' experience in the real estate profession or men who are guided by real estate analysts, civil engineers, or consultants who have specialized in the highly complex field of land utilization. To train men for this specialized calling, programs of study are currently offered by leading schools of higher learning, particularly by colleges of business administration, architecture, and civil engineering.

Kinds of real estate developments

Broadly speaking, developments may be classified into two general types: those that involve land at the fringe of the community or border line of the urban area and those that involve areas in outlying districts called suburban. In recent years, rapid transportation has made possible a third type of living area called rur-urban. It is here that developers seek to attract those interested in truck gardening, estate ownership, small-scale ranching, and all who can afford the luxury of living in the wide and open spaces and still remain within commuting range of an urban, social, and cultural center. Development of the rur-urban areas is still in the formative stage; the social, political, and economic problems that affect such areas have not sufficiently crystallized to warrant special treatment or analysis.

Available land situated directly in line with community growth and adjacent to the border of urban areas presents no difficult problems to the real estate developer other than those concerned with marketing. As a rule, plans for the utilization of land in such fringe areas are fairly well defined before the developer does any work at all. By custom or pattern there exists a natural trend for the community to grow in that direction. In all probability, the type of people who will migrate there will be similar to those now living in bordering blocks. Street patterns, too, are generally well established, while the availability of essential service utilities governs the location and use of additional site improvements. In these urban fringe areas, the developer, in fact, is tied to the city's "apron strings"—conformity to community patterns is the rule rather than the exception.

In outlying or suburban areas, the developer enjoys greater freedom in planning the subdivision project because he may allow his development ideas a wider and more imaginary range. There he is much more in control of his situation. He can, to some extent, select the type of development he deems best for all concerned and is not forced to fit the suburban pattern into a preconceived or "straitjacket" city plan. He may, and generally does, preserve the natural contours of the land, establish winding roads to increase the amenities and privacy of living, and he may, within zoning limitations, subdivide the lots into whatever size he deems best under the long-range plan of development. Suburban areas, too, may be planned as self-contained units complete with neighborhood shopping, recreational, school, church, transportation, and essential service facilities, or they may be planned as "bedroom" or "dormitory" areas for nearby urban centers. In either case, adequate provisions for commuting to economic nerve centers must be carefully considered if the developing plans are to be successfully concluded. The developing of ever more distant suburban areas may be largely credited to the "escape" characteristics of the twentieth century commuter who has fittingly been defined as a "man who works where he would rather not live, and lives where he would rather not work."

Developing costs

Few purchasers of homesites realize the great amount of work and the expenditures that are required to "produce" land even in a modest urban or suburban development. Often inaccurate or unfair references are made to the seemingly large spread existing between the developer's land costs on a per acre basis and his asking price per front foot of a lot. Analysis of development costs reveals that the sale price of a site in an average development may yield three to four times the cost of the "raw" land if the undertaking is to prove financially successful. Although it is difficult to set forth with accuracy specific development costs that would apply to all the various economic areas of the nation, an attempt will be made to set forth concrete measures of the kind and amount of expenditures that may be anticipated when subdividing and developing a project area. Caution, however, need be exercised in accepting dollar expenditures as typical or representative. Costs obviously will vary with lot and street width, population density, kind and number of utility services, and mode and quality of development improvements. The cost figures presented below, nevertheless, should prove enlightening to those who are unaware of the expenses involved in such projects.

Assume that a forty-acre tract of land is planned as a residential development and that under the highest and best land use it appears best to subdivide the area into 120 lots, each measuring 100 feet by 120 feet, or about 3 lots per acre. Assuming further that the balance of the land is devoted to streets, traffic isles, and other public uses, then typical development cost per improved lot may be as follows:[1]

Type of Improvement	Development Cost per Lot
Water mains	$ 650
Sanitary sewers	800
Street grading and asphalt (30') paving	475
Curbs and gutters	200
Other costs including survey, legal, filing, sales, brokerage, and overhead	375
Total cost exclusive of land cost and developer's profits	$2,500
Add cost of raw land ($1,950 per acre)	650
Developer's profit—approximately 10%	350
Fair sales price—per lot	$3,500

Based on the above illustration, each lot in this hypothetical subdivision would have to sell for at least $2,500 to return the direct and "out-of-pocket" costs, assuming (as some people do) that land is "free"—a gift of God—and that the developer is not entitled to any reward for his efforts or for risking his capital in providing improvements. Assuming, for purposes of this illustration, a reasonable land cost of $1,950 per acre and a 10 percent return to the developer, the lots would have to bring $3,500 each to make the enterprise financially worthwhile. The above cost allocations indicate that the proportion of "raw" land costs to total lot improvements costs equal, in this case, 19 percent. Developers generally consider a 20 percent ratio a maximum for residential properties.

In the derivation of the above lot improvement costs, it is assumed that the water mains and sanitary sewer facilities serve lots on both sides of the street and that only one-half of the street paving and curbing costs are assignable to each lot. It is further assumed that no costs will be incurred

---

[1] Based on estimated land development costs by Hugh Edwards, Inc., Developers, 1605 NW 22nd Street, Gainesville, Florida.

by the developer for the installation of sidewalks, for the extension of gas, electric, or telephone utilities, and that no expenditures are required for other public or recreational facilities. Should further costs be incurred they must, of course, be added proportionally to the sales price of each lot.

As indicated above, density of population affects in an important way site development costs. Although utility service mains must be larger and streets wider and paving stronger as density increases, the utility service and street grading and paving costs decline on a per capita basis as the population per lot or acre increases. However, a point of diminishing returns is reached when "crowding" occurs and oversize installations are required to care for abnormal loads.

Subdividing and developing problems

The effective planning and execution of urban or suburban neighborhoods require detailed study and the application of the combined skills of urban planners, architects, civil engineers, real estate consultants, and financiers, all cooperating on a project which must merit the sanction of respective governmental agencies. Before proceeding with the acquisition of the land or the expenditure of any site development costs, the entire project must be worked out on paper. Estimates must be made of the known, as well as of the probable, investment, operating, and overhead costs. This should be followed by a market analysis which will show the extent of present and reasonably anticipated demand for building sites in the area under development. The market survey and cost analysis must also indicate the price at which lots must sell to make the project a profitable undertaking.

Subdividing as the first step in the developing program requires the application of the economic concept of highest and best land use to the area as a whole and to each site under development in particular. Highest and best use was defined (see Chapter 1) as that present and prospective legal use that will yield to land the highest present value. It is one problem to determine the highest and best use of a given site, and a much more intricate problem to determine the highest and best use of a great number of interrelated sites, or for the development as a whole. The subdividing and developing problems are especially difficult where the planned area is suburban in character and where the subdivision must be a "self-contained" neighborhood because of distance from the nearest city or urban center. Thus, where consideration must be given to residential and commercial site locations, as well as to the establishment and placement of schools, parks, churches, recreational, cultural, and civic service facilities, decisions governing land uses may have important and far-reaching consequences.

Since the discussions of city planning and zoning in Chapter 26 will further deal with the locations and site problems of self-contained neighborhoods, special stress will be laid in this chapter on subdividing and developing theories and practices applicable to smaller sites and neighborhood areas.

A case study. For purposes of illustrating some of the problems and considerations that arise in connection with the subdividing and developing of a small tract of land located at the outer edge of a community of forty thousand people, a case study made for the purchaser of a thirteen-acre tract is briefly summarized. The problems were (1) to determine the highest and best use of the land, (2) to prepare and submit alternate subdivision and development plans, (3) to ascertain by market analysis the prices that the developed sites would command if exposed for sale, and (4) to establish the price or value per acre of the tract.

The problem of land use was solved without great difficulty, for the area was zoned residence "A" and thus legally restricted to residential uses. Zoning laws further provided that building sites must contain a minimum area of 10,000 square feet or be approximately 100 feet wide by 100 feet in depth. Streets had to be graded and paved and essential utilities had to be provided to make the sites eligible for federally insured and guaranteed mortgage loans.

A physical inspection of the area disclosed that the contour of the land

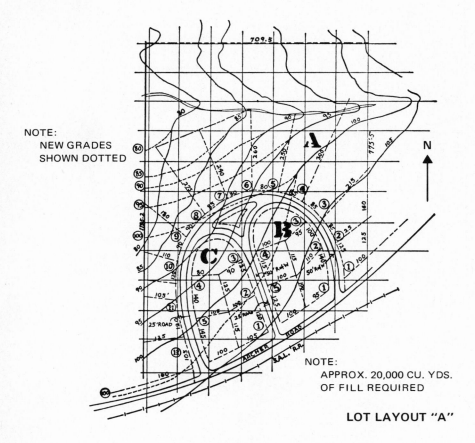

NOTE:
NEW GRADES
SHOWN DOTTED

N

NOTE:
APPROX. 20,000 CU. YDS.
OF FILL REQUIRED

LOT LAYOUT "A"

was uneven and that moving of earth for filling would be necessary to level low spots. The area as a whole drained toward a small clear creek near the north border of the tract. To ascertain the elevation and exact physical contour of the land, a civil engineer was engaged to survey the area and to prepare a contour map showing specific elevations. The map thus secured was then submitted to a consulting architect for preparation of alternative subdivision plats that would best conform to the contours of the land. Instructions, too, were given to determine the average amount of earth fill necessary to level the subdivision throughout to minimum required grades. The architect than superimposed his plat plans on the engineering contour map and presented his findings and suggestions for further analysis.

The two alternative plans submitted by the architect are reproduced for the reader's study. Plan "A" shows the tract fronting approximately 740 feet on Archer Road and extending due north for 1135.2 feet on its western and 775.5 feet on its eastern boundary. The northern tract boundary as shown is 709.5 feet in length. Plan "B," illustrated on the following page, called for a simple subdivision of the tract into nineteen lots. All land below an elevation of 80 feet (above sea level) was poorly drained, due to the existence of a high water table, and was deemed unfit for residential use. It was suggested that the creek area be landscaped and that the low areas be developed into a community park. To make Plan "B" feasible, 4,000 cubic yards of earth had to be moved and filled. To keep developing costs at a minimum, only one semicircular road 25 feet in width was proposed under Plan "B."

Alternative Plan "A" shows the same area with land contours and elevations altered after moving and filling 20,000 cubic yards of earth. Under this plan a more attractive subdivision was designed and lots available for homesite use were increased to twenty-two as shown. An additional center road, and the installation of a traffic isle, were suggested to increase pedestrian safety and to provide far greater privacy to home occupants.

Both plans were then subjected to a development cost analysis as follows:

Type of Improvement	Total Costs Under:	
	Plan "A"	Plan "B"
Water mains	$ 6,400	$ 5,000
Sanitary sewers	9,000	7,000
Street grading and paving	12,000	7,500
Curbs and gutters	7,500	5,000
Earth moving and filling at $.80 per cubic yard	16,000	3,200
Miscellaneous costs—legal, sales, and overheads	5,000	4,300
Total development costs, exclusive of cost of land and profits	$55,900	$32,000

With this information at hand, a market survey was then undertaken to determine the value of the developed sites if exposed for sale at the time of study. In the determination of the value data, reliance was placed on

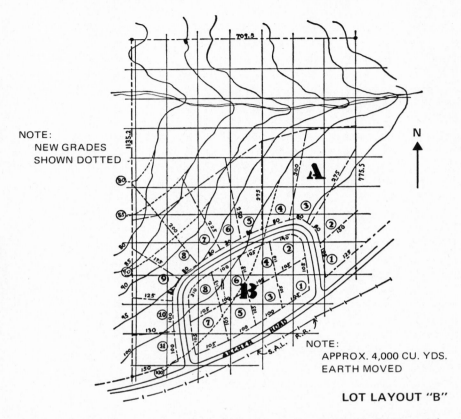

NOTE:
NEW GRADES
SHOWN DOTTED

N

NOTE:
APPROX. 4,000 CU. YDS.
EARTH MOVED

LOT LAYOUT "B"

comparable land sales and prices paid by buyers in equally desirable neighborhoods offering comparable homeside amenities. The technique employed was that illustrated in Chapter 24, "Real Estate Appraising."

The information secured via the market comparison approach to value indicated that lots sold under Plan "B" would average $2,750 per lot and yield a total of $52,250 for the nineteen lots. Under the more attractive layout of Plan "A" lots would yield an average price of $3,350 or a total of $73,700 for the twenty-two lots. Assuming that the purchaser or developer is entitled to a 10 percent profit based on actual development costs, the maximum price that could economically be offered to the owner for the tract of land was derived as follows:

	Plan "A"	Plan "B"
Total developing costs	$55,900	$32,000
Add developers' profit (10%)	5,590	3,200
Total costs and profits	$61,490	$35,200
Total market price of subdivision (based on lot sale values shown above)	73,700	52,250
Available for purchase of unimproved land	$12,210	$17,050

Although from a community and an aesthetic point of view, Plan "A" proves more attractive, Plan "B" indicates the highest and best use of the land. Since the tract in question contained approximately thirteen acres and Plan "B" supports a land value of $17,050, a purchase price at the rate of $1,300 per acre was recommended. This case study is presented to provide a practical guide to the problems incident to subdividing and development and to demonstrate a method under which the profitableness of an undertaking can be checked with a fair degree of accuracy—prior, of course, to the acquisition of the land and expenditures for subdivision improvements.

Subdividing and development practices

Before 1930, and particularly during the "boom" periods following World War I, land speculators took advantage of the naïveté of home buyers and the unconcern of community and governmental leaders, as evidenced during those years by lack of city planning, zoning, and subdivision controls. Subdivisions sprang up everywhere, principally in remote suburban places and often miles away from connecting utility service lines and community water, sewage, and transportation systems. Generally, imposing pillars were erected at the entrance to the proposed subdivision. Promotional schemes were then set in motion and supported by extravagant advertising campaigns. Municipal authorities often fell for the "bait" and agreed to extend municipal services, to pave and curb the streets, to install street lights, and to provide schools, police, and fire departmental services in order to meet the imminent "bandwagon" growth of the community. Many cities and hundreds of smaller incorporated communities burdened their citizens with long-term bonded debt to finance the ill-fated improvements, hoping by quick action to attract a greater share of the migrating city dwellers which the automobile was expected to set free. Except in isolated cases, the mad rush to the suburban hinterland never developed and thousands of once-imposing entrance pillars stand to this day as monuments to the fallacies of past subdivision practices.

The severe depression of the 1930–40 decade brought home to citizens everywhere the costly consequences of the hasty faith that municipal leaders placed in the overtures of fast-working real estate speculators. As an outcome of the debacle of the real estate boom, communities, with the aid of state *enabling acts* and indirect aid from federal agencies, have adopted safeguards to prevent a recurrence of the "runaway" subdivisions and their attendant civic burdens. Today most cities provide for strict subdivision controls. Whenever areas are to be subdivided, assurance must be given that all costs, including the grading and paving of streets and the installation of conduits for municipal services, can and will be borne by the owners or developers. Generally, necessary land for schools and other civic facilities must be dedicated to public use. Proof of subdivision demand, too, must be established in many jurisdictions before authority to proceed with site improvements is granted. In many states statutes have been enacted regulating the methods and practices governing subdivision land sales and placing the owners and developers under detailed supervision. Statutes in some instances provide that collections made on installment contracts for the purchase of lots—in developments that are subject to statutory control—be held as trust funds to cover the cost of releasing such lots from the liens of existing encumbrances. Under these statutes, violators are subject to criminal prosecution or may be restrained from further lot sales in the affected subdivision.

Agency controls

In addition to municipal subdivisions and development controls imposed through zoning ordinances under which street width, type, occupancy, and setback of structures are regulated, additional controls are exercised by health, fire, and building safety departments which inspect improvements to insure compliance with health and safety standards. Since 1935 one of the most effective, though indirect methods of assuring sound subdivision and development practices has been used by the Federal Housing Administration which is under legislative mandate to promote and encourage the development of basically sound residential areas. FHA indirect controls are achieved by threat of withholding mortgage loan insurance from any residential area that does not comply with minimum development standards. These regulations are applied with particular stringency in subdivisions that have been planned since World War II. The regulations are by no means arbitrary. In fact, they are quite flexible and subject to review and modification by regional offices to meet local needs, customs, and climatic conditions. Generally, the regulations are in the interest of all concerned and are designed to prolong the life of the area for residential use and to guard against practices that may hasten site deterioration or promote slum conditions. The following are some of the more important FHA minimum subdivision standards to which newly developed areas must conform to be eligible for mortgage loan insurance:

1. Streets must be of approved width and properly paved. Curved street patterns to avoid through-traffic and to promote greater privacy are recommended.
2. The area must be free from hazards caused by excessive dust, noise, heavy through-traffic, or other detrimental forces. Where the residential area is adjacent to nonconforming commercial or industrial uses, effective artificial barriers (parks or playgrounds) must be provided to shield and protect the area.
3. Subdivision must have ready access to adequate shopping and recreational facilities, schools, churches, and transportation service.
4. Essential utilities, such as water, electricity, sewage disposal, and area drainage, must be present and approved by city or county health authorities.
5. Lots must be of minimum size, generally at least 5,000 sq. ft. (50' × 100') in size, although the larger 100' × 120' plots are recommended.
6. Structures must be of approved design, must meet minimum construction standards, and must vary in elevation sufficiently to improve neighbor-

hood appearance. Row houses, for instance, except in areas classified as "temporary" or "emergency" would not be authorized for loan insurance.

7. Buildings must be uniform in setback from street or building property line. Lawns must be "sprigged" and a minimum of landscaping in front and on sides of the homes must be provided.

As a service to subdividers, developers, and builders, regional FHA offices furnish aid and offer helpful suggestions free of charge. Thus a developer may send the proposed subdivision and plot plans to the regional office for check or modification and approval. Trained specialists generally study the plan in relation to land contour, elevation, drainage, and the community environment and then offer changes intended to improve the subdivision layout and to increase the benefits to future homeowners. Even the placement of buildings, changes in the variety of design, and building color variation are suggested to make the appearance of structures pleasing to the eye and thus increase the amenities of living and pride of ownership among the occupants. Before approval is granted, proof must be supplied that the existing and potential demand for homesites warrants the proposed subdivision. The intention is to discourage purely speculative undertakings. In more recent years, the Loan Guarantee Division of the Veterans Administration has also adopted similar subdivision regulations in order to exercise control over developments where homesites are to be acquired by veterans under the GI Bill of Rights.

Private subdivision control

It is almost always customary to provide in the better subdivisions and developments private restrictions that govern land use and subject to which the land is sold to prospective users. Such restrictions are generally agreed upon by the owner or developer at the time of area subdivision and placed on public records.[2] All land subsequently deeded is then made subject to these restrictions and reference to the page and book of record will appear in each deed.

Deed restrictions are especially important where the subdivision is not improved in its entirety or where building sites are to be developed by future land owners. Private subdivision controls or deed restriction is intended to protect and safeguard the interests of present owners against willful or inadvertent misuse of the land. Deed restrictions attach to the land and are successively deeded with the land and run as a rule for a period of about twenty to thirty years, after which the restrictions, generally, may be continued by a majority or two-thirds vote of the landowners of record. Deed restrictions must be just, reasonable, and legal, that is, not contrary to public policy or in violation of constitutional or statutory rights. Typical deed restrictions in a fair quality development may provide as follows:

1. Building sites may be improved only with single-family residences, not to exceed two and one-half stories in height.

---

[2]See page 80.

2. Buildings must be set back not less than twenty feet from property building line, and not less than eight feet from property side lines.
3. Only buildings costing twelve thousand dollars or more and containing
one thousand square feet of living area or more may be erected on a
building site.
4. Occupancy of each structure is limited to a single family.
5. Re-subdivision of lots is prohibited and no more than one dwelling may
be erected on each lot.
6. Buildings must conform in design to the neighborhood and approval of
building plans must be secured from the subdivision building committee,
duly approved by a majority of property owners. Building sites may not
be used for erection of temporary residences, trailers, or structures moved
from other locations.
7. The keeping of animals, other than those classed as domesticated, is prohibited.
8. Observance of these covenants, subject to which the land is deeded, may
be enforced by any one or more owners of subdivision land through appropriate notice and court action.
9. These covenants shall remain in force from February 1, 1972, to February 1, 1992, and shall be subject to renewal for two additional twenty-
year periods, unless changed by a vote of two-thirds of the property
owners at the time of expiration.

Deed restrictions, well intended as they may be, do not automatically
enforce themselves. It is desirable, therefore, that a neighborhood or subdivision "Vigilance Committee" be appointed to guard against violations
and to secure court enforcement, if necessary, to protect the interests of
affected owners. Where size of the subdivision warrants it, a neighborhood
or civic organization may be founded not only to safeguard proper land
use in the area, as provided in the restrictions, but also to promote owners'
interests, as citizens, in matters of community-wide importance, or in matters concerning specific administrative or civic functions.

Nonresidential land uses

The discussions, thus far, have principally centered on the subdivision
and development of residential areas. The reason is that general principles
and practices concerning city planning and zoning for alternative land uses
will be given separate treatment in Chapter 26. Since some suburban areas,
however, necessitate development as "self-contained" projects, consideration should be given, if only briefly, to factors that govern nonresidential
land uses.

Whenever land is to be allocated to competing uses, care must be taken
not to violate the economic law of "highest and best land use." Since the
highest and best use is always determined by the present worth of *future*
rights to income or amenities, consideration must be given to the existence
of demand for the uses and purposes to which certain sites are dedicated
in the overall subdivision plan. Because business properties are known to
bring a much higher price per unit of land, it is a common error to over-
provide the amount of space required for commercial use. Simply design-
ing an area as business property does not make it one. There must be a

demand for business property, and that demand generally is in direct proportion to the number of people or better, families, residing in the area. The reasonable relationship of number of families to number and kind of retail and service establishments can best be judged by a study of the spending pattern of the people in the area under analysis. To illustrate the application of family spending pattern studies to subdivisions' needs for retail and service establishments, marketing data[3] for two selected states, New York and Florida, are presented below:

Sales by Type of Retail Establishment	*Family Dollar Expenditures in the Year 1969 for Selected States*	
	New York	*Florida*
Total Sales	$5,446	$5,808
Food	1,278	1,285
General merchandise	958	882
Apparel stores	450	296
Furniture and household	277	286
Automotive	724	1,238
Gas service stations	248	447
Lumber, building material, and hardware	188	238
Drugs	164	225

The spending pattern of families as noted above is important because such data can serve as a guide in determining the number of retail establishments best suited to an area. In comparing average family spending for the state of New York with the state of Florida, it is of interest to note that outlays for food and general merchandise are almost identical but that outlays for apparel stores, automotive, building material, and drugs are significantly different. This can be accounted for by differences in climate, geographic distances between cities, modes of construction (also influenced by climate), and average age of citizens, the latter influencing drugstore outlays.

Assuming the subdivision and developing of a "self-contained" neighborhood in a suburban area in which a maximum of one thousand families will reside, and further assuming a family spending pattern as shown above for New York State, then sound subdivision policy would provide for a maximum of twenty-three retail stores, distributed as follows:

Number of Stores	*Kind of Retail or Service Establishment*
3	Food stores
1	Bakery
2	Apparel stores
1	Drugstore
2	Eating places
1	Furniture and household
2	Automotive supplies

---
[2]See page 80.
Inc., (June 10, 1970), p. B–7.

Number of Stores	Kind of Retail or Service Establishment
2	Gas service station
1	Lumber, building materials, and hardware
1	Package liquor store
2	Barbershops
2	Beauty parlors
1	Shoe repair
1	Variety
1	Dry cleaning and pressing

The kind and number of retail establishments depend, of course, as previously stated, on community custom, climate, and general characteristics of the inhabitants.

Intelligent subdivision planning further requires an analysis of demand for the number and kind of rental and apartment units and for the number and kind of park, school, church, recreational, and civic facilities essential to make the development self-contained. Here, too, reference should be made to studies of other and similarly located suburban subdivisions, whose proven plans may serve as a guide in the proposed allocation of the subject land to alternative and often competing uses. In general, it is considered good policy to provide a buffer zone between the single-family residential and commercial areas. It is in this buffer zone that apartment, rental, and transient occupants may best be housed. Parks and recreational areas, too, provide effective protection against the "spilling" of inharmonious uses into the section reserved for single-family residential occupancy. The residents, it need be remembered, comprise the core or heart of the subdivision, and when their welfare is impaired, the development as a whole will suffer.

Financing

Only in exceptional instances is an urban or suburban area subdivided or developed without the aid of borrowed funds. Generally, the subdivider or real estate operator acquires the "raw" land with equity (owner) funds and then seeks aid through mortgage financing to carry out the development of the project area. The "raw" land, as was noted above, requires only a fraction of the total cost that the land and improvement in their final stage of development represent. Compared with total value of land and building improvements, suburban land in its "raw" stage represents generally not more than 3 to 5 percent of the entire development costs. To secure the remaining 95 to 97 percent of project funds poses the financial problem. There are many plans under which investment funds may be borrowed in the market. In some instances, the improvement funds are sought by individuals who assume personal liability for borrowed funds or by partnerships or syndicates that are organized for the purpose of carrying out the subdivision and development plans. In most instances, however, the corporate form of ownership is preferred, especially where the project involves large tracts of land. A typical and orderly procedure for financing land improvements may be carried out as follows:

1. The "raw" land is acquired with owner's or equity funds at a price substantiated by income and cost calculations as demonstrated above. The developer then proceeds with surveying, plotting, and filing of the proposed subdivision plan.
2. Once the plat is accepted and approved by municipal authorities and also by FHA regional representatives as a subdivision eligible for mortgage loan insurance (subject to completion of specified site improvements), the developer or developing company may borrow improvement funds over short-term periods of one to three years, offering the entire project land holdings as security under a "blanket" mortgage. Under this blanket mortgage, funds will be made available for land improvement purposes up to the maximum agreed upon. This mortgage customarily provides for the release of individual sites, from the lien of the mortgage, upon payment of agreed principal sums. This arrangement permits sale of building or improved homesites to individual buyers free and clear of mortgage encumbrances. This blanket mortgage, as a rule, also contains provisions under which it will assume a junior security position in case mortgage funds are obtained and invested for building construction on a given site or plot, either by the developer or by future homeowners.
3. Once the subdivision is improved with streets, utilities, and so forth, the developer may proceed with building financing plans as follows:
   a. He may offer the individual building sites for sale directly or through brokers, releasing each lot from the blanket mortgage as stated above.
   b. He may offer the sites to builders for a nominal down payment under a long-term land purchase contract which provides for payment of the balance of the purchase price upon erection and sale of the proposed structure. In most instances, builders require title to the land when they, too, seek mortgage funds for building construction purposes. Where this is the case, the developer takes back a junior mortgage or merely retains an equitable lien against the property. The building site under such arrangements must be freed from the blanket mortgage, or the latter, as provided, must assume a secondary lien position.
   c. The developer may hire his own contractors and subcontractors and proceed with the erection of a few model homes. The necessary funds are generally secured through construction mortgage loans or building loan mortgages where the improvements are built to order for approved mortgagors. The builder may also secure an FHA building mortgage loan commitment and borrow funds against the insurance thus offered to the lender. Where the market is active and a ready demand exists for homes in the proposed subdivision, the third method of financing the building improvements may prove most advantageous.

Marketing

The marketing of subdivided land is essentially a selling campaign which is more fully discussed in Chapter 20. Marketing begins as soon as the development is made presentable, that is, when the ground is cleared, streets and service utilities installed, signs and markers put in place, and other work completed to make the land attractive. It is always advisable to erect a few model homes—perhaps one house for every twenty lots—to invite inspection by prospects and curiosity seekers, and to provide a show of activity. Model homes have proved almost indispensable as selling aids in the marketing of homes and building sites of a development project.

Although most developers have their own regular sales force, cooperating real estate brokers often participate in the direct advertising and selling campaign. Compensation for them may be a fixed amount per unit or on a commission basis, derived as a percentage of the gross amount of sales. The goodwill and cooperation of real estate brokers in a community is often essential to the successful marketing of large subdivisions or when building improvements must be liquidated readily to secure necessary funds for payments of mortgage obligations or for further employment in the project development.

Development budget requirements

In recent years most of the land subdivided near large urban centers has been developed by operative builders who sell homes ready for occupancy. The builder usually erects a number of model homes, each with a different layout. From these basic plans, variation in structural appearance of additional buildings is achieved by slight changes in facades, dormers, orientation, and exterior finish. Such building practice avoids the monotony of structural design so often seen in older sections of most cities.

A modern large-scale development requires a careful analysis of all costs to be incurred from date of purchase of the raw land to date of sale of the finished residences. As an illustration of this type of development, the following actual case may be considered. The builder in this instance acquired fairly level suburban land at a cost of $6,500 per acre, each of which provided 4½ building plots 60′ × 100′ in size after meeting street and sidewalk requirements. The building plans called for a frame structure containing seven rooms, including three bedrooms and a basement playroom. The house was furnished with one bath, a 40-gallon automatic water heater, an oil burner, and a built-in garage. The structure was faced with a brick-and-wood front and asbestos shingle siding; it contained 22,500 cubic feet in volume. A budget to establish the selling price per property follows:

A. Developing Costs per Acre and per Plot
    1. *Engineering and survey fees*
       Outline survey
       Topographical map
       Subdivision map
       Test holes, etc. $ 225
    2. *Drainage dump area*
       Cost of land used for this purpose, excavation, earth moving, concrete curbs, and chain link fence   600
    3. *Subgrading of roads*   175
    4. *Drainage*
       Catch basins, manholes, underground pipes, concrete head walk required by Department of Public Works   625
    5. *Park area*   150
    6. *Road paving*
       Class A roads in conformity with county specifications   1,900
    7. *Sidewalks*   1,000
    8. *Curbs*   700
    9. *Water mains*   1,500

10. *Miscellaneous*
    Street signs
    Monuments
    County inspection fees, etc. 125

Total cost per acre	$ 7,000
Cost of raw land per acre	6,500
	$13,500
Cost per 60' × 100' plot (4½ to the acre)	$ 3,000

B. Total Cost per Structure

The dwelling was built to the specifications outlined above, excluding profit, at a cost of 80 cents per cubic foot, or $18,000 for the 22,500 cubic feet of the building. This may be broken down as follows:

Building (net cost)	$18,000
Profit—10%	1,800
	$19,800
Add land	3,000
Indicated selling price	$22,800

The profit margin noted may be altered by a number of factors, such as fortunate purchase of land at a lower price, extras added to suit some purchasers, competition in the area, and other conditions.

It must be remembered that this illustration above is of a typical dwelling on an average lot. Purchasers select the house from a model, contract for an identical house decorated to suit, often with extras such as fireplace, double garage, additional bath, and plumbing lines to attic for future expansion. A lot selected from the development plan, too, may cost much more or less than the average depending on orientation, shade trees, or elevation. These variable factors may contribute to the construction of a large number of properties each originating from one of the basic plans, but each differing in selling price from the others.

READING AND STUDY REFERENCES

1. HUSBAND, WILLIAM H., and FRANK RAY ANDERSON, *Real Estate*, Chapter 15. Homewood, Ill.: Richard D. Irwin, Inc., 1960.

2. KAHN, SANDERS A., FREDERICK CASE, and ALFRED SCHIMMEL, *Real Estate Appraisal and Investment*, Chapter 30. New York: The Ronald Press Company, 1963.

3. MARTIN, PRESTON, *Real Estate Principles and Practices*, Chapter 4. New York: The Macmillan Company, 1959.

4. RING, ALFRED A., *Questions and Problems in Real Estate Principles and Practices* (rev. ed.), Chapter 24. Englewood Cliffs, N.J.: Prentice-Hall, Inc., 1972.

5. UNGER, MAURICE A., *Real Estate* (4th ed.), Chapter 25. Cincinnati: South-Western Publishing Co., 1969.

6. WEIMER, ARTHUR M., and HOMER HOYT, *Real Estate* (5th ed.), Chapter 15. New York: The Ronald Press Company, 1966.

7. YOKLEY, E. C., *The Law of Subdivisions*, Chapters 2, 8, 10, and 11. Charlottesville, Va.: Michie Company, 1963.

26

CITY PLANNING
AND ZONING

Purpose

City planning and zoning functions and activities are intended to serve as means toward the accomplishment of desirable social and economic ends. City planning is the broader of the two governmental powers under which an attempt is made to secure economy in municipal operations and to direct the natural growth of the community in an orderly fashion. City planning is generally comprehensive and all-embracing in scope. Under it the social, economic, and political phases of municipal control are analyzed and plans are laid to operate and employ publicly owned resources in a manner that will yield the greatest possible long-run benefits for the community as a whole. The city plan, too, includes directives for control of privately owned land resources in order to promote and safeguard the health, welfare, and morality of the people. The governmental power involving supervision and control over the utilization of privately owned land, although a part of the overall city plan, is better known as zoning. Additional controls, of course, are exercised by municipal departments that are specifically charged with protecting public health, sanitation, safety, building maintenance, and construction.

The need for city planning

Although the planning of the growth of cities and towns in the United States in an orderly fashion begins in the twentieth century, city planning as an art and science dates back to the Middle Ages. The origin of the more recent and widespread need for the urban planning movement may be found in the very rapid growth of the United States urban population, along with the remarkable evolution in the mode of transportation and commercial intercourse.

The growth in the number of communities with a population of less than one hundred thousand is especially noteworthy, for the trend toward smaller cities is largely due to the decentralization movement in the metropolitan centers. Yet decentralization does not mean deurbanization. The trend is merely toward smaller satellite or dormitory suburban areas where the amenities of urban living can be enjoyed without the attendant disadvantages of congestion, dust, noise, smoke, and related ecological pollution which have become characteristic of the larger cities.

The rapid growth of the smaller urban communities has given impetus to the long-felt need for city planning. Since 1907 when the first city planning commission was organized in Hartford, Connecticut, 98 percent of all communities of ten thousand population and over, as of January 1970, have followed suit by establishing official planning agencies.[1] The founding of these planning agencies is a direct result of the realization that urban land is a resource of too great importance to be left at the mercy of chance development.

City planning aims

Communities are dynamic in character and must be sufficiently flexible in structural design to provide, if necessary, for sudden internal growth and orderly expansion beyond the city's limits. The aims of city planning are directed, therefore, not only toward the correction of existing urban structures but more so toward sound expansion of community service facilities in order to create a healthy and safe environment in which residents may enjoy life and carry on their business functions. In the accomplishment of these aims, planning commissions endeavor (1) to stimulate wider interest in community problems, (2) to coordinate civic developments, and (3) to stabilize property values by orderly city growth. In pursuit of these aims, city planning has developed as an applied science and as a practical art. As a science, city planning requires knowledge about human relationship as it affects the social, political, and economic development of the community. As an art, planning involves the structural development of the city's land space in relation to urban needs and in accordance with sound economic practices. To carry out these aims and to attain specific objectives, the community relies upon formulation and execution of a comprehensive *master plan*.

[1] *The Municipal Yearbook*, 1970. Chicago: The International City Managers.

Master planning requisites

A city may be considered a corporate entity offering cultural, social, and economic advantages superior to those offered to residents in competing urban, suburban, or rural areas. Like a business entity, a city as a whole must prosper if it is to continue as a going concern. In this effort the city must compete with other cities near and far which vie for national recognition and an ever greater share of the total urban market. The ability of a city to hold on to its present population and to continue to draw and attract new residents is thus of great concern to the city planner. As a requisite to good city planning, an inventory should be taken of the area's physical and economic growth potentials, and of the resources which underlie and justify the city's existence.

The *physical* survey involves the preparation of an official city plan. On this plan are delineated the legal boundaries, the pattern of the streets—in use and for expansion—the lay of the land in respect to elevation, sources of water supply, and character (weight-bearing quality) of the soil. The *economic* survey is generally more comprehensive in scope and more difficult to undertake. The following are some of the more important steps which must be followed in an economic analysis of a city. *First*, the origin and character of the city must be studied. What is the economic basis that warrants the city's continued existence? Is it principally industrial, commercial, recreational, political, or educational in character? Or does it serve two or more principal economic interests? The origin and future economic potentials of a city are important. The fact that a city prospers at present provides no guarantee that it will continue to do so. The many "ghost" towns in mining, farm, and mineral areas stand as monuments to costly errors made by city founders and real estate investors. Generally, the more diversified a city's commercial and industrial activities, the more stabilized is the economy and, hence, land values in the community. *Second*, the number, kind, and quality of the city's population must be analyzed. It is essential to study population in regard to density and migratory trends toward or from existing and potential urban centers. To plan adequately a city must know the needs arising from racial composition, number and age distribution of male and female population, professional and occupational practices, and employment opportunities. *Third*, the economic survey should reveal the city's standing in regard to volume of wholesale and retail trade, bank deposits and savings, number and value distribution of residential and commercial structures, number of automobiles, telephones, household appliances, and other indexes of economic well-being on a family or per capita basis as compared with like economic measures for the region, the state, and the nation as a whole. *Fourth*, the study should include survey information basic to the preparation of land utilization maps. Such survey maps should indicate the kind and amount of land used for public purposes (streets, parks, schools, and other public buildings) and privately owned, held for residential, commercial, or industrial uses. Value land maps based on market sales and property assessment rolls are also important as requisites to effective city planning.

The master plan

Careful analysis of the physical and economic survey data should furnish the basic information upon which the master plan is to be founded. This plan, comprehensive in its scope, must be sufficiently flexible to permit growth and economic adjustment to dynamic changes caused by city growth. As a rule the master plan provides a clear view of the existing pattern of public streets, arterial highways, traffic flow, and the relative adequacy of rail, water, air, and intercity highway transportation. In the preparation of the master plan, special attention is also given to intracity and suburban transit lines and to the adequacy of the transportation network system in relation to present and potential traffic demands.

To promote balanced community growth and efficient and most economical (highest and best) land uses, the master plan outlines the need for, and location of, public buildings, parks, recreational centers, parkways, and essential neighborhood developments. A well-conceived master plan is flexible, provides guided control over the future growth of the city, retards neighborhood blight, looks toward the elimination of city slums, and stimulates and guides private development in order to attain the greatest good for the greatest number among those who have a "stake" in the community.

Planning problems

Resistance to control of private property in the interest of the public good unfortunately delays the adoption and execution of a master plan in many communities until a time when symptoms of chaotic city growth arouse public attention and cause a demand for action to correct costly errors of the past. Thanks to the educational efforts of leading city planners, city managers' associations, and legislative interest on a state and federal level, community leaders have come to recognize that organized foresight is less expensive than hindsight and that wisely planned construction is preferable to costly reconstruction.

Although enlightened civic leaders can readily be convinced of the merits of good city planning, they find it difficult in practice to cope with the financial problems which preparation and execution of a master plan entail. Inevitably, improvements cost money and, even granting that citizens will assume the financial burden when shown that future benefits will outweigh present sacrifices, the immediate costs always seem large, if not prohibitive, when compared with probable benefits which are difficult to measure in terms of dollars. As a rule, the financial problems pose the greatest handicap to city planning. There are other problems, of course, concerned with legal, social, and technical aspects of guiding the orderly growth of a community, but these are generally subsidiary to the problem of financing the improvements that are called for in the master plan. Civic leaders may rightfully oppose a comprehensive city plan until the effect of proposed expenditures on real estate taxes and assessments are known. Investors, speculators, and homeowners, too, are interested in how the anticipated benefits and the incidence of the tax burden will influence the value of privately held land. It must also be determined whether improvement costs are to be borne by abutting landowners in accordance with the "benefit received" theory or whether they are to be borne by the citizens as a whole in accordance with "ability to pay." Many a comprehensive city plan lies dormant because of the failure to solve successfully the economic issues upon which, in the final analysis, the master plan depends.

Planning principles and practices

Principles of city planning serve as guides to the practical attainment of community objectives. A prime consideration of city planners is to reduce per capita urban costs, to improve the amenities of urban living, and to facilitate the flow of commerce. The success of such efforts is important, because property values depend upon the efficient and economical flow of goods and persons and the ready and convenient access to modes of transportation. To achieve the objective of traffic economy, a study must be made of traffic requirements and steps must be taken to provide adequate avenues of transport. Rapid and economical transportation offers significant opportunities to direct population flow in and about the city. No longer is it deemed good practice to follow population in congested areas with more means of transportation and thus generally increase or aggravate congestion problems. Rather it has been shown that people can be made to follow avenues of transport into areas that are planned and designed for better and more healthful living.

To facilitate the movement of goods and people in and about the city, streets should be designed and interconnected to meet normal as well as "rush hour" traffic requirements. Care should be taken to weigh the advantages and disadvantages of each of the several types of street patterns and to choose those that will facilitate travel and increase pedestrian and highway traffic safety. The proper design and layout of streets is important, because the very rapid development and use of the private automobile has created for city planners a real problem of easing traffic congestion in downtown areas or urban centers. The construction of belt highways, freeways, and turnpikes that skirt (bypass) the city proper has greatly contributed, in recent years, to a reduction of traffic hazards and a lessening in community costs which control of the through and intercity traffic necessitates. In residential areas it is, of course, best to discourage all except local traffic, and this can effectively be done by the use of winding streets.

The adequate provision for parks and recreational areas is next in importance as an objective of a sound city plan. The health, enjoyment, and welfare of the citizens necessitate that opportunities be provided for outdoor recreation. Parks should provide an aesthetic environment for those who seek relaxation; opportunity for play and sport should be available to those who seek more active recreation. It is important that neighborhood parks be readily accessible to residents of the various sections of the city.

A larger community park, preferably centrally located, may well serve major functions and at the same time provide the vital "breathing space" that every city should include in its master plan. The amount of land required for park and recreational uses depends largely on the density of urban population.

In determining the amount of land best suited for park and recreational purposes in a given community, consideration must be given to existing pattern of streets, the width of boulevards, the use of buildings, the cost of land, and the willingness of the people to pay for the improvements. No ready-made formula for this purpose can be suggested or employed. Location of the city, climate of the area, and characteristics of the population must also be given weight in the determination of this phase of city planning.

The proper location and grouping of public buildings is another important phase of city planning. Public buildings, such as city halls, court houses, post offices, and civic centers, attract population and influence to an important degree the value of surrounding land. Care must thus be taken to place such buildings where area utilization will permit ready access and where ample opportunity is given to commercial users to avail themselves of the higher business opportunities that such building locations may offer. Public buildings, particularly schools, fire stations, libraries, and amusement facilities, must be located near the center of population that such public structures are to serve. Since buildings of this type generally have an economic life of forty or more years, care must be taken to consider changes in population characteristics and future patterns of population distribution.

Patterns of land use in city planning involve the control of the use of public as well as private ownership in land. Because of the importance of *land use* control, a more detailed discussion will follow this phase of city planning under the subheading of *zoning*. It is an appropriate objective of the master plan to bring about an arrangement of residential areas into a homogeneous pattern of neighborhood units. Consideration should be given to the redevelopment of blighted areas into higher and better land uses and to the prevention of blight in other areas.

A practical and efficient solution must also be offered as part of the master plan for the elimination of slum housing conditions within the city. A flexible master plan must provide, as the city grows, a proper balance between the opportunities (advantages) and economic burdens (disadvantages) of centralization. At some point in the building-up process, civic costs in urban centers become burdensome to the extent that decentralization forces support a movement to another and generally "self-containing" urban or suburban area. This breaking-up of the central city into independent parts results in the creation of a metropolitan area and causes special problems of social, political, and economic coordination. The newest development in urban planning finds a solution to the complex problems of urban and suburban coordination through cooperation in planning on a county or regional basis and with aid, where needed, of the state itself. Since no city stands alone, nor constitutes a self-sufficient economic unit, regional and state planning is becoming of increasing importance.

City planning legislation

American cities are considered legal creatures of the state and are restricted in their powers to the rights delegated them in their charter of incorporation. Prior to the passage of broad *enabling acts*, communities could not alter their official city plan without express authorization and special act of the state legislature. This restriction to narrow charter powers explains why city planning was the exception rather than the rule during the nineteenth century. Increasing urban problems caused by the change from an agricultural to an industrial economy during the early years of the twentieth century induced state legislatures to pass enabling acts authorizing communities to engage in comprehensive planning within their borders. These acts have given to cities, towns, and villages of the state power to create and appoint a planning board with authority to employ the necessary experts and staff. In some communities, existing municipal departments took over planning functions; in most others, special commissions or planning boards were appointed to draft and execute the city plan.

The members of the planning board or commission are generally appointed by the city council, by the mayor, or by the city manager with the consent or confirmation of the city council. In a few cities authority is delegated to the mayor to create the commission upon his own initiative. The power of the planning commission differs considerably among the various communities. In some, the commission may merely exercise advisory powers. In such instances the commission members prepare the city plan but merely advise the legislative body in regard to the plan's execution. In other communities the planning commission has greater powers and may request adherence to its plans—subject to legislative veto—by other municipal departments or authorities.

Where city commission plans are operative, changes in the "official" city map or plan must be referred to the planning board by the legislative body, or the planning board may on its own initiative make such investigations, maps, reports, and recommendations as it deems desirable and in the city's interest. The underlying theory of urban planning and that of the commission entrusted with its functions is that its activities shall insure to the citizens an increased enjoyment of all the advantages that a well-organized municipality should supply and shall prevent such acts of private individuals or such use of private property as will in any way impede such enjoyment. The individual citizen is one member among many working and living in the city. What he does tends to have its effect upon the whole body of citizens whose interests, comforts, and conveniences are held to be paramount. Municipalities have a distinct responsibility for the manner in which cities develop, and the general public has a right to be protected from blighting influences and willful acts that impair the amenities of living and affect adversely investments in real property.

Zoning

Although zoning is a phase of city planning and is concerned with land use control of private property, zoning powers are better known, more generally applied, and in many communities predate the formulation of a master plan or even the formation of the planning commission itself. The widespread application of zoning powers is evident from a survey conducted by the International City Managers' Association. As reported in the 1970 *Municipal Yearbook*, 98 percent of all cities in excess of ten thousand population had enacted comprehensive zoning ordinances governing the utilization of privately owned land. Since more than 60 percent of all urban land is generally held under private ownership, the impact of zoning laws upon income and value of real property is most significant.

It can readily be seen that without comprehensive zoning control, the competition for diverse land uses would be unorganized and individual preferences, land income concepts, speculation, and possibly greed might cause "quilt work" land uses that ultimately would destroy not only land values but the usefulness of the city as a social, economic, and political unit. Yet the resistance to public controls over private land was so great among individual landholders that many controversial issues reached the highest court for judicial determination whether property under "zoning" was not taken contrary to the "due process" provisions of the Fourteenth Amendment of the U.S. Constitution. As a general rule, courts have upheld legislative rights granted communities under state law to regulate—in the public interest—the use of private property. The underlying concept in all court decisions was that cities must grow and that where individual rights interfere with those of the majority, individual prerogatives must give way.

Zoning powers

The legal basis for zoning is the police power under which a sovereign state, or its duly constituted "arms" and "branches" of government, may control the use of private property where the interests and protection of health, welfare, and morality of the citizens as a whole make such control necessary or even mandatory. Zoning powers specifically are conferred upon municipalities by state legislative enabling acts. To assure appropriate use of the police power for zoning purposes, a model or standard enabling act was drawn and suggested for use by the Advisory Committee on Zoning of the Department of Commerce. This standard act which has served as a model for most enabling acts now in force includes the following essential provisions:

1. A specific, definite, and clear grant of power
2. Safeguards in the preparation and adoption of the zoning ordinance through the provision of a public hearing of which sufficient notice is given

3. Prevention of too easy changes in the ordinance, so that it may not become a political weapon
4. Prevention of arbitrary operation of the ordinance, through provision of a Board of Adjustment or Board of Appeal whose decisions are subject to review by the Court
5. Provisions of means for the enforcement of the zoning ordinance, fines, imprisonment, the stopping of work on buildings, and so on

Since zoning as exercised under the police power of the state permits the taking of private property (by limiting its use) *without* compensation, zoning ordinances are applied with caution and only after due public hearings have convinced city officials that the rights taken away are adequately balanced, if not exceeded, by the value that accrues to the community as a whole.

Zoning practices

Zoning regulations affect private ownership in land as follows: (1) by regulating the right of the owner to employ the land for limited uses only, (2) by restricting the height of building structures that may be placed upon the land, and (3) by limiting the maximum land area that building improvements may occupy.

The first or *land use restrictions*, are best known. Urban areas that are subject to zoning control are generally divided into three main use classifications: (1) residential, (2) commercial, and (3) industrial. Each one of these main land use classes may then be further subdivided to permit greater homogeneity of land development. Thus, residential property may be classified as residence "A," "B," and "C." The "A" land may be limited to single detached residences, "B"' to semidetached residences and structures containing not more than four family dwelling units. "C" land may be employed for apartment houses, churches, private clubs, schools, hotels, and similar approved land uses. All structures are subject, of course, to height and area limitations as described below. Land use regulations also restrict the keeping of animals—other than those classed as domesticated —and prohibit use of billboards and professional signs exceeding specified dimensions.

Commercial land, too, may be subdivided into areas reserved for business "A" and "B." The "A" use may be restricted to office buildings, retail establishments, service shops, restaurants, and so forth, and the "B" areas to loft buildings and light manufacturing. Industrial areas which are generally open to all uses may be subclassified to segregate light industry from heavy industry. Some communities have taken steps to prohibit the erection of residential dwelling units on industrial or commercial zoned land. It is deemed, under modern zoning practice, equitable and essential to protect the large investment in industrial plants and buildings against possible future suits by residents based on claims that their health or welfare is affected by noxious odors, excessive dust, smoke, or other nuisances that normally may be accepted as characteristic of the industrial environment.

The selection of land classifications for zoning purposes is based on a study of highest and best land uses. Certain land, as is noted more fully in Chapter 1, is best adaptable for residential use, while other land possesses characteristics that make its employment for commercial or industrial purposes more suitable. In the selection of land uses, consideration is given to land contours, prevailing winds, drainage and sanitation problems, population trends, existing land uses (at time of zoning), soil characteristics, urban growth problems and population characteristics, and land use demands.

Zoning as a tool of city planning may be employed also to direct city growth and encourage land uses that are held in the best interest of the community at large. This type of zoning is known as *directive* zoning as distinguished from *restrictive* or *protective* zoning which safeguards established and, as a rule, higher land uses from encroachment by lower and nonconforming uses.

Land use zoning, it need be emphasized, does not by itself create land values. Land values are made by people and not by municipal decree. This has repeatedly been demonstrated in municipalities where public or political pressure caused an "over-zoning" of business properties. The intent, of course, was for private owners to dispose of such favorable zoned land at prices higher than those that residential use would warrant. Experience proved otherwise. These over-zoned business areas remained largely underdeveloped, and failure to use this land for residential purposes caused significant earnings losses to the misguided investment holders. Many communities have come to the aid of these blighted areas by revising the zoning ordinances and land use classification.

Contrary to popular belief, too, zoning does not prevent land value declines. It is true that intelligent zoning retards value decline, but it does not prevent it. The reason is that zoning regulates physical land uses but does not and constitutionally cannot regulate the classes or character of people who occupy the buildings. Thus, where lower income classes or different social groups settle in an area formerly used by a highly homogeneous group of professional people, value declines may reflect this change. Then, too, zoning cannot prevent the aging or depreciation of structures caused by physical, functional, or economic (demand) forces.

Whenever zoning ordinances are made applicable to improved city areas, permission is usually granted to owners of developed property to continue existing land uses until the structure has reached the end of its economic life, or until the property is abandoned for the uses to which the exemption applied. This practice of granting use exemptions and the maintenance of the property's *status quo* is known as *spot zoning*. The uses themselves are classified as "nonconforming." A structure so classified may be maintained and kept in good repair, but major remodeling or the enlargement or rebuilding of the structure is generally disallowed.

Building height restrictions are enforced under zoning ordinances and are intended to prevent the usurpation of sunlight, air, and ventilation.

Changes in design and building construction, the use of steel, and the perfection of air lifts and elevators made the erection of skyscrapers practical. It was feared that unrestricted building construction practices might bring about excessively tall buildings that would endanger the health and safety of their occupants and cause fire risks and street congestion which might impair the usefulness of neighboring structures.

Height limitations when first imposed were vigorously opposed by property owners as the taking of property without due process of law. Thus, it was argued that valuable land that physically and economically can support a twenty-story building is impaired in value if utilization is legally restricted to buildings of ten stories in height. The reduction of net income of a ten-story building as compared with that of a twenty-story structure was held to be confiscation of private income and thus confiscation of private property. Despite the merits of such arguments, courts upheld the constitutional right of a city to exercise the police power in the interest of community health, welfare, and safety.

In upholding the community's right to restrict building heights, courts ruled, however, that such zoning restrictions must be reasonable, equitable, and uniformly applicable to the area so controlled. Thus, limiting all structures in a commercial area to a given height without regard to area of the site or building setback practices would be held unreasonable under the law. To give effect to an equitable relationship of building height to width and depth of building sites, many communities have developed depth-width-height formulas applicable to each district and which are made a part of the zoning regulations. Other communities limit building height in direct proportion to the importance and width of adjacent public streets. Where such regulations are in force, the height districts are referred to in multiples of 1½, 2, or 3 times the street width. To illustrate, where building height is limited to two times the width of a thirty-foot street, the ordinance would work as follows: An imaginary line is drawn from the center of the street to the permissible height of sixty feet (2 × 30′ street width) at the property building line and no part of the proposed structure may transect this building height line. The diagram shown below demonstrates the application of this type of zoning practice.

Under the application of this ordinance, buildings may vary in height depending on size of lot and setback building practices. Yet the law is equitable in providing for uniform land utilization in relation to building height, volume, and the amount of air, light, and sunshine that may penetrate to street levels. In residential areas no special height formulas are applied. Buildings are generally limited to a given number of stories, i.e., 1½, 2, 2½, or higher; volume, or the size of building, is controlled under area or bulk regulations as explained below.

Area or bulk regulations are principally applicable to residential areas and are intended to regulate the density of population, to prevent congestion and crowding, to safeguard health standards, and to increase the

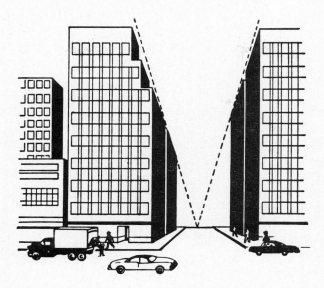

amenities of living. In effect, area and bulk regulations accomplish in residential areas what height limitations do in commercial and industrial areas. In most communities area regulations specify the following:

1. The percentage of the total building site that may be occupied by the improvements
2. Minimum setback from the building or street frontage line
3. Minimum setbacks from side and rear yard lines
4. Minimum size of inner and outer courts
5. Setback requirements for nonresidential structures, such as tool sheds and garages.

Thus typical area regulations may provide for land utilization by building improvement not in excess of 35 or 40 percent of the total building site. Under this regulation a large ranch house, for instance, may require a double lot to qualify for approval under the zoning law. Front setback regulations for residences may vary from twenty to forty feet from the street or building line. The required setback assures orderly and uniform improvement standards and permits the possible widening of streets without costly destruction of buildings, as is the case in many old residential districts that were developed prior to regulations which presently govern the orderly growth of neighborhoods.

Side and rear lot setback regulations are intended to assure a minimum of light, air, and sunshine to each residence and, incidentally, to protect privacy of occupancy. The size of inner and outer courts is controlled in relation to building heights (applicable to apartments and hotels) and is a health protective measure designed to minimize risks from fire and poor ventilation. Nonresidential structures, such as tool sheds and garages, are, as a rule, subject to special size and location regulations.

Other building and land use controls

Whereas city planning and zoning are principally concerned with the city of tomorrow and future urban land uses, other controls under the government's police power are employed to insure sound building construction and to prevent health and fire hazards that may result from poor structural maintenance and substandard housing. Enforcement of building codes and those governing safe and sanitary occupancy of city structures are entrusted to municipal building, sanitation, and fire departments. The building department as a rule establishes building codes which serve as minimum construction standards and under which strict supervision is exercised to assure the erection of structurally strong, sound, sanitary, and safe buildings. In many communities no building construction may be started nor may a building be torn down without express approval, as evidenced by the issuance of a building permit. Periodic inspections are made to detect changes in occupancy or use contrary to the *certificate of occupancy* which the plans of the building called for and which were approved when the permit was issued and the building was constructed. "Violations" are punished (where not promptly remedied) by fine or imprisonment of the owner, or other person responsible, or, if dangerous, by enforced emptying of the building or its demolition.

Strong efforts are now being made by the Federal Housing Administration to standardize building codes and to streamline building construction practices in order to reduce housing costs. Although significant progress has been made toward the accomplishment of this goal, it will take many more years before public enlightenment will compel the building trades and responsible city officials to eliminate local construction prejudices that hamper progress by continuing wasteful, inefficient building practices and time-wasting construction methods and by obstructing use of new and more satisfactory materials, design, and technology.

The fire and sanitation departments as a rule are empowered to make periodic inspections and to order compliance with directives to insure safe and sanitary use and occupancy of buildings. Proper enforcement of fire control and sanitation ordinances may go a long way toward retarding housing blight and toward the elimination of unsightly and unsafe city slums.

READING AND STUDY REFERENCES

1. BROWN, ROBERT K., *Real Estate Economics*, Chapter 19. Boston: Houghton Mifflin Company, 1965.
2. FUTTERMAN, ROBERT A., *The Future of Our Cities*, Chapter 1. Garden City, N.Y.: Doubleday & Company, Inc., 1961.
3. HUSBAND, WILLIAM H., and FRANK RAY ANDERSON, *Real Estate*, Chapter 27. Homewood, Ill.: Richard D. Irwin, Inc., 1960.

4. KRATOVIL, ROBERT, *Real Estate Law*, Chapters 21 and 27. Englewood Cliffs, N.J.: Prentice-Hall, Inc., 1969.

5. LUSK, HAROLD F., *Law of the Real Estate Business*, Chapter 19. Homewood, Ill.: Richard D. Irwin, Inc., 1965.

6. PERLOFF, HARVEY S., *Planning and the Urban Community*, Chapters 1, 4, 5, 7, 9, 10, and 11. Pittsburgh, Pa.: University of Pittsburgh Press, 1961.

7. RING, ALFRED A., *Questions and Problems in Real Estate Principles and Practices* (rev. ed.), Chapter 25. Englewood Cliffs, N.J.: Prentice-Hall, Inc., 1972.

8. UNGER, MAURICE A., *Real Estate* (4th ed.), Chapter 27. Cincinnati: South-Western Publishing Co., 1969.

27

HOUSING LEGISLATION

Importance

Community needs for adequate shelter, along with food and clothing, have always been recognized as essential to human welfare. Since the days of the early settlers in this country, shelter problems have been considered as "group" problems which must be solved collectively to assure the health and safety of the whole community.

In the American tradition of free enterprise and "rugged individualism," shelter or housing problems, at least until the 1930–40 decade, have been held to be of local interest and concern and were acted upon accordingly. It is true that during periods of war, or periods of emergency, reliance was placed on aid from state or federal governments, but even then such aid was temporary and transitional in nature and any interference with "local" plans for housing reconstruction and repairs was looked upon as a breach of sanctity and sovereignty of community "home rule."

Effects of industrialization and urbanization

The division and mechanization of labor, the discovery of electricity, and the invention of the telegraph, telephone, and internal combustion engine made possible the rapid industrialization and urbanization of the American economy. The rapid shift from diversified farming to manufacturing and commerce as a mode of livelihood caused an equally rapid

456

movement of population from farming regions to urban centers. Since 1880 when industrialization began in earnest, the urban population has increased nearly tenfold and outnumbers the rural population approximately three to one. Because of the relative fixity of land and the practical immobility of housing, the sudden migration, that is, internal shifting of population, brought about a serious unbalancing of local and regional housing supply and demand.

The necessity to provide shelter for a population, almost literally on wheels, caused cities to grow sporadically and generally without fore-thought or community plan. The hasty development of residential, com-mercial, and industrial areas and the inadequacy of interconnecting high-ways, byways, and modes of transport underlie most of the urban housing "ills" which state and federal legislation during the past two decades has been attempting to alleviate and cure. There are other causes, of course, which hampered normal urban growth. Two world wars, the conflict in Korea, and the present military actions in Vietnam have caused people to shift and settle where their activities or specialized training contributed most to national safety and the winning of the war. Changes in social and political attitudes, too, influenced people to seek shelter elsewhere. Federal subsidies to encourage farming or educational training are examples. To-day, a significant further shift in population is under way from urban to suburban areas where living conditions by many are found more whole-some and less costly. This condition of "flux" in urban population is re-sponsible for most of the more serious housing problems which many cities have been unable to solve or shoulder without state or federal aid and subsidy.

Kinds of housing problems

Housing problems no doubt differ in magnitude and intensity among the various regions, areas, and communities, but everywhere these prob-lems may be traced to one or more of the following:

1. The existence of neighborhood blight and slums and their effect on com-munity housing, health, and safety
2. Inability of low income family groups to secure adequate and decent housing facilities
3. Lack of organized home financing facilities, policies, and practices
4. Need for safeguards against loss of home, tenant eviction, and possible rent profiteering during periods of severe housing shortages or war emer-gencies

Although these conditions, to which our housing ills and legislative cures are traceable, will, for sake of clarity, be analyzed separately in the following discussions, the reader should keep in mind the interrelation and interactions of these conditions in the overall housing problem of a given community.

The problem of urban blight and slums

Practically every city in the United States, both large and small, con-tains slums and other blighted or deteriorated areas. Most people know what a slum area is when they see one and few indeed would not want to do away with them. Cities generally are aware of the unsound social and economic effects of slums and blight, but few cities are financially able or politically strong enough to cope with this major civic liability.

Studies of blight and slum conditions in major urban areas conducted by local housing authorities and planning commissions in such representative cities as Cleveland, Newark, New York, Birmingham, Indianapolis, and Atlanta have disclosed ratios as high as ten to one in civic costs expended in "servicing" slums as compared with tax revenues collected from these areas. Many of these reports emphasize that slums are breeding grounds for major crimes and juvenile delinquency and that the menace to community health and safety warrants the designation of such slum areas as the "cancer of the body politic." The late Herbert Hoover voiced his concern by stating that "slums have no excuse for being and should be eliminated by wise and concerted effort." The late Senator Robert A. Taft had often and publicly stated that "America cannot afford slums" and that "the Government must see that every family has a minimum standard of decent shelter." President Nixon openly declared "war on poverty" and committed himself to the awesome task of stamping out ignorance, racial inequality, technological unemployment, and the many other causes and harbingers of crime.

Slum clearance legislation

One of the main obstacles to clearance of blighted areas and slums is cost. Replacing an area by another means eliminating buildings, street paving, existing storm and sanitary sewers, water, electric, and other utilities. The cost to acquire the land area to raze it, clear it, re-subdivide it, and improve it generally far exceeds the value of the land when redeveloped for the highest and best use. Then, too, private means of acquiring and assembling the land are inadequate and costly and only in exceptional cases can cities afford to subsidize such private efforts.

Failure of cities to cope successfully with urban redevelopment problems caused civic and business leaders to urge "enabling" legislation on a state level. The proposal was to invest private corporations with the power of eminent domain in order to acquire land in slums. The areas would then be cleared and improved with modern, but simple, apartment buildings to house the displaced and low income groups. The city, under such legislation, would exercise control over rentals, design, density, location, and the method of selecting tenants. The development corporation in turn would be allowed tax concessions and permitted to earn up to a maximum rate of return on its depreciated investment. Such legislation was enacted as early as 1926 by the state of New York, and similar legislation in later years was adopted by Illinois, Michigan, Utah, and California. The initial success of the redevelopment projects encouraged larger cities everywhere to seek state aid and to impress their congressional representatives with the need for federal legislation and subsidy support. These collective efforts culminated in the passage of the comprehensive Housing Act of 1949, under which most states passed qualifying enabling acts that permitted cities of given population size to appoint local housing authorities and to administer the redevelopment of slum and blighted areas.

Federal aid for slum clearance

The Housing Act of 1949 recognizes slums as a national problem. Under this act, Title I, federal loans and grants are made available to clear the following kinds of urban land:

1. Residential slum and blighted areas for purposes of redeveloping the land for any locally approved residential, commercial, industrial, or a combination of such uses.
2. Nonresidential blighted areas, provided such areas are to be redeveloped predominantly for residential purposes.
3. Predominantly open areas which, because of obsolete plotting or faulty site improvements, are impeding sound city growth. Redevelopment of such areas, too, must be principally for residential purposes.

Under Title I of the Housing Act of 1949 qualifying communities may apply for a temporary loan to finance the initial cost of planning the slum clearing project and to assemble, clear, and prepare the land for sale or lease. After the area is cleared, redeveloped, and sold to private purchasers, the net project cost, that is, the difference between total redevelopment cost and proceeds from land sale, is then shared as follows: Two-thirds will be absorbed by the federal government out of funds authorized as grants (gifts); one-third must be borne by the local city government. City expenditures in the forms of city labor, land donations, and improvements may be offered in lieu of cash for part or all of the one-third city share of the net development costs.

To qualify for federal assistance under Title I, there are certain statutory requirements which the community must meet. The more important requirements are as follows:

1. A local public agency must be established under state law and fully authorized to undertake the project.
2. A detailed plan (approved by the governing body of the locality in which the project is situated) for the redevelopment of the project area must conform to the general master plan for the development of the community as a whole.
3. Findings by the local governing body that federal assistance is necessary to enable the project area to be redeveloped in accordance with the locally approved plan.
4. Maximum opportunity, consistent with the sound needs of the locality, for the redevelopment of the project areas by private enterprise.
5. A public hearing, prior to the acquisition of the land, after notice of the date, time, place, and purpose of such hearing.
6. Ability to furnish the required amount of local (one-third of total) grants-in-aid.
7. A feasible method for the temporary relocation of families displaced from the project area.
8. Assurance that there is or will be permanent housing at rents or prices

within the financial means of the families displaced from the project area equal to the number of and available to such displaced families in areas not generally less desirable in regard to public utilities and facilities, and reasonably accessible to their places of employment.

Provisions 7 and 8 under which the community must provide housing to care for displaced slum families have caused many of the smaller communities, particularly those located in the South and West, to reject federal aid under this housing act. A number of states, too, have held unconstitutional, and prohibited the use of, power of eminent domain for the acquisition and resale of land for private purposes, thus making the provisions of this act inapplicable.

Faced with the consequences of enforcement of civil rights legislation and the increasing voting strength of the black population, governments in most communities are "rethinking" their expressed attitudes toward improving urban slum areas. To encourage a new and more vigorous approach to slum clearance, Congress broadened and strengthened provisions of Public Law 89 with passage of the Housing and Urban Development Act of 1965. Under this act, the Federal Housing Authority is now authorized to insure mortgages to acquire and develop land for residential and related uses, provided such development is consistent with a comprehensive plan already developed or being developed for the area. Improvements financed could include water and sewer facilities, roads, streets, sidewalks, and other site improvements. The intent is to encourage the provision of a large supply of properly planned and improved building sites to small as well as to large builders.

The FHA insured mortgage could cover up to (1) 75 percent of the estimated value of the property when developed or (2) 50 percent of the value before development plus 90 percent of the cost of the site improvements whichever is less. The insured mortgage amount, however, cannot exceed $10 million. The 1965 act, as amended, further provides for grants as follows:

1. *Grants for Basic Sewer and Water Facilities*: Grants are authorized to public bodies to finance up to 50 percent of the cost of expanding, enlarging, and improving basic public water and sewer facilities, in accordance with an area-wide or comprehensive plan. Grants could not be used to finance ordinary repairs or to maintain existing facilities. During the fiscal year 1969, 366 grants were approved for this purpose. The budgeted amount to further this program during the fiscal year 1970 was $150 million. Equal amounts are scheduled to be allocated in future years.

2. *Grants for Open-Space Land Acquisition and Development*: Provisions of this act are intended to help communities acquire and develop land to be used as permanent open space in order to help curb urban sprawl, prevent the spread of urban blight, encourage more economic and desirable urban development, and provide needed park, recreation, conservation, scenic, and historic areas. These grants are predicated on com-

munity financial matching dollar requirements up to at least 50 percent of total costs of acquisition and development. Progress reports are required every six months and evidence must be submitted that construction of the facilities would contribute to the economy, efficiency, and comprehensively planned development of the area. During the fiscal year 1969, 395 grants were awarded ranging from $4,900 to $2 million. The amount budgeted for the fiscal year 1970 was $50 million.

3. *Grants for Neighborhood Facilities*: Grants are authorized to public bodies to finance projects for neighborhood facilities, such as community or youth centers, health stations, or similar public buildings. Emphasis would be placed on projects that would support a community action program under the Economic Opportunity Act (antipoverty program), and on projects that are so located as to be of special benefit to low-income families. Grants could cover up to two-thirds of the project cost, or 75 percent in areas approved under the Area Redevelopment Act or any act supplemental to it. The act, as amended, provides for assistance up to $1 million (maximum, under given circumstances, may be waived). In the fiscal year 1970, $40 million was committed for this purpose.

4. *Grants for Urban Beautification and Improvement*: Matching grants are authorized to assist localities in programs of beautification and improvement of open space and other public lands. Programs could be included for such things as street landscaping, park improvements, tree planting, and upgrading of malls and squares. Ordinarily, grants could not exceed 50 percent of the cost over and above the locality's average previous expenditures for such activities. In addition, to encourage experimentation and innovation, the act authorizes a $5 million demonstration grant program under which grants could cover up to 90 percent of the total cost of experimental activities. The general range of assistance per project is $1 million, depending upon the number of people within the community. The budgeted amount for the fiscal year 1969 was $13.3 million; for 1970, grants budgeted were $15.4 million. In 1969 alone, 110 grants for urban beautification were approved.

Urban renewal

The slum clearance and urban redevelopment program authorized by Title I of the Housing Act of 1949 first underwent a major revision with passage of the Housing Act of 1954. This broader act, which was intended not only to eliminate existing slums but also to prevent potential slums, authorized a new housing agency known as the Urban Renewal Administration which was charged with the responsibility by Congress to use forceful measures to prevent slums and to remove, with effective local aid, the causes of urban blight.

In framing the 1954 Housing Act, Congress followed closely the recommendations made by the President's Advisory Committee on Housing Policies and Programs. The aims of this committee were well stated in their report which read in part as follows:

A piecemeal attack on slums simply will not work—occasional thrusts at slum pockets in one section of a city will only push slums to other sections unless an effective program exists for attacking the entire problem of urban decay. Programs for slum prevention, for rehabilitation of existing houses and neighborhoods, and for demolition of wornout structures and areas must advance along a broad unified front to accomplish the renewal of our towns and cities. This approach must be vigorously carried out in the localities themselves, and will require local solutions which vary widely from city to city.[1]

To implement this expanded approach to urban renewal, the 1954 act continued the financial aids made available to communities by Title I and added the following further assistance:

The Urban Renewal Service
Special Demonstration Grants
Special Grants for Urban Planning Assistance
Special FHA Mortgage Insurance under Sections 220 and 221 of Title II

Under the Urban Renewal Service, communities may obtain technical and other professional aid for the preparation of local slum clearance programs. The 1954 act authorized $5 million for the developing, testing, and reporting of slum prevention and slum elimination techniques. To this end local community housing authorities may obtain grants up to two-thirds of cost, provided these studies will be valuable in solving urban renewal problems. State planning agencies may obtain cash grants for the provision of planning assistance to localities with population less than twenty-five thousand which lack funds to carry out effective urban planning. A grant for urban planning assistance may be made up to one-half the estimated cost of such planning expenditures. Five million dollars was initially appropriated for this purpose. The FHA special assistance program provides 100 percent insured loans under Section 220 of FHA Title II to encourage new buildings and rehabilitation of old ones in urban renewal areas. Under Section 221 the Federal Housing Administration provides 100 percent insurance on mortgages for low-cost housing to families displaced from urban renewal areas.

The 1954 Housing Act was substantially strengthened by provision of the comprehensive Housing Act of 1965.[2] This latter act increased the authorization for urban renewal grants by $675 million on enactment, $725 million on July 1, 1966, and $750 million on July 1 of both 1967 and 1968. In addition, it permitted 35 percent (compared with the prior 30 percent of earlier authorization) of the amount of new capital grant authority provided by the act to be used for nonresidential renewal to promote economic improvement. Grants for the fiscal year 1969 totaled $553 million, and loans for the same period aggregated $372 million. The estimated expenditures for the fiscal year 1970 were budgeted at $775 million for grants and $473 million for loans at subsidized rates of interest.

---

[1]U.S. Housing and Home Finance Agency, 8th Annual Report, 1954, p. 449.
[2]See Summary of the Main Provisions of Public Law 89—The Housing and Urban Development Act of 1965, Office of the HHFA Administrator, Washington, D.C. Also, Catalog of Federal Domestic Assistance, April 1970.

The act increased the authorization for low-interest rehabilitation loans for improving structures in urban renewal areas by $50 million for 1965–66 and $100 million for each of the next four fiscal years.

The act authorizes grants to localities to assist them in carrying out concentrated code enforcement programs in deteriorating areas. These grants can be up to two-thirds (three-fourths for towns of fifty thousand or less) of the cost of code enforcement activities. The act also authorizes two-thirds grants to localities to cover the cost of demolition of unsound structures in urban renewal areas, or, in certain cases, outside of urban renewal areas.

Urban renewal activity under the Urban Renewal Program has continued to spread throughout the nation as more and more communities began or stepped up the fight to attain the goal of "a decent home in a suitable environment for every American family."

Model cities program

The model cities program was enacted by Congress in 1966. Under this program, the federal government provides a grant-in-aid subsidy up to 80 percent of local government costs in approved model city areas. Emphasis is placed on community (neighborhood) *rehabilitation* rather than *clearance* as under the urban renewal program.

The objective of the program, as amended, is to demonstrate how the environment and the general welfare of people living in slums and blighted urban areas in cities of all sizes and in all parts of the country can be substantially improved through a comprehensive attack on social, economic, and physical problems in selected areas, utilizing federal, state, local, and private resources in a coordinated and concentrated manner.

Originally sixty-three cities were selected and were granted planning funds to begin area improvements. The range of financial assistance varied during the first year of implementation from $750,000 for a city of six thousand to $65 million for the largest city. The number of grants made in 1969 totaled thirty-five. The budgeted obligations for the fiscal year 1970 were $571.2 million. This program is still in its initial stages, but expectations are high that coordinated public and private efforts may succeed in eradicating the urban cancer of civic misery caused by neighborhood blight and widespread slums.

Federal aid for housing of low income families

Perhaps the most controversial legislation sponsored by the federal government is that concerned with low-rent public housing. Under this form of legislation, housing is erected with public funds and is owned and operated by government or an instrumentality of government, such as a municipal housing authority. All but six states have passed laws permitting communities to form housing authorities that will have whatever powers are necessary to meet the requirements for federal aid. These local bodies can purchase land (through condemnation proceedings when necessary), borrow money, and build and operate housing for low-income families who otherwise would have to live in substandard housing. This program, contrary to common belief, is local in origin, locally owned and operated for the benefit of local residents. The federal government merely provides financial assistance to make this program possible.

Federal aid to communities was first authorized under the United States Housing Act of 1937. Under this act the Federal Public Housing Authority (now the Public Housing Administration, headed by the Housing and Home Finance Agency, which also controls the Federal Housing Administration and the Federal Home Loan Bank) made available low-interest loans and grants (subsidies) to local housing agencies that qualified under federal law—the object being to provide decent, safe, and sanitary dwellings for families in the lowest income group who could not afford to avail themselves of proper and decent privately owned and operated housing. Under the 1937 act, a total of 191,700 dwelling units were provided in 268 localities. The public housing portions of the Housing Act of 1949 (Title III) amended the 1937 act to authorize financial assistance for construction and operation of 810,000 additional low-rent dwellings over a six-year program.

Congress, in the interest of national economy and for other reasons, opposed executive authority to provide federal assistance for the construction of 35,000 additional units of public housing as planned by the administration for the fiscal year 1954–55. The Housing Act of 1955, however, authorized the PHA to enter new contracts for construction of 45,000 housing units, and the Housing Act of 1956 authorized 35,000 units annually through June 1959. The Housing Act of 1959 continued low-rent housing authorization provided that units under contract plus additional dwelling units covered by new contracts did not exceed 37,000 units.

Significant further aid for housing of low income families was provided under the 1965 Housing Act. This act provided for 60,000 low-rent public housing units a year, or a total of 240,000 units over the four-year period 1965 to 1969, with an estimated 35,000 units a year to be new construction, 15,000 to be bought and rehabilitated if necessary from existing housing, and 10,000 units to be leased for low-rent use from private owners.

The innovation authorized by Congress in 1961, to provide housing at below market interest rates for low- and moderate-income families, was extended and continued under provisions of the act of 1965. The maximum interest rate was reduced to 3 percent to assure lower rents to needy families. Under this act, housing aid for the elderly and the handicapped was provided by authorization of $150 million as loans for construction of nonprofit housing at a maximum mortgage loan interest rate of 3 percent.

A controversial provision of the 1965 act calls for rent supplements direct to landlords for rent payments in excess of 25 percent of family income. This provision of the act activated some 375,000 units of nonprofit cooperative or limited dividend housing over the years 1966 through 1970. An estimated half million families are on the public housing waiting list and some six million families still have incomes below $4,000 a year. The units thus authorized will still fall far short of need for the low-income segment of the U.S. population.

Under the rent-supplement plan, eligible tenants would pay 25 percent of their income toward the established fair market rents. The rent supplement would pay any difference above that percentage. As family income rises, the supplement will be reduced, and when the family can pay the full rent, it can continue to live in the same unit without a supplement. If the housing is adapted for individual purchase, the family can also have an opportunity to buy it when its income permits. The 1965 act authorized $30 million for rent supplement payments in the fiscal year 1966, and additional amounts of $35 million in fiscal 1967, $45 million in fiscal 1968, $63 million in 1969, and $111 million in fiscal 1970. The face value of loans under this public housing program reached $600 million for the year 1970. As an experiment, the act as amended authorizes up to 10 percent of the rent supplement grants to be used on housing provided under FHA's below market interest rate program, FHA's elderly housing program, and housing for the elderly or handicapped built with direct 3 percent federal loans. The below market interest rate program will receive half the grants under this program, with the other half going to the other two programs.

Operation of the Public Housing Act

The local housing authority presents its application for federal loans and subsidies to the Public Housing Administration. It must be shown on the application that the local governing body has approved the project and will do its part in meeting the requirements of the federal act. Among such requirements are elimination of slum dwellings and provision that municipal services will be supplied and tax exemption will be granted. The application should show the need for the proposed housing and that it cannot be provided by private capital. Information should be furnished on the site or sites selected, preliminary building plans, an estimate of costs and a schedule of the rents to be charged, and other pertinent data.

If the application is approved, a contract will be entered into whereby the PHA agrees to make loans, both temporary and permanent, to finance the operation. The PHA also contracts to grant annual subsidies to the local authority for a long period of years. The subsidies by the federal government are what make such projects possible, for the projects are distinctly low-rental housing and the income would not be sufficient to operate and maintain the buildings and at the same time pay interest and amortization to service the debt incurred to produce them. The local community is, however, expected to contribute one-fifth as much as the federal contribution, but this contribution can be made by exemption from local taxation. The project, although tax exempt, pays an annual amount to the municipality for services.

Upon approval of the application, the municipal housing authority proceeds with the project construction employing local architects, engineers, and building contractors. The cost of the project is limited by law. Building and equipment costs must not exceed $1,750 per room except in certain high construction cost areas where an additional expenditure up to $750 per room may be allowed. Room costs for the elderly and for the handicapped have been authorized at $4,000 and $4,500 respectively.

Permanent financing is obtained by issuance of local authority long-term serial bonds which are secured by the federal government's pledge to pay annual contributions equal to the going federal rate plus 2 percent for debt amortization. It is calculated that most obligations with aid of project earnings can thus be retired over periods not exceeding forty years.

Public housing, occupancy, and rental payments

To guard against occupancy by other than low-income families, the law provides as follows:

1. To be eligible for admission, a family must not earn in excess of the maximum income set locally. Except for veterans, the family must come from slum housing, or be displaced by a slum-clearance project or another public-housing project, or actually be without housing through no fault of its own. Among eligible families, preference for initial occupancy is given first to families displaced from cleared areas, and second, to other low-income families, with veterans given first preference in each of these two groups.
2. The top rent for admission must be at least 20 percent below the rents at which private enterprise is providing a substantial supply of available standard housing, either new or old (for similar housing).
3. The net income of families at admission (less a $100 exception for each minor member as an aid to large families) cannot exceed five times the annual rent to be charged, including utilities.
4. Local authorities must set maximum income limits, both for admission to the project and for continued residence in it. These limits are subject to PHA approval.
5. The authority must make a written report to PHA showing that incomes of families admitted are within the limit.
6. The authority must reexamine the incomes of all tenant families periodically to adjust rents if necessary and to evict those families whose incomes have risen above the limit.

The maximum income limits for admission are set by the authority after a careful study of local needs. Factors considered include the incomes of families forced to live in slum housing, the lowest incomes earned by regularly employed workers, and income levels permitted by relief agencies for their clients. Maximum income limits for continued occupancy are generally set 20 to 25 percent above the admission limits to allow some increase in family income without necessitating eviction.

The rent to be charged a given family is based on its income and not on the size of the dwelling it requires. Each family is required to pay not less than 20 percent of its income for rent, including utilities.

So that public housing projects shall bear a share of the cost of such municipal services as schools and streets, the law permits local authorities to make payments in lieu of taxes up to 10 percent of the shelter rents charged in the projects.

Evaluation of public housing policies

Public housing is one of the most hotly debated legislative issues. Proponents sincerely believe that the maintenance of minimum standards of decent housing and the elimination of slums are essential to the preservation of democracy and the American way of life. Opponents, equally sincere, believe that public housing is another step toward centralization of government and toward socialization of family life and that such a step strikes at the very root of liberty and of American democracy.

The question is further raised to what extent, if any, public housing competes with private housing. Proponents claim that continued and active demand for private housing, particularly in areas where large public housing projects have successfully operated for ten or more years, refutes such arguments. Competition, proponents claim, is limited to slum housing which the public wants to eliminate anyway. The law, it is pointed out, wisely sets a wide gap between private and public rentals to insure occupancy of public housing only by those families who cannot afford even the cheapest of available decent private housing. Since the tenants of public housing will be families who cannot afford standard housing, proponents say, they are not part of the market that private housing serves.

Opponents of public housing hold such arguments as theoretical. They point to flagrant abuses of the law, to evidence of affluence of public housing tenants, to political subterfuge, to use of public facilities for private gain, and to instances of subsidy to the kind of people who are deemed least deserving as public beneficiaries. Opponents further lament the high cost of public home construction and the long-range conflict with private aims, individual initiative, and the American philosophy of free enterprise.

Undoubtedly the truth lies somewhere between these two opposing views. Slums do affect the health, welfare, and morality not only of the occupants but also of the city as a whole. As long as private and social gains equal or exceed the public costs as contemplated under the law, no harm can possibly have been done. The cry of "wolf" is raised whenever, under any form of legislation, freedom of private action is restricted. The very concept of democracy is based on a nicety of balance between individual rights and obligations, and it is the preservation of this balance that our elected representatives are charged to maintain. No doubt the pendulum of private versus public rights swings often to extremes, but reaction by the general public, as a rule, reestablishes the social-economic equilibrium that distinguishes and preserves the American way of life.

Federal home financing policies and practices

The need for government supervision and indirect control of home financing policies and practices became urgently apparent during the Great Depression following the stock market collapse in 1929. By 1933, hundreds of thousands of homeowners found themselves unable to meet their "term" mortgage obligations and were threatened with foreclosure of their homes. In fact, foreclosures were taking place at the rate of a thousand a day[3] when Congress established, by almost unanimous vote, the Home Owners' Loan Corporation as a temporary mortgage finance agency to aid distressed homeowners who were unable to refinance their mortgages or meet high interest and amortization installments during the depression years.

The magnitude of the task and the importance of the services rendered by the Home Owners' Loan Corporation can best be judged by the fact that the corporation refinanced over one million defaulted home loans during the period 1933 to 1936, which is equivalent to one out of five of all the mortgages on owner-occupied homes in the nation's nonfarm areas that were outstanding at that time. Home Owners' Loan Corporation refinancing of term mortgages at low interest rates of 5 percent, over maturity periods ranging up to fifteen years, averted foreclosure action for about four out of five borrowers who sought the corporation's aid.

Many collateral benefits can be attributed to Home Owners' Loan Corporation operations. Hard-pressed banks and other lending institutions, as well as individual lenders, received nearly $3 billion in exchange for frozen mortgages. One-half billion more was disbursed to local cities and towns in payment of delinquent taxes of its borrowers and taxes on the Home Owners' Loan Corporation's acquired properties. No doubt these indirect benefits strengthened the economy during the worst period of the depression years and aided in restoring the collapsed values of residential real estate.

The Home Owners' Loan Corporation as a temporary agency ceased making loans in 1936 and its operations were liquidated as of May 28, 1951. By congressional action, dissolution was authorized under Public Law 94 of the Eighty-third Congress on June 30, 1953.

Permanent home financing aids

To further bolster and preserve the social and economic stability that has been found inherent in a large home-owning population, a permanent federal agency, the Federal Housing Administration, was created in 1934 to underwrite and insure mortgages on residential properties. The operational activities of this federal mortgage insurance agency, as well as federal mortgage guarantee provisions authorized under the Servicemen's Readjustment Act of 1944, as amended, and the functions of the Federal National Mortgage Association, are more fully explained in Chapters 13 and 15.

Other federal housing legislation

In an attempt to coordinate the considerable body of existing knowledge and research in the field of housing, and to bring about a progressive reduction of housing costs and expansion of the private housing market, Congress authorized under the Housing Act of 1949 the operation of a housing research program. The act permits economic and technical research in the housing field under supervision of a research director and his specially trained operating staff. Congress wisely provided that the research

---

[3]Home Loan Bank Board release dated May 29, 1951, p. 2, Washington, D.C.

agency should not compete with private research activities but rather should avail itself of such independent sources and storehouses of knowledge and should negotiate on a contract basis preferably with public, educational, and other nonprofit organizations for the carrying out of research projects designed to achieve the broad congressional housing aims. The scope of the research program is indicated by the following objectives:

1. Improved and standardized building codes and regulations and more uniform administration
2. Standardized dimensions and methods for the assembly of home-building materials and construction
3. Improved residential home design and modes of construction
4. Sound techniques for the testing of materials, the types of construction, and for the determination of adequate performance standards
5. Economic data concerning housing needs, demand and supply, appraisal, credit, finance, investment, and other housing market data
6. Study of zoning and other laws, codes, and regulations as they apply to housing, land costs, use and improvement, site planning, and utilities

The research agency has promptly undertaken important studies in the fields of housing law, technology, design, and economics. Leading universities throughout the nation have readily cooperated in lending their research and laboratory facilities, and their findings have been channeled to public, industrial, and trade organizations through the medium of housing research papers published by the HHFA. Unfortunately, curtailments in appropriations authorized by the Eighty-third Congress (deemed necessary in the attempt to balance the national budget) have limited agency operating funds to a point where suspension of "contract" activities of the research agency became mandatory effective with the fiscal year of 1954.

To raise the standards of farm and rural housing, Congress passed necessary legislation under Title V of the Housing Act of 1949, under which the secretary of the Department of Agriculture is authorized to provide loans to farm owners who are otherwise unable to provide decent farm dwellings and buildings for themselves, their tenants, lessees, sharecroppers, or laborers. The law explicitly limits such financial assistance to those farm owners who are without sufficient resources to provide the necessary housing on their own account and who are unable to secure credit necessary for such housing from other sources on terms and conditions that they could reasonably expect to fill. Under this law as amended, the face value of direct loans made in the fiscal year 1970 reached $7 million, and insured loans $719 million. The range of financial assistance to farm owners averaged $4,000 in direct loans and $10,000 for insured loans in support of low- to moderate-income families in rural areas.

The 1965 act also requires certain procedures to be followed in cases where real property is taken by eminent domain in the following federally assisted urban development programs: urban renewal, public housing, urban mass transportation, public facility loans, open-space land, basic public works, neighborhood facilities, and advance acquisition of land. These procedures require that every reasonable effort be made to acquire property by negotiated purchase; that no owner be required to surrender possession of his property before being paid the purchase price reached by negotiation or 75 percent of the appraised value of the property if only the purchase price is in dispute; and that no occupant of property be required to surrender possession without ninety days' written notice.

The act also authorizes the FHA and VA to provide mortgage moratorium relief for homeowners who are unemployed as a result of the closing of a federal installation. In addition, the secretary of defense is authorized to acquire homes near military bases closed after November 1, 1964, where the owner's employment has been terminated as a result of the closing of the base.

The acquisition and development of land and building improvements is further assisted and subsidized in fields of national interest such as education, agriculture, small-business development, environmental improvement, hospital and institutional facilities, transportation, and national resources. A full discussion of the applicable laws and stipulations concerning these federal programs is beyond the scope of this publication. Those interested in one or more of the above economic support categories should refer to the *Catalog of Federal Domestic Assistance*, compiled by the Office of Economic Opportunity and distributed at modest cost by the Superintendent of Documents, Washington, D.C. For an abbreviated listing and description of individual housing programs by numbers and sections of the National Housing Act, see Appendix, page 591.

The Federal Home Loan Bank

To assure a steady flow of savings into banking institutions that are principally organized to provide an outlet for mortgage funds, Congress established in 1932 the Federal Home Loan Bank, patterned on the Federal Reserve System and serving the purpose among mortgage lending institutions (principally building or savings and loan associations) that the Federal Reserve System does among commercial banks. Twelve regional banks lend money to member institutions, accepting mortgages or collateral for such loans. To place the building and loan associations further on a par with their commercial sister banks, the Federal Savings and Loan Insurance Corporation was established and is now authorized to insure public savings and shareholder deposits up to an amount of $20,000 per account.

Federal Home Loan Bank backing of the building and loan associations fulfilled the objectives of its sponsors. Although the legislation was originally conceived as a depression measure intended to stave off foreclosures, encourage thrift, and stimulate building activity, government supervision of mortgage lending operations has increased the prestige of the savings and loan associations to a position where, in the field of residential mortgage lending, they now occupy a leading role. For specific regulations governing the mortgage lending power of these "hometown" institutions, reference should be made to Chapter 15, "The Mortgage Market."

Rent control

Realty, because of fixity in investment, immobility in location, and necessity for shelter purposes, lends itself readily to economic controls when such are deemed essential to serve social or political ends, or where the interest of health, safety, and morality of community population or the nation at large warrants it. Realty has consistently been recognized as a form of private property which is sufficiently invested with public interest to warrant its control either under the police power of a sovereign state and its branches of government or by direct and statutory legislation enacted within the framework of the governmental constitution.

Whenever war or catastrophe causes a sudden shifting of population or suspension of building operations, or both, an imbalance is brought about in the demand and supply of housing. This imbalance in housing demand and supply creates conditions of insecurity and instability among the tenants who fear indiscriminate eviction or unwarranted upward rental adjustments. The fact that a few landlords cannot resist the urge to violate the range of reason and equity during periods of emergency caused widespread fear of wholesale eviction and rent gouging by many. It is this background of possible exploitation during times of economic stress and strain that underlies the enaction of emergency rent control legislation.

Although rent control has been in effect in many communities, particularly the larger metropolitan communities, since World War II, the attitude of all levels of government is to view this form of legislation as temporary and to hasten, as far as their power permits, a return to normal relations between landlords and tenants.

Rent control prior to World War II

Rent control legislation was introduced in selected communities as an emergency measure immediately following American entry into World War I. During the years 1917 and 1918, state war rent control measures were adopted by Maine, Massachusetts, Connecticut, New Jersey, Nevada, and Virginia. State laws generally were enacted to safeguard the interests of servicemen and war personnel against landlord action at law until their discharge from war or military service. More stringent and broader rent control measures were enacted by the larger and war-affected communities, such as Newark, Philadelphia, Cleveland, New York, and Chicago. The federal government, too, took measures to protect dependents of servicemen by enacting the Soldiers' and Sailors' Civil Relief Act of 1918 under which eviction of dependents of men in the service was prevented unless the rental paid exceeded $50 per month or the eviction action was specifically authorized by court order. All of these early rent control laws expired prior to 1930.

Rent control since World War II

Housing imbalance caused by World War II and the relative lack of building construction during the depression years immediately preceding the war brought pressure for federal rent control legislation. Congress in January 1942 authorized rent control as a pattern of general price control, setting rental levels prevailing in April 1940 as guiding. This federal control extended only to residential properties. Where rent ceilings were placed on commercial properties, the authority for such controls originated from state or municipal governments.

The broad objectives of rent controls are as follows:

1. To fix rent ceilings as of the effective date of control.
2. To protect tenants against undue increases in rent by permitting upward adjustment only in "hardship" cases or where substantial improvements were necessary. The burden of proof always fell on the landlord when an upward adjustment in rental was petitioned by or on behalf of the owner.
3. To prevent tenant eviction except in the following instances:
   a. Bona fide occupancy of premises by owner.
   b. Complete remodeling of property (conversion, enlargement, major modernization).
   c. Sale of property and occupancy by purchaser.
   d. Breach of contract (nonpayment of rent, and so on).

Administration of rent control

To permit effective administration of rent control legislation, landlords were compelled, under penalty of law, to register their rental property at local rent control offices. Under registration requirements, the landlord had to stipulate the amount of rental charged and the services (utilities, furnishings, and so forth) rendered. Tenants were mailed separate forms on which rental payments and service data were supplied for check and filing purposes by the rent control administrator.

Rent control laws, at best, could only stabilize (not equalize) existing rentals. Since, in many instances, the rentals charged at the "effective" date were not representative of a fair return on the property's investment, rent adjustments were permitted where hardship cases could be proven to the administrator's satisfaction. Recourse could always be had to courts of jurisdiction where equity appeared to warrant such action. On the other hand, where landlords failed to continue rendering of specified services, rental decreases were ordered.

Effects of rent control

Rent legislation, at best, constitutes "negative" control. Although as an emergency measure rent control is justified, remedial legislation must be sponsored to alleviate, speedily, the housing shortage, or else the existing supply of rental units will diminish and the housing shortage will be aggravated, and for the following reasons:

1. Rent control does not produce houses. In fact, it discourages investment operation of private homes and encourages owners to sell at "uncontrolled" prices. Many tenants, in fact, were forced to buy their rental quarters at inflationary prices or face eviction by the purchaser who, under the law, could secure personal occupancy.
2. Rent control without "space" control increases the demand for housing, thus relatively worsening the shortage of housing. Whenever rent control or price control causes the underpricing of a good or service—in relation

to other goods or services which are uncontrolled—the demand, i.e., the consumption of the underpriced service, must increase. This is the result of the inevitable operation of the economic law of supply and demand. In the field of housing, many single people found it suddenly within their budget to enjoy the luxury of a private apartment—at a bargain price. Well-to-do country residents acquired extra dwelling space in urban centers to enjoy the "bargain" quarters during workday or shopping trips. "Undoubling" was encouraged. Why live with in-laws when apartments or homes could be had at rent controlled prices? Unless a workable system of space control can accompany rent control, this emergency legislation, if extended over many years, can have serious effects on the housing economy, as housing conditions in France and England, where rent controls have been in effect since 1914, indicate.

3. The ever-rising standard of living in the United States makes purchase of homes possible at an earlier age during the life of the breadwinner. The purchase of a home is high on the "wanted" list of most people. Since income rises faster during war emergencies, the urge for ownership will be more readily exercised at a time when tenant rent controlled space usually is in short supply. Then, too, while one federal agency "husbands" the rental space, other federal agencies make purchase of available housing supply attractive by decreasing down payment requirements and encouraging mortgage lending at marginal rates of interest.

The greater the disparity between controlled rents and market rents, the more difficult becomes rent control enforcement. This is due to "black market" operations. Tenants often, and particularly when in desperate need of rental space, will suggest means and ways to "beat" the law. Sale and rental of furniture or similar collateral facilities have been frequently used as a subterfuge to circumvent the law and to provide for indirect rent adjustment.

Rent control, where still applicable, is principally locally controlled and locally administered under state enabling acts. Continued high construction building programs should free most of the nation from this emergency form of legislation except, perhaps, in the large metropolitan centers where rent control may linger as a political rather than an economic expedient.

Perhaps one of the most far-reaching laws affecting housing and home ownership was signed into law by President Johnson in April 1968. This law, known as the "open housing" law, was passed as part of the 1968 Civil Rights Act, and its provisions are spelled out under Title VIII of this act. Because of the impact that the law is bound to have on existing as well as future so-called exclusive subdivisions, the full text of Public Law No. 90–284 is reproduced for reader's reference in the Appendix of this text beginning on page 595.

The aim of this legislation is to prevent, under penalty of up to one thousand dollars or up to one year imprisonment for each misdemeanor, the exclusion, preference, limitation of use, or discrimination in the sale or rental of dwellings to anyone because of race, color, religion, or national origin. This law is particularly aimed at brokers who act as agents for others in the sale or rental of real estate. The law took full effect on January 1, 1970. After that date no housing is exempted from the act where rental or sale is negotiated through a broker or his employee agent.

So-called exclusive or restricted subdivisions must now be open to all regardless of race, color, religion, or national origin except where the owner of no more than three houses or an owner of a multiple dwelling unit of not more than four units, one of which he occupies, markets the property himself and the sale, as advertised, is without direct or inferred discrimination.

No doubt the constitutional validity of this law will be tested in the years to come, but in light of the June 17, 1968, U. S. Supreme Court decision in which the court ruled that federal law prohibits, under the Civil Rights Act of 1866, racial discrimination, private or public, in the sale or rental of all real or personal property, the constitutionality of the open housing act appears assured.

READING AND STUDY REFERENCES

1. BROWN, ROBERT K., *Real Estate Economics*, Chapters 19, 20, 21, and 22. Boston: Houghton Mifflin Company, 1965.
2. HUSBAND, WILLIAM H., and FRANK RAY ANDERSON, *Real Estate,* Chapter 28. Homewood, Ill.: Richard D. Irwin, Inc., 1960.
3. RING, ALFRED A., *Questions and Problems in Real Estate Principles and Practices* (rev. ed.), Chapter 26. Englewood Cliffs, N.J.: Prentice-Hall, Inc., 1972.
4. UNGER, MAURICE A., *Real Estate* (4th ed.), Chapter 28. Cincinnati: South-Western Publishing Co., 1969.
5. WEIMER, ARTHUR M., and HOMER HOYT, *Real Estate* (5th ed.), Chapter 9. New York: The Ronald Press Company, 1966.

28

REAL ESTATE
AND THE MOBILE HOME

Ever since the pioneering days when migrant settlers felt the need for a mobile home while en route toward a more permanent place of settlement, efforts have been made to improve the construction, safety, and livability of shelter on wheels. The covered wagon, which played such a historic role in the settling of America, may be viewed as the first, though crude, effort to provide the protection and comforts of a home-away-from-home. Today, in the twentieth century, the economic motives that pressed a migrant population to move during the formative years of this country are as strong as they have ever been. In place of pioneers, we find an ever-increasing number of our dynamic and characteristically restless people living in mobile homes, which now have the permanency of real estate.

At the outset, a distinction must be made between the two types of successors to the covered wagon: the less-expensive travel trailers, and the modern mobile homes which contain up to four bedrooms and two baths and which measure up to fourteen feet in width (expandable to twenty-eight feet) and up to seventy feet in length. Although travel trailers and mobile homes are often built by the same manufacturing plant, the former are strictly personal fixtures with some of the features of an automobile, whereas the latter, once positioned in place, have been declared by statutory provisions of a number of states to possess the characteristics of realty. As such, they are held subject to restriction and *ad valorem* taxation as is other real estate within the community. Some states—like Florida—require annual purchase of mobile license tags. The cost of these tags varies with the size of the unit. In addition, counties may levy personal property taxes on these mobile homes. Statistics now indicate that mobile home residents pay, in the aggregate, equal or greater amounts in taxes than do residents of conventional homes of comparable value. The Western Mobile Home Association, representing owners in California, reports that mobile home owners in their state pay over $8 million annually in license taxes to the Department of Motor Vehicles. Of this amount, it is estimated that all but the 2 percent used to cover administrative costs is distributed to the counties, school districts, and incorporated communities.

The modern mobile home, which has been in great demand in recent years, owes its popularity to two important developments. First, the mass production has made possible the manufacture of mobile homes, complete with appliances and furniture, at approximately two-thirds the cost of similar-sized homes built in place, using local labor and materials. Second, construction of four-lane highways and limited access interstate highways has led an increasing number of states to modify restrictions on the movement of mobile homes.

Travel standards adopted in 1954 made possible the production of the "ten-wide" models. In recent years, industry's efforts to permit movement of the fourteen-foot-wide models have met with increasing success. Movement, however, is largely restricted to designated four-lane highways.

The size and significance of the mobile home industry and the impact of its product on local real estate development may best be judged from statistical surveys which disclose that in 1965 one out of every six new single-family homes was a mobile unit. In 1970 this ratio increased to one mobile unit out of every three new single-family homes. To state it differently, out of a total of 1,200,000 new single-family homes reported built in 1970, 400,000 were preconstructed by mobile home manufacturers and delivered to individually owned or mobile park homesites.

The National Institute of Real Estate Brokers in its newsletter of September 1970 reported that nearly seven million people live in mobile homes. This constitutes an increase of three million so domiciled over a five-year span from 1965 to 1970. Housing economists estimate that shipments of mobile homes will reach 450,000 in 1971 and 1,000,000 in 1975. These mobile homes are expected to be produced by the more than one thousand manufacturers that specialize in the field of mobile home construction. This industry currently accounts for 93 percent of all housing priced under fifteen thousand dollars and, as housing costs continue to skyrocket, all new housing under twenty thousand dollars by 1975 will be either a mobile home or one of prefabricated (modular) construction. More than one hundred thousand persons are employed in the various branches of the mobile home industry, including production of parts and materials. Retail sales of mobile homes and their smaller relatives, the travel trailers, are estimated to be in excess of $2 billion by 1975.

Among the people who prefer mobile homes are military personnel, construction workers, student couples, retired citizens, economy-minded couples, and vacationers who like a home away from home. In the latter category, especially, a significant increase in demand for mobile homes is anticipated. Just as the ownership of two cars per family has become the rule rather than the exception, so the ownership of two homes is rapidly becoming an accepted status symbol among members of the affluent society. According to findings published by the National Association of Real Estate Brokers in September 1970, more than twenty-five thousand mobile home parks with more than two million spaces are established in designated subdivisions of towns and cities of the United States. These parks are expanding by some eleven hundred parks each year. Some of these parks house as many as two thousand mobile homes and form separate and incorporated communities complete with mayor, councilmen, police and fire departments, and related community utilities and services.

The mobile home industry

Records indicate at least one manufacturer of mobile homes in each of forty states. The bulk of construction, however, about 60 percent of total mobile home production, is concentrated in four states ranked in order of size of operations: California, Indiana, Michigan, and Florida. Elkhart, a community located in northern Indiana, is commonly referred to as the capital of the mobile home industry. Within a twenty-five-mile radius of Elkhart there are over fifty manufacturers and over forty dealers of mobile home units. These firms employ more than four thousand persons at full production. Because of increasing costs of delivering the finished mobile home to the sales point, the mobile industry has been forced to decentralize, locating service and assembly branches near potential markets, especially in the Southwest and Southeast. The greater size and weight of newer models makes decentralization even more necessary. It is no longer unusual to see a mobile home that weighs over three tons and is almost seventy feet long, containing a flush toilet, tub or shower bath, complete kitchen facilities, and built-in sleeping accommodations. These homes arrive at the owner's site virtually ready for occupancy, except for incidental assembly operations, placement on temporary or permanent foundations, and connection to utilities on the site.

In addition to mobile homes, some manufacturers will build transportable school rooms, offices, hospitals, and other types of modular units. These auxiliary mobile structures should promote the development of park communities independent of conventional "on-site" construction for operation of commercial and professional service facilities.

In terms of mobile home sales, Florida is moving in front of top-rated California. A survey made by Frederick H. Bair, Jr., noted planning consultant and authority on the mobile home industry, shows that mobile home shipments to Florida nosed out those to California during 1965. Sales of mobile homes in Florida increased from six thousand in 1960 to twenty thousand in 1970. A continued increase at the rate of 25 percent a year is anticipated.

The prices of mobile homes range from $4,500 to $9,000, averaging, in January 1971, $6,500 furnished. For luxury models of the "double wide" variety, where two fourteen-foot-wide models are placed side by side and combined to form one mobile home with over fourteen hundred square feet of floor space, the price of the home, delivered and assembled, has reached a high of $22,500. Because of trucking, these so-called mobile homes are no longer truly mobile. In fact, judging by the quality of construction and the sumptuousness of interior furnishings, the motto of the mobile home industry appears to be: Less Mobility and More Home for Your Money. Therefore, mobile homes should legally be classified as realty rather than personalty as is currently the case in most jurisdictions.

Financing of mobile homes

Loans for mobile homes are as readily obtainable as loans for the purchase of automobiles. As as rule, large sales agencies, as well as commercial banks, finance mobile homes freely. The dealer of mobile homes generally is able to obtain loans of 90 percent of his cost including transportation of the mobile home, or he may elect to pay cash where the manufacturer's price concessions warrant it. Some manufacturers have their own financing subsidiaries to facilitate sale and promotion of their products. Approximately 80 percent of mobile homes are purchased on credit by the user, as are 80 percent of conventional homes. Loan maturities are relatively short, however, and range from four to six years at rates comparable to automobile loan rates. Like automobile dealers, mobile home dealers arrange for trade-ins, and an increasing number of dealer transactions involve used mobile homes. Trade-ins for new models, however, represent only a small fraction of mobile home sales.

A major boost to the mobile home industry was the enactment of the 1970 Emergency Housing Act. The provisions of the mobile home section of this act increased the supply of housing for lower income families to enable thousands of younger and older veterans to buy mobile homes—in many cases the only type of housing they can afford. Under this legislation, the Veterans Administration is authorized to guarantee 30 percent of mobile home loans that do not exceed the following:

1. $10,000 for twelve years and thirty-two days for a loan covering the purchase of a mobile home only, and such additional amount as is determined by the administrator to be appropriate to cover the cost of necessary site preparation where the veteran owns the lot, or
2. $15,000 (but not to exceed $10,000 for the mobile home) for fifteen years and thirty-two days for a mobile home and undeveloped lot and additional amount as determined appropriate for necessary site preparation, or

3. $17,500 (but not to exceed $10,000 for the mobile home) for fifteen years and thirty-two days for a loan covering the purchase of a mobile home and suitably developed lot on which to place such home.

Use of the mobile home loan guarantee benefit precludes the use of any home loan guarantee entitlement under any other section of the Veterans Act until the mobile home loan guaranteed has been paid in full. After the loan has been repaid, a veteran may use, in addition, his regular $12,500 entitlement to purchase a conventional home, if he so desires. The new act provides that "the Administrator shall establish such rate of interest for mobile home loans as he determines to be necessary in order to assure a reasonable supply of mobile home loan financing for veterans under this section." If lenders in the area will not extend the loans at these rates, the VA will make the loan directly to the GI applicant.

The VA administrator is charged with the responsibility of setting standards for planning, construction, and general acceptability of mobile homes and mobile home lots. Specifically, the standards are to be designed "to encourage the maintenance and development of sites for mobile homes which will be attractive residential areas and which will be free from, and not substantially contribute to, adverse scenic and environmental conditions." The act requires that the administrator, from time to time, inspect the manufacturing process of mobile homes to be sold to veterans and conduct random on-site inspection of such mobile homes.

The mobile home section of the 1970 Housing Act also authorizes the Federal Housing Administration to insure mobile home loans up to $10,-000 (exclusive of the price of the homesite) over repayment periods up to twelve years and thirty-two days. Interest rates on such loans are higher than those stipulated for conventional loans because mobile home construction is governed under Title I—the housing improvement section of the law. At present, FHA interest rates range from a low of 8 percent to a high of 11 percent depending on the amount of the loan and the repayment terms. The federal truth-in-lending law, as explained in the chapter on real estate financing, requires lenders as well as mobile home dealers to state clearly the simple annual interest rate on this type of loan.

The down payment required for an FHA insured loan is 5 percent of the first $5,000 of the mortgage and 10 percent of the amount above $6,000. No mobile home loan is insured by the FHA unless it meets construction standards set by the American National Standards Institute in Washington. A list of manufacturers complying with these standards can be obtained from the Mobile Homes Manufacturers Association, 6650 Northwest Highway, Chicago, Illinois 60631.

A mobile home costing $6,000 is generally purchased under conventional terms with a down payment of 25 percent, or $1,500. If the home is financed by a loan, the balance of $4,500 is repaid over five years. Payments to liquidate this debt, including interest on remaining debt balances at 8 percent, come to $91.26 a month. To arrive at the total cost of mobile

home ownership, such items as taxes, trailer space, rent or cost of homesite, utilities, and maintenance should be added to this amount.

The trailer park

The popularity of mobile homes and the increasing demand for space
and facilities needed to supply the necessary services have made the development and management of modern mobile home parks a profitable venture. According to W. W. Welch, president of Mobile Home Park Development Corporation, as reported in Prentice-Hall's *Real Estate Guide*, the
average net return to trailer park operators is 12 to 22 percent, varying
with land and community improvement costs and the availability of mortgage loans at favorable rates of interest.

Mobile homes, as previously stated, are no longer solely a means of
temporary shelter. They have come to be recognized as a permanent means
of shelter much like conventional homes in competing residential environ-
ments except for density of housing. Of the estimated twenty-five thousand
mobile parks the greatest number are concentrated in Florida, California,
and the southwestern states. The maximum density, unless otherwise controlled by zoning laws, is ten trailer spaces per acre. The Mobile Home
Manufacturers Association estimates park development cost at $1,500-
$2,500 per space, depending on number and quality of utility facilities in-
cluding paving, landscaping, and community recreation facilities. As a rule,
these mobile parks are situated at the fringe of the urban community where
raw land costs do not exceed $500 to $1,000 per acre. Although in some
instances spaces for mobile homes can be purchased outright, the general
practice is to rent the space at costs averaging $40 to $50 per month, varying with the number of service facilities provided, exclusive of utility costs
for water, gas, telephone, and electricity which are paid by the renter. In a
few luxury locations, such as seashore or golf club areas, monthly rentals
are as high as $100 or even more. Park owners often derive additional in-
come from the sale of bottled gas, from coin operated laundries, and from
food vending machines.

Financing of trailer parks follows the practices of financing conventional
real estate and residential developments. As a rule, the bulk of financing is
arranged through local financing institutions and individual lenders. In
recent years the Federal Housing Administration has made its insured loan
program available for mobile park developments, and a few loans have
been authorized by the Small Business Administration. Under FHA financing, the maximum loan for trailer or mobile parks with a minimum
of fifty trailer spaces is $2,500 per space, with a maximum loan of $1,-
000,000 per project. In areas where cost levels so require, loan limits may
be increased up to $3,265 per space and $1,450,000 per project. In no
event can the loan exceed 90 percent of the estimated value of the project
after completion. The maximum mortgage term is forty years or not ap-
preciably in excess of three-fourths of the economic life of the project,
whichever is less. The prevailing rate of interest is that authorized by the

FHA and is applicable on the real estate proper. The mobile home itself is financed separately as explained above.

Mobile park planning

The design of a mobile park must be undertaken with as great care as the planning of a permanent subdivision if the venture is to prove financially successful. Not more than half of the available raw land, and preferably no more than a third, should be allocated for mobile home or trailer spaces. The balance of the land is needed for access roads, community facilities, and open spaces to beautify the area. The Mobile Home Manufacturers Association, to improve the public image of mobile parks (and of course to market its products), offers help with the planning and design of a park. Information secured from this association is based on the wide experience of owner-operators throughout the country.

Until recently, obstacles have been placed in the way of the development of mobile parks in most communities. The reasons are many. First, the old trailer parks were often unsightly areas housing transients who seldom took part in community life. Second, the density of housing per acre was often triple the density allowed for residences in the lowest zoning classification. This high density increased the cost and burden of servicing trailer parks. Third, and most important, mobile homes in many jurisdictions were and still are taxed as motor vehicles or personal property, thus escaping the share of local property taxes that encumber the conventional home. To a large extent the image of the mobile home is rapidly improving. Taxes are being equalized by statutory action, and zoning requirements place limits on space density. Construction plans, too, must be submitted in advance to planning departments of city or county governments. As a rule, assurance must be given that proper steps will be taken to shield the park from other areas whose value may suffer from its improper location and operation.

Nevertheless, the stigma of a few years ago persists in most parts of the country—notably, in the Northeast. Local attitudes in New Jersey, for instance, remain largely hostile, as reported by the state Department of Health. Two-thirds of the nearly six hundred municipalities in the Garden State prohibit mobile home parks by ordinance. People seem to think of mobile homes as "unattractive, not well run, and generally disorderly."

The blame for untidy trailer park areas does not fall entirely on developers who are seeking profit. Zoning restrictions, until recent years, have more or less kept mobile home parks in nonresidential, often in industrial, areas. Such practices fortunately are diminishing, and in many jurisdictions mobile home parks are now considered appropriate for residential zones.

Mobile home manufacturers are spearheading drives to encourage country-wide adoption of uniform zoning ordinances to regulate orderly development of mobile home parks. P. M. Roberts, director of the Boise, Idaho, Department of Building and Zoning, recommends that subdivision regulations be prepared so that entire residential areas can be devoted to mobile homes and that no use of the land be permitted other than neighborhood shopping and utility areas to serve the inhabitants of mobile homes.

The problems of urban blight and obsolescence that plague most older communities also confront owners of long-established mobile parks. As the units increased in size from the standard eight-wide and ten-wide to the current fourteen-wide models, many parks became severely handicapped. Many of the older parks cannot accommodate the wider mobile homes. Rebuilding a park is prohibitive in cost and was labeled an "excursion into urban renewal" by officials of the Housing and Home Finance Administration.

To prevent obsolescence the Mobile Home Manufacturers Association adopted several years ago a rigid manufacturing code which binds all members. These standards closely parallel national standards adopted by the Federal Housing Administration and state building codes governing standards for plumbing, heating, electrical installations, and general soundness of construction essential to safe and maintenance-free occupancy.

Mobile home market

The mobile home industry offers the breadwinner in search of a modest home an opportunity to avail himself of economies of mass production which, in the conventional house market, are largely unavailable. Manufacturers of "shell" homes (complete except for interior finishing) and prefabricated homes, it is true, have attempted to introduce production-line methods into housing construction. However, overrestrictive local building codes, backed by craft unions who fear loss of their jobs to outside workers, have negated the savings that could result from home preconstruction. The mobile home, because it is classified as *personalty* rather than as *realty* in most jurisdictions, has so far escaped and promises to continue to escape the restrictions to which other prefabricated housing is subjected.

Mobile home advantages

The mobile home also differs from conventional housing in that it is finished inside and out to the last detail before leaving the factory. All furniture and furnishings, including rugs, draperies, and blinds, are in place and contained in the quoted and delivered price. Savings obtained through belt-line assembly are further increased by wholesale pricing of kitchen, heating, and cooling equipment. Mobile homes, as stated previously, are designed luxuriously to offer more and more home quality and less and less mobility. This trend is borne out by statistics gathered by the M.H.M.A. to show that the typical "mobile" home stays in place, on the average, for over five years. Surveys indicate that 80 percent of those living in mobile homes have not moved in the preceding five years, and of those who moved, 44 percent did so because of job changes.[1] Mobile home living ap-

---

[1] See Art S. Leitch "The Mobile Home Boom," *Successful Sales Slant*, No. 17, September 1970, National Institute of Real Estate Brokers, Chicago, Ill.

peals to the younger married couples and to the above middle-aged group in the semiretired or retired class. Statistics indicate that 55 percent of mobile home residents are skilled workers or persons of professional background. Questionnaires confirm that the compactness of mobile home construction offers more utility and convenience in the use of space than does the construction of conventional homes. Because of the welded unit body construction, upkeep is more economical. Built-in bureaus, beds, and appliances make housekeeping easier for senior citizens and for busy working couples.

The appeal of mobile home living is widespread. To large numbers of retired persons, mobile parks are a kind of new Eden, offering community spirit and friendly atmosphere generated by like-minded neighbors, a feeling unmatched in any area containing conventional homes of similar size and number. Young couples, too, find mobile living an ideal way to begin their homemaking adventure. A single purchase includes not only the roof over their heads but all the furniture and bulky appliances such as stove, refrigerator, washing machine, and many optional extras. Surveys of mobile parks indicate fewer children than in conventional homes, but higher income per family and more formal education than the national average.

Each year, manufacturers of mobile homes stage a major exhibition in the Midwest, West, and Southeast where the newest models and innovations are shown. These exhibits attract large crowds of present and potential mobile home users. The new models grow more luxurious each year. Many contain cushioned floors, oversize double beds, marble-top vanities, and wall-to-wall carpeting. A few of the larger models have one and one-half and even two bathrooms. Emphasis is also placed on expandable twenty-eight-foot-wide models (two fourteen-foot-wides joined together) which are equipped with central air conditioning, sliding glass doors, and built-in dressers. Flexibility further permits expansion of living space through the addition of carports and porches or patios. These innovations explain the popularity of this form of mobile housing. It is of interest to note that space of mobile home living has grown to such an extent that 85 percent of all mobile homes are now twelve feet wide. In California, 50 percent of mobile homes are double width, with sixty by twenty-four feet a common home size.[2] Further, eleven states now permit transportation and placement of fourteen-foot-wide mobile homes.

The future of mobile homes

The outlook for continued expansion of the mobile home industry and for increased use of this mode of housing in all states throughout North America is excellent. Planning agencies, too, encourage mobile park developments as a means of slowing community obsolescence and decay. Some planners go so far as to refer to mobile housing as "renewable hous-

[2]Reported by Robert J. Weis, general manager of the Mobile Home Division of Boise Cascade Corporation, Atlanta, Georgia, at a seminar sponsored by the American Institute of Real Estate Appraisers in Washington, D.C., March 13, 1970.

ing" which tends to self-modernize a park community. The theory is that residents will be more likely to trade old models for new, thus upgrading the environment as it ages. Only the future can show whether this theory is valid.

As the "great society" develops under the guiding hand of the federal government (average family income is expected to reach $9,500 by 1975), more emphasis will be placed on construction of mobile homes that offer more than mere shelter, and on built-in conveniences at a price the average family can afford. Mobile homes should find a ready market among those in search of convenience of living, economy of operation, and perhaps a second home for recreation, if not a "castle by the sea."

READING AND STUDY REFERENCES

1. BAIR, FREDERICK H., JR., *Mobile Homes and the General Housing Supply, Past, Present, and Outlook.* Mobile Homes Research Foundation, June 1966.
2. BEITLER, RICHARD K., "The Right Park for Your Home," *Mobile Home Life*, 1966.
3. *Federal Domestic Assistance Catalog*, U.S. Office of Economic Opportunity. Washington, D.C., 1970.
4. JONES, LESLIE M., "Financing Your Mobile Home," *Mobile Home Life*, 1966.
5. "Mobile Homes and Mobile Home Parks—1965—Florida Survey," *Florida Planning and Development*, June 1966.
6. "More New Families and Retirees: Mobile Homes' Demand Will Continue to Flourish," *Nation's Cities*, August 1965.
7. RING, ALFRED A., *Questions and Problems in Real Estate Principles and Practices* (rev. ed.), Chapter 27. Englewood Cliffs, N.J.: Prentice-Hall, Inc., 1972.

29

HOME
OWNERSHIP

A way of life

Home ownership cannot be effectively evaluated on economic grounds alone. Therefore, considering family shelter problems, it is essential to differentiate between the economic functions of a house and the social functions of a home. Unfortunately, most of the dwellings to which we are accustomed fall into the category of houses rather than homes. A house, if well built, provides the essentials of shelter and thus gives adequate protection from sun, rain, and the actions of the elements. A home, however, is a place that not only provides safety from the elements but offers, in addition, opportunities for a well-rounded and coordinated family life, for character building, and for the upbringing of healthy and happy children. It is for these reasons that a home is appropriately referred to as a *way of life*. In order to promote the building of homes rather than the construction of houses, an attempt will be made in this chapter to present and analyze the essentials and principles of home ownership, and to discuss practices that will lead to the purchase and development of well-designed and attractively located homes.

Home ownership trends

The widespread use of the long-term amortization mortgage at high loan-to-value ratios has brought about a significant evolution in the distri-

485

bution and acquisition of owner-occupied homes. There was a time hardly two decades ago when only those who had accumulated substantial savings could afford the risks that home ownership entailed. It was the necessity to purchase homes largely out of "savings" that placed home ownership out of reach of millions of otherwise qualified and potential purchasers.

Today a home, like any other consumer goods, may be purchased on time; mortgage credit is based largely on stability of future income rather than on accumulated savings. This significant change in the mode of home buying was made possible by federal mortgage insurance and guarantee provisions under which the government itself does not lend any funds but rather underwrites to the lender the integrity of the loan and the discharge of all financial obligations under the terms of the mortgage. Legislative requirements under which insured or guaranteed mortgages must be amortized on a monthly basis, over periods ranging up to thirty years, popularized the use of the installment plan of home acquisition or home construction. Federal savings and loan associations were also authorized to make amortized (uninsured) loans up to 90 percent of appraised value. Other lending institutions have followed in accepting the amortization mortgage as best suited to home financing. As a result of the "pay as you go" home purchase plan, over two-thirds of all dwelling units constructed since World War II are owner occupied, and in the years since 1945 a majority of families have attained home ownership status.

Unfortunately, the "easy" purchase plan, often government backed and secured, has tempted many families prematurely into undertaking the responsibilities that home ownership entails, and many, to their sorrow, have learned that home ownership is an important venture and must be carefully planned and timed. Too often it is not the initial cost but the "upkeep" that causes the amenities or pleasures of home ownership to end in financial grief. Since home ownership is currently and potentially within reach of every income producer who can muster the necessary but relatively small down payment, it is doubly important that careful and thoughtful consideration be given to each and all the principles of home ownership set forth in detail below.

Why own a home?

The case for home ownership, generally, is well stated and, if based on social and political considerations alone, unquestionably deserves strong support. Aside from the basic instinct and desire to own a home, there are many other compelling reasons—the most important of which are as follows:

1. *Adventure.* Home ownership, as well as the selection of a home, is one of the most interesting adventures in family life. It involves, in most instances, the largest single financial transaction that a family undertakes. It is indeed adventurous not only to invest one's life savings but also to roam around the community or countryside to find the best location, to choose a plot, and to select the design and layout of a home, if one is

to be built, or to look at the innumerable buildings already constructed in anticipation of the home purchaser's demands.

2. *Education.* With home ownership, an entirely new world is opened to the buyer. He learns about values and prices, contracts and building materials. As he considers his tax bill and governmental action that directly or indirectly touch upon his home, he is led to inquire into civic affairs —how government is run and its local problems—and sooner than he realizes the homeowner develops a feeling of "belonging" which induces him to take active part in community affairs.

3. *Credit.* Home ownership improves one's credit standing. It makes for stability and better employment relations and discourages the restless, wasteful practice of frequent moving about. As a homeowner reduces his mortgage, he comes to be known as a "property owner." His patronage is solicited and his credit rating may be counted as a financial asset.

4. *Thrift and saving.* Home ownership encourages saving, unwittingly as a rule, for the mortgage amortization provisions are specifically designed to increase the owner's equity or property at a rate faster than the counteracting losses incurred through wear and tear, depletion or other forces contributing to depreciation, i.e., loss in the value of the home. The homeowner, too, must set aside sums to meet his various payments, and the thrift habit becomes ingrained.

5. *Security.* The renter is always insecure. His rent may be raised, or the landlord may want possession. The homeowner is "set." Conditions may change, the economic cycle may go up or down, but he has his roof over his head and if he meets his payments regularly no one can disturb him; he will be subject to no eviction notice.

6. *Citizenship.* The ownership of a home brings with it an entirely different attitude toward social, economic, and political problems. Home ownership as a rule contributes to better citizenship by promoting civic pride. Homeowners tend to be politically conservative and prove more resistant to the introduction of "isms" or measures that may lead to a totalitarian state.

7. *Purpose.* Many people are drifters. They have no definite goal or purpose. Buying a home supplies the stimulant they need. It gives them something to work for. They must meet the payments, and each one met stiffens their confidence.

8. *Independence.* It is a wonderful feeling indeed for a homeowner to stand on a segment of mother earth and call it his own; to be king of his castle no matter how modest the realm. To a large extent the owner can do as he wishes. There is no landlord to restrict him.

9. *Peace of mind.* As soon as the initial payment on the home is made, the owner commences building up an equity, and this gives him peace of mind. To be sure, he has payments to make, but the renter also has his obligations each month. The great difference is that the renter is building up nothing for himself. The homeowner, by making equal or slightly higher payments, is slowly paying off his debts, and after a while the home is paid for and becomes a real refuge.

10. *Character development.* A community where homes are largely owner-occupied reflects better care of properties, better landscaping, cleaner thoroughfares, and stability of home and property investments. As a rule, a homeowner wants a nice home. Therefore he must save and can ill afford to be shiftless.

11. *Fun.* It is a delight to own one's home; to have a place in which to en-

tertain and do the things that a tenant may be prohibited from doing. The children can play about as they please without any complaint from landlords.

12. *Creative instinct.* The ownership of a home gives the owner an opportunity to play with his ideas. People do not design or build their rented quarters—they take them as they find them—and very often simply because they are the best they can get for the price or most conveniently located. Homeowners are people who satisfy their instinctive desire to develop their own background. If building, the architectural design and layout may be what the homeowner wishes. Even if he is purchasing an old house, he may bring into play his ideas of alteration and remodeling. He gets an opportunity to work in his garden. He landscapes his grounds. He may have, even without a large expenditure, a delightfully balanced home, set in most attractive surroundings.

To buy or rent

It is often urged that it is better to rent than to own. From the aesthetic point of view, no doubt, home ownership is more desirable. From the financial side the argument is a little keener. It is sometimes said that home ownership costs more than renting, but actually one is probably no more expensive than the other.

Unfortunately, there are special groups or interests that stand to benefit materially by a community of homeowners, and their active advertising appears to support the impression that the homeowner can "have his cake and eat it too." Yes, home ownership has merits, but it would constitute grave folly to urge it on each and all—though the means are available—unless the principles of home ownership can reasonably be applied.

Some people have neither socially nor economically "ripened" to undertake the duties and responsibilities which home ownership necessitates. To illustrate—a young man seeking employment opportunities should be free to move about wherever and whenever opportunity knocks and should not be tied by the confining cares and bonds that home ownership imparts. Other and older persons may find ties to a home most burdensome if the nature of their jobs necessitates possible moving about. In the latter class can be placed those engaged as sales representatives, field workers of social and federal agencies, and others who seek a career in the military branches of government.

Further consideration should be given to the fact that tenancy not only has its rightful place in our economy but as a rule is competitively priced and thus comparable in value per dollar to like home investment or expenditure. The renter will find that his rent includes all the costs of maintenance of the property, such as taxes, interest on the mortgage, and depreciation. He pays in his rent, also, such amounts as the landlord expects to expend for repairs and a fair return on the amount that the landlord has invested in the property. It is on these latter two points that the financial variation may occur. The renter cannot get all the repairs that he wants because the landlord, naturally, will not expend more on repairs than the rent includes. It is also true that the landlord counts on a return on the money he invests at a rate higher than that which accrues to bank savings accounts, but such higher returns are generally more than offset by efficiency of property management and economies due to large-scale purchase and maintenance operations. The homeowner, on the other hand, will have exactly the same items to calculate in figuring what his home actually costs him, but he can spend as much or as little on repairs as he wishes—without impairing his home investment—paying only for the items that he gets; and he can calculate, of course, the return on his investment at any rate he considers fair.

The costs of home ownership

It is amazing how many homeowners fail to consider the "real" costs of operating a home. Among the financial sacrifices to be counted as a cost of home ownership should be the following:

1. Income foregone on equity investment in the home
2. Interest on borrowed capital
3. Depreciation of home investment
4. Maintenance and repairs of home
5. Real estate taxes and assessments
6. Fire and other hazard insurance
7. Utilities—such as water, garbage, and sewage disposal where not included as part of the tax-paid city services

Assuming the purchase of a $25,000 home, where the buyer paid $5,000 down and $800 in title closing charges and assumed a $20,000 mortgage that is to be amortized monthly over a twenty-five year period with interest at 8 percent per annum, typical monthly costs of home ownership would be as follows:

1. Income foregone on equity and purchase (closing costs) investment of $5,800 at 8 percent per annum	$ 38.70
2. Interest on borrowed capital (mortgage) at 8 percent on $20,000	133.30
3. Depreciation of building improvements 1½ percent per year on $20,000 (building-to-land ratio is assumed as 4 to 1)	25.00
4. Maintenance and repairs—based on average monthly expenditures during life of home	30.00
5. Real estate taxes (these vary widely; for this illustration $600 per annum is estimated)	50.00
6. Fire and hazard insurance	9.00
7. Water, garbage, and sanitary sewage	6.00
Total Monthly Costs of Owning a $25,000 Home	$292.00

It is important to differentiate between *costs* and *expenses* of home ownership. Costs are the sum total of all the sacrifices in terms of dollars whether paid for or not by the homeowner during a given period. Expenses, on the other hand, are comprised only of those charges that the homeowner actually expends. The above-priced house, for instance, would be advertised as $5,000 down and $154.40 per month (covering monthly interest and mortgage amortization charges). No mention is made, as a rule, of closing costs nor of maintenance, repairs, taxes, or insurance expenditures. Even when the out-of-pocket payments covering taxes and insurance are included, the expenses of home ownership fall 20 to 25 percent short of real ownership costs as shown above.

Attention is also called to the fact that mortgage amortization payments should not be considered as home ownership costs. As the mortgage principal declines, the equity interest of the homeowner increases, at least to the extent that payments on the mortgage exceed accrued depreciation on the home. Overall costs, however, remain relatively constant; savings in mortgage interest—as the mortgage principal diminishes—are offset by corresponding losses in income foregone on the increasing equity investment. But even when considering the real costs of home ownership, the amenities to those who purchase wisely make home ownership a sound investment. This is especially true during periods of inflation when "big" dollars borrowed under a fixed interest mortgage are paid off with "small" dollars out of future and generally higher (inflated) dollar incomes.

Who can afford a home?

A rule for buying which has gained widespread acceptance particularly by agencies of the FHA is that the price of a home should not exceed 2 to 2½ times the buyer's annual income. This rule, as well as the cost of home maintenance rule which follows, is relied upon almost exclusively by federal insurance and private lending agencies as a cardinal guide to successful home ownership. Under this rule, a person earning $8,000 per annum should limit his search for a home to those offered at $20,000, or less, in the current market. A price in excess of the 2 to 2½ times income rule has proved to impose a burdensome strain on a family's operating budget.

The above rule was formulated after long investigation and study which disclosed that home expenditures average about 9 to 10 percent of the purchase price (value) of the house per year. Departures from this rule are in order, of course, depending on the size of the family and living habits of the individuals. A household without children can afford to allocate more for household expenses than can families who must provide for the health, welfare, and education of their children. Exceptions, however, should be held closely to the 20 percent maintenance rule which requires that the total outlay for maintaining a home and maintaining the investment in a home should not exceed 20 percent of the buyer's current and reasonably anticipated future income.

Strict adherence to this latter rule by the FHA and lending institutions in general is held accountable for the unusually low rate of home foreclosures in recent years. In the derivation of the 20 percent cost of maintenance rule, consideration is given to such items of expense as real estate taxes, assessments, interest on the mortgage indebtedness, amortization of the mortgage principal, fire and windstorm insurance, and costs of utilities —nonpayment of which may cause a lien to be placed on the owner's property. This rule, too, was formulated after investigation and field study of millions of homes. In making all the above prorated expenditures payable monthly to the lending agency, the chances for debt accumulation, which was the chief cause of foreclosures in depression years, is thus mitigated. Then, too, the lending agency can advise the homeowner as soon as a monthly default occurs and can see him through periods of temporary distress by extending or adjusting the periodic payments. Experience in recent years has proved the income rule to be highly successful. In the final analysis it is the income of the buyer—more so than the price paid for the home —that governs his ability to carry through the financial obligations which home ownership imposes.

Often attempts are made to circumvent the 20 percent maintenance rule by those who advocate home ownership—at any cost—by de-emphasizing indirect cost such as deferred maintenance and costs of home replacements. A favorite scheme, too, is to encourage the lengthening of the period over which the mortgage indebtedness is to be recouped. No doubt attempts will again be made to have Congress authorize longer insured mortgage lending periods, particularly for GI loans, from the customary twenty-five- or thirty-year period to one that will spread mortgage amortization over forty years. If such legislation were approved, an actual disservice would be rendered to the veterans, for real home ownership free from all mortgage debt would rarely be realized in their lifetime.

The fallacy of supporting extension of mortgage indebtedness over a period of forty years is further emphasized when consideration is given to the relatively small savings that accrue to the borrower by assuming debt obligations beyond the customary lending period of twenty-five years now in force. The table below which records the payments necessary to amortize a $1,000 debt at selected rates of interest for a given number of years supports the above conclusions.

PERIODIC MONTHLY PAYMENTS TO AMORTIZE A $1,000 MORTGAGE DEBT AT RATES OF 7½ AND 8 PERCENT INTEREST OVER SELECTED PERIODS OF YEARS

Debt Period in Years	Periodic Monthly Payments at: 7½%	8%
20	$7.50	$7.82
25	7.39	7.72
30	7.00	7.34
35	6.75	7.11
40	6.58	6.96

Inspection of the above table will disclose that at 8 percent interest an extension of the mortgage loan period from twenty-five to forty years will constitute a reduction of $0.76 per month in the debt burden per $1,000 of debt. Thus, while the mortgage loan period is increased from twenty-five to forty years, or by 60 percent, the mortgage debt burden is decreased only from $7.72 to $6.96, or approximately 10 percent. Is this "saving" of

10 percent in current mortgage costs worth the shouldering of the home indebtedness for an additional period of fifteen years Then, too, who will be happy in the thought of assuming equal payment burdens over a life period of forty years? It seems that tampering with the established rules or principles of home ownership may be at times politically expedient, but economically questionable.

Although homes are largely paid for out of income, a wise rule provides that the purchaser's accumulated savings should be equal, at the time of purchase, to not less than 20 percent of the price of the home. It is true that 10 percent of the purchase price may suffice as a minimum recommended down payment, but there are many hidden and unexpected costs connected with the purchase of a home. There are closing fees, legal fees, and costs of title insurance. Taxes, too, are prorated and are often payable in advance. Insurance for fire and windstorm is payable in advance and at the time of purchase. Essentials, such as cooking and heating equipment, must often be acquired. Refrigeration facilities, too, are seldom part of a home and must be secured. There are fuel expenses, alterations, moving costs, and innumerable small expenditures necessary to adapt one's living habits to the new environment. Defects in plumbing, heating, electrical or roofing structures, and equipment may call for sudden and unexpected outlays, and unless the recommended savings are available the ship of home may founder at the start, thereby robbing one of the joys of home ownership for many years to come. Homeowners, too, use more household gadgets, more water (watering lawns, and so on), more electricity, and more fuel than are used by those renting comparable apartment quarters, and such costs must be considered either as home maintenance or as immediate capital outlays.

When to buy a home

There is no specific time, period, or age at which home ownership can be recommended to any individual or group. The price of a home reflects market conditions as influenced by the supply and demand for housing, but the value of the home to the owner necessitates an analysis of personal factors and a consideration of subjective elements that enter into the evaluation process and the price to be paid for the home. There are, however, a few general rules that are presented here to guide the home purchaser. They are:

1. A home should not be purchased or built during periods of active housing or building demand or at any time when a housing shortage encourages the payment of premiums to gain immediate possession. It should be remembered that homes purchased at inflated prices generally impose equally inflated monthly financial obligations which must be borne over long debt periods (twenty or more years) irrespective of hardships that may occur during depression years. The specter of wholesale foreclosures of homes ill purchased and ill financed is bound to haunt the buyer if this rule is disregarded.
2. Prospective home purchasers who have heretofore lived in apartments should, where possible, rent a home first before undertaking a hasty pur-

chase. Home ownership imposes many obligations in regard to home care and maintenance which the purchaser may not be physically or emotionally prepared to undertake. Unless an abode means more than a mere place in which to sleep and eat, homeownership may prove both irritating and burdensome.

3. Before purchasing a home at any time, consideration should be given to the permanency of employment and stability of income. Purchasing late in life, too, is a hazard if a decrease in earning power comes with age.

4. Further consideration should be given to the purchaser's willingness to live in the selected spot for many years to come, because the resale of the property may prove expensive. Unfortunately and too often the purchase of a home is considered an investment. In reality a home is a consumer's item which diminishes in value (not necessarily in price) with age and use as do other consumer commodities. Consequently little provision is generally made for the replacement of the "investment" and, to the consternation of the purchaser, the full loss or cost of home ownership is not realized until the date of sale, or when extensive repairs require large capital outlays.

Where to buy a home

A prominent real estate broker was once asked to name three principles that should guide a purchaser in the selection of a home. His answer was as follows: (1) location, (2) location, and (3) location. At first impression it may appear that this answer was lightly and perhaps facetiously formulated, but when consideration is given to some of the peculiar characteristics of real estate the answer becomes meaningful.

Real estate is immobile. Though man may move some of the substance, the extent of land is geographically fixed and cannot be moved. The improvements, too, for all practical purposes, are stationary. It is of course possible to move a home physically, but such action, as a rule, is economically inadvisable. The point to be remembered by the prospective home buyer, however, is that while the land and the improvements are stationary, the city and the neighborhood are in a constant state of flux and literally move about it. Changes in the environment must ever be considered: ingress or egress of industry or commerce; increase or decrease in population; dangers to welfare, health, or morality; influx or encroachment by undesirable groups—all are bound to be reflected in the desirability and value of a property. It is location, thus, that can contribute to making or breaking the conditions that are conducive to maximum enjoyment of the pleasures and amenities of living that arise out of home ownership.

There is no one scale of values that can be recommended as a guide to all present or prospective homeowners. Likes and dislikes, tastes and conditions vary depending upon size of family, type of employment, costs of transportation, price of land, utility requirements, social habits, and personal characteristics of the purchaser. Proximity to place of work, no doubt, is of prime importance to all breadwinners, but other factors, both economic and social, may make living in the country and commuting to the city preferable to the confinement and lack of privacy that are the lot of the urban dweller.

In order to create an awareness of the more significant conditions to which careful consideration should be given by the purchaser, a listing of important items is presented as a guide to effective and successful evaluation of the home location. By comparing the relative value weights of two or more suggested and available locations in relation to family needs and living comforts, the home owner can wisely make an effective choice. The relative weights assigned to location factors as seen through the eyes of a typical home owner are itemized as follows:

Item	Relative Weight
Proximity to place of work	15
Quality of available schools	10
Distance to school	5
Nearness to church of own choice	5
Neighborhood—reputation and characteristics	10
Degree of owner occupancy and owner's pride in area	5
Quality and proximity of shopping area	5
Transportation (public) facilities and cost	5
City tax structure	10
Zoning stability	5
Availability of necessary utilities	5
Recreation opportunities	5
Extent of neighborhood development	5
Nature of terrain—drainage and topography	5
Absence of noise, traffic, smoke, and dust	10
Effective fire and police protection	10

Each family, of course, has problems of its own and the weights suggested above are purely relative and should be varied according to the specific needs with which each purchaser is confronted. In any event, a scale of values carefully selected and considered should act as a deterrent to hasty purchase and forestall the sweat and tears that otherwise may blot the joys that should be inherent in a home of one's own.

The financing of a home

A problem of deep concern to prospective home buyers is how best to finance a home and how to derive a mode of payment that will cause the least strain on the family budget and will not terminate in financial grief. A secondary problem generally arises out of the purchaser's desire to safeguard the investment into which he, like most homeowners, has poured the bulk of his life savings. Broadly speaking, home purchasers fall into two groups. The one includes those who have accumulated limited savings and thus are unable to provide a substantial down payment. The other is composed of those more fortunate in their financial standing who are able and willing to acquire a substantial equity in the home or pay all cash. For each group there are several plans and combinations of plans that lend themselves to suit their purpose. Only the most prevalent and the soundest are presented here for study and consideration.

Those who can least afford to see their savings dissipated and who must husband well each dollar of investment are best advised to seek their aid in home financing through an insured mortgage loan. Although the actual lending of money against a home mortgage security is undertaken by a private concern (generally a local bank, building and loan association, or similarly approved lending agency) the government (FHA) guarantee provisions necessitate, in the interest of all concerned, a careful study of the attending risk factors, the presence of which can make or break a home. This analysis principally evolves about:

1. *The Mortgagor*:
   His ability to meet without undue stress or strain the obligatory financial burdens to be imposed under the home purchase plan
2. *The Property*:
   a. The value of the home in relation to the purchase price
   b. The economic life of the structure in relation to the mortgage debt period
   c. The soundness of construction in relation to anticipated expenditures for maintenance and repairs
3. *The Location*:
   a. The economic stability of the location in relation to population changes, commerce, and industry
   b. The nature, stability, and kind of employment opportunities that prevail in the regional environment

Under provision of Section 203(b) of the Housing Act of 1970, the FHA financing plan enables a qualified buyer to borrow as follows:

97 percent of the first $15,000 of home cost,
90 percent of the next $10,000, and
80 percent of the amount above $25,000, with a maximum mortgage loan of $33,000 for a one-family home.

Veterans can get larger mortgages than nonveterans under FHA regulations. A qualified GI can borrow as follows:

100 percent of the first $15,000 (less $200 cash investment),
 90 percent of the next $10,000, plus
 85 percent of the excess over $25,000, with a maximum mortgage loan of $33,000 for a one-family home.

The loan-to-value ratio is based on *appraised* value by FHA staff or by certified independent fee appraisers.

The prevailing interest rate is 7.5 percent plus one-half percent for mortgage insurance, or a combined rate of 8 percent per annum on outstanding balances of the mortgage debt. To these monthly carrying charges must be added, of course, other costs of housing as previously noted.

Those able and willing to invest an equity aggregating 20 percent or more of the value of the home will find numerous private lending institutions ready to serve them. Care should be taken, however, that the mortgage contract selected contains suitable amortization provisions at reasonable rates of interest that are applied to the periodically declining balances of the mortgage, and also an agreement that will enable the purchaser to refinance his mortgage debt when an opportunity presents itself to do so at substantial savings.

A novel and interesting plan for home financing, combining mortgage lending and life insurance, is offered by some of the leading insurance companies. Under this plan, should death overtake the borrower any time during the mortgage contract period, the widow or estate of the deceased will be freed from the mortgage debt and from further mortgage payments and will receive a return of all payments on mortgage principal made during the life period of the borrower. In effect the plan provides for an accumulation of cash value and dividend earnings on the life insurance policy which accrues in accordance with policy provisions but which in case of the borrower's death matures to the face amount of the policy.

The mortgage life insurance plan deserves careful consideration by potential homeowners and others who deem it necessary or advisable to refinance their present mortgage debt. The plan appears suited to those who are financially strong enough to meet the increased payments which, on the average, aggregate 25 percent in excess of mortgage payments where no provision is made for insurance protection.

Pros and cons of mortgage debt financing

The question is often raised as to the advisability of "all cash" payments where the purchaser is financially able to do so. There was a time when debts and particularly mortgage debts on a home were considered ill advised. Times, however, have changed and with them our modes of living. The "pay as you go" home purchase plan, for three decades now, has proved to be sound in principle and a strong incentive toward the promotion of thrift and general "good housekeeping" among those who have adopted it.

Even where a home buyer has accumulated the required savings, the purchase of a home free from mortgage debt may not always prove advisable for the following reasons:

1. The purchase of a home converts savings from liquid assets into a relatively fixed and immobile form. Sudden or emergency needs for cash may arise and with "all the eggs in one basket" the raising of large sums over a relatively short period of time may prove costly and embarrassing.
2. Mortgage amortization payments constitute a form of regular and consistent savings which, as a rule, increase an owner's equity faster than the resulting losses accounted for by wear and tear, action of the elements, and other causes that contribute to the decline in the value of the home investment. Mortgage amortization thus indirectly contributes to stability and enhancement of the initial investment depending on the extent and rate at which amortization exceeds accrued depreciation.
3. A home can be more readily sold—when need arises—if it is subject to a mortgage debt, assuming that the mortgage bears a fair ratio to price of property and that it is financed at currently available low rates of interest. The reason for greater marketability arises out of the fact that a prospec-

tive purchaser need not finance the total purchase price, but merely raise the equity required over and above the existing mortgage debt.

There are, of course, laudable benefits that flow from "outright" home ownership. Among the more prominent advantages of 100 percent equity financing are counted the following:

1. Satisfaction or civic pride of undisputed ownership in a home of one's own—free and clear
2. Freedom from fear of monetary complications which may terminate in foreclosure of the home
3. Greater flexibility in the disposition of current income
4. A haven to which the unemployed, the ailing, or aged owners may retreat without fear of interference by "unfeeling" mortgagees

Yet, despite these advantages, an all cash purchase of a home is not advisable where such cash outlay necessitates delay in home acquisition for many years to come (in order to accumulate the necessary savings) or where such cash requirements bankrupt a purchaser's savings or obscure the real costs of home ownership. It should be remembered that homes, like automobiles, furniture, and fixtures, are consumer goods which deteriorate and lessen in value with use and with changes in design and changes in the environment of which the homestead is an inseparable part. And yet somehow, the concept that a home is an investment prevails, causing distress to homeowners who are faced with the necessity of meeting ever-increasing bills for home repair or who suffer accelerated home destruction caused by wear and tear and action of the elements. Well-financed homes, too, are easier to sell, since prospective buyers need only raise the cash (equity) above the mortgage debt and generally save both the time and the expense incurred in the placement of a new mortgage where debt refinancing is a necessity.

To buy or to build

Once the price range of a home and the neighborhood in which it is to be located are decided upon, the typical homeseeker is confronted with the query whether to build or whether to purchase a ready-made new or old home. There is no one answer to this problem. Due consideration must be given first to the financial ability of the purchaser and second to the advantages and disadvantages that underlie each purchase plan.

In building a new home, the purchaser must be prepared to meet the hazards of unexpected outlays which often prove the "killjoy" of the thrills that normally accompany the construction of a home. It is difficult to conceive of other investment ventures in which so large a share of a family's savings or income is involved and in which cost understatements prevail so commonly as in the building trades. The difficulty generally rests in the misunderstanding arising from a builder's conception of a house and an owner's conception of a home. To the average purchaser, a house is not a home unless it contains the basic requisites, including blinds, cabinets, stoves, landscaping, and utilities that are deemed essential to agreeable living. The aspirations, hopes, fears, and anxiety that are the lot of the typical home builder are well set forth, though in caricature, in Eric Hodgins's *Mr. Blandings Builds His Dream House*, to which the reader is referred.

Those more budget-minded and who must know beforehand the costs that home ownership necessitates are best served through the purchase of an existing house. Though the joy of planning and the thrill of watching the new home take form are foregone, the savings and economies resulting from the purchase of an already built house and the comforting ability to inspect the investment before dollar commitments are made often prove quite rewarding.

The reasons why a ready-built new home may prove more satisfactory to the average purchaser are as follows:

1. A builder can erect a number of houses cheaper than he can an isolated one. Part of this saving, which may amount to 5 percent or more of the total purchase price, is generally passed on to the buyer.
2. Builders, as a rule, secure better lot locations and at more favorable prices.
3. A planned "dream house" may turn out to be a financial nightmare. The cost of a ready-built house is readily known.
4. The home buyer has no "headaches" during home construction. Ready-made homes are available for inspection, and if the purchaser does not like it, he need not buy it.
5. Flaws in ready-built homes have matured and can be detected without difficulty by an expert architect or builder, either of whom should be called upon in an advisory capacity by the buyer.

If the building is old there are further economies that accrue to the purchaser:

1. Prices of old homes reflect a discount for lack of newness (and conversely there is an absence of premium for new conditions).
2. General sales resistance resulting from changes in modes of construction and home design causes old homes to sell at lowered prices.
3. Old homes show settlement and other flaws which have developed as the house matures, and allowance is made in the price to reflect such shortcomings.

There are, of course, disadvantages in purchasing a ready-built home which the wise buyer should also consider. For instance:

1. Homes built in anticipation of demand are built for profit, hence speculation.
2. The design of ready-built homes is standard and intended to please the average buyer, that is, every "Tom, Dick, and Harry." There is little individuality or homelike quality in mass-produced homes.
3. In ready-built homes, the needs of families must be subordinated to available space and design.
4. The quality of construction of mass-produced homes may be inferior to that obtained where construction is supervised by an architect representing the buyer.

Types of homes

When one approaches the problem of acquiring a home, no better advice can be given him than that he do just what he and his family will instinctively do, namely, look at all the papers, pamphlets, and literature they can find on the subject of houses. Many magazines feature home construction, design, and layout. It is always the desire of a home buyer that he have a home that is popular and in the current mode. He will find, very soon after he commences to study the pictures, that he is developing a style and popularity consciousness. It is also desirable to note the cost so that he may keep to the type and size of building that will fit his purse.

Not only must the type that the home buyer selects fit his purse and his own family's requirements but he should never finally fix on a type of building until he has selected the lot on which he intends to build. The topography of the lot will often have an important bearing. For example, a lot that has considerable contour, with a difference in ground level of as much as one story between the front and back of the house, will make entirely different the handling of the basement. On a flat lot, the basement will be simply for service, whereas on a lot that is a story different in level, the basement will be so arranged that the service rooms will be segregated and several rooms for real family use will be placed in the basement. Then, too, the home buyer must carefully bear in mind a number of the elements of value, such as the necessity of having a fair ratio of land cost to building cost, and the further necessity of selecting a type of building that is harmonious with the neighborhood as to both type and cost of other homes.

Prefabricated houses

This is a subject that is engaging the very serious attention of everyone in the building construction business and should be of concern to real estate men and home buyers. Simply stated, the prefabricated house is a building cut and constructed for the most part in a factory, then shipped to the plot upon which it is to be erected and there put together on the foundation. There are many variations of the method and scheme of prefabrication, and a brief explanation may be helpful. Let it be assumed that the owner of a lot intends to erect a frame building. Ordinarily he would have plans and specifications prepared and would submit them to a building contractor who would give an estimate of the cost of supplying the material and erecting the building. If the estimate is satisfactory, a contract is entered into for the building construction. The contractor then orders the material, and to a large extent the material is delivered at the location of the house in standard sizes and lengths. The carpenters then cut the lumber and put the house together. This process, of course, means that each building operation is a separate unit. It is about the most expensive way to construct a building.

Considerable expense is saved by developers who erect a number of buildings at a time, all following about the same general plan. Even the builder erecting one building will have certain parts of the work handled "at the mill." These would be such items as window frames and sash, doors and door frames.

The theory of prefabrication is that a great deal of the work ordinarily done on the job can be done in a factory in wholesale quantities and sold to the homeowner at a great saving. The homeowner selects the type of house he wants. Most of the prefabrication organizations have a number of designs. The owner, having selected a certain design, receives all the lumber needed for the erection of that house "ready cut," so that to a very large extent all that the carpenters have to do is fit the various pieces together and erect the house very rapidly. Some of the companies undertake as a part of their service the actual erection of the house. In the case of a garage, a truck with workmen and materials will appear in the morning and before the end of the day the garage is completed and has its first coat of paint. Some of the organizations will supply not only the ready-cut lumber but the proper amount of every single item, such as nails, plaster, and paint. Many organizations go to the extent of supplying the walls, both interior and exterior, in completed panels ready to be fastened together.

The market for and manufacture of prefabricated housing is steadily expanding. The one thing, more than any other, delaying progress is the opposition of organized labor as to how and where it may be used and as to what extent prefabrication of interior fixtures may be carried. Then, too, there is the unreadiness of the general public to accept the "ready-to-wear" idea of a home. Homes, as a matter of fact, are about the only things that have not yet been standardized. People still seem to desire individuality. As soon as the public realizes the great savings that may be had, there will be many more houses of the prefabricated type.

The obstacles to prefabricated houses are being slowly disposed of, but some of them may well be pointed out. Lightweight materials must be devised, or else transportation difficulties and expenses will eat up too much of the saving. Lots are of various shapes and sizes, and the contour of the ground is often not level. This condition creates engineering problems that cannot be overcome by prefabricated house plans that are too rigid. The house designs must be many and varied so as to take into consideration the fundamentally different types desirable in various parts of the country. The companies that sell these houses will have to give careful thought to the problem of financing and distribution. In many localities, building and other ordinances are so drawn (sometimes intentionally) as to make it almost impossible to erect prefabricated homes.

Importance of professional aid

The home purchaser is well advised to have his steps toward home ownership guided by competent professional aid which real estate brokers, appraisers, architects, and lawyers are prepared to offer. The real estate brokers are generally first contacted, because most lots and houses are offered for sale through their intervening services. The question is often raised,

Why deal through a broker? Can't the commission be saved by negotiating directly with the seller? Those who take this narrow view fail to realize that the broker renders necessary and important economic services for which the commission paid represents well-earned compensation. Some of the more important brokerage services which benefit the buyer and seller may be stated as follows:

Broker's Services Benefiting Buyer

1. Aid in speeding the selection of a home by offering valuable advice regarding city growth, neighborhood pattern, population and housing characteristics, value range, and kind of homes offered in the market.
2. Limiting inspection of homes to those that fit the pocketbook of the purchaser.
3. Safeguarding overpayment—for few brokers will waste time and money marketing overpriced properties.
4. Satisfaction of purchaser is in mind, for each satisfied buyer is a potential seller and client for other related services which brokers are prepared to offer in fields of management, insurance, financing, leasing, and selling.

Broker's Services Benefiting Seller

1. Advising as to reasonable asking price for the property offered for sale.
2. Reaching wider market through contacts with established brokers' and co-brokers' channels in other communities.
3. Separating the "suspects" from the "prospects" and thus saving annoyance resulting from sightseers and curiosity seekers who enjoy "house window-shopping."
4. Limiting visits to inspect homes to prearranged hours, thus saving inconvenience and possible embarrassment to occupying family.
5. Attending to actual negotiations, contract preparations, and details concerned with closing of title and transfer of property rights.

Although the intervening services of an established broker mitigate the chances of paying more than the property is worth, it should be remembered that the broker, in his capacity as agent, is duty bound to secure for his principal—the seller—the highest price that market conditions warrant. How then should the purchaser proceed to safeguard his interests? The answer, of course, lies in the employment of professional aid that will directly serve the buyer. After all, homes currently average well above $20,000 in price and no such sum should be committed without independent check as to the marketability of the investment at the offered price.

Perhaps one of the best safeguards that the buyer may adopt is to make the purchase contract contingent upon procurement of a maximum FHA, VA, or conventional mortgage loan. For where such loans are offered and bear a fair relation to purchase price, the buyer can rest assured that the sales price is fair and represents a conservative long-term value estimate. Where such contract provisions are denied, the purchaser should take recourse to employment of an independent appraiser who should be requested to submit a narrative report setting forth fully the reasoning underlying his value estimate and the conditions and assumptions of his value judgment. Since such professional services can be secured at fees that rarely exceed one-half of 1 percent of the purchase price of a home, it appears foolhardy to make a large and significant investment without the professional aid of a competent appraiser. The valuation of the home should, of course, take place in advance of contract commitments, for, once the purchaser signs on the dotted line, a change of mind may prove costly and legally burdensome.

Title search and title insurance

Under no circumstances should a buyer of real property sign a purchase agreement unless provision is made therein for the seller to deliver an unencumbered, good, and marketable title and one that a reputable title company or lawyers' title guild is willing to insure. This title should be subject to no other restrictions than those imposed by governmental authorities (zoning, building setback, and so forth) or deed restrictions that are intended to protect the property from inharmonious uses or undesirable occupation. The buyer should ever remember that even a warranty deed provides little protection unless the seller has a clear and conveyable title. Legally the seller cannot dispose of more than he rightfully owns, and if his title to land is faulty his possession may be effectively contested by the rightful owner. Of course, legal recourse may be had against the seller for damages in case of error, fraud, or negligence, but little consolation does that offer for the loss of one's home. It is assumed, too, that the seller can be brought before the bar of justice and that he still has means at his disposal with which to satisfy a judgment.

Even the formidable legal instrument known as an *Abstract of Title*, which a seller, in some states, is customarily required to bring up to date and to deliver to the purchaser for inspection, offers little protection to the prospective owner. In the first place, few men not legally trained can follow with understanding the technical language employed and fewer still are able to search and examine the required records to ascertain the validity of the statements made or whether title legally or even equitably can be conveyed. The wise buyer will insist that the purchase agreement is conditional upon delivery of a good, marketable, and insurable title subject to no other restrictions than those indicated above.

Since a purchase contract establishes the legal framework within which the transfer of property occurs, too much emphasis cannot be placed on the care with which this legal document should be drawn. At no stage of the purchase cycle does legal advice seem more important; every care should be taken to secure competent aid from an attorney.

The work of the architect

Whenever a home is to be erected in the conventional way, or a larger building for commercial or industrial use is contemplated, the work of the architect is important. He is consulted by those who wish to erect a building on land they own and by those who contemplate the purchase of land for a building operation. The owner determines the type of building to be erected, that is, whether it is to be a private dwelling, an apartment house, or a commercial building, and he furnishes the architect with a diagram or description of the plot. From this information, the architect advises concerning the size and shape of the proposed building, the arrangement of the rooms, and its probable cost. The information furnished by him often assists in determining whether or not the building will be a success commercially, or meet the needs of the homeowner.

The architect is employed to draw finished plans and specifications for proposed buildings and for alterations and additions to existing buildings. He prepares and approves contracts for the work to be performed; he approves payments to contractors and watches the progress of the building during construction. He guards the interests of his employer against fraud, overcharges, inferior work, delays, and violations of law. His work is sometimes in the interests of the mortgagee, reporting to the mortgagee on the quality of the material and the workmanship of the building. The architect often furnishes figures to be used as a basis for fixing the amount to be loaned. If the mortgage is advanced as a building loan, the advances are often made on certificates of the architect.

Decisions by the architect

When the architect is employed to superintend the construction, he may reject any part of the work not conforming to the specifications. In considering the rejection of any work, or in deciding any controversy between owner and contractor, he must be impartial. His judgment should be fair to both sides, even though he is retained and paid by the owner.

Necessary certificates

In many places, the authorities require certain certificates to be issued before a new building may be used for the purpose for which it was constructed. These may include a building department certificate, showing that the building code has not been violated; a tenement house department certificate, permitting occupancy of the building by three or more families; certificates of boards of fire underwriters and departments of gas and electricity as to electric wiring, motors, and fixtures; and, in the case of factories and loft buildings, certificates showing the weight that the various floors will sustain.

Home ownership and the role of government

Although land and its ownership, since time immemorial, has been subject to the powers of eminent domain, the police power, and the power of taxation, it is the ever-widening interpretation of these powers that causes concern to an increasing number of homeowners.

Under the power of eminent domain a government, local, state, or federal, may take private property provided it is to be used for public purposes and just compensation is paid the rightful owner. Under the police power the rights in property, its use, and occupation may be restricted—without any compensation whatsoever—when government deems such restrictions or seizure necessary in the interest of the welfare, morals, or safety of its citizens. It is to this power that citizens take recourse for city planning and zoning as well as for urban and subdivision control. But this power, it must be remembered, is also used by totalitarian states to socialize, or even sovietize, the home and other holdings.

Perhaps of greatest and most imminent interest to homeowners is the local government's power of taxation. It is this power that judges have held as equivalent to a power to destroy in instances where its abuse was deemed tantamount to property confiscation; for it is the net income residual to land that serves as a measure of land value, and any diminution of this amount through inequitable taxation should alert the owner to appropriate civic counteraction.

The role of government in housing should "point up" to homeowners their individual civic responsibilities. The home purchaser, in effect, acquires stock in an incorporated entity of which he and his fellow co-owners of land are an integral part. Like any other corporate undertaking, a community must organize and function with businesslike precision, for the resulting net income or losses in civic government are directly reflected in the desirability, marketability, and value of the community's homes and lands. To safeguard his interests, a homeowner thus should actively participate in general civic affairs by:

1. Intelligently discharging his right to vote
2. Attending public hearings concerning morals, health, and welfare
3. Joining and cooperating with civic organizations that promote city growth, civic pride, and cooperative city planning
4. Displaying civic-mindedness through proper home care and home maintenance
5. Increasing the amenities of home ownership through courtesy, neighborliness, and a wholesome display of hometown pride

Summary and conclusions

Home ownership constitutes to most people a significant step in life and undoubtedly represents the most important, if not the largest, single expenditure ever to be made by the typical home buyer. For this reason, the ways and means to sound home ownership should be carefully explored and well understood.

In this chapter an attempt has been made to highlight those principles and rules for buying that should guide the purchaser in the acquisition of a home and are deemed essential in assuring the enjoyments that follow a safe and sound investment. The more important principles of home ownership may be summarized as follows:

1. The pros and cons of owning versus renting a home should be thoroughly investigated and careful thought should be given to the care, both physical and mental, that home ownership imposes.

2. The ability to cope with the financial obligations without budgetary embarrassment or neglect of essential family and education requirements, too, is most important. There are many hidden costs which the prospective homeowner should unearth before saying "I do" on the dotted line of a purchase agreement. Home financing and budget calculations se-

cured or checked through local lending institutions may well serve as a safeguard against financial pitfalls that, too often in the past, have undermined both home and family security.

3. Timing, also, is a most important ingredient in the home purchase plan. There are short and extended hills and valleys in business activities, and purchase obligations undertaken in the wake of a postwar boom or during periods of short supply may impose a price that spells serious financial handicaps or may even lead to home investment losses when the inflationary honeymoon comes to an end.

4. The urge for home ownership, further, should be sufficiently controlled to permit selection of a place conducive to family and home contentment. A house should be viewed as more than mere mortar and stone, and every precaution should be taken to ascertain that present and prospective family life blends with the environment and generally absorbs from it a wholesome influence.

5. Because of the sacrifice and magnitude of savings necessary to back the purchase of a home, care should be taken to consider thoughtfully and without haste the steps and problems that precede home ownership. Whether a house is built or bought, the planning, examining, and evaluating of the structure and the land upon which it stands should not be undertaken without professional aid.

6. In all instances, prior consideration should be given to the utility of a home as a means to more enjoyable and all-around better living; only secondary consideration should be given to the enhancement or speculative possibilities of the home investment. Where design for living is paramount in the purchaser's mind, the chances are greatly improved to promote his active and constructive participation in essential civic and community affairs.

READING AND STUDY REFERENCES

1. HESS, NANCY R., "Economics of Home Ownership," Volume XXIV. Economic Leaflet, University of Florida, Gainesville, Florida, November 1965.

2. ———, "Preliminary Decisions in Planning a Home," Volume XXIV. Economic Leaflet, University of Florida, Gainesville, Florida, August 1965.

3. KENDALL, LEON T., Thrift and Home Ownership, United States Savings and Loan League, 1962.

4. RATCLIFF, RICHARD U., Real Estate Analysis, Chapter 8. New York: McGraw-Hill Book Company, 1961.

5. RING, ALFRED A., Questions and Problems in Real Estate Principles and Practices (rev. ed.), Chapter 28. Englewood Cliffs, N.J.: Prentice-Hall, Inc., 1972.

6. UNGER, MAURICE A., Real Estate (4th ed.), Chapter 10. Cincinnati: South-Western Publishing Co., 1969.

PLOT PLAN AND DRAINAGE PLAN
LOT 32, LIBBY HEIGHTS S/D
ALACHUA COUNTY, FLORIDA
(SCALE: 1″ = 10′)

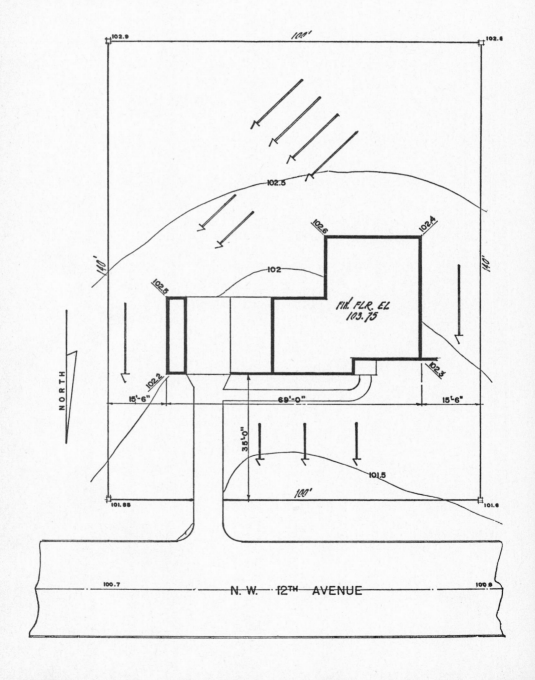

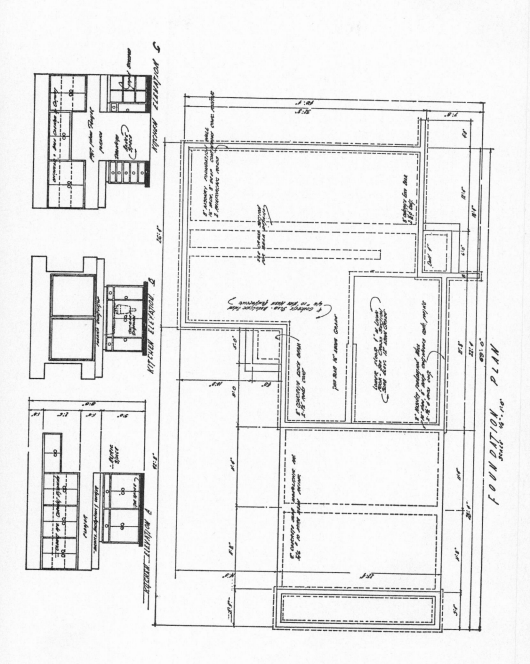

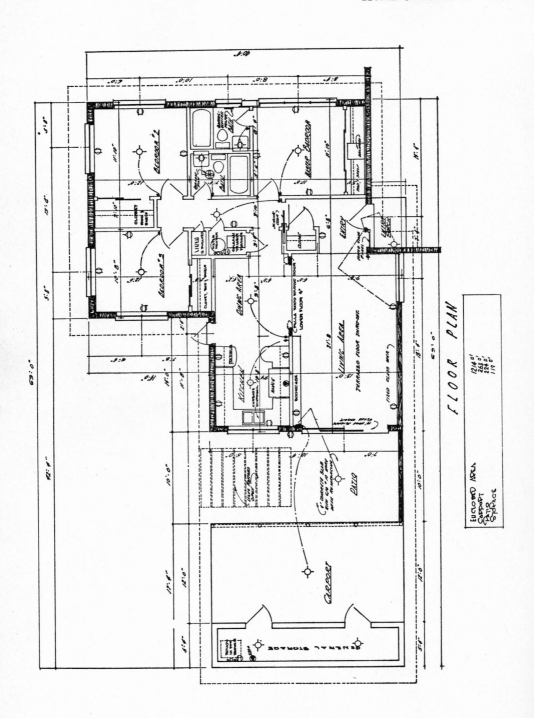

FLOOR PLAN

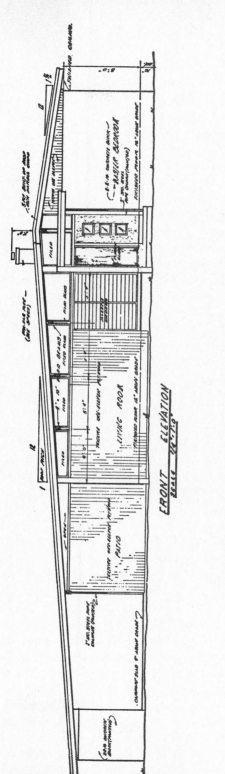

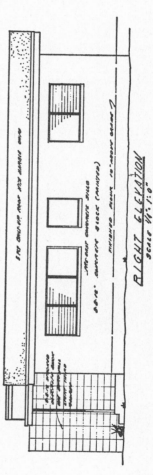

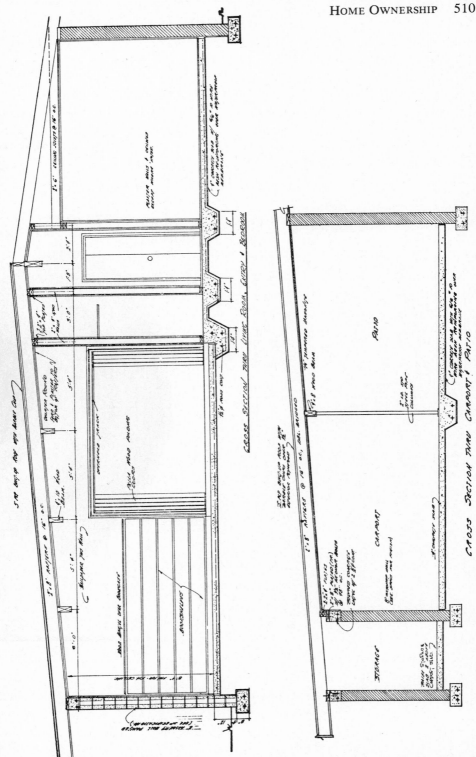

CROSS SECTION THRU LIVING ROOM, ENTRY & BEDROOM

CROSS SECTION THRU CARPORT & PATIO

VA Form VB4-1852
FHA Form 2005
Jan. 1955

For accurate register of carbon copies, form
may be separated along above fold. Staple
completed sheets together in original order.

Form approved.
Budget Bureau No. 63–R055.9

☐ Proposed Construction

☐ Under Construction

DESCRIPTION OF MATERIALS

No. ....
(To be inserted by FHA or VA)

Property address _Lot 26 Block A_ _First Addition to Church Estates_ City _Gainesville_ State _Florida_

Mortgagor or Sponsor _Hugh Edwards Inc_ _1 NW 10th Ave_
(Name) (Address)

Contractor or Builder _Hugh Edwards Inc_ _1 NW 10 Ave_
(Name) (Address)

INSTRUCTIONS

1. For additional information on how this form is to be submitted, number of copies, etc., see the instructions applicable to the FHA Application for Mortgage Insurance or VA Request for Determination of Reasonable Value, as the case may be.

2. Describe all materials and equipment to be used, whether or not shown on the drawings, by marking an X in each appropriate check-box and entering the information called for in each space. If space is inadequate, enter "See misc." and describe under item 27 or on an attached sheet.

3. Work not specifically described or shown will not be considered unless required, when the minimum acceptable will be assumed. Work exceeding

minimum requirements cannot be considered unless specifically described.

4. Include no alternates, "or equal" phrases, or contradictory items. (Consideration of a request for acceptance of substitute materials or equipment is not thereby precluded.)

5. Include signatures required at the end of this form.

6. The construction shall be completed in compliance with the related drawings and specifications, as amended during processing. The specifications include this Description of Materials and the applicable Minimum Construction Requirements.

1. EXCAVATION:
Bearing soil, type _Sandy Loam_

2. FOUNDATIONS:
Footings: Concrete mix _2500 psi_ Reinforcing _2 ½" 4 bars (cont)_
Foundation wall: Material _8·8·16 Concrete Block_ Reinforcing ....
Interior foundation wall: Material .... Party foundation wall ....
Columns: Material and size .... Piers: Material and reinforcing ....
Girders: Material and sizes .... Sills: Material ....
Basement entrance areaway .... Window areaways ....
Waterproofing .... Footing drains ....
Termite protection _Soil Treated_
Basementless space: Ground cover .... Insulation .... Foundation vents ....
Special foundations ....

3. CHIMNEYS:
Material _Metal Asbestos_ Prefabricated (make and size) _6" Vibracoler_
Flue lining: Material .... Heater flue size .... Fireplace flue size ....
Vents (material and size): Gas or oil heater .... Water heater ....

4. FIREPLACES:
Type: ☐ Solid fuel; ☐ gas-burning; ☐ circulator (make and size) .... Ash dump and clean-out ....
Fireplace: Facing ....; lining ....; hearth ....; mantel ....

5. EXTERIOR WALLS:
Wood frame: Grade and species .... ☐ Corner bracing. Building paper or felt ....
Sheathing ....; thickness ....; width ....; ☐ solid; ☐ spaced ...." o. c.; ☐ diagonal; ....
Siding ....; grade ....; type ....; size ....; exposure ...."; fastening ....
Shingles ....; grade ....; type ....; size ....; exposure ...."; fastening ....
Stucco ....; thickness ...." Lath ....; weight .... lb.
Masonry veneer .... Sills .... Lintels ....
Masonry: Facing _Conc Blk_; backup _Conc Blk_ thickness _8_". Bonding _½ Mortar_
Door sills _Concrete_ Window sills _Precast_ Lintels _Blocks & Formed (cont)_
Interior surfaces: Dampproofing _2_ coats of _Plaster_; furring _1 x 2 treated @ 16" oc_
Exterior painting: Material _Waterproofing_; number of coats ....
Gable wall construction: ☐ Same as main walls; ☐ other _¼" tempered masonite_

R FRAMING:
s: Wood, grade and species _____; other _____; bridging _____; anchors _____
ete slab: □ Basement floor; □ first floor; □ ground supported; □ self-supporting; mix _____; thickness ____"
nforcing _____; insulation _____; membrane _____
nder slab: Material _____; thickness ____".

LOORING: (Describe underflooring for special floors under item 21.)
rial: Grade and species _____; size _____; type _____
□ First floor; □ second floor; □ attic _____ sq. ft.; □ diagonal; □ right angles. _____

H FLOORING: (Wood only. Describe other finish flooring under item 21.)

OCATION	ROOMS	GRADE	SPECIES	THICKNESS	WIDTH	BLDG. PAPER	FINISH
floor							
nd floor							
floor	sq. ft.						

TITION FRAMING:
s: Wood, grade and species *2 Yellow Pine* Size and spacing *2"x4"@16" O.C.* Other
TERMITE 2x6 STUDS FOR ALL VENT & WASTE LINES

ING FRAMING:
s: Wood, grade and species *#2 Yellow Pine* Other _____ Bridging *1"x3" WHERE NEEDED*

F FRAMING:
ers: Wood, grade and species *#2 Yellow Pine* Roof trusses (see detail): Grade and species _____

FING:
thing: Grade and species *CD Plywood*; size *½"x4'x8'*; type *CD*; ☑solid; □ spaced ____" o.c.
ng *ASPHALT*; grade ____; weight or thickness ____; size ____; fastening ____
a or paint ____ Underlay ____
up roofing *ASPHALT*; number of plies *5*; surfacing material *MARBLE CHIPS*
hing: Material *GALVANIZED IRON*; gage or weight *26*; ☑gravel stops; □ snow guards

TERS AND DOWNSPOUTS:
ers: Material *GALV IRON*; gage or weight *26*; size *5"*; shape *O.G.*
nspouts: Material *GALV IRON*; gage or weight *26*; size *4*; shape *SQUARE*; number *SEE PLAN*
nspouts connected to: □ Storm sewer; □ sanitary sewer; □ dry-well. ☑Splash blocks: Material and size *CONCRETE 16x16"*

I AND PLASTER:
☑walls, ☑ceilings: Material *ROCKLATH*; weight or thickness *3/8"* Plaster: Coats *2*; finish *SAND GENERALLY EXCEPT KITCH. & BATH*
wall □ walls, □ ceilings: Material ____; thickness ____; finish ____; joint treatment ____

RATING: (Paint, wallpaper, etc.)

ROOMS	WALL FINISH MATERIAL AND APPLICATION	CEILING FINISH MATERIAL AND APPLICATION
en	Undercoat & 1 Co. Enamel (Washable)	Plaster
	Undercoat & 1 Co. Enamel (Washable)	Plaster
t of House	Undercoat & 1 coat Oil	Plaster

RIOR DOORS AND TRIM:
s: Type *FLUSH*; material *LAUAN MAHOGANY*; thickness *1 3/8"*
trim: Type *STOCK*; material *LARCH* Base: Type *STOCK*; material *LARCH*; size *4"*
h: Doors *1 co. shellac & 1 co. varnish*; trim *SAME*
r trim (item, type and location) *Note: Cover all surfaces completely and thoroughly*

17. WINDOWS:

Windows: Type _Jalousie_; make _No. Air_; material _Aluminum_; sash thickness _____

Glass: Grade _Sheet or Plate_; ☐ sash weights; ☐ balances, type _____; head flashing _____

Trim: Type _Std._; material _Aluminum_   Paint _____; number coats _____

Weatherstripping: Type _____; material _Neo-Prene_   Storm sash, number _____

Screens: ☒ Full; ☐ half; type _____; number _See Plans_; screen cloth material _Aluminum_

Basement windows: Type _____; material _____; ☐ screens, number _____; ☐ Storm sash, number _____

Special windows _____

18. ENTRANCES AND EXTERIOR DETAIL:

Main entrance door: Material _Jalousie_; width _3'0"_; thickness _1¾"_. Frame: Material _Edge Grain Fir_; thickness _¾"_

Other entrance doors: Material _Jalousie_; width _2'8"_; thickness _¾"_. Frame: Material _Same_; thickness _¾"_

Head flashing _____   Weatherstripping: Type _Neo-Prene_; saddles _Aluminum_

Screen doors: Thickness _____"; number _____; screen cloth material _____   Storm doors: Thickness _____"; number _____

Combination storm and screen doors: Thickness _____"; number _____; screen cloth material _____

Shutters: ☐ Hinged; ☐ fixed.   Railings _____   Louvers _____

Exterior millwork: Grade and species _____   Paint _Lead & Oil_; number coats _2_

19. CABINETS AND INTERIOR DETAIL:

Kitchen cabinets, wall units: Material _Wood_; lineal feet of shelves _See Plans_; shelf width _12_

Base units: Material _Wood_; counter top _Formica_; edging _Sta. Steel_

Back and end splash _Formica_   Finish of cabinets _Color Baked Enamel_; number coats _2_

Medicine cabinets: Make _Std. Mfg._; model _____

Other cabinets and built-in furniture _Linen Closet - 5 Shelves and Laundry Hamper_

20. STAIRS:

Stair	Treads		Risers		Strings		Handrail		Balusters	
	Material	Thickness	Material	Thickness	Material	Size	Material	Size	Material	Size
Basement										
Main										
Attic										

Disappearing: Make and model number _____

21. SPECIAL FLOORS AND WAINSCOT:

	Location	Material, Color, Border, Sizes, Gage, Etc.	Threshold	Base	Underfloor
Floors	Kitchen	TERRAZZO		WOOD	CONC.
	Bath	TERRAZZO		TILE	CONC.
	REST. OF HOUSE TERRAZZO			WOOD	CONC.

	Location	Material, Color, Border, Cap, Sizes, Gage, Etc.	Height	Height at Tub	Height at Shower
Wainscot	Bath	CERAMIC TILE	48"	72"	72"

Bathroom accessories: ☒ Recessed; material _Tile_; number _5_; ☐ attached; material _____; number _____

22. PLUMBING:

Fixture	Number	Location	Make	Mfgr's Fixture Identification No.	Size	Color
Sink	1	Kitchen	American Std.	7016	32" x 21	White
Lavatory	2	Baths	"	P 4100	19" x 17"	White
Water closet	2	Baths	"	P 2112 (Cadet)	–	White
Bathtub	2	Baths	"	P 225	60" x 32"	White
Shower over tub*	2	Baths	"			
Stall shower**						
Laundry trays						

*☑ Curtain rod **☐ Door ☐ Curtain rod
Water supply: ☑ Public; ☐ community system; ☐ individual (private) system. ★
Sewage disposal: ☑ Public; ☐ community system; ☐ individual (private) system. ★
★*Show and describe individual system in complete detail in separate drawings and specifications according to requirements.*
House drain (inside): ☑ Cast iron; ☐ tile; ☐ other _____ House sewer (outside): ☑ Cast iron; ☐ tile; ☐ other _____
Water piping: ☑ Galvanized steel; ☐ copper tubing; ☐ other _____ Sill cocks, number *2*
Domestic water heater: Type *ROUND* _____ ; make and model *GENERAL ELECTRIC* _____
  recovery _____ gph. 100° rise. Storage tank: Material *GALV. STEEL* _____ ; capacity *90* _____ gallons.
Gas service: ☐ Utility company; ☐ liq. pet. gas; ☐ other _____ Gas piping: ☐ Cooking; ☐ house heating.
Footing drains connected to: ☐ Storm sewer; ☐ sanitary sewer; ☐ dry well. Sump pump _____

23. HEATING:
☐ Hot water. ☐ Steam. ☐ Vapor. ☐ One-pipe system. ☐ Two-pipe system.
  ☐ Radiators. ☐ Convectors. ☐ Baseboard radiation. Make and model _____
  Radiant panel: ☐ Floor; ☐ wall; ☐ ceiling. Panel coil: Material _____
  ☐ Circulator. ☐ Return pump. Make and model _____ ; capacity _____ gpm.
  Boiler: Make and model _____ Output _____ Btuh.; net rating _____ Btuh.

Warm air: ☐ Gravity. ☑ Forced. Type of system *RADIAL DUCTS (OVERHEAD)*
  Duct material: Supply *ROUND* ; return *ROUND* Insulation *FIBERGLAS* thickness *1"* ☑ Outside air intake.
  Furnace: Make and model *COLEMAN # 2701- 759* Input *80,000* Btuh.; output *64,000* Btuh.
  THERMOSTAT CONTROLLED
☐ Space heater; ☐ floor furnace; ☐ wall heater. Input _____ Btuh.; output _____ Btuh.; number units _____
  Make, model _____

Controls: Make and types *COLEMAN AUTOMATIC*

Fuel: ☐ Coal; ☐ oil; ☐ gas; ☑ liq. pet. gas; ☐ electric; ☐ other _____ ; storage capacity *250 GAL.*

Firing equipment furnished separately: ☐ Gas burner, conversion type. Stoker: ☐ Hopper feed; ☐ bin feed.
  Oil burner: ☐ Pressure atomizing; ☐ vaporizing
  Make and model _____ Control _____

Electric heating system: Type *WALL TYPE MARKEL* Input *1000* watts; @ *120* volts; output *3800* Btuh.
  HEATER LOCATED IN MASTER BATH (THERMOSTAT CONTROLLED)
Ventilating equipment: Attic fan, make and model _____ ; capacity _____ cfm.
  Kitchen exhaust fan, make and model *10" NUTONE EXHAUST FAN OVER RANGE*
Other heating, ventilating, or cooling equipment _____

24. ELECTRIC WIRING:
Service: ☑ Overhead; ☐ underground. Panel: ☐ Fuse box; ☑ circuit-breaker _____ Number circuits *PER CODE*
Wiring: ☐ Conduit; ☐ armored cable; ☑ nonmetallic cable; ☐ knob and tube; ☐ other _____
Special outlets: ☑ Range; ☑ water heater; ☐ other _____
☑ Doorbell. ☐ Chimes. Push-button locations _____

25. LIGHTING FIXTURES:
Total number of fixtures *SEE BLDR* Total allowance for fixtures, typical installation, $ *60.00*
Nontypical installation _____

26. INSULATION:

LOCATION	THICKNESS	MATERIAL, TYPE, AND METHOD OF INSTALLATION	VAPOR BARRIER
Roof			
Ceiling	*2" MIN*	*ROCKWOOL BATTS BETWEEN CEILING JOISTS*	
Wall			
Floor			

27. MISCELLANEOUS:
(*Describe any main dwelling materials, equipment, or construction items not shown elsewhere*):_____

HARDWARE: (*Make, material, and finish*) *Weiser Brass - Aluminum Finish*

SPECIAL EQUIPMENT: (*State material or make and model.*)
Venetian blinds *Aluminum* — Number *See Plans* — Automatic washer _____
Kitchen range _____ Clothes drier _____
Refrigerator _____ Other _____
Dishwasher _____
Garbage disposal unit *Model FA 60, General Electric*

PORCHES: (*ENTRY*)
Reinforced concrete footing. Concrete block foundation and 4" concrete slab with 6/6 10 wire mesh. 2" ID steel column supports. Ceiling to be ¼" tempered masonite (painted). 5 ply built up roof with marble chips.

TERRACES:

GARAGES:
Concrete footing, 4" conc slab (reinf) ceiling to be ¼" tempered masonite, roof same as house.

WALKS AND DRIVEWAYS:
Driveway: Width *8'* Base material *Sand*; thickness ... Surfacing material *Concrete*; thickness *4"*
Front walk: Width *3* Material *Concrete*; thickness *4"*. Service walk: Width ___ Material ___; thickness ___"
Steps: Material ___; treads ___"; risers ___". Cheek walls ___"
8'0 wide drive to street; 3'0" wide walk to drive

OTHER ONSITE IMPROVEMENTS:
(*Specify all exterior onsite improvements not described elsewhere, including items such as unusual grading, drainage structures, retaining walls, fence, railings, and accessory structures.*)

LANDSCAPING, PLANTING, AND FINISH GRADING:
Topsoil ___" thick; ☐ Front yard; ☐ side yards; ☐ rear yard to ___ feet behind main building.
Lawns (*seeded, sodded, or sprigged*): ☒ Front yard *Sprigged* ☒ side yards *Sprigged*; ☒ rear yard *15' rear of house*
Planting: ☐ As specified and shown on drawings; ☐ as follows:
1 — Shade trees, deciduous, ___" caliper.
___ Low flowering trees, deciduous, ___' to ___'
___ High-growing shrubs, deciduous, ___' to ___'
12-15 Medium-growing shrubs, deciduous, *1* to *1½'*
___ Low-growing shrubs, deciduous, ___' to ___'
___ Evergreen trees, ___' to ___', B & B.
___ Evergreen shrubs, ___' to ___', B & B.
___ Vines, 2-year

IDENTIFICATION.—This exhibit shall be identified by the signature of the builder, or sponsor, and/or the proposed mortgagor if the latter is known at the time of application.

Date _____ Signature _____

APPENDICES

FACTS TO ASCERTAIN BEFORE DRAWING
A CONTRACT OF SALE

1. Date of contract.
2. Name and address of seller.
3. Is seller a citizen, of full age, and competent?
4. Name of seller's wife and whether she is of full age.
5. Name and residence of purchaser.
6. Description of the property.
7. The purchase price.
   a. Amount to be paid on signing contract.
   b. Amount to be paid on delivery of deed.
   c. Existing mortgage or mortgages and details thereof.
   d. Purchase money mortgage, if any, and details thereof.
8. What kind of deed is to be delivered: full covenant, quitclaim, or bargain and sale?
9. What agreement has been made with reference to any specific personal property, i.e., gas ranges, heaters, machinery, partitions, fixtures, coal, wood, window shades, screens, carpets, rugs, and hangings?
10. Is purchaser to assume the mortgage or take the property subject to it?
11. Are any exceptions or reservations to be inserted?
12. Are any special clauses to be inserted?
13. Stipulations and agreements with reference to tenancies and rights of persons in possession, including compliance with any governmental regulations in force.

14. Stipulations and agreements, if any, to be inserted with reference to the state of facts a survey would show: i.e., party walls, encroachments, easements, and so forth.
15. What items are to be adjusted on the closing of title?
16. Name of the broker who brought about the sale, his address, the amount of his commission and who is to pay it, and whether or not a clause covering the foregoing facts is to be inserted in the contract.
17. Are any alterations or changes being made, or have they been made, in street lines, name, or grade?
18. Are condemnations or assessment proceedings contemplated or pending, or has an award been made?
19. Who is to draw the purchase money mortgage and who is to pay the expense thereof?
20. Are there any covenants, restrictions, and consents affecting the title?
21. What stipulation or agreement is to be made with reference to Tenement Building Department and other violations?
22. The place and date on which the title is to be closed.
23. Is time to be of the essence in the contract?
24. Are any alterations to be made in the premises between the date of the contract and the date of closing?
25. Amount of fire and hazard insurance, payment of premium, and rights and obligations of parties in case of fire or damage to premises from other causes during the contract period.

UPON THE CLOSING OF TITLE, THE SELLER SHOULD BE PREPARED WITH THE FOLLOWING

1. Seller's copy of the contract.
2. The latest tax, water, and assessment receipted bills.
3. Latest possible meter readings of water, gas or electric utilities.
4. Receipts for last payment of interest on mortgages.
5. Originals and certificates of all fire, liability, and other insurance policies.
6. Estoppel certificates from the holder of any mortgage that has been reduced showing the amount due and the date to which interest is paid.
7. Any subordination agreements that may be called for in the contract.
8. Satisfaction pieces of mechanic's liens, chattel mortgages, judgments, or mortgages that are to be paid at or prior to the closing.
9. List of names of tenants, amounts of rents paid and unpaid, dates when rents are due, and assignment of unpaid rents.
10. Assignment of leases.
11. Letters to tenants to pay all subsequent rent to the purchaser.
12. Affidavit of title.
13. Authority to execute deed if the seller is acting through an agent.
14. Bill of Sale of personal property covered by the contract.
15. Seller's last deed.
16. Any unrecorded instruments that affect the title, including extension agreements.
17. Deed and other instruments that the seller is to deliver or prepare.

UPON THE CLOSING OF TITLE, THE PURCHASER SHOULD DO THE FOLLOWING

1. Have purchaser's copy of contract.
2. Obtain abstract of title.
3. Obtain report of title.
4. Examine deed to see if it conforms to the contract.

5. Compare description.
6. See that deed is properly executed.
7. Have sufficient cash or certified checks to make payments required by contract.
8. See that all liens which must be removed are properly disposed of.
9. Obtain names and details with reference to tenants and rents.
10. Obtain assignment of unpaid rents and assignment of leases.
11. Obtain and examine estoppel certificates with reference to mortgages that have been reduced.
12. Obtain letter to tenants.
13. Obtain affidavit of title.
14. Obtain and examine authority if the seller acts through an agent.
15. Obtain Bill of Sale of personal property covered by the contract.
16. Examine survey.
17. See if report of title shows any covenants, restrictions, or consents affecting the title or use of the property.
18. Have bills for any unpaid tax, utilities, or assessments, and have interest computed up to the date of closing.
19. Make adjustments as called for in the contract.
20. Examine purchase money mortgage and duly execute same.
21. Have damage award, if any, for public improvements assigned to the purchaser.
22. Obtain any unrecorded instruments affecting the title, including extension agreements.

LAND MEASUREMENT TABLE

ACREAGE

Acres	Square Feet	1 Acre Equals Rectangle	
		Width	Length
1	43,560		
2	87,120	16.5	2640.
3	130,680	33.	1320.
4	174,240	50.	871.2
5	217,800	66.	660.
6	261,360	75.	580.8
7	304,920	100.	435.6
8	348,480	132.	330.
9	392,040	150.	290.4
10	435,600	208.71	208.71

RULES FOR MEASURING LAND

The following rules will be found of service in many cases that may arise in land parceling, particularly in the computation of areas:

To find the area of a four-sided tract, whose sides are perpendicular to each other (called a rectangle): Multiply the length by the width, and the product will be the area.

To find the area of a four-sided tract, whose opposite sides are parallel, but whose angles are not necessarily right angles (called a parallelogram): Multiply the base by the perpendicular height, and the product will be the area.

To find the area of a three-sided tract (called a triangle): Multiply the base by half of the perpendicular height, and the product will be the area.

To find the area of a four-sided tract, having two of its sides parallel, called a trapezoid): Multiply half the sum of the two parallel sides by the perpendicular distance between these sides, and the product will be the area.

To ascertain the contents of a tract bounded by four straight lines, and in which no two lines are parallel to each other, the length of each line is known, and the two opposite angles are supplements of each other (called a trapezium): Add all the four sides together, and halve their sum; subtract separately each side from that sum; and the four remainders thus obtained multiply continually together, and extract the square root of the last product. The result will be the contents or area of the tract. Or, divide the tract by lines into triangles and trapezoids, and ascertain and add together their several areas, the sum of which will be the area of the tract proposed.

Land bounded by an irregular line, such as a stream of water or a winding road, is measured as follows: Draw a base line as near as practicable to the actual line of the road or stream; at different places in the base line, equidistant from each other, take the distance to the line of the stream or road. Add the sum of all the intermediate lines (or breadths) to half the sum of the first breadth and the last breadth, and multiply the sum thus obtained by the common distance between the breadths. The result will be the area of the land in question.

Should the breadths be measured at unequal distances on the base line, add all the breadths together, and divide their amount by the number of breadths for the mean breadth, and multiply the quotient so obtained by the length of the base line.

MEASUREMENT TABLES

Table of Linear Measure

12 inches (in.)	= 1 foot	ft.
3 feet	= 1 yard	yd.
5½ yards or 16½ feet	= 1 rod	rd.
40 rods	= 1 furlong	fur.
8 furlongs, 320 rods, or 5,280 feet ...	= 1 statute mile	mi.

Table of Square Measure

144 square inches (sq. in.)	= 1 square foot	sq. ft.
9 square feet	= 1 square yard	sq. yd.
30¼ square yards	= 1 square rod	sq. rd.
40 square rods	= 1 rood	R.
4 roods or 43,560 square feet	= 1 acre	A.
640 acres	= 1 square mile	sq. mi.

Table of Surveyor's Linear Measure

7.92 inches (in.)	= 1 link	l.
25 links	= 1 rod	rd.
4 rods or 66 feet	= 1 chain	ch.
80 chains	= 1 mile	mi.

Table of Surveyor's Square Measure

625 square links (sq. l.)	= 1 pole	P.
16 poles	= 1 square chain	sq. ch.
10 square chains	= 1 acre	A.
640 acres	= 1 square mile	sq. mi.
36 square miles (6 mi. square)	= 1 township	Tp.

Note: 1 acre in square form equals 208.71 feet on each side.

FUTURE WORTH OF A DEPOSIT OF $1.00 COMPOUNDED
AT ½ PERCENT INTEREST
PER PERIOD

Number of Periods	Growth of $1.00*	Growth of $1.00 Per Period**	Deposit Needed to Accumulate $1.00†
1	1.005 000	1.000 000	1.000 000
2	1.010 025	2.005 000	.498 753
3	1.015 075	3.015 025	.331 672
4	1.020 151	4.030 100	.248 133
5	1.025 251	5.050 251	.198 010
6	1.030 378	6.075 502	.164 595
7	1.035 529	7.105 879	.140 729
8	1.040 707	8.141 409	.122 829
9	1.045 911	9.182 116	.108 907
10	1.051 140	10.228 026	.097 771
11	1.056 396	11.279 167	.088 659
12	1.061 678	12.335 562	.081 066
13	1.066 986	13.397 240	.074 642
14	1.072 321	14.464 226	.069 136
15	1.077 683	15.536 548	.064 364
16	1.083 071	16.614 230	.060 189
17	1.088 487	17.697 301	.056 506
18	1.093 929	18.785 788	.053 232
19	1.099 399	19.879 717	.050 303
20	1.104 896	20.979 115	.047 666
21	1.110 420	22.084 011	.045 282
22	1.115 972	23.194 431	.043 114
23	1.121 552	24.310 403	.041 135
24	1.127 160	25.431 955	.039 321
25	1.132 796	26.559 115	.037 652

*How $1 left at compound interest will grow (deposit made at beginning of period). Formula: $s = P(1 + i)^n$

**How $1 deposited periodically will grow (deposit made at end of period). For deposits made at the beginning of the period, subtract 1 from the amount shown in the following period.
Formula: $S_n = \dfrac{(1 + i)^n - 1}{i}$

†Periodic deposit that will grow to $1 at a future date (deposits made at end of period). Formula: $\dfrac{1}{S_n} = \dfrac{i}{(1 + i)^n - 1}$

AT ½ PERCENT INTEREST

Number of Periods	Growth of $1.00*	Growth of $1.00 per Period**	Deposit Needed to Accumulate $1.00†
26	1.128 460	27.691 911	.036 112
27	1.144 152	28.830 370	.034 686
28	1.149 873	29.974 522	.033 362
29	1.155 622	31.124 395	.032 129
30	1.161 400	32.280 017	.030 979
31	1.167 207	33.441 417	.029 903
32	1.173 043	34.608 624	.028 895
33	1.178 908	35.781 667	.027 947
34	1.184 803	36.960 575	.027 056
35	1.190 727	38.145 378	.026 215
36	1.196 681	39.336 105	.025 422
37	1.202 664	40.532 785	.024 671
38	1.208 677	41.735 449	.023 960
39	1.214 721	42.944 127	.023 286
40	1.220 794	44.158 847	.022 646
41	1.226 898	45.379 642	.022 036
42	1.233 033	46.606 540	.021 456
43	1.239 198	47.839 572	.020 903
44	1.245 394	49.078 770	.020 375
45	1.251 621	50.324 164	.019 871
46	1.257 879	51.575 785	.019 389
47	1.264 168	52.833 664	.018 927
48	1.270 489	54.097 832	.018 485
49	1.276 842	55.368 321	.018 061
50	1.283 226	56.645 163	.017 654

*How $1 left at compound interest will grow (deposit made at beginning of period). Formula: $s = P(1 + i)^n$

**How $1 deposited periodically will grow (deposit made at end of period). For deposits made at the beginning of the period, subtract 1 from the amount shown in the following period.
Formula: $S_n = \dfrac{(1 + i)^n - 1}{i}$

†Periodic deposit that will grow to $1 at a future date (deposits made at end of period). Formula: $\dfrac{1}{S_n} = \dfrac{i}{(1 + i)^n - 1}$

FUTURE WORTH OF A DEPOSIT OF $1.00 COMPOUNDED
AT 3 PERCENT INTEREST
PER PERIOD

Number of Periods	Growth of $1.00*	Growth of $1.00 per Period**	Deposit Needed to Accumulate $1.00†
1	1.030 000	1.000 000	1.000 000
2	1.060 900	2.030 000	.492 611
3	1.092 727	3.090 900	.323 530
4	1.125 509	4.183 627	.239 027
5	1.159 274	5.309 136	.188 355
6	1.194 052	6.468 410	.154 598
7	1.229 874	7.662 462	.130 506
8	1.266 770	8.892 336	.112 456
9	1.304 773	10.159 106	.098 434
10	1.343 916	11.463 879	.087 231
11	1.384 234	12.807 796	.078 077
12	1.425 761	14.192 030	.070 462
13	1.468 534	15.617 790	.064 030
14	1.512 590	17.086 324	.058 526
15	1.557 967	18.598 914	.053 767
16	1.604 706	20.156 881	.049 611
17	1.652 848	21.761 588	.045 953
18	1.702 433	23.414 435	.042 709
19	1.753 506	25.116 868	.039 814
20	1.806 111	26.870 374	.037 216
21	1.860 295	28.676 486	.034 872
22	1.916 103	30.536 780	.032 747
23	1.973 587	32.452 884	.030 814
24	2.032 794	34.426 470	.029 047
25	2.093 778	36.459 264	.027 428

*How $1 left at compound interest will grow (deposit made at beginning of period). Formula: $s = P(1+i)^n$

**How $1 deposited periodically will grow (deposit made at end of period). For deposits made at the beginning of the period, subtract 1 from the amount shown in the following period.
Formula: $S_n = \dfrac{(1+i)^n - 1}{i}$

†Periodic deposit that will grow to $1 at a future date (deposits made at end of period). Formula: $\dfrac{1}{S_n} = \dfrac{i}{(1+i)^n - 1}$

AT 3 PERCENT INTEREST

Number of Periods	Growth of $1.00*	Growth of $1.00 per Period**	Deposit Needed to Accumulate $1.00†
26	2.156 591	38.553 042	.025 938
27	2.221 289	40.709 634	.024 564
28	2.287 928	42.930 923	.023 293
29	2.356 566	45.218 850	.022 115
30	2.427 262	47.575 416	.021 019
31	2.500 080	50.002 678	.019 999
32	2.575 083	52.502 759	.019 047
33	2.652 335	55.077 841	.018 156
34	2.731 905	57.730 177	.017 322
35	2.813 862	60.462 082	.016 539
36	2.898 278	63.275 944	.015 804
37	2.985 227	66.174 223	.015 112
38	3.074 783	69.159 449	.014 459
39	3.167 027	72.234 233	.013 844
40	3.262 038	75.401 260	.013 262
41	3.359 899	78.663 298	.012 713
42	3.460 696	82.023 196	.012 192
43	3.564 517	85.483 892	.011 698
44	3.671 452	89.048 409	.011 230
45	3.781 596	92.719 861	.010 785
46	3.895 044	96.502 457	.010 363
47	4.011 895	100.396 501	.009 961
48	4.132 252	104.408 396	.009 578
49	4.256 219	108.540 648	.009 213
50	4.383 906	112.796 867	.008 865

*How $1 left at compound interest will grow (deposit made at beginning of period). Formula: $s = P(1 + i)^n$

**How $1 deposited periodically will grow (deposit made at end of period). For deposits made at the beginning of the period, subtract 1 from the amount shown in the following period. Formula: $S_n = \dfrac{(1 + i)^n - 1}{i}$

†Periodic deposit that will grow to $1 at a future date (deposits made at end of period). Formula: $\dfrac{1}{S_n} = \dfrac{i}{(1 + i)^n - 1}$

FUTURE WORTH OF A DEPOSIT OF $1.00 COMPOUNDED AT 4 PERCENT INTEREST PER PERIOD

Number of Periods	Growth of $1.00*	Growth of $1.00 per Period**	Deposit Needed to Accumulate $1.00†
1	1.040 000	1.000 000	1.000 000
2	1.081 600	2.040 000	.490 196
3	1.124 864	3.121 600	.320 349
4	1.169 859	4.246 464	.235 490
5	1.216 653	5.416 323	.184 627
6	1.265 319	6.632 975	.150 762
7	1.315 932	7.898 294	.126 610
8	1.368 569	9.214 226	.108 528
9	1.423 312	10.582 795	.094 493
10	1.480 244	12.006 107	.083 291
11	1.539 454	13.486 351	.074 149
12	1.601 032	15.025 805	.066 552
13	1.665 974	16.626 838	.060 144
14	1.731 676	18.291 911	.054 669
15	1.800 944	20.023 588	.049 941
16	1.872 981	21.824 531	.045 820
17	1.947 900	23.697 512	.042 199
18	2.025 817	25.645 413	.038 993
19	2.106 849	27.671 229	.036 129
20	2.191 123	29.778 079	.033 582
21	2.278 768	31.969 202	.031 280
22	2.369 919	34.247 970	.029 199
23	2.464 716	36.617 889	.017 309
24	2.563 304	39.082 604	.025 587
25	2.665 836	41.645 908	.024 012

*How $1 left at compound interest will grow (deposit made at beginning of period). Formula: $s = P(1 + i)^n$

**How $1 deposited periodically will grow (deposit made at end of period). For deposits made at the beginning of the period, subtract 1 from the amount shown in the following period. Formula: $S_n = \dfrac{(1 + i)^n - 1}{i}$

†Periodic deposit that will grow to $1 at a future date (deposits made at end of period). Formula: $\dfrac{1}{S_n} = \dfrac{i}{(1 + i)^n - 1}$

AT 4 PERCENT INTEREST

Number of Periods	Growth of $1.00*	Growth of $1.00 per Period**	Deposit Needed to Accumulate $1.00†
26	2.772 470	44.311 745	.022 567
27	2.883 369	47.084 214	.021 239
28	2.998 703	49.967 583	.020 013
29	3.118 651	52,966 286	.018 880
30	3.243 398	56.084 938	.017 830
31	3.373 133	59.328 335	.016 855
32	3.508 059	62.701 469	.015 949
33	3.648 381	66.209 527	.015 104
34	3.794 316	69.857 909	.014 315
35	3.946 089	73.652 225	.013 577
36	4.103 933	77.598 314	.012 887
37	4.268 090	81.702 246	.012 240
38	4.438 813	85.970 336	.011 632
39	4.616 366	90.409 150	.011 061
40	4.801 021	95.025 516	.010 523
41	4.993 061	99.826 536	.010 017
42	5.192 784	104.819 598	.009 540
43	5.400 495	110.012 382	.009 090
44	5.616 515	115.412 877	.008 665
45	5.841 176	121.029 392	.008 262
46	6.074 823	126.870 568	.007 882
47	6.317 816	132.945 390	.007 522
48	6.570 528	139.263 206	.007 181
49	6.833 349	145.833 734	.006 857
50	7.106 683	152.667 084	.006 550

* How $1 left at compound interest will grow (deposit made at beginning of period). Formula: $s = P(1 + i)^n$

** How $1 deposited periodically will grow (deposit made at end of period). For deposits made at the beginning of the period, subtract 1 from the amount shown in the following period. Formula: $S_n = \frac{(1 + i)^n - 1}{i}$

† Periodic deposit that will grow to $1 at a future date (deposits made at end of period). Formula: $\frac{1}{S_n} = \frac{i}{(1 + i)^n - 1}$

FUTURE WORTH OF A DEPOSIT OF $1.00 COMPOUNDED
AT 5 PERCENT INTEREST
PER PERIOD

Number of Periods	Growth of $1.00*	Growth of $1.00 per Period**	Deposit Needed to Accumulate $1.00†
1	1.050 000	1.000 000	1.000 000
2	1.102 500	2.050 000	.487 805
3	1.157 625	3.152 500	.317 209
4	1.215 506	4.310 125	.232 012
5	1.276 282	5.525 631	.180 975
6	1.340 096	6.801 913	.147 017
7	1.407 100	8.142 008	.133 820
8	1.477 455	9.549 109	.104 722
9	1.551 328	11.026 564	.090 690
10	1.628 895	12.577 893	.079 505
11	1.710 339	14.206 787	.070 389
12	1.795 856	15.917 127	.062 825
13	1.885 649	17.712 983	.056 456
14	1.979 932	19.598 632	.051 024
15	2.078 928	21.578 564	.046 342
16	2.182 875	23.657 492	.042 270
17	2.292 018	25.840 366	.038 699
18	2.406 619	28.132 385	.035 546
19	2.526 950	30.539 004	.032 745
20	2.653 298	33.065 954	.030 243
21	2.785 963	35.719 252	.027 996
22	2.925 261	38.505 214	.025 971
23	3.071 524	41.430 475	.024 137
24	3.225 100	44.501 999	.022 471
25	3.386 355	47.727 099	.020 952

*How $1 left at compound interest will grow (deposit made at beginning of period). Formula: $s = P(1 + i)^n$

**How $1 deposited periodically will grow (deposit made at end of period). For deposits made at the beginning of the period, subtract 1 from the amount shown in the following period. Formula: $S_n = \dfrac{(1 + i)^n - 1}{i}$

†Periodic deposit that will grow to $1 at a future date (deposits made at end of period). Formula: $\dfrac{1}{S_n} = \dfrac{i}{(1 + i)^n - 1}$

AT 5 PERCENT INTEREST

Number of Periods	Growth of $1.00*	Growth of $1.00 per Period**	Deposit Needed to Accumulate $1.00†
26	3.555 673	51.113 454	.019 564
27	3.733 456	54.669 126	.018 292
28	3.920 129	58.402 583	.017 123
29	4.116 136	62.322 712	.016 046
30	4.321 942	66.438 848	.015 051
31	4.538 029	70.760 790	.014 032
32	4.764 941	75.298 829	.013 280
33	5.003 189	80.063 771	.012 490
34	5.253 348	85.066 959	.011 755
35	5.516 015	90.320 307	.011 072
36	5.791 816	95.836 323	.010 434
37	6.081 407	101.628 139	.009 840
38	6.385 477	107.709 546	.009 284
39	6.704 751	114.095 023	.008 765
40	7.039 989	120.799 774	.008 278
41	7.391 988	127.839 763	.007 822
42	7.761 588	135.231 751	.007 395
43	8.149 667	142.993 339	.006 993
44	8.557 150	151.143 006	.006 616
45	8.985 008	159.700 156	.006 262
46	9.434 258	168.685 164	.005 928
47	9.905 971	178.119 422	.005 614
48	10.401 270	188.025 393	.005 318
49	10.921 333	198.426 663	.005 040
50	11.467 400	209.347 996	.004 777

*How $1 left at compound interest will grow (deposit made at beginning of Period). Formula: $s = P(1 + i)^n$

**How $1 deposited periodically will grow (deposit made at end of period). For deposits made at the beginning of the period, subtract 1 from the amount shown in the following period. Formula: $S_n = \dfrac{(1 + i)^n - 1}{i}$

†Periodic deposit that will grow to $1 at a future date (deposits made at end of period). Formula: $\dfrac{1}{S_n} = \dfrac{i}{(1 + i)^n - 1}$

FUTURE WORTH OF A DEPOSIT OF $1.00 COMPOUNDED
AT 6 PERCENT INTEREST
PER PERIOD

Number of Periods	Growth of $1.00*	Growth of $1.00 per Period**	Deposit Needed to Accumulate $1.00†
1	1.060 000	1.000 000	1.000 000
2	1.123 600	2.060 000	.485 437
3	1.191 016	3.183 600	.314 110
4	1.262 477	4.374 616	.228 591
5	1.338 226	5.637 093	.177 396
6	1.418 519	6.975 319	.143 363
7	1.503 630	8.393 838	.119 135
8	1.593 848	9.897 468	.101 036
9	1.689 479	11.491 316	.087 022
10	1.790 848	13.180 795	.075 868
11	1.898 299	14.971 643	.066 793
12	2.012 196	16.869 941	.059 277
13	2.132 928	18.882 138	.052 960
14	2.260 904	21.015 066	.047 585
15	2.396 558	23.275 970	.042 963
16	2.540 352	25.672 528	.038 952
17	2.692 773	28.212 880	.035 445
18	2.854 339	30.905 653	.032 357
19	3.025 600	33.759 992	.029 621
20	3.207 135	36.785 591	.027 185
21	3.399 564	39.992 727	.025 005
22	3.603 537	43.392 290	.023 046
23	3.819 750	46.995 828	.021 278
24	4.048 935	50.815 577	.019 679
25	4.291 871	54.864 512	.018 227

*How $1 left at compound interest will grow (deposit made at beginning of period). Formula: $s = P(1 + i)^n$

**How $1 deposited periodically will grow (deposit made at end of period). For deposits made at the beginning of the period, subtract 1 from the amount shown in the following period. Formula: $S_n = \dfrac{(1 + i)^n - 1}{i}$

†Periodic deposit that will grow to $1 at a future date (deposits made at end of period). Formula: $\dfrac{1}{S_n} = \dfrac{i}{(1 + i)^n - 1}$

AT 6 PERCENT INTEREST

Number of Periods	Growth of $1.00*	Growth of $1.00 per Period**	Deposit Needed to Accumulate $1.00†
26	4.549 383	59.156 383	.016 904
27	4.822 346	63.705 766	.015 697
28	5.111 687	68.528 112	.014 593
29	5.418 388	73.639 798	.013 580
30	5.743 491	79.058 186	.012 649
31	6.088 101	84.801 677	.011 792
32	6.453 387	90.889 778	.011 002
33	6.840 590	97.343 165	.010 273
34	7.251 025	104.183 755	.009 598
35	7.686 087	111.434 780	.008 974
36	8.147 252	119.120 867	.008 395
37	8.636 087	127.268 119	.007 857
38	9.154 252	135.904 206	.007 358
39	9.703 507	145.058 458	.006 894
40	10.285 718	154.761 966	.006 462
41	10.902 861	165.047 684	.006 059
42	11.557 033	175.950 545	.005 683
43	12.250 455	187.507 577	.005 333
44	12.985 482	199.758 032	.005 006
45	13.764 611	212.743 514	.004 700
46	14.590 487	226.508 125	.004 415
47	15.465 917	241.098 612	.004 148
48	16.393 872	256.564 529	.003 898
49	17.377 504	272.958 401	.003 664
50	18.420 154	290.335 905	.003 444

*How $1 left at compound interest will grow (deposit made at beginning of period). Formula: $s = P(1+i)^n$

**How $1 deposited periodically will grow (deposit made at end of period). For deposits made at the beginning of the period, subtract 1 from the amount shown in the following period.
Formula: $S_n = \dfrac{(1+i)^n - 1}{i}$

†Periodic deposit that will grow to $1 at a future date (deposits made at end of period). Formula: $\dfrac{1}{S_n} = \dfrac{i}{(1+i)^n - 1}$

FUTURE WORTH OF A DEPOSIT OF $1.00 COMPOUNDED AT 7 PERCENT INTEREST PER PERIOD

Number of Periods	Growth of $1.00*	Growth of $1.00 per Period**	Deposit Needed to Accumulate $1.00†
1	1.070 000	1.000 000	1.000 000
2	1.144 900	2.070 000	.483 092
3	1.225 043	3.214 900	.311 052
4	1.310 796	4.439 943	.225 228
5	1.402 552	5.750 739	.173 891
6	1.500 730	7.153 291	.139 796
7	1.605 781	8.654 021	.115 553
8	1.718 186	10.259 803	.097 468
9	1.838 459	11.977 989	.083 486
10	1.967 151	13.816 448	.072 378
11	2.104 852	15.783 599	.063 357
12	2.252 192	17.888 451	.055 902
13	2.409 845	20.140 643	.049 651
14	2.578 534	22.550 488	.044 345
15	2.759 032	25.129 022	.039 795
16	2.952 164	27.888 054	.035 858
17	3.158 815	30.840 217	.032 425
18	3.379 932	33.999 033	.029 413
19	3.616 528	37.378 965	.026 753
20	3.869 684	40.995 492	.025 393
21	4.140 562	44.865 177	.022 289
22	4.430 402	49.005 739	.020 406
23	4.740 530	53.436 141	.018 714
24	5.072 367	58.176 671	.017 189
25	5.427 433	63.249 038	.015 811

*How $1 left at compound interest will grow (deposit made at beginning of period). Formula: $s = P(1 + i)^n$

**How $1 deposited periodically will grow (deposit made at end of period). For deposits made at the beginning of the period, subtract 1 from the amount shown in the following period.
Formula: $S_n = \dfrac{(1 + i)^n - 1}{i}$

†Periodic deposit that will grow to $1 at a future date (deposits made at end of period). Formula: $\dfrac{1}{S_n} = \dfrac{i}{(1 + i)^n - 1}$

AT 7 PERCENT INTEREST

Number of Periods	Growth of $1.00*	Growth of $1.00 per Period**	Deposit Needed to Accumulate $1.00†
26	5.807 353	68.676 470	.014 561
27	6.213 868	74.483 823	.013 426
28	6.648 838	80.697 691	.012 392
29	7.114 257	87.346 529	.011 449
30	7.612 255	94.460 786	.010 586
31	8.145 113	102.073 041	.009 797
32	8.715 271	110.218 154	.009 073
33	9.325 340	118.933 425	.008 408
34	9.978 114	128.258 765	.007 797
35	10.676 581	138.236 878	.007 234
36	11.423 942	148.913 460	.006 715
37	12.223 618	160.337 402	.006 237
38	13.079 271	172.561 020	.005 795
39	13.994 820	185.640 292	.005 387
40	14.974 458	199.635 112	.005 009
41	16.022 670	214.609 570	.004 660
42	17.144 257	230.632 240	.004 336
43	18.344 355	247.776 496	.004 036
44	19.628 460	266.120 851	.003 758
45	21.002 452	285.749 311	.003 500
46	22.472 623	306.751 763	.003 260
47	24.045 707	329.224 386	.003 037
48	25.728 907	353.270 093	.002 831
49	27.529 930	378.999 000	.002 639
50	29.457 025	406.528 929	.002 460

---

*How $1 left at compound interest will grow (deposit made at beginning of period). Formula: $s = P (1 + i)^n$

**How $1 deposited periodically will grow (deposit made at end of period). For deposits made at the beginning of the period, subtract 1 from the amount shown in the following period.
Formula: $S_n = \dfrac{(1 + i)^n - 1}{i}$

†Periodic deposit that will grow to $1 at a future date (deposits made at end of period). Formula: $\dfrac{1}{S_n} = \dfrac{i}{(1 + i)^n - 1}$

FUTURE WORTH OF A DEPOSIT OF $1.00 COMPOUNDED
AT 7½ PERCENT INTEREST
PER PERIOD

Number of Periods	Growth of $1.00*	Growth of $1.00 per Period**	Deposit Needed to Accumulate $1.00†
1	1.075 000	1.000 000	1.000 000
2	1.155 625	2.075 000	.481 928
3	1.242 297	3.230 625	.309 538
4	1.335 469	4.472 922	.223 568
5	1.435 629	5.808 391	.172 165
6	1.543 302	7.244 020	.138 045
7	1.659 049	8.787 322	.113 800
8	1.783 478	10.446 371	.095 727
9	1.917 239	12.229 849	.081 767
10	2.061 032	14.147 087	.070 686
11	2.215 609	16.208 119	.061 697
12	2.381 780	18.423 728	.054 278
13	2.560 413	20.805 508	.048 064
14	2.752 444	23.365 921	.042 797
15	2.958 877	26.118 365	.038 287
16	3.180 793	29.077 242	.034 391
17	3.419 353	32.258 035	.031 000
18	3.675 804	35.677 388	.028 029
19	3.951 489	39.353 192	.025 411
20	4.247 851	43.304 681	.023 092
21	4.566 440	47.552 532	.021 029
22	4.908 923	52.118 972	.019 187
23	5.277 092	57.027 895	.017 535
24	5.672 874	62.304 987	.016 050
25	6.098 340	67.977 862	.014 711

*How $1 left at compound interest will grow (deposit made at beginning of period). Formula: $s = P (1 + i)^n$

**How $1 deposited periodically will grow (deposit made at end of period). For deposits made at the beginning of the period, subtract 1 from the amount shown in the following period.
Formula: $S_n = \dfrac{(1 + i)^n - 1}{i}$

†Periodic deposit that will grow to $1 at a future date (deposits made at end of period). Formula: $\dfrac{1}{S_n} = \dfrac{i}{(1 + i)^n - 1}$

AT 7½ PERCENT INTEREST

Number of Periods	Growth of $1.00*	Growth of $1.00 per Period**	Deposit Needed to Accumulate $1.00†
26	6.555 715	74.076 201	.013 500
27	7.047 394	80.631 916	.012 402
28	7.575 948	87.679 310	.011 405
29	8.144 144	95.255 258	.010 498
30	8.754 955	103.399 403	.009 671
31	9.411 577	112.154 358	.008 916
32	10.117 445	121.565 935	.008 226
33	10.876 253	131.683 380	.007 594
34	11.691 972	142.559 633	.007 015
35	12.568 870	154.251 606	.006 483
36	13.511 536	166.810 476	.005 994
37	14.524 901	180.332 012	.005 945
38	15.614 268	194.856 913	.005 132
39	16.785 339	210.471 181	.004 751
40	18.044 239	227.256 520	.004 400
41	19.397 557	245.300 759	.004 077
42	20.852 374	264.698 315	.003 778
43	22.416 302	285.550 689	.003 502
44	24.097 524	307.966 991	.003 247
45	25.904 839	332.064 515	.003 011
46	27.847 702	357.969 354	.002 794
47	29.936 279	385.817 055	.002 592
48	32.181 500	415.753 334	.002 405
49	34.595 113	447.934 835	.002 232
50	37.189 746	482.529 947	.002 072

*How $1 left at compound interest will grow (deposit made at beginning of period. Formula: $s = P(1 + i)^n$

**How $1 deposited periodically will grow (deposit made at end of period). For deposits made at the beginning of the period, subtract 1 from the amount shown in the following period. Formula: $S_n = \dfrac{(1 + i)^n - 1}{i}$

†Periodic deposit that will grow to $1 at a future date (deposits made at end of period). Formula: $\dfrac{1}{S_n} = \dfrac{i}{(1 + i)^n - 1}$

FUTURE WORTH OF A DEPOSIT OF $1.00 COMPOUNDED AT 8 PERCENT INTEREST PER PERIOD

Number of Periods	Growth of $1.00*	Growth of $1.00 per Period**	Deposit Needed to Accumulate $1.00†
1	1.080 000	1.000 000	1.000 000
2	1.166 400	2.080 000	.480 769
3	1.259 712	3.246 400	.308 034
4	1.360 489	4.506 112	.221 921
5	1.469 328	5.866 601	.170 456
6	1.586 874	7.335 929	.136 315
7	1.713 824	8.922 803	.112 072
8	1.850 930	10.636 628	.094 015
9	1.999 005	12.487 558	.080 080
10	2.158 925	14.486 562	.069 019
11	2.331 639	16.645 487	.060 076
12	2.518 170	18.977 126	.052 695
13	2.719 624	21.495 297	.046 522
14	2.937 194	24.214 920	.041 297
15	3.172 169	27.152 114	.036 830
16	3.425 943	30.324 283	.032 977
17	3.700 018	33.750 226	.029 629
18	3.996 019	37.450 244	.026 702
19	4.315 701	41.446 263	.024 128
20	4.660 957	45.761 964	.021 852
21	5.033 834	50.422 921	.019 832
22	5.436 540	55.456 755	.018 032
23	5.871 464	60.893 296	.016 422
24	6.341 181	66.764 759	.014 978
25	6.848 475	73.105 940	.013 679

*How $1 left at compound interest will grow (deposit made at beginning of period). Formula: $s = P(1+i)^n$

**How $1 deposited periodically will grow (deposit made at end of period). For deposits made at the beginning of the period, subtract 1 from the amount shown in the following period. Formula: $S_n = \frac{(1+i)^n - 1}{i}$

†Periodic deposit that will grow to $1 at a future date (deposits made at end of period). Formula: $\frac{1}{S_n} = \frac{i}{(1+i)^n - 1}$

AT 8 PERCENT INTEREST

Number of Periods	Growth of $1.00*	Growth of $1.00 per Period**	Deposit Needed to Accumulate $1.00†
26	7.396 353	79.954 415	.012 507
27	7.988 061	87.350 768	.011 448
28	8.627 106	95.338 830	.010 489
29	9.317 275	103.965 936	.009 619
30	10.062 657	113.283 211	.008 827
31	10.867 669	123.345 868	.008 107
32	11.737 083	134.213 537	.007 451
33	12.676 050	145.950 620	.006 852
34	13.690 134	158.626 670	.006 304
35	14.785 344	172.316 804	.005 803
36	15.968 172	187.102 148	.005 345
37	17.245 626	203.070 320	.004 924
38	18.625 276	220.315 945	.004 539
39	20.115 298	238.941 221	.004 185
40	21.724 521	259.056 519	.003 860
41	23.462 483	280.781 040	.003 561
42	25.339 482	304.243 523	.003 287
43	27.366 640	329.583 005	.003 034
44	29.555 972	356.949 646	.002 802
45	31.920 449	386.505 617	.002 587
46	34.474 085	418.426 067	.002 390
47	37.232 012	452.900 152	.002 208
48	40.210 573	490.132 164	.002 040
49	43.427 419	530.342 737	.001 886
50	46.901 613	573.770 156	.001 743

*How $1 left at compound interest will grow (deposit made at beginning of period). Formula: $s = P(1+i)^n$

**How $1 deposited periodically will grow (deposit made at end of period). For deposits made at the beginning of the period, subtract 1 from the amount shown in the following period. Formula: $S_n = \dfrac{(1+i)^n - 1}{i}$

†Periodic deposit that will grow to $1 at a future date (deposits made at end of period). Formula: $\dfrac{1}{S_n} = \dfrac{i}{(1+i)^n - 1}$

FUTURE WORTH OF A DEPOSIT OF $1.00 COMPOUNDED AT 8½ PERCENT INTEREST PER PERIOD

Number of Periods	Growth of $1.00*	Growth of $1.00 per Period**	Deposit Needed to Accumulate $1.00†
1	1.085 000	1.000 000	1.000 000
2	1.177 225	2.085 000	.479 616
3	1.277 289	3.262 225	.306 539
4	1.385 859	4.539 514	.220 288
5	1.503 657	5.925 373	.168 766
6	1.631 468	7.429 030	.134 607
7	1.770 142	9.060 497	.110 369
8	1.920 604	10.830 639	.092 331
9	2.083 856	12.751 244	.078 424
10	2.260 983	14.835 099	.067 408
11	2.453 167	17.096 083	.058 493
12	2.662 686	19.549 250	.051 153
13	2.887 930	22.210 936	.045 023
14	3.133 404	25.098 866	.039 842
15	3.399 743	28.232 269	.035 420
16	3.688 721	31.632 012	.031 614
17	4.002 262	35.320 733	.028 312
18	4.342 455	39.322 995	.025 430
19	4.711 563	43.665 450	.022 901
20	5.112 046	48.377 013	.020 671
21	5.546 570	53.489 059	.018 695
22	6.018 028	59.035 629	.016 939
23	6.529 561	65.053 658	.015 372
24	7.084 574	71.583 219	.013 970
25	7.686 762	78.667 792	.012 712

*How $1 left at compound interest will grow (deposit made at beginning of period). Formula: $s = P (1 + i)^n$

**How $1 deposited periodically will grow (deposit made at end of period). For deposits made at the beginning of the period subtract 1 from the amount shown in the following period. Formula: $S_n = \dfrac{(1 + i)^n - 1}{i}$

†Periodic deposit that will grow to $1 at a future date (deposits made at end of period). Formula: $\dfrac{1}{S_n} = \dfrac{i}{(1 + i)^n - 1}$

AT 8½ PERCENT INTEREST

Number of Periods	Growth of $1.00*	Growth of $1.00 per Period**	Deposit Needed to Accumulate $1.00†
26	8.340 137	86.354 555	.011 580
27	9.049 049	94.694 692	.010 560
28	9.818 218	103.743 741	.009 639
29	10.652 766	113.561 959	.008 806
30	11.558 252	124.214 725	.008 051
31	12.540 703	135.772 977	.007 365
32	13.606 663	148.313 680	.006 742
33	14.763 229	161.920 343	.006 176
34	16.018 104	176.683 572	.005 660
35	17.379 642	192.701 675	.005 189
36	18.856 912	210.081 318	.004 760
37	20.459 750	228.938 230	.004 368
38	22.198 828	249.397 979	.004 010
39	24.085 729	271.596 808	.003 682
40	26.133 016	295.682 536	.003 382
41	28.354 322	321.815 552	.003 107
42	30.764 439	350.169 874	.002 856
43	33.379 417	380.934 313	.002 625
44	36.216 667	414.313 730	.002 414
45	39.295 084	450.530 397	.002 220
46	42.635 166	489.825 480	.002 042
47	46.259 155	532.460 646	.001 878
48	50.191 183	578.719 801	.001 728
49	54.457 434	628.910 984	.001 590
50	59.086 316	683.368 418	.001 463

*How $1 left at compound interest will grow (deposit made at beginning of period). Formula: $s = P(1 + i)^n$

**How $1 deposited periodically will grow (deposit made at end of period). For deposits made at the beginning of the period, subtract 1 from the amount shown in the following period. Formula: $S_n = \dfrac{(1 + i)^n - 1}{i}$

†Periodic deposit that will grow to $1 at a future date (deposits made at end of period). Formula: $\dfrac{1}{S_n} = \dfrac{i}{(1 + i)^n - 1}$

FUTURE WORTH OF A DEPOSIT OF $1.00 COMPOUNDED
AT 9 PERCENT INTEREST
PER PERIOD

Number of Periods	Growth of $1.00*	Growth of $1.00 per Period**	Deposit Needed to Accumulate $1.00†
1	1.090 000	1.000 000	1.000 000
2	1.188 100	2.090 000	.478 469
3	1.295 029	3.278 100	.305 055
4	1.411 582	4.573 129	.218 669
5	1.538 624	5.984 711	.167 092
6	1.677 100	7.523 335	.132 920
7	1.828 039	9.200 435	.108 691
8	1.992 563	11.028 474	.090 674
9	2.171 893	13.021 036	.076 799
10	2.367 364	15.192 930	.065 820
11	2.580 426	17.560 293	.056 947
12	2.812 665	20.140 720	.049 651
13	3.065 805	22.953 385	.043 567
14	3.341 727	26.019 189	.038 433
15	3.642 482	29.360 916	.034 059
16	3.970 306	33.003 399	.030 300
17	4.327 633	36.973 705	.027 046
18	4.717 120	41.301 338	.024 212
19	5.141 661	46.018 458	.021 730
20	5.604 411	51.160 120	.019 546
21	6.108 808	56.764 530	.017 617
22	6.658 600	62.873 338	.015 905
23	7.257 874	69.531 939	.014 382
24	7.911 083	76.789 813	.013 023
25	8.623 081	84.700 896	.011 806

*How $1 left at compound interest will grow (deposit made at beginning of period). Formula: $s = P(1 + i)^n$

**How $1 deposited periodically will grow (deposit made at end of period). For deposits made at the beginning of the period, subtract 1 from the amount shown in the following period. Formula: $S_n = \dfrac{(1 + i)^n - 1}{i}$

†Periodic deposit that will grow to $1 at a future date (deposits made at end of period). Formula: $\dfrac{1}{S_n} = \dfrac{i}{(1 + i)^n - 1}$

AT 9 PERCENT INTEREST

Number of Periods	Growth of $1.00*	Growth of $1.00 per Period**	Deposit Needed to Accumulate $1.00†
26	9.399 158	93.323 977	.010 715
27	10.245 082	102.723 135	.009 735
28	11.167 140	112.968 217	.008 852
29	12.172 182	124.135 356	.008 056
30	13.267 678	136.307 539	.007 336
31	14.461 770	149.575 217	.006 686
32	15.763 329	164.036 987	.006 096
33	17.182 028	179.800 315	.005 562
34	18.728 411	196.982 344	.005 077
35	20.413 968	215.710 755	.004 636
36	22.251 225	236.124.723	.004 235
37	24.253 835	258.375 948	.003 870
38	26.436 680	282.629 783	.003 538
39	28.815 982	309.066 463	.003 236
40	31.409 420	337.882 445	.002 960
41	34.236 268	369.291 865	.002 708
42	37.317 532	403.528 133	.002 478
43	40.676 110	440.845 665	.002 268
44	44.336 960	481.521 775	.001 077
45	48.327 286	525.858 734	.001 902
46	52.676 742	574.186 021	.001 742
47	57.417 649	626.862 762	.001 595
48	62.585 237	684.280 411	.001 461
49	68.217 908	746.856 648	.001 339
50	74.357 520	815.083 556	.001 227

*How $1 left at compound interest will grow (deposit made at beginning of period). Formula: $s = P (1 + i)^n$

**How $1 deposited periodically will grow (deposit made at end of period). For deposits made at the beginning of the period, subtract 1 from the amount shown in the following period. Formula: $S_n = \dfrac{(1 + i)^n - 1}{i}$

†Periodic deposit that will grow to $1 at a future date (deposits made at end of period). Formula: $\dfrac{1}{S_n} = \dfrac{i}{(1 + i)^n - 1}$

FUTURE WORTH OF A DEPOSIT OF $1.00 COMPOUNDED AT 9½ PERCENT INTEREST PER PERIOD

Number of Periods	Growth of $1.00*	Growth of $1.00 per Period**	Deposit Needed to Accumulate $1.00†
1	1.095 000	1.000 000	1.000 000
2	1.199 025	2.095 000	.477 327
3	1.312 932	3.294 025	.303 580
4	1.437 661	4.606 957	.217 063
5	1.574 239	6.044 618	.165 436
6	1.723 791	7.618 857	.131 253
7	1.887 552	9.342 648	.107 036
8	2.066 869	11.230 200	.089 046
9	2.263 222	13.297 069	.075 205
10	2.478 228	15.560 291	.064 266
11	2.713 659	18.038 518	.055 437
12	2.971 457	20.752 178	.048 188
13	3.253 745	23.723 634	.042 152
14	3.562 851	26.977 380	.037 068
15	3.901 322	30.540 231	.032 744
16	4.271 948	34.441 553	.029 035
17	4.677 783	38.713 500	.025 831
18	5.122 172	43.391 283	.023 046
19	5.608 778	48.513 454	.020 613
20	6.141 612	54.122 233	.018 477
21	6.725 065	60.263 845	.016 594
22	7.363 946	66.988 910	.014 928
23	8.063 521	74.352 856	.013 449
24	8.829 556	82.416 378	.012 134
25	9.668 364	91.245 934	.010 959

*How $1 left at compound interest will grow (deposit made at beginning of period). Formula: $s = P (1 + i)^n$

**How $1 deposited periodically will grow (deposit made at end of period). For deposits made at the beginning of the period, subtract 1 from the amount shown in the following period. Formula: $S_n = \dfrac{(1 + i)^n - 1}{i}$

†Periodic deposit that will grow to $1 at a future date (deposits made at end of period). Formula: $\dfrac{1}{S_n} = \dfrac{i}{(1 + i)^n - 1}$

AT 9½ PERCENT INTEREST

Number of Periods	Growth of $1.00*	Growth of $1.00 per Period**	Deposit Needed to Accumulate $1.00†
26	10.586 858	100.914 297	.009 909
27	11.592 610	111.501 156	.008 969
28	12.693 908	123.093 766	.008 124
29	13.899 829	135.787 673	.007 364
30	15.220 313	149.687 502	.006 681
31	16.666 242	164.907 815	.006 064
32	18.249 535	181.574 057	.005 507
33	19.983 241	199.823 593	.005 004
34	21.881 649	219.806 834	.004 549
35	23.960 406	241.688 483	.004 138
36	26.236 644	265.648 889	.003 764
37	28.729 126	291.885 534	.003 426
38	31.458 393	320.614 659	.003 119
39	34.446 940	352.073 052	.002 840
40	37.719 399	386.519 992	.002 587
41	41.302 742	424.239 391	.002 357
42	45.226 503	465.542 133	.002 148
43	49.523 020	510.768 636	.001 958
44	54.227 707	560.291 656	.001 785
45	59.379 340	614.519 364	.001 627
46	65.020 377	673.898 703	.001 484
47	71.197 313	738.919 080	.001 353
48	77.961 057	810.116 393	.001 234
49	85.367 358	888.077 450	.001 126
50	93.477 257	973.444 808	.001 027

*How $1 left at compound interest will grow (deposit made at beginning of period). Formula: $s = P (1 + i)^n$

**How $1 deposited periodically will grow (deposit made at end of period). For deposits made at the beginning of the period, subtract 1 from the amount shown in the following period. Formula: $S_n = \dfrac{(1 + i)^n - 1}{i}$

†Periodic deposit that will grow to $1 at a future date (deposits made at end of period). Formula: $\dfrac{1}{S_n} = \dfrac{i}{(1 + i)^n - 1}$

FUTURE WORTH OF A DEPOSIT OF $1.00 COMPOUNDED
AT 10 PERCENT INTEREST
PER PERIOD

Number of Periods	Growth of $1.00*	Growth of $1.00 per Period**	Deposit Needed to Accumulate $1.00†
1	1.100 000	1.000 000	1.000 000
2	1.210 000	2.100 000	.476 190
3	1.331 000	3.310 000	.302 115
4	1.464 100	4.641 000	.215 471
5	1.610 510	6.105 100	.163 797
6	1.771 561	7.715 610	.129 607
7	1.948 717	9.487 171	.105 405
8	2.143 589	11.435 888	.087 444
9	2.357 948	13.579 477	.073 641
10	2.593 742	15.937 425	.062 745
11	2.853 117	18.531 167	.053 963
12	3.138 428	21.384 284	.046 763
13	3.452 271	24.522 712	.040 779
14	3.797 498	27.974 983	.035 746
15	4.177 248	31.772 482	.031 474
16	4.594 973	35.949 730	.027 817
17	5.054 470	40.544 703	.024 664
18	5.559 917	45.599 173	.021 930
19	6.115 909	51.159 090	.019 547
20	6.727 500	57.274 999	.017 460
21	7.400 250	64.002 499	.015 624
22	8.140 275	71.402 749	.014 005
23	8.954 302	79.543 024	.012 572
24	9.849 733	88.497 327	.011 300
25	10.834 706	98.347 059	.010 168

*How $1 left at compound interest will grow (deposit made at beginning of period). Formula: $s = P(1 + i)^n$

**How $1 deposited periodically will grow (deposit made at end of period). For deposits made at the beginning of the period, subtract 1 from the amount shown in the following period.
Formula: $S_n = \dfrac{(1 + i)^n - 1}{i}$

†Periodic deposit that will grow to $1 at a future date (deposits made at end of period). Formula: $\dfrac{1}{S_n} = \dfrac{i}{(1 + i)^n - 1}$

AT 10 PERCENT INTEREST

Number of Periods	Growth of $1.00*	Growth of $1.00 per Period**	Deposit Needed to Accumulate $1.00†
26	11.918 177	109.181 765	.009 159
27	13.109 994	121.099 942	.008 258
28	14.420 994	134.209 936	.007 451
29	15.863 093	148.630 930	.006 728
30	17.449 402	164.494 023	.006 079
31	19.194 342	181.943 425	.005 496
32	21.113 777	201.137 767	.004 972
33	23.225 154	222.251 544	.004 499
34	25.547 670	245.476 699	.004 074
35	28.102 437	271.024 368	.003 690
36	30.912 681	299.126 805	.003 343
37	34.003 949	330.039 486	.003 030
38	37.404 343	364.043 434	.002 747
39	41.144 778	401.447 778	.002 491
40	45.259 256	442.592 556	.002 259
41	49.785 181	487.851 811	.002 050
42	54.763 699	537.636 992	.001 860
43	60.240 069	592.400 692	.001 688
44	66.264 076	652.640 761	.001 532
45	72.890 484	718.904 837	.001 391
46	80.179 532	791.795 321	.001 263
47	88.197 485	871.974 853	.001 147
48	97.017 234	960.172 338	.001 041
49	106.718 957	1057.189 572	.000 946
50	117.390 853	1163.908 529	.000 859

*How $1 left at compound interest will grow (deposit made at beginning of period). Formula: $s = P(1 + i)^n$

**How $1 deposited periodically will grow (deposit made at end of period). For deposits made at the beginning of the period, subtract 1 from the amount shown in the following period.
Formula: $S_n = \dfrac{(1 + i)^n - 1}{i}$

†Periodic deposit that will grow to $1 at a future date (deposits made at end of period). Formula: $\dfrac{1}{S_n} = \dfrac{i}{(1 + i)^n - 1}$

PRESENT WORTH OF A FUTURE AMOUNT OF $1.00
DISCOUNTED AT ½ PERCENT INTEREST
PER PERIOD

Number of Periods	Present Worth of $1.00*	Present Worth of $1.00 per Period**	Partial Payment per $1.00 of Loan†
1	.995 025	.995 025	1.005 000
2	.990 075	1.985 099	.503 753
3	.985 149	2.970 248	.336 672
4	.980 248	3.950 496	.253 133
5	.975 371	4.925 866	.203 010
6	.970 518	5.896 384	.169 595
7	.965 690	6.862 074	.145 729
8	.960 885	7.822 959	.127 829
9	.956 105	8.779 064	.113 907
10	.951 348	9.730 412	.102 771
11	.946 615	10.677 017	.093 659
12	.941 905	11.618 932	.086 066
13	.937 219	12.556 151	.079 642
14	.932 556	13.488 708	.074 136
15	.927 917	14.416 625	.069 364
16	.923 300	15.339 925	.065 189
17	.918 707	16.258 632	.061 506
18	.914 136	17.172 768	.058 232
19	.909 588	18.082 356	.055 303
20	.905 063	18.987 419	.052 666
21	.900 560	19.887 979	.050 282
22	.896 080	20.784 059	.048 114
23	.891 622	21.675 681	.046 135
24	.887 186	22.562 866	.044 321
25	.882 772	23.445 638	.042 652

*What $1 due in the future is worth today. Formula: $p = \dfrac{s}{(1 + i)^n}$

**What $1 payable periodically is worth today (payments made at end of period). For payments made at the beginning of the period, add 1 to the amount shown for the previous period. Formula: $a_n = \dfrac{1 - (1 + i)^{-n}}{i}$

†Periodic payment necessary to pay off a loan of $1. Formula: The sinking fund factor plus the rate of interest.

DISCOUNTED AT ½ PERCENT INTEREST

Number of Periods	Present Worth of $1.00*	Present Worth of $1.00 per Period**	Partial Payment per $1.00 of Loan†
26	.878 380	24.324 018	.041 112
27	.874 010	25.198 028	.039 686
28	.869 662	26.067 689	.038 362
29	.865 335	26.933 024	.037 129
30	.861 030	27.794 054	.035 979
31	.856 746	28.650 800	.034 903
32	.852 484	29.503 284	.033 895
33	.848 242	30.351 526	.032 947
34	.844 022	31.195 548	.032 056
35	.839 823	32.035 371	.031 215
36	.835 645	32.871 016	.030 422
37	.831 487	33.702 504	.029 671
38	.827 351	34.529 854	.028 960
39	.823 235	35.353 089	.028 286
40	.819 139	36.172 228	.027 646
41	.815 064	36.987 291	.027 036
42	.811 009	37.798 300	.026 456
43	.806 974	38.605 274	.025 903
44	.802 959	39.408 232	.025 375
45	.798 964	40.207 196	.024 871
46	.794 989	41.002 185	.024 389
47	.791 034	41.793 219	.023 927
48	.787 098	42.580 318	.023 485
49	.783 182	43.363 500	.023 061
50	.779 286	44.142 786	.022 654

*What $1 due in the future is worth today. Formula: $p = \dfrac{s}{(1+i)^n}$

**What $1 payable periodically is worth today (payments made at end of period). For payments made at the beginning of the period, add 1 to the amount shown for the previous period. Formula: $a_n = \dfrac{1-(1+i)^{-n}}{i}$

†Periodic payment necessary to pay off a loan of $1. Formula: The sinking fund factor plus the rate of interest.

PRESENT WORTH OF A FUTURE AMOUNT OF $1.00
DISCOUNTED AT 3 PERCENT INTEREST
PER PERIOD

Number of Periods	Present Worth of $1.00*	Present Worth of $1.00 per Period**	Partial Payment per $1.00 of Loan†
1	.970 874	.970 874	1.030 000
2	.942 596	1.913 470	.522 611
3	.915 142	2.828 611	.353 530
4	.888 487	3.717 098	.269 027
5	.862 609	4.579 707	.218 355
6	.837 484	5.417 191	.184 598
7	.813 092	6.230 283	.160 506
8	.789 409	7.019 692	.142 456
9	.766 417	7.786 109	.128 434
10	.744 094	8.530 203	.117 231
11	.722 421	9.252 624	.108 077
12	.701 380	9.954 004	.100 462
13	.680 951	10.634 955	.094 030
14	.661 118	11.296 073	.088 526
15	.641 862	11.937 935	.083 767
16	.623 167	12.561 102	.079 611
17	.605 016	13.166 118	.075 953
18	.587 395	13.753 513	.072 709
19	.570 286	14.323 799	.069 814
20	.553 676	14.877 475	.067 216
21	.537 549	15.415 024	.064 872
22	.521 893	15.936 917	.062 747
23	.506 692	16.443 608	.060 814
24	.491 934	16.935 542	.059 047
25	.477 606	17.413 148	.057 428

*What $1 due in the future is worth today. Formula: $p = \dfrac{s}{(1+i)^n}$

**What $1 payable periodically is worth today (payments made at end of period). For payments made at the beginning of the period, add 1 to the amount shown for the previous period. Formula: $a_n = \dfrac{1-(1+i)^{-n}}{i}$

†Periodic payment necessary to pay off a loan of $1. Formula: The sinking fund factor plus the rate of interest.

DISCOUNTED AT 3 PERCENT INTEREST

Number of Periods	Present Worth of $1.00*	Present Worth of $1.00 per Period**	Partial Payment per $1.00 of Loan†
26	.463 695	17.876 842	.055 938
27	.450 189	18.327 031	.054 564
28	.437 077	18.764 108	.053 293
29	.424 346	19.188 455	.052 115
30	.411 987	19.600 441	.051 019
31	.399 987	20.000 428	.049 999
32	.388 337	20.388 766	.049 047
33	.377 026	20.765 792	.048 156
34	.366 045	21.131 837	.047 322
35	.355 383	21.487 220	.046 539
36	.345 032	21.832 252	.045 804
37	.334 983	22.167 235	.045 112
38	.325 226	22.492 462	.044 459
39	.315 754	22.808 215	.043 844
40	.306 557	23.114 772	.043 262
41	.297 628	23.412 400	.042 712
42	.288 959	23.701 359	.042 192
43	.280 543	23.981 902	.041 698
44	.272 372	24.254 274	.041 230
45	.264 439	24.518 713	.040 785
46	.256 737	24.775 449	.040 363
47	.249 259	25.024 708	.039 961
48	.241 999	25.266 707	.039 578
49	.234 950	25.501 657	.039 213
50	.228 107	25.729 764	.038 865

*What $1 due in the future is worth today. Formula: $p = \dfrac{s}{(1 + i)^n}$

**What $1 payable periodically is worth today (payments made at end of period). For payments made at the beginning of the period, add 1 to the amount shown for the previous period. Formula: $a_n = \dfrac{1 - (1 + i)^{-n}}{i}$

†Periodic payment necessary to pay off a loan of $1. Formula: The sinking fund factor plus the rate of interest.

PRESENT WORTH OF A FUTURE AMOUNT OF $1.00
DISCOUNTED AT 4 PERCENT INTEREST
PER PERIOD

Number of Periods	Present Worth of $1.00*	Present Worth of $1.00 per Period**	Partial Payment per $1.00 of Loan†
1	.961 538	.961 538	1.040 000
2	.924 556	1.886 095	.530 196
3	.888 996	2.775 091	.360 349
4	.854 804	3.629 895	.275 490
5	.821 927	4.451 822	.224 627
6	.790 315	5.242 137	.190 762
7	.759 918	6.002 055	.166 610
8	.730 690	6.732 745	.148 528
9	.702 587	7.435 332	.134 493
10	.675 564	8.110 896	.123 291
11	.649 581	8.760 477	.114 149
12	.624 597	9.385 074	.106 552
13	.600 574	9.985 648	.100 144
14	.577 475	10.563 123	.094 669
15	.555 265	11.118 387	.089 941
16	.533 908	11.652 296	.085 820
17	.513 373	12.165 669	.082 199
18	.493 628	12.659 297	.078 993
19	.474 642	13.133 939	.076 139
20	.456 387	13.590 326	.073 582
21	.438 834	14.029 160	.071 280
22	.421 955	14.451 117	.069 199
23	.405 726	14.856 842	.067 309
24	.390 121	15.246 963	.065 587
25	.375 117	15.622 080	.064 012

*What $1 due in the future is worth today. Formula: $p = \dfrac{s}{(1 + i)^n}$

**What $1 payable periodically is worth today (payments made at end of period). For payments made at the beginning of the period, add 1 to the amount shown for the previous period. Formula: $a_n = \dfrac{1 - (1 + i)^{-n}}{i}$

†Periodic payment necessary to pay off a loan of $1. Formula: The sinking fund factor plus the rate of interest.

DISCOUNTED AT 4 PERCENT INTEREST

Number of Periods	Present Worth of $1.00*	Present Worth of $1.00 per Period**	Partial Payment per $1.00 of Loan†
26	.360 689	15.982 769	.062 567
27	.346 817	16.329 586	.061 239
28	.333 477	16.663 063	.060 013
29	.320 651	16.933 715	.058 880
30	.308 319	17.292 033	.057 830
31	.296 460	17.588 494	.056 855
32	.285 058	17.873 551	.055 949
33	.274 094	18.147 646	.055 104
34	.263 552	18.411 198	.054 315
35	.253 415	18.664 613	.053 577
36	.243 669	18.908 282	.052 887
37	.234 297	19.142 579	.052 240
38	.225 285	19.367 864	.051 632
39	.216 621	19.584 485	.051 061
40	.208 289	19.792 774	.050 523
41	.200 278	19.993 052	.050 017
42	.192 575	20.185 627	.049 540
43	.185 168	20.370 795	.049 090
44	.178 046	20.548 841	.048 665
45	.171 198	20.720 040	.048 262
46	.164 614	20.884 654	.047 882
47	.158 283	21.042 936	.047 522
48	.152 195	21.195 131	.047 181
49	.146 341	21.341 472	.046 857
50	.140 713	21.482 185	.046 550

*What $1 due in the future is worth today. Formula: $p = \dfrac{s}{(1+i)^n}$

**What $1 payable periodically is worth today (payment made at end of period). For payments made at the beginning of the period, add 1 to the amount shown for the previous period.
Formula: $a_n = \dfrac{1-(1+i)^{-n}}{i}$

†Periodic payment necessary to pay off a loan of $1. Formula: The sinking fund factor plus the rate of interest.

PRESENT WORTH OF A FUTURE AMOUNT OF $1.00
DISCOUNTED AT 5 PERCENT INTEREST
PER PERIOD

Number of Periods	Present Worth of $1.00*	Present Worth of $1.00 per Period**	Partial Payment per $1.00 of Loan†
1	.952 381	.952 381	1.050 000
2	.907 029	1.859 410	.537 805
3	.863 838	2.723 248	.367 209
4	.822 702	3.545 951	.282 012
5	.783 526	4.329 477	.230 975
6	.746 215	5.075 692	.197 017
7	.710 681	5.786 373	.172 820
8	.676 839	6.463 213	.154 722
9	.644 609	7.107 822	.140 690
10	.613 913	7.721 735	.129 505
11	.584 679	8.306 414	.120 389
12	.556 837	8.863 252	.112 825
13	.530 321	9.393 573	.106 456
14	.505 068	9.898 641	.101 024
15	.481 017	10.379 658	.096 342
16	.458 112	10.837 770	.092 270
17	.436 297	11.274 066	.088 699
18	.415 521	11.689 587	.085 546
19	.395 734	12.085 321	.082 745
20	.376 889	12.462 210	.080 243
21	.358 942	12.821 153	.077 996
22	.341 850	13.163 003	.075 971
23	.325 571	13.488 574	.074 137
24	.310 068	13.798 642	.072 471
25	.295 303	14.093 945	.070 952

*What $1 due in the future is worth today. Formula: $p = \dfrac{s}{(1 + i)^n}$

**What $1 payable periodically is worth today (payments made at end of period). For payments made at the beginning of the period, add 1 to the amount shown for the previous period.
Formula: $a_n = \dfrac{1-(1 + i)^{-n}}{i}$

†Periodic payment necessary to pay off a loan of $1. Formula: The sinking fund factor plus the rate of interest.

DISCOUNTED AT 5 PERCENT INTEREST

Number of Periods	Present Worth of $1.00*	Present Worth of $1.00 per Period**	Partial Payment per $1.00 of Loan†
26	.281 241	14.375 185	.069 564
27	.267 848	14.643 034	.068 292
28	.255 094	14.898 127	.067 123
29	.242 946	15.141 074	.066 046
30	.231 377	15.372 451	.065 051
31	.220 359	15.592 811	.064 132
32	.209 866	15.802 677	.063 280
33	.199 873	16.002 549	.062 490
34	.190 355	16.192 904	.061 755
35	.181 290	16.374 194	.061 072
36	.172 657	16.546 852	.060 434
37	.164 436	16.711 287	.059 840
38	.156 605	16.867 893	.059 284
39	.149 148	17.017 041	.058 765
40	.142 046	17.159 086	.058 278
41	.135 282	17.294 368	.057 822
42	.128 840	17.423 208	.057 395
43	.122 704	17.545 912	.056 993
44	.116 861	17.662 773	.056 616
45	.111 297	17.774 070	.056 262
46	.105 997	17.880 066	.055 928
47	.100 949	17.981 016	.055 614
48	.096 142	18.077 158	.055 318
49	.091 564	18.168 722	.055 040
50	.087 204	18.255 925	.054 777

*What $1 due in the future is worth today. Formula: $p = \dfrac{s}{(1 + i)^n}$

**What $1 payable periodically is worth today (payments made at end of period). For payments made at the beginning of the period, add 1 to the amount shown for the previous period.
Formula: $a_n = \dfrac{1 - (1 + i)^{-n}}{i}$

†Periodic payment necessary to pay off a loan of $1. Formula: The sinking fund factor plus the rate of interest.

PRESENT WORTH OF A FUTURE AMOUNT OF $1.00
DISCOUNTED AT 6 PERCENT INTEREST
PER PERIOD

Number of Periods	Present Worth of $1.00*	Present Worth of $1.00 per Period**	Partial Payment per $1.00 of Loan†
1	.943 396	.943 396	1.060 000
2	.889 996	1.833 393	.545 437
3	.839 619	2.673 012	.374 110
4	.792 094	3.465 106	.288 591
5	.747 258	4.212 364	.237 396
6	.704 961	4.917 324	.203 363
7	.665 057	5.582 381	.179 135
8	.627 412	6.209 794	.161 036
9	.591 898	6.801 692	.147 022
10	.558 395	7.360 087	.135 868
11	.526 788	7.886 875	.126 793
12	.496 969	8.383 844	.119 277
13	.468 839	8.852 683	.112 960
14	.442 301	9.294 984	.107 585
15	.417 265	9.712 249	.102 963
16	.393 646	10.105 895	.098 952
17	.371 364	10.477 260	.095 445
18	.350 344	10.827 603	.092 357
19	.330 513	11.158 116	.089 621
20	.311 805	11.469 921	.087 185
21	.294 155	11.764 077	.085 005
22	.277 505	12.041 582	.083 046
23	.261 797	12.303 379	.081 278
24	.246 979	12.550 358	.079 679
25	.232 999	12.783 356	.078 227

*What $1 due in the future is worth today. Formula: $p = \dfrac{s}{(1 + i)^n}$

**What $1 payable periodically is worth today (payments made at end of period). For payments made at the beginning of the period, add 1 to the amount shown for the previous period.
Formula: $a_n = \dfrac{1 - (1 + i)^{-n}}{i}$

†Periodic payment necessary to pay off a loan of $1. Formula: The sinking fund factor plus the rate of interest.

DISCOUNTED AT 6 PERCENT INTEREST

Number of Periods	Present Worth of $1.00*	Present Worth of $1.00 per Period**	Partial Payment per $1.00 of Loan†
26	.219 810	13.003 166	.076 904
27	.207 368	13.210 534	.075 697
28	.195 630	13.406 164	.074 593
29	.184 557	13.590 721	.073 580
30	.174 110	13.764 831	.072 659
31	.164 255	13.929 086	.071 792
32	.154 957	14.084 043	.071 002
33	.146 186	14.230 230	.070 273
34	.137 912	14.368 141	.069 598
35	.130 105	14.498 246	.068 974
36	.122 741	14.620 987	.068 395
37	.115 793	14.736 780	.067 857
38	.109 239	14.846 019	.067 358
39	.103 056	14.949 075	.066 894
40	.097 222	15.046 297	.066 462
41	.091 719	15.138 016	.066 059
42	.086 527	15.224 543	.065 683
43	.081 630	15.306 173	.065 333
44	.077 009	15.383 182	.065 006
45	.072 650	15.455 832	.064 700
46	.068 538	15.524 370	.064 415
47	.064 658	15.589 028	.064 148
48	.060 998	15.650 027	.063 898
49	.057 546	15.707 572	.063 664
50	.054 288	15.761 861	.063 444

*What $1 due in the future is worth today. Formula: $p = \dfrac{s}{(1 + i)^n}$

**What $1 payable periodically is worth today (payments made at end of period). For payments made at the beginning of the period, add 1 to the amount shown for the previous period. Formula: $a_n = \dfrac{1 - (1 + i)^{-n}}{i}$

†Periodic payment necessary to pay off a loan of $1. Formula: The sinking fund factor plus the rate of interest.

PRESENT WORTH OF A FUTURE AMOUNT OF $1.00
DISCOUNTED AT 7 PERCENT INTEREST
PER PERIOD

Number of Periods	Present Worth of $1.00*	Present Worth of $1.00 per Period**	Partial Payment per $1.00 of Loan†
1	.934 579	.934 579	1.070 000
2	.873 439	1.808 018	.553 092
3	.816 298	2.624 316	.381 052
4	.762 895	3.387 211	.295 228
5	.712 986	4.100 197	.243 891
6	.666 342	4.766 540	.209 796
7	.622 750	5.389 289	.185 553
8	.582 009	5.971 299	.167 468
9	.543 934	6.515 232	.153 486
10	.508 349	7.023 582	.142 378
11	.475 093	7.498 674	.133 357
12	.444 012	7.942 686	.125 902
13	.414 964	8.357 651	.119 651
14	.387 817	8.745 468	.114 345
15	.362 446	9.107 914	.109 795
16	.338 735	9.446 649	.105 858
17	.316 574	9.763 223	.102 425
18	.295 864	10.059 087	.099 413
19	.276 508	10.335 595	.096 753
20	.258 419	10.594 014	.094 383
21	.241 513	10.835 527	.092 289
22	.225 713	11.061 240	.090 406
23	.210 947	11.272 187	.088 714
24	.197 147	11.469 334	.087 189
25	.184 249	11.653 583	.085 811

*What $1 due in the future is worth today. Formula: $p = \dfrac{s}{(1 + i)^n}$

**What $1 payable periodically is worth today (payments made at end of period). For payments made at the beginning of the period, add 1 to the amount shown for the previous period. Formula: $a_n = \dfrac{1 - (1 + i)^{-n}}{i}$

†Periodic payment necessary to pay off a loan of $1. Formula: The sinking fund factor plus the rate of interest.

DISCOUNTED AT 7 PERCENT INTEREST

Number of Periods	Present Worth of $1.00*	Present Worth of $1.00 per Period**	Partial Payment per $1.00 of Loan†
26	.172 195	11.825 779	.084 561
27	.160 930	11.986 709	.083 426
28	.150 402	12.137 111	.082 392
29	.140 563	12.277 674	.081 449
30	.131 367	12.409 041	.080 586
31	.122 773	12.531 814	.079 797
32	.114 741	12.646 555	.079 073
33	.107 235	12.753 790	.078 408
34	.100 219	12.854 009	.077 797
35	.093 663	12.947 672	.077 234
36	.087 535	13.035 208	.076 715
37	.081 809	13.117 017	.076 237
38	.076 457	13.193 473	.075 795
39	.071 455	13.264 928	.075 387
40	.066 780	13.331 709	.075 009
41	.062 412	13.394 120	.074 660
42	.058 329	13.452 449	.074 336
43	.054 513	13.506 962	.074 036
44	.050 946	13.557 908	.073 758
45	.047 613	13.605 522	.073 500
46	.044 499	13.650 020	.073 260
47	.041 587	13.691 608	.073 037
48	.038 867	13.730 474	.072 831
49	.036 324	13.766 799	.072 639
50	.033 948	13.800 746	.072 460

*What $1 due in the future is worth today. Formula: $p = \dfrac{s}{(1 + i)^n}$

**What $1 payable periodically is worth today (payments made at end of period). For payments made at the beginning of the period, add 1 to the amount shown for the previous period. Formula: $a_n = \dfrac{1 - (1 + i)^{-n}}{i}$

†Periodic payment necessary to pay off a loan of $1. Formula: The sinking fund factor plus the rate of interest.

PRESENT WORTH OF A FUTURE AMOUNT OF $1.00
DISCOUNTED AT 7½ PERCENT INTEREST
PER PERIOD

Number of Periods	Present Worth of $1.00*	Present Worth of $1.00 per Period**	Partial Payment per $1.00 of Loan†
1	.930 233	.930 233	1.075 000
2	.865 333	1.795 565	.556 928
3	.804 961	2.600 526	.384 538
4	.748 801	3.349 326	.298 568
5	.696 559	4.045 885	.247 165
6	.647 962	4.693 846	.213 045
7	.602 755	5.296 601	.188 800
8	.560 702	5.857 304	.170 727
9	.521 583	6.378 887	.156 767
10	.485 194	6.864 081	.145 686
11	.451 343	7.315 424	.136 697
12	.419 854	7.735 278	.129 278
13	.390 562	8.125 840	.123 064
14	.363 313	8.489 154	.117 797
15	.337 966	8.827 120	.113 287
16	.314 387	9.141 507	.109 391
17	.292 453	9.433 960	.106 000
18	.272 049	9.706 009	.103 029
19	.253 069	9.959 078	.100 411
20	.235 413	10.194 491	.098 092
21	.218 989	10.413 480	.096 029
22	.203 711	10.617 191	.094 187
23	.189 498	10.806 689	.092 535
24	.176 277	10.982 967	.091 050
25	.163 979	11.146 946	.089 711

*What $1 due in the future is worth today. Formula: $p = \dfrac{s}{(1 + i)^n}$

**What $1 payable periodically is worth today (payments made at end of period). For payments made at the beginning of the period, add 1 to the amount shown for the previous period. Formula: $a_n = \dfrac{1 - (1 + i)^{-n}}{i}$

†Periodic payment necessary to pay off a loan of $1. Formula: The sinking fund factor plus the rate of interest.

DISCOUNTED AT 7½ PERCENT INTEREST

Number of Periods	Present Worth of $1.00*	Present Worth of $1.00 per Period **	Partial Payment per $1.00 of Loan†
26	.152 539	11.299 485	.088 500
27	.141 896	11.441 381	.087 402
28	.131 997	11.573 378	.086 405
29	.122 788	11.696 165	.085 498
30	.114 221	11.810 386	.084 671
31	.106 272	11.916 638	.083 916
32	.098 839	12.015 478	.083 226
33	.091 943	12.107 421	.082 594
34	.085 529	12.192 950	.082 015
35	.079 562	12.272 511	.081 483
36	.074 011	12.346 522	.080 994
37	.068 847	12.415 370	.080 545
38	.064 044	12.479 414	.080 132
39	.059 576	12.538 989	.079 751
40	.055 419	12.594 409	.079 400
41	.051 553	12.645 962	.079 077
42	.047 956	12.693 918	.078 778
43	.044 610	12.738 528	.078 502
44	.041 498	12.780 026	.078 247
45	.038 603	12.818 629	.078 011
46	.035 910	12.854 539	.077 794
47	.033 404	12.887 943	.077 592
48	.031 074	12.919 017	.077 405
49	.028 906	12.947 922	.077 232
50	.016 889	12.974 812	.077 072

*What $1 due in the future is worth today. Formula: $p = \dfrac{s}{(1+i)^n}$

**What $1 payable periodically is worth today (payments made at end of period). For payments made at the beginning of the period, add 1 to the amount shown for the previous period. Formula: $a_n = \dfrac{1-(1+i)^{-n}}{i}$

†Periodic payment necessary to pay off a loan of $1. Formula: The sinking fund factor plus the rate of interest.

PRESENT WORTH OF A FUTURE AMOUNT OF $1.00
DISCOUNTED AT 8 PERCENT INTEREST
PER PERIOD

Number of Periods	Present Worth of $1.00*	Present Worth of $1.00 per Period**	Partial Payment per $1.00 of Loan†
1	.925 926	.925 926	1.080 000
2	.857 339	1.783 265	.560 769
3	.793 832	2.577 097	.388 034
4	.735 030	3.312 127	.301 921
5	.680 583	3.992 710	.250 456
6	.630 170	4.622 880	.216 315
7	.583 490	5.206 370	.192 072
8	.540 269	5.746 639	.174 015
9	.500 249	6.246 888	.160 080
10	.463 193	6.710 081	.149 029
11	.428 883	7.138 964	.140 076
12	.397 114	7.536 078	.132 695
13	.367 698	7.903 776	.126 522
14	.340 461	8.244 237	.121 297
15	.315 242	8.559 479	.116 830
16	.291 890	8.851 369	.112 977
17	.270 269	9.121 638	.109 629
18	.250 249	9.371 887	.106 702
19	.231 712	9.603 599	.104 128
20	.214 548	9.818 147	.101 852
21	.198 656	10.016 803	.099 832
22	.183 941	10.200 744	.098 032
23	.170 315	10.371 059	.096 422
24	.157 699	10.528 758	.094 978
25	.146 018	10.674 776	.093 679

*What $1 due in the future is worth today. Formula: $p = \dfrac{s}{(1 + i)^n}$

**What $1 payable periodically is worth today (payments made at end of period). For payments made at the beginning of the period, add 1 to the amount shown for the previous period. Formula: $a_n = \dfrac{1 - (1 + i)^{-n}}{i}$

†Periodic payment necessary to pay off a loan of $1. Formula: The sinking fund factor plus the rate of interest.

DISCOUNTED AT 8 PERCENT INTEREST

Number of Periods	Present Worth of $1.00*	Present Worth of $1.00 per Period**	Partial Payment per $1.00 of Loan†
26	.135 202	10.809 978	.092 507
27	.125 187	10.935 165	.091 448
28	.115 914	11.051 078	.090 489
29	.107 328	11.158 406	.089 619
30	.099 377	11.257 783	.088 827
31	.092 016	11.349 799	.088 107
32	.085 200	11.434 999	.087 451
33	.078 889	11.513 888	.086 852
34	.073 045	11.586 934	.086 304
35	.067 635	11.654 568	.085 803
36	.062 625	11.717 193	.085 345
37	.057 986	11.775 179	.084 924
38	.053 690	11.828 869	.084 539
39	.049 713	11.878 582	.084 185
40	.046 031	11.924 613	.083 860
41	.042 621	11.967 235	.083 561
42	.039 464	12.006 699	.083 287
43	.036 541	12.043 240	.083 034
44	.033 834	12.077 074	.082 802
45	.031 328	12.108 402	.082 587
46	.029 007	12.137 409	.082 390
47	.026 859	12.164 267	.082 208
48	.024 869	12.189 136	.082 040
49	.023 027	12.212 163	.081 886
50	.021 321	12.233 485	.081 743

*What $1 due in the future is worth today. Formula: $p = \dfrac{s}{(1 + i)^n}$

**What $1 payable periodically is worth today (payments made at end of period). For payments made at the beginning of the period, add 1 to the amount shown for the previous period. Formula: $a_n = \dfrac{1 - (1 + i)^{-n}}{i}$

†Periodic payment necessary to pay off a loan of $1. Formula: The sinking fund factor plus the rate of interest.

PRESENT WORTH OF A FUTURE AMOUNT OF $1.00
DISCOUNTED AT 8½ PERCENT INTEREST
PER PERIOD

Number of Periods	Present Worth of $1.00*	Present Worth of $1.00 per Period**	Partial Payment per $1.00 of Loan†
1	.921 659	.921 659	1.085 000
2	.849 455	1.771 114	.564 616
3	.782 908	2.554 022	.391 539
4	.721 574	3.275 597	.305 288
5	.665 045	3.940 642	.253 766
6	.612 945	4.553 587	.219 607
7	.564 926	5.118 514	.195 369
8	.520 669	5.639 183	.177 331
9	.479 880	6.119 063	.163 424
10	.442 285	6.561 348	.152 408
11	.407 636	6.968 984	.143 493
12	.375 702	7.344 686	.136 153
13	.346 269	7.690 955	.130 023
14	.319 142	8.010 097	.124 842
15	.294 140	8.304 237	.120 420
16	.271 097	8.575 333	.116 614
17	.249 859	8.825 192	.113 312
18	.230 285	9.055 476	.110 430
19	.212 244	9.267 720	.107 901
20	.195 616	9.463 337	.105 671
21	.180 292	9.643 628	.103 695
22	.166 167	9.809 796	.101 939
23	.153 150	9.962 945	.100 372
24	.141 152	10.104 097	.098 970
25	.130 094	10.234 191	.097 712

*What $1 due in the future is worth today. Formula: $p = \dfrac{s}{(1 + i)^n}$

**What $1 payable periodically is worth today (payments made at end of period). For payments made at the beginning of the period, add 1 to the amount shown for the previous period.
Formula: $a_n = \dfrac{1 - (1 + i)^{-n}}{i}$

†Periodic payment necessary to pay off a loan of $1. Formula: The sinking fund factor plus the rate of interest.

DISCOUNTED AT 8½ PERCENT INTEREST

Number of Periods	Present Worth of $1.00*	Present Worth of $1.00 per Period**	Partial Payment per $1.00 of Loan†
26	.119 902	10.354 093	.096 580
27	.110 509	10.464 602	.095 560
28	.101 851	10.566 453	.094 639
29	.093 872	10.660 326	.093 806
30	.086 518	10.746 844	.093 051
31	.079 740	10.826 584	.092 365
32	.073 493	10.900 078	.091 742
33	.067 736	10.967 813	.091 176
34	.062 429	11.030 243	.090 660
35	.057 539	11.087 781	.090 189
36	.053 031	11.140 812	.089 760
37	.048 876	11.189 689	.089 368
38	.045 047	11.234 736	.089 010
39	.041 518	11.276 255	.088 682
40	.038 266	11.314 520	.088 382
41	.035 268	11.349 788	.088 107
42	.032 505	11.382 293	.087 856
43	.029 959	11.412 252	.087 625
44	.027 612	11.439 864	.087 414
45	.025 448	11.465 312	.087 220
46	.023 455	11.488 767	.087 042
47	.021 617	11.510 384	.086 878
48	.019 924	11.530 308	.086 728
49	.018 363	11.548 671	.086 590
50	.016 924	11.565 595	.086 463

*What $1 due in the future is worth today. Formula: $p = \dfrac{s}{(1+i)^n}$

**What $1 payable periodically is worth today (payments made at end of period). For payments made at the beginning of the period, add 1 to the amount shown for the previous period.
Formula: $a_n = \dfrac{1-(1+i)^{-n}}{i}$

†Periodic payment necessary to pay off a loan of $1. Formula: The sinking fund factor plus the rate of interest.

PRESENT WORTH OF A FUTURE AMOUNT OF $1.00
DISCOUNTED AT 9 PERCENT INTEREST
PER PERIOD

Number of Periods	Present Worth of $1.00*	Present Worth of $1.00 per Period**	Partial Payment per $1.00 of Loan†
1	.917 431	.917 431	1.090 000
2	.841 680	1.759 111	.568 469
3	.772 183	2.531 295	.395 055
4	.708 425	3.239 720	.308 669
5	.649 931	3.889 651	.257 092
6	.596 267	4.485 919	.222 920
7	.547 034	5.032 953	.198 691
8	.501 866	5.534 819	.180 674
9	.460 428	5.995 247	.166 799
10	.422 411	6.417 658	.155 820
11	.387 533	6.805 191	.146 947
12	.355 535	7.160 725	.139 651
13	.326 179	7.486 904	.133 567
14	.299 246	7.786 150	.128 433
15	.274 538	8.060 688	.124 059
16	.251 870	8.312 558	.120 300
17	.231 073	8.543 631	.117 046
18	.211 490	8.755 625	.114 212
19	.194 490	8.950 115	.111 730
20	.178 431	9.128 546	.109 546
21	.163 698	9.292 244	.107 617
22	.150 182	9.442 425	.105 905
23	.137 781	9.580 207	.104 382
24	.126 405	9.706 612	.103 023
25	.115 968	9.822 580	.101 806

*What $1 due in the future is worth today. Formula: $p = \dfrac{s}{(1 + i)^n}$

**What $1 payable periodically is worth today (payments made at end of period). For payments made at the beginning of the period, add 1 to the amount shown for the previous period.
Formula: $a_n = \dfrac{1 - (1 + i)^{-n}}{i}$

†Periodic payment necessary to pay off a loan of $1. Formula: The sinking fund factor plus the rate of interest.

DISCOUNTED AT 9 PERCENT INTEREST

Number of Periods	Present Worth of $1.00*	Present Worth of $1.00 per Period**	Partial Payment per $1.00 of Loan†
26	.106 393	9.928 972	.100 715
27	.097 608	10.026 580	.099 735
28	.089 548	10.116 128	.098 852
29	.082 155	10.198 283	.098 056
30	.075 371	10.273 654	.097 336
31	.069 148	10.342 802	.096 686
32	.063 438	10.406 240	.096 096
33	.058 200	10.464 441	.095 562
34	.053 395	10.517 835	.095 076
35	.048 986	10.566 821	.094 636
36	.044 941	10.611 763	.094 235
37	.041 231	10.652 993	.093 870
38	.037 826	10.690 820	.093 538
39	.034 703	10.725 523	.093 236
40	.031 838	10.757 360	.092 960
41	.029 209	10.786 569	.092 708
42	.026 797	10.813 366	.092 478
43	.024 584	10.837 950	.092 268
44	.022 555	10.860 505	.092 077
45	.020 692	10.881 197	.091 902
46	.018 984	10.900 181	.091 742
47	.017 416	10.917 597	.091 595
48	.015 978	10.933 575	.091 461
49	.014 659	10.948 234	.091 339
50	.013 449	10.961 683	.091 227

*What $1 due in the future is worth today. Formula: $p = \dfrac{s}{(1+i)^n}$

**What $1 payable periodically is worth today (payments made at end of period). For payments made at the beginning of the period, add 1 to the amount shown for the previous period.
Formula: $a_n = \dfrac{1-(1+i)^{-n}}{i}$

†Periodic payment necessary to pay off a loan of $1. Formula: The sinking fund factor plus the rate of interest.

PRESENT WORTH OF A FUTURE AMOUNT OF $1.00
DISCOUNTED AT 9½ PERCENT INTEREST
PER PERIOD

Number of Periods	Present Worth of $1.00*	Present Worth of $1.00 per Period**	Partial Payment per $1.00 of Loan†
1	.913 242	.913 242	1.095 000
2	.834 011	1.747 253	.572 327
3	.761 654	2.508 907	.398 580
4	.695 574	3.204 481	.312 063
5	.635 228	3.839 709	.260 436
6	.580 117	4.419 825	.226 253
7	.529 787	4.949 612	.202 036
8	.483 824	5.433 436	.184 046
9	.441 848	5.875 284	.170 205
10	.403 514	6.278 798	.159 266
11	.368 506	6.647 304	.150 437
12	.336 535	6.983 839	.143 188
13	.307 338	7.291 178	.137 152
14	.280 674	7.571 852	.132 068
15	.256 323	7.828 175	.127 744
16	.234 085	8.062 260	.124 035
17	.213 777	8.276 037	.120 831
18	.195 230	8.471 266	.118 046
19	.178 292	8.649 558	.115 613
20	.162 824	8.812 382	.113 477
21	.148 697	8.961 080	.111 594
22	.135 797	9.096 876	.109 928
23	.124 015	9.220 892	.108 449
24	.113 256	9.334 148	.107 134
25	.103 430	9.437 578	.105 959

*What $1 due in the future is worth today. Formula: $p = \dfrac{s}{(1 + i)^n}$

**What $1 payable periodically is worth today (payments made at end of period). For payments made at the beginning of the period, add 1 to the amount shown for the previous period.
Formula: $a_n = \dfrac{1 - (1 + i)^{-n}}{i}$

†Periodic payment necessary to pay off a loan of $1. Formula: The sinking fund factor plus the rate of interest.

DISCOUNTED AT 9½ PERCENT INTEREST

Number of Periods	Present Worth of $1.00*	Present Worth of $1.00 per Period**	Partial Payment per $1.00 of Loan†
26	.094 457	9.532 034	.104 909
27	.086 262	9.618 296	.103 969
28	.078 778	9.697 074	.103 124
29	.071 943	9.769 018	.102 364
30	.065 702	9.834 719	.101 681
31	.060 002	9.894 721	.101 064
32	.054 796	9.949 517	.100 507
33	.050 042	9.999 559	.100 004
34	.045 700	10.045 259	.099 549
35	.041 736	10.086 995	.099 138
36	.038 115	10.125 109	.098 764
37	.034 808	10.159 917	.098 426
38	.031 788	10.191 705	.098 119
39	.029 030	10.220 735	.097 840
40	.026 512	10.247 247	.097 587
41	.024 211	10.271 458	.097 357
42	.022 111	10.293 569	.097 148
43	.020 193	10.313 762	.096 958
44	.018 441	10.332 203	.096 785
45	.016 841	10.349 043	.096 627
46	.015 380	10.364 423	.096 484
47	.014 045	10.378 469	.096 353
48	.012 827	10.391 296	.096 234
49	.011 714	10.403 010	.096 126
50	.010 698	10.413 707	.096 027

*What $1 due in the future is worth today. Formula: $p = \dfrac{s}{(1 + i)^n}$

**What $1 payable periodically is worth today (payments made at end of period). For payments made at the beginning of the period, add 1 to the amount shown for the previous period.
Formula: $a_n = \dfrac{1 - (1 + i)^{-n}}{i}$

†Periodic payment necessary to pay off a loan of $1. Formula: The sinking fund factor plus the rate of interest.

PRESENT WORTH OF A FUTURE AMOUNT OF $1.00
DISCOUNTED AT 10 PERCENT INTEREST
PER PERIOD

Number of Periods	Present Worth of $1.00*	Present Worth of $1.00 per Period**	Partial Payment per $1.00 of Loan†
1	.909 091	.909 091	1.100 000
2	.826 446	1.735 537	.576 190
3	.751 315	2.486 852	.402 115
4	.683 013	3.169 865	.315 471
5	.620 921	3.790 787	.263 797
6	.564 474	4.355 261	.229 607
7	.513 158	4.868 419	.205 405
8	.466 507	5.334 926	.187 444
9	.424 098	5.759 024	.173 641
10	.385 543	6.144 567	.162 745
11	.350 494	6.495 061	.153 963
12	.318 631	6.813 692	.146 763
13	.289 664	7.103 356	.140 779
14	.263 331	7.366 687	.135 746
15	.239 392	7.606 080	.131 474
16	.217 629	7.823 709	.127 817
17	.197 845	8.021 553	.124 664
18	.179 859	8.201 412	.121 930
19	.163 508	8.364 920	.119 547
20	.148 644	8.513 564	.117 460
21	.135 131	8.648 694	.115 624
22	.122 846	8.771 540	.114 005
23	.111 678	8.883 218	.112 572
24	.101 526	8.984 744	.111 300
25	.092 296	9.077 040	.110 168

*What $1 due in the future is worth today. Formula: $p = \dfrac{s}{(1 + i)^n}$

**What $1 payable periodically is worth today (payments made at end of period). For payments made at the beginning of the period, add 1 to the amount shown for the previous period.
Formula: $a_n = \dfrac{1 - (1 + i)^{-n}}{i}$

†Periodic payment necessary to pay off a loan of $1. Formula: The sinking fund factor plus the rate of interest.

DISCOUNTED AT 10 PERCENT INTEREST

Number of Periods	Present Worth of $1.00*	Present Worth of $1.00 per Period**	Partial Payment per $1.00 of Loan†
26	.083 905	9.160 945	.109 159
27	.076 278	9.237 223	.108 258
28	.069 343	9.306 567	.107 451
29	.063 039	9.369 606	.106 728
30	.057 309	9.426 914	.106 079
31	.052 099	9.479 013	.105 496
32	.047 362	9.526 376	.104 972
33	.043 047	9.569 432	.104 499
34	.039 143	9.608 575	.104 074
35	.035 585	9.644 159	.103 690
36	.032 349	9.676 508	.103 343
37	.029 408	9.705 917	.103 030
38	.026 735	9.732 651	.102 747
39	.024 304	9.756 956	.102 491
40	.022 095	9.779 051	.102 259
41	.020 086	9.799 137	.102 050
42	.018 260	9.817 397	.101 860
43	.016 600	9.833 998	.101 688
44	.015 091	9.849 089	.101 532
45	.013 719	9.862 808	.101 391
46	.012 472	9.875 280	.101 263
47	.011 338	9.886 618	.101 147
48	.010 307	9.896 926	.101 041
49	.009 370	9.906 296	.100 946
50	.008 519	9.914 814	.100 859

*What $1 due in the future is worth today. Formula: $p = \dfrac{s}{(1+i)^n}$

**What $1 payable periodically is worth today (payments made at end of period). For payments made at the beginning of the period, add 1 to the amount shown for the previous period.
Formula: $a_n = \dfrac{1-(1+i)^{-n}}{i}$

†Periodic payment necessary to pay off a loan of $1. Formula: The sinking fund factor plus the rate of interest.

LIABILITY TO REPLACE
A MEASURE OF INCURABLE PHYSICAL DEPRECIATION
BASED ON INCREASING EFFECTIVE AGE —
FOR PROPERTIES WITH ECONOMIC LIFE OF 5 TO 50 YEARS
AT SELECTED RATES OF INTEREST

Percent Liability at Interest Rates of:

End of Year	7%	8%	9%	10%	11%	12%
			5-Year Economic Life			
1	17.39	17.05	16.71	16.38	16.06	15.74
2	36.00	35.46	34.92	34.40	33.88	33.37
3	59.90	55.34	54.77	54.22	53.66	53.12
4	77.21	76.81	76.81	76.02	75.62	75.23
5	100.00	100.00	100.00	100.00	100.00	100.00
			10-Year Economic Life			
1	7.24	6.90	6.58	6.27	5.98	5.70
2	14.98	14.36	13.76	13.18	12.62	12.08
3	23.27	22.41	21.58	20.77	19.99	19.23
4	32.14	31.11	30.10	29.12	28.17	27.23
5	41.62	40.50	39.39	38.31	37.24	36.20
6	51.77	50.64	49.52	48.41	47.32	46.24
7	62.64	61.59	60.56	59.53	58.51	57.49
8	74.26	73.42	72.59	71.75	70.92	70.09
9	86.69	86.20	85.70	85.20	84.70	84.20
10	100.00	100.00	100.00	100.00	100.00	100.00
			15-Year Economic Life			
1	3.98	3.68	3.41	3.15	2.91	2.68
2	8.24	7.66	7.12	6.61	6.13	5.69
3	12.79	11.96	11.17	10.42	9.71	9.04
4	17.67	16.60	15.58	14.61	13.69	12.82
5	22.89	21.61	20.38	19.22	18.10	17.04
6	28.47	27.02	25.62	24.28	23.00	21.77
7	34.44	32.86	31.34	29.86	28.44	27.06
8	40.83	39.17	37.56	35.99	34.47	32.99
9	47.67	45.99	44.35	42.74	41.17	39.63
10	54.98	53.35	51.75	50.16	48.60	47.07
11	62.81	61.30	59.81	58.32	56.86	55.40
12	71.19	69.89	68.60	67.30	66.02	64.74
13	80.15	79.17	78.18	77.18	76.18	75.19
14	89.74	89.18	88.62	88.05	87.47	86.89
15	100.00	100.00	100.00	100.00	100.00	100.00
			20-Year Economic Life			
1	2.44	2.19	1.96	1.75	1.56	1.39
2	5.05	4.55	4.09	3.67	3.29	2.94
3	7.84	7.09	6.41	5.78	5.21	4.68
4	10.83	9.85	8.94	8.10	7.34	6.63
5	14.03	12.82	11.70	10.66	9.70	8.82
6	17.45	16.03	14.71	13.46	12.33	11.26
7	21.11	19.50	17.98	16.56	15.24	14.00
8	25.03	23.24	21.56	19.97	18.47	17.07
9	29.22	27.29	25.45	23.71	22.06	20.51
10	33.70	31.66	29.70	27.83	26.05	24.36

Percent Liability at Interest Rates of:

End of Year	7%	8%	9%	10%	11%	12%

20-Year Economic Life – (Continued)

End of Year	7%	8%	9%	10%	11%	12%
11	38.50	36.37	34.32	32.35	31.47	28.67
12	43.64	41.47	39.37	37.34	35.38	33.49
13	49.13	46.97	44.87	42.82	40.83	38.90
14	55.01	52.92	50.86	48.84	46.87	44.96
15	61.30	59.33	57.39	55.47	53.59	51.74
16	68.03	66.27	64.51	62.77	61.04	59.34
17	75.23	73.75	72.27	70.79	69.31	67.84
18	82.93	81.84	80.73	79.61	78.49	77.37
19	91.18	90.57	89.95	89.32	88.69	88.05
20	100.00	100.00	100.00	100.00	100.00	100.00

25-Year Economic Life

End of Year	7%	8%	9%	10%	11%	12%
1	1.58	1.37	1.18	1.02	.87	.75
2	3.27	2.85	2.47	2.14	1.84	1.59
3	5.08	4.44	3.87	3.37	2.92	2.53
4	7.02	6.16	5.40	4.72	4.12	3.58
5	9.09	8.03	7.07	6.21	5.44	4.77
6	11.31	10.04	8.88	7.85	6.92	6.09
7	13.68	12.21	10.86	9.65	8.55	7.57
8	16.22	14.55	13.02	11.63	10.37	9.23
9	18.94	17.07	15.37	13.81	12.38	11.08
10	21.84	19.82	17.94	16.21	14.62	13.16
11	24.96	22.77	20.73	18.84	17.10	15.49
12	28.28	25.96	23.78	21.74	19.85	18.10
13	31.84	29.40	27.10	24.93	22.91	21.02
14	35.65	33.12	30.72	28.35	26.30	24.23
15	39.73	37.14	34.66	32.31	30.07	27.96
16	44.09	41.48	38.96	36.55	34.25	32.07
17	48.76	46.17	43.65	40.23	38.89	36.66
18	53.75	51.26	48.76	46.37	44.05	41.81
19	59.10	56.69	54.33	52.02	49.77	47.58
20	64.82	62.60	60.40	58.24	56.11	54.04
21	70.93	68.97	67.02	65.08	63.16	61.27
22	77.48	75.86	74.23	72.60	70.98	69.38
23	84.49	83.29	82.09	80.88	79.67	78.45
24	91.98	90.63	90.66	89.99	89.30	88.62
25	100.00	100.00	100.00	100.00	100.00	100.00

30-Year Economic Life

End of Year	7%	8%	9%	10%	11%	12%
1	1.06	.88	.73	.61	.50	.41
2	2.19	1.84	1.53	1.28	1.06	.88
3	3.40	2.87	2.41	2.01	1.68	1.40
4	4.70	3.98	3.36	2.82	2.37	1.98
5	6.09	5.18	4.39	3.71	3.13	2.63
6	7.57	6.48	5.52	4.69	3.98	3.36
7	9.16	7.88	6.75	5.77	4.92	4.18
8	10.86	9.39	8.09	6.95	5.96	5.10
9	12.68	11.02	9.55	8.26	7.12	6.12
10	14.63	12.79	11.15	9.69	8.40	7.27
11	16.71	14.69	12.88	11.27	9.83	8.56
12	18.94	16.75	14.78	13.00	11.41	10.00
13	21.32	18.98	16.84	14.91	13.17	11.61
14	23.87	21.38	19.09	17.01	15.12	13.42
15	26.60	24.97	21.54	19.32	17.29	15.45

Percent Liability at Interest Rates of:

End of Year	7%	8%	9%	10%	11%	12%

30-Year Economic Life – (Continued)

End of Year	7%	8%	9%	10%	11%	12%
16	29.52	26.77	24.21	21.85	19.69	17.72
17	32.65	29.79	27.13	24.65	22.36	20.26
18	35.99	33.06	30.30	27.72	25.33	23.10
19	39.57	36.59	33.76	31.10	28.61	26.29
20	43.40	40.40	37.53	34.82	32.26	29.86
21	47.50	44.51	41.64	38.91	36.31	33.85
22	51.88	48.95	46.13	43.41	40.81	38.33
23	56.57	53.75	51.01	48.35	45.80	43.34
24	61.59	58.94	56.34	53.80	51.34	48.96
25	66.96	64.53	62.14	59.79	57.49	55.25
26	72.70	70.58	68.47	66.37	64.31	62.25
27	78.85	77.11	75.36	73.62	71.89	70.18
28	85.43	84.16	82.88	81.59	80.30	79.02
29	92.47	91.77	91.07	90.36	89.64	88.92
30	100.00	100.00	100.00	100.00	100.00	100.00

35-Year Economic Life

End of Year	7%	8%	9%	10%	11%	12%
1	.72	.58	.46	.37	.29	.23
2	1.50	1.21	.97	.77	.62	.49
3	2.33	1.88	1.52	1.22	.98	.78
4	3.21	2.62	2.12	1.71	1.38	1.11
5	4.36	3.40	2.78	2.25	1.82	1.46
6	5.18	4.26	3.49	2.85	2.32	1.88
7	6.26	5.18	4.27	3.50	2.86	2.34
8	7.42	6.17	5.11	4.22	3.47	2.85
9	8.67	7.25	6.04	5.01	4.15	3.41
10	10.00	8.41	7.04	5.88	4.90	4.07
11	11.42	9.66	8.14	6.84	5.73	4.79
12	12.94	11.01	9.34	7.89	6.65	5.59
13	14.57	12.47	10.64	9.05	7.67	6.49
14	16.31	14.05	12.06	10.32	8.81	7.50
15	18.18	15.76	13.61	11.72	10.07	8.64
16	20.18	17.60	15.30	13.26	11.47	9.90
17	22.31	19.59	17.14	14.96	13.03	11.32
18	24.60	21.73	19.15	16.82	14.75	12.92
19	27.04	24.05	21.33	18.88	16.67	14.70
20	29.66	26.56	23.72	21.13	18.80	16.69
21	32.46	29.26	26.32	23.61	21.16	18.93
22	35.45	32.18	29.15	26.35	23.78	21.43
23	38.66	35.34	32.23	29.35	26.68	24.23
24	42.09	38.75	35.60	32.65	29.91	27.37
25	45.75	42.43	39.27	36.29	33.49	30.89
26	49.68	46.40	43.26	40.28	37.47	34.83
27	53.88	50.69	47.62	44.68	41.89	39.33
28	58.38	55.32	52.36	49.52	46.79	44.18
29	63.19	60.33	57.55	54.84	52.23	49.71
30	68.33	65.74	63.19	60.69	58.26	55.91
31	73.84	71.58	69.34	67.13	64.97	62.85
32	79.73	77.89	76.05	74.21	72.40	70.62
33	86.04	84.70	83.35	82.00	80.66	79.33
34	92.78	92.06	91.32	90.57	89.83	89.08
35	100.00	100.00	100.00	100.00	100.00	100.00

Percent Liability at Interest Rates of:

End of Year	7%	8%	9%	10%	11%	12%
			40-Year Economic Life			
1	.50	.39	.30	.23	.17	.13
2	1.04	.80	.62	.47	.36	.28
3	1.61	1.25	.97	.75	.58	.44
4	2.22	1.74	1.35	1.05	.81	.62
5	2.88	2 26	1.77	1.38	1.07	.83
6	3.58	2.83	2.23	1.74	1.36	1.06
7	4.34	3.44	2.72	2.14	1.68	1.32
8	5.14	4.11	3.26	2.58	2.04	1.60
9	6.00	4.82	3.85	3.07	2.44	1.93
10	6.92	5.59	4.50	3.60	2.87	2.29
11	7.91	6.43	5.20	4.19	3.36	2.69
12	8.96	7.33	5.96	4.83	3.90	3.15
13	10.09	8.30	6.79	5.54	4.51	3.65
14	11.30	9.35	7.70	6.32	5.17	4.22
15	12.59	10.48	8.69	7.18	5.91	4.86
16	13.97	11.71	9.77	8.12	6.74	5.57
17	15.45	13.03	10.94	9.16	7.65	6.17
18	17.03	14.46	12.22	10.30	8.66	7.27
19	18.72	16.00	13.62	11.56	9.79	8.27
20	20.54	17.67	15.14	12.94	11.04	9.39
21	22.47	19.46	16.80	14.46	12.42	10.65
22	24.55	21.41	18.61	16.13	13.96	12.06
23	26.77	23.51	20.58	17.97	15.67	13.64
24	29.14	25.77	22.73	20.00	17.56	15.40
25	31.68	28.22	25.07	22.22	19.67	17.38
26	34.40	30.86	27.62	24.67	22.00	19.60
27	37.32	33.72	30.40	27.36	24.59	22.08
28	40.42	36.80	33.43	30.32	27.47	24.86
29	43.75	40.13	36.74	33.58	30.66	27.97
30	47.32	43.73	40.34	37.37	34.21	31.46
31	51.13	47.61	44.27	41.11	38.14	35.37
32	55.21	51.81	48.55	45.45	42.51	39.73
33	59.58	56.34	53.21	50.22	47.36	44.64
34	64.25	61.23	58.30	55.46	52.74	50.13
35	69.24	66.52	63.84	61.24	58.71	56.27
36	74.59	72.22	69.88	67.59	65.34	63.16
37	80.32	78.39	76.47	74.57	72.70	70.87
38	86.44	85.05	83.65	82.25	80.87	79.50
39	92.99	92.24	91.47	90.70	89.94	89.17
40	100.00	100.00	100.00	100.00	100.00	100.00
			45-Year Economic Life			
1	.35	.26	.19	.14	.10	.07
2	.73	.54	.40	.29	.21	.16
3	1.13	.84	.62	.46	.34	.25
4	1.55	1.17	.87	.65	.48	.35
5	2.01	1.52	1.14	.85	.63	.47
6	2.50	1.90	1.43	1.07	.80	.60
7	3.03	2.31	1.75	1.32	.99	.74
8	3.59	2.75	2.10	1.59	1.20	.81
9	4.19	3.23	2.48	1.89	1.44	1.09
10	4.84	3.75	2.89	2.22	1.70	1.29

Percent Liability at Interest Rates of:

End of Year	7%	8%	9%	10%	11%	12%

45-Year Economic Life – (Continued)

End of Year	7%	8%	9%	10%	11%	12%
11	5.52	4.31	3.34	2.58	1.98	1.52
12	6.26	4.91	3.83	2.97	2.30	1.78
13	7.05	5.56	4.37	3.41	2.66	2.06
14	7.89	6.27	4.95	3.89	3.05	2.39
15	8.79	7.03	5.58	4.42	3.49	2.74
16	9.76	7.85	6.28	5.00	3.97	3.15
17	10.79	8.73	7.03	5.64	4.51	3.60
18	11.90	9.69	7.85	6.34	5.11	4.10
19	13.08	10.72	8.75	7.12	5.77	4.67
20	14.35	11.84	9.73	7.97	6.51	5.31
21	15.70	13.05	10.80	8.90	7.32	6.02
22	17.15	14.35	11.96	9.93	8.23	6.81
23	18.70	15.76	13.22	11.06	8.24	7.70
24	20.36	17.27	14.60	12.31	10.36	8.70
25	22.14	18.91	16.11	13.68	11.60	9.82
26	24.03	20.69	17.75	15.19	12.97	11.07
27	26.07	22.60	19.53	16.85	14.50	12.47
28	28.24	24.67	21.48	18.67	16.20	14.04
29	30.57	26.90	23.61	20.67	18.18	15.80
30	33.06	29.31	25.92	22.88	20.17	17.77
31	35.72	31.91	28.44	25.31	22.49	19.97
32	38.57	34.73	31.19	27.98	25.07	22.44
33	41.62	37.76	34.19	30.92	27.93	25.21
34	44.89	41.04	37.46	34.15	31.10	28.31
35	48.37	44.58	41.02	37.70	34.62	31.78
36	52.11	48.41	44.90	41.61	38.53	35.67
37	56.11	52.54	49.13	45.91	42.87	40.02
38	60.39	56.00	53.75	50.64	47.69	44.90
39	64.97	61.82	58.77	55.84	53.04	50.36
40	69.86	67.03	64.25	61.56	58.97	56.48
41	75.10	72.65	70.23	67.86	65.56	63.33
42	80.71	78.72	76.74	74.79	72.87	71.00
43	86.71	85.27	83.83	82.40	70.99	79.60
44	93.13	92.35	91.57	90.78	90.00	89.22
45	100.00	100.00	100.00	100.00	100.00	100.00

50-Year Economic Life

End of Year	7%	8%	9%	10%	11%	12%
1	.25	.18	.12	.09	.06	.04
2	.51	.36	.26	.18	.13	.09
3	.79	.57	.40	.28	.22	.14
4	1.19	.79	.56	.40	.28	.20
5	1.41	1.02	.74	.52	.37	.27
6	1.76	1.28	.92	.66	.47	.34
7	2.13	1.56	1.13	.82	.59	.42
8	2.52	1.85	1.35	.98	.73	.51
9	2.95	2.18	1.60	1.17	.85	.62
10	3.40	2.53	1.86	1.37	1.00	.73
11	3.83	2.90	2.16	1.59	1.17	.86
12	4.40	3.31	2.47	1.84	1.36	1.01
13	4.96	3.75	2.82	2.11	1.57	1.17
14	5.55	4.22	3.19	2.40	1.80	1.35
15	6.18	4.73	3.60	2.73	2.06	1.55

Percent Liability at Interest Rates of:

End of Year	7%	8%	9%	10%	11%	12%
			50-Year Economic Life – (Continued)			
16	6.86	5.29	4.05	3.09	2.35	1.78
17	7.59	5.88	4.54	3.48	2.67	2.04
18	8.36	6.53	5.07	3.92	3.02	2.32
19	9.20	7.22	5.65	4.40	3.41	2.64
20	10.08	7.98	6.27	4.92	3.85	3.00
21	11.04	8.79	6.97	5.50	4.33	3.40
22	12.06	9.67	7.71	6.13	4.87	3.85
23	13.15	10.62	8.53	6.83	5.46	4.36
24	14.31	11.64	9.42	7.60	6.12	4.92
25	15.56	12.74	10.39	8.45	6.86	5.56
26	16.89	13.94	11.45	9.38	7.67	6.26
27	18.32	15.22	12.60	10.40	8.57	7.06
28	19.85	16.62	13.86	11.53	9.58	7.95
29	21.49	18.12	15.23	12.77	10.69	8.94
30	23.24	19.74	16.72	14.13	11.93	10.06
31	25.11	21.50	18.35	15.63	13.30	11.30
32	27.11	23.39	20.13	17.28	14.82	12.70
33	29.26	25.44	22.05	19.10	16.51	14.27
34	31.55	27.65	24.17	21.09	18.39	16.02
35	34.00	30.03	26.47	23.29	20.47	17.99
36	36.63	32.61	28.97	25.70	23.78	20.19
37	39.44	35.39	31.70	28.36	25.35	22.65
38	42.45	38.10	34.68	31.28	28.20	25.41
39	45.67	41.64	37.92	34.49	31.36	28.50
40	49.11	45.15	41.45	38.03	34.87	31.96
41	52.79	48.94	45.31	41.91	38.76	35.84
42	56.73	53.03	49.51	46.19	43.08	40.18
43	60.95	57.44	54.09	50.90	47.88	45.05
44	65.46	62.21	59.08	56.06	53.21	59.49
45	70.29	67.36	64.52	61.77	59.12	56.59
46	75.46	72.93	70.45	68.03	65.69	63.43
47	80.98	78.93	76.91	74.92	72.97	71.07
48	86.90	85.42	83.95	82.50	81.05	79.65
49	93.23	92.43	91.63	90.83	90.04	89.25
50	100.00	100.00	100.00	100.00	100.00	100.00

MONTHLY PAYMENTS INCLUDING PRINCIPAL AND INTEREST REQUIRED TO LIQUIDATE A MORTGAGE LOAN OF $1,000 AT VARIOUS RATES FOR ANNUAL PERIODS FROM 5 TO 30 YEARS

Mortgage Loan Period No. Years	6%	7%	7½%	8%	8½%	9%	10%
5	$19.35	$19.81	$20.04	$20.28	$20.52	$20.76	$21.25
6	16.58	17.05	17.29	17.54	17.78	18.03	18.53
7	14.61	15.10	15.34	15.59	15.84	16.09	16.61
8	13.15	13.64	13.89	14.14	14.40	14.65	15.18
9	12.01	12.51	12.77	13.02	13.28	13.55	14.08
10	11.11	11.61	11.87	12.14	12.40	12.67	13.22
11	10.37	10.85	11.15	11.42	11.69	11.96	12.52
12	9.76	10.29	10.56	10.83	11.10	11.38	11.95
13	9.25	9.78	10.06	10.33	10.62	10.90	11.48
14	8.82	9.36	9.64	9.92	10.20	10.49	11.09
15	8.44	8.99	9.27	9.56	9.85	10.15	10.75
16	8.12	8.68	8.96	9.25	9.55	9.85	10.46
17	7.84	8.40	8.69	8.99	9.29	9.59	10.22
18	7.59	8.16	8.45	8.75	9.06	9.37	10.00
19	7.36	7.95	8.24	8.55	8.86	9.17	9.82
20	7.17	7.76	8.06	8.37	8.68	9.00	9.65
21	6.99	7.59	7.90	8.21	8.53	8.85	9.51
22	6.83	7.44	7.75	8.07	8.39	8.72	9.39
23	6.69	7.30	7.62	7.94	8.26	8.60	9.28
24	6.56	7.18	7.50	7.82	8.15	8.49	9.18
25	6.45	7.07	7.39	7.72	8.06	8.40	9.09
26	6.34	6.97	7.30	7.63	7.97	8.31	9.01
27	6.24	6.88	7.21	7.55	7.89	8.24	8.94
28	6.16	6.80	7.13	7.47	7.82	8.17	8.88
29	6.07	6.73	7.06	7.40	7.75	8.11	8.83
30	6.00	6.66	7.00	7.34	7.69	8.05	8.78

SCHEDULE OF AMORTIZATION
FOR A $10,000 MORTGAGE UNDER
LEVEL PAYMENTS AT 7 PERCENT INTEREST

Based on a $10,000 mortgage—amortized over 25 years at 7 percent interest, constant payments of $70.70 each, over 300 monthly periods.

Time of Payment Month	Year	Amount of Interest	Amount of Amortization	Balance of Principal $10,000.00
1	1	$58.30	$12.40	$ 9,987.60
2	"	58.30	12.40	9,975.20
3	"	58.20	12.50	9,962.70
4	"	58.10	12.60	9,950.10
5	"	58.00	12.70	9,937.40
6	"	58.00	12.70	9,924.70
7	"	57.90	12.80	9,911.90
8	"	57.80	12.90	9,899.00
9	"	57.70	13.00	9,886.00
10	"	57.70	13.00	9,873.00
11	"	57.60	13.10	9,859.90
12	"	57.50	13.20	9,846.70
1	2	57.40	13.30	9,833.40
2	"	57.40	13.30	9,820.10
3	"	57.30	13.40	9,806.70
4	"	57.20	13.50	9,793.20
5	"	57.10	13.60	9,779.60
6	"	57.00	13.70	9,765.90
7	"	57.00	13.70	9,752.20
8	"	56.90	13.80	9,738.40
9	"	56.80	13.90	9,724.50
10	"	56.70	14.00	9,710.50
11	"	56.60	14.10	9,696.40
12	"	56.60	14.10	9,682.30
1	3	56.50	14.20	9,668.10
2	"	56.40	14.30	9,653.80
3	"	56.30	14.40	9,639.40
4	"	56.20	14.50	9,624.90
5	"	56.10	14.60	9,610.30
6	"	56.10	14.60	9,595.70
7	3	56.00	14.70	9,581.00
8	"	55.90	14.80	9,566.20
9	"	55.80	14.90	9,551.30
10	"	55.70	15.00	9,536.30
11	"	55.60	15.10	9,521.20
12	"	55.50	15.20	9,506.00
1	4	55.50	15.20	9,490.80
2	"	55.40	15.30	9,475.50
3	"	55.30	15.40	9,460.10
4	"	55.20	15.50	9,444.60
5	"	55.10	15.60	9,429.00
6	"	55.00	15.70	9,413.30
7	"	54.90	15.80	9,397.50
8	"	54.80	15.90	9,381.60
9	"	54.70	16.00	9,365.60
10	"	54.60	16.10	9,349.50
11	"	54.50	16.20	9,333.30
12	"	54.40	16.30	9,317.00

AMORTIZATION FOR A $10,000 MORTGAGE
(Continued)

Time of Payment		Amount of Interest	Amount of Amorti- zation	Balance of Principal
Month	Year			
1	5	54.30	16.40	9,300.60
2	,,	54.30	16.40	9,284.20
3	,,	54.20	16.50	9,267.70
4	,,	54.10	16.60	9,251.10
5	,,	54.00	16.70	9,234.40
6	,,	53.90	16.80	9,217.60
7	,,	53.80	16.90	9,200.70
8	,,	53.70	17.00	9,183.70
9	,,	53.60	17.10	9,166.60
10	,,	53.50	17.20	9,149.40
11	,,	53.40	17.30	9,132.10
12	,,	53.30	17.40	9,114.70
1	6	53.20	17.50	9,097.20
2	,,	53.10	17.60	9,079.60
3	,,	53.00	17.70	9,061.90
4	,,	52.90	17.80	9,044.10
5	,,	52.80	17.90	9,026.20
6	,,	52.70	18.00	9,008.20
7	6	52.50	18.20	8,990.00
8	,,	52.40	18.30	8,971.70
9	,,	52.30	18.40	8,953.30
10	,,	52.20	18.50	8,934.80
11	,,	52.10	18.60	8,916.20
12	,,	52.00	18.70	8,897.50
1	7	51.90	18.80	8,878.70
2	,,	51.80	18.90	8,859.80
3	,,	51.70	19.00	8,840.80
4	,,	51.60	19.10	8,821.70
5	,,	51.50	19.20	8,802.50
6	,,	51.30	19.40	8,783.10
7	,,	51.20	19.50	8,763.60
8	,,	51.10	19.60	8,744.00
9	,,	51.00	19.70	8,724.30
10	,,	50.90	19.80	8,704.50
11	,,	50.80	19.90	8,684.60
12	,,	50.70	20.00	8,664.60
1	8	50.50	20.20	8,644.40
2	,,	50.40	20.30	8,624.10
3	,,	50.30	20.40	8,603.70
4	,,	50.20	20.50	8,853.20
5	,,	50.10	20.60	8,562.60
6	,,	49.90	20.80	8,541.80
7	,,	49.80	20.90	8,520.90
8	,,	49.70	21.00	8,499.90
9	,,	49.60	21.10	8,478.80
10	,,	49.50	21.20	8,457.60
11	,,	49.30	21.40	8,436.20
12	,,	49.20	21.50	8,414.70
1	9	49.10	21.60	8,393.10
2	,,	49.00	21.70	8,371.40
3	,,	48.80	21.90	8,349.50
4	,,	48.70	22.00	8,327.50
5	,,	48.60	22.10	8,305.40
6	,,	48.40	22.30	8,283.10

AMORTIZATION FOR A $10,000 MORTGAGE
(Continued)

Time of Payment		Amount of	Amount of	Balance of
Month	Year	Interest	Amortization	Principal
7	9	$48.30	$22.40	$ 8,260.70
8	,,	48.20	22.50	8,238.20
9	,,	48.10	22.60	8,215.60
10	,,	47.90	22.80	8,192.80
11	,,	47.80	22.90	8,169.90
12	,,	47.70	23.00	8,146.90
1	10	47.50	23.20	8,123.70
2	,,	47.40	23.30	8,100.40
3	,,	47.30	23.40	8,077.00
4	,,	47.10	23.60	8,053.40
5	,,	47.00	23.70	8,029.70
6	,,	46.80	23.90	8,005.80
7	,,	46.70	24.00	7,981.80
8	,,	46.60	24.10	7,957.70
9	,,	46.40	24.30	7,933.40
10	,,	46.30	24.40	7,909.00
11	,,	46.10	24.60	7,884.40
12	,,	46.00	24.70	7,859.70
1	11	45.80	24.90	7,834.80
2	,,	45.70	25.00	7,809.80
3	,,	45.60	25.10	7,784.70
4	,,	45.40	25.30	7,759.40
5	,,	45.30	25.40	7,734.00
6	,,	45.10	25.60	7,708.40
7	,,	45.00	25.70	7,682.70
8	,,	44.80	25.90	7,656.80
9	,,	44.70	26.00	7,630.80
10	,,	44.50	26.20	7,604.60
11	,,	44.40	26.30	7,578.30
12	,,	44.20	26.50	7,551.80
1	12	44.10	26.60	7,525.20
2	,,	43.90	26.80	7,498.40
3	,,	43.70	27.00	7,471.40
4	,,	43.60	27.10	7,444.30
5	,,	43.40	27.30	7,417.00
6	,,	43.30	27.40	7,389.60
7	12	43.10	27.60	7,362.00
8	,,	42.90	27.80	7,334.20
9	,,	42.80	27.90	7,306.30
10	,,	42.60	28.10	7,278.20
11	,,	42.50	28.20	7,250.00
12	,,	42.30	28.40	7,221.60
1	13	42.10	28.60	7,193.00
2	,,	42.00	28.70	7,164.30
3	,,	41.80	28.90	7,135.40
4	,,	41.60	29.10	7,106.30
5	,,	41.50	29.20	7,077.10
6	,,	41.30	29.40	7,047.70
7	,,	41.10	29.60	7,018.10
8	,,	40.90	29.80	6,988.30
9	,,	40.80	29.90	6,958.40
10	,,	40.60	30.10	6,928.30
11	,,	40.40	30.30	6,898.00
12	,,	40.20	30.50	6,867.50

AMORTIZATION FOR A $10,000 MORTGAGE
(Continued)

Time of Payment Month	Year	Amount of Interest	Amount of Amorti- zation	Balance of Principal
1	14	40.10	30.60	6,836.90
2	,,	39.90	30.80	6,806.10
3	,,	39.70	31.00	6,775.10
4	,,	39.50	31.20	6,743.90
5	,,	39.30	31.40	6,712.50
6	,,	39.20	31.50	6,681.10
7	,,	39.00	31.70	6,649.30
8	,,	38.80	31.90	6,617.40
9	,,	38.60	32.10	6,585.30
10	,,	38.40	32.30	6,553.00
11	,,	38.20	32.50	6,520.50
12	,,	38.00	32.70	6,487.80
1	15	37.80	32.90	6,454.90
2	,,	37.70	33.00	6,421.90
3	,,	37.50	33.20	6,388.70
4	,,	37.30	33.50	6,355.30
5	,,	37.10	33.60	6,321.70
6	,,	36.90	33.80	6,287.90
7	15	36.70	34.00	6,253.90
8	,,	36.50	34.20	6,219.70
9	,,	36.30	34.40	6,185.30
10	,,	36.10	34.60	6,150.70
11	,,	35.90	34.80	6,115.90
12	,,	35.70	35.00	6,080.90
1	16	35.50	35.20	6,045.70
2	,,	35.30	35.40	6,010.30
3	,,	35.10	35.60	5,974.70
4	,,	34.90	35.80	5,938.90
5	,,	34.60	36.10	5,902.80
6	,,	34.40	36.30	5,866.50
7	,,	34.20	36.50	5,830.00
8	,,	34.00	36.70	5,793.30
9	,,	33.80	36.90	5,756.40
10	,,	33.60	37.10	5,719.30
11	,,	33.40	37.36	5,682.00
12	,,	33.10	37.60	5,644.40
1	17	32.90	37.80	5,606.60
2	,,	32.70	38.00	5,568.60
3	,,	32.50	38.20	5,530.40
4	,,	32.30	38.40	5,492.00
5	,,	32.00	38.70	5,453.30
6	,,	31.80	38.90	5,414.40
7	,,	31.60	39.10	5,375.30
8	,,	31.40	39.30	5,336.00
9	,,	31.10	39.60	5,296.40
10	,,	30.90	39.80	5,256.60
11	,,	30.70	40.00	5,216.60
12	,,	30.40	40.30	5,176.30
1	18	30.20	40.50	5,135.80
2	,,	30.00	40.70	5,095.10
3	,,	29.70	41.00	5,054.10
4	,,	29.50	41.20	5,012.90
5	,,	29.20	41.50	4,971.40
6	,,	29.00	41.70	4,929.70

AMORTIZATION FOR A $10,000 MORTGAGE

(Continued)

Time of Payment Month	Year	Amount of Interest	Amount of Amortization	Balance of Principal
7	18	$28.80	$41.90	$4,887.80
8	,,	28.50	42.20	4,845.60
9	,,	28.30	42.40	4,803.20
10	,,	28.00	42.70	4,760.50
11	,,	27.80	42.90	4,717.60
12	,,	27.50	43.20	4,674.40
1	19	27.30	43.40	4,631.00
2	,,	27.00	43.70	4,587.30
3	,,	26.80	43.90	4,543.40
4	,,	26.50	44.20	4,499.20
5	,,	26.20	44.50	4,454.70
6	,,	26.00	44.70	4,410.00
7	,,	25.70	45.00	4,365.00
8	,,	25.50	45.20	4,319.80
9	,,	25.20	45.50	4,274.30
10	,,	24.90	45.80	4,228.50
11	,,	24.70	46.00	4,182.50
12	,,	24.40	46.30	4,136.20
1	20	24.10	46.60	4,089.60
2	,,	23.90	46.80	4,042.80
3	,,	23.60	47.10	3,995.70
4	,,	23.30	47.40	3,948.30
5	,,	23.00	47.70	3,900.60
6	,,	22.80	47.90	3,852.70
7	,,	22.50	48.20	3,804.50
8	,,	22.20	48.50	3,756.00
9	,,	21.90	48.80	3.707.20
10	,,	21.60	49.10	3,658.10
11	,,	21.30	49.40	3,608.70
12	,,	21.10	49.60	3,559.10
1	21	20.80	49.90	3,509.20
2	,,	20.50	50.20	3,459.00
3	,,	20.20	50.50	3,408.50
4	,,	19.90	50.80	3,357.70
5	,,	19.60	51.10	3,306.60
6	,,	19.30	51.40	3,255.20
7	21	$19.00	$51.70	$3,203.50
8	,,	18.70	52.00	3,151.50
9	,,	18.40	52.30	3,099.20
10	,,	18.10	52.60	3,046.60
11	,,	17.80	52.90	2,993.70
12	,,	17.50	53.20	2,940.50
1	22	17.20	53.50	2,887.00
2	,,	16.80	53.90	2,833.10
3	,,	16.50	54.20	2,778.90
4	,,	16.20	54.50	2,724.40
5	,,	15.90	54.80	2,669.60
6	,,	15.60	55.10	2,614.50
7	,,	15.30	55.40	2,559.10
8	,,	14.90	55.80	2,503.30
9	,,	14.60	56.10	2,447.20
10	,,	14.30	56.40	2,390.80
11	,,	13.90	56.80	2,334.40
12	,,	13.60	57.10	2,276.90

AMORTIZATION FOR A $10,000 MORTGAGE

(Continued)

Time of Payment Month	Year	Amount of Interest	Amount of Amorti- zation	Balance of Principal
1	23	13.30	57.40	2,219.50
2	,,	12.90	57.80	2,161.70
3	,,	12.60	58.10	2,103.60
4	,,	12.30	58.40	2,045.20
5	,,	11.90	58.80	1,986.40
6	,,	11.60	59.10	1,927.30
7	,,	11.20	59.50	1,867.78
8	,,	10.90	59.80	1,808.80
9	,,	10.50	60.20	1,747.80
10	,,	10.20	60.50	1,687.30
11	,,	9,80	60.90	1,626.40
12	,,	9.50	61.20	1,565.20
1	24	9.10	61.60	1,503.60
2	,,	8.80	61.90	1,441.70
3	,,	8.40	62.30	1,379.40
4	,,	8.00	62.70	1,316.70
5	,,	7.70	63.00	1,253.70
6	,,	7.30	63.40	1,190.30
7	24	6.90	63.80	1,126.50
8	,,	6.60	64.10	1,062.40
9	,,	6.20	64.50	997.90
10	,,	5.80	64.90	933.00
11	,,	5.40	65.30	867.70
12	,,	5.10	65.60	802.10
1	25	4.70	66.00	736.10
2	,,	4.30	66.40	669.70
3	,,	3.90	66.80	602.90
4	,,	3.50	67.20	535.70
5	,,	3.10	67.60	468.10
6	,,	2.70	68.00	400.10
7	,,	2.30	68.40	331.70
8	,,	1.90	68.40	262.90
9	,,	1.50	69.20	193.70
10	,,	1.10	69.60	124.10
11	,,	.70	70.00	54.10
12	,,	.30	54.10	0.00

PERCENTAGE OF MORTGAGE DEBT REMAINING AT
END OF EACH YEAR FOR MORTGAGE LOAN PERIODS
OF 5 TO 30 YEARS AT 6 PERCENT INTEREST
UNDER MONTHLY CONSTANT PAYMENT DEBT AMORTIZATION

Age of Loan	Mortgage Loan Periods – Years					
	5	10	15	20	25	30
	Percent Mortgage Debt Remaining at End of Each Year*					
1	82.31	92.46	95.76	97.32	98.21	98.77
2	63.53	84.46	91.25	94.48	96.31	97.46
3	43.62	75.97	86.46	91.46	94.30	96.07
4	22.42	66.95	81.39	88.26	92.16	94.59
5	0.00	57.37	75.99	84.86	89.88	93.02
6		47.21	70.27	81.25	87.47	91.36
7		36.41	64.19	77.41	84.90	89.60
8		24.95	57.74	73.34	82.18	87.72
9		12.79	50.89	69.02	79.30	85.72
10		0.00	43.62	64.44	76.23	83.61
11			35.90	59.56	72.97	81.37
12			27.70	54.39	69.52	78.99
13			18.99	48.90	65.85	76.46
14			9.76	43.08	61.95	73.77
15			0.00	36.89	57.82	70.92
16				30.32	53.43	67.89
17				23.35	48.77	64.68
18				15.94	43.82	61.27
19				8.08	38.57	57.64
20				0.00	32.99	53.80
21					27.07	49.72
22					20.78	45.38
23					14.11	40.78
24					7.02	35.90
25					0.00	30.71
26						25.20
27						19.36
28						13.15
29						6.56
30						0.00

*To find remaining mortgage debt for remaining life period of a loan, multiply the monthly constant mortgage loan payment by "Present Worth of $1.00" factor – use fractional monthly interest rate for number of remaining monthly payments.
Formula: $a_n = \dfrac{1 - V^n}{i}$

PERCENTAGE OF MORTGAGE DEBT REMAINING AT
END OF EACH YEAR FOR MORTGAGE LOAN PERIODS
OF 5 TO 30 YEARS AT 6½ PERCENT INTEREST
UNDER MONTHLY CONSTANT PAYMENT DEBT AMORTIZATION

Mortgage Loan Periods – Years

Age of Loan	5	10	15	20	25	30
	Percent Mortgage Debt Remaining at End of Each Year[*]					
1	82.50	92.65	95.92	97.47	98.34	98.87
2	63.83	84.81	91.56	94.78	96.57	97.67
3	43.91	76.44	86.91	91.90	94.68	96.38
4	22.65	67.52	81.95	88.83	92.66	95.01
5	0.00	57.99	76.66	85.56	90.51	93.55
6		47.83	71.01	82.07	88.21	91.99
7		36.99	64.98	78.34	85.76	90.32
8		25.42	58.55	74.36	83.14	88.54
9		13.08	51.69	70.12	80.35	86.65
10		0.00	44.38	65.59	77.38	84.62
11			36.57	60.76	74.20	82.46
12			28.23	55.60	70.81	80.16
13			19.34	50.10	67.20	77.70
14			9.86	44.24	63.34	75.08
15			0.00	37.97	59.22	72.28
16				31.30	54.83	69.30
17				24.17	50.14	66.11
18				16.56	45.14	62.72
19				8.45	39.81	59.09
20				0.00	34.12	55.22
21					28.05	51.09
22					21.57	46.69
23					14.65	41.99
24					7.28	36.98
25					0.00	31.63
26						25.92
27						19.83
28						13.33
29						6.39
30						0.00

[*]To find remaining mortgage debt for remaining life period of a loan, multiply the monthly constant mortgage loan payment by "Present Worth of $1.00" factor – use fractional monthly interest rate for number of remaining monthly payments.

Formula: $a_n = \dfrac{1 - V^n}{i}$

PERCENTAGE OF MORTGAGE DEBT REMAINING AT END OF EACH YEAR FOR MORTGAGE LOAN PERIODS OF 5 TO 30 YEARS AT 7 PERCENT INTEREST UNDER MONTHLY CONSTANT PAYMENT DEBT AMORTIZATION

Age of Loan	Mortgage Loan Periods – Years					
	5	10	15	20	25	30
	Percent Mortgage Debt Remaining at End of Each Year*					
1	82.68	92.83	96.09	97.61	98.47	99.07
2	64.11	85.14	91.89	95.05	96.82	97.99
3	44.19	76.90	87.39	92.31	95.06	96.84
4	22.84	68.06	82.57	89.36	93.17	95.60
5	0.00	58.58	77.40	86.21	91.15	94.27
6		48.41	71.85	82.82	88.98	92.84
7		37.51	65.91	79.19	86.65	91.31
8		25.82	59.53	75.30	84.15	89.67
9		13.29	52.69	71.12	81.47	87.91
10		0.00	45.36	66.65	78.60	86.02
11			37.49	61.85	75.52	84.00
12			29.07	56.71	72.22	81.84
13			20.03	51.19	68.68	79.51
14			10.33	45.27	64.88	77.02
15			0.00	38.93	60.81	74.34
16				32.13	56.44	71.48
17				24.83	51.76	68.40
18				17.01	46.74	65.11
19				8.62	41.36	61.57
20				0.00	35.59	57.78
21					29.40	53.71
22					22.77	49.35
23					15.65	44.68
24					8.02	39.67
25					0.00	34.29
26						28.53
27						22.36
28						15.73
29						8.63
30						0.00

*To find remaining mortgage debt for remaining life period of a loan, multiply the monthly constant mortgage loan payment by "Present Worth of $1.00" factor – use fractional monthly interest rate for number of remaining monthly payments.

Formula: $a_n = \dfrac{1 - V^n}{i}$

PERCENTAGE OF MORTGAGE DEBT REMAINING AT END OF EACH YEAR FOR MORTGAGE LOAN PERIODS OF 5 TO 30 YEARS AT 7½ PERCENT INTEREST UNDER MONTHLY CONSTANT PAYMENT DEBT AMORTIZATION

Mortgage Loan Periods – Years

Age of Loan	5	10	15	20	25	30
			Percent Mortgage Debt Remaining at End of Each Year[*]			
1	82.87	93.01	96.24	97.75	98.58	99.16
2	64.41	85.47	92.18	95.33	97.06	98.18
3	44.52	77.35	87.81	92.72	95.41	97.12
4	23.09	68.60	83.10	89.91	93.64	95.97
5	0.00	59.17	78.02	86.87	91.73	94.74
6		49.01	72.55	83.61	89.67	93.41
7		38.05	66.65	80.09	87.45	91.98
8		26.25	60.30	76.29	85.06	90.44
9		13.53	53.45	72.21	82.48	88.78
10		0.00	46.07	67.80	79.71	86.99
11			38.12	63.06	76.72	85.06
12			29.56	57.94	73.49	82.99
13			20.32	52.42	70.02	80.75
14			10.38	46.48	66.28	78.33
15			0.00	40.09	62.24	75.73
16				33.18	57.89	72.93
17				25.75	52.21	69.91
18				17.73	48.16	66.65
19				9.10	42.72	63.15
20				0.00	36.86	59.37
21					30.54	55.29
22					23.73	50.90
23					16.39	46.17
24					8.48	41.08
25					0.00	35.58
26						29.66
27						23.28
28						16.40
29						8.99
30						0.00

[*]To find remaining mortgage debt for remaining life period of a loan, multiply the monthly constant mortgage loan payment by "Present Worth of $1.00" factor – use fractional monthly interest rate for number of remaining monthly payments.

Formula: $a_n = \dfrac{1 - V^n}{i}$

PERCENTAGE OF MORTGAGE DEBT REMAINING AT
END OF EACH YEAR FOR MORTGAGE LOAN PERIODS
OF 5 TO 30 YEARS AT 8 PERCENT INTEREST
UNDER MONTHLY CONSTANT PAYMENT DEBT AMORTIZATION

Mortgage Loan Periods – Years

Age of Loan	5	10	15	20	25	30
			Percent Mortgage Debt Remaining at End of Each Year [*]			
1	83.05	93.19	96.40	97.88	98.69	99.23
2	64.70	85.81	92.50	95.58	97.27	98.33
3	44.82	77.81	88.28	93.10	95.73	97.36
4	23.29	69.16	83.70	90.40	94.07	96.30
5	0.00	59.78	78.75	87.49	92.26	95.16
6		49.63	73.38	84.33	90.31	93.92
7		38.64	67.56	80.91	88.19	92.57
8		26.73	61.27	77.20	85.90	91.12
9		13.83	54.45	73.19	83.42	89.54
10		0.00	47.07	68.84	80.73	87.83
11			39.08	64.13	77.82	85.99
12			30.42	59.04	74.66	83.99
13			21.04	53.52	71.25	81.82
14			10.89	47.54	67.55	79.47
15			0.00	41.06	63.55	76.93
16				34.05	59.21	74.17
17				26.47	54.51	71.19
18				18.23	49.43	67.96
19				9.32	43.20	64.46
20				0.00	37.95	60.67
21					31.49	56.58
22					24.49	52.13
23					16.91	47.32
24					8.71	42.11
25					0.00	36.47
26						30.36
27						23.74
28						16.57
29						8.81
30						0.00

---

[*]To find remaining mortgage debt for remaining life period of a loan, multiply the monthly constant mortgage loan payment by "Present Worth of $1.00" – use fractional monthly interest rate for number of remaining monthly payments.

Formula: $a_n = \dfrac{1 - V^n}{i}$

PERCENTAGE OF MORTGAGE DEBT REMAINING AT END OF EACH YEAR FOR MORTGAGE LOAN PERIODS OF 5 TO 30 YEARS AT 8½ PERCENT INTEREST UNDER MONTHLY CONSTANT PAYMENT DEBT AMORTIZATION

Mortgage Loan Periods – Years

Age of Loan	5	10	15	20	25	30
	Percent Mortgage Debt Remaining at End of Each Year*					
1	84.68	93.94	96.84	98.18	98.90	99.31
2	66.56	86.77	93.11	96.03	97.60	98.49
3	46.84	78.96	89.05	93.68	96.18	97.60
4	25.38	70.47	84.63	91.13	94.63	96.63
5	0.00	61.23	79.82	88.36	92.95	95.58
6		51.17	74.58	85.34	91.12	94.43
7		40.22	68.88	82.05	89.12	93.18
8		28.30	62.68	78.47	86.96	91.82
9		15.32	55.93	74.57	84.60	90.34
10		0.00	48.58	70.33	82.03	88.73
11			40.58	65.72	79.23	86.97
12			31.88	60.69	76.19	85.06
13			22.40	55.23	72.88	82.98
14			12.09	49.28	69.28	80.72
15			0.00	42.80	65.35	78.26
16				35.75	61.08	75.58
17				28.08	56.44	72.67
18				19.73	51.38	69.50
19				10.65	45.88	66.04
20				0.00	39.89	62.28
21					33.37	58.19
22					26.27	53.74
23					18.55	48.89
24					10.14	43.61
25					0.00	37.87
26						31.63
27						24.82
28						17.42
29						9.36
30						0.00

*To find remaining mortgage debt for remaining life period of a loan, multiply the monthly constant mortgage loan payment by "Present Worth of $1.00" factor – use fractional monthly interest rate for number of remaining monthly payments.

Formula: $a_n = \dfrac{1 - V^n}{i}$

PERCENTAGE OF MORTGAGE DEBT REMAINING AT END OF EACH YEAR FOR MORTGAGE LOAN PERIODS OF 5 TO 30 YEARS AT 9 PERCENT INTEREST UNDER MONTHLY CONSTANT PAYMENT DEBT AMORTIZATION

Mortgage Loan Periods – Years

Age of Loan	5	10	15	20	25	30
	Percent Mortgage Debt Remaining at End of Each Year [*]					
1	84.86	94.09	96.99	98.29	98.98	99.37
2	66.85	87.07	93.40	96.25	97.78	98.63
3	47.16	79.39	89.48	94.02	96.45	97.81
4	25.61	70.99	85.19	91.59	95.01	96.92
5	0.00	61.80	80.50	88.92	93.43	95.94
6		51.75	75.37	86.00	91.70	94.87
7		40.76	69.76	82.81	89.81	93.70
8		28.74	63.62	79.32	87.74	92.42
9		15.59	56.91	75.51	85.48	91.02
10		0.00	49.56	71.33	83.00	89.49
11			41.53	66.77	80.29	87.82
12			32.74	61.78	77.33	85.99
13			23.13	56.32	74.09	83.98
14			12.61	50.34	70.55	81.79
15			0.00	43.81	66.67	79.40
16				36.66	62.43	76.78
17				28.84	57.79	73.91
18				20.29	52.72	70.78
19				10.94	47.17	67.35
20				0.00	41.10	63.60
21					34.46	59.50
22					27.20	55.01
23					19.26	50.11
24					10.57	44.74
25					0.00	38.87
26						32.44
27						25.42
28						17.74
29						9.33
30						0.00

---

[*]To find remaining mortgage debt for remaining life period of a loan, multiply the monthly constant mortgage loan payment by "Present Worth of $1.00" factor – use fractional monthly interest rate for number of remaining monthly payments.

Formula: $a_n = \dfrac{1 - V^n}{i}$

PERCENTAGE OF MORTGAGE DEBT REMAINING AT
END OF EACH YEAR FOR MORTGAGE LOAN PERIODS
OF 5 TO 30 YEARS AT 9½ PERCENT INTEREST
UNDER MONTHLY CONSTANT PAYMENT DEBT AMORTIZATION

Mortgage Loan Periods – Years

Age of Loan	5	10	15	20	25	30
	*Percent Mortgage Debt Remaining at End of Each Year**					
1	85.02	94.25	97.11	98.39	99.06	99.44
2	67.13	87.38	93.66	96.48	97.93	98.76
3	47.47	79.83	89.87	94.37	96.70	98.02
4	25.85	71.53	85.70	92.05	95.34	97.20
5	0.00	62.41	81.12	89.50	93.84	96.30
6		52.38	76.08	86.70	92.20	95.32
7		41.36	70.55	83.62	90.39	94.24
8		29.24	64.46	80.23	88.41	93.05
9		15.92	57.77	76.51	86.23	91.74
10		0.00	50.42	72.42	83.83	90.30
11			42.33	67.92	81.19	88.72
12			33.45	62.98	78.29	86.98
13			23.68	57.54	75.11	85.07
14			12.94	51.57	71.60	82.97
15			0.00	45.01	67.75	80.66
16				37.79	63.52	78.12
17				29.85	58.87	75.33
18				21.13	53.76	72.26
19				11.55	48.14	68.89
20				0.00	41.59	65.19
21					35.16	61.11
22					27.69	56.64
23					19.49	51.71
24					10.46	46.30
25					0.00	40.36
26						33.82
27						26.63
28						18.73
29						10.04
30						0.00

*To find remaining mortgage debt for remaining life period of a loan, multiply the monthly constant mortgage loan payment by "Present Worth of $1.00" factor – use fractional monthly interest rate for number of remaining monthly payments.

Formula: $a_n = \dfrac{1 - V^n}{i}$

PERCENTAGE OF MORTGAGE DEBT REMAINING AT
END OF EACH YEAR FOR MORTGAGE LOAN PERIODS
OF 5 TO 30 YEARS AT 10 PERCENT INTEREST
UNDER MONTHLY CONSTANT PAYMENT DEBT AMORTIZATION

Mortgage Loan Periods — Years

Age of Loan	5	10	15	20	25	30
			*Percent Mortgage Debt Remaining at End of Each Year**			
1	85.19	94.39	97.23	98.49	99.13	99.49
2	67.40	87.67	93.90	96.68	98.09	98.87
3	47.76	80.24	90.23	94.68	96.94	98.19
4	26.06	72.03	86.17	92.46	95.67	97.44
5	0.00	62.96	81.68	90.02	94.26	96.61
6		52.94	76.73	87.32	92.71	95.70
7		41.87	71.25	84.34	91.00	94.69
8		29.64	65.21	81.05	89.10	93.57
9		16.14	58.53	77.41	87.01	92.33
10		0.00	51.15	73.39	84.70	90.97
11			43.00	68.95	82.15	89.46
12			33.99	64.04	79.33	87.80
13			24.04	58.62	76.21	85.96
14			13.05	52.64	72.77	83.93
15			0.00	46.02	68.97	81.68
16				38.72	64.77	79.20
17				30.65	60.13	76.47
18				21.73	55.01	73.44
19				11.88	49.34	70.10
20				0.00	43.09	66.41
21					36.17	62.33
22					28.54	57.82
23					20.10	52.84
24					10.79	47.34
25					0.00	41.26
26						34.55
27						27.14
28						18.95
29						9.90
30						0.00

*To find remaining mortgage debt for remaining life period of a loan, multiply the monthly constant mortgage loan payment by "Present Worth of $1.00" factor — use fractional monthly interest rate for number of remaining monthly payments.

Formula: $a_n = \dfrac{1 - V^n}{i}$

**PRESENT WORTH OF AN ANNUITY OF 1 TABLE
FOR SELECTED INTEREST RATES
BASED ON STRAIGHT LINE THEORY OF DEPRECIATION
UNDER THE DIRECT-RING METHOD OF CAPITALIZATION***

Period	6%	7%	8%	9%	10%
1	.94340	.93458	.92593	.91743	.90909
2	1.78571	1.75439	1.72414	1.69492	1.66667
3	2.54237	2.47934	2.41935	2.36222	2.30771
4	3.22581	3.12500	3.03030	2.94118	2.85714
5	3.84615	3.70370	3.57143	3.44828	3.33333
6	4.41176	4.22535	4.05405	3.89560	3.74995
7	4.92958	4.69799	4.48718	4.29448	4.11765
8	5.40541	5.12821	4.87805	4.65116	4.44444
9	5.84416	5.52147	5.23256	4.97240	4.73687
10	6.25000	5.88235	5.55555	5.26316	5.00000
11	6.62651	6.21469	5.85106	5.52761	5.23809
12	6.97674	6.52174	6.12245	5.76934	5.45464
13	7.30337	6.80624	6.37255	5.99089	5.65227
14	7.60870	7.07071	6.60377	6.19464	5.83328
15	7.89474	7.31707	6.81818	6.38284	5.99999
16	8.16327	7.54717	7.01754	6.55738	6.15385
17	8.41584	7.76256	7.20339	6.71953	6.29644
18	8.65835	7.96460	7.37705	6.87002	6.42855
19	8.87850	8.15451	7.53968	7.01262	6.55308
20	9.09091	8.33333	7.69231	7.14286	6.66667
21	9.29204	8.50202	7.83582	7.26639	6.77415
22	9.48276	8.66142	7.97101	7.38253	6.87500
23	9.66387	8.81226	8.09859	7.49182	6.96966
24	9.83607	8.95522	8.21918	7.59492	7.05882
25	10.00000	9.09091	8.33333	7.69231	7.14286

*What $1 payable periodically for the remaining economic life of an investment and with annual interest paid on the entire investment is worth today.
Formula: Ring Factor = $\frac{1}{\text{Str. Line Rate}}$ or $\frac{1}{\text{Int. Rate} + \text{Depre. Rate}}$

PRESENT WORTH OF AN ANNUITY OF 1 TABLE
FOR SELECTED INTEREST RATES
BASED ON STRAIGHT LINE THEORY OF DEPRECIATION
UNDER THE DIRECT-RING METHOD OF CAPITALIZATION*

Period	6%	7%	8%	9%	10%
26	10.15625	9.21986	8.44156	7.78452	7.22230
27	10.30534	9.34256	8.54430	7.87154	7.29714
28	10.44776	9.45946	8.64197	7.95456	7.36844
29	10.58394	9.57096	8.73494	8.03329	7.43594
30	10.71429	9.67742	8.82353	8.10833	7.50019
31	10.83916	9.77918	8.90805	8.17942	7.56098
32	10.95890	9.87654	8.98876	8.24742	7.61905
33	11.07382	9.96979	9.06593	8.33333	7.69231
34	11.18421	10.05917	9.13978	8.37444	7.72732
35	11.29032	10.14492	9.21053	8.43377	7.77780
36	11.39240	10.22727	9.27835	8.49055	7.82607
37	11.49068	10.30640	9.34343	8.54504	7.87234
38	11.58536	10.38251	9.40594	8.59734	7.92823
39	11.67664	10.45576	9.46602	8.64745	7.95919
40	11.76470	10.52632	9.52381	8.69565	8.00000
41	11.84971	10.59431	9.57944	8.74202	8.03923
42	11.93181	10.65989	9.63303	8.78665	8.07696
43	12.01117	10.72319	9.68469	8.82963	8.11326
44	12.08791	10.78431	9.73451	8.87099	8.14817
45	12.16216	10.84337	9.78261	8.91091	8.18197
46	12.23404	10.90047	9.82906	8.94943	8.21429
47	12.30366	10.95571	9.87395	8.98665	8.24565
48	12.37113	11.00917	9.91736	9.02258	8.27588
49	12.43654	11.06094	9.95935	9.05731	8.30510
50	12.50000	11.11111	10.00000	9.09091	8.33333

*What $1 payable periodically for the remaining economic life of an investment and with annual interest paid on the entire investment is worth today.

Formula: Ring Factor = $\dfrac{1}{\text{Str. Line Rate}}$ or $\dfrac{1}{\text{Int. Rate + Depre. Rate}}$

THE NATIONAL HOUSING ACT
CONDENSED LISTING OF NUMBERS AND SECTIONS
OF INDIVIDUAL HOUSING PROGRAMS*

Title I	Housing renovation and modernization
Title II	Mortgage Insurance
Sec. 203(b)	Homeownership, regular program
Sec. 203(i)	Low-cost homes in outlying areas and farm homes
Sec. 203(k)	Repair of homes not in urban renewal areas
Sec. 203(m)	Seasonal homes
Sec. 207	Rental housing, regular program
Sec. 213	Cooperative housing
Sec. 220	New and rehabilitated homes and rental housing in urban renewal areas
Sec. 220(h)	Repair and rehabilitation of homes and multi-family housing in urban renewal areas
Sec. 221	New or rehabilitated homes and rental housing for displaced families or low- or moderate-income families
Sec. 221(d)(3)	New or rehabilitated rental housing for displaced or low- or moderate-income families with mortgages bearing below-market interest rates (BMIR) and purchased by GNMA under its special assistance program
Sec. 221(h)	Nonprofit rehabilitation of deteriorating or substandard housing for resale to low-income home purchaser at below-market interest rates
Sec.221(i)	Conversion of 221(d)(3) BMIR projects to condominium ownership
Sec. 221(j)	Conversion of 221(d)(3) BMIR projects to cooperative ownership
Sec. 222	Homeownership for servicemen
Sec. 231	New or rehabilitated housing for the elderly
Sec. 232	New or rehabilitated nursing homes
Sec. 233	Experimental housing, homes and rental
Sec. 234	Condominium housing
Sec. 235	Homeownership for lower income families with aid of "mortgage assistance payments"
Sec. 235(j)	Nonprofit or public rehabilitation of deteriorating or substandard housing for resale to lower income families
Sec. 236	Rental housing for lower income families with the aid of "interest reduction payments"
Sec. 237	Credit assistance and counseling for low- and moderate-income purchasers
Sec. 240	Purchases by lessees of fee simple title to property on which their homes are located
Sec. 241	Supplemental loans for multi-family projects
Sec. 242	Nonprofit hospitals
Sec. 608	World War II housing and veterans' rental housing (inactive)
Sec. 803	Military ("Capehart") housing (inactive)
Sec. 809	Homes for civilian employees at a research or development installation of military department, NASA, AEC, or a contractor thereof
Sec. 810	Single- and multi-family rental housing for military personnel and essential civilian personnel serving or employed in connection with a defense installation

The Mortgage Banker, March 1969, published by the Mortgage Bankers Association of America, Washington, D.C.

BASIC CONSTRUCTION SPECIFICATIONS FOR STANDARD HOUSE

1,000 SQ. FT.

DESCRIPTION: 5-room, 2-bedroom, 1-bath
Slab floor construction—finished floor and
bathroom tiling must be added

1. EXCAVATION	Sand, trench
2. FOUNDATION	Concrete 1:2:4 mix, footing reinf. 2—5/8" bars
3. CHIMNEY	Metal or brick
4. EXTERIOR WALLS	Concrete block—8 x 8 x 16 painted, furred
	Gables—concrete block
5. FLOOR CONSTRUCTION	Slab—4" Concrete, wire mesh reinf., steel trowel-Sand fill 8", 2—15# Felt mopped
6. PARTITIONS	Wood studs 2 x 4 x 16" o.c. #2 Y.P. P.T. plate
7. CEILING FRAMING	2 x 6 x 16" o.c. #2 Y.P.
8. ROOF FRAMING	2 x 6 x 16" o.c. #2 Y.P., Purlins & Braces 2 x 4 x 48" o.c.
	Wood sheathing 1 x 6 solid 4 in 12 pitch
9. ROOFING	210# Asphalt Shingles and 2—15# Felt (boxed in cornice 12" roof overhang)
10. GUTTERS & DOWNSPOUTS	None
11. WINDOWS	Steel casement—10
12. ENTR. & EXT. DETAIL	Stock entrance door, screen door, combination rear door
13. INSULATION	4" rock wool
14. STAIRS	None
15. LATH & PLASTER	Rock lath and plaster, sand finish—2 coats
16. FINISH FLOORING	None—add as specified
17. TILE & RESILIENT FLOOR	Asphalt in kitchen, greaseproof
18. INTERIOR DOOR & TRIM	Flush 9 interior doors, 2 exterior doors
19. CABINET WORK	Kitchen cabinets factory finish, tile or formica top, 24 lin. feet wall & 6' of base cabinets, 1 linen closet. Coat closets, shelf and rod
20. PAINTING & DECORATING	Kitchen & bath 3 ct. Enamel, other 2-ct. oil base paint
21. PLUMBING	Sink, Tub, W.C. & Lav. connect to sewer 1—30 gal. Auto. Water Heater
22. HEATING	Forced air, 64,000 B.T.U.
23. ELECTRIC	Overhead service for range and water heater, nonmetallic cable, average fixtures, 100 amps. electric service

BUILDING COST ESTIMATING

Base Unit Cost per Square Foot of
Standard 1,000 sq. ft. House

Typical Construction: Concrete Block

DESCRIPTION: *5-room, 2 bedroom, 1-bath; CB painted; concrete slab only; interior walls, ceiling and roof frame construction; furred and plastered walls, painted 2 coats 1 undercoat & 1 coat enamel, except kitchen and bath which will have 3 coats enamel; steel casement windows; no tiling in bath; 30 gal. automatic electric water heater; weather-stripped exterior doors; 201# asphalt roof with 2-15 # felt underlayers tintagged.*
Base Unit Cost—Gainesville, Florida, January 1972
Concrete Slab Floor

Base Unit Cost Variations
Resulting from Changes in Building Size

Building Size in Sq. Ft.	Base Unit Cost per Sq. Ft.	Percent Variation from Standard	Perimeter Exterior Wall, Lin. Ft.
700	$ 13.80	115	105
750	13.44	112	109
800	13.08	109	113
850	12.72	106	117
900	12.48	104	121
950	12.24	102	125
1,000	12.00	100	130
1,050	11.88	99	134
1,100	11.64	97	138
1,150	11.52	96	142
1,200	11:40	95	147
1,250	11.28	94	151
1,300	11.16	93	155
1,350	11.04	92	159
1,400	10.92	91	163
1,450	10.80	90	167
1,500	10.68	89	171
1,550	10.56	88	175
1,600	10.56	88	180
1,650	10.44	87	184
1,700	10.32	86	188
1,800	10.20	85	197
1,900	10.20	85	205
2,000	10.08	84	213
2,100	9.96	83	221
2,200	9.96	83	228
2,300	9.84	82	236
2,400	9.84	82	244
2,500	9.72	81	252

TYPICAL COST VARIATIONS
FOR DIFFERENT STRUCTURAL ELEMENTS

Exterior Construction	*Per Sq. Ft.*
Frame (wood) siding	$ 1.00
Brick veneer	1.30
Brick-solid	1.65

Wall Perimeter—Complete exterior and interior finish	*Per Lin. Ft.*
Concrete block—slab floor	$ 16.00
Concrete block—suspended floor	18.50
Frame—slab floor	20.00
Frame—suspended floor	21.00
Brick veneer—slab floor	23.00
Brick veneer—suspended floor	24.00
Brick solid—slab floor	23.50
Brick solid—suspended floor	25.00

Roof Construction	*Per Sq. Ft.*
Built-up roof (5 ply)	$ .10
Asbestos shingled roof	.20
Hip roof	.09
Boxed eaves—each ft. over 1st ft.	.10
Overhang—each ft. over 1st ft.	.15
Roof pitch—more or less than 4″ in 12″ (per inch of pitch)	.09
Insulation—2″	.12
—3″	.14
—4″	.20

Floor Construction	
Asphalt tile "B" net floor area	.24
"C" " " "	.26
"D" " " "	.32
Greaseproof	.50
Cork tile 5/16″	.90
Terrazzo—monolithic	.70
Terrazzo—strip	1.10
Parquet floor	.90
Quarry tile	1.20
Rubber tile 3/16″	1.40
" " 1/8″	1.10
Ceramic tile	2.25
Select oak—suspended floor construction	.90
Vinyl tile 1/16″	.50
" " 1/8 ″	.65

Other Improvements	*Per Unit*
Full tiling in bathroom	$ 400.00
Tile over tub only	125.00
Tile on floor only (5′ x 8′)	90.00
Tile per sq. ft.	2.50
Fireplace—extra chimney (no mantel facing)	600.00
Extra bath	560.00
Extra 1/2 bath—including stack	350.00
*Extra windows—each (casement)	52.00
*Extra doors—each	88.00
Tile window stools—each	10,00
Electric outlets—each	9.00
Aluminum awning window (added cost)—each	25.00
Kitchen exhaust fan 10″	75.00

NOTE: For variations in exterior walls and roof construction the base cost of a standard house should be increased by amounts shown above.

*Basic 1,000 sq. ft. house has 10 interior doors and 11 window. Unit sq. ft. cost includes one additional door and window for each 100 sq. ft. increase in building size.

TYPICAL COST VARIATIONS (Continued)

Sky vent—each	$ 50.00
Mercury switches—each	1.50
Space heater—65,000 B.T.U. & 55 gal. tank	150.00
Septic tank	180.00
Stoop (4' x 6') and storage closet	200.00

	Per.Lin.Ft.
Gutter and downspout	$ 1.50

	Per Sq.Ft.
Patio	$ 2.25
Carport (sealed ceiling)	4.50
Garage—Concrete block	6.00
Screened porch—concrete floor	4.75
suspended floor	5.50
Open porch	4.00
Entrance porch	6.00
Walks and driveway—concrete	.80
Paneled walls—add cost of lumber over and above cost of plaster in place	

	Board Ft.
Cypress # 1	$ .55
Spruce # 2	.35
Plaster in place	$ 2.35

THE OPEN HOUSING LAW OF 1968

(Public Law No. 90-284)

Because of the economic impact of the Civil Rights Act, Title VIII (commonly referred to as the open housing law) upon real estate transactions in general and the real estate business in particular, the complete text of the law as enacted by Congress, approved by President Johnson, and stated in the Congressional Record of March 11, 1968, is quoted below.

This open housing law is intended to ban all reference, limitations, or discrimination in the sale, use, or rental of housing throughout the United States, its territories and possessions, because of race, color, religion, or national origin of the individual buyer or tenant.

Housing financed under Veterans Administration guaranty loan programs or under Federal Housing Administration insured legislation are immediately subject to the law where such dwellings are sold by real estate brokers or their salesmen and employees. During 1969 all housing, whether privately or publicly financed, if sold by real estate agents, was subject to the law except for single-family homes and structures containing not more than four units.

Beginning January 1, 1970, there are no exemptions to the law so far as the real estate agent is concerned. Exemptions to the law apply only to individual owners who sell their single-family dwelling or housing of not more than four units, one of which they occupy, without the use of a real estate broker and without advertising that indicates a discriminatory preference. An individual owner, too, is subject to the law if he owns or has an interest in more than three residential dwellings or sells more than one home of which he is not an occupant in any twenty-four-month period.

The penalty for violation is deemed a misdemeanor and upon conviction is punishable by a fine up to $1,000 or imprisonment for not more than one year. Where, because of law defiance, bodily injury results, the penalty is stepped up to $10,000 or imprisonment for not more than ten years. Where the injury culminates in death, the imprisonment may be for any term of years or for life.

Although the effect of the open housing law in the early years of its enactment seems more psychological than real in practice, nevertheless those who own, rent, sell, or deal as agents in real estate are advised to read and study the provisions of the law as stated here in full:

CIVIL RIGHTS ACT, TITLE VIII—FAIR HOUSING
Policy

Sec. 801. It is the policy of the United States to provide, within constitutional limitations, for fair housing throughout the United States.

Definitions

Sec. 802. As used in this title—

(a) "Secretary" means the secretary of Housing and Urban Development.

(b) "Dwelling" means any building, structure, or portion thereof which is occupied as, or designed or intended for occupancy as, a residence by one or more families, and any vacant land which is offered for sale or lease for the construction or location thereon of any such building, structure, or portion thereof.

(c) "Family" includes a single individual.

(d) "Person" includes one or more individuals, corporations, partnerships, associations, labor organizations, legal representatives, mutual companies, joint-stock companies, trusts, unincorporated organizations, trustees, trustees in bankruptcy, receivers, and fiduciaries.

(e) "To rent" includes to lease, to sublease, to let, and otherwise to grant for a consideration the right to occupy premises not owned by the occupant.

(f) "Discriminatory housing practice" means an act that is unlawful under section 804, 805, or 806.

(g) "State" means any of the several states, the District of Columbia, the Commonwealth of Puerto Rico, or any of the territories and possessions of the United States.

Effective Dates of Certain Prohibitions

Sec. 803. (a) Subject to the provisions of subsection (b) and section 807, the prohibitions against discrimination in the sale or rental of housing set forth in section 804 shall apply:

(1) Upon enactment of this title, to—

(A) dwellings owned or operated by the federal government;

(B) dwellings provided in whole or in part with the aid of loans, advances, grants, or contributions made by the federal government, under agreements entered into after Nov. 20, 1962, unless payment due thereon has been made in full prior to the date of enactment of this title;

(C) dwellings provided in whole or in part by loans insured, guaranteed, or otherwise secured by the credit of the federal government, under agreements entered into after Nov. 20, 1962, unless payment thereon has been made in full prior to the date of enactment of this title: *Provided,* that nothing contained in subparagraphs (B) and (C) of this subsection shall be applicable to dwellings solely by virtue of the fact that they are subject to mortgages held by an FDIC or FSLIC institution; and

(D) dwellings provided by the development or the redevelopment of real property purchased, rented, or otherwise obtained from a state or local public agency receiving federal financial assistance for slum clearance or urban renewal with respect to such real property under loan or grant contracts entered into after Nov. 20, 1962.

(2) After Dec. 31, 1968, to all dwellings covered by paragraph (1) and to all other dwellings except as exempted by subsection (b).

(b) Nothing in section 804 (other than subsection (c)) shall apply to—

(1) any single-family house sold or rented by an owner: *Provided,* that such private individual owner does not own more than three such single-family houses at any one time: *Provided further,* that in the case of the sale of any such single-family house by a private individual owner not residing in

such house at the time of such sale or who was not the most recent resident of such·house prior to such sale, the exemption granted by this subsection shall apply only with respect to one such sale within any 24 month period: *Provided further,* that such bona fide private individual owner does not own any interest in, nor is there owned or reserved on his behalf, under any express or voluntary agreement, title to or any right to all or a portion of the proceeds from the sale or rental of, more than three such single-family houses at any one time: *Provided further,* that after Dec. 31, 1969, the sale or rental of any such single-family house shall be excepted from the application of this title only if such house is sold or rented (A) without the use in any manner of the sales or rental facilities or the sales or rental services of any real estate broker, agent, or salesman, or of such facilities or services of any person in the business of selling or renting dwellings, or of any employee or agent of any such broker, agent, salesman, or person and (B) without the publication, posting or mailing, after notice, of any advertisement or written notice in violation of section 804(c) of this title; but nothing in this proviso shall prohibit the use of attorneys, escrow agents, abstractors, title companies, and other such professional assistance as necessary to perfect or transfer the title, or

(2) rooms or units in dwellings containing living quarters occupied or intended to be occupied by no more than four families living independently of each other, if the owner actually maintains and occupies one of such living quarters as his residence.

(c) For the purposes of subsection (b), a person shall be deemed to be in the business of selling or renting dwellings if—

(1) he has, within the preceding 12 months, participated as principal in three or more transactions involving the sale or rental of any dwelling or any interest therein, or

(2) he has, within the preceding 12 months, participated as agent, other than in the sale of his own personal residence in providing sales or rental facilities or sales or rental services in two or more transactions involving the sale or rental of any dwelling or any interest therein, or

(3) he is the owner of any dwelling designed or intended for occupancy by, or occupied by, five or more families.

Discrimination in the Sale or Rental of Housing

Sec. 804. As made applicable by section 803 and except as exempted by sections 803(b) and 807, it shall be unlawful—

(a) To refuse to sell or rent after the making of a bona fide offer, or to refuse to negotiate for the sale or rental of, or otherwise make unavailable or deny, a dwelling to any person because of race, color, religion, or national origin.

(b) To discriminate against any person in the terms, conditions, or privileges of sale or rental of a dwelling, or in the provision of services or facilities in connection therewith, because of race, color, religion, or national origin.

(c) To make, print, or publish, or cause to be made, printed, or published any notice, statement, or advertisement, with respect to the sale or rental of a dwelling that indicates any preference, limitation, or discrimination based on race, color, religion, or national origin, or an intention to make any such preference, limitation, or discrimination.

(d) To represent to any person because of race, color, religion, or national origin that any dwelling is not available for inspection, sale, or rental when such dwelling is in fact so available.

(e) For profit, to induce or attempt to induce any person to sell or rent any dwelling by representations regarding the entry or prospective entry into the neighborhood of a person or persons of a particular race, color, religion, or national origin.

Discrimination in the Financing of Housing

Sec. 805. After Dec. 31, 1968, it shall be unlawful for any bank, building and loan association, insurance company or other corporation, association, firm or enterprise whose business consists in whole or in part in the making of commercial real estate loans, to deny a loan or other financial assistance to a person applying therefor for the purpose of purchasing, constructing, improving, repairing, or maintaining a dwelling, or to discriminate against him in the fixing of the amount, interest rate, duration, or other terms or conditions of such loan or other financial assistance, because of the race, color, religion, or national origin of such person or of any person associated with him in connection with such loan or other financial assistance or the purposes of such loan or other financial assistance, or of the present or prospective owners, lessees, tenants, or occupants of the dwelling or dwellings in relation to which such loan or other financial assistance is to be made or given: *Provided,* that nothing contained in this section shall impair the scope or effectiveness of the exception contained in section 803(b).

Discrimination in the Provision of Brokerage Services

Sec. 806. After Dec. 31, 1968, it shall be unlawful to deny any person access to or membership or participation in any multiple-listing service, real estate brokers' organization, or other service, organization, or facility relating to the business of selling or renting dwellings, or to discriminate against him in the terms or conditions of such access, membership, or participation, on account of race, color, religion, or national origin.

Exemption

Sec. 807. Nothing in this title shall prohibit a religious organization, association, or society, or any nonprofit institution or organization operated, supervised, or controlled by or in conjunction with a religious organization, association, or society, from limiting the sale, rental, or occupancy of dwellings which it owns or operates for other than a commercial purpose to persons of the same religion, or from giving preference to such persons, unless membership in such religion is restricted on account of race, color, or national origin. Nor shall anything in this title prohibit a private club not in fact open to the public, which as an incident to its primary purpose or purposes provides lodgings which it owns or operates for other than a commercial purpose, from limiting the rental or occupancy of such lodgings to its members or from giving preference to its members.

Administration

Sec. 808. (a) The authority and responsibility for administering this act shall be in the secretary of Housing and Urban Development.

(b) The Department of Housing and Urban Development shall be provided an additional assistant secretary. The Department of Housing and Urban Development Act (Public Law 89-174, 79 Stat. 667) is hereby amended by—

(1) striking the word "four," in section 4(a) of said Act (79 Stat. 668; 5 U.S.C. 624 (a)) and substituting therefor "five,"; and

(2) striking the word "six," in section 7 of said Act (79 Stat. 669; 5 U.S.C. 624 (c)) and substituting therefor "seven."

(c) The secretary may delegate any of his functions, duties, and powers to employees of the Department of Housing and Urban Development or to boards of such employees, including functions, duties, and powers with respect to investigating, conciliating, hearing, determining, ordering, certifying, reporting, or otherwise acting as to any work, business, or matter under this title. The persons to whom such delegations are made with respect to hearing functions, duties, and powers shall be appointed and shall serve in the Department of

Housing and Urban Development in compliance with section 3105, 3344, 5362, and 7521 of title 5 of the United States Code. Insofar as possible, conciliation meetings shall be held in the cities or other localities where the discriminatory housing practices allegedly occurred. The secretary shall by rule prescribe such rights of appeal from the decisions of his hearing examiners to other hearing examiners or to other officers in the department, to boards of officers or to himself, as shall be appropriate and in accordance with law.

(d) All executive departments and agencies shall administer their programs and activities relating to housing and urban development in a manner affirmatively to further the purposes of this title and shall cooperate with the secretary to further such purposes.

(e) The secretary of Housing and Urban Development shall—

(1) make studies with respect to the nature and extent of discriminatory housing practices in representative communities, urban, suburban, and rural, throughout the United States;

(2) publish and disseminate reports, recommendations, and information derived from such studies;

(3) cooperate with and render technical assistance to federal, state, local, and other public or private agencies, organizations, and institutions which are formulating or carrying on programs to prevent or eliminate discriminatory housing practices;

(4) cooperate with and render such technical and other assistance to the Community Relations Service as may be appropriate to further its activities in preventing or eliminating discriminatory housing practices; and

(5) administer the programs and activities relating to housing and urban development in a manner affirmatively to further the policies of this title.

Education and Conciliation

Sec. 809. Immediately after the enactment of this title the secretary shall commence such educational and conciliatory activities as in his judgment will further the purposes of this title. He shall call conferences of persons in the housing industry and other interested parties to acquaint them with the provisions of this title and his suggested means of implementing it, and shall endeavor with their advice to work out programs of voluntary compliance and of enforcement. He may pay per diem, travel, and transportation expenses for persons attending such conferences as provided in section 5703 of title 5 of the United States Code. He shall consult with state and local officials and other interested parties to learn the extent, if any, to which housing discrimination exists in their state or locality, and whether and how state or local enforcement programs might be utilized to combat such discrimination in connection with or in place of, the secretary's enforcement of this title. The secretary shall issue reports on such conferences and consultations as he deems appropriate.

Enforcement

Sec. 810. (a) Any person who claims to have been injured by a discriminatory housing practice or who believes that he will be irrevocably injured by a discriminatory housing practice that is about to occur (hereafter "person aggrieved") may file a complaint with the secretary. Complaints shall be in writing and shall contain such information and be in such form as the secretary requires. Upon receipt of such a complaint the secretary shall furnish a copy of the same to the person or persons who allegedly committed or are about to commit the alleged discriminatory housing practice. Within 30 days after receiving a complaint, or within 30 days after the expiration of any period of reference under subsection (c), the secretary shall investigate the complaint and give notice in writing to the person aggrieved whether he intends to resolve it. If the secretary decides to resolve the complaint, he shall proceed to try to eliminate or correct the alleged discriminatory housing practice by informal methods of conference, conciliation, and persuasion. Nothing said or done in the course of such informal endeavors may be made public or used as evidence in a subsequent proceeding under this title without the written consent of the persons concerned. Any employee of the secretary who shall make public any information in violation of this provision shall be deemed guilty of a misdemeanor and upon conviction thereof shall be fined not more than $1,000 or imprisoned not more than one year.

(b) A complaint under subsection (a) shall be filed within 180 days after the alleged discriminatory housing practice occurred. Complaints shall be in writing and shall state the facts upon which the allegations of a discriminatory housing practice are based. Complaints may be reasonably and fairly amended at any time. A respondent may file an answer to the complaint against him and with the leave of the secretary, which shall be granted whenever it would be reasonable and fair to do so, may amend his answer at any time. Both complaints and answers shall be verified.

(c) Wherever a state or local fair housing law provides rights and remedies for alleged discriminatory housing practices which are substantially equivalent to the rights and remedies provided in this title, the secretary shall notify the appropriate state or local agency of any complaint filed under this title which appears to constitute a violation of such state or local fair housing law, and the secretary shall take no further action with respect to such complaint if the appropriate state or local law enforcement official has, within 30 days from the date the alleged offense has been brought to his attention, commenced proceedings in the matter, or, having done so, carries forward such proceedings with reasonable promptness. In no event shall the secretary take further action unless he certifies that in his judgment, under the circumstances of the particular case, the protection of the rights of the parties or the interests of justice require such action.

(d) If within 30 days after a complaint is filed with the secretary or within 30 days after expiration of any period of reference under subsection (c), the secretary has been unable to obtain voluntary compliance with this title, the person aggrieved may, within 30 days thereafter, commence a civil action in any appropriate United States district court, against the respondent named in the complaint, to enforce the rights granted or protected by this title, insofar as such rights relate to the subject of the complaint: *Provided,* that no such civil action may be brought in any United States district court if the person aggrieved has a judicial remedy under a state or local fair housing law which provides rights and remedies for alleged discriminatory housing practices which are substantially equivalent to the rights and remedies provided in this title. Such actions may be brought without regard to the amount in controversy in any United States district court for the district in which the discriminatory housing practice is alleged to have occurred or be about to occur or in which the respondent resides or transacts business. If the court finds that a discriminatory housing practice has occurred or is about to occur, the court may, subject to the provisions of section 812, enjoin the respondent from engaging in such practice or order such affirmative action as may be appropriate.

(e) In any proceeding brought pursuant to this section, the burden of proof shall be on the complainant.

(f) Whenever an action filed by an individual, in either federal or state court, pursuant to this section or section 812, shall come to trial the secretary shall immediately terminate all efforts to obtain voluntary compliance.

Investigations; Subpenas; Giving of Evidence

Sec. 811. (a) In conducting an investigation the secretary shall have access at all reasonable times to premises, records, documents, individuals, and other evidence or possible sources of evidence and may examine, record, and copy such materials and take and record the testimony or statements of such persons as are reasonably necessary for the furtherance of the investigation: *Provided, however,* that the secretary first complies with the provisions of the Fourth Amendment relating to unreasonable searches and seizures. The secretary may issue subpenas to compel his access to or the production of such materials, or the appearance of such persons, and may issue interrogatories to a respondent, to the same extent and subject to the same limitations as would apply if the subpenas or interrogatories were issued or served in aid of a civil action in the United States district court for the district in which the investigation is taking place. The secretary may administer oaths.

(b) Upon written application to the secretary, a respondent shall be entitled to the issuance of a reasonable number of subpenas by and in the name of the secretary to the same extent and subject to the same limitations as subpenas issued by the secretary himself. Subpenas issued at the request of a respondent shall show on their face the name and address of such respondent and shall state that they were issued at his request.

(c) Witnesses summoned by subpena of the secretary shall be entitled to the same witness and mileage fee as are witnesses in proceedings in United States district courts. Fees payable to a witness summoned by a subpena issued at the request of a respondent shall be paid by him.

(d) Within five days after service of a subpena upon any person, such person may petition the secretary to revoke or modify the subpena. The secretary shall grant the petition if he finds that the subpena requires appearance or attendance at an unreasonable time or place, that it requires production of evidence which does not relate to any matter under investigation, that it does not describe with sufficient particularity the evidence to be produced, that compliance would be unduly onerous, or for other good reason.

(e) In case of contumacy or refusal to obey a subpena, the secretary or other person at whose request it was issued may petition for its enforcement in the United States district court for the district in which the person to whom the subpena was addressed resides, was served, or transacts business.

(f) Any person who willfully fails or neglects to attend and testify or to answer any lawful inquiry or to produce records, documents, or other evidence, if in his power to do so in obedience to the subpena or lawful order of the secretary, shall be fined not more than $1,000 or imprisoned not more than one year, or both. Any person who, with intent thereby to mislead the secretary, shall make or cause to be made any false entry or statement of fact in any report, account, record, or other document submitted to the secretary pursuant to his subpena or other order, or shall willfully neglect or fail to make or cause to be made full, true, and correct entries in such reports, accounts, records, or other documents, or shall willfully mutilate, alter, or by any other means falsify any documentary evidence, shall be fined not more than $1,000 or imprisoned not more than one year, or both.

(g) The Attorney General shall conduct all litigation in which the secretary participates as a party or as amicus pursuant to this act.

Enforcement by Private Persons

Sec. 812. (a) The rights granted by sections 803, 804, 805, and 806 may be enforced by civil actions in appropriate United States district courts without regard to the amount in controversy and in appropriate state or local courts of general jurisdiction. A civil action shall be commenced within 180 days after the alleged discriminatory housing practice occurred: *Provided, however,* that the court shall continue such civil case brought pursuant to this section or section

810(d) from time to time before bringing it to trial if the court believes that the conciliation efforts of the secretary or a state or local agency are likely to result in satisfactory settlement of the discriminatory housing practice complained of in the complaint made to the secretary or to the local or state agency and which practice forms the basis for the action in court: *And provided, however,* that any sale, encumbrance, or rental consummated prior to the issuance of any court order issued under the authority of this act, and involving a bona fide purchaser, encumbrancer, or tenant without actual notice of the existence of the filing of a complaint or civil action under the provisions of this act shall not be affected.

(b) Upon application by the plaintiff and in such circumstances as the court may deem just, a court of the United States in which a civil action under this section has been brought may appoint an attorney for the plaintiff and may authorize the commencement of a civil action upon proper showing without the payment of fees, costs, or security. A court of a state or subdivision thereof may do likewise to the extent not inconsistent with the law or procedures of the state or subdivision.

(c) The court may grant as relief, as it deems appropriate, any permanent or temporary injunction, temporary restraining order, or other order, and may award to the plaintiff actual damages and not more than $1,000 punitive damages, together with court costs and reasonable attorney fees in the case of a prevailing plaintiff: *Provided,* that the said plaintiff in the opinion of the court is not financially able to assume said attorney's fees.

Enforcement by the Attorney General

Sec. 813. (a) Whenever the Attorney General has reasonable cause to believe that any person or group of persons is engaged in a pattern or practice of resistance to the full enjoyment of any of the rights granted by this title and such denial raises an issue of general public importance, he may bring a civil action in any appropriate United States district court by filing with it a complaint setting forth the facts and requesting such preventive relief, including an application for a permanent or temporary injunction, restraining order, or other order against the person or persons responsible for such pattern or practice or denial of rights, as he deems necessary to insure the full enjoyment of the rights granted by this title.

Expedition of Proceedings

Sec. 814. Any court in which a proceeding is instituted under section 812 or 813 of this title shall assign the case for hearing at the earliest practicable date and cause the case to be in every way expedited.

Effect on State Laws

Sec. 815. Nothing in this title shall be construed to invalidate or limit any law of a state or political subdivision of a state, or of any other jurisdiction in which this title shall be effective, that grants, guarantees, or protects the same rights as are granted by this title; but any law of a state, a political subdivision, or other such jurisdiction that purports to require or permit any action that would be a discriminatory housing practice under this title shall to that extent be invalid.

Cooperation with State and Local Agencies Administering Fair Housing Laws

Sec. 816. The secretary may cooperate with state and local agencies charged with the administration of state and local fair housing laws and, with the consent of such agencies, utilize the services of such agencies and their employees and, notwithstanding any other provision of law, may reimburse such agencies and their employees for services rendered to assist him in carrying out this title. In furtherance of such cooperative efforts, the secretary may enter into written agreements with such state or local agencies. All agreements and terminations thereof shall be published in the Federal Register.

Interference, Coercion, or Intimidation

Sec. 817. It shall be unlawful to coerce, intimidate, threaten, or interfere with any person in the exercise or enjoyment of, or on account of his having exercised or enjoyed, or on account of his having aided or encouraged any other person in the exercise or enjoyment of, any right granted or protected by section 803, 804, 805, or 806. This section may be enforced by appropriate civil action.

Appropriations

Sec. 818. There are hereby authorized to be appropriated such sums as are necessary to carry out the purposes of this title.

Separability of Provisions

Sec. 819. If any provision of this title or the application thereof to any person or circumstances is held invalid, the remainder of the title and the application of the provision to other persons not similarly situated or to other circumstances shall not be affected thereby.

TITLE IX
Prevention of Intimidation in Fair Housing Cases

Sec. 901. Whoever, whether or not acting under color of law, by force or threat of force willfully injures, intimidates or interferes with, or attempts to injure, intimidate, or interfere with—

(a) Any person because of his race, color, religion, or national origin and because he is or has been selling, purchasing, renting, financing, occupying, or contracting or negotiating for the sale, purchase, rental, financing, or occupation of any dwelling, or applying for or participating in any service, organization, or facility relating to the business of selling or renting dwellings; or

(b) any person because he is or has been, or in order to intimidate such person or any other person or any class of persons from—

(1) participating, without discrimination on account of race, color, religion, or national origin, in any of the activities, services, organizations, or facilities described in subsection 901(a); or

(2) affording another person or class of persons opportunity or protection so to participate; or

(c) any citizen because he is or has been, or in order to discourage such citizen or any other citizen from lawfully aiding or encouraging other persons to participate, without discrimination on account of race, color, religion, or national origin in any of the activities, services, organization, or facilities described in subsection 901(a), or participating lawfully in speech or peaceful assembly opposing any denial of the opportunity to so participate—

shall be fined not more than $1,000, or imprisoned not more than one year, or both; and if bodily injury results shall be fined not more than $10,000, or imprisoned not more than 10 years, or both; and if death results shall be subject to imprisonment for any term of years or for life.

CODE OF ETHICS
NATIONAL ASSOCIATION OF REAL ESTATE BOARDS
Preamble

Under all is the land. Upon its wise utilization and widely allocated ownership depend the survival and growth of free institutions and of our civilization. The

Realtor is the instrumentality through which the land resource of the nation reaches its highest use and through which land ownership attains its widest distribution. He is a creator of homes, a builder of cities, a developer of industries and productive farms.

Such functions impose obligations beyond those of ordinary commerce. They impose grave social responsibility and a patriotic duty to which the Realtor should dedicate himself, and for which he should be diligent in preparing himself. The Realtor, therefore, is zealous to maintain and improve the standards of his calling and shares with his fellow-Realtors a common responsibility for its integrity and honor.

In the interpretation of his obligations, he can take no safer guide than that which has been handed down through twenty centuries, embodied in the Golden Rule:

"Whatsoever ye would that men should do to you, do ye even so to them."

Accepting this standard as his own, every Realtor pledges himself to observe its spirit in all his activities and to conduct his business in accordance with the following Code of Ethics:

PART I
Relations to the Public

ARTICLE 1.

The Realtor should keep himself informed as to movements affecting real estate in his community, state, and the nation, so that he may be able to contribute to public thinking on matters of taxation, legislation, land use, city planning, and other questions affecting property interests.

ARTICLE 2.

It is the duty of the Realtor to be well informed on current market conditions in order to be in a position to advise his clients as to the fair market price.

ARTICLE 3.

It is the duty of the Realtor to protect the public against fraud, misrepresentation or unethical practices in the real estate field.
He should endeavor to eliminate in his community any practices which could be damaging to the public or to the dignity and integrity of the real estate profession. The Realtor should assist the board or commission charged with regulating the practices of brokers and salesmen in his state.

ARTICLE 4.

The Realtor should ascertain all pertinent facts concerning every property for which he accepts the agency, so that he may fulfill his obligation to avoid error, exaggeration, misrepresentation, or concealment of pertinent facts.

ARTICLE 5.

The Realtor should not be instrumental in introducing into a neighborhood a character of property or use which will clearly be detrimental to property values in that neighborhood.

ARTICLE 6.

The Realtor should not be a party to the naming of a false consideration in any document, unless it be the naming of an obviously nominal consideration.

ARTICLE 7.

The Realtor should not engage in activities that constitute the practice of law and should recommend that title be examined and legal counsel be obtained when the interest of either party requires it.

ARTICLE 8.

The Realtor should keep in a special bank account, separated from his own funds, monies coming into his possession in trust for other persons, such as escrows, trust funds, client's monies and other like items.

ARTICLE 9.

The Realtor in his advertising should be especially careful to present a true picture and should neither advertise without disclosing his name, nor permit his salesmen to use individual names or telephone numbers, unless the salesman's connection with the Realtor is obvious in the advertisement.

ARTICLE 10.

The Realtor, for the protection of all parties with whom he deals, should see that financial obligations and commitments regarding real estate transactions are in writing, expressing the exact agreement of the parties; and that copies of such agreements, at the time they are executed, are placed in the hands of all parties involved.

PART II

Relations to the Client

ARTICLE 11.

In accepting employment as an agent, the Realtor pledges himself to protect and promote the interests of the client. This obligation of absolute fidelity to the client's interest is primary, but it does not relieve the Realtor from the obligation of dealing fairly with all parties to the transaction.

ARTICLE 12.

In justice to those who place their interests in his care, the Realtor should endeavor always to be informed regarding laws, proposed legislation, governmental orders, and other essential information and public policies which affect those interests.

ARTICLE 13.

Since the Realtor is representing one or another party to a transaction, he should not accept compensation from more than one party without the full knowledge of all parties to the transaction.

ARTICLE 14.

The Realtor should not acquire an interest in or buy for himself, any member of his immediate family, his firm or any member thereof, or any entity in which he has a substantial ownership interest, property listed with him, or his firm, without making the true position known to the listing owner, and in selling property owned by him, or in which he has such interest, the facts should be revealed to the purchaser.

ARTICLE 15.

The exclusive listing of property should be urged and practiced by the Realtor as a means of preventing dissension and misunderstanding and of assuring better service to the owner.

ARTICLE 16.

When acting as agent in the management of property, the Realtor should not accept any commission, rebate or profit on expenditures made for an owner, without the owner's knowledge and consent.

ARTICLE 17.

The Realtor should not undertake to make an appraisal that is outside the field of his experience unless he obtains the assistance of an authority on such types of property, or unless the facts are fully disclosed to the client. In such circumstances the authority so engaged should be so identified and his contribution to the assignment should be clearly set forth.

ARTICLE 18.

When asked to make a formal appraisal of real property, the Realtor should not render an opinion without careful and thorough analysis and interpretation of all factors affecting the value of the property. His counsel constitutes a professional service.

The Realtor should not undertake to make an appraisal or render an opinion of value on any property where he has a present or contemplated interest unless such interest is specifically disclosed in the appraisal report. Under no circumstances should he undertake to make a formal appraisal when his employment or fee is contingent upon the amount of his appraisal.

ARTICLE 19.

The Realtor should not submit or advertise property without authority, and in any offering, the price quoted should not be other than that agreed upon with the owners as the offering price.

ARTICLE 20.

In the event that more than one formal written offer on a specific property is made before the owner has accepted an offer, any other formal written offer presented to the Realtor, whether by a prospective purchaser or another broker, should be transmitted to the owner for his decision.

PART III
Relations to His Fellow-Realtor

ARTICLE 21.

The Realtor should seek no unfair advantage over his fellow-Realtors and should willingly share with them the lessons of his experience and study.

ARTICLE 22.

The Realtor should so conduct his business as to avoid controversies with his fellow-Realtors. In the event of a controversy between Realtors who are members of the same local board, such controversy should be arbitrated in accordance with regulations of their board rather than litigated.

ARTICLE 23.

Controversies between Realtors who are not members of the same local board should be submitted to an arbitration board consisting of one arbitrator chosen by each Realtor from the real estate board to which he belongs or chosen in accordance with the regulations of the respective boards. One other member, or a sufficient number of members to make an odd number, should be selected by the arbitrators thus chosen.

ARTICLE 24.

When the Realtor is charged with unethical practice, he should place all pertinent facts before the proper tribunal of the member board of which he is a member, for investigation and judgment.

ARTICLE 25.

The Realtor should not voluntarily disparage the business practice of a competitor, nor volunteer an opinion of a competitor's transaction. If his opinion is sought it should be rendered with strict professional integrity and courtesy.

ARTICLE 26.

The Agency of a Realtor who holds an exclusive listing should be respected. A Realtor cooperating with a listing broker should not invite the cooperation of a third broker without the consent of the listing broker.

ARTICLE 27.

The Realtor should cooperate with other brokers on property listed by him exclusively whenever it is in the interest of the client, sharing commissions on a previously agreed basis. Negotiations concerning property listed exclusively with one broker should be carried on with the listing broker, not with the owner, except with the consent of the listing broker.

ARTICLE 28.

The Realtor should not solicit the services of an employee or salesman in the organization of a fellow-Realtor without the knowledge of the employer.

ARTICLE 29.

Signs giving notice of property for sale, rent, lease or exchange should not be placed on any property by more than one Realtor, and then only if authorized by the owner, except as the property is listed with and authorization given to more than one Realtor.

ARTICLE 30.

In the best interest of society, of his associates and of his own business, the Realtor should be loyal to the real estate board of his community and active in its work.

CONCLUSION

The term Realtor has come to connote competence, fair dealing and high integrity resulting from adherence to a lofty ideal of moral conduct in business relations. No inducement of profit and no instructions from clients ever can justify departure from this ideal, or from the injunctions of this Code.

The Code of Ethics was adopted in 1913. Amended at the Annual Convention in 1924, 1928, 1950, 1951, 1952, 1955, 1956, 1961, and 1962. No further amendments have been made since 1962.

GLOSSARY OF
REAL ESTATE TERMS

Abstract of Title A condensed history of the title, consisting of a summary of the various links in the chain of title, together with a statement of all liens, charges, or encumbrances affecting a particular property.

Acre A measure of land, 160 square rods (4,840 square yards; 43,560 square feet).

Adverse Possession The right of an occupant of land to acquire title against the real owner, where possession has been actual, continuous, hostile, visible, and distinct for the statutory period.

Agent One who represents another from whom he has derived authority.

Agreement of Sale A written agreement whereby the purchaser agrees to buy certain real estate and the seller agrees to sell upon terms and conditions set forth therein.

Amortization The liquidation of a financial obligation on an installment basis.

Annuity A sum of money or its equivalent that constitutes one of a series of periodic payments.

Appraisal An estimate of quantity, quality, or value. The process through which conclusions of property value are obtained; also refers to the report setting forth the estimate and conclusion of value.

Assessed Valuation   Assessment of real estate by a unit of government for taxation purposes.

Assessment   A charge against real estate made by a unit of government to cover the proportionate cost of an improvement, such as a street or sewer.

Binder   An agreement to cover a down payment for the purchase of real estate as evidence of good faith on the part of the purchaser; in insurance: a temporary agreement given to one having an insurable interest, and who desires insurance subject to the same conditions that will apply if, as, and when a policy is issued.

Blanket Mortgage   A single mortgage that covers more than one piece of real estate.

Bond   Any obligation under seal. A real estate bond is a written obligation, usually issued on security of a mortgage or a trust deed.

Broker   One employed by another, for a fee, to carry on any of the activities listed in the license law definition of the word.

Building Code   Regulating the construction of buildings within a municipality by ordinance or law.

Chattel   Personal property, such as household goods or fixtures.

Cloud On the Title   An outstanding claim or encumbrance which, if valid, would affect or impair the owner's title; a mortgage or judgment.

Commission   Sum due a real estate broker for services in that capacity; the administrative and enforcement tribunal of real estate license laws.

Common Law   Body of law that grew up from custom and decided cases (English law) rather than from codified law (Roman law).

Condemnation   Taking private property for public use, with compensation to the owner, under the right of eminent domain.

Condominium   Full ownership of a part or space unit of developed land and an undivided interest to use the common land or space areas on an equal basis with other condominium owners.

Constructive Eviction   Breach of a covenant of warranty or quiet enjoyment; for example, the inability of a purchaser or lessee to obtain possession by reason of a paramount defect in title, or a condition making occupancy hazardous.

Cooperative Ownership   Ownership of shares in a cooperative venture entitling the owner to use, rent, or sell a specific space unit (apartment).

Covenant An agreement between two or more persons, by deed, whereby one of the parties promises the performance or nonperformance of certain acts or that a given state of things does or does not exist.

Cubage Front or width of building multiplied by depth of building and by the height, figured from the basement floor to the outer surfaces of walls and roof.

Curtesy The right that a husband has in his wife's estate at her death.

Dedication An appropriation of land by an owner to some public use together with acceptance for such use by or on behalf of the public.

Deed A writing by which lands, tenements, and hereditaments are transferred, which writing is signed, sealed, and delivered by the grantor.

Defeasance An instrument that nullifies the effect of some other deed or of an estate.

Deficiency Judgment The difference between the indebtedness sued upon and the sale price or market value of the real estate at the foreclosure sale.

Depreciation Loss in value, brought about by deterioration through ordinary wear and tear, action of the elements, or functional or economic obsolescence.

Dispossess To deprive one of the use of real estate.

Dower The right that a wife has in her husband's estate at his death.

Earnest Money Down payment made by a purchaser of real estate as evidence of good faith.

Easement The right, liberty, advantage, or privilege that one individual has in lands of another (a right-of-way).

Economic Life The period over which a property may be profitably utilized.

Eminent Domain The right of the people or government to take private property for public use upon payment of compensation.

Encroachment A building, part of building, or obstruction that intrudes upon or invades a highway or sidewalk or trespasses upon property of another.

Encumbrance A claim, lien, charge, or liability attached to and binding upon real property, such as a judgment, unpaid taxes, or a right-of-way; defined in law as any right to, or interest in, land that may subsist in another to the diminution of its value, but consistent with the passing of the fee.

Equity The interest or value that an owner has in real estate over and above the mortgage against it; system of legal rules administered by courts of chancery.

Erosion   The wearing away of land through processes of nature as by streams and winds.

Escheat   Reversion of property to the sovereign state owing to lack of any heirs capable of inheriting.

Escrow   A deed delivered to a third person for the grantee to be held by him until the fulfillment or performance of some act or condition.

Estate   Quantity of interest a person has in property.

Eviction   A violation of some covenant in a lease by the landlord, usually the covenant for quiet enjoyment; also refers to process instituted to oust a person from possession of real estate.

Exclusive Agency   The appointment of one real estate broker as sole agent for the sale of a property for a designated period of time.

Fee Simple   The largest estate or ownership in real property.

Fixture   A personal chattel that does not pass with the land but may be removed by the owner, such as awnings, carpets. Also real fixtures, such as furnaces or plumbing fixtures, that are a part of realty or real estate.

Foreclosure   A court process instituted by a mortgagee or lien creditor to defeat any interest or redemption that the debtor-owner may have in the property.

Freehold   An estate in fee simple or one held for life.

Front Foot   A standard of measurement, one foot wide, extending from street line for a depth, generally conceded to be one hundred feet.

Grantee   A person to whom real estate is conveyed; the buyer.

Grantor   A person who conveys real estate by deed; the seller.

Holdover Tenant   A tenant who remains in possession of leased property after the expiration of the lease term.

Homestead   Real estate occupied by the owner as a home; the owner enjoys special rights and privileges.

Installment Contract (also known as *land contract*)   Purchase of real estate upon an installment basis; upon default, payments are forfeited.

Joint Tenancy   Property held by two or more persons together with the distinct character of survivorship.

Judgment   Decree of court declaring that one individual is indebted to another and fixing the amount of such indebtedness.

Junior Mortgage   A mortgage second in lien to a previous mortgage.

Land Contract (or *installment contract*)   A contract for the purchase of real estate upon an installment basis; upon payment of last installment, deed is delivered to purchaser.

Landlord   One who rents property to another.

Lease   A contract, written or oral, for the possession of lands and tenements on the one hand and a recompense of rent or other income on the other.

Leasehold   An estate in realty held under a lease.

Lessee   A person to whom property is rented under a lease.

Lessor   *See* Landlord.

Lien   A hold or claim that one person has upon property of another as security for a debt or charge; judgments, mortgages, taxes.

Life Estate   An estate or interest held during the term of some certain person's life.

Listing   Oral or written employment of broker by owner to sell or lease real estate.

Market Value   The highest price that a buyer, willing but not compelled to buy, would pay, and the lowest a seller, willing but not compelled to sell, would accept.

Mechanic's Lien   A species of lien, created by statute, in favor of persons who have performed work or furnished materials in the erection or repair of a building.

Metes and Bounds   A description in a deed of the land location, in which the boundaries are defined by directions and distances.

Mortgage   A conditional transfer of real property as security for the payment of a debt or the fulfillment of some obligation.

Mortgagee   A person to whom property is conveyed as security for a loan made by such person (the creditor).

Mortgagor   An owner who conveys his property as security for a loan (the debtor).

Multiple Listing   The arrangement among real estate board or exchange members whereby each broker brings his listings to the attention of the other members so that if a sale results, the commission is divided between the broker bringing the listing and the broker making the sale with a small percentage going to the multiple listing board.

Net Listing   A price, which must be expressly agreed upon, below which the owner will not sell the property and at which price the broker will not receive a commission; the broker receives the excess over and above the net listing as his commission. The excess must represent a reasonable brokerage charge.

Obsolescence   Impairment of desirability and usefulness brought about by physical, economic, or other changes.

Open Housing Law   A law passed by Congress in April 1968 prohibiting discrimination in the sale of real estate because of race, color, or religion of buyers.

Open Listing   An oral or general listing.

Option   The right to purchase or lease a property at a certain price for a certain designated period, for which right a consideration is paid.

Over-Improvement   An improvement that is not the highest and best use for the site on which it is placed by reason of excess in size or cost.

Percentage Lease   A lease of property in which the rental is based upon the volume of sales made upon the leased premises.

Plottage   Increment in unity value of a plot of land created by assembling smaller ownerships into one ownership.

Police Power   The inherent right of a government to pass such legislation as may be necessary to protect the public health and safety and/or to promote the general welfare.

Principal   The employer of an agent; the person who is ordinarily liable primarily.

Principal Note   The promissory note that is secured by the mortgage or trust deed.

Property   The right or interest that an individual has in lands and chattels to the exclusion of all others.

Purchase Money Mortgage   A mortgage given by a grantee to the grantor in part payment of the purchase price of real estate.

Quitclaim Deed   A deed given when the grantee already has, or claims, complete or partial title to the premises and the grantor has a possible interest that otherwise would constitute a cloud upon the title.

Realtor   A coined (patented) word to designate an active member of a local real estate board affiliated with the National Association of Real Estate Boards.

Release of Lien   The discharge of certain property from the lien of a judgment, mortgage, or claim.

Remainder Estate   An estate in property created at the same time by the same instrument as another estate and limited to arise immediately upon the termination of the other estate.

Replacement Cost   Sacrifice or cost necessary to replace the function or utility (service) of an improvement.

Reproduction Cost   Normal cost of exact duplication of a property, as of a certain date.

Restriction   A device in a deed for controlling the use of land for the benefit of the land.

Reversion   The residue of an estate left to the grantor, to commence after the determination of some particular estate granted out by him.

Riparian Owner   One who owns lands bounding upon a river or water-course. This includes rights for contiguous use and enjoyment of water rights.

Satisfaction Piece   An instrument for recording and acknowledging payment of an indebtedness secured by a mortgage.

Seizin   Possession of real estate by one entitled thereto.

Specific Performance   A remedy in a court of equity compelling the defendant to carry out the terms of the agreement or contract that was executed.

Subdivision   A tract of land divided into lots suitable for home building purposes.

Subletting   A leasing by a tenant to another, who holds under the tenant.

Survey   The process by which a parcel of land is measured and its area ascertained.

Tenancy at Will   A license to use or occupy lands and tenements at the will of the owner.

Tenancy in Common   Form of estate held by two or more persons, each of whom is considered as being possessed of the whole or an undivided part.

Tenant   A person who holds real estate under a lease (lessee).

Tenant at Sufferance   One who comes into possession of lands by lawful title and keeps it afterward without any title at all, but with implied consent of the owner.

Title   Evidence of ownership, which refers to the quality of the estate.

Title Insurance   A policy of insurance that indemnifies the holder for any loss sustained by reason of defects in the title.

Trust Deed   A conveyance of real estate to a third person to be held for the benefit of a cestui que trust (beneficiary).

Usury   Charging more than the legal rate of interest for the use of money.

Vendee   The purchaser of real estate under an agreement.

Vendor   The seller of real estate, usually referred to as the party of the first part in an agreement of sale.

Warranty Deed   One that contains a covenant that the grantor will protect the grantee against any claimant.

Zoning Ordinance   Exercise of police power of a municipality in regulating and controlling the character and use of property.

INDEX